Reinsurance

WRITTEN BY TWENTY-THREE AUTHORITIES

Edited by
Robert W. Strain, CLU, CPCU
Dean
The College of Insurance

THE COLLEGE OF INSURANCE
123 William Street
New York, New York 10038

1980

Library of Congress Cataloging in Publication Data

Reinsurance.

   Includes index.
   1.   Reinsurance.   I.   Strain, Robert W.   II.   New
York.   College of Insurance.
HG8059.R4R44   368'.012   80-14442

Printed in the United States of America

First Printing, May 1980
Second Printing, January 1981
Third Printing, May 1984

Contents

REINSURANCE FORMS AND RATES

William G. Clark
Senior Vice President, General Reinsurance Corporation

The purpose of Facultative Reinsurance, Characteristics of Facultative Reinsurance, Facultative Pricing and Structuring (the layering concept, ratemaking procedures, structuring property excess coverages), The Facultative Certificate, Summary.

Walter J. Coleman
Senior Vice President, The Reinsurance Corporation of New York

Types of Pro Rata Treaties (the quota share treaty: portfolio v. running account, net v. gross account, the "guaranteed-profit" quota share agreement; the surplus treaty: premium volume guidelines, the surplus treaty and other reinsurances), Significant Concepts and Practices, Pricing: The Reinsurance Commission, Summary.

Stanford Miller
Chairman, Employers Reinsurance Corporation

Purpose and Function, Working Excess Variations, Special Cases (the advance deposit premium cover, the combination pro rata excess plan, inflation and the working excess of loss reinsurance treaty), Rating the Working Excess, Summary.

Robert S. Gilliam, Jr.
Chairman, Excess and Treaty Management Corporation

Purposes of Catastrophe Reinsurance, Designing the Catastrophe Program (objectives, proper catastrophe retention, catastrophe reinsurance limit, catastrophe programs for selected companies, continuity), Catastrophe Perils, Catastrophe Contracts, Claims and Claims Expenses, Rating, Summary.

LeRoy J. Simon, FCAS
Senior Vice President, Prudential Reinsurance Company

Principal Types, Rating Casualty Treaties (pricing factors, rating plans), Evaluating the Casualty Excess Reinsurer and Reinsured, Punitive and Extra-Contractual Damages, Summary.

THE USERS OF REINSURANCE

THE TECHNIQUES OF THE REINSURER

THE REINSURER AS A BUSINESS CONCERN

Preface

Never before in the history of reinsurance literature has there been an effort such as this. Twenty-three reinsurance authorities (fourteen of them chief executives), chosen by their peers for their knowledge and the success with which it has been applied, have written twenty-one chapters. While any one of them could have written a book on reinsurance, no one of them could spare the time. Indeed, in some cases more than a year was required in the preparation of a single chapter. Only through the combined effort of many was the work done: initiated by the needs of the business, structured by a committee of reinsurance leaders, produced by more than one hundred persons (writers, reviewers, and critics), orchestrated and shaped by three editors, and finally approved by the committee as having met its objectives. Four years in the making, it was truly a labor of love. In most cases, the work had to be done after employment responsibilities had been met for the day.

The method of production should be equally effective in other disciplines, especially those in which the premier people whose knowledge is sought are too busy to write an entire volume alone. The planning for this book commenced in 1976 and required a year of development before a format was determined. Over that period, numerous meetings were held by the Reinsurance Advisory Committee of The College of Insurance in New York. Co-Chairmen of the Committee were Henry Kramer (President of The Risk Exchange, Inc. and author of Chapter 1) and John L. Baringer (Chairman of Rochdale Insurance Company and author of Chapter 11). They were ably assisted by Alan Brightman (Vice President of Employers Reinsurance Corporation), David G. Christie (Senior Vice President of Duncanson & Holt), and N. David Thompson (President of North American Reinsurance Corporation). The College was indeed fortunate to have the dedication and distinguished services of these reinsurance executives.

The chief architect for the work was Mr. Kramer. He prepared the initial outline for the entire book, which was then modified and improved by Mr. Baringer and the Committee. Both gentlemen are widely known for their competency as technicians and executives, and for being keen interpreters of the major issues affecting reinsurance. My particular gratitude and respect go to Henry Kramer for serving as a tower of strength to this writer throughout the entire project. A gentleman of the first rank, he consistently urged us in his gracious way to do more, to do it better, and to do it now.

The textbook outline proposed the major contents of each chapter as a guide for each author and to avoid duplication among them. However, each author was asked to paint the picture as he saw it. The object was to maintain objectivity in sharing with the reader those truths gained from a lifetime of accomplishment. If that goal has been achieved, the reader is exposed to a vast amount of knowledge and experience brought together in one volume. Indeed, the chief value of such diverse authors is their expertise as reinsurance practitioners. These are not theoreticians who pluckily plow their isolated furrows.

With so many writers contributing, the reader will need to shift gears occasionally at the varied styles of writing. However, the diligent student of reinsurance will find such variety interesting, especially when it reveals differences of opinion among authors. And the reinsurance fraternity has not been known for its reticence in pursuing competitive goals, so the reader can look forward to some lively discussions.

Once the authors were selected, each was asked to choose two chapter reviewers from outside his organization and from among those considered equally knowledgeable in the assigned subject. Each author was encouraged to benefit from any help his business associates could render, both in saving the author's time and in augmenting his contribution. The reviewers examined the first draft and reported to the author any omissions, errors, or needed improvements in technical matters. A second draft was then prepared and sent to the three editors, two of whom were to serve as associate editors in looking for technical accuracy and balance, and the other to read the chapter as a layman. The author was then asked to take those suggested changes which he considered as improvements and prepare a third draft. That version was then inspected by this writer (who also served as the layman editor) before submitting it to the Committee for its final approval. By the time the third draft reached the Committee, the thoroughness with which it had been prepared assured its approval in most cases.

Throughout the production, each person involved in the project was kept informed by monthly mailings of a progress report, with dated entries for each chapter as it moved through its stages. The report had another important purpose besides revealing progress: to stimulate, psychologically, busy people to push the work along to its next step. Similar to water dripping on a stone, the reminder eventually made its mark. The progress report also helped develop momentum for the entire project in fostering among its many participants an *esprit de corps.*

The following persons served as reviewers of the chapters, in most cases two reviewers per chapter. In addition, they helped their authors in numerous supportive roles, and their total contributions were vital in moving the project to completion.

ALLEN, STANLEY W., Vice President, INA Reinsurance Company, 1600 Arch Street, Philadelphia, Penna. 19101.

ALVERSON, DWIGHT F., Vice President, Firemans Fund Insurance Company, 3333 California Street, P.O. Box 3395, San Francisco, Calif. 94119.

BINNEY, R. IVOR, Chairman and Chief Executive, C.T. Bowring (Insurance) Holdings Ltd., Box 745, Tower Place, London EC3P 3BE, England.

BUNAES, BARD E., President and Chief Executive Officer, Constitution Reinsurance Corporation, 110 William Street, New York, New York 10038.

COLE, DONALD L., Second Vice President, Reinsurance Operation, Travelers Insurance Companies, One Tower Square, Hartford, CT 06115.

DeWITT, CLYDE, President, Employers Reinsurance Corporation, P.O. Box 2088, Kansas City, MO 64142.

DITTMER, NORMAN, Vice President, Employers Reinsurance Corporation, P.O. Box 2088, Kansas City, MO 64142.

ELWELL, ALAN C., President and Chief Executive Officer, Crum & Forster Insurance Company (Bermuda), 840 Rock Rimmon Road, North Stamford, Connecticut 06903.

ENGLISH, CLIFFORD, Senior Vice President, Intere Intermediaries Inc., 127 John Street, New York, New York 10038.

ESTES, JAMES M., Senior Vice President, Employers Reinsurance Corporation, P.O. Box 2088, Kansas City MO 64142.

GARRETT, JOSEPH, 40 Prospect Avenue, Basking Ridge, New Jersey 07920.

GEHRLEIN, WILLIAM C., Senior Vice President, North American Reinsurance Corporation, 245 Park Avenue, New York, New York 10017.

GSCHWIND, A. EDWARD, President, American Overseas Management Corporation, 40 Wall Street, New York, New York 10005.

HAFTL, FRANKLIN D., Vice President, Metropolitan Reinsurance Company, P.O. Box 17, 1 Madison Avenue, New York, New York 10010.

HANSEN, NIEL, Treaty Group Vice President, North American Reinsurance Corporation, 245 Park Avenue, New York, New York 10017.

HASSING, ANTON J. C., President, Philadelphia Reinsurance Corporation, 3 Girard Plaza, Philadelphia, Penna. 19102.

JOHNSON, DONALD E., Vice President, Nationwide Insurance Company, 1 Nationwide Plaza, Columbus, Ohio 43216.

KELLY, AMBROSE, General Counsel, American Mutual Reinsurance Co., One East Wacker Drive, Chicago, Ill. 60601.

KELLY, DANIEL M., Salomon Brothers, One New York Plaza, New York, New York 10004.

KENNEY, ROGER, Harvard Club of Boston, 374 Commonwealth Avenue, Boston, Mass. 02215.

LeSTRANGE, KENNETH J., Vice President, General Reinsurance Corporation, 600 Steamboat Road, Greenwich, Conn. 06830.

MacKAY, DONALD R., 3535 North Meridian Road, Tallahassee, Florida 32303. (retired President, American Re-Insurance Company).

MAVROS, PAUL S., Senior Vice President, E. W. Blanch, 444 N. Michigan Avenue, Suite 3560, Chicago, Ill. 60611.

MENEGAY, LESTER A., Codfish Hill Road, Bethel, Conn. 06801. (retired Vice President of American Re-Insurance Company).

MORAHAN, JOSEPH E., JR., Chairman, Shand, Morahan & Company, Inc., 1 American Plaza, Evanston, Ill. 60201.

MUNSON, FRANK, President, General Reinsurance Corporation, 600 Steamboat Road, Greenwich, Conn. 06830.

NEWHOUSE, ROBERT J., JR., President, Marsh & McLennan Companies, Inc. 1221 Avenue of the Americas, New York, New York 10020.

PRIOR, FRANCIS, Secretary, MONY Reinsurance Corporation, 127 John Street, New York, New York 10038.

RATCLIFFE, GEORGE E., Senior Vice President, Skandia America Reinsurance Corporation, 280 Park Avenue, New York, New York 10017.

REARDEN, WILLIAM B., President, Winterthur Swiss Insurance Company, 1 World Trade Center, New York, New York 10048.

RONDEPIERRE, EDMOND, ESQ., Vice President, General Counsel and Corporate Secretary, General Reinsurance Corporation, 600 Steamboat Road, Greenwich, Conn. 06830.

SEMPLE, T. DARRINGTON, JR., ESQ., Resident Counsel and Secretary, American Re-Insurance Company, 1 Liberty Plaza, New York, New York 10006.

SHEPARD, RAYMOND, 747 Woodleave Road, Bryn Mawr, Pennsylvania 19010. (retired Vice President of Reliance Insurance Company).

SUDEKUM, LOTHAR, Deputy Chairman of Mercantile and General Reinsurance Company of America, R.D. Box 188C, Staats Road, Bloomsbury, New Jersey 08804. (retired President of Constellation Reinsurance Company).

TAYLOR, W. E., President, John F. Sullivan Company, 14th Floor, People's National Bank Building, Seattle, Washington 98171.

THOMPSON, N. DAVID, President, North American Reinsurance Corporation, 245 Park Avenue, New York, New York 10017.

TOTSCH, MARVIN D., President, Totsch Enterprises, Inc., 18 South Michigan Avenue, Chicago, Ill. 60603.

WHITE, JAMES P., Executive Vice President, American Re-Insurance Company, One Liberty Plaza, 91 Liberty Street, New York, New York 10006.

WOODBURY, MARION, President, Reinsurance Corporation of New York, 99 John Street, 19th Floor, New York, New York 10038.

ZECH, JOHN R., President, The National Reinsurance Corporation, 123 William Street, New York, New York 10038.

Assisting the Committee and me were two associate editors, Andrew Barile, CPCU, and Jean Webb, CPCU. They were selected by me because of their technical competence in the subject, because of their having served The College for years as adjunct professors of insurance, and because of their conscientious devotion to improved reinsurance education. Indeed, the three of us cooperated in creating the "Brief Course in Reinsurance," a six-hour instructional offering which has been given bi-monthly since 1975, each time to a capacity audience. Barile and Webb have served as the distinguished faculty in teaching that course.

Mr. Barile is President of ANECO Group of America, Inc. A graduate of The College of Insurance (BBA in insurance, cum laude), he received the MBA in international business and finance from New York University. He has been in the insurance and reinsurance business for over twenty years, serving with North American Reinsurance Corporation, American Re-Insurance Company, and as executive vice president of Howden Reinsurance Corporation prior to his current affiliation. We were fortunate to have Mr. Barile's editorial help with approximately half of the book before his busy activities required more of his time.

Mr. Webb is Vice President of North American Reinsurance Corporation in New York and is in charge of their property treaty underwriting. Following graduation from Amherst College in 1958, he served with Great American Insurance Companies and INA in Pennsylvania and New York before joining The National Reinsurance Corporation in 1969, where he served until 1980. In addition to editing all chapters in the book, Mr. Webb helped immeasurably in preparing the glossary of reinsurance terms in the appendix. He also served as the reinsurance lexicographer in the latest edition of *Insurance Words and Their Meanings* (Rough Notes Co.), which this writer also edited.

All of us hope that this book will serve all persons interested in reinsurance at any level of achievement or professional standing, from the highly expert to the literal beginner. As befits a work produced by individuals of the kind concerned here, no attempt has been made deliberately to talk down to the level of the unskilled or unfamiliar. Reinsurance as it is practiced does not lend itself easily to simple categories, rules, or standard procedures even though there are strong similarities with insurance in form and methods. A few useful facts underlying the practice or reinsurance may make this book more useful and easier to understand.

The purpose of reinsurance begins with the desire and ability to insure with others part or all of what one has already insured. The object may be one essentially of sharing risk, and this objective is how reinsurance first began. The reinsurance of part or all of a risk insured under a single policy is called facultative, or specific reinsurance. In keeping with this object of sharing, all reinsurance was originally arranged on a proportional (or "pro rata") basis. An agreed percentage of a policy (and loss falling to it) was reinsured in return for the same percentage of the original premium (the "reinsurance" premium). Ordinarily, the reinsurer reimbursed the insurer for its allocable cost of acquiring and producing the policy by allowing a "ceding commission" appropriate to that cost or expense, expressed as the percentage of the reinsurance premium. Ceding commissions remain a frequent characteristic, an almost universal one with proportional reinsurance.

In later years, it was found possible and convenient to define certain kinds and amounts or shares of policies which could be reinsured routinely or as a group (or "portfolio") under a general or wholesale agreement at much less cost than reinsuring them one by one, and with a far higher degree of certainty that the reinsurance would be available. With this concept, the so-called reinsurance "treaty," or "agreement," or "contract" came into general use. The need for facultative was not eliminated because some policies were too large, which is to say they required more "reinsurance capacity" than the treaty allowed, or the policies were of a kind that was not acceptable or not contemplated under the treaty. But most reinsurance came to be done in this treaty manner, and still is.

Still later, the principle of using a deductible, or first-loss retention, was developed and the concept of "excess of loss" or "non-proportional" reinsurance was formulated. This development was more or less as a consequence of the search for more efficient ways to reinsure against the background of a steadily growing insurance industry, one increasingly able to carry the burden of small losses regardless of policy size or accumulations of risk subject to common loss. This approach rested on the fact that a contract of reinsurance is not an extension of or part of the contract of insurance from which it springs, nor does reinsurance extinguish or supersede the original insurance which continues in all respects as originally issued, reinsured or not. Accordingly, while it had always been possible to reinsure some rather than all policy risks, perils, or coverages on a proportional or pro rata basis, it was now possible to reinsure, on an excess of loss basis, part or all of only those losses which exceeded an agreed amount per loss event.

The disassociation of the reinsurance and insurance contracts now permitted the reinsurance of insurance liability in the form of actual loss in ways directly concerned with the way losses from policies fall to an in-

surer: a) from loss under a single policy as a matter of facultative reinsurance, b) from loss affecting one or more policies insuring the same
risk, accident, event, or interest as a matter of a so-called "working excess" cover, c) from loss affecting a great many policies or risks exposed
to the same cause of loss as a matter of catastrophe reinsurance,
or d) from overall unsatisfactory excessive accumulations of losses in an
agreed period of time as a loss ratio or aggregate excess of loss reinsurance. All of these ways take different forms within the very general
outline given here. For example, when insuring risks or perils where the
sum insured bears no particular relationship to the likelihood of serious
losses (measured by the total amount insured, as in many forms of casualty insurances written for large limits of liability), the excess of loss
form has shown itself particularly well suited, since damages at law have
no direct connection with amounts of insurance purchased.

In short, it can now be said that all reinsurance is written either as
facultative (one policy reinsurance) or treaty (more than one policy), and
each of them is going to be either proportional (pro rata) or excess of loss
(non-proportional). This is a generalization the beginner can rely upon in
reading the detailed treatment of reinsurance given in this book. Beyond
this point, standardization and routine yield to particular needs and solutions desired.

One more aspect of reinsurance relating to professionalism deserves
a word. One who is unfamiliar with the practice of reinsurance may be
struck by the seeming informal and casual manner in which it is administered. As a part of this informality, three principles of professionalism
tend to mislead the uninitiated: the fact of reinsurance as an utmost good
faith relationship, together with the traditional regard of reinsurance as
an honorable engagement and the equally venerable principle of a reinsurer "following the fortunes" of its reinsured. These principles spring
from practical considerations of great value to reinsured and reinsurer
alike which it is the purpose of this book to describe properly. Moreover,
it is that professionalism to which this book has been dedicated by all
those concerned with it—not only in the hope that it may assist those
who would learn what reinsurance is and how it is done, but to serve as a
guide for those who would use it constructively.

In conclusion, the future is likely to bring even greater reliance on
the stability of reinsurers' service and advice to reinsureds in the years
ahead—as values escalate monetarily, as giant risks increase in number
and size, as inflation increases the difficulty of maintaining adequate rate
levels, as loss reserve updating becomes more essential to insurer solvency, and as changes in personnel make it difficult to cope with such a

dynamic future for the primary market. As we enter the Eighties, the relevant question to ask of the system of reinsurance in this country, indeed the world, is not whether it succeeds in its immediate purpose—in being profitable, in being used widely, and in generating a large currency flow. The question instead is whether the society it serves has derived maximum benefits from its services at the lowest possible cost, as measured by a cost-benefit relationship. For only those institutions which accomplish that result will continue in a free market, and the system of reinsurance deserves no favoritism in its competitive zeal to serve its clients well.

This book was written to help all users of reinsurance recognize its sophistications and realize from responsible practice the maximum benefits they fully deserve. All of us who shared in its creation hope that our labors will prove helpful. Of all entitled to gratitude from this writer, my greatest thanks go to my lovely secretary, Miss Ann Walters, whose near perfection on the job and enormous patience with me have served as inspirations for years now.

Robert W. Strain

Deer Ridge Road
Wingdale, New York 12594
January 8, 1980

Dedicated to
students of reinsurance everywhere
especially those at
The College of Insurance

1

The Nature of Reinsurance

by Henry T. Kramer*

The parties to a reinsurance contract are insurers, and the contracts they employ are frequently sophisticated. Indeed, they may be as sophisticated and distinctive as the parties wish them to be, because there are no standard or uniform forms either required by law or regulation or established by common preference. As might be expected, however, considerable similarities in wording and form are nevertheless found if for no more reason than to identify intent with commonly accepted principles and practices, and to make specific adaptations or deviations from common practice readily identifiable. Usual or not, these wordings do not readily speak for themselves any more than the practices, customs, and usages of reinsurance do, all of which is mysterious to the uninformed. It is the purpose of this book to remove that mystery, beginning in this chapter with certain aspects of the nature of reinsurance that underly or illustrate its use, value and purpose in any situation.

Introduction

Reinsurance was once described as a mystery not worth the solving. The humor, if any, in the remark served mainly to suggest that few people were in the reinsurance business, and that except for those few, the rewards for the newcomer were likely to be slow in coming, if they came at all. For a very long period of time, this was true. Indeed, the practice of reinsurance as a separate business did not begin until the 19th century. For the most part, reinsurance was something that was done between insurance underwriters. All insurers didn't have access to all risks being in-

*President, The Risk Exchange, Inc., Ambest Road, Oldwick, New Jersey 08858.

2 Reinsurance

sured, and larger risks posed a problem by concentrating possibilities of loss, so insurers fell into the practice of persuading one another to assume portions of their own insurances, as reinsurances of one another. Shares of risk so reinsured reduced loss exposures while also serving as a trade-off for equal amounts of incoming reinsurance. This practice of requiring replacement reinsurance became known as "reciprocity," or the recipro-cal exchange of reinsurance, allowing an insurer to keep the same amount of original premium gained by its production efforts while achieving a larger number of insured risks within tolerable loss limits, or in other words resulting in a better "spread of risk." In a sense, this prac-tice inhibited further development of reinsurance so long as the insur-ance marketplace was well served by it. Yet, as in one country after an-other the insurance industry grew beyond the limits of personal coopera-tive efforts of this sort, reinsurance began to expand, an expansion that included the development of so-called "professional" reinsurers, those whose business was limited entirely or principally to reinsurance as such, and also the development of the reinsurance treaty under which numbers of risks are more or less automatically reinsured under a sort of wholesale agreement controlling the kind and size of risks involved.

As it was, the development of reinsurance as a separate business did not become significant until this century, particularly in the second half. The number of reinsurance persons, those who specialize in it as a separate business, has become large compared to only a few years ago. Accompanying the development of a substantial reinsurance market among professional reinsurance companies, captive insurance companies and primary insurers which have established separate, virtually free-standing reinsurance departments operating independently within the parent company also now play an important role.

In short, reinsurance today is far from being a mystery not worth the solving, but to many people it remains a mystery, or at least associated with a number of concepts and practices that do not quickly speak for themselves. But it is something eminently worth solution, both because it is now a large business and also because of the constructive, imaginative ways in which reinsurance can be used to achieve results nothing else will do as well.

The history of reinsurance is an interesting subject, because its development has followed the growth and development of insurance. Reinsurance is the creature of insurance. "Here," an insurer has said, "is something I want to do as an insurer." "Here," a reinsurer has said, "is the way reinsurance can help you do it." Reinsurance is first and foremost an arrangement between those who assume insurable risk. It is a means of distributing risk in ways that support and enhance the activity of insurers. The act of reinsuring part or all of a risk does not make that risk more or less liable to suffer loss. It has the effect of sharing the original amount of loss with another insurer. This, in turn, means that reinsurance is mainly concerned with the large risk, as well as large accumulations of risk subject to common loss. From this, the concept of reinsurance as a source of what has come to be called "underwriting capacity" follows directly. As presently used and understood, underwriting capacity is a more subtle thing than a given amount of dollars a reinsurer is willing to assume on an individual risk. By assuming portions of an insurer's business, a very close continuing business interest in common has been created between the reinsurer and the insurer because they are both at risk on the same thing. The relationship of the reinsurer to the reinsured extends to all areas of the insurer's insurance operations one way or another, as they take place with respect to reinsured policies.

In the end, the need of insurers for a broad kind of operational "capacity," the capacity to sustain and survive catastrophic losses, the capacity to achieve statistically predictable loss behaviour, the capacity to carry costs of acquiring larger and larger amounts of new insurance, these and other interests in common set the stage for what reinsurance is and what reinsurers do today.

It is the purpose of this chapter to consider the inherent nature of reinsurance as the first and logical place to start in the solution of what these alleged mysteries of reinsurance might be. Reinsurance is not the only way by which the things it is used to do can, in fact, be done, but there are differences, indeed frequently significant differences, between these choices. So a discussion of the nature of reinsurance begins with its definition. Its definition is made meaningful and easier to understand by comparisons of reinsurance to insurance, certain ways of doing insurance, and other comparisons and distinctions which, if ignored, can easily and incorrectly blur or distort the true nature of the subject of this book. Reinsurance is not a dead language. All that can be done with reinsurance has not been done. New applications, conceptual enhancements — in short, new ideas in reinsurance remain to be discovered or conceived. The development of reinsurance will not cease until the development of insurance has ceased and become an automatic routine, and that is so unlikely as not to be worth considering. In the years to come, as always, the development of reinsurance will be within an insurance context. But just as the increasing sophistication of a variety of insurance forms and practices has caused greater individuality of reinsurance forms and practices, so will the future development of reinsurance continue to appear less like insurance. Yet, the basic definition of what reinsurance is as a concept and as a legal distinction from insurance has hardly changed at all during the hundreds of years it has been practiced. These basic concepts and principles are not likely to change in the future, however the forms in which they appear do change.

It is in this context, that of the unchanging nature of reinsurance, that the bulk of this chapter is to be considered. It is, of course, useful and necessary to explain aspects of reinsurance in terms of modern-day, perhaps temporary, applications in order to make any discussion of the generalities of reinsurance meaningful in terms of current practice. It is suggested, however, that a good working understanding of the inherent nature of reinsurance is essential to its use today and always will be as long as private enterprise in a free society has a need for insurance as we know it.

What is Reinsurance?

REINSURANCE AND INSURANCE

Reinsurance is a form of insurance. As such, a contract of reinsurance is an insurance contract. It is so established in law, and the general characteristics that distinguish a contract of insurance from other contracts are required and found in contracts of reinsurance. One of those essential elements of an insurance is that the insured must have an insurable interest in the subject of the insurance. Discussed in more detail later in this chapter, it is the insurable interest of the party being reinsured that constitutes the distinction between reinsurance and any other kind of insurance contract, and any definition of reinsurance must include a suitable reference to this point.

A discussion of reinsurance begins here because some forms of reinsurance contracts so resemble other policies of insurance purchased by insurance companies as to suggest little if any difference between them except as to specific application. A case in point is catastrophe reinsurance under which the reinsurer agrees to indemnify the insurer for loss suffered under all policies not otherwise reinsured from certain defined perils and exceeding an agreed amount in all. In this, as in all other reinsurances, the losses in question must first have fallen to the insurer by reason of its role as an insurer of others, or in other words under its insurance business, not its business as an insurer. Thus, the insurer may reinsure its losses under policies issued as an insurer, but must obtain insurance as such to protect or indemnify itself with respect to owned property or interests other than those of others assumed as an insurer.

DEFINITION

Many definitions of reinsurance exist. None is commonly accepted by everyone as uniquely correct. When one may be regarded as falling short in some respect, it is usually because a particular feature or characteristic of reinsurance is being stressed. Thus, a typical definition of "to reinsure" in a dictionary will state: "1: to insure again by transferring to another insurance company all or part of a liability assumed; 2: to insure again by assuming all or part of the liability of an insurance company already covering a risk." Both are acceptable as far as they go, but they leave open certain possibilities such as syndicating insurance among insurers, which is not reinsurance. Other brief definitions exist such as "the insurance of insurance" or the "insurance of insurance companies," and so forth, all of which have a ring of truth. A better definition, perhaps, follows: "Reinsurance is a form of insurance, being the insurance of one insurer (the "reinsured") by another insurer (the "reinsurer") by means of which the reinsured is indemnified for loss under insurance policies issued by the reinsured to the public."

The above is lengthy, but it established the following points: 1: that reinsurance is "an insurance," 2: that as such only one empowered to insure may reinsure, 3: that the insurable interest of the reinsured/insurer is insurance liability, 4: that as such the reinsured must also be empowered to insure, and 5: that a contract of reinsurance is properly a contract of indemnity and not a "promise to pay." All of these will be discussed later. All are crucial to a definition of reinsurance. Another, somewhat briefer definition is perhaps as complete and useful, but also serves to illustrate how these various essentials become more implied than expressed as the definition shortens: "A reinsurance is a contract under which one insurer agrees to indemnify another with respect to actual loss sustained under the latter's policy or policies of insurance."

Several points already raised deserve further comment; insurable interest is one. Never fully defined, insurable interest in the case of insurance may be any of a variety of circumstances or facts touching on a person or legal entity including a) ownership or interest in property, b) legal liabilities, c) legal obligations or rights as debtor or creditor or contracting party, d) life or personal injury or earning power, and so forth. The presence of one or more of these things is necessary as a matter of direct interest to the purchaser of insurance. In the case of reinsurance, the insurable interest of the entity reinsured is always insurance liability, something an original insured can never have and which the reinsured cannot have until an insurance has been made.

From this comes a basic characteristic in the nature of reinsurance: one cannot reinsure what was not first insured.

Another aspect of reinsurance already defined is its being a separate agreement from the original insurance, the parties to which do not include the original insured. As such, several additional characteristics may be noted: a) as reinsurance is a separate agreement, the original insurance is not abridged, or modified, or superseded, or strengthened by right of direct access to the reinsurer, or affected in any other way. There is no privity of contract between the original insured and the reinsurer. b) As a separate agreement, where insurance liability is the insurable interest, a reinsurer may reinsure less than originally insured, but not more. Neither may it reinsure that for which insurance liability no longer exists. Thus, reinsurance may be limited in scope, or changed in form or otherwise adapted to need; but it may not go beyond or outside the original insurance, nor may it indemnify for known or final loss that has already happened (although it can apply to possible—but not certain—additional loss from known or unknown past events).

From the foregoing, it may be correctly concluded that each reinsurance is a thing unto itself, separately negotiated, arranged, priced, and memorialized within the principles of insurance generally and the principles of reinsurance as well, which is the purpose of this book to set forth.

The Purpose Of Reinsurance

It is in the nature of reinsurance to share—by means of indemnification—the insurance liabilities of the insurer. Outright sharing as such, by means of separate policies issued to the same insured by separate insurers, covering the same risks and perils has long been known and practiced and still is. It may be termed syndication, or the horizontal distribution of risk. Reinsurance, in this context, is a vertical distribution of risk. In a similar situation, where an insurer is unwilling to assume at its own risk the whole of the insurance offered, it nevertheless does so, and reinsures so much of it in such form as it deems suitable and necessary to reduce its own ultimate exposure to loss to proper limits. Reinsurers may do the same, using reinsurance with others, or retrocession, to reduce their exposures appropriately. There are various reasons behind this wish to limit exposure to loss which will be dealt with directly later, but reinsurance has advantages over other methods and they will be dealt with directly later also. It comes down to reinsurance being a means by which an insurer can assume larger amounts of liability under individual policies or a number of them than its own resources permit, a limitation which is both a matter of fact as well as one of actuarial judgement translated into questions of unacceptable variations of loss behaviour over discreet periods of time, as well as solvency *per se*. In normal practice, it is the credible operation of the law of large numbers that is the immediate concern, initiating the use of reinsurance as well as other essentials of the insurance process. In recognizing this, the question of time periods over which this law is to work is fundamental, given the objective of achieving underwriting profit over the same periods. It may be accepted that unless reinsurers too can achieve underwriting profit, reinsurance will become unavailable, so the question of how much reinsurance to use becomes one of available premium to pay for it as well as the insurer's ability to balance its own portfolio of exposures through the use of various kinds and degrees of reinsurance.

Origin Of Reinsurance

The idea of reinsurance and its practice in some form are probably as old as the commercial practice of insurance. Initially, the problem of insurance was no different from the problem today—to make the law of large numbers work within a portfolio of risks assumed. Put another way, reinsurance allowed the insurer to assume risks in such a way that its assumptions were no longer a series of wagers, but rather insurance.

As early as the 16th century, reinsurance was described as a class of contract separate and distinct from the insurance giving rise to it. It was said then that "the risks of the insurer form the object of the reinsurance which is a new, independent contract not at all concerning the insured who consequently can exercise no power or authority with respect to it," and that it was a "distinguishing character of this class of contract that notwithstanding a reinsurance, the first contract subsists as at first without change or amendment." Both these quotations, which were found in a collection of judicial rules composed in Northern France in the late 16th century ("Le Guidon de la Mer"), are as valid to the concept of reinsurance today as then, particularly with reference to the lack of privity of contract of the original insured.

This is not to say that reinsurance has always meant the same thing in all places. For example, at one time the word described the practice of re-selling more than the original risk for less than the original premium, thus guaranteeing a profit to the insurer whether a loss occurred or not, a practice soon outlawed. Only one alternative meaning for reinsurance is known to survive from earlier centuries. That meaning is now so rare as to permit its being ignored, but reinsurance was also considered to be the purchase of additional insurance on the same risk.

Reinsurance almost certainly grew out of the practice of offering risk to more than one insurer when the first insurer could not accept it all. This practice of syndicating insurance or issuing a number of policies, each from a separate insurer covering the same risk survives today. Examples are policies issued by Underwriters at Lloyd's, London, policies of certain U.S. joint underwriting pools and associations, and the practice of some agents and brokers in placing large risks directly with a number of carriers, using separate, parallel policies from each or a subscription policy for all. However, when this sort of syndication is accomplished today, the practice is usually not a preferred alternative to the use of reinsurance, rather, such syndication is used for other reasons, such as to concentrate underwriting expertise or specially dedicated capacity for the purpose of insuring special kinds of risks.

CONTROL

A significant practical difference between reinsurance and the syndication of direct policies to achieve the same effect lies in the matter of control by the insurer. Because the original insured is not a party to reinsurance, the insurer who writes the whole of a risk and then reinsures part of it retains (rather than shares) control of the insurer-insured relationship. It is also simpler for the agent or broker to obtain the desired insurance for the insured from one insurer than many. Another difference is that reinsurance as a "back up" to one policy also assures same-premium insurance coverage. These and other attributes of one policy coverage are commercially desirable to both insured and insurer in most situations. The desire to use a single policy in place of several or many is almost certainly responsible for reinsurance having become a viable commercial activity, and for the consequent development of reinsurance as a separate business including the development of broad, non-specific forms of reinsurance treaties such as catrastrophe contracts.

CAPACITY

Reinsurance is a means by which an insurer can assume more original insurance liability than its own resources permit, as determined either by judgment or fact. Reinsurance is not the only way the same effect can be achieved, but it is by far the most common way it is done. In the process, the concept of "partnership" or "sharing" between reinsured and reinsurer is present in one degree or another. The concept may be stated as contractual provisions in some cases. and it may also appear as tacitly agreed behaviour and a traditional subordination of otherwise inherent rights in all forms of reinsurance (unless officially stated to the contrary). These manifestations of the partnership concept are all practical outgrowths of desired relationships, many of which have acquired the strength and standing of binding principles (unless specifically set aside).

Behind every custom and usage that distinguish reinsurance from insurance, a practical business reason can be found. This background implies an intimate relationship and concurrence of interests between insurer and reinsurer which is, indeed, the most distinguishing characteristic of this business. If reinsurance were done entirely at arm's length, the resulting costs of monitoring, verifying, and otherwise supervising the substantial transactions that characterize reinsurance would effectively destroy its utility as we know it today.

Utmost Good Faith

It is the position of reinsurers that their contracts are those of "utmost good faith." Utmost good faith contracts of any kind are so delicate in character and so susceptible of abuse that unusual precautions must be observed by both parties in their implementation. Contracts of reinsurance may surely be so described.

As used in reinsurance, utmost good faith means that the maxim of *caveat emptor* has no application to either party in the relationship. Furthermore, utmost good faith in reinsurance is not a duty of only one party toward the other, but a mutual duty each party owes the other. The duty exists with respect to any action necessary or desirable in order to place and maintain both parties within a fair and equitable bargain. In its simplest terms, the reinsurer intends to assume risk for the purpose of making a profit, and the ceding insurer intends to be indemnified in respect of loss when it happens. Neither party may mislead or baulk the other in the legitimate realization of these goals, notwithstanding the goals are mutually exclusive. The subjective interests of each need not be the same, the treatment of each by the other must be. A case in point is the fact and meaning of "adequate disclosure," as an exercise in good faith in reinsurance.

A basic duty of the reinsured is to disclose to the reinsurer all known information touching on the risk of loss. Failing in that duty, the reinsured may be called upon by a court of arbitration or law to grant to the reinsurer appropriate relief in equity. Or the reinsurance contract may be rescinded or cancelled. In the case of misrepresentation by the reinsured, relief may also be had if the effect is to seriously injure the reinsurer, even if (depending on the circumstances) the misrepresentation is innocent. These are demanding considerations but they are tempered by the obligation of utmost good faith.

Subtle gradations in the operative responsibilities of each party within a proper exercise of good faith are encountered according to the kind of reinsurance concerned. The good faith expected of the treaty reinsurer with respect to disclosure, for example, is necessarily implemented in a different way than in the case of the facultative reinsurer. In facultative reinsurance, adequate disclosure is primarily addressed to disclosure of facts ordinarily known at the time concerning the insurance risk of the property or interest to be reinsured. In the case of a (new) treaty, most policies to be reinsured thereunder are yet to be issued, and the underwriting information required to be disclosed concerning them when the agreement is negotiated must inescapably be dealt with in general and anticipatory terms. Disclosure for a treaty becomes a broader duty, in respect to terms of the proposed treaty, its interplay with other reinsurances and the nature of primary policies to be produced, and its probable use in the future, as well as all pertinent information about past loss experience to which the treaty as a whole is likely to be subject.

As practical examples of where the utmost good faith maxim may lead, a ceding insurer may give a promise to take a certain action which the reinsurer may require as a condition of acceptance. Failure to keep that promise would normally permit rescission of the agreement. And yet there are all kinds of promises, the fulfullment of which may not be seen alike by both parties. For instance, the failure of the promisee to enforce or to monitor satisfactory compliance of a condition — if such failure were negligent or if it served to demonstrate an actual indifference to the condition — may either waive the right to rescind or stop the party seeking rescission from enforcing it.

The concept of utmost good faith may be seized too quickly as a lever to enforce one party's will. It is a powerful weapon and should be invoked with care. The point here is twofold. Both parties to a reinsurance have traditionally been regarded as sophisticated and knowledgeable in the business of insurance and reinsurance. They may usually be regarded as equally skilled in its practice and in the interpretation of contracts of reinsurance. On this generally accepted understanding, most of the practical differences in law and regulation between insurance and reinsurance rest. Secondly, the cession or acceptance of insurance liability is not to be given or taken lightly. In the event of voidance or rescission affecting many cessions in force for many years and all losses occurring under them in the meantime, the consequences can be far more severe than the immediate consequences of an isolated violation of good faith. In such cases the complaining party must weigh carefully whether such consequences are justified by the violation, or whether its own conduct contributed to the violation in any respect, in which event voidance or repudiation could very well involve doing wrong through exercising a right.

In reinsurance a person's word is good, assumed to be given in good faith, and it will be relied upon. In giving it, the person is necessarily assumed to be authorized to do so and to be sufficiently knowledgeable and skilled to preclude its groundless disavowal later. Were this not so, the cost of transacting reinsurance would be significantly increased, and it is doubtful it would survive as we know it today.

Utmost good faith speaks to fair dealing. On the one hand, it legitimatizes an agreement to perform routine reformation of mere technical and inadvertent errors in the ceding of reinsurance under treaties before and after loss, but rejects a unilateral decision to cede a larger cession after a loss than would have been made before it. On the other hand, good faith is not a shelter against the bad judgement or carelessness of either party. Yet it frequently animates an agreement to cancel or reform when a reinsurance is shown to be manifestly unfair or unreasonably burdensome to either party, regardless of reason or fault. A party to a reinsurance contract is expected to go outside the literal terms of an agreement in any situation, if necessary, to enforce the original meeting of the minds. And that meeting of the minds must have been accomplished within a full and complete exercise of good faith. It is for this latter reason that arbitration in reinsurance is preferred to settling disputes in courts of law in the belief that impartial practitioners of insurance or reinsurance are likely to judge utmost good faith in reinsurance more equitably than those whose special talents lie outside reinsurance. In the end, utmost good faith in reinsurance is given priority in cases of doubt, and it invariably prevails in situations about which the agreement is effectively silent. By its nature, a contract of reinsurance cannot anticipate every contingency which can arise. If it could, the utmost good faith maxim and others of the same invocatory nature ("following the fortunes," and the reinsurance contract as an "honorable engagement") would have no traditional place in reinsurance.

"FOLLOW THE FORTUNES"

It is the traditional and normal position of the parties to a reinsurance, that quite apart from the principle of utmost good faith between them, a reinsurer shall also and in any case "follow the fortunes" of the insured as if the reinsurer were a party to the original insurance. This seems to speak for itself, but in practical usage problems can arise. The difficulty usually lies in determining precisely what kind of fortunes the reinsurer has agreed to follow.

It is clear that this understanding (which may or may not be expressed in an agreement of reinsurance but nevertheless exists for all) does not supersede stated limitations or exclusions in a reinsurance agreement. Neither is it a means by which a reinsurer can be taken right outside the contract of reinsurance on a matter about which the contract is silent or allegedly ambiguous. This understanding carries no contradiction within it that weakens the equally well established principle that both parties to a reinsurance contract are sophisticated and equally skilled in its interpretation. Instead, "following the fortunes" stems from the need for a guide to certain practical considerations within the desired relationship. Such a guide helps to resolve those of the reinsurer's duties and obligations which cannot usefully be anticipated in specific terms or for which the answer cannot be given in absence of the event.

Perhaps no feature of the reinsurance relationship is more subject to ingenuous exaggeration than the duty to follow fortunes, largely because of the conceptual language in which it is expressed and the identity it is all too often given with utmost good faith. A striking distinction is that 'follow the fortunes' sets a responsibility on one party alone, the reinsurer, and not on both parties as good faith does. The duty to follow fortunes is basically intended to identify the obligations of the reinsurer to the reinsured as those of the insurer to the insured, according to the actual discharge of the reinsured policy obligations by the reinsured.

It must be recalled that each contract of reinsurance is a separate contract, and not an extension of an insurance contract. Within the concept of following fortunes, a reinsurer usually agrees as a specific contractual provision not to exercise a separate defense to policy loss as between reinsured and reinsurer. Otherwise, as a matter of separable interest, such a separate defense could be made by the reinsurer. While this agreement is implicit under following fortunes, its practical application is found in clauses dealing with loss settlements. A practical example of what "follow the fortunes" is meant to accomplish in this respect is found in the case where an insurer formally denies liability to its insured, and in so doing denies liability to the reinsurance involved too, but nevertheless agrees to pay the insured for the "loss." In such a case, "follow the fortunes" as implemented in the normal loss clause would oblige the reinsurer to pay also. How far outside pure indemnification or payment of an insured loss to, or on behalf of the insured, this absolute reinsurance liability goes has never been fully spelled out, because insurance itself is not that cut and dried and because the exercise of proper self-interest of the reinsured tends to avoid abuse.

On the other hand, a reinsurer would not be obliged to pay for insurance coverage made retroactive by the insurer prior to a loss event (i.e., where the insurance and reinsurance either did not exist earlier, or the insurance did not cover the peril or risk concerned). Nevertheless, a reinsurer could agree to accept coverage and to pay the loss anyway in a good faith context.

In a word, the concept of follow fortunes cannot create a reinsurance where none exists. Thus, the good faith expected of a reinsurer is partially established by the reinsurer's duty to "follow the fortunes" of the reinsured under the policy obligations the reinsurer has assumed, while no specific amplification is necessarily to be found with respect to other areas of utmost good faith each owes the other.

Misconceptions

PARTNERSHIP

It is normal and usual for both parties in reinsurance to want many of the attributes of partnership to characterize the 'exchange' or 'sharing' or reinsurance. The quota-share form of reinsurance is frequently indistinguishable from a partnership, but this is the result of terms and conditions carefully chosen to have that effect. This notion of 'partnership' is frequently reflected, but not actually created, in contract language. Examples are the expression of the principle that the reinsurer shall "follow the fortunes" of the insurer under the policies reinsured (or words to that effect), or the normal provision that the reinsurer will be bound by the loss settlements of the ceding insurer, including compromise, *ex gratia* payments, and the like. Such examples do create a community of interest characteristic of some aspects of a partnership in its ordinary sense. But the extent and meaning of such language must be gauged against the traditional customs and usages of the reinsurance business which they are intended to invoke.

CO-VENTURE

A venture is defined as an undertaking involving chance, risk, or danger, especially a speculative business enterprise. This describes insurance and it describes the reinsurance of that insurance. But because the original insured is not a party to the reinsurance, reinsurance cannot be or create a co-venture. One should not be too quick, however, in dismissing the existence of a separate co-venture arising out of the implementation of a reinsurance. For example, many casualty reinsurance agreements permit a reinsurer to intervene or "join" the reinsured in the settlement of claims made by the original insurer, and oblige the reinsured to cooperate with the reinsurer as a result of which a (separate) joint venture in the loss settlement may come to exist. As another (rare) example, the reinsurer may agree to guarantee payment of direct policy obligations of the ceding insurer (such as for an affiliate). In still another respect, a reinsurer may agree as a condition of the reinsurance to provide certain services to the insured which are normally performed by the insurer, such as loss adjustment or underwriting services associated with the reinsured policies.

All these and other actions the parties can take may involve something more than a pure reinsurance relationship, but always as a separate matter. When this extra relationship occurs, the basic reinsurance rights and duties of the parties tend to become blurred. Good practice requires clear agreement and provision for such ancillary obligations before performance if serious possibilities of dispute are to be avoided.

CO-INSURANCE

Co-insurance describes the assumption, by separate insurers, of shares of the same insurance risk, or joint-insurance (it also describes the assumption of a share of an insured risk by the assured). The insurable interest remains the same. Reinsurance is not a co-insurance. This too is established by the original insured's not being a party to the reinsurance. Yet, uncertainty on this point may well be encountered if a reinsurer has agreed to pay direct on a policy loss under "reinsurance assumption" or "mortgagee guarantee" endorsements of one kind or another. Such endorsements, properly drawn, are usually contingent in nature and do not change a reinsurance into a co-insurance, or anything else, before the contemplated contingency occurs.

BANKING

Reinsurance is not banking, nor the loaning of money. However, reinsurance does fulfill a financing function by providing a "banking" function for the amortization of insurance losses. Depending on the form and terms agreed to, reinsurance may have the effect of banking, but it is an effect rather than a change in the nature of reinsurance. Reinsurance frequently will "finance" the growth of the ceding insurer as a valuable attribute of reinsurance when properly used. The financing effect is derived from correct accounting procedures for the kind of reinsurance ceded. For many insurers this financing effect may be the only reason for doing a reinsurance in the first place. But as long as the reinsurance contains the elements essential to it, including specifically the risk of loss to the reinsurer, it is not a loan or a financing contract, it remains a reinsurance.

Risk of loss in reinsurance must be real and reasonably probable. This is not to say that certain kinds of reinsurances are inadmissible merely because the kind or extent of loss reinsured has never happened, or because the premium or commission is capable of retroactive adjustment based on past experience. However, if the terms of the reinsurance reflect a clear intent that the reinsurer's losses shall not exceed its premium regardless of events, so effectively guaranteeing against net underwriting loss to the reinsurer, then the contract is improper. Hold harmless provisions of any kind, so expressed or not, may be enforceable once put into effect. But they are not reinsurance.

The subject matter or insurable interest out of which the reinsurer's risk springs must also be fortuitous, which is to say, outside the reinsured's control. Thus, a reinsurance of an insurer's entrepreneurial risk is as improper as one under which the reinsurer may fairly be judged to have no risk of suffering net underwriting loss. That a general purpose of all reinsurance is, in fact, to enhance the entrepreneurial risk of the reinsured does not conflict with the point of this discussion, so long as the risks or interests reinsured do not go beyond those first insured.

The difference between reinsuring risk of loss and entrepreneurial risk lies in their purposes: the former deals with chances of loss to property or interest of others, while the latter is a guarantee of one's own business success. And business success is a matter of self-created risks and entrepreneurial performance, which it is against the theory of social interest to insure or reinsure (quite apart from practical considerations of moral risk in avoiding or preventing loss). The straightforward reinsurance of certain forms of policies such as mortgage guarantee or municipal bond guarantees may bring the reinsurer into the arena of banking, credit, and performance guarantees and warranties. But the reinsurances of such policies are neither financing agreements nor loan contracts between the ceding and assuming reinsurers, and therefore they are proper subjects of reinsurance so long as the insurable interest of the reinsured is insurance liability.

Security

Reinsurance is not a security, such as a stock certificate or bond used as evidence of debt or property. It has been decided at law that a reinsurance is not an "investment" or security, at least as defined in U.S. securities legislation.[1] The propriety of this finding is upheld by the nature of the risk assumed, a nature falling properly in the field of insurance — not that of entrepreneurship or finance, and not that of the earning power of money or of the future profits of the reinsured's business. In any case, the initial (and so far the only) test of reinsurance as an investment was apparently made in an attempt to disavow coverage on the grounds that a prior compliance with security regulations was lacking. If nothing else, such an attempt illustrates the desirability of looking after fine points of definition when engaged in the reinsurance business.

SYNDICATION

Reinsurance is not a syndication, as syndication is distinguished from a co-venture. Nor is reinsurance the association of parties in a common enterprise. Especially in the case of reinsurance treaties, it may appear that an overriding agreement having the nature of a syndication or association in common has been reached. But it is not so, because the relationship between reinsured and reinsurer remains unchanged with respect to each individual reinsurance of each policy, so achieved.

The reinsurance treaty is animated by actual, individual cessions of policy liabilities even in the case of quota share treaties administratively handled by the reinsured on a summary account basis. This animation occurs even though the precise amounts of liability or loss reinsured may not be known until loss has taken place, and even though those amounts may change as more than one loss in the same loss event affects the same policy or policies.

One may search in vain for a right or duty, created by the act of reinsurance, by which the reinsurer comes to stand in the shoes of the reinsured; saving only such ancillary but separate agreements to do this in addition to or accompanied by a reinsurance.

Special Cases

PORTFOLIO REINSURANCE

When an insurer proposes to stop doing business before all its outstanding insurance obligations have been discharged, a special problem is created with respect to the continuing contract rights of its policyholders.

---

[1]American Mutual Reinsurance Co. vs. Calvert Fire Insurance Co., No. 74L10737 (Circuit Court of Cook County, Illinois, Law Division); and Calvert Fire Insurance Co. vs. American Mutual Reinsurance Co., No. 75C103 (U.S. Dist. Court, No. District of Illinois, Eastern Division).

One way to avoid injuring them is to substitute another insurer willing to assume 100 % of those policy liabilities as its own. Reinsurance is a convenient framework within which this substitution may be done. Here we have a situation where the exclusive privity of contract between reinsurer and reinsured is, at a point in time, to be set aside, because the intent is for the reinsurer to replace the original insurer in all respects. By accomplishing this replacement through a reinsurance technique, rather than the cancellation of old policies and the issuance of new ones, a great simplification and saving may usually be accomplished. But nothing in reinsurance gives the parties the right or duty to supersede or transfer direct policy obligations and rights from the reinsured to the reinsurer without the consent of those policyholders and others whose interests are involved. To the extent such agreement is obtained and the policies (wholly) reinsured in this way, a special kind of reinsurance will have taken place. The true nature of the arrangement has, however, become one of insurance and it is thereafter treated accordingly. As one might suppose, such reinsurance assumptions will normally require the prior consent of state insurance department authorities. In fact, the method is frequently sponsored informally by such authorities when an insurer ceases doing business, or wishes to withdraw from a whole class of insurance with immediate effect. All of an insurer's business may be so reinsured, or all of certain kinds, with many variations in between.

In a similar set of circumstances, when two insurers merge, both companies may decide either to "take over" the policies of one by the other or to continue to issue policies in their respective names, but with the added security of a guarantee of payment by the stronger insurer added to the weaker. Either may be done by way of a portfolio reinsurance. The latter, is, in fact, a one-way "joint reinsurance," as described below, for which no common term of its own exists.

The term "portfolio" reinsurance has a more common meaning, being the simultaneous reinsurance of a defined group of policies in force (whether already reinsured elsewhere or not). As such, it frequently describes the application of a quota share reinsurance or another reinsurance treaty to business already reinsured by a treaty which is being cancelled and which is not to continue to apply to cessions in force after cancellation, as those cessions and reinsured policies "run-off" to the named expiration of each. This usage of "portfolio" is not a special case, and is far more common usage than the others described here.

JOINT REINSURANCE

When insurance is provided within a single policy of insurance which is issued by or on behalf of two or more insurers, with a cross-guarantee of liability between them, the policy is sometimes termed a "joint reinsurance." It is usually so termed when the cross-guarantee is referred to in the policy as a "reinsurance" of each insurer by the other(s). Basically, however, the issued policy is itself an insurance. The insured is a party to the joint reinsurance policy and as such has the right of direct action against all or any of the insurers involved. The insured is not a party to the reinsurance agreement between the insurers, however, and has no right of selective direct action against anyone under it *as reinsurers*. The reinsurance agreement animating this kind of arrangement will usually have current effect through achieving an agreed distribution of premium and loss among joint insurers, and it will always have the contingent effect of requiring the other joint reinsurers to make good on the default of any one of them.

Rarely defined adequately, joint reinsurance is a kind of insurance cited in some insurance statutes. The citation is of particular interest because it appears in the context of bringing this form of "reinsurance" back under the rate and policy form regulatory provisions applicable to insurance, but not ordinary reinsurance. Joint reinsurance differs from portfolio reinsurance in that it contemplates new as well as renewal policies running full term, as well as that the parties to it reinsure each other with respect to their interests in the same policies.

CUT-THROUGH ENDORSEMENTS

In many states, reinsurers are permitted to make payments direct to claimants or any other party having an insurable interest in the original insurance (usually a mortgagee) rather than paying such claims to the estate or liquidator of a bankrupt reinsured. The direct payments are accomplished by separate agreements, typical titles of which are "cut-through" or "mortgagee assumption" endorsements. The cut-through endorsement is so named, because it "cuts through" the usual route of claim payment from reinsurer-to-insurer, and substitutes instead reinsurer-to-claimant. By whatever name, the forms are issued by the reinsurer or on its behalf to such payees in advance. These endorsements usually are contingent upon the insurer being unable to pay claims, but there is no standard form. The use of cut-through endorsements occurs only on request of mortgagees or some insureds, and is a practice which ceding insurers would rather avoid.

The strict legalities of cut-through endorsements cannot be generalized, because the wordings vary and must be judged on their own merits. Many have appeared to contain the seeds of future conflict with existing law or the rights of others, depending on the circumstances at the time. But the contingencies provided against and actual disputes arising therefrom have not occurred with sufficient frequency to serve as reliable precedent. Inasmuch as the effect of such endorsements may run from merely paying the same amounts to someone other than a liquidator, to becoming in fact a direct insurer of the holder of such an endorsement, the reinsurer is well advised to use care in wording, issuing and keeping track of them.

AGENCY REINSURANCE

Agency or "general agency" reinsurance is worth noting, because its title erroneously suggests that an insurance agent can either reinsure or be reinsured. While an agent may bind insurance on behalf of an insurer and so give (the insured) the impression of issuing insurance, the agent cannot assume insurance liabilities as such. Therefore, the agent can neither insure nor reinsure, and has no insurable interest in the insurance liability of its issuing company.

An agency reinsurance is a normal contract of reinsurance between an insurer and a reinsurer that is confined to business produced by a named agent of the ceding insurer, and is usually generated by that agent and administered directly with the reinsurer, with permission of the insurer. While there are other reasons for the practice, the principal intent is to allow the agent to issue larger policies than the insurer would otherwise permit for that agent, or for any agent. Usually, agency reinsurance is written as proportional reinsurance on property or other first-party insurances. So doing gives the effect desired, that of limiting the effective amount of insurance (issued by the agent) to a stipulated company maximum with respect to the usual gross policy or risk capacity normally available to the insurer with or without other available reinsurance of its own.

Properly arranged, agency reinsurance is a valid and correct form as herein defined. For such an agreement to be proper, it is necessary only to verify that the normal rights and obligations of the ceding insurer and reinsurer, however modified by delegation, nevertheless remain. The agent must possess authority from the ceding company to initiate and execute cessions in the company's name and on its behalf. Unless the agent is authorized in all necessary respects to act for the ceding insurer, the reinsurance agreement is defective.

CO-REINSURANCE

As a term, "co-reinsurance" describes the relationship between more than one reinsurer sharing the same cession, or cessions under the same treaty or facultative cession. The relationship may be applied to a joint assumption (i.e., each reinsurer for all) but is more commonly used for separate (concurrent) assumptions (i.e., each reinsurer for itself and not one for the others). Either way, co-reinsurance is usually made on identical terms and conditions applying to each cession.

RETROCESSION

A retrocession is a reinsurance of reinsurance liability, which is to say that one reinsurer assumes the reinsurance obligations already assumed by another reinsurer. All the definitions of reinsurance apply to retrocession, which may be used to describe any number of reinsurances of the same reinsurance. Thus, if a retrocession is in turn reinsured, it becomes known as the "first" retrocession. If reinsured again, the "second", and so on. The ceding reinsurer is called the "retrocedent" and the assuming reinsurer the "retrocessionaire." These two are designated "first," "second," retrocessionnaire, etc., just as the cession is a "first," "second," etc., retrocession. Retrocessions need not follow the form of the original reinsurance any more than that reinsurance must follow the form of the insurer. Frequently they won't.

Who May Reinsure?

AUTHORITY TO REINSURE

Terminology in insurance and reinsurance is loose and capable of serious misconstruction if care is not taken. For example, the question "Who may reinsure?" may refer to who may cede reinsurance to another (or reinsure someone else). Ordinarily, the powers to cede and assume reinsurance co-exist as a general proposition, but not always. The power to cede reinsurance is generally implicit in the right to insure and assume the insurance liabilities of doing so. The insurable interest created in the form of insurance liability taken by the insurer becomes as much a proper subject for reinsurance as the value of real property owned by an insured in the case of insurance. Statutory, regulatory, or charter restrictions on the assumption of reinsurance are rare, but the power to assume reinsurance ought not to be taken for granted. In all cases, however, an insurer may not reinsure with others those kinds of insurance its charter or license would not permit to be insured. While it is beyond the scope of this work to detail the limitations on ceding and assuming reinsurance, most of those limitations which continue to exist are archaic and disappearing. The trend is to afford the free exchange of reinsurance, including the easing of qualifications for authorized status of foreign and alien reinsurers. On the international scene, reinsurance flows easily and freely across the borders of most countries, including the U.S., because underwriting capacity is a demanding mistress and cannot be created by an act of will.

The basic power to cede or assume reinsurance in any regulatory jurisdiction lies first in those corporations, associations, syndicates or other entities authorized to do an insurance business as defined in that jurisdiction. Such definitions of insurance are essentially the same in all jurisdictions in the U.S., and the key is the power to assume risk or indemnify as an insurer. Without that capability, the power to reinsure does not exist. Inasmuch as reinsurance is a contract of insurance, the company chartered only to do a reinsurance business must have the underlying powers of an insurance company, and will ordinarily be obliged to meet the same qualifications.

This is not to say that some plans or arrangements erroneously described as reinsurance are not put forward sometimes by non-insurers. With such plans, the word "reinsurance" is intended merely to describe an objective or procedure comparable to that of a true reinsurance. The exception is the governmental body which has empowered itself to act as a reinsurer, in which case the distinction is merely technical as between private and public reinsurance. "Reinsurance" plans put forward by financial organizations such as factoring firms are rare, but they must not be confused with true reinsurance. At the same time, reinsurances put forward by pools, associations, and other underwriting or servicing organizations or affiliations of insurers or reinsurers, are usually true reinsurances even though the named reinsured or policy issuing organization may not in its own right be an insurer or reinsurer. If it is a true reinsurance (and not an insurance or something else), a study of the wording in the agreement will show the power to cede or assume running from or to the insurers or reinsurers comprising the issuing organization, in one way or another.

For the U.S. reinsurer ceding business to an alien reinsurer from outside this country, the only considerations are those attached to "unauthorized" reinsurance and (depending on applicable tax conventions between a given country and the U.S.A.) the requirement that a 1 % federal tax on such premiums be paid. For the U.S. reinsurer assuming alien business, the only considerations are that the reinsurance be of a kind that does not take the reinsurer outside its powers in the U.S. Compliance with the other country's laws or regulations, even if not enforceable at the time, is nevertheless good business against the possibility that a more direct presence in that country may be desired later.

To sum up, the power to cede or assume reinsurance generally walks hand-in-hand with the power to insure. A carrier may bar itself from either. In any case, just as a reinsurer cannot reinsure that which was not first insured, neither can an insurer assume as reinsurance any kinds of insurance it has not been given powers to insure. Exceptions to the latter exist in some states, however, for life insurance companies.

New York Insurance Exchange

As this chapter was in preparation, the New York Insurance Exchange was also in the course of being organized. A creature of the New York Legislature, the New York Insurance Exchange is intended to be a market for insurance and reinsurance of all kinds, except that the kinds of insurance that may be transacted are limited to risks located entirely outside the United States, and those submitted to insurers under Section 168-d of the New York Insurance Law (the so-called Free Trade Zone) and rejected by them. As such, the New York Insurance Exchange, when operational, will be of direct interest to those interested in reinsurance as a reinsurance marketplace, the ultimate nature and significance of which cannot be meaningfully described now. Generally speaking, the Exchange is being modeled on Underwriters at Lloyd's, London, with underwriting members and recognized brokers transacting business with one another under its rules.

However, certain exemptions and regulations from New York insurance law that have already been promulgated deserve mention here. It has been established that   1) while a licensed insurer (or reinsurer) in New York, or in any other state or country may not be an underwriting member of this Exchange,   2) a licensed insurer may form or own a subsidiary corporation for the purpose, and   3) that when such a corporation (formed as a subsidiary of a licensed insurer or by anyone else) is admitted as an underwriting member of the Exchange, such admission will not constitute authorization or licensure for it to transact an insurance business in the state of New York (and, probably, anywhere else as a result).

On its face, this legalism would seem to contradict what has been said about the required power to insure as a prerequisite to the ability to reinsure. On closer examination, however, the meaning of these regulations may be seen as unexceptional in this respect. The assumptions of liability as reinsurance by underwriting members of the Exchange are to be done as specially authorized actions of the Exchange and under its authority, a concept quite clearly supported by a provision in the legislation establishing the Exchange, that reinsurances arranged there will be "authorized" reinsurances (see directly below) in the state of New York. In short, it is the Exchange itself that has been given the power to reinsure, which is exercised by its underwriting members writing through the Exchange, powers those members may not exercise in any other way because they do not possess any powers to insure or reinsure in their own right.

Authorized vs. Unauthorized Insurance

An insurer (or reinsurer) is automatically "authorized" in its domiciliary state where it was organized or incorporated, and where it is (first) licensed for the purpose. In that state, it is referred to as a domestic insurer. If the insurer conducts business in other states, it is known there as a foreign insurer. And if the insurer is domiciled outside the U.S., it is then called an alien insurer. In this context, a U.S. branch of an alien insurer gives that insurer the status of a domestic insurer in the state where it was entered and (first) licensed in the U.S., and the status of a foreign insurer in other States — all as respects business transacted in the U.S. by that U.S. branch.

The significance of a reinsurer's authorized status in any state is that ceded reinsurance transactions with that reinsurer (with particular reference to undischarged liabilities) are recognized as valid by that state. More specifically, in all states and the District of Columbia, a ceding company reinsuring with an authorized reinsurer is permitted to reduce its gross liabilities for unearned premiums and for unpaid losses and loss expenses, to show reinsurance losses recoverable on paid losses as a valid asset, to recognize unearned reinsurance ceded commissions received as deductions from acquisition expenses, and to recognize all other transactions allocable to pertinent reinsurance transactions. But the reductions are permitted only if the reinsurer is authorized and if the actual dollar reduction in those liabilities (or offset to assets) is carried and reported to the same state(s) by the authorized reinsurer as a liability or liabilities of its own.

Further, in complying with the general requirement that an insurer may not carry an amount of insurance on any risk in excess of 10 % of its policyholder surplus, only authorized reinsurance in force is recognized as a valid reduction to such gross policy sums insured. For example, an insurer with $10 million in policyholder surplus may insure a single risk for more than $1 million, but only if the surplus or excess is reinsured by an authorized reinsurer.

In brief, the effect of authorized reinsurance (with respect to gross policy obligations and liabilities) when the ceding insurer reports its financial condition is the same as if the reinsured portions of policies had not been insured in the first place, while the effect of unauthorized reinsurance on the undischarged liabilities of the ceding insurer is the same as if no reinsurance had taken place. The practical value of this distinction will vary according to the circumstances of the ceding insurer and the kind of reinsurance concerned, with particular reference to the financing effects of authorized reinsurance discussed elsewhere. Ordinarily, as a practical matter of acceptability, authorization in all states is essential for any reinsurer wishing to conduct a substantial business.

The principal accounting effects of authorized reinsurance (i.e., the reductions allowed the ceding insurer for unearned premiums, unpaid claims, etc., on reinsurance ceded) may in large part be achieved when ceding reinsurance to an unauthorized reinsurer — if that reinsurer is willing to leave or provide sums or assets on deposit with the ceding company as offsetting assets to liabilities that could otherwise have been reduced. The deposit practice is commonplace in reinsurance overseas where the exact counterpart of authorized reinsurance does not exist.

However, while this "funds held for offset" alternative goes a long way to duplicate the effects of authorized reinsurance, it will not go the whole way. To the extent reinsurance is required to reduce net exposures in order to comply with statutory limitations of risk (10% of policyholder surplus), actual funds held for unauthorized reinsurance either may not satisfy the limitation or would be impractical because of the amounts required for all such risks. A further disadvantage is that funds to be held for offset have to be made available as needed, and practical difficulties may impede or delay such availability beyond critical dates, particularly in the case of large loss reserves concerning losses happening prior to current reporting dates but reported later, before the report is filed.

In the end, the acceptability of assets in any form used to offset ledger liabilities is subject to regulatory approval, and the burden of proof lies on the ceding insurer. As a general rule, anything short of cash or its full equivalent, and any restriction on the ceding insurer's right to dispose of that asset as the ceding insurer's own property, risks disapproval.

LICENSED REINSURERS

At least eighteen states require a full license to transact all kinds of insurance directly as insurance if the same kinds are to be assumed as reinsurance, although at least one of those states also permits a special license for reinsurance only (without power to insure at all in that state) to be substituted. In all other states, recognition of authorized status is generally given any foreign reinsurer without a full license — if the requirements for full licensure as an insurer (for the lines of business desired) are substantially the same and have been met by the reinsurer where domiciled (or, in the case of an alien reinsurer, where entered into the U.S.). It is necessary to apply for such recognition in some but not all of those states. Special provisions exist in some states for Lloyd's type of operations as well as for government reinsurance. Underwriters at Lloyd's, London, for example, do enjoy authorized status in all states now, notwithstanding the lack of a full insurance license.

Even when not required, authorization by way of license is nevertheless frequently desirable for a number of reasons. A license gives the status of resident or citizen for purposes of recourse to the courts of that state. This status may be regarded as an advantage by either the insurer or reinsurer in the insurer's home state. As another reason, while the right to transact business without a license in person (instead of by telephone or mail) is unlikely to be challenged on the grounds of licensure, the strict application of most insurance regulations requires licenses or authorized status for company personnel physically present in that state.

INSOLVENCY CLAUSE

In the event of insurer insolvency, the liability of the reinsurer does not run directly to the original insured but to the "estate" of the bankrupt insurer. Any reinsurance payments due the insurer are thus payable to its liquidator, trustee-in-bankruptcy, or statutory successor. In the U.S. certain other legal requirements touching on the insolvency of the reinsured must be met if the reinsurance is to qualify as "authorized" reinsurance: such reinsurance must not only be payable to the liquidator or statutory successor of a reinsured but payable in full, without diminution because of such insolvency and without regard to the portions of direct loss settlements ultimately paid to original insureds under the (original) reinsured policies. Without such requirement, which is fully established by Section 77 of the New York Insurance Law, and expressed in a reinsurance contract by an Insolvency Clause, a reinsurer may take the position that it is not obliged, under a contract of strict indemnity, to pay more than its share of actual loss paid by or on behalf of the bankrupt reinsured. In such a case, if no losses were to be paid by or for a bankrupt insurer, the reinsurer could seek to avoid any liability for such unpaid claims. While this result would heavily underscore the "separate contract" nature of reinsurance, the insurance laws of the several states take the view that any such reduction in the liability of a reinsurer to a bankrupt insurer is contrary to public policy and would be in the nature of a windfall to the reinsurer. Accordingly, such laws discourage or prohibit the practice within their jurisdictions, and require specific contractual provisions to that effect, because so long as the reinsurance is written as an unmodified contract of indemnity (as distinguished from a "promise to pay"), the residual power of the reinsurer to fix its liability in terms of actual loss paid by the reinsured remains.

"Authorized" or not, the failure of a reinsurer does not diminish or vacate a (solvent) ceding insurer's liability for gross loss payable to its insureds (to the extent that reinsurance recovery on such losses cannot be made). Further, in the event a bankrupt reinsurer is also engaged in the insurance business, it is likely that its direct insureds will be given priority (total or partial) over its reinsureds in the distribution of assets against outstanding claims.

The above possibilities have been overshadowed by the institution of so-called guarantee funds in various states which are to pay the unpaid claims of citizens or residents in that state in full. Such funds pre-empt the filing of claims against a bankrupt carrier's estate for (gross) unpaid insurance losses, but as yet they do not honor claims against a bankrupt reinsurer made by anyone. This partiality is a practical recognition of the priority mentioned and, as such, an acceptance of the practical distinctions between reinsurance and other forms of insurance. These funds have, however, opened the question of privity of reinsurance contract through claiming direct payment by reinsurers to such funds of losses otherwise payable to the bankrupt carrier's estate. This usually conflicts with normal insolvency clauses and will ultimately be decided through litigation. The principal issue to reinsurers is that, regardless of who succeeds to the recovery rights of the bankrupt carrier, the liability of the reinsurer in each case is specific to the contract of reinsurance and not general to the estate as well, and that, therefore, the reinsurer may not be required to pay the same reinsurance claim twice.

U.S. Treasury Department Regulations

Whether a reinsurer engages in the reinsurance of surety bonds or not, certain U.S. Treasury requirements are sooner or later going to affect that reinsurer even if the consequences of non-compliance are no more than a certain (possible) constraint on the reinsurer's acceptability in the marketplace. One may begin the explanation with the required underwriting practice which any surety company must follow with respect to bonds running to the credit or interest of the U.S. Government. Under Treasury regulations, only surety companies (insurer or reinsurer) which have been approved by the Treasury Department may issue such bonds. And an approved surety company may not issue the bonds for a gross amount of indemnity or face value larger than 10% of the company's policyholder surplus (as the Treasury determines that surplus) whether the company reinsures any portion of such bonds or not. Out of this general requirement three consequences flow. First, if the reinsurer desires to reinsure surety and fidelity business generally, its reinsureds are likely to want to issue such bonds running to the credit or interest of the U.S. Government, and will look to their reinsurers for capacity on these as well as other kinds of bonds. Some are going to exceed the "Treasury limit" of the reinsured (i.e., 10% of surplus as fixed by the Treasury). As the surety cannot issue a bond in excess of that limit regardless of reinsurance, the reinsurer will usually be asked to issue its own bond as co-surety (up to its Treasury limit). So the reinsurer needs to be approved as a surety insurer and obtain an approved limit of liability through being listed by the U.S. Treasury for this purpose.

Second, in determining compliance with the 10% of surplus risk limitation rule, all other kinds of insurance or reinsurance risks and perils assumed by the surety company are concerned, and where reinsurance is used to comply, only reinsurance placed with approved or authorized reinsurers on a "second" Treasury list will be recognized. As the 10% rule applies to *all* risks — surety, property, casualty, or any other kind — a surety bond insurer will not want to place reinsurance *of any kind* with a reinsurer who is not on the second Treasury list of approved reinsurers (unless there is no chance at all that disregard of that reinsurance by the Treasury would cause the 10% rule to be violated). Some reinsurers, otherwise enjoying authorized status in any or all of the various states, may not obtain such recognition by the Treasury in any case (principally in the case of alien companies — U.S. Branches do not qualify).

Third, to be approved by the Treasury for its second list of approved reinsurers, a reinsurer must apply, showing among other things that it complies with the 10% surplus risk limitation rule on all its business which, in turn, means that its retrocessionnaires must also be on the "second" list, at least to the extent that retrocessions made to them do reduce gross per-risk exposures to less than the critical limit. As a generality, therefore, any reinsurer contemplating development of its business generally across the insurance industry scene will confront the need to apply for listing on one or both of these lists sooner or later.

Returning to the role of a reinsurer acting as co-surety, such bonds may, as a practical matter be brought back under the general terms of a reinsurance treaty by special agreement between the surety company and the reinsurer. But the U.S. Government takes no account of that agreement, since it is not a party to the reinsurance arrangement. Instead, the government retains direct access to the surety and all co-sureties. It also follows that the reinsurer in acting as a co-surety must have full license powers for the purpose wherever the bond is issued anywhere in the U.S.

How Reinsurance Affects Underwriting Capacity

Underwriting capacity is the same thing for reinsurance as for insurance. It is a phrase of art, describing a concept without suggesting its precise meaning, since the phrase itself may be used in different situations. At its simplest, underwriting capacity is the maximum amount of money an insurer or reinsurer is willing to risk—as maximum permissible limits of liability per policy, per insured, or per risk, per event, or even for the entire insurance portfolio itself. The determination of this amount involves many considerations more appropriate to a work on the theory of insurance risk. That is to say, the determination of a suitable per-risk underwriting capacity involves: the particular risks themselves as they may be exposed to loss from other risks insured, the loss exposures as they may affect the anticipated underwriting experience from all risks insured (or any sub-group of risks), and the financial resources of the company available to cover unusual or catastrophic loss behaviour of risk portfolios.

Reinsurance cannot make a good risk out of a bad one. All reinsurance can do in this context is to lessen the dollar impact of a loss, whether the risk was good or bad. Thus, reinsurance can reduce the chances of an insurer's overall underwriting loss in a given period of time (or, in extreme circumstances, the chance of insolvency) when "too much" underwriting capacity is deployed by the insurer in the first place. Put another way, reinsurance is not well suited for controlling an insurer's frequency of loss, which is better controlled by proper underwriting in selecting good risks. On the other hand, reinsurance by its nature is well used to control an insurer's severity of loss. As such the gross underwriting capacity of the reinsurer may be said to have been added to that of the ceding insurer, allowing it to accept more liability than it could otherwise safely assume alone. The underwriting capacity of the reinsurer becomes the channel through which more even distribution of risk is achieved for the insurer.

The control of an insurer's severity of loss by reinsurance is less a matter of theory or convenience than a necessity. The gross capacity demands of the insurance marketplace are unyielding. As a practical marketing matter, most insurers are obliged to accept sums insured which exceed the net retained limits within which the law of large numbers will work, at least over periods as short as one year or less. Viewed this way, reinsurance is a commercial activity that permits an insurer to do what it wants: to issue policies in the amounts required by its insureds. This increased capacity provides the basis for two significant underlying characteristics of the relationship between insurer and reinsurer: the continuing need for the reinsurer's capacity, and the concurrency of business interests between them as a result. This use of reinsurance as a marketing capability is the reason why 'shopping' one's reinsurance among reinsurers for short-term advantage is often unwise.

Fundamentally, the choice of a reinsurance program is in the context of an underwriting and marketing support function. When reinsurance is ceded primarily for other purposes (i.e., financial reasons, or as a source of profit by itself), the role of the assuming reinsurer is changed and a host of new considerations intrude. A full explanation of these possibilities is a subject in itself, but the most common example is found when a primary insurer reinsures so much of its business that the reinsurer is in fact, if not form, an insurer. The use of reinsurance for purposes other than to support direct underwriting activity has many pitfalls. For example, the overuse of reinsurance should be avoided by reinsurer and reinsured alike, either because it places too heavy a burden on the profitability of the primary portfolio or because serious distortions in the ceding insurer's financial statements can occur (even though technically correct).

In particular, the leverage effect of commission-bearing reinsurance should be understood when the proportion of total business reinsured is high. The leverage effect is revealed when the proportion of policyholder surplus attributable to unearned commissions received on reinsurance ceded is growing faster than total policyholder surplus. The significance of this effect lies in the downward leverage imposed on policyholder surplus if, for any reason, this proportion can be reduced involuntarily. Depending on the terms of the reinsurance, such a reduction can be caused by a variety of things. Among the less obvious are downward adjustments to earned commisions on account of poor experience, or essentially the same thing in more dramatic form when the reinsurance can be and is cancelled and all in-force or mid-term cessions as well as new and renewal must then be reinsured at a (materially) lower rate of ceding commission.

Conclusion

Reinsurance is the creature of insurance. It exists to support and expand the practice of insurance as a means of reconciling and rationalizing the demands and characteristics of the three corners of the insurance industry: a) the public need for insurance in widely differing kinds and amounts to be satisfied in a free, commerical marketplace, b) the amount of capital (or free policyholder surplus) and flow of premium available to carry the assumption of risk, and c) the actuarial realities in the predictable operation of the law of large numbers applied to discreet portfolios of risk over arbitrary periods of time.

In short, reinsurance is a necessary and advantageous means by which small insurers may effectively compete with large ones, and large ones grow larger. In the same process both large and small insurers can use free resources ("capital") effectively, and achieve a viable spread of risk out of an otherwise unbalanced and untenable portfolio or risk as (may) originally be presented to each insurer by the insuring public.

For insurers in an underdeveloped country, reinsurance obtained from other countries provides an essential source of contingent or emergency capital for the purpose of replacing local economic loss beyond the resources of local companies. For insurers in a developed country, growth and progress commensurate with the constantly expanding growth of assets and interests in other industries and endeavors in that country and elsewhere is made possible through the agency of reinsurance. Reinsurance, accordingly, has grown with insurance — always according to need at the time; sometimes more, sometimes less. But as societies and economies have produced ever increasing demands for insurance, the use of reinsurance in distributing risk, balancing portfolios or risk, and protecting solvency, has also continued to grow.

Reinsurance allows the insurer to control its own business and so preserve each insurer's development of its own business. The key to the ability of reinsurance to do this lies in the nature of what is reinsured which, by definition, must first have been insured, so creating an insurance liability which, in turn, may become and constitute the substance of a separate transaction of concern and effect to the insurer and reinsurer alone, that of reinsurance.

Because it is the creature of very sophisticated businessmen, created by and for their use, the practice of reinsurance is attended with many informal formalities, evidenced notably by the concepts or maxims of "a gentleman's agreement," "utmost good faith," and "following fortunes." Because the insuring public is not involved, regulation of reinsurance in the public interest exists, but is limited. Regulation is significantly lower in the absence of policy form and rate control, a freedom given reinsurers which underscores the unique, "stand alone" substance and nature of each reinsurance as well as the assumed sophistication of the parties to it.

*   *   *   *   *   *

About the Author of Chapter 1

Henry T. Kramer was born April 8, 1917, in Chicago, Illinois. He was educated at the Sheffield Scientific School of Yale University and received in 1940 the Bachelor of Science Degree in industrial administration. Shortly thereafter he served in the U.S. Navy from 1941 until 1946, returning to civilian life after becoming a lieutenant commander.

His reinsurance career began with American Mutual Reinsurance Company from 1946 to 1951. The next five years were spent with Obrion Russell & Company in Boston as a reinsurance broker from 1951 to 1956, followed by one year as vice president of the Fire and Casualty Insurance Company of Connecticut. He became reinsurance manager for Allstate Insurance Company in 1957, leaving it in 1965 as vice president in charge of reinsurance and special accounts. In 1965 he joined the SwissRe group of companies in New York, becoming president of North American Reinsurance Corporation the following year. He retired in 1976 from North American Re and became president of the Risk Exchange, Inc. ("REX") in Oldwick, New Jersey.

2

The Purpose of Reinsurance

by Robert A. Baker*

Basic Functions

Reinsurance as a technique is capable of being used for a variety of reasons. It may be used for purposes both worthy and unworthy and for risks both insurable and non-insurable. Its flexibility can be a strength or weakness, depending on the knowledge and skill of those using it. Regardless of the nature and motivation of its application, however, all reinsurance must fulfill one or more of a limited number of basic functions.

Historically, reinsurance users have been primarily insurance companies engaged in private enterprise. Lately, however, governments have found in reinsurance a means of accomplishing some of their purposes. It has been used as a tool to achieve certain social aims and as an instrument of national fiscal policy. It is even used by associations of governments on a regional basis as a means of developing a certain region economically.

PRIVATE ENTERPRISE USERS

Regardless of who uses reinsurance, and for what purpose, certain basic functions are provided the reinsured. The first is to improve an insurer's capacity to serve its market (the marketing purpose). The second and third are to protect the insurer from a catastrophe and to provide an element of stabilization to its performance (the managerial purpose). The fourth and last is to increase the insurer's financial strength (the financial

*President, Hudson Underwriting, Limited, P.O. Box 168, Flatts 3, Bermuda.

purpose). Reinsurance literature summarizes these functions as capacity, catastrophe protection, stabilization, and financial.

Marketing with Improved Capacity. Reinsurance is useful for marketing reasons because it enables an insurance company to write policies for monetary amounts substantially greater than those it could afford to write in the absence of reinsurance. Almost any insurer is limited in the amount of insurance it can write on any one risk, since the law of averages makes it safer to write a large number of small risks rather than a few large risks. The larger the insurer, the larger that amount can be. Reinsurance, by adding to that amount, thereby grants the company "capacity" and enhances its position in the marketplace when competing with other companies. Moreover, the importance of reinsurance to a primary company's marketing efforts can be more appreciated when comparing total capacity after reinsurance with the company's net capacity. For example, the ratio of such added reinsurance capacity to the company's net capacity may be as much as 10-to-1 in economically developed countries, and as high as 100-to-1 in undeveloped countries.

Currently the so-called "captive" insurance companies provide a testimonial to the necessity of reinsurance and its ability to provide capacity. These are insurance companies established by non-insurance parents solely for the purpose of insuring the parent company's exposures. Most of these have tended to be located offshore and to be capitalized for much smaller amounts than conventional insurance companies. For this reason their net retained amount of risk is usually less than that of the conventional insurance company which would otherwise write the business (although not necessarily in relation to its assets), and reinsurance is even more essential to its operation. That this captive company concept is a significant element in today's market (particularly for large risks) is borne out by the number of insurance companies incorporated in Bermuda, a center of captive company activity. Such companies totalled 675 in 1977.[1] It can safely be said that at least 75% of these are captive companies. While the reasons for establishing a captive company are many and varied, without the availability of reinsurance one of the most interesting developments in the insurance business in the last twenty years would never have occurred.

Managing for Better Results: Stabilization and Catastrophe Protection. The second most important obligation of insurance company management (the first being to pay all of the policyholders' claims upon it) is to

---

[1]Budget Statement, 1978/79, The Hon. J. D. Gibbons, M. P., J. P., Minister of Finance.

avoid wide swings in profit and loss and to reduce variances from budget to a minimum. This stabilization is essential both for public relations purposes (marketing again) and to demonstrate to the stockholders and policyholders that they are identified with a well-managed enterprise.

Underwriting results can be de-stabilized in two ways — by the accumulation of day-to-day losses of an unexceptional nature and by the occurrence of a "catastrophe," which though not unanticipated is nevertheless impossible to predict exactly. Reinsurance of the appropriate type may be deployed to meet each of these contingencies.

ORDINARY STABILIZATION. This is sought to be achieved in the following ways:

1) By control of exposure-to-loss on each individual risk;

2) By further control of the total accumulated losses arising during the course of the year from the net retained liability on each risk (exclusive of catastrophic occurrences);

3) By adjusting the mix of business; and

4) By maximizing spread of risk.

Control of exposure-to-loss on each individual risk will be discussed in detail later in this chapter. For purposes here, it is sufficient to say that the insurance company decides in advance the maximum amount of loss it would wish to bear on each insured risk and reinsures out the remainder. The amount of potential loss it keeps is known as its "net retained liability." Theoretically, the net retained liability on each risk is low enough so that, if a total loss does occur on that risk, it will not be large enough to de-stabilize the expected underwriting results for that year.

While the loss per risk can be controlled, it is apparent that the company's total losses for the year will be the accumulation of the amounts of loss incurred on its net retained liability on each risk it insures, and this accumulation is much more difficult to control than the per risk exposure. There is a type of reinsurance (the so-called "stop loss" variety) that can be used for this purpose very effectively. However, its use tends to be restricted to specialized lines of business such as crop-hail and, it is usually not available to apply to a company's whole account, at least in the area where profit shades into loss. It may be more available for the purpose of reducing a very substantial underwriting loss to a more moderate amount of loss. As a general rule, however, it is not available for the purpose of guaranteeing a company a profit on its overall operations, since it is not one of the functions of reinsurance to remove all elements of commercial risk from an insurance enterprise.

In the nature of things, the different lines or classes of business such as fire, workers' compensation, automobile liability, and inland marine tend to vary in profitability at any given time. A primary company, therefore, can attempt to stabilize its results by reducing the production emphasis on unprofitable lines and increasing it on profitable lines. This does not require the use of reinsurance, except perhaps to the extent the more profitable business could be acquired by way of reinsurance rather than primary insurance, if that should be feasible for the company to do.

An effective way to stabilize results is to increase the spread of risk; reinsurance is an excellent way to do this. One company may trade a portion of its own reinsurance-ceded program or net retained account for a participation in another company's program ("reciprocity"). If the other company is operating in another country, or in an area not subject to the same conditions which determine underwriting results for the first company, the probable variation in results is reduced for both companies. This is the reason why reciprocity is such an important element in the international reinsurance market. It is not as important in the United States which essentially is one market as contrasted with, for example, Europe, which consists of a number of distinct markets following national boundaries. Even in the United States, however, the practice is not unheard of. For example, a small county mutual writing business only within the confines of one county will usually try to swap business with similar companies in other counties for the same reason — to widen the spread of risk.

CATASTROPHE PROTECTION. Preventing de-stabilization of results arising from the impact of a catastrophic event such as a windstorm or conflagration is a much simpler task than preventing de-stabilization from normal underwriting operations. All that needs be done is for the primary company to decide the maximum amount of losses it wishes to incur as the result of one occurrence and to buy excess of loss reinsurance indemnifying it for losses in excess of that amount per occurrence. The reinsurance obtained should be sufficient in amount to cover any foreseeable loss, otherwise the company could find itself responsible for more losses than it anticipated.

While the company can limit the amount of loss it wishes to incur from one catastrophic event, it is difficult for it to forecast with any degree of certainty how many, if any, such events there might be in any one year. Here again uncertainty may be replaced and stabilization achieved by structuring the catastrophe cover reinsurance so that the company's net retention is either reduced or eliminated after the occurrence of an agreed-upon number of events. In such cases, the events must be closely defined in terms of the minimum size necessary to qualify as a catastrophe.

Before leaving the subject of catastrophe stabilization, a form of catastrophe protection known as a "funding plan" should be acknowledged. It differs from normal catastrophe reinsurance in that the function of the reinsurer is merely to hold funds in the form of premiums on behalf of the ceding company, releasing them as and when a catastrophe occurs. For the ceding company, it is a way of self-insuring (through the medium of a reinsurer) without incurring the federal income tax penalties arising from self-insurance reserves, or contravening generally accepted accounting principles (GAAP).

Under Internal Revenue Service regulations, self-insurance reserves are not tax-deductible and, if established, must be done from after-tax income. This is one of the reasons for the past development of the captive company concept, since premiums paid to a captive were, until recently, tax deductible. Likewise GAAP regulations, as laid down by the Financial Accounting Standards Board and binding on accounting firms, do not permit the erection of contingency reserves for possible catastrophic events. Funding plans, since they involve payment of premiums which are tax deductible, and since the reserves are held by a reinsurer, qualify on both counts. The probability of loss on the part of the reinsurer is less in funding plans than in normal catastrophe covers, but there must be some element of risk of loss to the reinsurer present in such plans.

Strengthening the Financial Structure. The financial purposes of reinsurance are many and varied. Reinsurance is a proven method of increasing a company's ratio of assets to liabilities (with the term "liabilities" understood not to include share capital and policyholder surplus). A company may wish to do this to meet the demands of regulatory authorities, for purposes of floating securities for additional capital, or for reflecting an increase in return on assets.

A simple example will illustrate how a company's financial position may be strengthened by the use of reinsurance, using the ratio of assets to liabilities as an index of financial strength. Assume an insurance company at the end of the year has the following position:

$1000 Assets	$ 500 Liabilities (Losses and Unearned Premium Reserve)
	500 Policyholder Surplus
$1000	$1000

The company then writes a policy for an annual premium of $100, with initial expenses of $40. Immediately the assets increase by $60 (the amount of cash actually received by the company), while the entire $100 premium must be put into the unearned premium reserve. The initial expenses must decrease surplus, leaving the picture:

$1060 Assets	$ 600 Liabilities
	460 Surplus
$1060	$1060

The ratio of assets to liabilities has decreased from 2:1 to 1.77:1.

However, if the company decides to reinsure 50% of that policy when it is written, then its assets will increase by only $30, while its liabilities will decrease by $50, and surplus increase by the $20 commission allowed by the reinsurer, giving the following situation:

$1030 Assets	$ 550 Liabilities
	480 Surplus
$1030	$1030

The ratio of assets to liabilities has improved from 1.77:1 to 1.87:1.

While the above example illustrated the effect of reinsuring new business, the same result will be obtained by reinsuring existing business. For example, say the position of the company as at December 31st is as follows:

$1000 Assets	$ 300 Loss Reserves
	200 Unearned Premium Reserve
	500 Surplus
$1000	$1000

If the company decides to reinsure 50% of its business, and is allowed a commission of 40% by the reinsurer, the unearned premium reserve would go down by $100, the surplus would go up by the commission allowed of $40, and the assets would decrease by $60, resulting as follows:

$ 940 Assets	$ 300 Loss Reserves
	100 Unearned Premium Reserve
	540 Surplus
$ 940	$ 940

It can be seen that the ratio of assets to liabilities has instantly been improved from 2:1 to 2.35:1.

Reinsuring a portion of the unearned premium reserve in this fashion is known as a "financing quota share." Reinsurance treaties of this nature are resorted to whenever the primary insurer feels the necessity to strengthen its financial position. This usually happens at the end of the year, since the Annual Statement of the company filed with the regulatory authorities reflects the position as at December 31. Since the effect of such a transaction is instantaneous, the desired improvement in the balance sheet can be achieved immediately. Such a treaty would be dated to incept on December 31 rather than January 1, since the reinsurance cession producing the desired improvement in the Annual Statement must be in effect by midnight December 31. To eliminate the problem of unearned premium calculation, a time of 11:59 p.m. would normally be chosen.

It was mentioned earlier that reinsurance could be used for unworthy purposes, and the financing quota share supplies an illustration of a possible abuse. When government regulators were less sophisticated than now, it was not unheard of for such an agreement to go into effect at 11:59 p.m. on December 31, only to be reversed at 12:01 a.m. on January 1. The effect, of course, was to produce the desired figures for the Annual Statement without actually changing anything at all. It can reasonably be stated that such accounting legerdemain is now a thing of the past, at least in this particular form.

Although reinsurance premiums paid out are properly considered an expense to a ceding company, reinsurance may nevertheless be used as a source of income. For example, if a primary company obtains commissions on its ceded reinsurance that are in excess of its actual costs in producing the business, it has made a profit (known as the "turn"). Reinsurance also may be used to reduce taxes when business is reinsured into a geographic area having lower tax rates than the area where the business was originally written. On a governmental level, the national banks of countries afflicted with a weak currency encourage the inflow of hard currencies into their country arising from the assumption by local companies of reinsurance ceded in hard currency areas.

GOVERNMENT USERS

While private enterprise has used reinsurance to perform the four basic functions just discussed, governments are now using it as a tool to achieve desired aims. It could be maintained that examples of governmental use of reinsurance are not illustrations of the true purposes of reinsurance but rather illustrations of its misuse or misapplication.

Whatever the conclusions on this point, they will not alter the fact that governments find reinsurance a useful mechanism.

Government may use reinsurance to accomplish goals both fiscal and social in nature. For example, a government might decide to reduce the (presumed) outflow of its currency for reinsurance premiums by establishing a nationally owned reinsurer. The typical requirement in such cases is that all or a portion of any reinsurance ceded by insurance companies operating in that country must be directed to the nationally owned reinsurer. In many cases, this reinsurance is then pooled and some of it redirected back to local markets, with the surplus placed abroad. Examples of countries with national reinsurance companies are Brazil, Argentina, Peru, Taiwan, Indonesia, and Malaysia.

An example of a social aim of government is to guarantee availability of certain types of insurance by mandating a joint reinsurance arrangement among all companies for certain lines of business that are consistently unprofitable. An example of this is the Automobile Reinsurance Facility in South Carolina. Other lines of business such as flood insurance may be considered non-insurable according to normal criteria of insurability in the private sector, and in such cases the government may provide governmental reinsurance to private insurance companies to enable them to market these lines of business. Indeed, in the specific case of flood insurance the federal government took over in 1978 the whole insurance function from the private companies.

Principally through the medium of the United Nations and its affiliated organizations such as UNCTAD, reinsurance has been utilized on a regional basis by associations of government in under-developed areas as a means of hastening the economic development of these areas. The aim is to do on a regional basis what individual governments have been trying to do on their own. A recent example of this is the Asian Reinsurance Corporation (ARC), set up in 1977 by the governments of India, Iran, Bangladesh, Sri Lanka, Afghanistan, Thailand, and the Philippines. Initially five per cent of the reinsurance placed overseas in each of these countries will be ceded to the ARC, with the funds invested by the ARC in projects in the member countries. The premise underlying these arrangements is that reinsurance in these areas results in a large outflow of cash. Since premiums are not remitted but rather balances (premiums less commissions and paid losses), and since often the cash flow is the other way (e.g., Australia after Typhoon Tracy in 1974), the validity of this premise is open to question. What is not open to question is the fact that reinsurance has become a key mechanism in the economic development not only of countries but of whole areas of the world.

Limitations of Reinsurance

Reinsurance has many useful functions and purposes but it also has its limitations. The chief of these is that, in itself, it cannot change the inherent nature of the business being reinsured. In other words, the mere operation of the reinsurance mechanism does not render an inherently uninsurable risk insurable. Nor can the mechanism convert an under-rated risk into an adequately-rated risk. In the terminology of the marketplace, reinsurance cannot convert "bad" business into "good" business. While this limitation may seem obvious, some regulatory authorities nevertheless seem to believe that a critical insurance problem can be solved merely by introducing a reinsurance mechanism somewhere along the line.

An illustration of this kind of thinking can be found in the various reinsurance pools for automobile liability and malpractice liability formed in some states during the past few years. In such pools it is typical to require all licensed primary insurers in the state to participate, by way of reinsurance, in the writing of such business, the participation being in proportion to each company's writings in that state. The advantages of such a reinsurance pool would appear to be guaranteed placement of poor risks, proportional sharing by all primary insurers of such undesirable business, and avoidance of other serious political alternatives for dealing with the problem. The real disadvantage is that this approach does nothing to solve the basic problems which cause the condition of non-availability of insurance in the first place. It merely spreads the loss evenly among all insurers. By so doing, the insurance and reinsurance mechanism has been used, at an economic cost to the insurers and reinsurers, to achieve social aims of government.

A further limitation of reinsurance is that it is capable of being misused or overused ("dollar-swapping") if the ceding company and the reinsurer are not sufficiently knowledgeable about their business. For example, for reinsurance written on an excess of loss basis, the retention of the primary company should always be set at the point where the size of the loss begins to be unpredictable. Losses below that point should be treated as normal costs of doing business. Otherwise, the primary company will find itself ultimately paying back those losses plus the reinsurer's costs as well.

Another limitation of reinsurance is its vulnerability to being used for improper or even fraudulent purposes. Through reinsurance, liquid funds can be siphoned by unscrupulous operators from one insurer they control to another, for illegal purposes. Reinsurance can also be used as a device to bilk reinsurers and others of funds. An example of the latter was the Equity Funding case in California a few years ago, involving life insurance policies fraudulently created and "placed" with life reinsurers in return for financial "advances." The fraud continued for some time until detected, involved millions of dollars and dozens of companies, and was perpetrated by the collusion of many employees of that company acting in concert.

Finally, the question arises as to whether there are any kinds of insurance being sold in the marketplace that are not proper subjects for the techniques of reinsurance (i.e., pure financial guarantees where the ability or willingness to pay a debt is being insured). The question of what is a proper insurable risk is a thorny one, and it is safe to say that the actions of the marketplace in this connection do not necessarily accord with the theories of academicians. Reinsurance as a technique can be applied just as readily to a form of insurance conceptually unsound as to a form about which there is no disagreement, and this may be regarded either as a limitation or as an advantage. How one feels about this will depend upon the extent to which one is a pragmatist.

Control of Exposures to Loss

Reinsurance accomplishes its purposes by controlling first the primary insurer's exposure to loss, and second the financial results of that insurer if a loss does occur. Loss exposure may arise from individual risks or from both known and unknown concentrations of individual risks. Individual risks may be dealt with either by facultative reinsurance (which is specific reinsurance for a particular policy issued to the public by a primary insurer), or by treaty reinsurance (which applies to all such policies of a particular kind written by the primary insurer). In either case the insurer's exposure to loss from individual risks is controlled.

Both facultative and treaty reinsurance on individual risks will be either of the proportional (pro rata) variety or of the non-proportional (excess of loss) variety. Under pro rata reinsurance a percentage of the entire risk is reinsured ("ceded") to the reinsurer, which then becomes, in effect, a co-insurer with the primary insurer. The reinsurer receives its proportional share of the premium and pays its proportional share of any loss which might occur, regardless of size. Under excess of loss, however, there is no cession of any portion of the risk — the reinsurer merely agrees to reimburse the primary insurer if a loss on that risk exceeds a certain amount. It can be seen that the exposure to loss for the primary insurer, therefore, is limited under pro rata reinsurance by the size of the percentage of risk reinsured, and under excess of loss by the point at which the reinsurance commences. The percentage of the risk which the primary insurer retains in the first instance and the size of the loss which it retains in the second instance constitutes in each case its "net retained liability."

A further exposure to loss arises, however, from the accumulation or concentration of the company's net retained liability on individual risks. Where such concentrations are known, either facultative or treaty reinsurance can be used. Where such concentrations cannot be determined, obviously only treaty reinsurance is suitable. Treaties that deal with the problem of the company's exposure to loss arising from the accumulation of net retained liability on individual policies in a single occurrence are generally known as "catastrophe covers." They are always written on an excess-of-loss basis.

It is also possible for an insurance company to become more exposed to loss on an individual risk than is called for by its underwriting policy. This increased exposure can come about through honest error in the underwriting department or through unavoidable duplications arising from different production sources. All primary insurance underwriting departments operate according to instructions contained in an underwriting guide (or line guide) specifying the maximum amount of liability to be retained for the company's own account on each particular risk. This amount will vary according to the particular conditions, internal and external, affecting that risk. Misinterpretation of the underwriting guide can result in an "overline" on a particular risk. In addition, an agent of the company might write a policy of insurance on a portion of a risk at the same time an underwriter is accepting facultative reinsurance from another company on another portion of the risk. These overlines can be dealt with satisfactorily by treaty reinsurance if such provision is made in the treaty contract.

Control of Underwriting Results

An insurance company's underwriting results are generally regarded as profitable if the total of its loss ratio (losses incurred divided by earned premiums) and its expense ratio (expenses incurred divided by written premiums) is less than 100%. While techniques employed to control exposure to loss can successfully cope with the problem of severity of loss, they cannot affect the frequency of loss, since that is determined by factors always out of control of the reinsurer (for example, a severe winter) and often out of the control of the insurance company itself.

The problem of controlling underwriting results arising from the frequency of losses can only be completely solved through reinsuring the loss ratio over a certain level. This would be done through the use of treaties known as excess-of-loss ratio, or stop-loss covers (referred to earlier in this chapter). It can also be done by reinsuring the aggregate total of losses in absolute amounts, rather than expressed as a loss ratio.

Since a primary company's loss ratio and therefore its combined ratio (loss ratio plus expense ratio) can be so easily controlled by the stop-loss form or reinsurance, the question might arise as to why the company would not simply purchase this arrangement as its only form of reinsurance rather than utilizing different forms of reinsurance to limit the loss on each individual risk and then to limit the loss per occurrence on its accumulated net retained liabilities per risk. The answer is that reinsurers would not participate in such an arrangement except for a specialized class of business such as crop-hail. The reason is that abandonment of the per risk and per occurrence loss controls would lead to a technically unsound position by violating the homogeneity requirement of the law of large numbers that all risks be essentially the same as respects probability of loss times the amount insured. This would in turn expose reinsurers unduly to loss.

When such covers are provided, they should be tailored so that the primary company cannot make a profit while the reinsurer is incurring a loss. Since the covers usually apply only to the loss ratio and not the expense ratio, substantial reduction of the expense ratio might produce an overall profit for the primary company even though it had exceeded the loss ratio at which the stop-loss provisions began to operate. For example, assume a cover where the primary company was protected for a loss ratio exceeding 65%, while its normal expense ratio was 35%. If the company reduced its expenses by 5% and had an actual loss ratio of 68%, the reinsurer would pick up 3%, leaving the primary company with a combined ratio of 65% loss and 30% expense, or 95%. For this reason, such covers are normally constructed so that the ceding company must absorb a loss (usually at least 5%) before the stop loss cover comes into effect. As mentioned before, it is not one of the functions of reinsurance to remove entirely all elements of commercial risk of profit or loss from the insurance enterprise.

Sharing of Insurance

THE REINSURER AS A BUSINESS "PARTNER"

It is apparent by now that the reinsurer and the ceding company are very much in a form of business "partnership" in sharing the insurance to the public. Indeed, in addition to help in pure reinsurance, the insurance company may look to the reinsurer for advice and counsel in areas as disparate as the following:

1) Underwriting guidance and information on forms, rates and loss experience on lines of business the company is considering entering;

2) Investments;

3) Personnel recruiting;

4) Claims reserving;

5) Engineering; and

6) Acquisitions of other companies.

When an insurance company enters a new line of business, the line may represent a total innovation to the market or simply be a well-established line that the company had never written. Either way, the availability of reinsurance may be essential in allowing the company to take such a step at an acceptable risk to itself. Clearly, the risk of the new enterprise is shared between primary company and reinsurer and their financial interests are parallel.

THE REINSURER AS A BANKER

Reinsurance is sometimes compared to banking, and in fact there are so-called "banking" or "funding" plans, as mentioned earlier in this chapter. In such cases, the reinsurer acts as a banker, holding funds for the ceding company until it needs them to pay losses arising from a specific disaster. The difference between these covers and normal catastrophe covers is that the actual risk of loss to the reinsurer is much less. It cannot, however, be non-existent, or the arrangement would not qualify as reinsurance in the eyes of regulators.

The analogy with banking is usually drawn because customers of banks ultimately repay monies advanced to them, and (in theory, at least) primary insurers ultimately repay to reinsurers any reinsurance loss payments in excess of premiums charged by the reinsurers. While everyone is familiar with the fact that banks expect to be repaid for the loans they make, the idea that reinsurers have the same expectations may be novel. But if one looks at the insurance market as a whole, and over a long period of time, the validity of this theory is apparent. Reinsurers could not continue to exist if they continually paid out more money in losses than they took in by way of premiums. Interest received by reinsurers on premiums advanced and on loss reserves established for future payment is an additional source of income which is needed if the reinsurer is to grow, assuming that losses completely offset premiums.

While losses must not exceed premiums in the long run, they certainly can in the short run, or else there would be little need for reinsurers. When that happens, the reinsurer is in the position of advancing funds to a client, much as a bank. The big difference is that reinsurers do not collect a rate of interest on these payments (although it can be argued that they have been collecting a similar rate of interest on the premiums advanced to them which go to pay all or a portion of these loss payments). Another dissimilarity is that there is no collateral pledged as a hostage to fortune for the sums advanced.

The Reinsurer as a Guarantor

In the partnership referred to earlier, the reinsurer is very much a silent partner of the ceding company as far as the individual policyholder of the primary company is concerned. Most people do not know, nor do they necessarily need to know, that a reinsurer is behind many of the obligations spelled out in their policies. However, in the case of insolvency of the primary company, this cloak of privacy does not remove the reinsurer from responsibility for its share of the reinsured's obligations. In the event of insolvency of the primary company, reinsurance in force is payable by the reinsurer to the company, or to its liquidator receiver or statutory successor. Such payments are on the basis of the liability of the reinsurer to the primary company under policies reinsured without diminution because of the insolvency.

An exception to this general rule is where the reinsurance agreement specifically provides another payee of such reinsurance in the event of the insolvency of the primary insurer. Such a situation may come about because banks and other financial institutions, as mortgagees, are often unwilling to accept policies of certain insurers as protection for collateral unless an insurer is satisfactorily rated by A. M. Best Company, the financial rating organization of the insurance industry. While the absence of a satisfactory rating may indicate an insurer is weak financially, often a rating is withheld only because a company is too young or too small to qualify. To assuage such mortgagees, and to improve the marketability of their client reinsureds' policies, many reinsurers will offer to issue "cut-through" endorsements for the primary insurer's policies. Upon insolvency of such an insurer, the endorsements "cut through" the usual route of claim payment and provide for reinsurer reimbursement direct to mortgagee or other party specified, instead of reinsurer-payment-to-liquidator followed by liquidator-payment-to-claimant. Because the normal route usually results in payment by the liquidator to claimants for less than 100 cents on the dollar of claims made, since other claimants share legally in the remaining funds of the insolvent insurer, the use of the cut-through endorsement is not only more advantageous to mortgagees but has assuaged their concerns about insurer financial strength. Some reinsurers issue such endorsements reluctantly as a competitive necessity, done at reinsurer expense, but still considered a proper purpose of reinsurance.

Summary

While reinsurance may be resorted to for a variety of reasons, it has a limited number of basic functions. These are summarized as providing capacity, stabilizing results (including protection from catastrophes), and increasing the financial strength of the reinsured.

The increased capacity furnished by reinsurance is essential for marketing purposes. It has also been essential for the growth of the "captive" company concept in recent years.

The stabilization of underwriting results (of which protection against catastrophic occurrences is a component) is required for managerial purposes. Erratic operating results do not engender confidence in the company on the part of either stockholders or the general public.

Ordinary stabilization can be achieved by way of reinsurance that:

1. Controls exposure-to-loss on each individual risk,

2. Controls total accumulated loss during the year arising from non-catastrophic occurrences,

3. Adjusts the mix of business by line, and

4. Increases spread of risk geographically.

Since catastrophe protection is purchased on an excess of loss basis, if a sufficient amount of protection is purchased the company can effectively limit the amount of loss it wishes to incur from one event. It may even be able to limit the total aggregate losses it incurs as a result of its net retentions under each of several catastrophic events during the year.

An increase in the financial strength of a company can be obtained through reinsurance that serves to increase its ratio of assets to liabilities (net of policyholder surplus). All pro rata reinsurance does this on individual risks but it can be accomplished for whole blocks of business through the medium of "financing quota share" treaties.

While reinsurance originated in the private sector, governments have seized upon it as a mechanism for achieving certain goals, both fiscal and social in nature. National reinsurance companies have been set up by governments for the purpose of preventing the outflow of reinsurance premiums from the country. Regional associations of governments have mandated area reinsurance arrangements for the purpose of retaining funds for economic development. Governments also attempt to improve availability of reinsurance for certain problem lines of insurance by directing the establishment of joint reinsurance arrangements that spread risks among all insurance companies in their jurisdictions.

Reinsurance has its limitations. It cannot change the inherent nature of the business being reinsured. It can be misused and overused. It is vulnerable to being used for improper or fraudulent purposes. Companies can be stripped of their assets through the improper use of reinsurance. It can even be used to reinsure risks that in themselves may not be insurable according to conventional theories of risk.

Reinsurance seeks to control first the exposure to loss and second the financial results if a loss does occur. Loss exposure originates both from individual risks and concentrations of individual risks, both known and unknown. Both pro rata reinsurance and excess of loss reinsurance restrict exposure to loss, the former by the sharing of the individual risk and the latter by indemnification of the loss.

Controlling the financial results of loss, as expressed in the loss ratio, can be done most effectively through the medium of stop-loss forms of reinsurance. For various technical reasons, such arrangements are normally not available for a company's overall operation.

Besides the functions already mentioned, reinsurers assist their client companies in many other ways, including underwriting advice, and assistance in the areas of investments, personnel acquisition, claims reserving, and engineering.

While reinsurance is similar to banking in some respects, the principal difference is that reinsurers do not have collateral for the monies they advance to their clients as a result of poor experience, nor does the client pay interest on such sums.

In the event of insolvency of a primary company, reinsurers will remain liable for the portion of the risk reinsured with them, even though the ceding company is bankrupt. While most policyholders remain unaware of the extent to which they are reinsured, in certain cases through the medium of so-called "cut-through" endorsements, the policyholder is guaranteed payment directly by the reinsurer for its liability in the case of insolvency of the primary company.

*   *   *   *   *   *

About the Author of Chapter 2

Robert Alexander Baker was born in Buffalo, New York, on January 10, 1923. His secondary schooling was taken in the Father Ryan High School of Nashville, Tennessee, and the St. Joseph's Collegiate Institute of Buffalo. He received the B.A. Degree in international relations from Yale University in 1944 and the professional designation of Chartered Property and Casualty Underwriter in 1951. He served in the United States Navy from 1943 to 1946 as commanding officer of SC-1013 in the Atlantic theater and SC-722 in the Philippines, being discharged as lieutenant.

His insurance career started in 1947 with The Travelers, and the following eight years included service with that company in its Providence, Buffalo, Charleston, and New York City offices. From 1955 to 1962 he was with Chubb and Son in New York, becoming manager of its commercial casualty department. The next ten years were spent with the North American Reinsurance Corporation in New York where he established the facultative casualty department and became underwriting vice president in 1969. In 1972 he moved to Bermuda where he was associated for the next seven years with the Security Reinsurance Corporation, serving as its president and chief executive officer. He also was chairman of the board in Bermuda for The London Security Reinsurance Corporation, a subsidiary of Security Re. In 1979 he became president of Hudson Underwriting, Limited, also in Bermuda.

3

The Bases of Reinsurance

by Ronald E. Ferguson*

In this chapter, the bases or various types of reinsurance will be discussed. Reinsurance can serve many roles, both technical and financial. The roles of reinsurance fall into four principal categories—financing, capacity, stabilization, and catastrophe protection. Some or all of these functions may be provided in some degree by a reinsurance plan. It is important to have these functions of reinsurance in mind as the bases or forms of reinsurance are discussed. After setting out a framework of the various forms of reinsurance, examples will be given and the advantages and disadvantages of each form will be discussed. Having defined terms for an understanding of the basic forms of reinsurance in this chapter, practical applications and the subtleties of reinsurance will be dealt with in succeeding chapters.

The student or buyer of reinsurance is confronted with a bewildering array of reinsurance plans. Many of these plans are described with language that is not always descriptive, and in some cases the terminology is arcane. Unfortunately, the reinsurance business suffers from a lack of standardized vocabulary, as well as practitioners often disposed to coin new phrases or "buzz" words. Nevertheless, most of the terminology can be deciphered once a few principles are established.

There are probably several hundred different reinsurance plans in place at any given moment. Like fingerprints, no two reinsurance programs are identical. Reinsurance needs vary from company to company, as well as within a company over time; thus, reinsurance programs are constantly being invented and modified. Somewhere along the line, each

* Senior Vice President, General Reinsurance Corporation, 600 Steamboat Road, Greenwich, Connecticut 06830.

version takes on a name or shorthand description. Despite the great number of plans in existence, they can be distilled into two types of reinsurance—proportional and non-proportional. The variations on these two basic forms are seemingly endless and often complex, but any reinsurance plan can be taken apart, analyzed, and categorized as either proportional or non-proportional.

The terms "proportional" and "non-proportional" are not commonly used in the United States and require definition. Proportional reinsurance describes a reinsurance plan where, in return for a predetermined proportion or share of the insurance premium, the reinsurer pays a predetermined proportion or share of the loss plus allocated loss adjustment expenses. For example, the insurer might cede 50% of its premiums to the reinsurer, and similarly, recover 50% of its losses from the reinsurer. The important point here is that the reinsurer's participation in the losses is known or set without regard to the actual frequency and severity of losses.

Non-proportional reinsurance describes plans where the reinsurer's portion of the loss depends on the size of the loss. The loss may be defined as that arising out of an individual risk or policy, or an event or occurrence. However defined, the insurer retains all losses up to a predetermined amount, and then recovers the losses beyond that amount (subject to some limit) from the reinsurer. The most straightforward form of non-proportional reinsurance provides for recoveries excess of a fixed retention, say $50,000 on an individual risk or policy. In other words, the first $50,000 of loss from each occurrence will be retained by the primary insurance company. The premium charge for non-proportional reinsurance is, of course, appropriate for the exposures undertaken, but unlike proportional reinsurance, the relationship between the premium and the loss recoveries is not obvious.

Even though the words proportional and non-proportional appear to be precise and descriptive, they are not frequently used in the United States. In the U. S., reinsurance practitioners more often use the words "pro rata" to describe proportional reinsurance and "excess of loss" to describe non-proportional reinsurance. Although the words pro rata and excess of loss are used frequently in the reinsurance business (and indeed throughout this textbook), it will be helpful for the reader to keep in mind the more rigorous and precise definitions of proportional and non-proportional reinsurance.

While in its purest form, reinsurance can be categorized as proportional or non-proportional, it is helpful to have some sub-categories.

Proportional reinsurance can be conveniently divided into two categories, while four categories are required to fully describe the various types of non-proportional plans. Drawing on the published works of Feay,[1] Vajda,[2] and Bjerreskov,[3] reinsurance will be (sub)divided into six general classes.

"CLASS A" — Each claim for each risk is shared in the same predetermined proportions. Reinsurance plans of this type are usually referred to as quota share plans.

"CLASS B" — Each claim for risk is shared in a proportion determined by reference to the policy limit and a line guide. This type of plan is usually referred to as surplus share reinsurance.

"CLASS C" — For each claim for each risk, the insurer pays the amount of the claim up to a predetermined amount, and the reinsurer pays any amount of the claim in excess of the retained portion subject to whatever limit is stated in the reinsurance agreement. This class of reinsurance is generally referred to as per risk excess of loss.

"CLASS D" — For a collection of risks which have claims as a result of an event or occurrence, the insurer pays all claims up to a predetermined total limit for the event and the reinsurer pays amounts in excess of that limit. This type of plan is called a per event or occurrence excess of loss plan.

"CLASS E" — For each risk, the insurer pays the total amount of all claims in a specified period of time up to a predetermined limit for the period, and the reinsurer pays the amount in excess of the limit for the period. This form is rarely used.

---

[1] Herbert L. Feay, "Introduction to Nonproportional Reinsurance," *Transaction* Society of Actuaries, Vol. XII (Chicago, 1960), p. 22.

[2] *Non-Proportional Reinsurance* edited by Dr. S. Vajda (London), published by Arithbel, S.A., Brussels, Belgium.

[3] S. Bjerreskov (Denmark), *Transactions* XIVth International Congress of Actuaries, Vol. I, p. 715.

"CLASS F" — For a collection of risks, the insurer pays all claims in a specified period of time up to a predetermined limit for the period, and the reinsurer pays the amounts in excess of the limits for the period. This type of reinsurance plan is (usually) referred to as an aggregate excess program.

The six classes represent subdivisions of the two basic forms of reinsurance—proportional and non-proportional. The first two classes are both variations of proportional reinsurance. In "Class A," proportions retained (or ceded) are the same for all risks in a portfolio whereas in surplus share or "Class B" plans, the amount of the cession varies from risk to risk depending on policy limit and an underwriting guide. Once the cession parameters are fixed, the reinsurance operates on a quota share basis. The four remaining classes ("C, D, E, and F") are all forms of non-proportional reinsurance, and reflect four ways in which a non-proportional plan can operate. Non-proportional reinsurance can attach on a per risk basis with or without a time dependency, or it can attach on an occurrence basis, again with or without a time element. The two basic forms of reinsurance and the six subdivisions can be set forth in chart form as shown in Exhibit 1.

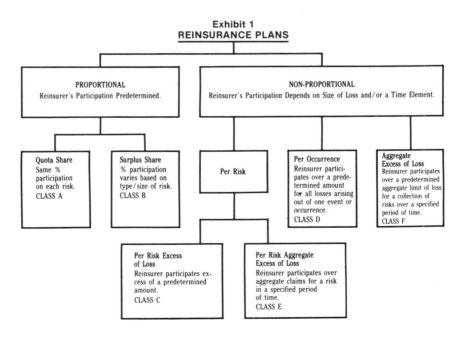

Exhibit 1
REINSURANCE PLANS

PROPORTIONAL
Reinsurer's Participation Predetermined.

NON-PROPORTIONAL
Reinsurer's Participation Depends on Size of Loss and/or a Time Element.

Quota Share
Same %
participation
on each risk.
CLASS A

Surplus Share
% participation
varies based on
type/size of risk.
CLASS B

Per Risk

Per Occurrence
Reinsurer partici-
pates over a prede-
termined amount
for all losses arising
out of one event or
occurrence.
CLASS D

Aggregate
Excess of Loss
Reinsurer participates
over a predetermined
aggregate limit of loss
for a collection of
risks over a specified
period of time.
CLASS F

Per Risk Excess
of Loss
Reinsurer participates excess of a predetermined
amount.
CLASS C

Per Risk Aggregate
Excess of Loss
Reinsurer participates over
aggregate claims for a risk
in a specified period
of time.
CLASS E

Proportional Reinsurance

QUOTA SHARE ("CLASS A")

Quota share reinsurance is probably the oldest and in many respects the simplest form of reinsurance. Under quota share reinsurance agreements, the insurer cedes a predetermined fixed percentage of all premiums to the reinsurer, and the reinsurer in turn pays a predetermined fixed percentage of all loss and loss adjustment expenses.

Quota share reinsurance can be written to cover all of the ceding company's business, or it may cover only certain lines of business, or it may apply to specified areas of business. Quota share reinsurance may be a one-time arrangement designed to cover a particular risk (a single cession) expiring when that policy expires. Or, it may be an ongoing relationship (continuing) whereby, under the terms of the contract, all coverage is automatically renewed until the quota share agreement itself is canceled.

Under quota share arrangements, the reinsurer pays a ceding commission to the originating or ceding company. The ceding commission is designed to compensate the ceding company for its acquisition costs, administrative expenses, and premium taxes. Sometimes, the ceding commission will be set at a level that will more than cover routine expense items, thereby giving the ceding company its profit on retained business, and an automatic profit on the ceded portion of the business.

The reinsurer, of course, carries its proportional share of all the reserves flowing from the insurance transaction. In the reinsurer's balance sheet, its share of the case losses, loss adjustment expenses, and incurred but not reported (IBNR) reserves will be posted as liabilities. In addition, the reinsurer will post as a liability its share of the unearned premium reserves.

If a ceding commission were allowed, the asset items associated with these reserves will be insufficient (to offset the liabilities) under statutory accounting requirements, and the reinsurer will have a surplus penalty. If the reinsurer is "admitted" in the state for which the ceding company is filing an Annual Statement, the ceding company can take credit for the liabilities ceded to and carried by the reinsurer. The ceding company's accounting entries are, of course, the mirror image of the reinsurer's accounting entries, thus its surplus will be enhanced by the amount of the ceding commission allowed on the unearned premium reserve. This statutory balance sheet effect is illustrated by the following examples from a publication of the Munich Reinsurance Company.

Single Cession Quota Share. An insurance company has developed, at the end of the year, $1,000,000 in gross unearned premium reserves (before reinsurance). It wants to increase its surplus from $500,000 to $700,000; so it purchases a 50% quota share treaty applying only to net business in force as of that date, with the reinsurance treaty to be in force for one year. The ceding commission is 40%.

Prior to the quota share reinsurance, the company's Statement of Assets and Liabilities showed:

Assets		Liabilities and Surplus	
Cash	$ 750,000	Unearned Premium Reserves .	$1,000,000
Other Assets . . .	2,250,000	Other Liabilities	1,500,000
		Surplus	500,000
Total Assets	$3,000,000	Total Liabilities and Surplus . .	$3,000,000

Under the 50% quota share reinsurance arrangement, the reinsurer assumes $500,000 of the company's unearned premium reserve, and the company pays $300,000 to the reinsurer ($500,000 less the 40% commission, or $200,000). Cash is reduced $300,000 (the payment to the reinsurer), the unearned premium reserve is reduced $500,000 and surplus is increased by the commission allowance of $200,000.

The company's Statement of Assets and Liabilities after the transaction shows:

Assets		Liabilities and Surplus	
Cash	$ 450,000	Unearned Premium Reserves .	$ 500,000
Other Assets . . .	2,250,000	Other Liabilities	1,500,000
		Surplus	700,000
Total Assets	$2,700,000	Total Liabilities and Surplus . .	$2,700,000

In the ensuing year the reinsurer will pay its 50% quota share of losses occurring on and after the effective date of reinsurance on those policies which were in force at the beginning of the treaty year and for which the gross unearned premium reserve was $1,000,000. Assuming that all such policies expire during the year, and assuming further that the loss ratio on such policies is 56%, by the end of the year all of the premiums on these policies have been earned and the reinsurer's experience is as follows:

Premiums ceded to the reinsurer . . . . (50% of unearned premium reserve of $1,000,000 beginning of treaty year)	$ 500,000
Less commission allowed of 40%	200,000
Net payment to reinsurer	$300,000
Less losses recovered from reinsurer during treaty year . . . . (56% of $500,000 premiums earned during treaty year)	$280,000

Reinsurer's gross underwriting profit (4% of earned
   premiums of $500,000, or company's cost). . . . . $ 20,000

   Continuing Quota Share Reinsurance. The initial transaction involving
unearned premium reserves is identical to that described for a single cession
quota share. However, during the ensuing year or years, the reinsurer also
assumes 50% of premiums on all new and renewal business, less a 40%
ceding commission, and pays 50% of all the company's losses. At termination of such a contract, the reinsurer returns to the company the full unearned premium reserve on the 50% quota share reinsurance, as of the date of
termination, less the 40% ceding commission.

Assume the contract is in force for two years, and during the two years the
company writes an increasing volume of profitable business. With the help
of investment income and stock appreciation, the company is able to add
$300,000 to surplus. The Statement of Assets and Liabilities immediately
prior to the termination of the reinsurance contract shows:

Assets		Liabilities and Surplus	
Cash	$ 500,000	Unearned Premium Reserves	$ 600,000
Other Assets. . . .	2,900,000	Other Liabilities.	1,800,000
		Surplus	1,000,000
Total Assets	$3,400,000	Total Liabilities and Surplus . .	$3,400,000

At termination, the reinsurer returns the unearned premium reserve on the
quota share business, $600,000, but actually pays the company $360,000
($600,000 less a 40% commission of $240,000). The company's Statement
of Assets and Liabilities then becomes:

Assets		Liabilities and Surplus	
Cash	$ 860,000	Unearned Premium Reserves .	$1,200,000
Other Assets. . . .	2,900,000	Other Liabilities.	1,800,000
		Surplus	760,000
Total Assets	$3,760,000	Total Liabilities and Surplus . .	$3,760,000

The transactions between the company and the reinsurer are as follows:

INITIAL CESSION

Premiums ceded to the reinsurer at the inception
   of the treaty, 50% of $1,000,000 gross
   unearned premium reserve. $500,000
Less commission allowed of 40%   200,000

Net payment to reinsurer $300,000

TRANSACTIONS DURING TWO-YEAR TERM

Premiums ceded to the reinsurer	
50% of company's gross written premium of	
$4,700,000	$2,350,000
Less commission allowed of 40%	940,000
	$1,410,000
Less losses recovered from reinsurer	
50% of $2,520,000 losses occurring during	
term..	$1,260,000
Net payment to reinsurer during term...................	$ 150,000

TRANSACTIONS AT TERMINATION

Premiums returned by reinsurer	
50% of $1,200,000 gross unearned premium	
reserve...	$ 600,000
Less commission of 40%	240,000
Net payment to company	$ 360,000

SUMMARY

Initial premium cession...............................	$ 500,000
Premiums ceded during term..........................	2,350,000
Total premiums ceded	$2,850,000
Less premiums returned at the termination of	
treaty...	600,000
Premiums earned by reinsurer during term...............	$2,250,000
Commission on initial cession	$ 200,000
Commission on interim premiums ceded	940,000
	$1,140,000
Less commission returned by reinsurer at	
termination....................................	$ 240,000
Commission allowed by reinsurer......................	$ 900,000
Total premiums earned by reinsurer	$2,250,000
Less commission allowed by reinsurer..................	900,000
	$1,350,000
Less losses paid by reinsurer..........................	1,260,000
Reinsurer's gross underwriting profit	
(4% of $2,250,000)................................	$ 90,000[4]

---

[4]"Reinsurance and Reassurance," published by Munich Reinsurance Co., Book II, (New York, 1963).

Effects. *Statutory Underwriting Results.* As noted in the above examples, the cession of reinsurance on a written basis with a ceding commission affects the statutory balance sheet. Perhaps less obvious—but of equal importance—there is a similar effect on statutory underwriting results. Other things being equal, the statutory underwriting results for a fiscal period will be affected by the change in the (provisional) ceding commissions allowed on the ceded unearned premium reserve. If the (level of) ceding commissions on the ceded unearned premium reserve increases, the statutory underwriting result will be enhanced by that amount. On the other hand, if the (level of) ceding commissions allowed on the unearned premium reserve are declining, statutory results will be adversely affected.

Federal Income Taxes. Taking the income statement one step further, it will be seen that these transactions also affect the incidence or timing of federal corporate income taxes. Generally speaking, federal corporate income tax rules apply to property and liability insurance companies just as they would to any other corporation, although there are a few special provisions outlined in Parts 2 and 3 of Sub-chapter L in the Internal Revenue Code. The starting point in the tax computation is underwriting income, and the other important element is taxable investment income. The NAIC prescribed Annual Statement or so-called statutory accounting is used to determine underwriting income for tax purposes. From time to time, the IRS has challenged particular aspects of statutory accounting, but in general statutory accounting is accepted for tax purposes. Thus, to the extent that reinsurance affects the statutory underwriting results, there will be a related tax effect. Indeed, it is theoretically possible to structure arrangements where the only purpose is to affect the incidence of taxes. Reinsurance arrangements that have a substantial tax effect but otherwise lack economic substance or business purpose will be challenged by tax authorities.

GAAP Accounting. In discussing the impact reinsurance has on statutory accounting and indirectly on taxation, it is important to recognize another set of accounting standards—generally accepted accounting principles (GAAP). Until September 30, 1974, the insurance industry, for the most part, only reported results on a statutory basis. However, as far back as the early 1950's, in filings with the Securities and Exchange Commission, it was necessary to present five-year adjusted earnings statements and two-year adjusted capital stock equity statements which were an attempt to reflect GAAP results. Some publicly held companies included such GAAP type statements in reports to shareholders.

In July 1974, the Auditing Standards Division of the American Institute of Certified Public Accountants (AICPA) issued a Statement of Position with respect to auditors' reports on financial statements of fire and casualty insurance companies for periods ending September 30, 1974. This Statement of Position stated the preferable method of financial statement presentation—to avoid the need for qualification of the auditors' report—was to present the financial statements in accordance with generally accepted accounting principles. Thus, in reports issued for years ending December 31, 1974, GAAP accounting was required in order to avoid a "qualified" report.

GAAP accounting is based on a going-concern concept and results in several important differences from statutory accounting:

1.   Under GAAP accounting, certain assets which are considered "non-admitted" under statutory accounting are "admitted."

2.   Under statutory accounting, a ceding company is unable to take credit for reinsurance placed with "unauthorized" reinsurers. Under GAAP accounting, the ceding company can generally take credit for these ceded reserves.

3.   Under GAAP accounting, a company is required to establish reserves for federal income taxes on the unrealized appreciation of investments and for taxes related to prepaid acquisition costs.

4.   The handling of prepaid acquisition costs is perhaps the most important difference between GAAP and statutory accounting. Under statutory accounting, all acquisition costs are charged against the current period. Under GAAP accounting, most of these costs are considered a prepaid asset and are amortized over the policy (exposure) period.

Since prepaid acquisition costs less applicable taxes are an allowed asset under GAAP accounting, it follows that the effect reinsurance has on statutory balance sheets and results does not flow through to GAAP accounting. Since under GAAP accounting the company gets credit for its prepaid acquisition costs, the cession of an unearned premium reserve with corresponding ceding commission (which commission is roughly equal to the company's acquisition cost) will not have a material effect on the GAAP balance sheet, and the only effect on the (GAAP) income statement is the minor impact of the (GAAP basis) profit (or loss) of the reinsurer.

Follow-the-Fortunes. The setting of the ceding commission is extremely important and can be a complex matter. The original idea behind quota share reinsurance was probably for both parties to have the same potential for profit or loss in proportion to their interests. In other words, the reinsurer was expected to "follow the fortunes" of the primary company as respects contractual obligations. This being the case, it is impor-

tant for the ceding company to allocate its costs fairly to the business subject to the reinsurance agreement. In a slight digression, a current example offers a case in point: extra contractual obligations (ECO's). Such
obligations are defined as punitive and/or compensatory damages assessed
against the insurer as a consequence of the insurer's tortious conduct.
ECO's have, in recent years, become a vexing problem for the insurance
industry and controversial as respects reinsurance.

When ECO's arise, it can be argued that the subject matter of a reinsurance contract is the original or underlying policy, and that only the
damages covered by that original policy are covered by the reinsurance
agreement. Consequently, losses which are extra contractual, i.e., not
arising directly out of the original policy, are not covered by reinsurance
agreements. An analogy can be made to the automobile and general
liability exposures arising out of the insurance company's operations (i.e.,
the company's own auto fleet, as well as its premises liability exposure)
which are not covered by the reinsurance agreement. In the case of
automobile and general liability exposures, insurance companies generally purchase insurance in the open market, or if large enough, perhaps
self insure.

There is now available in a limited number of markets insurance
company errors and omission policies which provide coverage for
punitive and compensatory damages. As a result of market pressure,
some reinsurers have agreed to cover ECO's in their contracts; however,
many questions remain. Are extra contractual obligations automatically
covered by reinsurance? If so, to what extent? Does the reinsurance contract cover only ECO on policies which are otherwise covered under the
contract? Does the reinsurance contract limit apply separately to ECO
and to the original loss, or to the combined original loss plus ECO?
Should they be covered by reinsurance? If so, at what cost? There does
not appear to be a consensus on these issues, and the reinsurer and reinsured must deal with them on a case-by-case basis.

Quota share reinsurance is normally thought of as a partnership, but
in fact, that analogy is not really appropriate. There are two reasons why
quota share reinsurance does not create a partnership. First of all, the
ceding company does in fact own or control the underlying business and
thus has a greater stake in it. The parties then have somewhat different
interests which will not always coincide. Since the ceding company controls the business, it normally expects to receive more than its pro rata
share of any profits. (Profit-sharing arrangements will be discussed later.)
The second reason is that the reinsurer's administrative expenses are
rarely taken into account when setting the terms for the quota share

agreement. Even if the commission is set precisely at the level required to reimburse the ceding company for its expenses, the two parties to the transaction will have different results. The following example illustrates this situation:

QUOTA SHARE REINSURANCE — A PARTNERSHIP?

Assumptions:

Gross Primary Company Premium		$1,000,000	
Ceding company retains	25%	Reinsurer assumes	75%
Ceding company expense ratio	23%	Reinsurer's expense ratio	6%

I.   Traditional ceding commission arrangement.

Ceding Company			Reinsurer		
Net premium	$250,000		Net premium	$750,000	
Net expense	$ 57,500	23%	Net expense (a)	$172,500	23%
			(b)	45,000	6%
				$217,500	
Break-even loss ratio	77%		Break-even loss ratio	71%	

II.   For both parties to have the same break-even loss ratio, the ceding company would have to, in effect, reimburse the reinsurer for a portion of its overhead.

Ceding Company			Reinsurer		
Net premium	$250,000		Net premium	$750,000	
Net expense (a)	$ 57,500	23%	Net expense (a)	$172,500	
(b)	11,250	25%	(b)	45,000	
		of $45,000	(c)	(11,250)	
	$ 68,750			$206,250	
Break-even loss ratio	72.5%		Break-even loss ratio	72.5%	

As noted above, competitive pressures often enter into the setting of the ceding commission. The reinsurer will often reduce its profit potential on the assumed book of business by setting the commission at a level greater than the expenses of the ceding company. There are many other ways to redistribute the profits between the two parties to the contract. Many proportional reinsurance arrangements and some non-proportional arrangements contain provisions for varying the ceding commission based on actual loss experience. Two of the most common adjustable commission schemes are the sliding scale commission and the contingent commission.

Sliding Scale Commission. Assume that a reinsurance agreement carries a provisional commission of 40 %, and the commission is subject to adjustment in line with the loss ratio according to the following scale:

Loss Ratio	Commission Ratio	
63 % or above	34.00 %	Minimum
62	34.75	
61	35.50	
60	36.25	
59	37.00	
58	37.75	
57	38.50	
56	39.25	
55	40.00	Provisional
54	40.75	
53	41.50	
52	42.25	
51	43.00	
50	43.75	
49	44.50	
48	45.25	
47 or below	46.00	Maximum

Using earned premiums and incurred losses, the commission is adjusted upward or (slides) downward 3/4 of 1 % for each percentage point the loss ratio deviates from 55 %.

Contingent Commission. Assume a company ceded premiums of $1,000,000 with paid losses and loss adjustment expenses of $400,000, which in turn are recovered from the reinsurer. The unearned premium reserve was $500,000 at the beginning of the year, and $550,000 at the end of the year. The unpaid loss reserves were $250,000 at the beginning of the year, and $200,000 at the end of the year. The ceding commission was 35 %. The contingent commission is computed on the following basis:

PREMIUMS EARNED:

Net Premiums Written	$1,000,000
Add: Premium Reserve End of Previous Period	500,000
Deduct: Premium Reserve End of Current Period	550,000
	$950,000

LOSSES INCURRED:

Losses Paid Including Loss Expense.	$ 400,000	
Add: Losses Outstanding End of Current Period	200,000	
Deduct: Losses Outstanding End of Previous Period . .	250,000	
		$350,000

EXPENSES INCURRED:

Commission at 35 % of $950,000.	$ 332,500	
Management Expense at 5 % of $950,000	47,500	
		$380,000

PROFIT OR LOSS CURRENT YEAR.	$220,000
DEFICIT FROM PREVIOUS YEAR	0
CONTINGENT PROFIT (or Loss).	$220,000
CONTINGENT COMMISSION AT 25 %	$ 55,000

Administration. The administration of a quota share program is relatively simple since each premium and loss transaction is factored in the same way. In the past, premium and losses were reported on a bordereau (usually monthly) which listed each policy and each claim separately with most indicative data (term, expiration, etc.). From this detail, the reinsurer could develop all the statistics necessary (in-force and unearned premium by line or sub-line; paid and unpaid losses by line or sub-line, accident date, policy date, etc.). However, this reporting format is now used infrequently.

To alleviate the administrative burden, current reporting techniques usually call for the monthly summarization and reporting of premiums written and losses paid by line or sub-line. In-force premium information is supplied in summary form by line, term month and year of expiration, or the actual unearned premium reserve segregated by line or sub-line is supplied. These reports would usually be rendered to the reinsurer on a quarterly basis. Similarly, unpaid losses will usually be reported on a quarterly basis segregated by line, accident date, and possibly policy year. Occasionally, the reinsurer will request additional information such as state, territory, and sub-line.

Advantages and Disadvantages. One advantage of quota share reinsurance is that it is relatively simple to handle. Also, quota share reinsurance is well suited to helping a ceding company enter a new class of business or a new area. Quota share reinsurance can also be used to scale back underwriting commitments to a level commensurate with the company's financial resources. Oftentimes, quota share reinsurance will have a material impact on statutory results and the incidence of federal income taxes as shown earlier.

As a disadvantage, quota share reinsurance can be the most expensive form of reinsurance—both from the point of view of underwriting income and total return. Under a quota share agreement, the reinsurer is developing a profit on each and every risk and is holding substantial reserves with the associated-invested-assets.

SURPLUS SHARE ("CLASS B")

Surplus share reinsurance is a form of proportional reinsurance and a variation of quota share reinsurance. The proportion retained and the proportion reinsured vary from risk to risk depending on the policy limit and type of risk. For a given type of risk, the ceding company determines the maximum retention or "line" it wishes to keep. Risks which have policy limits within the retention or line are retained 100%. If the policy limit is greater than the retention — the "surplus" amount is ceded on a quota share basis to the reinsurer — in such an amount as to bring the ceding company's retained exposure down to the desired level.

A ceding company might have a fairly complex retention or line guide. The company might, for example, wish to have a retention or line of $20,000 on apartment house business and a $10,000 retention on restaurant business. In the process of underwriting the risk, the underwriter will refer to the underwriting manual/line guide and determine the maximum retention or line. This in turn determines the parameters of the cession. Using the hypothetical lines from above, the underwriter would compute cessions as follows:

Original Amount of Insurance	Percent Reinsured	
	Restaurant	Apartment House
$ 5,000	0	0
10,000	0	0
20,000	50%	0
30,000	66-2/3	33-1/3%
40,000	75	50
50,000	80	60

Once the cession percentage is determined (by the amount of original insurance), the reinsurance operates just as it would on a quota share basis: the entire risk is shared proportionately as to premiums and losses. In fact, surplus share can be thought of as quota share reinsurance with the quota share percentage varying by type of risk and policy limit. In other words, the percentages shown in the above example are set by the ceding company to produce the desired retention for each risk insured.

The capacity of a surplus share reinsurance arrangement is often expressed in terms of the number of lines. As noted above, a line is the maximum retention/loss the ceding company is willing to retain/suffer. A reinsurance arrangement might, for example, provide for fifteen lines. If the retention or line is $10,000, the reinsurer(s) will take at most $150,000 surplus of $10,000. Thus, on a $160,000 policy, the ceding company retains one sixteenth of all premiums and losses with the balance ceded. If additional capacity is required, there can be second, third, etc., surplus share reinsurance arrangements fitted over the first one.

Sometimes one encounters a variable line limit—based on probable maximum loss (PML). A company might retain "one PML" and cede the "surplus." Usually, the reinsurance arrangement will contain some restriction on the PML determination (e.g., PML to be not less than 20% of policy limit) to prevent adverse selection and contain capacity. An example of surplus share reinsurance may be helpful:

Assume a first surplus property reinsurance treaty with capacity for nine lines, that is, nine times the company's net retained liability on a risk. The company keeps net lines of up to $100,000, so the nine-line first surplus treaty then provides reinsurance capacity of $900,000. Let us further assume the company has a second surplus treaty which provides reinsurance capacity up to another five lines, another five times its net retained liability, or $500,000. Additional capacity is obtained facultatively on a pro rata basis.

Using the example of a $2,000,000 risk, the reinsurance would then be distributed as follows:

Distribution	Amount of Liability	Percentage to total
Net retained line..................	$ 100,000	5%
First surplus treaty		
(nine times net retained line).......	900,000	45
Second surplus treaty		
(five times net retained line).......	500,000	25
Facultative reinsurance.............	500,000	25
Total amount insured by company	$2,000,000	100%

The $20,000 premium on this risk would then be distributed:

Net retained by company . . . . $20,000 x 5%	=	$ 1,000
First surplus treaty . . . . 20,000 x 45	=	9,000
Second surplus treaty . . . . 20,000 x 25	=	5,000
Facultative . . . . 20,000 x 25	=	5,000
		$20,000

Payments to the reinsurers are reduced by the commission allowance to the company.

Assuming a $1,000,000 loss on the risk, the distribution is as follows:

Gross loss on risk before reinsurance			$1,000,000
Less reinsurance loss recoveries:			
First surplus treaty	45%	=	$450,000
Second surplus treaty	25	=	250,000
Facultative	25	=	250,000
Total loss recoveries from reinsurers			950,000
Net loss to company after reinsurance . . . . $			50,000[5]

As might be expected, commission arrangements and reporting requirements on surplus share business are identical to those described in the preceding quota share section. Similarly, the advantages and disadvantages of surplus share reinsurance generally track those mentioned for quota share reinsurance. The advantages and disadvantages of surplus reinsurance were summarized by one author as follows:

> The great advantage of surplus share is that it enables the company to maintain the sharing principle of reinsurance without the necessity of reinsuring small risks on which reinsurance is not required. Its fundamental disadvantages lie in the fact that it (1) is the most complicated in application, (2) requires extensive detail work on the part of the reinsured, (3) is subject to errors both of judgment and oversight, and (4) provides a false crutch for some underwriters who either fear or lack knowledge to face the responsibilities of their job.[6]

Non-Proportional Reinsurance

Per Risk and Per Occurrence Excess of Loss ("Classes C and D")

Non-proportional or excess of loss reinsurance is probably the newest form of reinsurance. Non-proportional reinsurance was developed in response to a need for catastrophe or high-limit reinsurance coverage. At the same time, ceding companies had an understandable desire to retain as much as possible of their premium and loss reserves on their own books.

---

[5] Ibid, p. 12.

[6] R. L. Braddock, "Reinsurance" Chapter in Long and Gregg, Property and Liability Handbook, R. D. Irwin, Inc (1965) p. 958.

Non-proportional reinsurance responds for losses excess of a pre-determined deductible or retention. There is not a proportional relationship between the reinsurance and primary premium and the reinsurance and primary loss. The reinsurance can attach on a risk or claim basis or on an occurrence basis, or on an aggregate basis (covered in the next section). On a risk basis, the ceding company recovers losses in excess of a retention which applies to each risk or line involved in an event or occurrence. If the reinsurance attaches on an occurrence (sometimes called an event or accident) basis, the retention applies to the occurrence. For example, consider an accident involving a passenger car and an at-fault commercial vehicle insured by the ceding company. Suppose the liability imposed on the owner/insurer of the at-fault vehicle was $200,000 for a bodily injury claim and that the driver of the at-fault vehicle has a workers' compensation claim of $80,000. If the reinsurance agreement afforded coverage on a risk or line basis, the company would have two retentions. If the reinsurance for each line were $900,000 excess $100,000, there would be a $100,000 recovery on the bodily injury claim but no recovery on the workers' compensation claim. If the reinsurance were $900,000 excess of $100,000 but attached on an accident basis, the reinsurance claim would be $180,000 ($280,000 less the retention of $100,000).

A more complicated example of non-proportional reinsurance may help to highlight the differences between risk basis and occurrence basis. Suppose that a company insured a number of properties in an area and had per risk reinsurance of $900,000 excess of $100,000 and had catastrophe or occurrence reinsurance that paid up to 90% of $3,000,000 excess of $400,000. Also, assume that as a result of a catastrophe or event, there are losses on these various risks of $2,500,000. Further, assume the $2,500,000 losses were made up from one loss of $200,000 and the balance being smaller than $100,000 each. To further complicate matters, also assume that on a certain class of risks that produced losses under $100,000 each, there was some proportional reinsurance that allowed the company to recover $200,000. The loss recoveries are computed as follows:

Gross occurrence loss	$2,500,000
Less proportional reinsurance recoveries of	$ 200,000
Less per risk excess of loss reinsurance recoveries	$ 100,000
Losses subject to the catastrophe reinsurance	$2,200,000
Less the retention of	$ 400,000
100% loss of catastrophe recovery	$1,800,000
Less the company's 10% participation	$ 180,000
Recovery from catastrophe cover	$1,620,000

Pricing. Premiums for non-proportional reinsurance covers are normally expressed in either of two ways. A premium can be developed by applying a flat rate to the entire subject book of business, without reference to the fact that some of the risks in the book expose the excess of loss treaty while others do not. In that class of risks exposing the treaty, there will be varying levels of exposures. The second approach is to develop a charge for each subclass of the book of business that has the same approximate exposure to loss. In other words, there will be no rate charged against those risks which do not expose the reinsurance cover, but rates are applied to an exposed class on a graduated basis commensurate to the level of exposure. As might be expected, the process of developing the appropriate charge for rates for non-proportional reinsurance is a rather difficult one. The pricing process usually involves one or more of the following approaches:

Exposure Rating. An attempt is made to measure the possible exposure to loss for each subclass within the book of business. Sometimes there are aspects of the primary pricing that can be used directly or indirectly to measure this exposure. For many casualty lines of business, factors used by the insurer for pricing higher policy limits (i.e., increased limits factors)[7] can be used directly or indirectly. In workers' compensation, the excess loss premium factors used in retrospective rating can be a starting point for measuring exposure. In other lines, one must rely on actual or hypothetical loss distributions including modeling and theoretical loss distributions. Examples are given in papers by Simon[8] and Bickerstaff.[9]

Experience Rating. To the extent that data are credible and relevant, ordinary actuarial rate making techniques can be employed to develop reinsurance rates. The data, of course, must be adjusted so as to account for those things that have changed since the data were developed. For example, an increase (or decrease) in the frequency and/or severity of loss will necessitate adjustments to the data. One rarely has a complete historical picture, and it is important to ascertain and provide for losses that have occurred but have not been reported.[10,11]

---

[7] Ronald E. Ferguson, "Allocating Premium to Layer by the Use of Increased Limits Tables," *Proceedings* of the Casualty Actuarial Society, Vol LIX, (Boston: Sperry Rand Corp., 1972), pp. 43-50.

[8] Leroy J. Simon, "Actuarial Applications in Catastrophe Reinsurance," *Proceedings* of the Casualty Actuarial Society, Vol. LIX, (Boston: Sperry Rand Corp., 1972), pp. 196-202.

[9] David R. Bickerstaff, "Automobile Collision Deductibles and Repair Cost Groups: The Lognormal Model," *Proceedings* of the Casualty Actuarial Society, Vol. LIX, (Boston: Sperry Rand Corp., 1972), pp. 68-102.

[10] Ronald L. Bornhuetter and Ronald E. Ferguson, "The Actuary and IBNR," *Proceedings* of the Casualty Actuarial Society, Vol. LIX, (Boston: Sperry Rand Corp., 1972), pp. 181-195.

[11] T. W. Fowler, "Liability IBNR Reserves," *IBNR*, (Nederlandse Reassurantie Group N. V., Amsterdam, 1972), p. 30.

Self-rating. One frequently encounters self-rating plans (i.e., either prospectively or retrospectively oriented) for at least a lower layer or level of reinsurance arrangements. Just as in primary arrangements, such plans provide for the premium which will be adjusted in accordance with actual losses subject to a minimum and maximum premium.

Judgment Rating. Oftentimes, non-proportional reinsurance will involve exposures lacking credible or relevant statistics and where the only rating approach is drawn from the experience and judgment of the reinsurance underwriter.

In general, pricing non-proportional reinsurance is extraordinarily difficult—for at least three reasons. First, relevant and credible data may not be readily available. Second, the measurement of the incurred but not reported liabilities is difficult and subject to great error. Third, inflation, both economic and social, has a substantial effect on non-proportional reinsurance losses.

The effect of inflation on non-proportional reinsurance is explained in detail in the following paragraphs taken from a paper, "Nonproportional Reinsurance and the Index Clause."

One of the most vexing problems the non-proportional reinsurer faces is the leveraged effect of inflation. If losses are insured over a fixed retention, say $50,000, all losses that exceeded the retention before inflation will, with inflation, treat the excess writer to a double dose of inflation. The excess writer will experience an increased cost on its part of the claim and also will bear the inflation on the retention, for on this type of loss, all the inflation is passed on to the excess area. The excess carrier experiences yet a more insidious inflation effect. Some losses that would not have pierced the retention without inflation now will, because of inflation, become excess losses. For example, with 10% inflation the $48,000 claim which formerly produced no excess loss, would now generate a $2,800 excess loss. Inflation increases the severity of losses that already exceeded the retention *and* increases the frequency of claims by actually creating new excess losses.

The leveraged effect of inflation does vary greatly by retention. This phenomenon was studied by Mr. L. H. Roberts, who prepared a lengthy, technical report, although a summary did appear in the trade press. Mr. Roberts started with actual loss distributions to which he fitted a sequence of connected second and third degree polynomials and used a Pareto type curve for the last (top) group. Various inflation rates were assumed and run against the loss model. A sample of the results is set forth below:

TABLE II

OVERALL INFLATION RATE 8.6% PER ANNUM[12]

(1) Retention	(2) Effects on Losses (limited to retention)	(3) Effect on Excess Losses
$ 10,000	7.27%	17.95%
15,000	7.67	18.94
20,000	7.83	21.21
25,000	7.97	23.02
50,000	8.35	29.59

As the retention increases, Column (2) will approach 8.6% and Column (3) will increase without bound.

The great and relentless pressure on excess rates can be seen in the following example. For purposes of this example, a loss distribution was constructed (losses below $30,000 are not shown since they are not germane to the point) and the following assumptions employed:

1. Losses take four years to settle.
2. There is no loss development other than that caused by inflation.
3. Gross losses inflate by 10% per annum.
4. The initial total limits (or subject) premium is $10,000,000.

TABLE III

Losses	1974 Initial Gross Losses $29,999 and Over	1974 Accidents Settled at 1978 Values	1975 Accidents Settled at 1978 Values	1976 Accidents Settled at 1978 Values
10	$ 30,000	$ 43,923	$ 48,315	$ 53,147
5	40,000	58,564	65,520	70,862
3	50,000	73,205	80,526	88,578
2	60,000	87,846	96,631	106,294
1	80,000	117,128	128,841	141,725
1	100,000	146,410	161,051	177,156
Losses excess of $50,000	$100,000	$351,665	$446,832	$582,983

---

[12] L. H. Roberts, *Best's Review;* Property/Liability Edition, "The Impact of Inflation on Reinsurance Costs," March 1973, p. 16.

	Total Limits Premium	Pure Loss Cost or Excess Rate Before Expense and Profit
1974	$10,000,000	3.52%
1975	11,000,000	4.06%
1976	12,100,000	4.82%

The leveraged effect of inflation is without a doubt one of the most serious problems faced by any carrier writing long-tail business over fixed retentions or significant deductibles.

Even if properly rated and nothing else changes (the legal climate, underwriting, accident frequencies, and product mix are all stable, and the primary carrier properly reflects inflation in his total limits ratemaking), the excess rate cannot hold up under the attack of inflation. The excess carrier must—even if the exposure was properly priced in the first year—constantly reassess his pricing and seek rate increases every year. In this example, the subject premium and the excess premium increased 10% each year, but *in addition,* the excess writer needs a 15% increase for the second year and a 19% increase for the third year. If inflation can be predicted with reasonable accuracy, and if both the ceding company and the assuming carrier understand the forces eroding the adequacy of the excess rate, there is no reason why the excess coverage cannot be written over a fixed retention. Both parties would simply have to become accustomed to the need for frequent rate increases.

There is a way to achieve stability in the excess rate, even in the face of inflation. The only way stability can be achieved is for the ceding company and the excess carrier to share the effects of inflation. This can be accomplished by adjusting the retention over time in phase with changing economic conditions.

The part of the contract that spells out the terms of the adjustable retention is usually called "Index Clause," although it is sometimes referred to as a "Stability Clause." The contractual language is neither long nor complicated. It may state that it is the intent of the parties that the company's retention and the excess carrier's limit of liability retain their relative monetary value (by means of the index clause). It could be and often is stated in a different way—but, of course, the end result is the same. Another example—it is intended to equitably share the effect of inflation or deflation between the ceding and assuming carrier (by means of the index clause).

In the case of a single claim (payment) the operation is very simple, the retention is merely adjusted in direct proportion to the change in the selected index between the time coverage was *priced* (i.e., inception of a reinsurance treaty), and the date of claim *settlement.* If for example, the index went up 20% (say from 100 to 120 or from 150 to 180), the retention would be increased by 20%.

For example, suppose a retention of $50,000 was selected and priced when a certain type of gross claim was expected to cost $65,000. If such a claim occurred and was settled not for $65,000 but $78,000 by reason of inflation, the excess carrier without an index clause would have a claim severity 87% greater than expected, while the ceding carrier's loss would have stopped at $50,000 for a 0% effect. With the index clause, the retention would go to $60,000 (50,000 x 1.20) and both carriers would have experienced a 20% claims inflation. In other words, the two carriers would have ratably shared the effects of inflation.

Returning to the rating problem and assumption discussed earlier (Table III) with a $50,000 retention, it was demonstrated that:

TABLE IV

No Inflation	Losses Excess of $50,000	Pure Loss Cost or Excess Rate Before Expenses
	$100,000	1.00%

10% Per Annum Inflation

	Losses Excess of $50,000	Pure Loss Cost or Excess Rate Before Expenses
1974 Accidents (settled 1978)	$351,665	3.52%
1975 Accident Year (settled 1979)	446,832	4.06
1976 Accident Year (settled 1980)	582,983	4.82

Assuming the index selected went up 10% per annum (just as the losses), the retention as respects cases settled in 1978 would be $73,205, $80,526 in 1979, and $88,578 in 1980. Under these circumstances, the expected excess losses and rate would be:

TABLE V

	Losses Excess of Indexed Retention	Losses Related to Exposure Base
1974 Accident Year	$146,410	1.46%
1975 Accident Year	161,050	1.46
1976 Accident Year	177,157	1.46

Thus, it can be seen that, other things being equal, the index clause can create a stable excess rate by sharing inflation between the two carriers. Both carriers under the index clause are liable for the same percentage of the total limits losses they would have had without inflation. In other words, the retention and limit have been adjusted so as to maintain relative monetary values consistent with those obtained when the business was originally underwritten and priced.[13]

Commissions. Usually, reinsurance pricing is done on a "net" basis, that is, the reinsurance underwriter or actuary will use one or more of the pricing approaches described earlier to develop the premium/rate required for covering the loss and allocated loss adjustment expense—the so-called pure loss cost. The next step, of course, is to add provisions for the reinsurer's expenses, profits, and contingency. Sometimes the process ends here, but frequently a commission allowance is factored in.

For example, if the pure loss cost is 10% and the loss conversion factor or profit and expense loading is 100/80ths, the net rate is 10% x 100/80 or 12.5%. If the rate is to be grossed up for a 40% commission, the net rate must be divided by $1 - \frac{\text{commission as }\%}{100}$ or in this case 12.5/.60 = 20.833%. Another way to look at this process is that the loss conversion factor becomes 100/48ths (i.e., $10\% \cdot 100/48 = 20.833$) derived from $\frac{100/80}{.60}$.

Contrary to most articles and discussions of this subject, many nonproportional reinsurance arrangements carry a ceding commission today. This, of course, means that there is a balance sheet effect. It is a widely and incorrectly held view that only proportional reinsurance has a balance sheet effect. In fact, any reinsurance arrangement that involves an unearned premium reserve and a ceding commission has a balance sheet effect similar to that described in the section dealing with proportional reinsurance.

Loss Adjustment Expense. When studying non-proportional reinsurance, one must pay particular interest to the way allocated loss adjustment expense is handled. It can be handled in one of two ways. Normally, allocated loss adjustment expense is shared between the ceding company and assuming carrier in the same proportion as the loss is distributed. For example, assume a company has an excess of loss arrangement that covers $900,000 excess of $100,000 each accident. The company

---

[13] Ronald E. Ferguson, "Nonproportional Reinsurance and the Index Clause," *Proceedings* of the Casualty Actuarial Society, Vol. LXI, (Boston: Sperry Rand, 1974), pp. 141-169.

has a loss of $900,000 with allocated loss adjustment expenses of $50,000. The recoveries from the reinsurer are computed as follows:

	Loss	Allocated Loss Adjustment Expense
Gross	$900,000	$50,000
Retention	100,000 (1/9)	5,555 (1/9)
Loss Recovery	$800,000 (8/9)	
Allocated loss adjustment expense recovery	44,445	$44,445
Total Recovery	$844,445	

The other approach, which complicates the pricing a bit, is to simply add the allocated expense to the gross loss before applying the retention. Under this approach, the recovery would be:

Gross loss	$900,000
Allocated loss expense	50,000
	$950,000
Retention	$100,000
Recovery	$850,000

Administration. Under non-proportional reinsurance arrangements, premium data are usually reported monthly on a summarized basis. This follows the same logic and procedures referred to earlier in the reporting section of Proportional Reinsurance. For per occurrence and aggregate excess of loss ("Classes D and F"), oftentimes deposit premiums are paid to the reinsurer with adjustments resulting after a predetermined period of time has elapsed.

Losses are usually reported individually with substantial detail as they arise. At a minimum, the reinsurer will require information on each loss by line, sub-line, accident date, and policy date. Since the non-proportional reinsurer is routinely dealing with large losses, a certain expertise has been developed and the reinsurer will be able to advise and counsel the ceding company on the management of large troublesome claims.

Advantages and Disadvantages. The advantage of non-proportional reinsurance is that the ceding company is getting a substantial amount of protection and stability in return for a relatively modest premium outlay.

Looked at from another perspective, the cash outflow is minimized under this form of reinsurance. The disadvantage is that non-proportional reinsurance produces only a modest financing effect and may be a little more complicated from an administrative point of view. With modern computing equipment, however, even complex non-proportional plans can be set up to run smoothly and effortlessly.

PER RISK AGGREGATE AND AGGREGATE EXCESS OF LOSS ("CLASSES E AND F")

Aggregate excess of loss has many of the identifying characteristics discussed in the preceding section — for per risk excess of loss reinsurance. However, because of the complexity of the plans, additional descriptions in a separate section are needed. There are so many variations of the aggregate excess of loss idea that it is difficult to develop a simple, short definition. The basic idea is that losses arising out of a collection of risks (or rarely a single risk such as "Class E") are aggregated, and retained to a certain predetermined level within a specified time period with losses in excess of that level recovered from the reinsurer. The two most frequently encountered aggregate excess plans are:

A. Loss Ratio Cover — Example

Primary premiums $10,000,000
Reinsurance loss ratio threshold 65% cover up to 110% (or 45 loss ratio points excess of 65)
Actual loss ratio 75%
Reinsurance recovery (.75 − .65) x $10,000,000 or $1,000,000.

B. Annual Aggregate Deductible — Example

Assume a reinsurance cover of $900,000 excess $100,000 subject to a $300,000 annual aggregate deductible. Each loss excess of $100,000 will be analyzed and the amount greater than $100,000 will be accumulated but retained by the ceding company until the accumulated excess amounts it has paid equal $300,000. After this point, losses in excess of $100,000 paid will be recovered from the reinsurer (over the balance of the period).

This type of cover (as well as certain other aggregate type covers) raises an interesting pricing question. If the expected losses for the reinsurance cover outlined above are $450,000 for a full cover (i.e., no deductible), what should the premium be with a $300,000 aggregate deductible? The tempting but technically incorrect answer is to reduce the expected losses by $300,000 and then apply loading factors to the $150,000 residual amount. Theoretically, the credit should be less than $300,000 since:

1. The expected value of the losses excess of a $300,000 annual aggregate deductible is not $150,000. Suppose the $450,000 expected value were developed as follows:

Losses Excess of $100,000	Probability*	Expected Value
$ 0	10%	$ 0
100,000	10	10,000
200,000	10	20,000
300,000	10	30,000
400,000	10	40,000
500,000	10	50,000
600,000	10	60,000
700,000	10	70,000
800,000	10	80,000
900,000	10	90,000
		$450,000

If the first $300,000 of each loss is removed (by operation of the deductible), the distribution is:

Excess Losses**	Probability	Expected Value
$ 0	40%	$ 0
100,000	10	10,000
200,000	10	20,000
300,000	10	30,000
400,000	10	40,000
500,000	10	50,000
600,000	10	60,000
		$210,000

2. The residual reinsurance cover is more volatile or unbalanced and requires larger profit and contingency loadings.

3. From a total return point of view, the reinsurance cover is less attractive since the reinsurer will have smaller reserves and less funds to invest.

* The probability factors used in this illustration can be conceptualized as follows: Suppose we knew or expected that if this reinsurance cover were in effect for 100 years — there would be ten years with no losses to the cover, ten years where the loss to the cover is $100,000 (each year), ten years where the loss to the cover is $200,000, ten years at $300,000, etc. It follows that each loss level would carry a probability of occurrence of 1 in 10 or 10%.

** $900,000 excess $100,000 subject to a $300,000 annual aggregate deductible.

Aggregate excess of loss programs have a valid role but sometimes are gimicky and poorly understood. For certain lines or perils where loss events are difficult to define (such as crop-hail), an aggregate loss ratio program may be appropriate. In general, aggregate programs are extremely difficult for the reinsurer to price and manage. The reinsurer's experience under an aggregate program is likely to be volatile, and as a result, the risk or profit and contingency loading will be heavy. The reinsurer will almost always insist that the reinsured co-reinsure (i.e., retain) a part (e.g., 10%) of the cover, and the reinsurance limit will usually be modest. Another disadvantage of most aggregate programs is that they do not provide the immediate cash flow support the company may need.

Summary

No one form of reinsurance can be characterized as best. In general, proportional forms of reinsurance provide greater financing and volume capacity than non-proportional forms. On the other hand, non-proportional forms provide greater limits, catastrophe protection, stabilization, and minimize cash outflow. It must be kept in mind that any form of reinsurance can provide some part of each of the four functions of reinsurance — capacity, financing, catastrophe protection, and stabilization — but the emphasis varies. There are no simple answers or solutions for the reinsurance needs of a company. Reinsurance needs vary from company to company and within a company over time. The reinsurance program is an important part of the primary company's operation and as such requires serious and continuous study.

*   *   *   *   *   *

About the Author of Chapter 3

Ronald E. Ferguson was born on January 16, 1942, in Chicago. In 1963 he graduated from Blackburn College in Carlinville, Illinois, receiving the B.A. Degree in mathematics and economics. Two years later he completed the M.A.S. Degree in actuarial science at the University of Michigan in 1965. He became a Fellow of the Casualty Actuarial Society in 1971 and is a member of the American Academy of Actuaries.

His insurance career began in Chicago immediately after completing his graduate work at the University of Michigan. From 1965 to 1969 he was a statistician with Lumbermens Mutual Casualty. In 1969 he joined General Reinsurance Corporation in its Chicago office as an actuarial assistant. The following year he moved to its home office as an assistant secretary, becoming vice president four years later in 1974. In 1975 he was put in charge of the management information department for the Corporation, and in 1977 he achieved his current title of senior vice president.

4

Reinsurance Contract Wording

by Robert F. Salm*

The long and well established tradition that reinsurance transactions are a matter of "utmost good faith" between the parties has had a predictable effect on the preparation of reinsurance contracts (sometimes called "treaties" or "agreements"). The typical reinsurance contract is a relatively short, concise document, noticeably lacking in the legalisms so characteristic of other types of contracts. This underlying assumption of utmost good faith allows the companies to draft a document that assumes both parties are so knowledgeable on the subject matter to be dealt with and possess such a degree of sophistication as to preclude the necessity for long, expository declarations of intent and implementation. There is also the tradition that, should a difference of opinion or interpretation arise, it will be settled by a court of artibration composed of experienced insurance and reinsurance personnel. It has been the intent of such tradition that the court of arbitration, so composed, will interpret the contract wording according to the customs and traditions of the business as an honorable engagement rather than a mere legal obligation.

These underlying assumptions and traditions should not, however, be so persuasive as to lead to the preparation of a contract that is carelessly drafted or ambiguous. To the extent practicable, the contract should contain terms and provisions which have a clearly established meaning within the industry and which lend themselves to ready and uniform interpretation.

The first section of this chapter discusses sixteen terms and clauses which are commonly used by reinsurance contract drafters. The second

---

* Assistant Vice President, Reinsurance Division, Continental Casualty Company, CNA Plaza, Chicago, Illinois 60685.

section then discusses several clauses applicable to excess reinsurance agreements. Thirdly, some tips useful in drafting treaties are offered, since many readers of this chapter will look to it for practical suggestions toward improvement. Finally, certain problem areas are highlighted because their effects are widespread, their solutions are sometimes elusive, and their importance commands the attention of all concerned with reinsurance.

Standard Provisions

There are certain provisions which are found in most reinsurance contracts, depending in some measure upon the type of reinsurance involved.

REINSURING CLAUSE

Unlike the common insurance policy which begins with an "Insuring Clause" summarizing the protection to be provided, reinsurance contracts may employ a variety of ways in outlining the essentials of the coverage and the intention of the parties. Some contract drafters prefer to incorporate these essentials in a Preamble to the contract or perhaps under a Business Covered Clause, and there is no fundamental objection to this approach as long as the necessary points are covered. Every contract must contain a reference to the nature of the contract, i.e., the type of reinsurance involved, whether it be pro rata or excess, and what the obligations of the parties are, so that a true contractual obligation is established.

Excess. An excess contract which makes use of a Reinsuring Clause in much the same manner as an Insuring Clause in an ordinary insurance policy might read as follows:

In consideration of the payment of the premium as provided herein, the Reinsurers agree to indemnify the Company in respect of the net excess liability which may accrue to the Company as a result of loss occurrences arising during the term of this Contract under any of its policies, binders, contracts of insurance or reinsurance (all hereinafter called "policies") or other evidences of liability (whether written or oral) heretofore issued or which may hereafter be issued by or on behalf of the Company, subject to the following conditions.

Pro Rata. A similar Reinsurance Clause applicable to a pro rata treaty (in this case an obligatory surplus treaty) might well read in the following manner:

By this Treaty, the Reinsurers obligate themselves to accept as reinsurance of the Company, and the Company
obligates itself to cede to the Reinsurers the whole of its first
surplus liability, as herein defined, under all policies of insurance or reinsurance issued through its Fire, Inland Marine,
and Multiple Line Departments in force at inception hereof or
issued or renewed during the period this Treaty remains in
force.

This pro rata wording clearly obligates the company to cede to the
treaty its first surplus liability (as defined elsewhere in the treaty). There
are also non-obligatory surplus treaties which allow the company the option of ceding to the treaty. Such non-obligatory treaties would contain
wording to the effect that the company "may cede," but the reinsurers
would still be obligated to assume the reinsurance. Also, this pro rata
Reinsuring Clause provides for coverage of business in force at the inception of the agreement. Such an arrangement will require elsewhere in the
agreement a statement to the effect that the reinsurers will assume the
portfolio of unearned premiums applicable to the business in force at the
inception of the reinsurance treaty.

EXCLUSIONS

Depending on how the Reinsurance Clause, the Preamble, or the
Business Covered Clause defines the business to be protected under the
contract, each contract will require a list of exclusions to clearly spell out
the classes of business or perils which are not intended to be protected or
reinsured. If these clauses have been particularly precise in identifying
exactly what business is to be protected, the list of exclusions will naturally be shorter. However, if the clauses are not definitive on this subject
(as in the excess of loss contract Reinsuring Clause cited above), it will be
extremely important to deal adequately and thoroughly with the exclusions. Even in those cases where the Reinsuring Clause relates the
business to be covered to policies issued in certain departments of the
company (as in the pro rata Reinsurance Clause quoted above), careful
thought must be given as to what classes of business are not to be
covered, as it is possible the company might issue certain types of
policies in one of its underwriting departments that the reinsurers wish
not to cover. Boiler and machinery business written in a company's fire
department is one example that comes quickly to mind.

The precise list of exclusions is generally a matter of negotiation between the two parties and is frequently a part of the underwriting information submitted along with the initial proposal for the reinsurance. The

Exclusion Clause often refers to business "classified" by the company as a certain type; this allows the company the option of making its own determination of exactly what business is or is not to be covered, but it does, by the same token, theoretically allow the company to classify arbitrarily certain lines of business in such a way that they will automatically fall under the coverage of the reinsurance contract. Again in this instance, the tradition of utmost good faith comes into play, and the reinsurer is assuming the company will not take advantage of such wording to cede business which has not been contemplated as a type of coverage to be reinsured.

Classes. Exclusion clauses are necessary to preclude coverage for whole classes of insurance, such as boiler and machinery and aviation, which were not contemplated under the contract. In the case of property treaties, all forms of "casualty" insurance would be excluded. It might be wise to interject at this point that if casualty insurance is to be excluded, it is well to define just what is meant by casualty insurance, as the term as used in the trade does not always encompass the same lines of business. Burglary and theft, for instance, is one example that normally requires clarification, since some companies classify it as a property peril, while others consider it a casualty risk.

Difficult Exposures. The Exclusion Clause will probably also exclude certain difficult exposures (underground coal mining, for instance) which the rate for the cover does not contemplate and which, therefore, the reinsurer does not wish to protect.

Perils. The same Exclusion Clause will probably also prohibit by specific reference certain perils, such as flood, hail on growing crops, and war; again, these normally represent exposures which are not reflected in the rate for the contract and which the reinsurer wishes to avoid.

Incidental Exposures. Exclusion clauses usually specify that certain exclusions, generally those relating to certain difficult exposures, shall not apply to policies issued to any insured where the excluded operations are "incidental" to the insured's business. Since the company must make the determination as to what operations are incidental, once again the reinsurer must rely on the good faith and conscience of the company not to abuse this privilege.

Temporary Coverage. A provision reading along the following lines also frequently appears as a part of the Exclusion Clause:

> In the event of the Company being interested in any such excluded risk, either by an existing insured expanding its operations or by an inadvertent acceptance by an agency or other-

wise, the Company shall be protected to the extent as if there were no exclusion but only until the Company is able to effect cancellation of such coverage and then not for more than forty-five days from the date of discovery of such excluded risk by the underwriting officials of the Home Office.

This wording is designed to deal with situations which come up normally in the course of routine underwriting by the company, and it represents common sense solutions to these situations.

Certain "Standard" Exclusions. Current practices dictate that the exclusion list include such "standard" exclusions in property treaties as the Target Risk Exclusion Clause (which is promulgated by the Lloyd's Non-Marine Association) and the Total Insured Value Exclusion Clause (which also originated in the London Market) and which is designed to exclude risks where, at the time of cession, the "total insured value" over all interests exceeds a certain figure, presently $100,000,000. There is also a standard Pools Associations and Syndicates Exclusion Clause (again largely the effort of the Lloyd's Market) which spells out which pool, association and syndicate-type insurance operations are protected or are not to be protected under property treaties. These specific exclusions were designed in large measure to protect the reinsurers from undue concentration on certain highly valued risks. The London market also developed Nuclear Incident Physical Damage, Liability, and Boiler and Machinery Exclusion Clauses which are obviously designed to avoid nuclear exposures and which have the effect of forcing the underwriting of such risks exclusively by the nuclear energy pools in this country.

A recent standard exclusion incorporated into the list is that of denying coverage for any assessments that might be made against the company by any state insolvency fund. This exclusion also originated in London and represents the opinion that such assessments are not a risk contemplated under any reinsurance agreements. To open reinsurance funds to such assessments by insolvency funds is to provide "insolvency insurance" to that extent to a ceding company and is not a function of the reinsurance contract of indemnity as designed.

All exclusions should be clearly stated to avoid ambiguity. Superfluous exclusions which are not really germane to the subject matter of the reinsurance are to be avoided. Careful attention to the terminology of the exclusion list will avoid differences of opinion that might well develop and should represent mutual agreement between the parties. For example, an equivocal term such as "explosive substance" should be clearly defined, so that both parties will know what the term encompasses and exactly what is intended to be excluded.

DEFINITIONS

The fact that well-drafted reinsurance contracts incorporate terminology considered fairly standard within the industry does not eliminate the need for definitions, especially if there is any possibility that the terms could be subject to different interpretations. For instance, in a surplus treaty it is important to define what is meant by the term "surplus liability," i.e., that portion of the company's gross liability on any one risk which exceeds the amount of the company's net retained liability thereon. The term "net retained liability" is construed as representing the amount of liability carried by the company for its own account on each risk reinsured. The same definition will probably include a reference to the company's privilege of determining what constitutes a single risk, a privilege which the company must retain in order to allow it sufficient flexibility in its underwriting and cession procedures. A prudent reinsurer will make sure it understands what the company's underwriting rules are for determining "one risk," since those rules could have an important effect on the liability being assumed under the reinsurance contract.

If the terms "earned premium" or "incurred losses" are used in the reinsurance contract, it is well to make sure that they are also defined. However, their definitions may appear in the clauses in which the terms appear rather than in a Definitions Article as such, although this is a matter of choice on the part of the drafter. There is some merit in the opinion, however, that all definitions should appear under one heading, for convenient reference by both parties. Later, in discussing provisions common to excess covers, it will become evident that there is an even greater need for a comprehensive set of definitions because of the many variables involved.

WARRANTIES

The reinsurer may wish to require in the reinsurance contract that the company "warrant" certain facts and figures that have a significant bearing on the liability assumed by the reinsurer. Such data are normally part of the underwriting information the reinsurer receives with the proposal, but it is not uncommon for the reinsurer to require that certain substantive representations be incorporated into the contract wording in the form of warranties. The effect is to make the information readily available, to eliminate any doubts as to what the ceding company's obligations are, and to highlight the significance of the warranted information.

Typical warranties deal with the maintenance of pro rata reinsurance (which has the effect of reducing the reinsurer's exposure under excess contracts) and with references to the maximum net lines the company will write on any one risk. In the case of pro rata treaties, the reinsurer may require the ceding company to warrant the maintenance of excess coverages in those cases where the reinsurer is to be protected by such excess contracts along with the ceding company. Another typical provision that frequently comes under the heading of warranties is the requirement that the company will purchase the reinsurance provided by the Department of Housing and Urban Development to cover riot losses.

There are no inflexible rules as to what the reinsurer will normally accept as underwriting representations or will require as contract warranties. Prudence suggests more vital data should be spelled out in the contract as obligations and agreements of the ceding company, and as essential facts having a significant effect on the risk being assumed by the reinsurer.

TERM

Reinsurance contracts can be issued either on a "term" basis, i.e., for a specified period of time, or on a continuous-until-cancelled basis; the latter is normally applicable to pro rata treaties. Either approach obviously requires a statement as to the time and date the reinsurance coverage is to become effective, and good practice dictates that this time and date be precise, i.e., 12:01 a.m. Central Standard Time, January 1, 1977. In the case of a term contract, the statement as to when the coverage expires should be equally precise.

With respect to catastrophe excess contracts which protect the company from a large loss arising out of an accumulation of losses from one event, it is particularly important to have the term contract become effective and terminate at a discreet point in time. Otherwise, losses that might occur before and after a time and date that are not precisely identified might fall within different time zones, with the result that the catastrophe excess contract might not incorporate all the losses arising out of the one event and thus defeat the purpose of the contract.[1] Pro rata and per risk excess contracts should, on the other hand, provide that the effective and termination date and time are those at the location of the risk.

CANCELLATION

In the event the reinsurance contract is issued on a continuous-until-

---

[1] Robert Salm, "Thinking About the Time of Day," *Reinsurance*, October, 1971. pp. 230-231.

cancelled basis, some provision must be made in the contract for giving notice of cancellation by one party to the other. Some advance notice is needed to allow the company sufficient time to negotiate replacement cover, and the reinsurer is also entitled to advance notice of the company's change in plans. The more common custom is to require either party to give to the other ninety days notice in writing, to be effective either at a quarter end or at year end.

Provisional Notice. There is some opinion within the industry that it is better practice to write catastrophe excess contracts on a term basis, which of course requires renegotiation at the renewal time. To issue such contracts on a continuous basis frequently puts the reinsurer in a position of having to issue a "provisional" cancellation notice in order to have sufficient time to review the renewal underwriting data. Such provisional notices are frequently unnerving to the company, which is naturally concerned with continuity of coverage. However, if the cover is issued on a term basis, at least the company is aware of the requirement for submitting renewal data in order to assure that the contract will be renewed. Depending on the time element involved, it is sometimes also necessary for the reinsurer to give provisional cancellation notice on pro rata treaties, the essential purpose of which is to review the latest available experience figure to determine the appropriate continuation terms.

Disposition of Liability. In the case of excess contracts, cancellation normally means that there is simply no reinsurance coverage for losses that occur after the termination date. Pro rata treaties, on the other hand, require a further elaboration of the cancellation provision to provide for disposition of liability ceded up to the point of cancellation. There are two alternatives, one being complete cancellation of the portfolio of inforce business with a return of the unearned premium to the company; in such situations, the reinsurer has no liability for losses that occur after the cancellation date. Alternatively, the cancellation provision can stipulate that the in-force book of business may be allowed to run off until natural expiry or at an agreed-upon earlier date. There are advantages to both methods, the selection of which is a matter of negotiation between the parties. The important point to be borne in mind is that the contract must state the procedure which applies in the event of cancellation, so that both parties are aware in advance of what action will be taken.

Arbitration

Much has been written on the subject of Arbitration Clauses, probably because they are such an essential component in the reinsurance transaction itself. They are designed to avoid taking a dispute to a court of law and can be an effective self-regulatory measure in the reinsurance business. This is true in spite of the fact that such clauses are not binding on the parties in all jurisdictions; rather, their effectiveness is determined by the law of the state in which the particular action is brought. Nevertheless, virtually all states (and the Federal Government) now recognize the enforceability of such clauses; Missouri is perhaps the most notable exception.

Those states which recognize the validity of the arbitration provision in reinsurance contracts usually provide in their statutes that their courts are required to grant a stay of the trial until the arbitration has been completed. Those statutes also provide limited grounds on which the decisions of the arbitrators may be vacated, with the grounds generally based upon misconduct or fraud by the arbitrators. The statutes further provide that the decision of the arbitrators is enforceable in a court of law.

A well drafted Arbitration Clause should contain certain specifics. It should state that the arbitrators should be present or prior officers of insurance or reinsurance companies, and that the arbitrators should not be under the control of either party to the arbitration. The Clause should provide for the selection of an umpire if the two arbitrators are unable to agree upon the selection of such an umpire. It should provide for the payment of the cost of the arbitration, and should state a time limit for the appointment of the arbitrators. The Clause should also provide that the arbitrators are not obliged to follow judicial formalities but shall instead make their decision according to the practice and customs of the business. Further, the Clause should provide that a decision rendered by a majority of the arbitrators shall be final and binding on both parties, and that judgement may be entered upon the final decision of the arbitrators in any court having jurisdiction. The site of the arbitration is normally the city and state of the home office of the ceding company, unless otherwise agreed by both parties.

It is important for the Arbitration Clause to clearly state that any dispute between the two parties to the reinsurance contract shall be settled by arbitration. This plainly expresses the wishes of both parties that arbitration shall be the sole vehicle for settling any differences that may arise, and thus is intended to avoid the alternative of taking the dispute to a court of law. It is interesting to note in this connection that the Arbitration Clause has been held to be inoperable if one party to the contract is contending that it is void *ab initio* (from inception), since such a position would have the effect of voiding the Arbitration Clause itself.[2]

Because of its vital significance and the fact that it goes to the very heart of the reinsurance business, the Arbitration Clause should receive the closest scrutiny of both parties to make sure that it clearly expresses their intent and wishes. A typical Arbitration Clause might read as follows:

> As a precedent to any right of action hereunder, if any dispute shall arise between the Company and the Reinsurers with reference to the interpretation of this Agreement or their rights with respect to any transaction involved, whether such dispute arises before or after termination of this Agreement, such dispute, upon the written request of either party, shall be submitted to three arbitrators, one to be chosen by each party, and the third by the two so chosen. If either party refuses or neglects to appoint an arbitrator within thirty days after the receipt of written notice from the other party requesting it to do so, the requesting party may appoint two arbitrators. If the two arbitrators fail to agree in the selection of a third arbitrator within thirty days of their appointment, each of them shall name two, of whom the other shall decline one and the decision shall be made by drawing lots. All arbitrators shall be executive officers of insurance or reinsurance companies not under the control of either party to this Agreement. The arbitrators shall interpret this Agreement as an honorable engagement and not as merely a legal obligation; they are relieved of all judicial formalities and may abstain from following the strict rules of law, and they shall make their award with a view to effecting the general purpose of this Agreement in a reasonable manner rather than in accordance with a literal interpretation of the language. Each party shall submit its case to its arbitrator within thirty days of the appointment of the third arbitrator. The decision in writing of any two arbitrators, when filed with the parties hereto, shall be final and binding on both parties. Judgment may be entered upon the final decision of the arbitrators in any court having jurisdiction. Each party shall bear the expense of its own arbitrator and shall jointly and equally bear with the other party the expense of the third arbitrator and of the arbitration. Such arbitration shall take place in the

---

[2] Legal Correspondent, "Scope of the Arbitration Clause," *Reinsurance*, January, 1972, pp. 385-389.

city in which the Company's Head Office is located unless some other place is mutually agreed upon by the Company and the Reinsurers.

TERRITORY

It is common to include in all reinsurance contracts a reference to the territorial limits of the coverage which is to be provided, since the reinsurer is concerned with knowing the territorial extent of his exposure. In some instances the territory may be limited to business written only in certain states, which makes the territory provision simpler. The fact that larger companies write business on a much wider scale requires, quite naturally, a broader Territory Clause.

A distinction must be made in the Territory Clause as to whether the exposure is limited to policies issued in certain geographical areas or whether the coverage is worldwide in scope, i.e., it covers business that the company may write in foreign countries. A not uncommon Territory Clause might read as follows: "This Contract shall cover wherever the Company's policies cover but is limited to policies issued in the United States of America and/or its territories and possessions and/or Canada and/or Puerto Rico and covering property normally located therein." If the reinsurer is already informed of the territory in which the company writes business and is satisfied with the situation, a simpler Clause might read: "This Agreement shall apply to losses occurring within the territorial limits of the Company's original policies."

SELF-INSURED OBLIGATIONS

It is not uncommon in modern reinsurance practice for a company to expect its reinsurer to cover under the reinsurance contract those obligations for which the company is self-insured. However, the wisdom of such coverage has been challenged. One of the more significant objections is that of a possible conflict of interest, since the self-insured company is actually settling claims under its own policy. But if the two parties do agree to provide such coverage, a typical Self-Insured Obligations Clause might read as follows:

As respects all business the subject matter hereof, this Agreement shall cover all obligations of the Company assumed by it as a self-insurer (or self-insured obligations in excess of any valid and collectible insurance available to the Company) to the same extent as if all types of insurance covered by this Agreement were afforded under the broadest form of agreements issued by the Company. The Company shall provide, upon request of Reinsurers, appropriate evidence of their self-insured obligations.

An insurance or reinsurance contract wherein the Company and/or its affiliated and/or subsidiary companies are named as the Insured or Reinsured party, either alone or jointly with some other party, shall be deemed to be an insurance or reinsurance coming within the scope of this Agreement, notwithstanding the fact that no legal liability may arise in respect thereof by reason of the fact that the Company and/or its affiliated and/or subsidiary Companies are named as the Insured or Reinsured party or one of the Insured or Reinsured parties.

In respect of all such business, the Company shall include in the "gross net premium income" hereunder the premiums that would be paid were such obligations covered by policies or bonds.

It is expected that the company will actually issue policy forms to evidence such self-insurance, for the reinsurer will want to know the nature of such exposures when underwriting the reinsurance agreement.

INSOLVENCY

Insolvency Clauses are now standard provisions in all reinsurance contracts because they are required by the statutes of several states, among which are California, Illinois, Louisiana, Massachusetts, New York, Tennessee, Utah, and Washington. Their history dates back to the Depression of the 1930's, when several insurance companies became insolvent and were unable to make full payment on the claims held against them. Some reinsurers at the time took the position that since an insolvent ceding company did not pay 100 cents on the dollar for each claim, the reinsurer should indemnify the company only to the extent that the company made actual payment on each claim. This meant that if the company paid, say, only $1,000 on a $5,000 claim, the reinsurer would pay only its proportionate share of the $1,000 payment.

As a result of this situation, New York passed in 1939 controlling legislation (Section 77 of the New York Insurance Law, as amended by Chapter 171, Laws 1952). That law required, in order for the ceding company to take credit in its Annual Statement for the reinsurance on its books, the reinsurance contract must specifically provide that, in the event of the insolvency of the company, the reinsurer must make full payment to the liquidator of the company for the reinsurer's liability under the reinsurance contract, without diminution because of insolvency of the company. Lack of the Clause in those jurisdictions which require it would mean that the state insurance department would disallow the reinsured unearned premiums and loss reserves shown in the company's Annual Statement. Accordingly, the reinsurance contract drafter should be absolutely certain to include an Insolvency Clause which meets the requirements of the particular state jurisdiction. In point of fact, the New York statute lays out wording which is satisfactory to all other jurisdictions, and as a consequence is the wording which appears most often in reinsurance contracts. An Insolvency Clause which incorporates the necessary features of the New York Clause is as follows:

> In the event of the insolvency of the Company, this reinsurance shall be payable directly to the Company, or to its liquidator, receiver, conservator or statutory successor on the basis of the liability of the Company without diminution because of the insolvency of the Company or because the liquidator, receiver, conservator or statutory successor of the Company has failed to pay all or a portion of any claim. It is agreed, however, that the liquidator, receiver, conservator or statutory successor of the Company shall give written notice to the Reinsurers of the pendency of a claim against the Company indicating the policy or bond reinsured which claim would involve a possible liability on the part of the Reinsurers within a reasonable time after such claim is filed in the conservation or liquidation proceeding or in the receivership, and that during the pendency of such claim the Reinsurers may investigate such claim and interpose, at their own expense, in the proceeding where such claim is to be adjudicated any defense or defenses that they may deem available to the Company or its liquidator, receiver, conservator, or statutory successor. The expense thus incurred by the Reinsurers shall be chargeable, subject to the approval of the court, against the Company as part of the expense of conservation or liquidation to the extent of a pro rata share of the benefit which may accrue to the Company solely as a result of the defense undertaken by the Reinsurers.
>
> Where two or more Reinsurers are involved in the same claim and a majority in interest elect to interpose defense to such claim, the expense shall be apportioned in accordance with the terms of the reinsurance agreement as though such expense had been incurred by the Company.

The reinsurance shall be payable by the Reinsurers to the Company or to its liquidator, receiver, conservator, or statutory successor, except as provided by Section 315 of the New York Insurance Law or except (a) where the Agreement specifically provides another payee of such reinsurance in the event of the insolvency of the Company, and (b) where the Reinsurers with the consent of the direct insured or insureds have assumed such policy obligations of the Company as direct obligations of the Reinsurers to the payees under such policies and in substitution for the obligations of the Company to the payees.

PREMIUM

All reinsurance contracts must contain a statement as to how the reinsurance premium is to be calculated. There are a number of variations and formulae that may be employed, depending upon the terms as agreed between the two parties. A minimum stipulation would provide in a pro rata treaty that the reinsurer is to receive its appropriate share of the gross original premium, from which is deducted an agreed upon ceding commission to cover the company's acquisition costs (including but not limited to agents' fees and state premium taxes).

Extraction Factors. Excess contracts, on the other hand, are normally rated on a percentage of the company's net written or net earned premiums; the definition of these terms should be specific as to what is to be included or excluded in the subject premium base. For instance, in property excess contracts which protect Homeowners policies but which exclude the third-party and perhaps the burglary portions thereof, there should be provision for an extraction factor. That factor is applied as a deduction from the company's subject premium in order to extract from the indivisible premiums of Homeowners policies the portions thereof applicable to the excluded perils. While there is always room for negotiation over the specifics of an extraction factor, a typical reinsurer might provide for a factor of 10% to exclude the third party liability exposure under a Homeowners policy, and 25% for the burglary and theft portion thereof. For ease and simplicity, excess contracts sometimes provide that the company's entire premium income shall be considered as the subject premium base, since the real concern of the reinsurer is what the reinsurance premium is going to be, and not necessarily the base on which the reinsurance premium is to be calculated.

Burning Cost Formula. There are numerous variations that might be employed in rating excess contracts. One of the more common is a "burning cost" formula, which determines the reinsurance premium by multiplying the company's losses by a loss conversion factor, and then dividing the result by the company's subject premium. Such rating formulae normally cover a span of years to average out (or "burn off") the cost of the reinsurance and also include a minimum and maximum rate. Great care must be used in drafting clauses applicable to such rating formulae so as to preclude any possible misunderstanding.

Sliding Scale Commissions. Pro rata treaties commonly provide for a profit commission (in addition to the ceding commission) to be paid by the reinsurer to the company in the event of good experience under the contract. This provision obviously encourages the company to produce good results under the treaty, and there are a number of different calculations that might be employed. Some contracts provide that the ceding commission to the company will be calculated on a sliding scale basis, depending on the loss experience under the treaty. Such a sliding scale might incorporate wording as follows:

The final ceding commission shall be determined by the loss experience under the Agreement for each Agreement Year in accordance with the other paragraphs of this Article, but in the event of termination no adjustment shall be made thereafter until the termination of all liability and the settlement of all losses under the Agreement.

Within forty-five days following each January 1st, the Company will calculate an adjusted ceding commission for the Agreement Year then expired based on premiums earned and losses incurred. The ceding commission shall then be adjusted between the parties in accordance with the following schedule:

Should the ratio of losses incurred to premiums earned be 65% or higher, then the adjusted Ceding Commission shall be 30%. Should the ratio of losses incurred to premiums earned be less than 65%, then the adjusted commission shall be determined by adding 1% to 30% for each 1% reduction of loss ratio, until a commission allowance of 35% is reached at a loss ratio of 60%, and then ½% for each 1% reduction of loss ratio, until a commission allowance of 37.5% is reached at a loss ratio of 55% and then adding ¾% for each 1% reduction in loss ratio, subject to a maximum ceding commission of 45% at a 45% loss ratio.

The term "Premiums Earned" means the premiums ceded

during the Agreement Year, plus the unearned premium reserve at the beginning of the Agreement Year, less the unearned premium reserve at the close of the Agreement Year.

The term "Losses Incurred" means losses and loss adjustment expenses paid during the Agreement Year, less salvages recovered, plus reserves outstanding on losses at the end of the Agreement Year, less losses and loss expense outstanding at the end of the preceding Agreement Year, and with consideration for any credit or debit carry forward from the previous Agreement Year.

If the ratio of losses incurred to premiums earned for any Agreement Year, including any debits or credits carried forward, is less than 45%, the difference in percent between the actual loss ratio and 45% shall be multiplied by the premiums earned for the Agreement Year and the product shall be carried forward to the next Agreement Year's commission adjustment calculation as a credit to losses.

If the ratio of losses incurred to premiums earned for any Agreement Year, including any debits or credits carried forward, is more than 65%, the difference in percent between the actual loss ratio and 65% shall be multiplied by the premiums earned for the Agreement Year and the product shall be carried forward to the next Agreement Year's commission adjustment calculation as a debit to losses.

Should this Agreement be terminated on a run-off basis, then the run-off period shall be considered as an Agreement Year for purposes of this Article.

Contingent Commissions. Other contracts include a formula for calculating the actual loss experience under the treaty, then applying an agreed-upon percentage factor to any profit that is produced by the experience, as follows:

The Company shall receive a further allowance of 25% contingent commission on the net profits accruing under this Treaty, computed in accordance with the following formula, it being understood and agreed that all calculations of unearned premium reserve shall be made on the monthly pro rata basis:

(A) NET PREMIUMS EARNED TO BE:

    (1) The unearned premium reserve at the close of the previous contingent period, if any;

    (2) Plus the net premiums ceded during the contingent period;

    (3) Less the unearned premium reserve at the close of the contingent period.

(B) NET LOSSES INCURRED TO BE:

    (1) Losses and loss adjustment expenses paid during the contingent period;

    (2) Less the reserve for outstanding losses and loss adjustment expenses at the close of the previous contingent period, if any;

    (3) Plus the reserve for outstanding losses and loss adjustment expenses at the close of the contingent period.

(C) NET EXPENSES INCURRED TO BE:

    (1) 40% ceding commission on net premiums earned, computed as in (A) above;

    (2) Plus management expenses of 7½% of net premiums earned, computed as in (A) above;

    (3) Plus deficit or underwriting loss at the close of the previous contingent period, if any.

(D) NET PROFIT TO BE:

    (1) Net premiums earned, as in (A) above;

    (2) Less net losses incurred, as in (B) above;

    (3) Less net expenses incurred, as in (C) above.

The term "contingent period" shall mean the twelve-month period commencing on each January 1 and ending on each December 31, both days inclusive. Calculations of contingent commission as respects each contingent period shall be made annually except that after termination of the treaty, no further calculation shall be made until the expiration of all liability and the settlement of all losses falling under this Treaty. Statements of net profit shall be prepared by the Company and shall be forwarded to the Reinsurers within three months after the close of each contingent period. Contingent commissions due shall be paid immediately upon verification by the Reinsurers that its records are in agreement with the statement as rendered.

TAXES

All states require the ceding company to pay state premium taxes on its written premium before deducting any reinsurance premiums ceded. Although this requirement makes unnecessary its repetition in the reinsurance agreement, it has remained, nevertheless, a common practice for the contract to contain a specific Tax Clause. The clause was introduced into reinsurance contracts at a time when states were revising their statutes requiring the payment of premium taxes on gross premiums, and some reinsurers felt it would be useful to include in the contract a reminder to the company that the company was no longer allowed to deduct ceded premiums in calculating state premium taxes. Therefore, the clause appears to be included more out of habit and tradition than for any other compelling reason, since the specific purpose for which it was originally intended no longer exists. Today a typical Reinsurance Tax Clause would read as follows:

> In consideration of the terms under which this Agreement is issued, the Company undertakes not to claim any deduction of the premium hereon when making Canadian tax returns or when making tax returns, other than Income or Profit Tax returns, to any State or Territory of the United States of America or to the District of Columbia.

CURRENCY

Since it is not uncommon for the ceding company to become involved in policy transactions in foreign currency (particularly Canadian), it is standard practice to incorporate a Currency Clause in the reinsurance contract. Such a clause deals with the methods of currency conversion to be followed by the parties and the procedure to be observed in the event of a loss requiring payment in more than one currency. A typical Currency Clause might read as follows:

> Wherever the word "Dollars" and the sign "$" appear in this Agreement, they shall be construed to mean United States Dollars, excepting in those cases where the policies are issued by the Company in Canadian Dollars, in which cases they shall mean Canadian Dollars.

> In the event of the Company being involved in a loss requiring payment in United States and Canadian Currency, the Company's retention and the amount recoverable hereunder shall be apportioned to the two currencies in the same proportion as the amount of ultimate net loss in each currency bears

to the total amount of ultimate net loss paid by the Company.

For the purposes of this Agreement, where the Company receives premiums or pay losses in currencies other than United States or Canadian Currency, such premiums and losses shall be converted into United States Dollars at the actual rates of exchange at which these premiums and losses are entered on the Company's books.

PREMIUM AND ACCOUNTS ARTICLE

Every reinsurance contract will contain a provision dealing with the reports and remittances that the company must make to the reinsurer. A catastrophe excess contract normally has a relatively simple Premium Clause, spelling out the reinsurance rate and defining the subject premium base. If the contract provides for a minimum and deposit premium, such a reference will also appear in this article. If it is the intent to provide premium extraction factors for original policies written on an indivisible premium basis, an appropriate provision should also be made in this article. A sample Premium Clause that might appear in a catastrophe excess contract is as follows:

The Company shall pay to the Reinsurers in respect of each annual period during the currency of this Agreement premium calculated by applying a rate of 2.50% to the Gross Net Written Premium Income of the Company during such annual period in respect of business the subject matter of this Agreement.

The term "Gross Net Written Premium Income" as used herein shall be understood to mean gross premiums written less returned premiums and less premiums paid for reinsurances, recoveries of which inure to the benefit of this Agreement. For purposes hereon, 90% of the Company's original premium in respect of Homeowners Policies, where the premium is indivisible, shall be considered subject matter premium.

The annual minimum and deposit premium for this Agreement shall be $150,000 payable in quarterly installments of $37,500 at the beginning of each calendar quarter commencing July 1, 1976. Within forty-five (45) days after the close of the fourth quarter of each annual period, the Company shall submit a statement showing the actual premium due for such annual period, calculated in accordance with the first paragraph of this article, and shall remit to the Reinsurers the amount by which the actual premium exceeds the minimum and deposit premium.

A typical Premium and Accounts Article in a pro rata treaty would probably include the following provisions, which provide for statistical data the reinsurer requires in order to record the business correctly on its books.

A. The Company shall furnish the Reinsurers with the following reports:

MONTHLY:

(1) Monthly account current consisting of total net written premiums in respect of cessions made during the month in question less a ceding commission of 35% and less losses and loss adjustment expenses (after deduction of salvages) paid during such month;

(2) Reserve for losses outstanding at the end of the month in question; and

(3) Summary of paid losses, loss adjustment expense, and salvages segregated by major class.

QUARTERLY:

(1) Total net written premiums in respect of cessions made during the quarter segregated by major class;

(2) In-force and unearned premiums as of the end of the quarter, segregated by term, month, and year of expiration; and

(3) Summary of outstanding losses segregated by major class.

B. Within thirty days after the close of each month, the Company shall render the monthly account current specified in Paragraph A (1) above, for such month, and the balance due thereunder shall be payable by the debtor within sixty days after the close of the month under adjustment. It is agreed, however, that the Company may make request for immediate settlement by the Reinsurers of individual losses which exceed $25,000.

ERRORS AND OMISSIONS

The Errors and Omissions Clause, which is a standard provision in all reinsurance contracts, expresses and illustrates in an important way the utmost good faith that underlies the agreement between the parties. It recognizes that errors may be made by either party, but it provides that such errors shall not relieve the parties of liability as long as such errors are corrected as soon as possible. It not only deals with errors and omissions, as such, but also allows for delays which might occur in such functions as preparing accounts and paying losses. Such a Clause would probably contain wording similar to the following: "Any inadvertent delay, omission, or error shall not be held to relieve either party hereto from any liability which would attach to it hereunder if such delay, omission, or error is rectified immediately upon discovery."

The origins of this Clause date back to the days when it was the custom to provide the reinsurer with elaborate bordereaux listing policy cessions, and was thus intended to assure that coverage was provided even though an item might be left off a bordereau inadvertently. The Clause does have limitations that should be kept in mind. It is not intended to apply if the error or omission results from a shortcoming or lack of system in the business organization of the ceding company, nor can it properly be invoked to allow the ceding company to change its retention on a particular policy after a loss has occurred — unless it can be clearly established that an "error" was involved and not merely a case of bad judgment.

Access To Records

Reinsurers typically require the right to inspect the company's books and records applicable to the reinsurance provided. One important reason for the requirement is the reinsurer's interest in the adequacy of the company's loss reserves. Another is the possibility of turning up losses that might involve the reinsurer but on which the company has not yet advised the reinsurer. This right also allows the reinsurer to ascertain whether the company is following the terms and conditions of the contract, especially in such matters as the accuracy of cessions and calculation of reinsurance premiums. Such an Access-to-Records Clause would probably be worded along these lines:

The Reinsurers or their duly accredited representatives shall have free access to the books and records of the Company on matters relating to this reinsurance at all reasonable times for the purpose of obtaining information concerning this Agreement or the subject matter hereof.

Honorable Engagement

The "utmost good faith" concept, which is the cornerstone of all reinsurance contracts, carries with it the important corollary that the contract is an "honorable engagement" between the two parties. This point is well established in reinsurance practice and usage, and the wording of a typical Arbitration Clause confirms this concept. The Errors and Omissions Clause is also illustrative of this same principle. The concept imposes an obligation on both parties to exercise their responsibilities in a manner reflecting the highest level of integrity and good faith.

Modern reinsurance practices require the ceding company to provide a minimum of accounting data to the reinsurer. The reinsurer must therefore assume that its client will exercise the utmost degree of diligence and honesty in fulfilling the contract requirements. The ceding company is obviously in a more advantageous position than the reinsurer in this respect, because it has first-hand information on the nature of its business and the exact subject matter insured.

The concept of an honorable engagement extends not only to the reporting requirements imposed on the ceding company but also to the defense and handling of claims. The company must retain the right to adjust and settle claims according to its own best judgment, and the reinsurer is obliged to pay as the company pays. This honorable engagement concept imposes on the ceding company an obligation to adjust claims in a highly professional manner, particularly in view of the fact that the reinsurer's money is at stake whenever the company's retention is exceeded.

It may be said that the obligation between the two parties to a reinsurance contract bears some resemblance to a fiduciary relationship, with all that term implies in the way of confidence and trust. The slightest suspicion that either the reinsurer or the client company is not treating the agreement as an honorable engagement puts the entire relationship in jeopardy and may very well lead to cancellation of the contract.

Provisions Common To Excess Covers

REINSURING CLAUSE

Earlier in this chapter a typical Reinsuring Clause in an excess of loss contract was cited, obligating the reinsurer to "indemnify" the company for losses under the contract. It is well established that a reinsurance contract is a contract of "indemnity," i.e., the contractual obligation is for the reinsurer to "reimburse" the company for losses. The reinsurer is not under obligation to put the company in funds for any loss it has not actually sustained, and in practice it is normally expected that the company has actually paid the loss before it seeks indemnification from the reinsurer. This indemnification principle is equally applicable to pro rata treaties, even though the word "indemnify" may not actually appear in the pro rata contract itself.

The excess of loss Reinsuring Clause quoted also made quite clear that the contract covered loss occurrences arising during the term of the contract. This date-of-loss provision is important and should appear clearly set forth either in the Reinsuring Clause or in some other appropriate place in the contract, perhaps in the commencement and termination provisions. Exceptions may be made with so-called "Claims-Made" or "Losses Discovered" policies, in which the reinsurance contract may specify the date of loss to be the date of the first report of the claim to the insured or to the company. It is important to make this distinction clear in excess contracts to avoid confusion as to how the date of loss is to be determined, depending upon the type of original policy involved in the loss. Good reinsurance practice is for the reinsurance contract to follow the original policy in establishing a loss date, for the reinsurance is intended to be concurrent with the terms and conditions of the policy reinsured.

RETENTION AND LIMITS

It is obviously necessary to spell out in an excess contract the retention the company is to keep, as well as the limit of the reinsurer's liability. This normally poses no particular problem and consists of a straightforward statement such as the following: "No claim shall be made hereunder unless the Company shall have first sustained, by reason of any one loss occurrence, a net loss the excess of $1,000,000. The Reinsurers shall then be liable for 90% of the amount of net loss the excess of $1,000,000 each loss occurrence, with a limit of liability to the Reinsurers of $900,000 in respect to any one loss occurrence."

One possible complication may occur in excess contracts (normally casualty covers) which provide for prorating the loss adjustment expenses between the ceding company and the reinsurer. The loss amount plus the pro rata share of loss adjustment expenses may possibly exceed the reinsurer's "limit of liability" in the contract. To avoid confusion in such cases, it is helpful to define the reinsurer's limit of liability as that amount stated in the contract, plus the reinsurer's share of such prorated expenses.

The example cited above provides for 90% coverage of excess losses. In such contracts it is common for the reinsurer to require a statement that the ceding company will retain the additional 10% for its own account and unreinsured in any way. Such a provision would obviously be unnecessary in a contract which provides for a 100 % recovery of losses.

DEFINITIONS

Excess of loss contracts, by their very nature, require a longer and more comprehensive list of definition than the normal pro rata treaty. This arises out of the necessity for describing exactly what constitutes a loss under the contract and has led to considerable discussion within the industry as to the precise terminology to be employed.

One Event. Since the typical property catastrophe excess contract is intended to protect the company against an accumulation of losses that, when combined together in one event, exceed the company's retention under the contract, it becomes important to consider how an "event" is to be defined. The subject becomes even more complicated when dealing with casualty losses, where it is often difficult to determine precisely when the loss occurred. For example, in third party property damage cases, the loss might extend over a considerable period of time, such as the pollution of a river or stream. Third party bodily injury losses also present such a problem, as in cases where a drug causes injury or death to a number of people over an extended time period.

In the case of either third party property damage or bodily injury, most reinsurers now content themselves with a definition stating that the terms "accident," "disaster," "casualty," and "occurrence" as used in the agreement shall mean each and every such accident, disaster, casualty, occurrence, or series of accidents, disasters, casualties, or occurrences "arising out of one event." Such an approach eliminates the need for lengthy discussions of how the actual occurrence date is to be determined, a determination which may be impossible to spell out precisely and comprehensively in the contract because of the variable circumstances of each case.

To rely simply on the term "arising out of one event" assumes that the parties will be able to reach a mutual agreement, according to the customs of the business and depending on the circumstances applicable to each situation. One rarely sees in current casualty excess contracts lengthy definitions of the formulae to be used in determining the date of loss, because such definitions in the past have frequently led to more confusion than clarity. Thus, the compromise approach is taken: referring to "one event" in the contract, and relying on the good faith of the parties to agree on an equitable solution.

Hourly Period. In addition to the "one event" terminology, property catastrophe excess contracts then go on to specify that certain hourly periods shall determine what is one event in the case of wind, riot, earthquake, and sometimes flood losses. This represents an attempt to confine such loss events to a specified time period, and, in the case of riot losses, to a geographical area. The reasoning behind such hourly provisions is to prevent the company from including as one event the losses for several events. For example, wind losses might go on for many days and inflict damage over a wide territory even though they did not arise out of one particular storm, which was the hazard the reinsurer had in mind when agreeing to provide the coverage. The reference to a geographical area along with the hourly limitation in the riot provisions was strongly influenced by the Dr. Martin Luther King riots in 1968. At that time, reinsurers became concerned that a ceding company might attempt to include as one event disturbances that occurred nationwide, which was not the hazard contemplated. A concise and typical hourly clause dealing with wind, riots, and earthquakes might read as follows:

Except as hereinafter provided the term "loss occurrence" shall mean any one accident, casualty, disaster or occurrence or series of accidents, casualties, disasters, or occurrences arising out of or following on one event.

As regards the perils of tornado, cyclone, windstorm, hurricane, or hail, the term "loss occurrence" shall mean all losses occasioned by tornadoes, cyclones, windstorms, hurricanes, or hailstorms arising from the same atmospheric disturbance and occurring during any continuous period of forty-eight hours.

As regards the peril of earthquake, the term "loss occurrence" shall mean all losses occasioned by earthquake, including ensuing fire, occurring during any continuous period of one hundred and sixty-eight hours.

As regards the perils of riot, civil commotion, vandalism, and malicious mischief, the term "loss occurrence" shall mean all losses occasioned by riot, civil commotion, vandalism, and malicious mischief including losses caused by fire, smoke, or explosion resulting therefrom, occurring during any continuous period of seventy-two hours and within the area circumscribed by one principal municipality or county and the municipalities or counties immediately abutting thereon.

The Company may elect the moment from which each of the specified periods shall be deemed to have commenced; provided, however, that such election shall not result in the inclusion of an individual loss within more than than one loss occurrence, as herein defined, and that no such period shall commence prior to the time of the first loss sustained by the Company as a result of the respective loss occurrence.

There are some shortcomings to these clauses, one of the more interesting being the use of the term "atmospheric disturbance" with reference to wind losses. Meteorologists tell us that such an expression is not a part of official meteorological terminology, but the term nonetheless appears in many reinsurance contracts and represents an attempt to deal with a situation for which there may be no better answer. The reference to "ensuing fire" in the earthquake provision also may raise a question as to whether such fire must have started and stopped within the 168-hour period. Common sense dictates, however, that the intent is to cover ensuing fires which incepted during the hourly period, even though the fires were actually still burning beyond the term period specified. In the case of fires, it is simply not realistic to assume a determination can always be made as to when damage actually stopped.

The provision that no hourly period shall commence prior to the time of the first loss sustained by the company as a result of the respective loss occurrence is a relatively new provision in this standard clause. The provision is used to prevent the ceding company from starting to count the 48-hour wind loss period, for instance, sometime before the first loss was sustained so that two separate loss occurrences could be claimed, thus enabling the company to take two retentions and to recover twice from the same wind loss.

Per risk excess contracts do not create a problem over hourly periods, since the reinsurance coverage is designed to protect the company against losses arising out of one risk only. The reinsurer is presumably aware from the underwriting data in its possession or in the contract itself of how the company, according to its underwriting practices, determines "one risk."

Ultimate Net Loss

The Ultimate Net Loss Clause in an excess contract states how allocated loss adjustment expenses are to be handled in determining recovery under the contract. The Clause also specified the procedure for dealing with salvage recoveries and recoveries from other reinsurers.

Until fairly recently in casualty excess contracts, it had been the tradition for loss adjustment expenses to be prorated between the company and the reinsurer according to their respective shares of the loss itself. Property excess contracts, on the other hand, usually provided that allocated loss adjustment expenses were to be included in the company's ultimate net loss. There is some indication that this tradition is changing, with more contracts (both property and casualty) now including allocated loss adjustment expenses in the ultimate net loss. The theory is that the company should be encouraged through indemnification from the reinsurer to incur as much legal expense as necessary in resisting a claim, where circumstances so dictate.

An Ultimate Net Loss Clause in an excess contract which provides for including allocated loss adjustment expenses in the company's ultimate net loss might read as follows:

> The term "ultimate net loss" shall be understood to mean the actual loss or losses sustained by the Company under its policies, such loss or losses to include expenses of litigation, if any, and all other loss expenses of the Company (excluding general office overhead and salaries of its officials and regular employees but including the pro rata share of salaries and expenses of the Company's outside employees according to the time occupied in adjusting such loss and also including expenses of the Company's officials incurred in connection with the loss, but such inclusion shall not apply to salaries of the Company's officials or any normal overhead charges) but salvages and any other recoveries, including recoveries under all reinsurance, whether collected or not, are first to be deducted from such loss to arrive at the amount of liability, if any, attaching hereunder.

> Nothing in this clause, however, shall be construed as meaning that losses are not recoverable hereunder until the ultimate net loss to the Company has been ascertained.

> Recoveries from underlying catastrophe excess contracts effected by the Company shall be entirely disregarded for all purposes of this contract and shall not be considered to be a recovery which reduces the loss under this contract.

It is important to keep in mind that the Ultimate Net Loss Clause should not refer to losses "paid" by the Company, as this wording has been held by some regulatory authorities to be in conflict with the intent and provisions of the Insolvency Clause in the contract.

NET RETAINED LINES

The Net Retained Lines Clause in an excess reinsurance contract is an amplification of the Ultimate Net Loss Clause and is intended to make clear that the reinsurance applies only to that portion of any insurance which the company retains net for its own account. This is a logical requirement, as otherwise the company could conceivably recover the same loss from two reinsurers.

The Ultimate Net Loss Clause quoted above made reference to underlying excess reinsurance which is to be disregarded in determining the company's net loss. Unless such a statement is made, there is obviously a conflict with the Net Retained Lines Clause, which states that only exposures which the company keeps net for its own account are to be protected. This statement is necessary only in those instances where the company actually carries underlying excess reinsurance. The clear intent is for the reinsurer on the particular layer of reinsurance in which he participates to ignore the fact that the company also carried reinsurance underneath that layer, such underlying layers to inure to the benefit of the company. A typical Net Retained Lines Clause is ordinarily a short statement reading somewhat as follows:

> This contract applies only to that portion of any insurance or reinsurance which the Company retains net for its own account, and in calculating the amount of loss hereunder and also in computing the amount or amounts in excess of which this contract attaches, only loss in respect of that portion of any insurance or reinsurance which the Company retains net for its own account shall be included.

> It is understood and agreed that the amount of the Reinsurer's liability hereunder in respect of any loss or losses shall not be increased by reason of the inability of the Company to collect from any other Reinsurer, whether specific or general, any amounts which may have become due from them, whether such inability arises from the insolvency of such other Reinsurer or otherwise.

Notice Of Loss And Loss Settlements

All excess reinsurance contracts include an obligation for the company to give notice to the reinsurer of a loss which may involve the reinsurance. However, this requirement is sometimes a source of difficulty between the company and the reinsurer, because the determination of whether a loss is large enough to involve the reinsurer is left to the discretion of the company. Claims adjusting is obviously an art, not a science, and considerable difference of opinion may arise as to the proper reserve for a particular claim. The typical Clause quoted below is actually a combination Notice of Loss Clause and Loss Settlements Clause, and it is logical to combine them in the same article.

> In the event of an accident, disaster, casualty, or occurrence occurring which either results in or appears to be of a serious nature as probably to result in a loss involving this Agreement, the Company shall give notice as soon as reasonably practicable to the Reinsurers, and the Company shall keep the Reinsurers advised of all subsequent developments in connection therewith.

> The Reinsurers agree to abide by the loss settlements of the Company, such settlements to be considered as satisfactory proofs of loss, and amounts falling to the share of the Reinsurers shall be immediately payable to the Company by them upon reasonable evidence of the amount paid or to be paid by the Company being presented to the Reinsurers.

If the reinsurer wishes to lay down a specific requirement for the point at which a loss is to be reported (perhaps when the company establishes a reserve equal to one half of its retention under the contract), such condition may be incorporated in the Notice of Loss Clause. Such a requirement would enable the reinsurer to keep a closer watch on its possible exposure and to take action to protect its own interests as necessary. Late reported losses are indeed a sensitive point with reinsurers, and the reinsured company is well advised to heed the loss reporting requirement with utmost conscientiousness.

In the loss settlement part of the Clause there must be a requirement that the reinsurer will abide by the loss settlements of the company. Otherwise, the company could never be confident its reinsurer would indemnify it for a particular loss, and the purpose of the reinsurance might well be defeated.

Under certain conditions, the reinsurer may also demand "claims cooperation" or "claims association" wording which will permit the reinsurer to join in the disposition of a claim. Such wording would probably read as follows:

> It is understood and agreed that, when requested, the Company will afford the Reinsurer an opportunity to be associated with the Company, at the expense of the Reinsurer, in the defense of any claim or suit or proceeding involving this reinsurance, and the Company will cooperate in every respect in the defense or control of such claim, suit, or proceeding.

REINSTATEMENT

Castastrophe excess contracts (particularly property covers) frequently provide for a reinstatement premium if a loss is sustained under the contract. On the other hand, if a contract is to be reinstated to its full limit without the payment of an additional premium, it is well for the contract to so specify in order to eliminate any possible misunderstanding between the parties. This is particularly true since reinstatement premium provisions are so common, and it might be construed that the lack of a reinstatement premium requirement was merely an oversight.

Reinstatement provisions are normally calculated on a pro rata basis, being pro rata as to the amount reinstated and to the unexpired term of the contract. An example is as follows:

> In the event of a claim under this contract, it is agreed that the amount of liability hereunder is reduced from the time of the occurrence of the loss by the sum payable on such claim. However, the amount so exhausted is immediately reinstated from the time of the occurrence of the loss. For each amount so reinstated, the Company agrees to pay an additional premium calculated at pro rata of the annual earned reinsurance premium hereon, being pro rata as to the fraction of the face value of this contract (i.e., the fraction of $9,000,000) so reinstated and as to the fraction of the unexpired term hereunder at the time of the occurrence. Nevertheless, the liability of the Reinsurers shall not exceed $9,000,000 in any one loss occurrence, nor $18,000,000 in the aggregate during the term of this contract for all perils combined.

This particular example of a Reinstatement Clause provides for one full reinstatement at pro rata premium. Other clauses may provide for different calculations, perhaps using an arbitrary time factor of 50% of the term of the contract, rather than figuring from the actual date of the loss. Sometimes provision for more than one reinstatement is made. The arrangements are negotiable and should be clearly established before the contract is completed.

EXTENDED TERMINATION

Catastrophe excess reinsurance contracts are intended to cover on an "occurrence" basis, so as to protect the company from all losses arising out of one event. The fact that such an event or occurrence might be in progress when the reinsurance contract expires does not relieve the reinsurer of its obligation to indemnify the company for the full loss arising from the event. This leads to the inclusion in such catastrophe contracts of an Extended Termination Clause reading essentially as follows: "Should this contract terminate while a loss occurrence covered hereunder is in progress, it is understood and agreed that, subject to the other conditions of this Contract, the Reinsurers shall be responsible for their proportion of the entire loss or damage caused by such loss occurrence."

Such provision properly appears only in catastrophe excess contracts which, by their nature, deal with all losses arising out of one event. If there were no such provision, it is conceivable that old and new reinsurers might each require the company to stand a separate retention under the expiring as well as under the new excess contract. This is not a proper provision in a per risk excess contract, where the "event" concept is lacking.

Good Practice in Treaty Drafting

BREVITY AND AVOIDANCE OF REDUNDANCY

The well drafted reinsurance contract need not be lengthy. In fact, the more concise the wording and the fewer instances of redundancy, the less likely it is that difference of opinion will arise. Superfluous provisions are particularly dangerous, because they may carry the implication that something was intended by the parties which was not really contemplated when the agreement was negotiated. One example of such superfluous provisions might be the attachment of the Nuclear Incident Liability Reinsurance Clause to a property contract. The fact that such a clause was attached may lead to the impression that perhaps liability exposures (as opposed to property only) were intended to be protected by the cover. The prudent contract drafter will say only what is necessary and appropriate in the contract and will not include any provisions which are not really required to establish clearly the intent of both parties.

Overlapping provisions can also be dangerous, since they may cause confusion as to which of the provisions is to govern the terms of the reinsurance. To the extent practicable, each provision of the contract should be self-contained and not require complicated and confusing cross references to other sections or provisions. The objective to be achieved is that of a straightforward statement of the terms and conditions that govern the reinsurance transactions, free from unnecessary elaborations and "frills." As has been seen, there is fairly uniform wording that covers many provisions in the standard reinsurance contract. The wise drafter will confine himself to the use of such uniform provisions which have over the years come to be well understood and uniformly interpreted by reinsurance practitioners.

STANDARD OR MODEL WORDINGS

The use of standard wording is intended for a sound purpose. That purpose is to assure that the contract is readily understood by both parties, or by arbitrators, or conceivably by a court that might be requested to settle a dispute.

Compliance with some statutory regulations also dictates the use of standard wording, perhaps the most important example of which is the Insolvency Clause. The statutory provisions governing the Insolvency Clause in certain states are quite clear as to what the Clause must provide; this particular provision is, however, the only current statutory requirement that lays out in clear-cut language what a reinsurance contract provision must contain.

Reinsurance contract wordings enjoy the rather unusual privilege of being virtually free of specific regulatory provisions. The assumption is that close regulation is not necessary, since the parties are considered to be knowledgeable and sophisticated in reinsurance matters. Hence, there is little need for statutory requirements to protect either of the parties. This is not to say that a reinsurance contract must not meet the essential requirements of commercial law. Such requirement of contractual law as the "intent to make the agreement," a "meeting of the minds" (which is accomplished through offer and acceptance), and "consideration" (which is commonly held to mean that a legal benefit to one party or a legal detriment to the other, or both, must be present) — are essential features of a reinsurance contract if it is to be enforceable at law.

AMENDMENTS AND ADDENDA

Reinsurance contracts frequently require changes whenever different requirements and revised terms arise by agreement. Such changes are normally made by means of formal amendments (or endorsements, as they are sometimes called) to the contract itself. Such amendments tend to follow a standard format which might be illustrated as follows:

Addendum Number 1

to

Reinsurance Contract No. 2819

"Fourth Casualty Excess of Loss Contract"

Between the ABC Reinsurance Company (hereinafter called the "Reinsurer") and the XYZ Insurance Company (hereinafter called the "Company"), originally effective January 1, 1976.

It is hereby mutually understood and agreed that, effective 12:01 A.M., Eastern Standard Time, January 1, 1977, the following paragraph is added to Article I, Exclusions:

"E. Underground coal mining."

All other terms and conditions remain unchanged.

Such an addendum would close with the signature clause as it appeared in the original reinsurance contract.

The use of an amendment is the most desirable way to effect changes in reinsurance contracts, for the addendum illustrated clearly identifies the contract which is being amended and leaves no doubt as to precisely what is being altered. An alternative to the amendment technique is a "letter agreement" dealing with changes by means of an exchange of correspondence between the parties. While such letter agreements apparently serve the same purpose as amendments and may appear to be easier, such agreements nevertheless are risky in effecting changes; letters may easily be incorporated in a large correspondence file and become lost in the process. The small extra effort required to prepare a formal addendum attached to the contract is worthwhile. The attachment provides ready reference and identification of any changes that have been made, without having to refer to the correspondence between the two companies.

Problem Areas

Judgments In Excess Of Policy Limits

It is not altogether uncommon for an insurance company to be held liable in third party claims for a judgment in excess of its policy limits. Such situations arise when a company fails to accept a settlement offer within its original policy limits or commits some act of alleged or actual negligence in handling the claims. The court may award a judgment against the original insured which is in excess of the company's policy limits, and the insured in turn sues the company on the grounds that the company did not handle the claim settlement properly.

There is still controversy as to how such situations should be handled in reinsurance contracts. For example, should the reinsurer follow the fortunes of the ceding company even though the reinsurer was not directly involved in the handling of the claim? Reinsurance custom is rapidly coming to the point where the reinsurer now accepts such liability under third party contracts. The reasoning is found in one of the essential principles underlying an excess of loss cover; the ceding company shall be assured that all losses over and above the retention point will be accepted by the reinsurer, within the reinsurance contract limit. In order to make this liability of the reinsurer clear, the majority of third party excess contracts now employ a "Loss in Excess of Original Policy Limits" Clause, reading essentially as follows:

> With respect to Third Party Liability Insurance of any kind, this Agreement shall protect the Company, within the limits hereof, in connection with any loss for which the Company may be legally liable to pay in excess of the limit of its original policy, such loss in excess of the limit having been incurred because of failure by it to settle within the policy limit or by reason of alleged or actual negligence, fraud, or bad faith in rejecting an offer of settlement or in the preparation of the defense or in the trial of any action against its Insured or in the preparation or prosecution of an appeal consequent upon such action.

Punitive Damages

There is perhaps no more vexing and complicated problem currently facing the reinsurance industry than that of punitive damages. Such damages are awards assessed by a court for intentional wrongdoing, reckless disregard of others, or outrageous, malicious, or fraudulent conduct. As the term implies, punitive damages are a "punishment" assessed against the guilty party. There has been a great deal written on this subject, and a comprehensive treatment of the topic could easily require a complete chapter in this book. The following, therefore, represents an attempt only to highlight the essential aspects of the problem in a few paragraphs.

In those cases where punitive damages are assessed against an insured for intentional injury or willful and wanton misconduct, some states hold it is against public policy to pass on such "punishment" to the insuring company. In other jurisdictions, punitive damages assessed against an insured are held to be covered by the insurance policy, unless specifically excluded. Some members of the insurance industry recently attempted to insert such a general exclusion in third party policies, but the attempt was defeated by the failure of several state insurance departments to approve the exclusion. As the situation now stands, there appears to be a general agreement that a reinsurer must indemnify the ceding company for punitive damages assessed against its insured (in those jurisdictions allowing for insurance coverage against such awards) unless the reinsurance contract specifically excludes such coverage.

A second question, and one more pertinent to this discussion, arises when punitive damages are assessed against an insurance company — if it is held that the company acted in an outrageous or malicious manner in the handling of a claim. Such instances arise when the policyholder can prove, for instance, that he suffered harm or financial loss as a consequence of the manner in which his claim was handled. The question then arises as to whether the ceding company, against whom the judgment is rendered, can seek indemnification from its reinsurer for such judgment.

At this writing, there is considerable difference of opinion in the industry on this point. Some in the reinsurance business maintain that punitive awards against a client company are a business risk, and, as such, not covered by the reinsurance contract. The reasoning is that such a tort committed by the reinsured company is more properly protected by the company's general liability insurer. In other words, such acts of misconduct or wrongdoing on the part of the ceding company or its employees fall outside the scope and intent of the reinsurance contract, which is limited to the insurance risks underwritten by the company.

The fact that punitive damage awards are becoming more common makes this subject a matter of considerable concern. Indeed, some reinsurers are incorporating specific exclusions in their contracts to clarify the situation. The precise wording suggested varies somewhat, but a typical example might be as follows: "Liability of the Reinsurer for any damages assessed against the Company arising out of its conduct in the investigation, negotiation, defense or handling of any claims or suits or in any dealings with its policyholders is specifically excluded under this contract." However, there is an indication that some reinsurers may be willing to provide the coverage, but at an additional cost. The status of the coverage or the lack of it in present and past reinsurance contracts remains in doubt, and will do so until arbitration or a court decision tests the wordings.

Because some confusion appears to exist on the subject, it may be well to attempt to clarify here the distinction between judgments in excess of the original policy limit and punitive damages for outrageous conduct. The essential difference to be kept in mind is that an action for outrageous conduct is an independent cause of action for "extra-contractual" damages with a goal of punishment. On the other hand, in excess judgment cases, recovery is sought first from the insured for his negligence, and the insured then sues his insurance carrier for breach of contract in handling and adjusting the claim under the insured's policy.

PROTECTING A COMPANY AND ITS QUOTA SHARE REINSURERS

A not uncommon practice is for an excess reinsurance contract to be so drawn as to protect a ceding company and its quota share reinsurers. Such a practice should be discouraged because it apparently establishes a contractual relationship between the excess reinsurers and an unnamed third party, i.e., the quota share reinsurers. This relationship is obviously not good practice in any type of contract. When utilized in the context noted above, the practice can create serious problems relating to the responsibility for collection of reinsurance premiums and the recovery of reinsured losses.

The same result can be achieved by simply including in the excess contract a statement to the effect that the company carries quota share reinsurance and that such reinsurance is to be ignored for all purposes of the excess contract. Such a statement eliminates any difficulties over the company's retention warranty in the excess contract and also precludes difficulties arising between the excess reinsurer and the quota share carriers over loss recoveries and premium collections. The statement does, in effect, eliminate any "fuzzy" contractual obligation between the excess reinsurer and the quota share reinsurer; it reduces the contractual relationship to one between the original ceding company and the company's excess reinsurers, which is the desirable objective.

In order to provide the quota share reinsurers with evidence of the excess protection they have agreed to purchase for joint account with the original ceding company, a warranty may be included in the quota share treaty. That warranty can confirm that excess reinsurance is being carried for the joint account of the two parties and can also authorize the original ceding company to deduct the pro rata cost of such excess protection from premiums paid to the quota share reinsurers.[3]

SEVERAL AND NOT JOINT LIABILITY

The Preamble or Reinsuring Clause in a tightly drawn reinsurance contract will make clear that the liability of a particular reinsurer signing the contract is "several and not joint" with the co-reinsurers on the contract. This clarity is appropriate to eliminate any possible interpretation that any one of the participating reinsurers in the contract is actually liable for the shares of the other co-reinsurers on a "joint" basis. The intent of several liability is that the particular reinsurer is assuming liability only for its specified percentage share of the entire coverage provided. Frequently these words are used: "The share of the Reinsurer shall be

---

[3]Robert Salm, "Quota Share Reinsurers in an Excess Contract," *Reinsurance*, August, 1973, p. 204.

separate and apart from the share of the other Reinsurers, and shall not be joint with those of other Reinsurers, and the Reinsurer shall in no event participate in the interest and liabilities of the other Reinsurers." A shorter and equally acceptable statement is as follows: "Under the terms of this contract the Reinsurer agrees to assume severally and not jointly with other participants a __% share of the liability described in the contract."

Package Policies

There has been a significant development in recent years within the insurance industry of so-called "package policies" which incorporate within one policy form various coverages formerly insured under individual policy forms. Perhaps the best known of these package policies is the Homeowners Policy, which incorporates property damage, third party liability, and burglary coverage into one policy. More recently there has been a similar development in the commercial field, where there is virtually no limit as to the types of coverage that might be included in a Commercial Multi-Peril Policy form. These package policies create problems for the contract drafter where the contract is intended to protect some, but not all, of the coverages encompassed in the package policy. This is particularly true if the ceding company is seeking reinsurance protection for property coverages under one reinsurance contract and casualty protection under a second contract with another reinsurer.

Such a situation obviously calls for careful and precise drafting, with particular reference to business covered and to the exclusions. It also calls for precise wording of the permium clause to make sure that the subject premium is properly identified, and that any necessary provisions are made for premium extraction factors with which to extract non-subject premiums if the package policy is written on a non-divisible premium basis.

Follow-the-Fortunes Clause

Reinsurance contracts sometimes contain a provision to the effect that "It is the intent of this agreement that the Reinsurer shall follow the fortunes of the Company in all matters falling under this agreement." This is a controversial statement and has unfortunately been the subject of many different interpretations. Editorial limitations do not permit an exhaustive discussion of these various interpretations, some of which are so broad as to imply that the reinsurer should accept and cover virtually every conceivable incident of bad fortune that might be suffered by the Company.

The true intent of the Clause can perhaps be summarized by drawing a distinction between the "insurance" fortunes of the ceding company as opposed to the company's "business" fortunes. It is the true intent that the reinsurer follow only the insurance fortunes of the company; for example, the risk that a loss will occur under a policy or that the company may, under certain circumstances, even be required to pay a claim for which it is, in fact, not liable. It is not the intent that the reinsurer follow the business fortunes of the company, such as the dishonesty of an employee or the inability of a producing agent to pay premiums.

These latter incidents are misfortunes that might befall any ordinary businessman, and, as such, are to be distinguished from the activities peculiar to the pure insurance operations of the company, which were those contemplated by the reinsurer when the reinsurance agreements were established. If this distinction can be borne in mind, the Follow-the-Fortunes Clause which appears in some reinsurance contracts becomes clearer and less likely to lend itself to misunderstanding or misinterpretation.[4]

Summary

This chapter has discussed how the utmost good faith tradition affects the drafting of reinsurance contracts and allows for the preparation of a relatively short, concise document. Several clauses commonly used by reinsurance drafters have been cited, giving examples and explaining the reasons behind them. Practical suggestions for the improvement of contract drafting have been discussed, as well as certain problem areas which require special attention. Familiarity with these principles and suggestions will hopefully prove of value to those responsible for the preparation of reinsurance documentation.

*   *   *   *   *   *

About the Author of Chapter 4

Robert F. Salm was born in Keokuk, Iowa, on July 15, 1921. After service in World War II as a master sergeant, he received his B.A. Degree in political science from Cornell College in 1949.

His entire insurance career has been with Continental Casualty's Reinsurance Department which he joined in 1952 as an administrative assistant. He became an assistant secretary of the company in 1965 and an assistant vice president in 1977.

---

[4]Rudolf H. Grossman, "The Limits of the Reinsurer's Obligation to 'Follow the Fortunes' of the Reinsured," *Reinsurance*, March, 1970, pp. 481-485.

5

Facultative Reinsurance: Reinsuring Individual Policies

by William G. Clark*

To the French, facultative is a baseball term meaning "fielder's choice." In reinsurance, it means much the same thing. Facultative reinsurance is a transaction between reinsurer and reinsured ceding company involving one specific policy. The primary insurer voluntarily offers a portion of its risk. Just as there is no obligation to offer, the reinsurer is under no obligation to accept. Risk characteristics, coverages, conditions, exclusions, retentions and limits are discussed by the reinsurer and the ceding company. A reinsurance premium quotation is made to the ceding company. The primary insurer may: 1) accept the quotation, or 2) reject the quotation and proceed to write the insurance without the benefit of facultative reinsurance, or 3) reject the quotation and advise the producer that it is unwilling to insure the risk, or 4) reject the quotation and advise the producer that it is only willing to write that portion of the risk which it intends to retain on a net basis — in most cases, simply a smaller limit of liability. Should the proposition prove to be marketable, coverage is bound and, in due course, a certificate reflecting the terms and conditions of the transaction is issued by the reinsurer. The facultative reinsurance certificate is simply a contract between the reinsurer and the ceding company to which the original insured is not a party. Indeed, the insured is usually completely unaware of the existence of the facultative reinsurance.

Facultative reinsurance is often referred to as one of the purest forms of underwriting. Property and casualty facultative reinsurance

* Senior Vice President, General Reinsurance Corporation, 600 Steamboat Road, Greenwich, Conn. 06830

both deal with risks which, because of the hazard or amount of insurance involved, fall outside the normal pattern of risks written by a primary insurance company — risks which for the particular ceding company are unique or unusual and which the company is either unwilling or unable to handle within its normal treaty reinsurance facilities. The very same risks, when offered to some other primary company, might prove to be entirely acceptable to it. Certainly, the occasional offbeat risk — a rock concert, a demolition contractor, some forms of professional liability, products liability on new or exotic products — demands innovative and creative underwriting approaches. Because such a risk is so unusual, its underwriting necessarily transcends existing actuarial and ratemaking techniques. The nature of facultative business requires an underwriting atmosphere where each risk is: 1) judged individually for coverage, and 2) priced at a rate which is commensurate with exposure.

Certain basic operating principles are followed by all facultative reinsurers. While the ceding company is relatively free to select its retention or participation and while the reinsurance may be purchased on either an excess of loss or pro rata basis, reinsurers seek to avoid involvement in areas of loss frequency. Thus, the approach to a property capacity problem on a pro rata basis would normally involve a significant deductible, and an automobile fleet would only be handled on an excess of loss basis. Facultative underwriting, therefore, not only involves consideration of the merits of a risk, but usually requires appraisal of exposures at varying levels of indemnity. Furthermore, as the ceding company controls loss settlement, it should reasonably have financial interest in the settlement. Hence, facultative underwriters are unwilling to provide reinsurance without a reasonable first loss or share participation on the part of the ceding company.

In the early post World War II years, Lloyd's was virtually the sole market for facultative reinsurance. It was rarely used, however, due to the difficulties of long distance communication coupled with the added cost of dealing through intermediaries. Facultative departments of reinsurance companies first appeared in the United States in the early 1950's, and the reinsurance was sold directly to primary companies without going through reinsurance brokers. It was an effort to offer more service to treaty clients by providing a domestic market for those risks which, for reason of capacity or loss potential, were better covered outside the treaty arrangement.

As the concept and utility of facultative reinsurance further evolved, primary companies found it a helpful tool in influencing their underwriting results. Through the reduction of net retained limits and the controlling of exposures, they found they could stabilize results without running the risk of jeopardizing a favorable treaty rate earned over a long period of time. Meeting production goals frequently included either the "not-so-average" risk or the large and difficult account. Not only could the primary underwriter buy capacity for either situation but, at the same time, a second underwriting opinion could be obtained from an underwriter who was skilled at analyzing the unique and unusual. Today, insurance companies use facultative reinsurance for many of the same reasons. While large accounts are often placed through reinsurance brokers, the vast majority of facultative placements are handled by direct writing reinsurers, those which deal directly with the primary companies. This saves brokerage commission and guarantees underwriter-to-underwriter communication, which is so vital on high hazard or complex risks.

The Purposes of Facultative Reinsurance

The purchase of facultative reinsurance may fulfill a variety of underwriting, production, financial, and management objectives. The following are the major reasons a primary company seeks facultative reinsurance:

1) Treaty Exclusions. As previously discussed, treaties frequently exclude certain classes of business. Facultative reinsurance provides the primary underwriter with an alternative to declining coverage on risks that do not qualify for inclusion in the treaty. For example, many treaties exclude volatile exposures such as blasting contractors, munitions manufacturers, or long-haul truckers.

2) Treaty Protection. If a ceding company feels that certain classes of risks, although not specifically excluded from the treaty, may have an adverse impact on the treaty experience, it may seek facultative reinsurance protection on those risks. While perhaps not excluded from a treaty, a school bus might be placed facultatively.

3) Net Protection. A primary company's "net" is that portion of a risk which it retains for its own account, exclusive of treaty arrangement. For example, an underwriter working with a $500,000 "net" may wish to protect it by purchasing facultative reinsurance in excess of a retained limit of only $100,000. Many high exposure risks might fall into this category — a ladder manufacturer, a pharmaceutical producer, or a sewer and water main contractor. Indeed, most companies buy facultative reinsurance over a limit smaller than their normal treaty retention.

4) Capacity. Treaty terms and company underwriting guidelines set

limitations on capacity. Facultative reinsurance can provide additional capacity, particularly on property business.

5) Accommodation. Business or agency accommodation occasionally requires that a primary insurance company accept substandard or less than desirable business, or business in which it simply has no experience, and therefore no confidence in its ability to write it profitably. Facultative reinsurance can assist the primary insurance company in such a situation. The classic example of accommodation business is the placement of automobile coverage for an eighteen-year-old who has had four accidents. Normally, the individual would be placed in "an assigned risk pool." Since the individual's father owns a large construction company currently being insured through ABC insurance company, ABC decides that it is in its own best interest to write the policy, but not without facultative reinsurance.

6) Catastrophe. An insurance company may conclude that an exposure is too potentially catastrophic to be written comfortably. The grandstand exposure of a college or university is typical, as is property damage on a fleet of rental cars, all stored on the same lot. Facultative reinsurance is an alternative to risk rejection.

7) New Lines. Volume and spread of risk on new lines of business should reach a certain point of maturity before normal net and treaty limits are exposed. Facultative underwriters can offer underwriting assistance as well as interim capacity for such lines of business. Many insurance companies are only now beginning to write medical malpractice or products liability coverages and often approach facultative reinsurance markets for underwriting advice and reinsurance assistance.

8) Expertise. The facultative underwriter is willing to share with the ceding company the knowledge gained in underwriting difficult or unusual risks — a knowledge that has been developed over many years and from a great variety of sources.

9) Competition. Facultative reinsurance permits a primary company to venture into unfamiliar coverage areas and to develop underwriting experience without shouldering unacceptably high liabilities.

10) Stability. Facultative reinsurance can help stabilize year-end results. It helps provide broader services, finds better ways to write coverage at a profit, and offers new lines of insurance, all adding to a company's full service image. Facultative reinsurers, as risk-bearing partners, play an important role in helping large and small companies alike to maintain that image.

Characteristics of Facultative Reinsurance

It is difficult to fully appreciate the distinct characteristics of facultative reinsurance without also discussing the nature of treaty reinsurance. While it is not the intent of this chapter to treat the latter subject in any depth, a basic knowledge of certain treaty concepts will provide a clearer understanding of the facultative process.

Reinsurance treaties are purchased to stabilize the underwriting results of an insurance company over a period of years. The reinsurer agrees to accept liability on a block of business. Close analysis of the company's underwriting philosophy, present book, claims handling ability, and cumulative experience will establish the terms of the treaty proposal. Once the treaty is accepted and written, the reinsurer is not involved in the day-to-day decisions involved in the evaluation or underwriting of individual risks covered by the treaty. It is generally agreed that the reinsurer's results may vary from year to year. Nevertheless, there exists a mutual understanding with the ceding company that the treaty terms will be adjusted to produce a modest profit over the long run.

A treaty is a reinsurance relationship which allows for the protection of a book of business and manifests the following characteristics: 1) no individual risk scrutiny by the reinsurer, 2) obligatory acceptance by the reinsurer of covered business, and 3) a long-term relationship in which the reinsurer's profitability is expected, but measured and adjusted over an extended time period. On the other hand, facultative reinsurance establishes a separate underwriting relationship with each and every risk. The reinsurer retains the faculty, or option, to accept or reject any risk. The reinsurer sets the price and the terms of coverage for each risk it does accept. Each risk, therefore, stands or falls on its own. Both the reinsurer and the ceding company agree that there is no expressed, or even implied, obligation for the company to restore the reinsurer if it should lose money on a given risk or on all the risks accepted. Therefore, the facultative underwriter must be sure that the reinsurance premium takes into consideration the short-term nature of the contract and adequately contemplates all exposures.

Under the facultative arrangement, the ceding company may choose to purchase reinsurance on an entire line or some portion thereof. Placement of only a portion of a given line may be illustrated by the following example. The ceding company wishes to insure a fleet of thirty-five vehicles. The fleet consists of thirty private passenger vehicles and five gasoline haulers. The ceding company decides to write a casualty limit of $1,000,000 on each vehicle in the fleet but wants to "lay off," or reinsure, part of the liability on the gasoline haulers. They decide to retain on $100,000 any one occurrence, and obtain reinsurance protection for the remaining $900,000. The fact that the ceding company had differentiated between the "innocuous" private passenger vehicles and the more volatile gasoline haulers had enabled the company to retain the more desirable portion of the risk, yet buy protection against the more severe loss potential presented by the gasoline haulers.

It is this process of differentiating between risks, or as in the above case between various portions of the same risk, that results in what the reinsurer terms "adverse selection" — the conscious and deliberate cession of those risks, segments of risks, or coverages that appear less attractive for retention by the ceding company. Facultatively reinsuring such items allows the company to ease the burden of the problem exposure for a one-time charge, which may perhaps only be a fraction of the account's total premium. While this differentiation between risks and between exposures is an example of the flexibility possible through the facultative process, it is also a clear illustration of the fact that facultative reinsurers do not share in the vast area of profitable (or at least more comfortably predictable) business written and retained by the ceding company. Indeed, the challenge to the facultative reinsurer is to profitably underwrite for its own account in spite of having invited adverse selection, essentially without redress. Facultative underwriting is an exceedingly volatile business.

Facultative Pricing and Structuring

It is important to an overall understanding of facultative business to discuss how the facultative underwriter prices the product. Pricing considerations usually include: 1) an analysis of the risk's characteristics and operations, 2) an assessment of the type and probability of loss, 3) a measure of potential loss frequency and severity, 4) consideration of the impact of inflationary forces on the eventual dollar amount of loss, and 5) the ceding company's expertise in the particular class of business. Most important is the reinsurer's ability to anticipate loss activity within the given layer of limits. This technique, known as layer rating, is one of the fundamental tools of the facultative underwriter.

THE LAYERING CONCEPT

The essence of the layering concept is the allocation of premium dollars to layers having the greatest exposure to loss. For conceptual purposes, any casualty risk may be arbitrarily sub-divided into four general levels, each of which lies directly on top of the one preceding it.

1) Primary Layer. This layer includes normal or expected losses and is the bailiwick of the primary insurer. On a broad base, losses within this layer are statistically predictable, i.e., trips and falls in a supermarket, fender-benders, or minor injuries on the job. Facultative reinsurers rarely, if ever, participate in this layer. It should be evident, moreover, that this layer contains the bulk of the premium that the insured ultimately pays.

2) Working Excess Layer. Here, losses are less frequent than in the primary layer, and the frequency with which it is penetrated is extremely sensitive to inflation. This working excess layer encompasses the area between frequency and catastrophe: occasional losses are anticipated. There is, however, a clearly less predictable or discernible pattern for such losses than for those in the primary layer. Reinsurers tread carefully in this layer, recognizing that its proximity to the primary layer provides great potential for loss penetration. Manual rate increases are usually inadequate for the working excess layer, especially on a facultatively placed risk which was nonstandard to begin with.

3) Catastrophe Layer. It might be said that this is the layer where a loss is possible and probably unlikely. The catastrophe layer contemplates the unanticipated and infrequent large shock loss — the school bus hit by a train, or the collapse of a warehouse roof. Umbrella policies with limits of $1,000,000 to $5,000,000 normally provide catastrophe protection.

4) Capacity Layer. Here, the probability of a loss is so remote as to be nearly unimaginable. Capacity insurance has been called "sleep" insurance, and is meant to guard against the truly unexpected disaster — the explosion of a nuclear plant, the collapse of a skyscraper.

RATEMAKING PROCEDURES.

Clearly, the ratemaking procedures used by the facultative reinsurer are not comparable to those used in the primary field. Rating of working excess and catastrophe layers presents a rather complicated problem to the reinsurer, as no reliable actuarial data is available for the classes of business and layers of coverage it reinsures. While the reinsurer may determine the premium for a specific layer as a function of the Insurance Services Office manual rates or as a function of loss experience from similar exposures, or combinations of both, the principal ingredient in the determination of an appropriate price is judgement. That judgement is the combination of the individual underwriter's own experience, the collective experience of the reinsurance company's total underwriting staff, the reinsurance company's previous years of experience on analogous business as well as the contribution of the reinsurer's claims and actuarial support staffs. It can certainly be said of the facultative business that two heads are always better than one.

Casualty facultative prices are almost always surcharged rates — i.e., they are greater than the "manual increased limits premium." This is principally due to adverse selection and the leveraged impact of inflation on excess writers. Moreover, inflation in the casualty business includes not just economic inflation, but social and legal inflation as well — increasingly more people sue each other, for more reasons, and with greater success.

Casualty facultative reinsurance is almost always placed on an excess of loss basis. If, however, the policy to be reinsured is itself an excess policy, then the reinsurer usually writes pro rata reinsurance, also called contributing excess. Umbrella policies are normally reinsured in this way. Excess of loss reinsurance is typically written on a net basis, that is, without a commission payable to the ceding company. The ceding company is, of course, free to adjust the net reinsurance quotation to cover its commission, taxes, expenses and profit in establishing the gross premium that the insured will pay.

Property facultative pricing practices tend to fit more comfortably into the manual pricing structure. There are two reasons for such suitability. The property business is more stable in being more predictable, and property facultative reinsurance is usually purchased to acquire additional capacity rather than to cede difficult exposures.

As mentioned, casualty facultative is almost always written excess of loss. Up to the limit of reinsurance purchased, the reinsurer indemnifies the ceding company for that portion of a loss which is excess of the ceding company's net, or net and treaty, retention. Property facultative reinsurance may either be arranged on a pro rata basis or on an excess of loss basis. In pro rata reinsurance, the primary company typically cedes a large percentage of risk to the reinsurer(s). They share the risk on a percentage basis. Less ceding and brokerage commissions, the primary company cedes to the reinsurer the same percentage of its premium as the percentage of the risk accepted by the reinsurer. Clearly, the cost of this type of facultative arrangement can be conceptually staggering. As an example, consider a ten-story office building of fire resistive construction, valued at $10,000,000. If a primary company wished never to actually lose more than $1,000,000 on this type or risk, to adequately protect itself in a total loss situation it would have to purchase $9,000,000 pro rata reinsurance. To do this it would give up 90% of its premium.

Although many companies still purchase pro rata reinsurance, it may be said that the excess of loss concept in property facultative has come of age. An excess of loss treatment of a facultative property placement is similar to a casualty placement. The property reinsurer analyzes the risk characteristics, assesses exposures, takes inflation into consideration, etc. The reinsurer vertically divides a risk into dollar areas of potential loss. Again, these areas are referred to as layers. Allocating reinsurance premium for a given layer is a direct function of the loss potential for the layer. For the vast majority of property risks, there is much greater potential for partial loss than for total loss. Lower layers of reinsurance are said to be closer to loss and are allocated more premium, or higher rates, than are the higher layers.

From an excess of loss point of view, a property risk can be divided into five layers of loss potential: frequency, estimated normal loss, probable maximum loss (PML), PML protection, and catastrophe.

Frequency. This is the area of small losses. It is properly handled by means of adequate deductibles, negotiated by the primary company with the insured.

Estimated Normal Loss. This is the layer in which most losses may be expected to occur. These are the losses which, for the most part, are contemplated in bureau rates.

Probable Maximum Loss (PML). After taking into consideration variables of the risk such as construction, occupancy, protection, and exposures, a property underwriter makes a determination that in the event of a fire, the loss should not go beyond this PML layer.

PML Protection. This is a safety layer. It is a buffer between a PML loss and a catastrophic loss. It takes into consideration that at the time of a loss, actual conditions may be somewhat worse than what the underwriter considered them to be when making a PML assessment. Determination of the dollar limit of this layer is subjective and judgemental, and its amount can vary considerably from risk to risk. This layer is impacted severely by inflation.

Catastrophe. In this layer, the probability of loss is extremely remote, the unforeseen total loss. Yet such a loss is still possible. For example, consider the warehouse risk where a heating system malfunctioned, a wet sprinkler system was frozen, and a fire company was delayed or unable to gain access. A severe loss such as that might exhaust lower layers and penetrate the catastrophe layer.

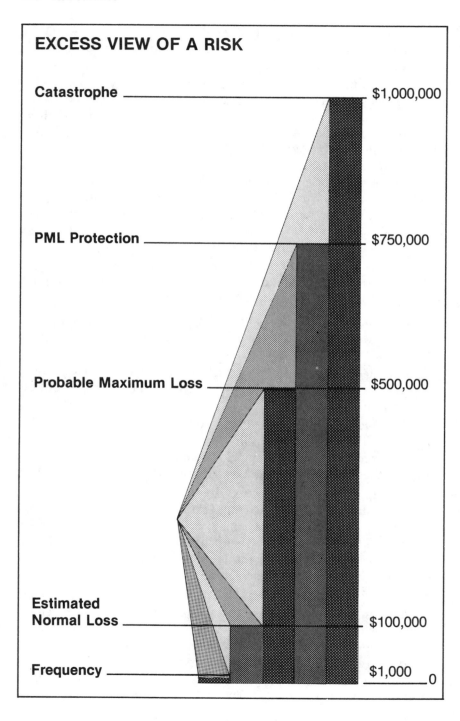

EXCESS VIEW OF A RISK

Catastrophe _____ $1,000,000

PML Protection _____ $750,000

Probable Maximum Loss _____ $500,000

Estimated
Normal Loss _____ $100,000

Frequency _____ $1,000 __ 0

As with casualty, experience and judgement are the keys to pricing and layer-rating excess of loss property facultative business. Layer-rating is, in effect, an exercise in analyzing loss distributions.

STRUCTURING PROPERTY EXCESS COVERAGES

There are basically four ways of arranging excess of loss property facultative reinsurance: pure excess, capacity excess, working excess, and mid-layer excess. With the pure excess method, facultative reinsurance is purchased excess of either a retention kept 100% net by the primary company or, as illustrated, a retention consisting of the company's net and its treaty which in this case is providing 66⅔% quota share coverage.

Pure Excess

Excess of entire net or net and treaty.

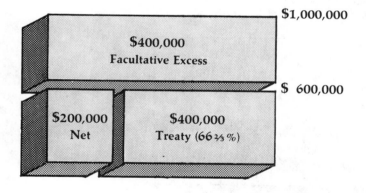

$1,000,000

$400,000
Facultative Excess

$ 600,000

$200,000
Net

$400,000
Treaty (66⅔%)

A loss to the reinsured risk in an amount of $600,000 or less would be borne by the primary company (33⅓%) and its treaty reinsurer (66⅔%). The amount of loss above $600,000 up to the policy limit of $1,000,000 would be borne by the facultative excess reinsurer(s).

With the capacity excess method, a facultative layer is purchased excess of the primary company's net retention, each sharing the treaty. A company's quota share property treaty might assume 40% of any risk covered under the treaty. On a $1,000,000 risk, the ceding company's share would be $600,000, and the treaty's share would be $400,000. If the ceding company only wished to retain, on a net basis, $200,000 of its $600,000 share, it could purchase $400,000 capacity excess. The $1,000,000 risk liability would be divided $400,000 to the treaty,

$200,000 net retention on the part of the ceding company, and $400,000 excess of the ceding company's $200,000 on the part of the facultative reinsurer. Whether a loss be partial or total, the treaty's share of the loss would always be 40%. The facultative excess would only become involved, or attach, after the ceding company's $200,000 was exhausted. To exhaust the $200,000 net retention of the ceding company, a loss would have to be at least $333,333. Loss settlement would be $200,000 (60%) paid by the ceding company and $133,333 (40%) by the treaty carrier(s). If a loss were greater than $333,333, the attachment point of the excess, that portion of the loss which was excess of $333,333, would be shared 60% by the facultative reinsurer and still 40% by the treaty.

Capacity Excess

Excess reinsurance over net, sharing with treaty.

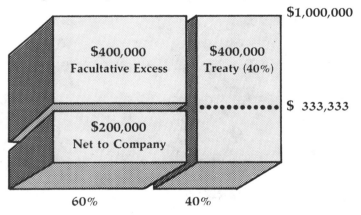

$1,000,000

| $400,000 Facultative Excess | $400,000 Treaty (40%) |

$ 333,333

| $200,000 Net to Company |

60%   40%

Similarly, with the working excess method, a facultative layer is purchased excess of only a portion of a primary company's net retention. The primary company commits the remainder of its retention, still sharing proportionately with the treaty, excess of the facultative and treaty layer. Very simply, a company may wish to protect its net retention by dividing it, and purchasing a facultative layer in between. Just as in capacity excess, these layers include a treaty share. Thus, in a working excess arrangement, a net and treaty layer is excess of a facultative and treaty layer, which is excess of a net and treaty layer.

Working Excess

**Excess in middle of net
retention, sharing with treaty.**

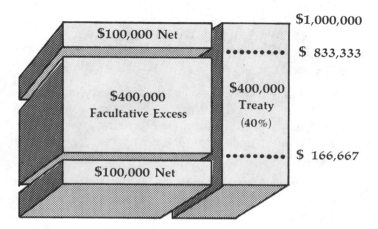

With the mid-layer excess method, net and treaty share a first layer and an upper layer with a facultative layer between.

Mid-Layer Excess

**Mid-layer excess with net
and treaty sharing in first loss and upper-layer.**

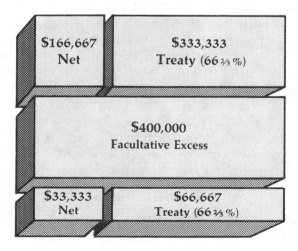

As in the case in working excess, there are at least three layers of coverage involved. There is a primary layer, shared in varying percentages (33⅓ and 66⅔ in the illustration) by the ceding company and its treaty, and two layers excess of the primary. In mid-layer excess, the middle layer is facultative reinsurance only. Only the top layer and the primary layer share with the treaty. In both working excess and in mid-layer excess, facultative coverage acts as a buffer. It protects the ceding company's net retention. Only a total loss could completely exhaust the ceding company's net retention. In mid-layer excess, the facultative provides like protection to the treaty.

To properly price the product, the facultative property underwriter must reconcile the potential loss characteristics of a given risk with the way the ceding company wishes the facultative layering arranged. This should entail a good deal of underwriter-to-underwriter negotiation in terms of limits allocation and rates.

Many primary companies use property facultative to limit their exposure on difficult risks. It is the size of property risks today, however, which lends itself particularly well to facultative treatment due to the additional capacity provided. Take, for example, a college with a schedule of nine buildings. Eight of the buildings are valued at less than $1,000,000 each and present no capacity problem for a given primary company. The library building is valued at $10,000,000, however, and the primary company is only willing to write $2,000,000 of it. There is a need for $8,000,000 facultative reinsurance, 80% of the value of the library. Since most reinsurers are unwilling to provide pro rata facultative on only one building of a schedule of buildings (the one building being termed a picked item), the primary company would probably have to reinsure 80% of the entire schedule. It would give up 80% of its total premium just to solve its problem with one building, the library. The solution to the problem would be for the primary company to buy excess of loss facultative only on the building where it needs it. Coverage for $8,000,000 x/s (excess) of $2,000,000 could be purchased on the library for a portion of the premium involved in the library exposure only. The primary company would retain the premium for the other eight buildings, which it is comfortable in writing net and treaty, without facultative.

It should be noted that inflation has had an enormous impact on insured values and limits. Inflation can transform an adequately rated PML protection layer into a dangerously underrated PML layer, particularly when a risk was initially undervalued. Property and casualty reinsurance underwriters are acutely aware that care must be exercised lest inflation erode and undermine the value of their decisions.

The Facultative Reinsurance Certificate

Sample reinsurance certificates appear in this chapter and should be self explanatory. There are, however, several aspects of the certificates which deserve comment.

Once an agreement to reinsure has been reached between the ceding (primary) company and its reinsurer, a certificate of reinsurance can be issued. Because of the nature of the business, the contractual relationship between facultative reinsurer and insurer must be one of utmost good faith (*uberrimae fidei*). Although this is the underlying principle of all insurance agreements, it is the cornerstone of a reinsurance transaction. The prospective ceding company is required to disclose all relevant information to the best of its knowledge. Considering the fact that the facultative reinsurer's relationship exists only with the ceding company and that it has no contact with the insured or the producer, it is imperative that the primary company promptly bring to the reinsurer's attention any material changes in the risk. Typical facultative certificate language provides that:

> The company shall furnish the reinsurer with a copy of its policy(ies) and all endorsements thereto and agrees to notify the reinsurer promptly of all changes which in any manner affect this certificate of reinsurance.

Fraud, mistake, misrepresentation and concealment can void the contract if the information in question materially affects the reinsurer, notwithstanding the fact that the reassured remains liable to the original insured. If the change in the risk is unknown to the primary insurer, however, the reinsurance contract will remain in force.

The contractual agreement between reinsurer and reinsured is bilateral with the reinsurer having no obligation to the insured except in the rarest of circumstances. Normally, there is a direct obligation on the part of the reinsurer to the insured only when the insured is specifically made a third party beneficiary of the contract between reinsurer and reassured. The vehicle for doing this is called a "cut-through" endorsement, treated elsewhere in this text.

In the event of the insolvency of the reinsured (the ceding company), the facultative reinsurance is still applicable, but only for its agreed upon share or in excess of the amount that was originally retained by the ceding carrier. On the other hand, should the reinsurer become insolvent, the entire risk and subsequent losses remain the responsibility of the reinsured. Accordingly, it is essential that proper selection of reinsurers be made before facultative cessions are made.

CERTIFICATE OF CASUALTY FACULTATIVE REINSURANCE ISSUED BY

GENERAL REINSURANCE CORPORATION

GREENWICH, CONNECTICUT 06830

CERTIFICATE NUMBER

F

RENEWS/REPLACES

DECLARATIONS

CEDING COMPANY AND ADDRESS

ATTENTION

GENERAL REINSURANCE

NAME OF INSURED

COMPANY POLICY NO.

COMPANY POLICY PERIOD

CITY   STATE

REINSURERS CERTIFICATE PERIOD

ITEM 1
TYPE OF INSURANCE

excluding all Benefits and Liabilities arising from State or Federal No-Fault Laws or Optional coverage extensions thereof.

ITEM 2 POLICY LIMITS AND APPLICATION	ITEM 3 COMPANY RETENTION	ITEM 4 REINSURANCE ACCEPTED	ITEM 5 BASIS OF ACCEPTANCE
			☐ EXCESS OF LOSS
			☐ CONTRIBUTING EXCESS
			☐ NON-CONCURRENT

THE REINSURERS NET PREMIUM FOR THIS CERTIFICATE SHALL BE $_____

☐ FIXED CHARGE

☐ DEPOSIT PREMIUM

THIS PREMIUM SHALL BE ADJUSTED ANNUALLY AT:

RATE	BASE	ESTIMATED EXPOSURE	REINSURERS ESTIMATED ANNUAL PREMIUM	MINIMUM PREMIUM FOR REINSURANCE PERIOD
			$	$

COUNTERSIGNED AT_____ THIS_____ DAY OF_____, 19____

GENERAL REINSURANCE CORPORATION

by:_____
Authorized Signature

PLEASE GIVE SPECIAL NOTICE OF THIS FACULTATIVE REINSURANCE TO YOUR CLAIM DEPARTMENT

C101A Rev. 10/77

GENERAL REINSURANCE CORPORATION
(A Delaware Corporation)
Greenwich, Connecticut 06830
(herein called the Reinsurer)

REINSURING AGREEMENTS AND CONDITIONS

In consideration of the payment of the premium, and subject to the terms, conditions and limits of liability set forth herein and in the Declarations made a part hereof, the Reinsurer does hereby reinsure the ceding company named in the Declarations (herein called the Company) in respect of the Company's policy(ies) as follows:

A.   The Company warrants to retain for its own account, subject to treaty reinsurance the, amount of liability specified in Item 3 of the Declarations. The liability of the Reinsurer, as specified in Item 4 of the Declarations, shall follow that of the Company, subject in all respects to all the terms, conditions, and limit(s) of the Company's policy(ies) except when otherwise specifically provided herein or designated as non-concurrent reinsurance in the Declarations. The Reinsurer's certificate period shall be as specified in the Declarations at 12:01 AM as to both dates at the place specified in the Company's policy(ies). The Company shall furnish the Reinsurer with a copy of its policy(ies) and all endorsements thereto and agrees to notify the Reinsurer promptly of all changes which in any manner affect this certificate of reinsurance. The Company shall make available for inspection, and place at the disposal of the Reinsurer at all reasonable times all records of the Company relating to this certificate of reinsurance or claims in connection therewith.

B.   In no event shall anyone other than the Company or, in the event of the Company's insolvency, its receiver, liquidator or statutory successor, have any rights under this agreement.

C.   The Company shall notify the Reinsurer promptly of any occurrence which in the Company's estimate of the value of injuries or damages sought, without regard to liability, might result in judgment in an amount sufficient to involve this certificate of reinsurance. The Company shall also notify the Reinsurer promptly of any occurrence in respect of which the Company has created a loss reserve equal to or greater than fifty (50) percent of the Company's retention specified in Item 3 of the Declarations; or, if this reinsurance applies on a contributing excess basis, when notice of claim is received by the Company. While the Reinsurer does not undertake to investigate or defend claims or suits, it shall nevertheless have the right and shall be given the opportunity, with the full cooperation of the Company, to associate counsel at its own expense and to join with the Company and its representatives in the defense and control of any claim, suit or proceeding involving this certificate of reinsurance.

D.   All loss settlements made by the Company, provided they are within the terms, conditions and limits of the original policy(ies) and within the terms, conditions and limit(s) of this certificate of reinsurance, shall be binding on the Reinsurer. Upon receipt of a definitive statement of loss, the Reinsurer shall promptly pay its proportion of such loss as set forth in the Declarations. In addition thereto, the Reinsurer shall pay its proportion of expenses (other than office expenses and payments to any salaried employee) incurred by the Company in the investigation and settlement of claims or suits and its proportion of court costs and interest on any judgment or award, in the ratio that the Reinsurer's loss payment bears to the Company's gross loss payment. If there is no loss payment, the Reinsurer shall pay its proportion of such expenses only in respect of business accepted on a contributing excess basis and then only in the percentage stated in Item 4 of the declarations in the first layer of participation.

E.   Definitions
As used in this certificate the following terms shall have the meaning set opposite each.

Excess of Loss - The limit(s) of liability of the Reinsurer, as stated in Item 4 of the Declarations, applies(y) only to that portion of loss within the policy limits, in excess of the applicable retention of the Company as stated in Item 3 of the Declarations.

Contributing Excess - The Company's policy(ies) applies(y) in excess of other valid insurance, reinsurance of a self-insured retention and the limit(s) of liability of the Reinsurer applies(y) proportionally to all loss settlements in the percentage(s) set forth in Item 4 of the Declarations.

Non-Concurrent - The reinsurance provided does not apply to any hazards or risks of loss or damage covered under the Company's policy other than those specifically set forth in the Declarations. The retention of the Company and liability of the Reinsurer shall be determined as though the Company's policy applied only to the hazards or risks of loss or damage specifically described in the Declarations.

F.   The Reinsurer will be paid or credited by the Company with its proportion of salvage, that is, reimbursement obtained or recovery made by the Company, less all expenses paid by the Company in making such recovery. If the reinsurance afforded by this certificate is on the excess of loss basis, salvage shall be applied in the inverse order in which liability attaches.

G.   The Company will be liable for all taxes on premiums ceded to the Reinsurer under this certificate of reinsurance.

H.   In the event of the insolvency of the Company, the reinsurance provided by this certificate shall be payable by the Reinsurer on the basis the liability of the Company under the policy(ies) reinsured, without diminution because of such insolvency, directly to the Company or its receiver, liquidator, or statutory successor. The Reinsurer shall be given written notice of the pendency of each claim against the Company on the policy(ies) reinsured hereunder within a reasonable time after such claim is filed in the insolvency proceedings. The Reinsurer shall have the right to investigate each such claim and interpose, at its own expense, in the proceeding where such claim is to be adjudicated, any defenses which it may deem available to the Company or its receiver, liquidator or statutory successor. The expense thus incurred by the Reinsurer shall be chargeable, subject to court approval, against the insolvent Company as part of the expense of liquidation to the extent of a proportionate share of the benefit which may accrue to the Company solely as the result of the defense undertaken by the Reinsurer.

I.   The Reinsurer may offset any balance(s), whether on account of premiums, commissions, claims, losses, adjustment expense, salvage or any other amount(s) due from one party to the other under this certificate of reinsurance or under any other agreement heretofore or hereafter entered into between the Company and the Reinsurer, whether acting as assuming reinsurer or as ceding company.

J.   Should the Company's policy be cancelled, this certificate shall terminate automatically at the same time and date. This certificate may also be cancelled by the Company or by the Reinsurer upon not less than thirty days prior written notice, one to the other, stating when thereafter the reinsurance afforded hereby shall terminate. Proof of mailing shall be deemed proof of notice and calculation of the earned premium shall follow the Company's calculation in the use of short rate or pro rata tables.

K.   The terms of this certificate of reinsurance shall not be waived or changed except by endorsement issued to form a part hereof, executed by a duly authorized representative of the Reinsurer.

L.   Any difference of opinion between the Reinsurer and the Company with respect to the interpretation of this certificate or the performance of the obligations under the certificate shall be submitted to arbitration. Each party shall select an arbitrator within one month after written request for arbitration has been received from the party requesting arbitration. These two arbitrators shall select a third arbitrator within ten days after both have been appointed. Should the arbitrators fail to agree on a third arbitrator, each arbitrator shall select one name from a list of three names submitted by the other arbitrator, and the third arbitrator shall be selected by lot between the two names chosen. The arbitrators shall be officials or former officials of other insurance or reinsurance companies. The arbitrators shall adopt their own rules and procedures. The decision of the majority of arbitrators shall be final and binding on the parties.

In Witness Whereof, GENERAL REINSURANCE CORPORATION has caused this certificate of reinsurance to be signed by its President and by its Vice President and Secretary at Greenwich, Connecticut, but the same shall not be binding upon the Reinsurer unless countersigned by an authorized representative of the Reinsurer.

President

Vice President and Secretary

136 Reinsurance

CERTIFICATE OF PROPERTY FACULTATIVE REINSURANCE ISSUED BY

CERTIFICATE NUMBER

GENERAL REINSURANCE CORPORATION **FF**

GREENWICH, CONNECTICUT 06830

NEW YORK • CHICAGO • ATLANTA • SAN FRANCISCO • TORONTO • DALLAS • HARTFORD • COLUMBUS

DECLARATIONS

CEDING COMPANY AND ADDRESS

ATTENTION

EXCESS PROPERTY FACULTATIVE REINSURANCE
FIRE - INLAND MARINE
MULTI PERIL - AUTO PHYSICAL DAMAGE

ASSURED   COMPANY POLICY NO.

LOCATION   CITY

STATE
FF

OUR CERT. NO.   REINS. EFFECTIVE   EXPIRATION   TERM

GENERAL REINSURANCE

RENEWAL OF CERT. NO.   REPLACES CERT. NO.

ITEM 2 POLICY LIMITS AND APPLICATION	ITEM 3 COMPANY RETENTION	ITEM 4 REINSURANCE ACCEPTED	ITEM 5 PREMIUM
			NET PREMIUM DUE OR FIRST INSTALLMENT
			FUTURE INSTALLMENTS NO. NEXT ANNIV. DATE

ITEM 1 TYPE OF INSURANCE AND PROPERTY COVERED	ITEM 6 BASIS OF ACCEPTANCE
	☐ EXCESS OF LOSS ☐ SHARE
	☐ CONTRIBUTING EXCESS ☐ NON-CONCURRENT

MINIMUM PREMIUM FOR REINSURANCE PERIOD $_____ MINIMUM PREMIUM FOR CERTIFICATE $_____

COUNTERSIGNED AT_____ THIS_____DAY OF_____, 19____

GENERAL REINSURANCE CORPORATION

by:_____
Authorized Signature

PLEASE GIVE SPECIAL NOTICE OF THIS FACULTATIVE REINSURANCE TO YOUR CLAIM DEPARTMENT

U104 REV. 10/78

GENERAL REINSURANCE CORPORATION
(A Delaware Corporation)
Greenwich, Connecticut 06830
(herein called the Reinsurer)

REINSURING AGREEMENTS AND CONDITIONS

In consideration of the payment of the premium, and subject to the terms, conditions and limits of liability set forth herein and in the Declarations made a part
hereof, the Reinsurer does hereby reinsure the ceding company named in the
Declarations (herein called the Company) in respect of the Company's policy(ies)
as follows:

A.   The Company warrants to retain for its own account, subject to treaty reinsurance or other facultative reinsurance if applicable, the amount of liability
specified in Item 3 of the Declarations. The liability of the Reinsurer, as specified in
Item 4 of the Declarations, shall follow that of the Company, subject in all respects
to all the terms, conditions, and limits of the Company's policy except when otherwise specifically provided herein or designated as non-concurrent reinsurance in
the Declarations. The Reinsurer's certificate period shall be as specified in the
declarations at 12:01 AM as to both dates at the place specified in the Company's
policy. The Company shall furnish the Reinsurer with a copy of its policy and all
endorsements thereto and agrees to notify the Reinsurer promptly of all changes
which in any manner affect this certificate of reinsurance. The Company shall
make available for inspection, and place at the disposal of the Reinsurer at all
reasonable times all records of the Company relating to this certificate of reinsurance or claims in connection therewith.

B.   In no event shall anyone other than the Company or, in the event of the Company's insolvency, its receiver, liquidator or statutory successor, have any rights
under this agreement.

C.   The Company shall notify the Reinsurer promptly of any occurrence which in
the Company's estimate of the value of injuries or damages sought, without
regard to liability, might result in judgment in an amount sufficient to involve this
certificate of reinsurance. The Company shall also notify the Reinsurer promptly
of any occurrence in respect of which the Company has created a loss reserve
equal to or greater than fifty (50) percent of the Company's retention specified in
Item 3 of the Declarations; or, if this reinsurance applies on a contributing excess
basis, when notice of claim is received by the Company. While the Reinsurer does
not undertake to investigate or defend claims or suits, it shall nevertheless have
the right and shall be given the opportunity, with the full cooperation of the Company, to associate counsel at its own expense and to join with the Company and
its representatives in the defense and control of any claim, suit or proceeding involving this certificate of reinsurance.

D.   All loss settlements made by the Company, provided they are within the
terms, conditions and limits of the original policy(ies) and within the terms, conditions and limits of this certificate of reinsurance, shall be binding on the Reinsurer.
Upon receipt of a definitive statement of loss, the Reinsurer shall promptly pay its
proportion of such loss as set forth in the Declarations. In addition thereto, the
Reinsurer shall pay its proportion of expenses (other than office expenses and
payments to any salaried employee) incurred by the Company in the investigation
and settlement of claims or suits and its proportion of court costs and interest on

any judgment or award, in the ratio that the Reinsurer's loss payment bears to the Company's gross loss payment. If there is no loss payment, the Reinsurer shall pay its proportion of such expenses only in respect of business accepted on a contributing excess basis and then only in the percentage stated in Item 4 of the declarations in the first layer of participation.

E.　Definitions
As used in this certificate the following terms shall have the meaning set opposite each.

Excess of Loss - The limit(s) of liability of the Reinsurer, as stated in Item 4 of the Declarations, applies(y) only to that portion of loss settlement(s), in excess of the applicable retention of the Company as stated in Item 3 of the Declarations.

Contributing Excess - The Company's policy applies in excess of other valid insurance, reinsurance of a self-insured retention and the limit of liability of the Reinsurer applies proportionally to all loss settlements in the percentage(s) set forth in Item 4 of the Declarations.

Non-Concurrent - The reinsurance provided does not apply to any hazards or risk of loss or damage covered under the Company's policy other than those specifically set forth in the Declarations. The retention of the Company and liability of the Reinsurer shall be determined as though the Company's policy(ies) applied only to the hazards or risks of loss or damage specifically described in the Declarations.

F.　The Reinsurer will be paid or credited by the Company with its proportion of salvage, that is, reimbursement obtained or recovery made by the Company, less all expenses paid by the Company in making such recovery. If the reinsurance afforded by this certificate is on the excess of loss basis, salvage shall be applied in the inverse order in which liability attaches.

G.　The Company will be liable for all taxes on premiums ceded to the Reinsurer under this certificate of reinsurance.

H.　In the event of the insolvency of the Company, the reinsurance provided by this certificate shall be payable by the Reinsurer on the basis the liability of the Company under the policy(ies) reinsured, without diminution because of such insolvency, directly to the Company or its receiver, liquidator, or statutory successor. The Reinsurer shall be given written notice of the pendency of each claim against the Company on the policy(ies) reinsured hereunder within a reasonable time after such claim is filed in the insolvency proceedings. The Reinsurer shall have the right to investigate each such claim and interpose, at its own expense, in the proceeding where such claim is to be adjudicated, any defenses which it may deem available to the Company or its receiver, liquidator or statutory successor. The expense thus incurred by the Reinsurer shall be chargeable, subject to court approval, against the insolvent Company as part of the expense of liquidation to the extent of a proportionate share of the benefit which may accrue to the Company solely as the result of the defense undertaken by the Reinsurer.

I.　The Reinsurer may offset any balance(s), whether on account of premiums, commissions, claims, losses, adjustment expense, salvage or any other amount(s) due from one party to the other under this certificate of reinsurance or under any other agreement heretofore or hereafter entered into between the Company and the Reinsurer, whether acting as assuming reinsurer or as ceding company.

J.   Should the Company's policy(ies) be cancelled, this certificate shall terminate automatically at the same time and date. This certificate may also be cancelled by the Company or by the Reinsurer upon not less than thirty days prior written notice, stating when thereafter the reinsurance afforded hereby shall terminate. This certificate may also be cancelled by the Reinsurer upon written notice to the Company, stating when thereafter the reinsurance afforded hereby shall terminate. The date of such termination shall be the earlier date of either: A) the date written notice is mailed plus the number of days required to cancel the Company's policy reinsured hereby plus fifteen days; or B) the date written notice is mailed plus forty-five days.

Proof of mailing shall be deemed proof of notice and calculation of the earned premium shall follow the Company's calculation in the use of short rate or pro rata tables.

K.   The terms of this certificate of reinsurance shall not be waived or changed except by endorsement issued to form a part hereof, executed by a duly authorized representative of the Reinsurer.

L.   Any difference of opinion between the Reinsurer and the Company with respect to the interpretation of this certificate or the performance of the obligations under the certificate shall be submitted to arbitration. Each party shall select an arbitrator within one month after written request for arbitration has been received from the party requesting arbitration. These two arbitrators shall select a third arbitrator within ten days after both have been appointed. Should the arbitrators fail to agree on a third arbitrator, each arbitrator shall select one name from a list of three names submitted by the other arbitrator, and the third arbitrator shall be selected by lot between the two names chosen. The arbitrators shall be officials or former officials of other insurance or reinsurance companies. The arbitrators shall adopt their own rules and procedures. The decision of the majority of arbitrators shall be final and binding on the parties.

In Witness Whereof, GENERAL REINSURANCE CORPORATION has caused this certificate of reinsurance to be signed by its President and by its Vice President and Secretary at Greenwich, Connecticut, but the same shall not be binding upon the Reinsurer unless countersigned by an authorized representative of the Reinsurer.

President

Vice President and Secretary

Generally, facultative certificates ask for notice of any occurrence which might involve the reinsurance. Some certificates require notice of all claims where the company's reserve is equal to 50% or more of its retention. As the claim investigation develops, it is the reinsured's duty to keep the reinsurer posted on all changes relevant to the claim. Although the reinsured is responsible for claim investigation and settlement regardless of the amount of the reinsurer's participation, the reinsurer reserves the right to participate in negotiations and defense. If the claim in question is not one contemplated by the facultative agreement, the reinsurer must promptly advise the reinsured of the coverage denial.

Should there be disputes between reinsured and reinsurer regarding the certificate, and should negotiations fail to resolve the controversy, the facultative certificate provides for arbitration. Most insurance companies and reinsurers greatly prefer arbitration to the more complicated, more expensive, and usually more unpleasant alternative of a lawsuit.

As with treaty reinsurance, salvage also applies to facultative transactions. If the reinsurance were written on an excess of loss basis, salvage is applied in the inverse order in which liability attached, i.e., from the top down.

In facultative reinsurance, the reinsured may execute cancellation at any time of its primary policy without prior notice to the reinsurer. In fact, if the reinsured's policy is cancelled either by the insured or reinsured, the reinsurance contract terminates at the same time. Cancellation of the certificate, however, requires notice from either party to the other.

Summary

Facultative reinsurance is a transaction between reinsurer and ceding company involving one specific risk. Each party has the faculty (or option) of offering a risk or accepting it. The contract between the two is evidenced by a reinsurance certificate which sets forth details of the agreement.

Facultative reinsurance differs from treaty reinsurance in several respects. While the treaty relationship provides for no individual risk scrutiny by the reinsurer, facultative reinsurance establishes a separate underwriting relationship with each risk involved. While a treaty relationship provides for an obligatory acceptance by the reinsurer of covered business, in facultative reinsurance the reinsurer has the option of accepting or rejecting any risk submitted. Lastly, while a treaty relationship is long-term in nature and provides for an expected profitability for the reinsurer over an extended time period, in facultative reinsurance the reinsurer sets the price and terms of coverage for each risk it accepts, seeking profitability from the aggregate of all such facultative risks accepted. Each risk, therefore, stands or falls on its own. In other words, both the reinsurer and the ceding company agree that there is no express, or even implied, financial obligation for the company to restore the reinsurer if it should lose money on a given risk or on all the risks accepted.

Although facultative reinsurance has existed for decades, facultative departments of reinsurance companies first appeared in the U.S. in the early 1950's. As facultative reinsurance has evolved, primary companies have found it a helpful tool in influencing their underwriting results. Net retained limits can be reduced and exposures can be controlled, both of which stabilize results without jeopardizing favorable reinsurance treaty experience. Aside from capacity considerations, primary insurers have benefited from a second opinion from an underwriter skilled at analyzing the unique and unusual risks which facultative reinsurance attracts. The reinsurer expects adverse selection from such risks and exercises care in pricing the appropriate cover.

Facultative pricing considerations usually include an analysis of the risk's characteristics and operations, an assessment of the type and probability of loss, a measure of potential loss frequency and severity, consideration of the impact of inflationary forces on the eventual dollar amount of loss, and the ceding company's expertise in the particular class of business. Ratemaking procedures, except for some proportionally reinsured property risks, are not comparable to those used in the primary field: the principal ingredient in the determination of an appropriate price is judgment. That judgment is the combination of the individual facultative underwriter's own experience, the collective experience of the reinsurance company's total underwriting staff, the reinsurance company's previous years of experience on analogous business as well as the contribution of the reinsurer's claims and actuarial support staff.

While there are clearly defined differences between facultative and treaty reinsurance, a major point of similarity should be emphasized here. Both forms of reinsurance are critical factors in the exacting task of forecasting and planning. They are essential tools through the responsible use of which primary insurance companies may more confidently guide their own destinies. Obviously, it is impossible to know what the future holds for the insurance industry. In a world of increasing technological complexity, and enormous inflationary pressures, primary insurance companies are faced with more challenges to their profit-making ability than at any time in their history. Clearly, their use of and reliance on both facultative and treaty reinsurance will be greater than ever.

The combined impact of increasing values, increasing court judgments, and increasing inflationary pressures stemming from both economic and social factors will continue to make traditional evaluations of experience patterns vastly more difficult, if not entirely obsolete. In this regard, the challenge will be to the primary insurer and its treaty reinsurer to evaluate their arrangements in an ongoing manner and adapt them to long-term needs and goals. More immediate needs for reinsurance protection on losses of an exceptional nature and size will be effectively addressed by the primary insurer through facultative placements.

Demands of the future will, as never before, tax the underwriting courage and financial resources of insurer and reinsurer alike. The entire insurance industry will meet all reasonable demands if there is commitment to the conviction that success requires sound underwriting to be the foremost factor in exercising risk acceptance.

*   *   *   *   *   *

About the Author of Chapter 5

William G. Clark was born in Englewood, New Jersey, on January 14, 1933. He was educated at Cornell University and received his B.A. in 1954 and M.B.A. in 1955. For the next four years he was a DC-6 pilot in the U.S. Air Force, flying overseas routes in Europe, Africa, and the Far East.

He began his reinsurance career in 1959 with General Reinsurance Corporation where he was appointed a casualty facultative underwriter. Seven years later he was promoted to vice president and became senior vice president in 1971 in charge of the company's facultative division. In 1978 he became a member of the newly created Office of Reinsurance Operations. In addition to his responsibilities with the parent company, in 1979 he was elected president of Herbert Clough, Inc., a wholly owned subsidiary rendering service as a reinsurance intermediary to clients of the General Re Group in all lines of business.

6

The Pro Rata Treaty in Property Insurance

by Walter J. Coleman*

Fundamentally, the term *pro rata* means an exact apportionment of the premium based on the same proportionate amount of risk assumed by the reinsurer from the ceding insurer. Losses, if any, would be shared in the same ratio. In brief, there are two types of treaties by which that exact apportionment is accomplished. One is the quota share treaty, in which a certain retention by the insurer, and a certain cession to the reinsurer, are agreed upon by both parties. The other is the surplus share treaty, in which the insurer decides for each risk offered to it the amount to be retained and the amount to be ceded to the reinsurer, with the reinsurer sharing proportionately only those risks having a surplus liability above the threshold agreed on in the treaty. An example of quota share is a split of 25-75 % between insurer and reinsurer of any risk up to a certain limit, or 50-50 %, or any other such division. Once agreed upon, the division of liability and premium and losses is automatic. On the other hand, an example of surplus share is a proportionate sharing of any risk whose liability taken by the insurer exceeds $25,000: a risk of $30,000 would be shared (premiums and losses) 25/30 by insurer, 5/30 by reinsurer.

The purpose of this chapter is to describe both pro rata treaties as they have evolved historically, to relate certain concepts and practices by which they are used by insurers to meet reinsurance needs, and to observe methods for improving results from their use.

The concept of the pro rata treaty in property insurance developed from the marine business, which in turn was an outgrowth of joint ven-

*Senior Vice President, The Reinsurance Corporation of New York, 99 John St., New York, N.Y. 10038.

tures in the ancient business marketplace. As commerce grew in volume among nations, merchants would simply divide their cargo with other merchants among several ships — instead of placing all cargo from one merchant on one ship. In dividing merchandise this way, the merchants decreased their chance of losing cargo at sea. In the unsophisticated joint ventures, originating in the idea of sharing, the basis of the agreement among merchants probably did not contemplate any more than a net sharing in the profit or loss of each venture, with no insurance premium consideration.

There is some historical evidence that the insurance mechanism originated in financial arrangements between bankers and borrowing merchants. Loans on ocean shipments were made on either of two bases: one requiring repayment, and another (at a higher interest rate than the first) requiring repayment only if the voyage proved successful. The slight increase in interest rate was the banker's measurement of the chance of losing the cargo, and thus relieving the borrower from having to repay the loan. The arrangement protected the merchant only against his interest as financed, however, and it was natural for him to look elsewhere for protection against loss to his remaining interests.

As the business transactions became more complex, insurance companies or associations came into being, whose sole function was to assume the risk involved for a premium and relieve the assured of his loss liability. This probably came about when an individual entrepreneur, who was familiar with the law of large numbers, decided that amalgamation of some or all these risks on an average basis would produce a profitable venture for a loaded charge later termed a "premium." He sold the idea to several other parties, and an insurance company was formed and capitalized. As these insurance transactions multiplied, the amount at risk in one company both on an individual basis and an aggregate basis created in turn a necessity to diversify and spread the risk. Hence, reinsurance was born. The first type of reinsurance of a pro rata nature was probably an individual facultative cession, followed by quota share, and then the other types of pro rata treaties as the business became more complex.

Types of Pro Rata Treaties

THE QUOTA SHARE TREATY

A quota share treaty provides that the ceding insurer cedes and the reinsurer accepts a proportionate interest in all the net retentions of the insurer ("net" after all other reinsurance), subject to a maximum dollar per risk limitation. This quota share arrangement can be modified with per risk and catastrophe reinsurance to include protection for both parties. The purpose of quota share reinsurance is, in effect, a partnership between the insurer and the reinsurer to share on a percentage basis the same fortunes resulting from insurance written. Of the two pro rata treaties in property insurance, the quota share treaty does not allow for selectivity, as does the surplus treaty, but like the surplus treaty it has unlimited treaty liability, subject only to a per-risk liability. It is the purest and simplest form of reinsurance and in essence reduces the ultimate net liability of the insurer to a substantial degree.

Over and above its effect on the ultimate liability of the insurer, there are several other advantages the quota share treaty can produce for the insurer, either on a quota share of the total portfolio of business or on a selected segment of the portfolio of business.

1. The treaty allows the insurer to replenish its policyholder surplus through recovering prepaid expenses (initial costs of underwriting and production) on business ceded. Such replenishment may be needed if the insurer has either overwritten its "book" in volume of premium dollars or had a depletion of its policyholder surplus — due to unfortunate underwriting or decline in investment asset values.

2. The treaty permits the insurer to embark on a new and unknown class of business by reducing its net risk through quota share reinsurance. That advantage prevails until the new business produces enough premium volume and profit to warrant a change.

3. The treaty provides the insurer an option to use a "fronting" arrangement on any business which is alien to its normal book of business. A fronting arrangement exists whenever an insurer retains only a nominal percentage of the business involved. The insurer is considered the organization in front of the insurance transaction, hence the term fronting.

4. In catastrophe areas or classes, the treaty reduces the insurer's net commitment by quota share reinsurance.

5. The quota share treaty increases the insurer's net retention for cessions to any other pro rata treaties by having the quota share form part of the net retention for other cession purposes. This may be achieved, for example, by increasing the limit of other surplus treaties, since they are based on the multiples of net retention.

"Portfolio" vs. "Running" Account. An assumed portfolio by itself means a takeover of an unearned premium reserve representing the in-force liability without new or renewal business, and the business is then allowed to run off. This assumption is rarely done, however, and certainly there is no true partnership here, as the overall results of the insurer will not track with the results of the runoff of the business. Additionally, a problem may be faced by the insurer on such initial portfolio cessions. Since there is generally a sizeable balance of funds due the reinsurer, it may be inopportune for the insurer to raise the cash from its investment portfolio due to investment market conditions at the time. Some payment basis may have to be worked out to alleviate this situation.

A second and similar situation can exist where only new and renewal business is accepted on a quota share basis. This limitation may be desired because the net experience for the ceding insurer from its inforce portfolio will be different from the reinsurer which accepts only new and renewal business. To truly track with the insurer's results, a combination of portfolio and continuing business is necessary. However, dependent on circumstances, any one of the three methods may be employed.

"Net" vs. "Gross" Account. Net account for the purposes of quota share reinsurance is the net retention of the insurer after all other reinsurance effected by the insurer. Since the reinsurer receives the greatest protection from this type of arrangement, it generally will give much better terms to the insurer because of it.

Gross quota share reinsurance can be divided into two parts: 1. The quota share is effected on the ceding insurer's net retention before application of per risk and catastrophe reinsurance. Here the terms given by the reinsurer are adjusted to recognize the higher risk involved in this arrangement and may not be as beneficial to the ceding insurer. 2. A quota share of the gross book of business before application of any reinsurance, either pro rata or excess, which is the least favorable situation usually for a reinsurer.

As an aside, reinsurers often apply the term "quota share" differently when using it among themselves. Reinsurers may use the term to mean also a "quota share of excess business" (which is really not primary business), and for various other quota share agreements between reinsurers themselves (which is not primary business), but in any event the same basic principles of quota share reinsurance are in effect. For example, if catastrophe reinsurance is pooled among several reinsurers on a quota share basis, those reinsurers may term such catastrophe business as being placed among themselves on a quota share basis.

The "Guaranteed-Profit" Quota Share Agreement. The guaranteed-profit quota share came into use to provide a financial relief to the insurer, with the reinsurer having very little risk and a correspondingly small profit margin. Over the years the agreement was refined until it became a bookkeeping transaction, with no risk to the reinsurer in some cases. It provided the insurer with an Annual Statement picture that in essence would disappear upon return of the portfolio or settlement of the account and, therefore, did not reflect the true financial position of the insurer. This temporary appearance was accomplished by inflated reinsurance commission rates on the portfolio of business assumed by the reinsurer, not setting forth the final settlement rate of commission which was substantially lower. As might be expected, state insurance commissioners have curbed such practices where no insurance risk is involved and also have limited the extent to which the provisional commission can exceed the minimum commission in the reinsurance contract.

THE SURPLUS TREATY

Definition. A surplus treaty is defined as an agreement between the insurer and the reinsurer whereby the reinsurer agrees to assume and the ceding insurer agrees to cede, on a pro rata basis, part of the liability on designated individual risks as set forth in the treaty for a pro rata part of the premium and to pay the same pro rata part of any loss and loss expense based on the proportion of the cession made. The "designated individual risks" are described in the treaty (by class or type) to include the reinsurer's pro rata participation only on risks insured by the ceding company above a certain amount, hence the use of "surplus."

Purpose. The purpose of the surplus treaty from an insurance standpoint is to provide the ceding insurer with increased capacity for individual risks beyond the amount it wishes to retain net. This improved capacity allows the ceding insurer to average more effectively incoming business, so that its net retained line on each risk is approximately the same, thus enabling the law of large numbers to work for it effectively. The reinsurer theoretically gets the same spread because it deals with a large number of insurance companies and sets its net line on a similar basis and uses retrocessions with other reinsurers to achieve this position.

However, in addition to improved capacity, there are at least four other facets that enter into the judgment of an insurer in determining the proper basis on which to cede business to a reinsurer.

1. Any insurer's policyholder surplus (assets less liabilities) limits the amount of new business it can write. That limitation exists for two reasons, regardless of the size of insurer or policyholder surplus. (a) Although the insurer receives premium at the start of protection for

the policyholder, the insurer is required by law to maintain all of that premium as reserve liability and to consider the premium as "earned" only with the passage of the policy coverage period, or with the reporting of a loss, whichever occurs sooner. (b) Initial underwriting costs, however, must be met immediately by a deduction in the policyholder surplus. In addition, several states limit the amount an insurer can retain net on a risk to a certain percentage of its policyholder surplus.

The use of a surplus treaty diminishes that policyholder surplus limitation and enables the insurer to offer its services to more assureds, or write more insurance for fewer assureds, or both. With a surplus treaty, credit is applied against the insurer's unearned premium reserve for the reinsurance ceded, and an offset to prepaid commission on expense is realized in the insurer's surplus for the commission received from the reinsurer on cessions made. A similar effect is achieved by a quota share treaty.

2. The use of surplus pro rata reinsurance improves the insurer's competitive ability with other insurance companies, since larger lines for assureds can then be written.

3. The exposure to catastrophe loss is minimized for the insurer because the surplus treaty has unlimited liability for repayment of losses from individual risks — compared to the established occurrence amount recoverable under a catastrophe or aggregate loss ratio cover.

4. The profit potential of the insurer is enhanced, because the surplus treaty allows the insurer to write a larger book of business and share in the profits either through a sliding scale commission or contingent commission arrangement without impacting its surplus position.

Function. The function of surplus pro rata reinsurance is to provide a leveling factor on the net results of the insurer, which is accomplished in the following ways.

1. A surplus treaty absorbs the brunt of large individual losses occurring during a given year and helps stabilize the insurer's results.

2. When rates charged to direct assureds as policyholders are insufficient, the pro rata treaty, being on the same premium base, reflects to some extent the same negative results, thus cushioning the impact on the insurer's results for a temporary period until the rates are adjusted.

3. When underwriting results are poor, the cash flow from reinsurer to ceding company in sharing losses alleviates the cash outgo from the insurer in any one year. This is especially important if a catastrophe is involved.

4. When underwriting results are positive, the net profitability of

the insurer's book of business is enhanced, either because of increased reinsurance commission or contingent commissions.

Premium Volume Guidelines. The premium volume in a pro rata treaty is generally a prime indicator of the risk, i.e., the limit the reinsurer will provide the ceding insurer. As a rule of thumb, the following guidelines may give an indication of practices followed.

Obligatory Method	*Premium Volume*
1st Surplus Treaty	2 to 4 times the limit of the treaty
2nd Surplus Treaty	1 to 2 times the limit of the treaty
3rd Surplus Treaty	½ to 1 times the limit of the treaty
Facultative or Semi-optional Agreement	Less than ½ times the limit of the treaty

While these guidelines seem clear, in actual practice they vary significantly. There is no set pattern, except for the reinsurer a first surplus should have the best ratio of premium-dollars-to-limit, and so on up the ladder of treaties.

The reasons for setting up first, second, or subsequent surplus treaties is that within the scope of the exposure, the first surplus would be the most stable, since it has the highest premium volume compared to its loss potential. The first surplus treaty would then have the best chance for profitability over a period of years and, therefore, command a higher commission and a better percentage of the reinsurer's profit on the results. The second surplus provides less consistent profit potential and more risk for the reinsurance underwriter on less premium volume, and so the commission and profit sharing are reduced to the insurer accordingly. The same reasoning applies as the surplus treaties increase in number, whether obligatory or facultative. The basic purpose for determining this allocation between treaties is to avoid, if possible, unfavorable results from a shock loss. Expressed another way, the purpose is to spread the risk of a shock loss among as many treaties as the reinsured considers desirable.

The Surplus Treaty and Other Reinsurances. The more sophisticated an insurer becomes, the more complex the reinsurance requirements will be. The insurer's protection may involve per risk coverages in various layers, catastrophe covers in various layers, agency reinsurance, facultative reinsurance, quota share reinsurance, aggregate loss ratio reinsurance, combination of excess and quota share reinsurance, and adaptations of these covers. Nevertheless, the surplus treaty has in most cases remained an important segment in the reinsurance business, because its advantages to an insurer are manifold.

CATASTROPHIC EXPOSURES. Generally the surplus treaty has unlimited exposure for catastrophic loss, which is one of the main attributes of this type of reinsurance. The reinsurer recognizes this inherent condition and covers it by means of its own retrocessional program with other reinsurers. The reinsurer also takes into consideration, when underwriting the treaty, the possibility of the catastrophic exposure and should set treaty terms accordingly. Any limitation of the catastrophic loss payment in the treaty by the reinsurer negates to a certain extent the purpose of the treaty, especially when the basic premise of the reinsurer is to share proportionately in the premium applicable to the same risks the insurer has underwritten.

PROTECTING THE SURPLUS TREATY. An insurer may wish to "protect" its treaty from heavy losses which can lead to increased rates or decreased participation in any profit-sharing arrangements with the reinsurer. This protection can be accomplished in two ways: (1) either reducing or not ceding on an individual risk where, in the underwriter's judgment, it may be detrimental to the treaty; or (2) providing an individual excess per risk cover which protects the insurer's net retention and the surplus treaty for common account on larger risks. This provision is not done on a blanket basis but only on occasional individual risks within the treaty, except where the cover is bought to protect only the surplus treaty.

Significant Concepts and Practices

THE TRANSFER OF RISK

The concept of insurance is that there must be a risk involved to issue an insurance policy. This basic tenet is also true of the reinsurance business; so, when a reinsurer accepts business from an insurer as reinsurance under a treaty arrangement which is designed for purposes other than risk assumption and where there is no foreseeable risk to the reinsurer, there is grave doubt at to whether this comes within the purview of insurance or reinsurance. As a matter of fact, state insurance regulatory authorities do not feel this is reinsurance at all.

COVERAGE AND LIMITS

The reinsurance contract should spell out the various types of perils to be covered, i.e., fire, extended coverage, homeowners, commercial multiple peril, inland marine, automobile physical damage, and any other classification needed. As a necessary attribute, the various exclusions and territory limitations should amend the business covered. For example, if no petrochemical plants are to be covered, the contract should so state in the exclusions.

Each treaty should have a dollar limit per risk, so that the reinsurer can determine its ultimate risk liability. Starting with this basic premise, modifications within the treaty perimeter usually take the following forms. 1. A quota share limit is usually determined as a percentage (generally subject to a dollar risk limit) of the insurer's net book of business which the quota share covers. The net book of business is considered to be the gross premium book, less surplus and facultative reinsurance premium. In addition, if there is per risk excess reinsurance or catastrophe reinsurance involved, it is a matter of agreement whether the applicable premium is deducted for the common account protection of the quota share reinsurer to arrive at the ultimate net subject to the quota share treaty. 2. Surplus treaties are geared to multiples of the insurer's net retention. The net retention of the insurer is the amount retained after all reinsurance is placed. However, by agreement the net retention can be before per risk excess or inclusive of a surplus treaty and/or quota share treaty, dependent upon the agreement between the ceding insurer and reinsurer.

For illustration purposes, if the ceding insurer wrote a $100,000 policy for an assured and ceded to a treaty with capacity of three lines, and kept a net retention of $25,000, the cession to the treaty would be $75,000. As long as the maximum per risk limit in the treaty is not exceeded, the above illustration would hold. A surplus treaty can also have a different number of lines dependent on class or net retained line of the ceding insurer. This is called a graded surplus treaty.

For example:

Net retention: $25,000	1 line to treaty
25,000 - $50,000	2 lines to treaty
and so forth.	

RETENTION WARRANTIES

The retention warranties within the treaty set forth the amount of risk the insurer must retain net to be in a position to cede to the treaty. A violation of this condition in effect abrogates the cession, since the reinsurer based its underwriting on such warranties. It is of paramount importance that the reinsurer know that the insurer has a part of the same risk and has kept net at least its minimum retention. Sometimes the insurer keeps its net on one section of the risk, such as the building, and cedes the reinsurer another part of the risk, such as the business interruption. If this is permitted, it should definitely be so stated in the treaty.

Where there is a schedule of risks for one assured, the net retention for the largest risk determines the net retention requirement and the percentage of allocation for premium and loss purposes over the schedule. If the insurer only wants to cede one item in the schedule, that item is handled as a separate risk cession.

RISK DEFINITION

The risk definition in an agreement has been a matter of debate for a long time. Usually the clause reads: "The insurer shall be the sole judge of what constitutes one risk." It has been modified in some cases to read: "A risk shall constitute any building within four walls," or "any one non-fire resistive building and its contents." Fire resistive risk cessions are a matter of agreement between the parties. As one gets into all the ramifications of what constitutes a single risk — not only the fire hazard, the tornado hazard, the earthquake hazard, the contents of a building, the adjacent exposures, the business interruption hazard, and others with which the direct underwriter on the risk is familiar but with which the reinsurer is not — in the final analysis one must depend on the underwriting ability of the ceding company to determine what is considered to be an individual risk exposure.

Even the terms PML (probable maximum loss) and MFL (maximum foreseeable loss) are judgment factors for the direct underwriter to determine, even when relying on engineering and inspection services used. Since there are still occasional large losses in excess of these amounts, the prudent reinsurer should always set a limit on the dollar amount of liability to be committed on any one loss.

Probable maximum loss (or what can occur under normal circumstances) is keyed to the idea that sometimes the normal insurable risk subject to loss is less than 100% and thus forms only a part of the total liability. Therefore, the underwriter can write a larger line than possible under conditions where the insurable risk is 100% subject to the loss and still maintain an average commitment over a book of business. For example:

Risk 100% PML: Limit $ 25,000
Risk 25% PML: Limit $100,000
Loss probabilities on both: $25,000

(Note: PML is always converted to % for convenience.)

Basically the underwriter considers the 25% PML as four sub-risks within the total risk. In accepting reinsurance the same principle is followed in some pro rata treaties, subject to maximum risk limitation in the treaty on a PML and/or a sum insured limit.

Maximum foreseeable loss is that loss which the underwriter envisages in the worst circumstances. It usually comes into consideration on a large plant or office building or plant site where the total amount of exposure involved is more than the MFL. The underwriter's commitment, then, is based on the MFL rather than the total sum insured. Here again, the principle is to break the risk down, so that more than one risk can be involved for underwriting purposes and more than one retention is held by the ceding insurer.

The basic difference between PML and MFL is that the PML represents the normal loss expectancy, whereas the MFL represents a loss due to unusual circumstances. The risk itself to a reinsurance underwriter should be the sum insured at a location. If the line is to be increased due to the PML or MFL factor, there should be in the agreement a line limit based on PML or MFL not to exceed the total dollar risk amount to be committed on the treaty in respect to any one risk or location.

The separate building and contents and location limits are again dependent on the agreement reached beforehand. Is the insurer to keep a net line on each building, on the contents in each buiding, or a net line on both? Will the insurer take one location with several buildings and consider them one risk or several risks? Will the ceding insurer divide one building into several risks? The reinsurer's decision will depend on its knowledge of and confidence in the ceding company's underwriter.

ATTACHMENT OF LIABILITY

The attachment of liability of the treaty commences at the inception date of the agreement. In the event a loss occurs during the term of the agreement before the reinsurance cession is made, the cession will be made and the loss collected in conformity with the usual cessions made on the same type of risk. The date of attachment of the treaty determines the original date from which the reinsurer assumes liability. The assumed liability can be on new and renewal business or can also include a portfolio assumption (a segment of the in-force business to be written in the treaty).

A portfolio assumption (which can take effect at the inception of the treaty) provides that an unearned premium reserve shall be accepted by the reinsurer and that all losses occurring from the inception date of the treaty shall be paid on the basis of the treaty terms. In the event the incoming portfolio is not constructed on the same cession basis as the new and renewal business, a supplemental agreement to handle it will have to be worked out.

AUTOMATIC (OBLIGATORY) TREATIES VS FACULTATIVE (OPTIONAL) TREATIES

The automatic (or blanket) reinsurance agreement allows the ceding insurer and the reinsurer to predetermine the circumstances under which cessions are to be made, and the predetermination then becomes binding on both parties to the agreement. In other words, the cessions must be made and accepted in accordance with contract terms, hence the term obligatory. This concept applies to quota share, as well as one or more obligatory surplus treaties.

The semi-automatic (or optional) treaty gives the ceding insurer the right to select what business it desires to place in the agreement, within the agreement's conditions, and the assuming reinsurer is bound thereby.

The facultative treaty provides that the ceding insurer has the "faculty" (or option) to cede, and the reinsurer also has the right to accept or decline an individual risk forming part of the treaty. Generally, the facultative treaty is an automatic binding facility for the ceding insurer; if a loss occurs before the ceding company is notified of rejection by the reinsurer of the risk, the reinsurer is bound for its share of the loss. However, if it is a facultative obligatory treaty, the reinsurer does not have the right to accept or decline an individual risk.

The automatic or obligatory treaty was supplemented originally by a detailed listing of each risk, the amount ceded, the term, location, premium, and other pertinent data. That listing was called a bordereau. Its purpose was not only to give a detailed accounting, but also provide the assuming reinsurer with necessary information on each risk ceded. On the basis of this information, the assuming reinsurer, where necessary, could then retrocede to a second reinsurer part of the business to protect its risk and aggregate exposure. As the business grew, this bordereau was phased out because of the multiplicity of the transactions and the new concept of bulk reinsurance underwriting instead of risk reinsurance underwriting as practiced in the facultative field.

As respects any surplus treaty, there is generally a provision granting permission for agency reinsurance, a practice more widespread in the past than today. Agency reinsurance occurs where the ceding insurer has granted permission to its agent to place reinsurance on a risk or risks in excess of the agent's permissible gross line authority from the ceding insurer; this reinsurance is not considered as part of the ceding insurer's gross or net retention for the purpose of pro rata treaty considerations.

Also, if the insurer in its underwriting judgment deems that it is to the benefit of the reinsurer not to cede any or less than the maximum to the surplus treaty on a specific risk, it is permitted to do so, but not on a wholesale basis.

REPORTING TRANSACTIONS

The reporting of treaty business by the insurer generally consists of a monthly account rendered within thirty days after the close of the particular month. The account sets forth the total gross premium, less return premium ceded, the paid losses and loss expenses chargeable to the reinsurer for the month, and the commissions allowed on the month's net premium. The balance of the account — net premium, less commission, less paid losses and loss expenses — is settled within an agreed period of time by the debtor party. The outstanding losses reserved at the end of the month are usually footnoted on the account. At least quarterly the unearned premium reserve is also footnoted — at the end of March, June, September, and December. The agreement usually provides for an advance loss payment on a large loss by the reinsurer at any time. Annually the necessary statistical breakdown for Annual Statement purposes is furnished by the insurer. The errors and omissions clause provides that any mistake made inadvertently within the confines of the treaty will be rectified immediately upon discovery, without invalidating the liability of the reinsurer.

Originally losses were reported on a loss bordereau which detailed all losses. However, under present practices only large losses over a stated sum are reported to the reinsurer on an individual basis. Such large loss reporting is done for the reinsurer to appraise the underwriting involved or else to determine if its accumulation on the same loss from other sources is collectible under the reinsurer's retrocessional program. Special reports on catastrophes are furnished to the reinsurer for the same purposes by catastrophe number where applicable.

TERMINATION

The termination notice provisions on a treaty are the same for both parties. A unilateral provisional notice is neither contemplated nor effective in the wording. The implementation of the cancellation provisions as respects the in-force liability at the date of cancellation varies, dependent on the original agreement between the parties. The more common provisions are as follows.

1. Return portfolio of unearned premium reserve on in-force cessions by the reinsurer at cancellation date with no further loss liability on losses occurring after the date of cancellation.

2. Return portfolio of unearned premium reserve by ceding insurer at its option, either at cancellation date or after a run off of the in-force business for one year, at which time there is a return of the portfolio if any is still in force.

3. Run off by both parties for one year, with return of any unearned portfolio still in force one year later.

4. Run off of all business until expiration. The run off usually excludes assumption of any increase in liability after the cancellation date by the reinsurer.

Usually the notice period for cancellation can vary from thirty days to one year, dependent upon the date on which the cancellation can be effected by agreement; and the notice can be delivered by regular mail, certified, or registered mail. In addition, most agreements also provide for cancellation in the event of a merger, liquidation, impairment of capital, or change of ownership — on immediate notice.

Pricing: The Reinsurance Commission

FLAT COMMISSION, WITH OR WITHOUT CONTINGENT COMMISSION

There are two generally accepted methods of commission reimbursement to the ceding insurer: a flat commission, or a sliding scale commission. A flat or fixed commission is applied to the net written premium developed under the treaty, usually coupled with a contingent commission based on the net profits of the reinsurer for a period. The period of the contingent is an agreed time span, usually one year, but can be for a longer period dependent upon the risk relationship to premium income. For instance, a risk exposure of $1,000,000 with a premium income of $250,000 would, if there were a contingent involved, be calculated over a period of years to allow the leveling of any shock loss which might occur. The basic formula for a contingent commission would be as follows.

INCOME:

Earned premium for the period (as defined under the sliding scale section below).

LESS OUTGO:

Losses and loss expenses incurred (net of salvage for the period), as defined under the sliding scale section before deficit or credit carryover;

Commissions at the stipulated rate applied to earned premiums;

Management expense of the reinsurer at a flat rate applied to earned premium; and

Deficit carryover, if any, from the previous contingent.

EQUALS NET PROFIT:

Insurer's share of net profit at an agreed percentage.

Generally, all contingent formulas provide that if the period's results produce a deficit instead of a profit, that deficit is carried forward as a charge in the next contingent calculation. The deficit can be carried forward indefinitely or for a maximum period of time, depending on the agreement between the parties. Therefore, while contingent formulas provide for deficit carryforwards, they do not provide credit carryforwards, since their purpose is to provide immediate returns to the ceding company by way of the contingent commissions formula.

The determination of the rate of commission and contingent commission is the bargaining area within a treaty and can range up and down the scale. The only basic factors which a reinsurer can start with in developing a fair basis are these: the original costs of production to the ceding insurer, the ceding insurer's overhead, and the ceding insurer's expertise in underwriting for a profit — coupled with the risk limit exposure and expected premium volume.

It should be noted that return portfolios of unearned premium reserve (reassumption by a ceding company of a portfolio) also embrace the refund of the flat commission paid by the reinsurer to the ceding company on the unearned premiums.

SLIDING SCALE COMMISSION

A sliding scale of commission is based on a predetermined range. The initial or provisional commission is then dependent on written premiums, and an adjustment of the provisional commission is made for each agreed period, based on loss ratio related to earned premiums as follows. If the agreed-upon slide provides a minimum commission of 35% at a loss-ratio-to-earned-premium of 60% for the period, and if the provisional commission paid on the written premium is 40%, a 5% adjustment on earned premium will be credited to the reinsurer if the loss ratio for the period is 60%. If the slide provides ½ of 1% increase in commission for each one percentage decrease in loss ratio from 60% subject to a maximum commission of 45% at a 40% loss-ratio-to-earned-premium, then at a 40% loss ratio the reinsurer credits the insurer with an additional 5% of earned premium. It should also be noted that on any return portfolio of unearned premium reserve to the ceding company, the provisional commission would be deducted.

In the above computation, the loss ratio incurred for a period is determined first by adding the losses and loss expenses, inclusive of salvage, together with the outstanding losses at the end of the period, and deducting the outstanding losses at the beginning of the period. Then the total result is adjusted for any deficit or credit carryover from the calculation of the previous period to secure a final total, which is then divided into the earned premiums for the period to secure the loss ratio. Likewise, the earned premiums for a period are determined by adding to the premiums written during the period the unearned premium at the beginning of the period, and deducting the unearned premium at the end of the period, which produces the earned premiums.

The deficit carryover is created when the loss ratio exceeds the 60% in the above example. The credit carryover is created when the loss ratio is less than the 40% in the example. As an illustration of the method by which the deficit or credit carryover is created for carryover to the next calculation, the following two examples are shown. Both A and B assume an earned premium of $1,000 for the year.

A	B
An actual loss ratio of 35% is realized.	An actual loss ratio of 65% is realized.
Permissible (or antici-pated) loss ratio was 40%, so the	Permissible (or antici-pated) loss ratio was 60%, so the
Credit carryover is: 5% of $1,000, or $50	Deficit carryover is: 5% of $1,000, or $50

The 5% differential in ths slide at the minimum commission is roughly equivalent to the reinsurer's management office expenses in the contingent formula. They both provide a minimum net profit to the reinsurer before profit sharing commences. The variety of these scales, like the flat commission plus contingent, is part of the bargaining or negotiating process, as is also the period which they encompass.

In further comparing the flat with the sliding approach, other differences can be noted. The sliding scale usually enables the insurer to receive a larger provisional commission than on a flat basis, which provides the company with more surplus income initially. It also provides a greater amount of commission as compared to a contingent if underwriting results are exceptionally good. Offsetting this consideration, a flat commission (except for a contingent commission calculation) requires no adjustment on an earned basis, whereas the sliding scale does. In periods of adversity, the insurer would have a decrease in surplus income in a poor year under the sliding scale basis. Again, the sliding scale provides not only for deficit carryforwards, but also credit carryforwards, as compared to the contingent basis which sets forth only deficit carryforwards. Deficit or credit carryovers can be for a set period of years or indefinitely, dependent on the treaty agreement.

In the event of cancellation, usually both methods provide for final settlement after all business is expired and all losses settled. Any deficit remaining is a loss to the reinsurer on both a flat and sliding scale basis. Any credit over the scale on the sliding scale basis is income to the reinsurer.

Summary

There are two pro rata treaties used in reinsuring property insurance: quota share and surplus share. In quota share, both parties (the ceding company and the reinsurer) agree on how the ceding company's net retention is to be divided between ceding company and reinsurer. Once agreed upon, the division of liability and premium and losses is automatic. In surplus share, the ceding company decides for each risk the amount to be retained as well as the amount to be ceded to the reinsurer, with the reinsurer then sharing proportionately only those risks having a surplus liability above the threshold agreed on in the treaty. While the surplus share treaty allows for selectivity by the ceding company, the quota share treaty does not. Both treaties, however, provide for unlimited treaty liability.

The quota share treaty offers to the ceding company certain advantages — the replenishment of its policyholder surplus, the encouragement of new classes of business writings, the availability of a fronting arrangement for risks alien to its normal book of business, the reduction of the catastrophe risk, and the increase of ceding company net retentions for any other pro rata treaties used. The surplus share treaty also offers certain advantages — the similar replenishment of policyholder surplus, improved competitive ability to write larger lines, reduced exposure to catastrophe loss, and enhanced profit potential from the leveling factor on the net results of the ceding company.

Under either quota share or surplus share reinsurance, there must be risk shifted from insurer to reinsurer for insurance to exist. Otherwise, the arrangement smacks of improper "fronting" and deserves the criticism of state insurance departments. The reinsurance contract should spell out the details of the risks being shifted, the dollar limits involved per risk, the inception of liability, the requirements for reporting transactions, and provisions for terminating the treaty.

Pricing the pro rata treaty is a function of the reinsurance commission. That commission may be either "flat" or based on a sliding scale formula. The flat commission is applied to the net written premium developed under the treaty and is usually coupled with a contingent commission based on the net profits of the reinsurer from the treaty for a given period. The sliding scale commission is determined by a formula applied to the ceding company's underwriting results for a given period. Whether flat or sliding scale, the variety of commission arrangments and the period they encompass are parts of the bargaining process between ceding company and reinsurer and continue throughout their reinsurance relationship.

*   *   *   *   *   *

About the Author of Chapter 6

Walter James Coleman was born in Flushing, New York, on February 1, 1914. He graduated from Xavier High School in New York City in 1930 and for the next nine years was employed by banking, real estate, and insurance agency firms in New York City. In 1941 he earned his B.S. Degree in accounting from New York University and later became a Certified Public Accountant in New York State.

His insurance career started with Joseph Froggett & Company, an insurance auditing firm in New York. Three years later he joined his current employer in 1942 as an accountant, serving successively as chief accountant, assistant treasurer and underwriter, secretary-underwriter, vice president, and senior vice president. In 1977 he helped organize the United Reinsurance Corporation of New York as an affiliate of his current employer and has since served as its president.

7

The Working Excess of Loss Treaty In Property Insurance

by Stanford Miller*

Excess reinsurance is that system of reinsurance which, subject to a specified limit, affords indemnity for loss sustained by the primary insurer in excess of a predetermined retention. Property excess reinsurance is frequently written in layers and the first layer is the "working excess," which is that area of excess reinsurance in which frequency of claims against the reinsurer is anticipated.

Purpose and Function

The working excess is primarily designed to perform the capacity and stabilization functions of reinsurance. The working excess accomplishes these functions economically because it involves a minimum amount of clerical detail and it permits the primary insurer to keep more of its premium.

With the exception of excess of line reinsurance, described later in this chapter, the working excess of loss reinsurance treaty is completely automatic and requires no cession of individual risks but applies to all of a specified class or classes of property business, subject to the exclusions and other terms of the treaty.

GENERAL CHARACTERISTICS

Excess reinsurance indemnifies against only that part of loss which exceeds the specified retention. The term "excess of loss" evolved to

---

* Chairman, Employers Reinsurance Corporation, P. O. Box 2088, Kansas City, Missouri 64142. The basic work for this chapter was done by June Austin Parrish, General Counsel of Employers Re, to whom a major share of the credit for this contribution should be directed.

emphasize the fact that excess reinsurance pertains to the amount of loss sustained by the primary insurer, as distinguished from pro rata reinsurance which pertains to the amount of each risk shared by the primary insurer and the reinsurer.

Working excess of loss reinsurance is divided into three basic classes which are examined in this chapter: 1) excess each risk, 2) excess each occurrence, and 3) aggregate excess. There may be various combinations and modifications of the three basic classes. The excess each occurrence reinsurance, which provides protection against catastrophe loss, is considered in Chapter 8.

RETENTION AND REINSURANCE LIMIT

Selections of the type of working excess property reinsurance to be used, the retention and the reinsurance limits depend upon such variables as class of property business under consideration, the exposure, the geographical spread, and the size of the primary insurer.

There are no established rules governing the method of fixing retentions, only broad principles which have developed. The first consideration is that the retention be set at an amount which the primary insurer can afford to bear in the event the occurrence insured against takes place. That amount depends not only on the sum insured, but the possibility of loss as a result of the occurrence being total or partial, a factor which cannot be precisely determined. The proper classification of the property risks according to the amount and frequency of probable loss is essential in establishing retentions. The amount of loss which the primary insurer determines to retain must have a reasonable relationship to its financial position as reflected in its premium income, policyholder surplus and reserves. By establishing the appropriate retention, the primary insurer realizes the stability function of reinsurance. As a result of selecting that level of retention which eliminates the inevitable large loss or so-called "high peak" in the experience curve and at the same time permitting the reinsurer to enjoy some of the primary insurer's profit in good years, the primary insurer is able to reflect a consistent experience applicable to its net retained business and at the same time have a reliable reinsurance market readily available.

The reinsurance limit applicable to the working excess of loss each-risk or each-occurrence property treaty should be set at a figure which will provide the primary insurer with a layer of protection adequate to cover the vast majority of the primary insurer's business. Ideally it should rarely be necessary for the primary insurer to seek additional reinsurance for capacity purposes. At the same time, the limit should be kept at a level which will eliminate the possibility that an occurrence resulting in substantial loss will have too great an impact on the rating structure of the treaty.

CALCULATIONS OF RECOVERABLES (EXCESS EACH RISK)

The retention, indemnity, and reinsurance limit under excess each-risk property reinsurance apply to loss sustained by the primary insurer as a result of damage to each risk involved in each occurrence. The purpose of the excess each risk reinsurance is to afford capacity. For example, if the primary insurer desires to establish an automatic capacity of $500,000 each risk and has determined that it can retain $100,000 on each risk involved in each occurrence, it will obtain an excess each risk working cover for $400,000 each risk each occurrence excess of $100,000 each risk involved in each occurrence. Assume that, as a result of fire, the risk is damaged to the extent of $250,000. The primary insurer and the reinsurer will bear loss as a result of the occurrence as follows:

Primary Insurer	Working Excess Each Risk Reinsurer	Total Loss
$100,000	$150,000	$250,000

In excess of loss reinsurance the reinsurer is not involved in loss as a result of any occurrence until loss exceeds the predetermined retention. Thus, if as a result of a fire, damage is $75,000 to the previously described $500,000 risk, the $75,000 loss will be borne by the primary insurer and the reinsurer as follows:

Primary Insurer	Working Excess Each Risk Reinsurer	Total Loss
$75,000	none	$75,000

Assume that the same primary insurer desires to insure a $1,000,000 property risk. The excess each risk reinsurance treaty sometimes provides that if the primary insurer assumes liability as respects any risk which exceeds an amount equal to the retention plus the reinsurance limit (the capacity), the primary insurer will either purchase pro rata reinsurance to the extent that its gross line exceeds such amount or become co-reinsurer to that extent. The primary insurer will then cede to a surplus share reinsurance treaty or purchase pro rata facultative reinsurance applicable to the $500,000 surplus of the $500,000 capacity of the excess each risk reinsurance treaty. Assume now that as a result of fire, the $1,000,000 risk is damaged to the extent of $250,000. The primary insurer, the excess each risk treaty reinsurer and the pro rata surplus facultative reinsurer will bear loss as a result of the occurrence as follows:

Primary Insurer	Working Excess Each Risk Reinsurer	Pro Rata Surplus Reinsurer	Total Loss
$100,000	$25,000	$125,000	$250,000

The primary insurer in this case first recovers from the pro rata reinsurance, and the working excess of loss applies to the net retained liability of the primary insurer.

If the $1,000,000 risk sustains damage to the extent of $75,000 as a result of an occurrence, the loss will be borne by the primary insurer, the excess each risk treaty reinsurer and the pro rata reinsurer as follows:

Primary Insurer	Excess Each Risk Reinsurer	Pro Rata Surplus Reinsurer	Total Loss
$37,500	none	$37,500	$75,000

In the absence of a requirement in the per risk working excess of loss treaty that the primary insurer must purchase pro rata reinsurance to the extent that any risk exceeds the working excess treaty capacity, the primary insurer is free to purchase excess reinsurance. The second excess facility may be on a facultative or automatic treaty basis, depending upon the particular requirements of the primary insurer. If the hypothetical primary insurer with the $1,000,000 property risk obtains second excess reinsurance to protect its exposure in excess of the working excess per risk capacity of $500,000, the recovery will be as follows in the event of the $250,000 damage previously considered:

Primary Insurer	Working Excess Each Risk Reinsurer	Second Excess Each Risk Reinsurer	Total Loss
$100,000	$150,000	none	$250,000

Usual Contract Provisions

RETENTION AND REINSURANCE

The retention and reinsurance provision of the working excess of loss treaty reflects the details of the indemnity afforded. Depending on the protection desired by the primary insurer, the retention will apply to each risk involved in each occurrence or to all risks involved in each occurrence. The reinsurance limit can apply to each risk involved in the occurrence, to each risk involved in the occurrence subject to an occurrence limit with respect to all risks involved in the occurrence, or solely to each occurrence regardless of the number of risks involved in the occurrence. The indemnity desired by the primary insurer can involve any combination of the foregoing units of retention and reinsurance limit. In property reinsurance the primary insurer is sometimes required to share some portion of the excess loss (usually 10%).

The introductory language of the retention and reinsurance clause of a working excess treaty can follow the same format regardless of the units of retention and reinsurance limit selected. The application of the retention and reinsurance limit can then be stated in the table which is a part of the clause. The following example of the retention and reinsurance treaty provision sets forth the alternative tables which may be used in a working excess treaty, depending on the specific type of reinsurance which is negotiated between the parties, and using hypothetical figures.

> RETENTION AND REINSURANCE. As respects loss sustained by the Company under such perils, the Company shall retain as its own net retention loss as indicated in the retention column of the following Table and the Reinsurer hereby agrees to indemnify the Company against loss as indicated in the reinsurance column of the following Table.

TABLE A

Retention	Reinsurance
$5,000 each risk involved in each occurrence plus 10% of loss each risk involved in each occurrence excess of $5,000	90% of loss each risk involved in each occurrence excess of $5,000 subject to a limit of 90% of $95,000 each risk involved in each occurrence

TABLE B

Retention	Reinsurance
$5,000 each risk involved in each occurrence plus 10% of loss each risk involved in each occurrence excess of $5,000	90% of loss each risk involved in each occurrence excess of $5,000 subject to a limit of 90% of $95,000 each risk involved in each occurrence and 90% of $190,000 all risks involved in each occurrence

TABLE C

Retention	Reinsurance
$5,000 each occurrence plus 10% of loss each occurrence excess of $5,000	90% of loss each occurrence excess of $5,000 subject to a limit of 90% of $95,000 each occurrence

The introductory language identifies "loss" (some reinsurers use the term "ultimate net loss") as the unit to which retention and reinsurance apply. The term "loss" is defined elsewhere in the treaty and is considered later in this chapter as it relates to the working excess treaty. The reference to "such perils" in the introductory language pertains to the specific exposures to which the treaty applies and which are itemized in a preceding clause of the working excess treaty. The agreement of the reinsurer to indemnify the primary insurer emphasizes the basic concept of reinsurance as an agreement to reimburse the primary company for "loss" and not an agreement to pay amounts on behalf of the primary company.

Per Risk Working Excess. The reinsurance under Table A is designed to afford the primary insurer capacity to write individual risks having a value up to $100,000 each. Recovery under the treaty is not limited by the number of risks involved in each occurrence. However, the primary insurer must retain loss as respects each risk involved in the occurrence. If the primary insurer has reinsured three houses for $100,000 each in the same city block and a windstorm damages each roof to the extent of $5,000, for a total of $15,000, the reinsurance is not involved. If one roof is damaged to the extent of $15,000, the reinsurance will afford indemnity for $9,000 (90% of $10,000) excess the retention of the first $5,000 plus $1,000 (10% of loss excess of $5,000).

Per Risk Working Excess Subject to a Per Occurrence Limit. The reinsurance afforded under Table B is designed to afford the capacity to write individual risks having a $100,000 value each subject to a limit as respects each occurrence. That limit is usually established at two or three times the amount of the each risk limit. Under a self-rated working excess of loss treaty the each occurrence limit is attractive to the primary insurer. If the occurrence involves loss in an amount greater than the each occurrence limit, the primary insurer will look to its catastrophe reinsurance treaty for protection, and such greater amount of loss will not be charged in the rating formula applicable to the per risk cover.

Per Occurrence Retention and Reinsurance Limit Working Excess. The reinsurance afforded under Table C can also be considered as a facility to afford capacity if it is supplemented by higher layers of excess reinsurance. Under this reinsurance program, if the primary insurer has insured three houses for $100,000 each in the same city block and a windstorm damages each roof to the extent of $5,000, for a total loss of $15,000 as respects the occurrence, the primary insurer will retain $6,000 ($5,000 + $1,000 [10% of loss excess of $5,000]), and the reinsurer will afford indemnity for $9,000 (90% of $10,000).

If as a result of a single occurrence, the three $100,000 houses located in the same block are totally damaged, the working excess of loss treaty 1) written on the basis of Table A would afford indemnity with respect to three houses, 2) written on the basis of Table B would afford indemnity with respect to two houses, and 3) written on the basis of Table C would afford indemnity with respect to one house.

The utilization in a working excess cover of the retention and reinsurance limit applicable to each occurrence usually takes place when the basic objective of the primary insurer is to seek protection against frequency of claims rather than capacity. When such a cover is used for reinsuring such lines as automobile physical damage, the terms of the treaty normally recognize that it may be used for capacity purposes in the case, e.g., of fleet and dealer risks, and will require the primary insurer to purchase pro rata reinsurance to the extent that its gross line exceeds the total of the retention and reinsurance limit or to become co-reinsurer to that extent.

NET RETAINED LINE CLAUSE

The net retained line clause reflects the intention of the parties that the excess of loss treaty is applicable only to that portion of any insurance or reinsurance which the primary company retains net for its own account. The clause is normally included in a catastrophe reinsurance treaty for the purpose of providing that recovery under any per risk facility inures to the benefit of the catastrophe treaty. The clause is included in a working excess of loss treaty so that the primary insurer may reinsure a surplus or quota share of certain risks or classes of risks, and it is clear that the excess of loss treaty applies only to that portion of the business retained by the primary company. The clause normally provides that:

> This agreement applies only to that portion of any insurance or reinsurance covered hereunder which the Company retains net for its own account, and in calculating the loss under any one occurrence only losses in respect of that portion of any insurance or reinsurance which the Company retains net for its own account shall be included, but the amount of the Rein-

surer's liability hereunder in respect of any occurrence shall not be increased by reason of the inability of the Company to collect from any other reinsurers, whether specific or general, any amounts which may become due from them, whether such inability arises from the insolvency of such other reinsurers or otherwise.

EXCLUSIONS

Generally, the exclusions in a working excess of loss property treaty depend upon the particular line or lines of property business being reinsured by the treaty. For example, a working excess of loss automobile physical damage reinsurance agreement might exclude such coverages as theft, robbery, pilferage, collision or upset, and wrongful conversion. Normally a working excess of loss property reinsurance treaty contains a war exclusion which provides that the treaty does not apply to:

loss, damage or liability arising from enemy attacks by armed forces including action taken by military, naval or air forces in resisting an actual or an immediately impending enemy attack, invasion, insurrection, rebellion, revolution, civil war, usurped power, or confiscation by order of any government or public authority.

The working excess of loss property reinsurance treaty also excludes all excess of loss reinsurance assumed by the primary carrier. The working excess of loss property treaty applies to the specified business of the primary insurer whether written as direct or accepted by reinsurance. The working excess of loss treaty must apply only to pro rata reinsurance accepted by the primary insurer which is rated on the basis of assuming a share of the original premium of the primary insurer. Reinsurance accepted on an excess of loss basis is rated at a percentage of the original premium; clearly the working excess of loss reinsurance premium rate would be inadequate if applied to that premium derived by the primary insurer from the excess of loss reinsurance it has assumed. The working excess cover may also exclude obligatory pro rata reinsurance assumed by the primary insurer, with the result that the treaty applies only to assumed pro rata reinsurance written on a facultative basis.

DEFINITIONS OF "LOSS" AND "CLAIMS EXPENSES"

"Loss," i.e., the amount paid by the primary company in settlement of claims, is the unit with respect to which indemnity is afforded by the reinsurer to the primary company. One important function of the definition of "loss" in a working excess of loss property treaty involves the manner in which the treaty is to afford indemnity against "claim expenses," i.e., court costs, interest upon judgments, and allocated investigation and adjustment expenses.

If a basic function of the working excess of loss treaty is to afford capacity, it is appropriate that indemnity for claim expenses be afforded by the reinsurer in the same share that the reinsurer bears of loss under the primary policy. This is achieved by defining "loss" as excluding claim expenses and including a separate provision pertaining to indemnity for claim expenses. If "claim expenses" are included in "loss," it is possible in the event the reinsured property is totally destroyed that the primary company would not have adequate reinsurance, and the purpose of having a capacity facility would be partially defeated. Assume, for example, that the working excess of loss treaty affords reinsurance for $95,000 each risk excess of $5,000 each risk, and that a $100,000 risk reinsured thereunder is totally destroyed by fire under suspicious circumstances. In an unsuccessful attempt to prove arson, assume that the primary insurer spends $10,000 in claim expenses. If claim expenses are included in loss under the reinsurance treaty, a total of $110,000 will have been paid by the primary company as a result of the claim, and the primary company will bear the entire $10,000 of claim expenses because the reinsurance limit will have been exhausted by the payment of $95,000 by the reinsurer. If the treaty affords pro rata indemnity as respects claim expenses, the primary company, which bears 5% of loss under the policy, would bear 5% or $500 of the claim expenses and the reinsurer would bear $9,500 of the claim expenses. Thus the total $110,000 pertaining to the claim would be distributed as follows:

	Primary Company	Reinsurer	Total
Loss	$5,000	$ 95,000	$100,000
Claim Expenses	$ 500	$ 9,500	$ 10,000
Total	$5,500	$104,500	$110,000

If the property risks insured by the primary insurer are of a type not exposed to total damage, e.g., fire and extended coverage applicable to fire resistant structures located in highly protected areas, the need for a reinsurance capacity facility which affords protection against exhaustion of policy limits is not so important. It would be appropriate in a treaty reinsuring such business to include claim expenses in the definition of loss, with the result that the reinsurance limit stated in the treaty applies to the total of payments made in settlement of the claim under the policy plus investigation and claim expenses.

The definitions of "loss" and "claim expenses" normally exclude the salaries of employees of the primary insurer. In computing loss, all subrogation, salvage and other recoveries are deducted. However, this does not prevent the primary carrier from making recovery from the reinsurer prior to the time that the actual amount of loss is ultimately determined and the treaty provision pertaining to the definition of "loss" reflects that fact.

The reinsurance treaty is designed to afford indemnity to the primary insurer with respect to loss sustained by the primary insurer under the particular primary policies it issues. In the absence of specific provisions to the contrary, it is not the intention of the parties to a reinsurance treaty that coverage be afforded to the primary insurer for its tortious conduct in the investigation or settlement of claims. In recent years the subject of compensatory and punitive damages imposed upon insurers as a result of bad faith or gross negligence in the investigation or settlement of claims has become increasingly important in the property insurance field. This has prompted the inclusion of treaty language defining "loss" and "claim expenses" which clarifies what has always been the intention of the parties with respect to such damages. The following examples of treaty language illustrate the method of handling these important subjects. If the reinsurer is to afford indemnity for claim expenses in the same share that it bears of policy loss, the treaty contains a separate clause affording indemnity for claim expenses, and the definitions of "loss" and "claim expenses" provide that:

> The unqualified word "loss" shall mean only such amounts as are actually paid by the Company in settlement of claims or in satisfaction of judgments; provided, however, that in the event of insolvency of the Company, "loss" shall mean the amount of loss which the insolvent insurer has incurred or is liable for, and payment by the reinsurer shall be made to the liquidator, receiver or other statutory successor of the Company in accordance with the provisions of the insolvency clause made a part of this agreement; but the word "loss" shall not include claim expenses.

> The term "claim expenses" shall mean court costs, interest upon judgments, and allocated investigation, adjustment and legal expenses.

If the "claim expenses" are included in "loss," the treaty will define "loss" as follows:

> The unqualified word "loss" shall mean only such amounts as are actually paid by the Company in settlement of claims or in satisfaction of judgments, and including court costs, interest upon judgments, and allocated investigation, adjustment, and legal expenses, paid by the Company; provided, however, that in the event of insolvency of the Company, "loss" shall mean the amount of loss which the insolvent insurer has incurred or is liable for, and payment by the reinsurer shall be made to the liquidator, receiver or other statutory successor of the Company in accordance with the provisions of the insolvency clause made a part of this agreement.

The treaty provision pertaining to salvage and subrogation clarifies the fact that indemnity may be provided by the reinsurer prior to the time that the total amount of loss is ultimately determined and states that:

> Net salvage, subrogation or any other recovery (after expenses) shall be used to reduce the loss and so much of such recovery shall be paid to the Reinsurer as will reduce the loss ultimately borne by the Reinsurer to what it would have been had the recovery preceded any payment of such loss by the Reinsurer.

The subject of salaries of employees of the primary insurer and damages for misconduct by the primary insurer in settling claims is covered under the working excess of loss treaty in the following clause, which is made a part of the definition of "loss" or the definitions of "loss" and "claim expenses," if the latter term is defined separately for reasons previously discussed:

> Neither the word "loss" nor the term "claim expenses" shall include:
> a) salaries paid to employees of the Company;
> b) any amount paid by the Company for punitive, exemplary or compensatory damages awarded to the insured, arising out of the conduct of the Company in the investigation, trial or settlement of any claim or failure to pay or delay in payment of any benefits under any policy;

provided, that this subparagraph b) shall not apply if the Reinsurer has, in advance of any such conduct by the Company, counseled with the Company and concurred in the Company's course of conduct;

c) any statutory penalty imposed upon the Company on account of any unfair trade practice or any unfair claim practice.

Working Excess Variations

THE EXCESS OF LOSS RATIO COVER

A working excess of loss reinsurance treaty applicable to a specific class of business can be in the form of aggregate excess reinsurance. Under such a cover the primary insurer's retention is fixed at a certain predetermined loss ratio of the primary insurer, computed annually on the business under consideration and the reinsurance applies only when that loss ratio is exceeded during the annual period. The reinsurance is subject to a fixed dollar limit or a loss ratio or both as respects each annual period. This form of reinsurance is called "excess of loss ratio reinsurance or, more frequently, "stop loss" reinsurance.

The excess of loss ratio cover is basically designed to protect the primary insurer's loss ratio as respects a particular class of business after deducting recoveries from all other reinsurance. The primary function of the cover is to afford stability with respect to the underwriting results of the primary insurer. Excess of loss ratio reinsurance is frequently applied to classes of business, such as hail insurance, which are subject to cyclical losses. Such reinsurance is obtained for the purpose of keeping the year-end results of the primary insurer for such class of business within fairly reasonable figures and not for the purpose of avoiding loss as a result of any particular occurrence. A working excess of loss per risk property treaty covering risks and classes of business subject to a high degree of frequency may also have an excess of loss ratio cover applicable to the net retention of the primary insurer so that the treaty affords capacity plus stability.

Under excess of loss ratio reinsurance, the reinsurer is not responsible for the excess of the amount by which any individual claim exceeds a fixed amount. The reinsurer is not responsible for any claims until the loss ratio for the year exceeds the predetermined percentage of the primary insurer's premiums. Thereafter the reinsurer is responsible for all claims, regardless of size until the reinsurance limit is reached. For example, the treaty may afford reinsurance with respect to loss excess of a

90% loss ratio, subject to a limit of a 120% loss ratio. The limit is usually also expressed in a dollar amount to protect the reinsurer against a substantial increase in the primary insurer's premium writings.

The loss ratio upon which the aggregate excess cover depends is computed by relating claims paid and outstanding to premiums earned during the annual period. At the close of each annual period, claims paid during the period are increased by claims outstanding at the end of the period and decreased by claims outstanding at the beginning of the period. Earned premiums are computed by adding to premiums written during the period the reserve for unearned premiums at the beginning of the period and deducting the unearned premium reserve at the close of the period. The loss ratio can also be computed by relating loss as a result of occurrences taking place during the annual period to premiums written during the period.

The stop loss cover usually provides that the primary insurer will retain 10% of loss excess of the predetermined loss ratio and that the reinsurer will indemnify against 90% of loss excess of the loss ratio. This safeguards the reinsurer against any relaxation by the primary insurer in the method of claim settlement after the predetermined loss ratio has been reached.

The stop loss cover is not designed to guarantee a profit. If the loss ratio is established at too low a percentage so as to allow an apparent margin to the primary insurer, the reinsurance premium rate would necessarily be increased and the margin to the primary insurer would be reduced accordingly. As in all forms of reinsurance, the total account must provide a reasonable opportunity for profit for both parties, with recognition that each party must from time to time be involved in loss and that profit cannot be guaranteed to either of them. The reinsurance premium rate for stop loss covers is a net percentage of the premium income. The rate depends on such factors as the class of business, primary limits, and previous experience. The method of determining claims cost over a three or five years' period with a loading for profit and contingencies is particularly appropriate for stop loss covers.

AGGREGATE RETENTION COVER (EXCESS LOSSES ONLY)

The working excess of loss property cover occasionally takes the form of aggregate reinsurance applicable to loss excess of a predetermined amount with respect to each occurrence. The retention and reinsurance can be established as a loss ratio, i.e., a percentage of earned premium or as a flat dollar amount applicable to all occurrences taking place during each calendar year.

The objective of such an aggregate treaty is to protect the primary insurer against an accumulation of large losses during any calendar year. Such a cover frequently applies to all lines of property insurance written by the primary insurer. Some of the separate lines may be subject to working excess of loss per risk treaties for the purpose of capacity with retentions thereunder further protected by aggregate cover applicable to the large losses for stability purposes. The following treaty language illustrates the manner in which the reinsurance is afforded:

> **AGGREGATE RETENTION AND REINSURANCE.** As respects such net retained loss in excess of $200,000 each occurrence, the Company shall retain such loss as a result of all such occurrences taking place during each calendar year as indicated in the aggregate retention column of the following Table and the Reinsurer hereby agrees to indemnify the Company against loss as indicated in the aggregate reinsurance column of the following Table:

TABLE

Aggregate Retention	Aggregate Reinsurance
$7,000,000	90% of loss in excess of the aggregate retention subject to a limit of 90% of $7,000,000 as respects all occurrences taking place during the calendar year.

The reinsurance premium rate is determined for such a cover by the same methods applicable to other forms of working excess of loss covers. Self-rating programs are particularly appropriate for this form of aggregate reinsurance.

THE EXCESS OF LINE COVER

The working excess each risk treaty written as an excess of line cover is a form of excess reinsurance which can strengthen the primary insurer's surplus as well and afford capacity. The primary insurer is permitted to select a retention which is usually subject to minimum and maximum dollar amounts as respects each risk. The reinsurance limit is expressed as a multiple of the primary insurer's retention, e.g., twenty-five times or 2500% of the retention, and usually subject to a dollar amount. The indemnity afforded by the treaty applies to each risk in excess of the retention selected by the primary insurer, subject to the dollar limit stated in the treaty. The indemnity in excess of the retention is usually for some percentage less than 100 % so that the primary insurer is kept very well involved in the excess loss.

For the purpose of illustrating how the excess of line treaty applies, assume that the treaty provides that the primary insurer's retention shall be an amount which shall not be less than $5,000 each risk nor more than $25,000 each risk, and that the reinsurance shall be 90 % of loss excess of the retention selected by the primary insurer, subject to a limit of 90 % of twenty-five times the retention so selected but not more than 90 % of $125,000 each risk. Under such a cover the primary insurer has a capacity of $150,000 each risk if it selects a retention of $25,000 as respects the risk. The treaty affords only five lines as respects the $150,000 risk and twenty-five lines as respects a $130,000 risk if the primary insurer selects a retention of $5,000 as respects such risk. Once the retention and reinsurance limit are established under an excess of line treaty, the allocation of loss between the primary insurer and the reinsurer is identical with any other excess each risk treaty.

If the excess of line reinsurance premium applies to the gross primary written premium income pertaining to the primary liability in excess of the retention, the facility affords capacity and at the same time operates to strengthen the primary insurer's surplus because part of the primary insurer's liability for unearned premium reserves is transferred to the reinsurer. The reinsurance premium is subject to a commission to the primary insurer as an allowance for taxes, acquisition and other expenses. The experience under such a treaty could be subject to a profit commission to the primary insurer. If strengthening the surplus of the primary insurer is not an objective, reinsurance premium for the excess line cover will be computed on the same basis subsequently described for other working excess reinsurance covers.

The excess of line cover is appropriate for large primary companies having a substantial variation in the size and probable maximum loss of risks they write. At the same time it affords the primary insurer maximum flexibility in establishing retention and reinsurance. The excess of line cover is the single exception to the initial advantage recited for the automatic nature of working excess of loss reinsurance, because the underwriting expense of primary insurer in determining the appropriate retention for each risk under the excess of loss cover could be expensive in the absence of well established underwriting rules. The summary reporting of premiums and loss follows the usual property excess of loss format and is inexpensive for the primary insurer.

Special Cases

THE ADVANCE DEPOSIT PREMIUM COVER

The reinsurance premium rate applicable to most working excess of loss treaties is a percentage of premiums written during the period of the treaty. If the treaty applies to occurrences taking place on or after the effective date of the treaty as respects business in force on the effective date of the treaty, the reinsurer will collect an unearned reinsurance premium pertaining to the business in force on the effective date of the agreement. Likewise, if the treaty is terminated on the so-called "cut-off" basis, with respect to loss as a result of occurrences taking place on or after the termination date, the reinsurer will return to the primary insurer the unearned reinsurance premium as of the termination date, less any commission previously allowed by the reinsurer to the primary insurer. This system of reinsurance is based on premiums earned during the period the reinsurance treaty is in force. The reinsurance premium is usually paid on a monthly or quarterly basis. If the premium is paid on an annual or semi-annual basis, a deposit premium is usually paid at the beginning of each annual or semi-annual period based on the anticipated writings for the year. Promptly after the close of the period the premium is adjusted on the basis of primary premium earned.

When the primary insurer's property business involves a class of fairly stable premium volume, that class of business may be reinsured under a working excess of loss treaty which is written on a "losses incurred basis." The reinsurance applies to loss as a result of occurrences taking place during the period of the agreement, regardless of effective date of the primary policies. The reinsurance premium is based on the net premiums earned by the primary insurer during the period of the agreement. Under this system the reinsurance is based upon annual periods and the years' premiums pay for the years' losses. When such treaties are entered into, it is generally with the intention that they are to be of a permanent nature and are to be renewed from year to year. This system usually involves an annual minimum advance deposit premium, sometimes payable in semi-annual or quarterly installments, based on the anticipated writings for the year. Promptly after the close of the year the actual reinsurance premium is computed by applying the agreed upon reinsurance premium rate to the primary premiums actually written during the year, and if the actual reinsurance premium is greater than the annual minimum advance deposit premium previously paid, the primary insurer will immediately pay the difference to the reinsurer. The rating system is not technically accurate because losses occurring during the year do not necessarily relate to premiums written during the year. The system does have the advantage of minimum expense to the primary insurer in computing reinsurance premium. While the reinsurance premium is based on premiums written during the period of the treaty, for the purposes of such a treaty, premiums are deemed earned when written and no unearned reinsurance premium exists to be returned to the primary insurer on the termination date, although the treaty does not apply to loss as a result of occurrences taking place on or after the termination date.

The term "advance deposit premium cover" is used by some reinsurers to identify a reinsurance premium which is subject to a higher than normal reinsurance premium rate. A predetermined percentage of the reinsurance premium, e.g., 25%, is allocated to the reinsurer to cover its fee for expenses and profit. The remaining 75% of the reinsurance premium is set up as unearned reinsurance premium and is used to pay loss under the reinsurance agreement. Any remaining amount is returned to the primary insurer as return reinsurance premium. This type of cover enables the primary insurer to use a portion of its reinsurance premium for loss reserves.

THE COMBINATION (PRO RATA EXCESS) PLAN

The combination plan is a useful reinsurance facility for assisting the primary insurer through the transitional period from pro rata to excess of loss each risk reinsurance. The facility may be particularly helpful to the primary insurer which has relied heavily on pro rata reinsurance to increase its policyholder surplus.

As its name implies, the combination pro rata excess plan involves both types of reinsurance. The reinsuring clause of the treaty is normally divided into two parts, excess reinsurance and quota share reinsurance.

The terms of the excess of loss per risk reinsurance are first stated, identifying a fixed-dollar retention applicable to each risk involved in each occurrence and providing for indemnity against loss excess of such retention subject to a specified limit applicable to each risk involved in each occurrence. Provision is next made for the quota share reinsurance which applies to the primary insurer's retention as respects each risk under the excess of loss per risk reinsurance. If the loss pertaining to the risk does not exceed the retention under the excess reinsurance, the quota share reinsurance will nevertheless apply to loss pertaining to the risk.

The following clause of a combination treaty describes the application of the reinsurance.

RETENTION AND REINSURANCE. §A. Excess Reinsurance. As respects loss sustained by the Company pertaining to each risk involved in each occurrence, the Reinsurer hereby agrees to indemnify the Company against loss excess of the amount indicated in the retention column of the following Table subject to the limit indicated in the reinsurance limit column of the following Table:

TABLE

Retention Each Risk Each Occurrence	Reinsurance Limit Each Risk Each Occurrence
$25,000	$250,000

§B. Quota Share Reinsurance. As respects loss retained by the Company under §A of this article the Reinsurer hereby agrees to indemnify the Company against 40% of such loss subject to a limit of $10,000 as respects each risk involved in each occurrence.

The following chart illustrates the manner in which loss is borne under the foregoing combination plan with respect to two hypothetical risks: X, a $100,000 loss as respects the occurrence, and Y, a $10,000 loss as respects the occurrence.

Risk	§A. Excess		§B. Quota Share		Total	
	Retention	Reinsurance	Retention	Reinsurance	Retention	Reinsurance
X—$100,000	$25,000	$75,000	$15,000	$10,000	$15,000	$85,000
Y—$ 10,000	$10,000	none	$ 6,000	$ 4,000	$ 6,000	$ 4,000

In view of the fact that the combination plan is a facility designed in part to provide financial assistance to the primary insurer, the reinsurance premium rate is normally on a gross basis subject to a sliding scale ceding commission, as discussed in Chapter 6. The automatic features of the combination plan result in inexpensive administration of the reinsurance program. The quota share feature presents the possible disadvantage that the primary insurer may be ceding premiums which it would normally retain under a first surplus pro rata program. A further disadvantage may exist if the provisional ceding commission is greater than the minimum ceding commission under the sliding scale commission formula because the stability feature is minimized in a year of large losses resulting in a decrease in the ultimate ceding commission.

INFLATION AND THE WORKING EXCESS OF LOSS REINSURANCE TREATY

The development of experience under working excess of loss property reinsurance treaties is usually fairly prompt. As a result the consequences of inflation on the reinsurer are not as severe as the experience of the reinsurer under casualty reinsurance covering third-party liability coverages.

The increased cost to the reinsurer of loss and claim expenses is substantially absorbed by the self-rating premium formulae previously discussed. However, it is essential for the reinsurer to keep the minimum and maximum reinsurance premium rates in those formulae properly reflecting the increased costs to the reinsurer as a result of inflation. At the same time it is important that retention under the working excess of loss covers be maintained at a level so that frequency of involvement of the reinsurer is not accelerated because of inflation.

Rating The Working Excess

Determination of the reinsurance premium for a working excess of loss property treaty depends on a number of variables, and it is not possible to establish any reliable set formula. In addition to the retention and reinsurance limit, consideration must be given to the types of risks and classes of property business involved, the geographical spread of the business, plus the risks and classes of business excluded from the treaty. The important factor in rating the working excess of loss property treaty is the past experience of the business reinsured. Usually the premium is developed by applying a percentage rate to the premium derived by the primary insurer from the business to which the treaty is applied.

RATING PLANS

During the years various plans have developed for rating the working excess of loss property treaty. The annual premium income earned during the annual period by the primary insurer from the property business subject to the treaty and the cost of all claims in excess of the retention as a result of occurrences taking place during the annual period provide the figures necessary for calculating that percentage of the premiums used to pay claims in excess of the retention. That pure claims cost (sometimes referred to as "burning cost") must then be loaded by some factor to produce a reinsurance premium rate. The loading (sometimes referred to as the "multiplier") does not normally involve a ceding commission, because working excess of loss property reinsurance is seldom used for the purpose of strengthening the financial position of the primary insurer by increasing its surplus. As a result, the excess property reinsurance premium rates are applicable to earned premium or written premium deemed earned and are usually quoted net. The loading includes allowances for administrative expenses, acquisition costs, incurred but not reported claims, inflation, reserve for catastrophe, and profit to the reinsurer.

PROSPECTIVE V. RETROSPECTIVE RATING

In lieu of a fixed reinsurance premium rate, a so-called self-rating plan can be used in the working excess of loss reinsurance treaty by application of a prospective or a retrospective rating formula. There are numerous variations of the basic self-rating formulas but the underlying principles are quite simple.

Under a prospective formula, the pure claims cost of the business is determined for a period of three years or five years immediately preceding the year for which the reinsurance premium rate is being determined. The pure cost is then loaded by an agreed margin for the reinsurer's expenses and profit. The basic principle of the prospective formula is that past results govern future costs. The working excess of loss reinsurance treaty rated on a prospective formula is sometimes called "spread loss reinsurance." The following table illustrates the application of the prospective rating formula over a three years' period:

Year	Premium Base	Excess Loss	Loss Cost
1980	$10,000,000	$ 750,000	7.50 %
1981	$11,000,000	$ 550,000	5.00 %
1982	$12,000,000	$1,020,000	8.50 %
	$33,000,000	$2,320,000	21.00 %

Average loss cost for the three years is 7 %.

If the profit and expense margin for the reinsurer is set at 25 % (of losses), then the reinsurance premium rate for 1983 is 8.75 % (7 % + 1.75 % [25 % x 7 %]). Assume that in 1983 the premium is $14,000,000 and excess loss totals $910,000 with a 6.50 % loss cost. In computing the reinsurance premium rate for 1984, these 1983 figures replace the 1980 figures producing new totals for the three years' experience period of $37,000,000 premium and $2,480,000 excess loss. The average loss cost for the three years is 6.66 ⅔ % and the reinsurance premium rate is 8.33 ⅓ %.

The loading factor for the reinsurer's profit, costs and expenses can also be expressed as a fraction, such as 100/75 or 100/80, applied to excess loss, as indicated in the following table:

Factor	Loss	Excess Cost	Margin
100/75	$750,000	$1,000,000	$250,000 (33 1/3 %)
100/80	$800,000	$1,000,000	$200,000 (25 %)

The retrospective self-rating premium plan provides for the computation of the actual premium for each year sometime after the close of such year, based upon the actual experience for such year. The initial premium for the year is estimated and is subsequently adjusted. The formula is the same, i.e., a predetermined margin for expenses and profit of the reinsurer applied to the cost of excess loss.

The advantage of prospective rating is that the reinsurance premium rate for the year is fixed in advance. Prospective rating does have the disadvantage of failing to accurately reflect the actual results of the year under consideration. Rapid change in the economy is not necessarily properly reflected in the prospective premium rate. The retrospective rating plan does reflect the actual experience for the year under consideration, but the delay in determination of the actual premium rate may be troublesome for the primary insurer in such matters as budgeting and establishing a reserve for the actual premium which will ultimately be due. Some underwriters consider the retrospective rating plan unattractive because it results in increased premiums as a result of increased loss. However, from a practical standpoint the increased premium, while applicable to the year of poor loss experience, is usually paid in the following year so the two increased items, loss and reinsurance premium, are not necessarily paid in the same year.

In evaluating the advantages and disadvantages of prospective and retrospective rating, consideration must be given to the fact that frequently the formula will recite a minimum premium rate and a maximum premium rate. This is particularly so if the treaty is not subject to termination for a specified period of years by the reinsurer if the reinsurance experience is in a credit position or by the primary insurer if the reinsurance experience is in a deficit position. The retrospective premium plan which has a minimum and maximum rate and a carryover of deficit and credit does not, of course, necessarily reflect the actual experience for the year under consideration.

From the standpoint of the primary insurer, the reinsurance premium is only one element of the cost of reinsurance. The expense of the underwriter in determining retention and reinsurance premium, the cost of processing reinsurance recovery on account of claims, and the loss of investment income on the reinsurance premium held by the reinsurer are all items to be considered by the primary insurer. The working excess of loss reinsurance treaty is usually more attractive than the pro rata reinsurance treaty, because it is simple to administer and uses a smaller amount of the primary premium dollar.

Summary

The basic function of the working excess of loss property reinsurance treaty is to provide capacity and stabilization to the primary insurer. The typical working excess of loss property reinsurance treaty does not require individual cessions but applies automatically to all of a specified class of property business, subject to the terms of the treaty.

The retention and reinsurance limit under the working excess of loss property reinsurance treaty can apply to each risk involved in each occurrence, all risks involved in each occurrence, a predetermined loss ratio of the primary insurer, or various combinations of the foregoing units, depending on the class of property business, its geographical spread, and the requirements of the primary insurer. Some loss frequency is expected under a working excess treaty. It is the underwriting intention that the experience under a working excess treaty will average out over a period of time. For this reason the reinsurance limits under the working excess treaty should not be so high that the experience could be distorted.

The reinsurance premium for a working excess of loss property treaty can be computed at a flat rate or on any one of various retrospective or prospective rating plans, which are based on minimum, provisional and maximum rates. The fundamental factor which determines the reinsurance premium is the experience on the business reinsured.

*   *   *   *   *   *

About the Author of Chapter 7

Stanford Miller was born in Kansas City, Missouri, on November 15, 1913. He attended the University of Arizona and received his B.A. Degree in economics from the University of Kansas in 1934. Four years later he received the Juris Doctor Degree from the University of Chicago.

Upon graduation from law school in 1938, he began his insurance career with his current employer, Employers Reinsurance Corporation. Since that time, he served in varying levels of responsibility with the company and has been active in its underwriting operations for over thirty-eight years. In 1962 he became a director of the company and has served since 1968 as its president and chief executive officer.

His contributions to the insurance community have been many, ranging from speaking and writing to serving in positions of leadership for insurance organizations. With Robert D. Brown, Mr. Miller was co-author of Health Insurance Underwriting, published in 1962 by the Eastern Underwriter and re-printed in 1968. He has written many articles for insurance and business publications on reinsurance and underwriting. Currently, he is a director for the University of Kansas City and a trustee for the American Institute for Property and Liability Underwriters and the Insurance Institute of America. He has also served as secretary and director of the Health Insurance Association of America and as chairman of the Reinsurance Association of America.

8

The Property Catastrophe Reinsurance Contract

by Robert S. Gilliam, Jr.*

Previous chapters have indicated that the pro rata treaty and the working excess-of-loss contract are directed primarily at protecting the individual risk. The catastrophe contract (treaty), on the other hand, is designed primarily to reinsure the insurer against an accumulation of losses, which generally are a result of a single large occurrence, such as a hurricane, tornado, flood, or earthquake. Catastrophe reinsurance is usually accomplished through the arrangement of a series of layers of coverage to provide indemnity for losses exceeding a predetermined figure (retention), subject to a predetermined maximum limit, and judged to be sufficient to protect the surplus of the insurer (which, of course, is also the reinsured in reinsurance parlance). Therefore, it is recommended that the reader not study this chapter to learn the role of the catastrophe contract in property reinsurance without having read the preceding chapters, particularly those covering the pro rata treaty and the working excess-of-loss contract, Chapters 6 and 7. Without such background it will be difficult to appreciate the final line of defense that the catastrophe treaty provides in the reinsurance program of an insurance company.

---

*Chairman, Excess and Treaty Management Corporation (underwriting manager of Excess and Casualty Reinsurance Association), 127 John Street, New York, New York 10038. While much of the initial planning on this chapter was done by Mr. Gilliam prior to his retirement, most of the technical work was completed by President Richard A. Hopkins, with the help of Executive Vice President R. M. Huggins and Vice President J. G. Lunz. To those three the author extends his sincere thanks for their contributions, their insights, and their cooperation in completing the chapter.

Purposes of Catastrophe Reinsurance

In the case of the smaller company or perhaps a company in a marginal financial condition without a geographically-balanced spread of business, there are two basic reasons for catastrophe reinsurance: to protect its policyholder surplus (henceforth referred to as "surplus") and to lessen large fluctuations in year-to-year operating results. With respect to the larger stock company in sound financial condition with a good spread of business, catastrophe reinsurance is purchased to level results, thereby protecting earnings per share and avoiding large fluctuations in loss ratio which would have an adverse effect on the market price of the company's stock.

The surplus of a company may be likened to a person's integrity — certainly something to be protected! Surplus is the true net worth of a company after taking into account all of its known and anticipated liabilities. It is an important gauge by which a company's strength is measured and by which one company is compared to another. Surplus also limits the amount of business a prudent company management will place on its books. If an insurer is to maintain its financial integrity and continue to meet the challenges of an ever-expanding economy, its surplus must grow at a comparable rate. Any serious disruption of growth in surplus may seriously hamper a company's ability to meet its production goals. The disruption may even force the company to reduce its market share of business which required years to obtain.

While a company's surplus may erode gradually for many reasons (such as from uncontrolled expenses, from faulty underwriting, or from an unusual frequency of small to medium-sized losses, or from weak stock and bond markets), the property catastrophe event can occur quickly and cause surplus reduction at lightning speed. Prudent management will naturally do its best to reduce a company's exposure to all of the situations both gradual and sudden which could have an adverse effect upon surplus. The catastrophe excess cover (or treaty) is the answer as respects indemnification for catastrophic property losses. Accordingly, a basic property catastrophe program is designed to protect a company from devastating losses which would reduce surplus. In order for this protection to be purchased at a reasonable cost, the coverage normally attaches at a level where there should be little loss activity (frequency). In other words, this protection is not generally designed to handle the routine tornado losses which a company incurs each year, but to take care of the large ones which are expected to occur every five to twenty years or more.

Since a catastrophe excess cover will eliminate the peaks of property catastrophe losses by lowering the company's net loss, it will tend to level out results. For example, instead of a company sustaining a disastrous loss once every ten years and perhaps showing a handsome profit in each of the other nine years, most managements would prefer to pay a reasonable catastrophe premium each year, thereby reducing profits a little in those nine years but enabling their companies to break even in the one year when the disaster occurs. The following graph will illustrate this leveling effect of catastrophe protection. Note that Chart 1 shows a combined ratio of 101 % and 104 % for two catastrophe years (1980 and 1984), which could have become 96 % and 97 % with catastrophe excess of loss reinsurance in Chart 2, at the expense of a slightly higher combined ratio for all the years shown.

Comparison of Insurance Company Results
Catastrophe Excess of Loss Reinsurance Protection
(shown as combined ratios anticipated)

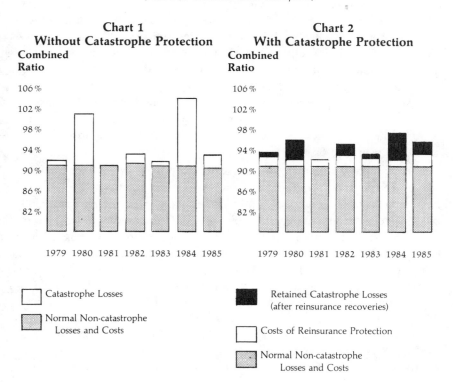

Some companies believe so much in the value of the leveling-device approach and place their retentions so low that their catastrophe programs sustain almost annual losses. Since those companies also purchase adequate coverage on the upper side (in addition to their low-level catastrophe cover), they still have reinsurance from the real disaster. The disadvantage of this program is its cost. Since such a program is designed to pay for the relatively modest as well as large catastrophes, reinsurance premiums are substantial. The only insurers which can afford this approach are those that have exceptionally good long-term records. There are not too many companies with such a record, so the very low-level catastrophe cover approach is not used extensively.

Designing the Catastrophe Program

OBJECTIVES

Having decided that catastrophe coverage is desirable, each company must then design a catastrophe program which will meet its needs. This is not an easy task, but company managements are able to obtain professional assistance and advice if they wish. Professional reinsurers who deal directly with primary companies can help design an effective program for their clients. Reinsurance intermediaries who are experienced in designing such programs and who have access to almost unlimited capacity with professional reinsurers throughout the world are also most willing to assist. Even some primary insurers have reinsurance assuming departments equipped to offer "programming" assistance. These services, by the way, are at no direct charge to the ceding company, although obviously their cost must eventually be included in overall reinsurance premiums.

A company's catastrophe coverage will be only one part of its overall reinsurance program, and each part must be meshed into a cohesive package to prevent any unintended gaps in coverage. For example, it is necessary to analyze the company's net losses over at least a ten-year period. It is important to reflect in such figures any significant changes in the company's underlying program (pro-rata and risk excess), plus the effect of using facultative reinsurance. Assume a loss history indicates a preponderance of relatively small losses which can be absorbed by the company, plus one large hurricane loss. This distribution of losses might well suggest a catastrophe program which would provide occurrence coverage over a relatively high retention. On the other hand, if the loss history shows no one disastrous loss but rather a frequency of relatively large losses which in total would seriously affect surplus, perhaps the catastrophe program should provide aggregate reinsurance protection. This type of coverage would aggregate these large losses and recovery would be based upon this aggregate total above a certain amount (retention) which the ceding company would retain. A third type of coverage, a loss-ratio excess-of-loss program, might also be appropriate for the company with the better loss history. Under this third approach it would not matter whether the losses were large or small, but merely that the gross loss ratio was high before the catastrophe cover would respond to lower the net loss ratio to a more acceptable figure.

One area which every company wants to control is its exposure to loss on an individual risk. Whereas pro rata and per risk treaties are basically intended to control per risk exposures, these treaties are often not sufficient. In many cases a company's per risk excess is designed to fully indemnify for the anticipated loss or "probable maximum loss" (PML) on an individual risk. A company may also want its catastrophe program to protect its failure to assess PMLs accurately, but this adds an additional cost factor. The cost may be eliminated, however, if the company wishes by agreeing to a "two-risk warranty." Under such a warranty, the catastrophe excess will not respond for an individual risk loss, since two or more risks must be involved in one loss occurrence for coverage to apply.

PROPER CATASTROPHE RETENTION

The purposes of catastrophe protection are to protect a company's surplus and level its operative results. These purposes must be kept in mind when decisions are made with respect to retention and limit. Also, the decision on proper retention and limit should be made by each company only after a careful analysis has been made of its own exposures and financial condition. For this reason it is not practical to present any formulae which all companies can apply to their own operations. There are certain basic considerations, however, which should be reviewed before retention and limit decisions are made.

How much catastrophe exposure should a company retain — in view of its reinsurance program otherwise, in view of its past catastrophe losses, and in view of any basic changes in its exposures? Factors to consider in establishing a company's retention before catastrophe reinsurance are as follows: the amount of loss the company can absorb; the risk protection, if appropriate; the underlying reinsurance program; the company's past loss history; and the company's exposure. Since catastrophe excesses are merely parts of an overall reinsurance program, a review of the underlying program is necessary. It must be recognized that if the company has basically an excess of loss underlying program, the net loss in a catastrophe may well be much higher than if the company has a substantial pro rata underlying program. The company will have to decide how much it is willing to lose on any one risk and whether any risk coverage will be desirable under the catastrophe program.

A review of the company's past catastrophe losses is essential. In doing this, one should begin with each gross loss and estimate what that loss would be today, if based upon today's values. The current underlying reinsurance program should then be taken into consideration to reduce the gross to net loss. A switch from mostly pro rata to mostly excess, or a large increase in net retention in the company's underlying program, may have a substantial increasing effect on its "as if" loss history. In reviewing past history, one must also keep in mind any basic change in the company's exposures. For example, has the company started a new line of business, e.g., mobile home business along the Gulf Coast, or taken on a large agency in Florida? Getting down to basics, the question really becomes: How much can the company afford to lose before the catastrophe excess responds? For a company with a small policyholder surplus, this decision may be fairly clear-cut. For the more secure company, however, it may be a question of preference, with the ultimate decision based primarily upon cost. What should be avoided is a situation where the retention is so low that there is too much "trading of dollars" between reinsured and reinsurer caused by a high frequency of losses.

CATASTROPHE REINSURANCE LIMIT

In deciding on its catastrophe retention, a company is more concerned with frequency of losses than severity. But in deciding on the catastrophe reinsurance limit it considers appropriate to its total portfolio of risks, the company is more concerned with severity of losses and the maximum, catastrophe loss it could bear financially.

Some of the considerations in deciding on the company's retention will also be appropriate in deciding how much upper limit of liability the company should purchase. Certainly a review of loss history and exposure is essential. As a starter, companies should review their largest historical claims and try to recast them in the light of today's values, taking into consideration not only inflation but changes in the basic reinsurance program, changes in the company's line guide, and increased or decreased activity in the area involved. If a company sustained a $1 million loss from a hurricane in Mississippi, where it wrote only 1% of its business, and its writings from the neighboring state of Louisiana represent 5% of its business—that should impact management's thinking, since the same size storm probably would have caused a $5 million loss in Louisiana! Basically, each company has to estimate its own exposure for each catastrophe peril. It may then choose to purchase catastrophe coverage in order to fully handle this estimated exposure, or else a percentage of same. Quotations are usually sought for varying limits in this general area, and the decision is then made based upon the company's evaluation of cost.

As catastrophe reinsurance costs are generally quite reasonable for the top layers, most companies which are not certain of the accuracy of their exposure evaluations will find it wise to secure more than seems necessary at the time. Even if catastrophe reinsurance limits appear excessive initially, they probably will be inadequate a few years later. This is another way of saying that a catastrophe program can never be put to bed for a long period, but rather must be constantly reviewed to make certain it is responsive to the needs of the ceding company. In fact, the trend today is to purchase much higher limits than heretofore. This trend applies to large as well as small companies and attests to the importance of the maintenance of strong reinsurance markets.

CATASTROPHE PROGRAMS FOR SELECTED COMPANIES

Since Chapter 12 is devoted in its entirety to arranging a reinsurance program, only a property catastrophe program for three hypothetical companies will be offered here. Unfortunately, there is no magic formula, so each company must evaluate its own exposures and determine its needs, taking into account cost and availability of coverage in the reinsurance marketplace.

Company A. Company A is a relatively young personal lines company operating only in the states of Nebraska and Kansas. It has a 33-1/3% quota share treaty (recently reduced from 50%) and a risk excess of $50,000/10,000. Its net premiums written on property lines are $2,500,000, and its policyholder surplus is $2,000,000.

The major catastrophe exposure to this company is from tornadoes. Since its writings are primarily personal lines and rural business, the conflagration hazard is deemed to be minimal. In analyzing its spread of business, it determines that in a severe tornado its maximum involvement would be 400 dwellings. Using an average loss per dwelling at $4,000, the company estimates that it could expect losses of $1,600,000. (Remember the company has a cap on any one risk loss of $10,000).

Because of the small surplus and the fact that the company is exposed to a number of tornado losses in any one year, it must select a low retention and decides on $50,000. To be on the safe side, it decides to purchase $2 million of coverage and concludes that it should not co-participate in this cover any more than its reinsurers will require. In the end the company might wind up with three layers of coverage as follows:

1st Excess -   95 % of $250,000/50,000

2nd Excess -   95 % of $750,000/300,000

3rd Excess - 100 % of $1,000,000/1,050,000

An occurrence loss which exhausted the limits of the 1st and 2nd excesses would cost the company a net loss of $100,000 ($50,000 retention plus $50,000 excess participation). Any further increase in the occurrence loss up to $2,000,000 would not increase the company's net involvement. The $100,000 net loss represents 5 % of surplus and about 3 % in loss ratio points, which the company concludes it can afford. The annual cost of this protection was roughly $125,000 for the 1st excess and $25,000 for the 2nd excess.

Company B. Company B has operated for many years in six states in the southeastern U.S. This company cedes $3 million annually to a surplus treaty and carries a working excess in the amount of $450,000/50,000. Coverage applies on a per-risk basis for the perils of windstorm, hail, and earthquake, and per occurrence for all other perils. This company has a policyholder surplus of $15,000,000 and net property writings of $20,000,000.

Writing its business in the Southeast, it is primarily concerned about hurricanes. While its business is spread throughout six states, it writes in Florida, Georgia, and South Carolina which can all be involved in one hurricane.

A review of its liabilities by county along the East and Gulf Coasts confirms that it is the storm that moves up the East Coast, starting in Florida, which poses the greatest threat. After reviewing past storm data and comparing notes with other companies in the area plus the advice of reinsurers and brokers, the company concludes that a loss of $6 million is conceivable. It decides on an $800,000 retention and a 10 % participation throughout. While the protection will be layered, the company decides to purchase coverage of 90 % of $5,000,000/800,000 which will cover virtually all of the potential exposure.

A $6 million loss would cost the company $1,500,000 as follows:

Retention	$800,000
10% Participation	500,000
Unreinsured	200,000
	$1,500,000

Such a net loss would represent 10% of surplus and almost 4% in loss ratio but this was tolerable. The premium for this coverage might be in the area of $450,000.

Company C. Company C is a company which operates in all states. It cedes $12 million to surplus treaty which reduces its gross volume down to $100,000,000. It carries no risk or working excess. This large company has an excellent distribution of business throughout the 48 continental United States. It codes all of its property business by construction and location (zip codes). With assistance from its computer, the company can determine its estimated hurricane losses, given the path of a "model" storm and its intensity. Using this technique it determined that a hurricane in the Houston, Texas, area could result in losses to the company of roughly $15,000,000. On the other hand, using a different computer model relating to earthquake exposure, the company determined that it had a larger exposure to earthquake in the Los Angeles area. Actually, using a model earthquake with an intensity of 7.5 on the Richter Scale indicated a shock loss of $14 million. Through some further analysis, and undoubtedly a large degree of guesswork, it was thought that with the inclusion of "fire following" the quake, total losses might be close to $20 million.

In view of its strong surplus ($50,000,000), the company selected a retention of $5,000,000. It then purchased coverage of 90% of $15,000,000/5,000,000. Since it has maintained similar coverage with the same reinsurers for many years, with no recoveries in the last ten years, it was able to secure a very reasonable quotation, namely $1¼ million.

CONTINUITY

Inasmuch as catastrophe reinsurance programs may be terminated upon expiration of term contracts, or for continuous contracts by either party giving proper cancellation notice at the end of the twelve months period, the reinsured has a frequent opportunity to change its current program to another reinsurer or groups of reinsurers. Such changes, however, may leave the current reinsurer in a bad loss position. For this reason reinsurers stress the value of long-term continuity between the two contracting parties. Both parties should try to agree upon an arrangement whereby a reasonable profit for each may be expected. Unless the catastrophe program is beneficial to each party, it will not serve their economic needs and will not be long-lasting. After a series of loss-free years, the reinsurer probably will be agreeable to make certain rate or premium concessions, thus sharing its good fortunes with its contracting partner and encouraging longevity in the relationship. Likewise, after a series of substantial losses, the reinsurer would expect additional premium to maintain a reasonable profit level, to continue a viable operation, and to be able to pay its losses when catastrophes occur. The reinsurer should play a role similar to that of a banker. Where this relationship exists, it is usually beneficial to both the reinsured and the reinsurer.

Catastrophe Perils

It is appropriate at this point to visualize the perils which could provoke a catastrophe, and to what extent losses could be prevented or controlled. Such perils would include fire, explosion, wind (whether in the form of windstorms, tornado, or hurricane), riot, flood, earthquake, and war. Fires most often result from man-made causes, against which loss prevention techniques normally reduce the likelihood of catastrophes. Conflagrations in modern cities are rare. On the other hand, forest fires are caused by lightning on occasion, which is beyond the control of man. When considered in economic terms, in other words, the cost of prevention and protection outweighs from an economic standpoint the consequences of potential catastrophes resulting from lightning-caused forest fires. The peril of explosion is normally within the control of man and can be either prevented or controlled by the use of proper techniques and equipment so that the likelihood of a catastrophe is minimized. However, experience has provided ample evidence of catastrophic loss potentials of explosions.

The peril of wind is probably the most dreaded by reinsurers, because of their vulnerability to its immunity from loss prevention and location, and its widespread destructiveness to concentrated property values. To provide protection against violent winds is often not economically feasible. For example, the wind velocity generated by tornadoes and hurricanes can range from 75 to over 200 miles per hour. Not all structures are suited to wind-resistant design either. Expensive industrial, commercial, and public buildings can be designed and constructed to withstand substantial winds, but it is not generally feasible for the homeowner to pay for building construction strong enough to endure a severe hurricane or a tornado; in fact, a tornado can destroy virtually the strongest of buildings. And location of the structure warrants no immunity either. While there are some geographical areas which are more susceptible to strong winds than others, experience has shown that disaster-producing winds can occur in almost every spot on the globe. Moreover, when they occur, windstorms usually cover an area large enough to include property values of substantial proportions. Wind is therefore a peril for which even the strongest insurers buy catastrophe reinsurance.

Hurricanes, which are usually formed in the Caribbean Sea and are occasionally formed off the western coast of Africa, frequently threaten the Gulf states from June through October. They are also a real threat to the East Coast of the U.S. Whereas hurricanes have been more frequent visitors to the Gulf Coast since 1965, storms which sweep up the East Coast and reach Long Island and New England are truly feared by reinsurance underwriters due to the enormous property values there.

The greatest incidence of tornadoes generally occurs along an alley from Texas to Michigan. The season for tornadoes begins in early Spring of each year and extends through late Fall. Unfortunately, these powerful funnels are also spawned by hurricanes, so that occasionally communities will be devastated by both a hurricane and a tornado in a one-two punch. Tornado winds do not affect as large an area as those generated by hurricanes, but they are much stronger and can level almost anything in their path.

The peril of riot, which for this discussion will include civil commotion, is one which should be controllable by man, if man had the will to do so. Unfortunately riots often result from social pressures which build up emotions exceeding the control of man. Normally it is not a severe peril, although in recent years riots have caused fires and explosions in many countries where public authorities simply were unable to cope with the rioting populace. It might be considered a peril which results from the breakdown of law and order, causing such chaos that the numbers of individual claims aggregate into catastrophic proportions. There is probably no practical way in today's political climate of preventing riots, unless progress is made in improving social conditions to remove the primary causes resulting in tempers reaching the stage of near-insanity. There is little the insurer and reinsurer can do to prevent riots, so it is a peril with which it is difficult to reckon.

The peril of flood has been minimized in many areas through irrigation and water control projects. However, cloud bursts, quick thawing of ice, sudden melting of snow, and forms of windstorms are often accompanied by heavy rains causing flooding more intense than flood control projects can handle. The peril of flood is insured under various forms of insurance, and therefore the reinsurer is susceptible to flood losses under catastrophe contracts. Insurers are normally aware of flood-prone areas and will control their premium volume accordingly so as not to have an out-of-balance flood exposure. Reinsurers, likewise, take means of assessing and limiting flood exposures.

The peril of earthquake is probably the most difficult of any to analyze and to underwrite properly when developing a catastrophe program. The frequency of sizable earthquakes is low. While earthquake faults are well known, there is insufficient statistical information upon which to base a sound analysis of the exposure. Man has learned how to build reasonably secure structures, from strong earthquakes, and the experience thus far justifies the additional costs involved in such "quake-proof" construction. Such buildings are now erected in known earthquake areas, but there exist many poorly constructed risks in those same areas. Nevertheless, it is not economically feasible to provide a large population with earthquake-proof homes, stores, shopping centers, and other commercial and industrial enterprises. Often residences are built on landfill in earthquake areas. Therefore, earthquake protection under catastrophe covers is important. Also, it is not only the earthquake shock exposure that is of concern. Fire and explosion exposures following earthquake shocks can cause a conflagration. With the use of natural gas and various liquefied gas and liquid petroleum products prevalent in large quantities today, it is difficult to assess the real exposure in any one earthquake area. Again, the ceding company covering risks in earthquake-prone areas must have catastrophe protection.

War is, in theory, a man-made and controllable peril. Because of this, insurers and reinsurers do not normally provide protection against war, such protection being afforded by federal governmental bodies. Nevertheless, during World War II there was at least one insurance company which underwrote U.S. property risks against the peril of war, presumably without reinsurance, and made many millions of dollars thereby. While the sanity of the underwriter was questioned, certainly its luck was not. It was the kind of gamble which responsible commercial insurance carriers feel ill-equipped to take on fixed property.

In summary, insurance becomes necessary for situations where perils cannot be controlled within safe limits and where financial indemnification is required for economic protection. Reinsurance then becomes necessary to lessen the catastrophe shock to the insurer. There are several perils which are largely outside the control of man and which present exposures so great that the individual insurance company will find it essential to have reinsurance for the catastrophic liabilities it assumes from the public.

Catastrophe Contracts

BASIC CONTRACTS

There are three general types of property catastrophe excess contracts (treaties): occurrence, aggregate, and loss-ratio or stop-loss covers. While the first two focus on events by size, the last deals with total losses of the ceding company. And the first two obviously protect against severity of losses, while the third is affected by the company's normal frequency of losses as well as the catastrophic loss. All three are widely used by reinsurers as the basic methods for protecting reinsureds against the shock losses of catastrophes. In addition, there are variations and combinations of these three types.

Occurrence. The first type, occurrence, is by far the most popular in the U.S. It is estimated that over 55% of the reinsurance placed by ceding companies is on that basis. Occurrence coverage is an excess of loss form of protection which applies to the ceding company's total ultimate net loss (UNL) from any one loss occurrence, as defined in the contract. Coverage under a typical contract might be described as "90% of $2,000,000 in excess of $500,000 per occurrence," which is often expressed as "90% up to $1,800,000/$500,000."[1] This means that for occurrence losses above the company's retention of $500,000, it would recover from its reinsurer 90% of its ultimate net loss (UNL) up to a maximum of $1,800,000. For example, if a company had an UNL from one occurrence of $3,000,000, the distribution of that loss would be as follows:

	Loss ($3,000,000)	Payments by Company	Reinsurer
First	$ 500,000	$ 500,000	—
Next	2,000,000	200,000	$1,800,000
Next	500,000	500,000	—
		$1,200,000	$1,800,000

Had the company purchased a second layer of protection for, say, 90% up to $1,800,000/$2,500,000, then the top $500,000 of the $3,000,000

---

[1] One reinsurer may assume 5% of 90% of $2,000,000/$500,000 or maximum of $90,000 which is different from 5% part of 90% $2,000,000/$500,000 or maximum of $100,000.

loss would have been reinsured. The distribution of the loss would have been:

		Payments by	
Loss ($3,000,000)		Company	Reinsurer
First $ 500,000		$ 500,000	—
Next 2,000,000		200,000	$1,800,000
Next 500,000		50,000	450,000
		$ 750,000	$2,250,000

As mentioned previously, the retention is normally set at a level above the frequency range, and yet low enough that the company is obtaining adequate protection of its surplus. Likewise, the amount of coverage to be purchased must be analyzed carefully and will be based upon the company's estimate of its exposure to loss. As might be expected, cost is often an important factor in how much limit will be purchased and how low the retention will be. Once losses are paid under the occurrence type of catastrophe coverage, the limits are usually reinstated automatically, subject to additional premiums.

Aggregate. Aggregate coverage may be described as the accumulating or collecting of certain loss amounts into a total mass, or aggregate, which then is subject to percentage and dollar limitations between reinsured and reinsurer. The coverage is provided in various arrangements and in practice is limited only by one's imagination. A widely used form is a contract providing that all loss amounts in the excess of $50,000 per loss be aggregated, and coverage would apply to 90% of said aggregate of excess losses up to $1,800,000 in excess of $500,000. Coverage applies on an annual basis, and during that period all losses over $50,000 from a peril covered by the agreement and arising out of various loss occurrences would be subject to application of the aggregate feature. When the phrase, "the excess of $50,000," is used in aggregate coverage, only that portion of each loss which is above $50,000 may be included in the aggregate. For example, if a company had several occurrence losses of $100,000, $275,000, $55,000, $425,000 and $1,000,000 during the annual period of an aggregate contract, the amounts to be aggregated are $50,000, $225,000, $5,000, $375,000 and $950,000 for a total of $1,605,000. This total would then be subject to the coverage of 90% up to $1,800,000/$500,000 in the same manner as the occurrence coverage applied. The reinsurer would therefore pay 90% of $1,105,000, or $994,500.

Compared with occurrence coverage, the aggregate coverage just described is much broader. Although $50,000 is deducted from each loss subject to the aggregate, the ability to accumulate even the "excess portion" of a number of losses (which are below the $500,000 retention of the occurrence cover, in comparison) is a distinct advantage to the ceding company. With such an advantage, one might ask why most catastrophe reinsurance is not purchased on an aggregate, instead of occurrence, basis. There are several good reasons. Cost would be the most important consideration, Also, generally the contract cannot be reinstated, and the limit is reduced by the amount of losses sustained by the reinsurer during the contract period. Should a company have a number of losses throughout the Spring and Summer, for example, and then get walloped by a hurricane in late August, it might exhaust its coverage with several months left before the expiration date of its contract. If this happened, only at a high cost would the company be able to purchase some emergency or temporary protection. The preferable alternative is to purchase sufficient coverage at contract inception, after it has been decided to use the aggregate-excess approach.

Loss Ratio. A very simple form of catastrophe coverage is the loss ratio excess. Such a contract might be described as covering for twenty percentage points of loss ratio in excess of seventy percentage points of loss ratio. This coverage also applies on an annual basis, and the ratios are applied to earned premiums (rather than written premiums) to eliminate distortions caused by incoming or outgoing premium portfolios. For a company with an earned premium of $5,000,000 and using the above ratios, the coverage would be $1,000,000/$3,500,000. It should be noted that all subject matter losses (i.e., losses on all properties covered by the contract reinsuring clause) of the company are applicable. Therefore, merely a frequency of small losses could easily trigger a reinsurance recovery, even without a true catastrophe incident. For example, if the company finished the year with a loss ratio of 73.5 % on the classes of business subject to this loss ratio protection, it would recover 3.5 % of its earned premiums, or $175,000. In conclusion, this form of coverage would be catastrophe protection only if expertly designed; otherwise, it would be more of a working excess.

The loss ratio excess might seem to be the most desirable form of protection in order to meet a company's objective. Is not the company trying to keep its loss ratio controlled, whether inundated with a frequency of small losses or a few catastrophes? The answer of course is, Yes, but again cost is a problem. Since all losses are in effect aggregated with no retention at all, this is the most expensive form of coverage. As with the aggregate cover, the limit of the loss ratio excess is not subject to reinstatement, which means that a large limit is a necessity for a company.

If a ceding company can afford the loss ratio excess, it can gain such stability in its operating results. Some years ago a reinsurer was offered a chance to participate on a loss ratio excess for a rather small company, which arrangement was an unusually good deal from the company's standpoint. The limit was adequate and the cover attached at a 60% loss ratio. The company's expense ratio was averaging about 31%, and the cost of the loss ratio coverage was about 4%, the company's expenses were therefore 35%. With the reinsurance, the company's losses could not exceed 60%; it had a 5% profit assured. Such an arrangement would have to be considered unusual, if not unique, for most loss ratio contracts are structured so that if reinsurers incur a loss, the ceding company must also.

Reinsurance and insurance underwriters and brokers are imaginative people who work under no governmental restrictions as to price and form of reinsurance contracts (treaties). Uniformity to some degree is desirable for ease and speed of placements and negotiations. The three types of property catastrophe reinsurance described already are widely used and suffice in most instances. However, at certain times and in special situations a catastrophe "banking plan" or an "advance deposit premium plan" may be appropriate.

A catastrophe banking plan provides for the ceding company to pay into the reinsurer "premiums" which are invested. Retention provisions are such as to minimize loss frequency. The ceding company may have the option of filing or not filing qualified claims. The reinsurer's overhead and expenses are thus very low, and the ceding company has an opportunity of recovering a substantial share of both total premiums paid and accumulated interest earned on the premiums. Such arrangements are more akin to banking than reinsurance, hence the term "banking plan."

An advance deposit premium plan uses the same general idea, except that an appreciable percentage of the advance deposit is returned to the ceding company if no loss occurs at contract termination or at each year end. Some question arises as to whether such a plan has enough risk assumption involved to qualify it as reinsurance.

CONTRACTUAL PROVISIONS

Percentage Coverage. In several examples above, the ceding company was a co-reinsurer. When the description of coverage is stated as

"90% of $2,000,000," it means that the ceding company has a 10% participation in the excess layer. The ceding company will share 10% of every excess loss up to the maximum, at which point the company would be responsible for $200,000 of any loss and the reinsurer would be liable for $1,800,000.

Most reinsurers believe strongly that keeping the reinsured involved in an excess loss will encourage conservative loss settlements. Occasionally co-participation is 5% rather than the more normal 10%. Sometimes 100% contracts (i.e., ceding companies do not assume any liability under the contract) are written by reinsurers, but often these tend to be expensive. Ceding companies are usually forced to pay a price for being excused from any participation in the reinsurance loss! Sometimes when examining a 100% contract, it is concluded that the ceding company has no stake after the retention is reached. Afterwards it is found the company has taken a participation in the reinsurance placement — which works out the same in the end. In other words, if a contract with a $2,000,000 limit is placed 100%, but the ceding company assumes 10% of the reinsurance placement, that is the same as having a 90% contract. In such situations reinsurers may ask that the contract contain a warranty stating that the ceding company will maintain its 10% position in addition to its retention.

Layered Coverages. If a company buys, for instance, $10 million of catastrophe coverage, sometimes the coverage will be placed in one layer (i.e., one retention and one limit), but more often it will be "layered" into two or more excesses. The basic reason for dividing a catastrophe program into layers is marketing. Some reinsurers want to commit their lines (or limits of liability) at a low level where the premium rates are high; some want to participate across-the-board; and some want to be in the upper layers, perhaps above the point where a foreseeable loss might occur. By layering a large program it can be marketed more successfully, since reinsurers will commit larger lines if they are offered what they want. There is another advantage of layering in lieu of one overall contract, which involves reinstatement provisions. If the catastrophe program is structured in one contract, the ceding company will pay smaller reinstatement premiums on partial losses.

Two-Risk Warranty. As was shown earlier, catastrophe covers may be used to protect a company's risk exposure when PML estimates prove to be inaccurate. Sometimes reinsurers do not wish to be exposed to single-risk losses and will then insist that a two-risk warranty be placed in the contract. A two-risk warranty requires that two or more risks must be involved in a loss occurrence for the catastrophe cover to be applicable. If there is no single-risk exposure under a catastrophe excess, the rate will naturally be less than if there is. Therefore, ceding companies will occasionally offer to accept this clause in order to get a lower rate, knowing that there is, in fact, no single risk exposure above the retention or that it is minimal and will be retained net.

Reinstatements. A catastrophe contract has a stated limit per occurrence (generally) and a stated rate or premium. The agreed-upon premium is for the limit stated in the contract; once that limit is exhausted, it must be reinstated for additional premium or else there is no further coverage. For the protection of the ceding company, a reinstatement clause is almost always inserted in catastrophe covers to provide for automatic reinstatement of the full limit in event the cover has been depleted. (For the formula to calculate the reinstatement premium see Chapter 4). As mentioned previously, occurrence forms of catastrophe coverage almost always are subject to reinstatement, whereas loss ratio and aggregate excesses seldom are. The reinsured naturally will desire at least one full reinstatement of a total loss under the catastrophe treaty, and without additional premium. The reinsurer, on the other hand, will prefer no reinstatements, except at pro rata premium based on time and amount. Normally, one full reinstatement at pro rata additional premium is agreed upon. In any event, the contract should provide for reinstatement if the program is to be maintained intact and provide the coverage the reinsured needs for proper protection of its assets after only one occurrence loss.

Exclusions. Three types of risks are normally excluded in property catastrophe reinsurance: nuclear incident risks, financial guarantees, and insurance pools. Nuclear incident risks are usually excluded because they are insured through special pools or syndicates comprised of most of the worldwide capacity available for such risks. This arrangement eliminates duplication of liability assumptions by reinsurers. Financial guarantees are considered business risks and are not ordinarily suitable for insurance nor reinsurance. Therefore, such exposures are usually excluded. Insurance and reinsurance pools, syndicates, and associations ordinarily have their own reinsurance programs. Thus, to avoid duplication of liability assumptions, members of such organizations cannot usually obtain coverage under their individual reinsurance programs for liabilities assumed as pool members. Lastly, the following classes of business are not subject to commercial reinsurance: war risks on fixed property, target risks, and insolvency funds. In time of war, the U.S. government provides war risk coverage on fixed property in the U.S. Target risks are bridges, tunnels, and other high-valued risks so designated by Lloyd's to avoid duplication of liability. Insolvency funds really provide financial guarantees protection under governmental supervision.

Application of Coverage. The property catastrophe contract provides coverage against a company's "ultimate net loss" from a particular loss occurrence. The ultimate net loss to the contract is calculated by starting with the gross loss, then deducting recoveries to the company from all reinsurances which inure to the benefit of reinsurers of the cover in question. For example, all facultative and pro rata treaty reinsurance would fall into the category of reinsurance inuring to the benefit of reinsurers on a first catastrophe excess. Other underlying excess of loss treaty reinsurance would also inure to reinsurers' benefit unless special permission had been secured to exempt such reinsurance. This permission is occasionally granted. As may be apparent, recoveries under a first catastrophe excess do not inure to the benefit of reinsurers on the higher layers. The ultimate net loss clause of all catastrophe excesses above the first excess will provide for the exemption of recoveries under the first excess from the UNL calculation.

In presenting previous examples of coverage, definite amounts have been used for limits and retentions (e.g., $2,000,000/$500,000). However, due to the effects of inflation it is becoming more popular, certainly with reinsurers, to have an adjustable retention and sometimes an adjustable limit as well. The retention (and limit) may be based upon a percentage of gross net earned premium income (GNEPI) for the year in question. Therefore, the retention (and limit) increase as the premium base increases, and automatically places the ceding company and reinsurer in a relative position as they were in the previous year. Ceding companies will often argue against this scheme, because of their not knowing exactly and at all times what retentions and limits apply, as the GNEPI will not be known exactly until after year end.

Definition of Loss Occurrence. The significance of catastrophe perils lies in their definitions, as revealed by the implementation of catastrophe coverage. In other words, what is a windstorm, an earthquake, a riot? Normally, the typical contract will stipulate that ". . . the term 'loss occurrence' shall mean all losses arising out of or caused by one event except as otherwise stipulated." Separate definitions are usual for windstorm, earthquake and riot, and occasionally the flood definition is separate also. The salient features of the numerous varying definitions are as follows:

A. Windstorm — includes all losses occurring during a 72-hour period and arising out of "one atmospheric disturbance." (Note: "one atmospheric disturbance" is frequently used in reinsurance contracts for lack of a better term. It has been the subject of many discussions, as the term defies precise definition.)

B. Earthquake — includes all losses occurring during a 72-hour period.

C. Riot — includes all losses occurring during a 72-hour period within a city, town, village or place and the areas adjacent thereto.

D. Flood — varies in language, but generally it is a straight, one-event definition; or a 72-hour, one-river basin definition.

The purpose of these specific definitions, such as they are, is to avoid unrelated losses being included in the one loss occurrence. As respect earthquake losses, the opposite intent prevails, so that after-shock losses will be reinsured and to avoid arguments over whether an earthquake in Los Angeles on April 1 is either the same or a separate loss occurrence (event) from an earthquake in San Francisco on April 2. Reinsurers will allow companies to claim for all earthquake losses occurring during any 72-hour period even if some should occur in Los Angeles and others in St. Louis.

Claims and Claims Expenses

Catastrophe reinsurance programs can cover many thousands of individual risks which may be involved in a single catastrophe. The amount of money involved is large, and it is therefore essential that the reinsured have proper claims handling staff and techniques (or contracts with those organizations which provide such services) in order to make speedy and economical settlements. The reinsurer's property claims department will work closely with the reinsured's claims personnel to assist in developing proof of loss information and advising in other areas to effect speedy settlements after the catastrophe.

Rating

CONSIDERATIONS

Each reinsurance underwriter has its own way of analyzing the rating of a catastrophe program. However, the basic factors which perhaps all experienced underwriters consider for individual reinsureds are the following: 1) exposure, 2) market conditions, 3) backlog of profits or accumulated deficits, 4) management reputation and financial position of the ceding company, and 5) the reinsurer's contractual experience with the ceding company.

Exposure. Before a reinsurance catastrophe program is designed, it is necessary to make an analysis of the exposure held by the insurance company to perils which create catastrophes. For the company which has been in business for ten years or more, developing exposure information should not be difficult. Such information would include for each year of a ten-year period and for each class of property insurance business the company's written premiums, earned premiums, expenses paid, and claims and claim expenses, together with statutory underwriting profits and losses, and combined loss and expense ratios. Premiums and claims statistics should be developed by state in order to determine the number and extent of concentrations of risks which could become involved in losses of catastrophic amounts. The catastrophe reinsurance underwriter should have no hesitancy to ask for such information, inasmuch as it was undoubtedly used by the insurance company in designing its basic reinsurance programs which are to be supplemented by catastrophe protection. Additionally, the reinsurer will have at its disposal industrywide statistical information published at least annually in several technical publications. Such published information will enable the underwriter to compare the exposures of a particular company with those of the average company writing similar classes of insurance in the same geographical areas, and thus determine where a particular company is more exposed or less exposed than the average company.

Market Conditions. Reinsurers are providing liability-assuming capacity and their rates must reflect this fact. When reinsurers' operating losses cause a shrinkage of capacity, reinsurance rates go up; and the opposite occurs when reinsurers' operating profits produce an excess of capacity: reinsurance rates decline. It is the balancing effect of supply and demand. If a reinsurer is offered a $75,000 premium from a new client for $1,000,000 of capacity, and the reinsurer receives only $50,000 from existing clients, one can understand the reinsurer's reluctance upon renewal to sell its capacity to existing clients for a $50,000 price. In practice, probably the capacity would be offered to existing clients in the range of $65,000. This type of increase for existing clients does occur even when those clients have had a loss-free track record, as the increase is caused solely by competitive market conditions. Needless to say, if the reinsurer has the capacity available, he will also accept the new client's offer and write the business for the $75,000 premium. This discussion assumes, of course, that the exposures and other conditions are comparable.

Accumulated Profit or Deficit Backlog. If a catastrophe contract has been in effect for several years without a loss, the ceding company has built up a "backlog" of profits with the reinsurer. This "bank" would not be the entire premiums paid in over the years but perhaps 50 % of same, after allowance for the reinsurer's expenses and profits. This backlog is not something that can be drawn down by the ceding company upon cancellation of the contract, but rather is a more nebulous item which both parties understand will affect future rating. On the other hand, when a reinsurer is in a deficit position, the rate has to be adjusted upward to bring the reinsurer back to a profit position. Otherwise, the reinsurer may not be financially healthy enough to pay for the next catastrophe. In practice this means that the client is charged a reinsuring rate for the cover, plus an additional loading (a "payback") to amortize the deficit over a reasonable period of years. Further, to an underwriter five years of loss-free experience means one thing under a first catastrophe excess, when the bank might amount to 80 % of the limit, and quite another under a sixth catastrophe excess when the bank might only amount to 5 % of the limit. In the latter situation, it would be doubtful if any credit would be given for the bank.

Reputation of Ceding Company. Some ceding companies have reputations either for leaving reinsurers in a deficit position or for constantly shopping their programs each year to strive for the lowest possible rates. Similarly, there are ceding companies which are known to try to make a profit at the expense of their reinsurers. On the other side of the coin, many companies have the reputation of never leaving their reinsurers in a loss position. Over a period of time a reinsurer learns from which ceding companies it has a good chance of reasonable profit, and from which it has little chance of breaking even. This information will affect rating practices as well as decisions on such matters as amount of capacity to be provided and underwriting restrictions.

RATING APPROACHES

Percentages or Flat Amounts. Most catastrophe rates are quoted as percentages (e.g., 2 %), which are to be applied to the ceding company's subject gross net written or earned premium income. Occasionally a flat premium (e.g., $100,000) is the fixed premium and there is no further adjustment. When a percentage rate is agreed upon, a minimum premium equal to 75-80 % of reinsurer's estimated annual earned premium under the contract is normally paid quarterly in advance. Following expiration the actual premium is computed once the company's premium income figures are known. The additional premium, if any, is then payable to the reinsurer.

Having analyzed the various considerations discussed above, the underwriter calls upon prior experience to decide whether the "payback" period needed should be, say, ten years (e.g., $100,000 liability limit and $10,000 premium), or whether a higher annual premium resulting in a more rapid payback is called for. The term "payback" merely describes the relationship between the limit and the premium. If an underwriter quotes a rate producing a 5-year payback (premium), he is in effect estimating that there will be a total loss in 3-1/2 to 4 years, with the additional premium representing his profit. Paybacks range from three years to as much as one hundred years, although in the upper range many reinsurers value their capacity more than the premium involved and will not participate in high levels of coverage where such extensive periods are involved. In the U.S., most underwriters use the term "payback," while overseas the term "rate on line" is more frequently used. In the above example the rate on line would be 20% ($20,000 ÷ $100,000), which is the same as a five-year payback.

Lines Individually Rated. Technically-oriented underwriters will individually rate the lines of business subject to the contract. Assume the estimated gross net written premium income (GNWPI) under a property catastrophe contract is as follows:

		Windstorm Premium*	
		%	Amount
Fire	$100,000	—	—
Estimated Extended Coverage	50,000	80%	$ 40,000
Earthquake	10,000	—	—
Inland Marine	20,000	10%	2,000
Commerical Multi-Peril (65%)**	150,000	15%	22,500
Homeowners (90%)**	270,000	25/90%	75,000
	$600,000		$139,500

*Percentages that reinsurers often use to arrive at windstorm premiums come.

**If casualty (third party liability) lines are excluded, normally a factor such as 90% will be used as the declarable premium income (i.e., 10% will be deemed to represent casualty).

The reinsurance underwriter would then reveal the major exposures to the contract as follows:

	GNWPI
Earthquake	$ 10,000
Windstorm	139,500
All Other (mostly fire)	450,500
	$600,000

With a catastrophe excess of $100,000/$50,000, the underwriter might rate the perils and the contract as follows:

Perils	GNWPI		Rates		Premium
Earthquake	$ 10,000	@	15%	=	$ 1,500
Windstorm	139,500	@	8%	=	11,160
Other	450,500	@	1%	=	4,505
	$600,000				17,165

With an indicated premium of approximately $17,000, one would convert that to a rate, namely 2.83% ($17,000 ÷ $600,000). A rate of 2.80% or 2.85% would probably be quoted.

The advantage of this approach is the ease of analyzing changes in exposure and of adjusting the rate accordingly. For example, assume the 2.85% rate was acceptable. When the first renewal came up for discussion, it was suggested by the client or its broker that the contract be renewed on the same terms and conditions. At first blush, this may seem reasonable if the GNWPI is also estimated at $600,000. However, after reviewing the makeup of this $600,000, the underwriter might come to a different conclusion as the following figures would suggest:

Perils	GNWPI		Rates		Premium
Earthquake	$ 15,000	@	15%	=	$ 2,250
Windstorm	185,000	@	8%	=	14,800
Other	400,000	@	1%	=	4,000
	$600,000				21,050

As one can see, rating the renewal on the same rate basis as the original cover produces a much higher rate, namely 3.5% ($21,050 ÷ $600,000), because of differences in peril proportions. Without analyzing the exposures in this manner, the underwriter might have very easily missed the increase exposure.

Special Techniques. Most underwriters are offered large selections of flat-rated occurrence coverages. They examine loss-ratio offerings much less frequently. There is a suggested way to convert a loss ratio into an occurrence cover for rating only. Assume the loss ratio excess covers for $1,000,000 over a 75% loss ratio. Also assume a gross net earned premium income (GNEPI) of $5,000,000. The loss ratios over the past ten years, with and without catastrophe losses, are as follows:

	Actual Loss Ratios	Loss Ratios Excluding Catastrophe Losses
1965	89%	69%
1966	60	60
1967	62	62
1968	58	58
1969	70	70
1970	63	63
1971	59	59
1972	75	65
1973	68	68
1974	95	72

In addition to the above ratios, annual earned premiums for each of the ten years are required so that a "mean" loss ratio may be calculated. Multiplying each annual earned premium by its corresponding loss ratio will provide annual losses which can be totaled and divided by the ten-year total earned premium (assume 68%). Since the cover attaches at a 75% loss ratio, the difference between the two ratios is seven percentage points. Under this suggested technique, it would be proper to consider the retention for rating purposes as being $350,000 (7% of $5,00,000). The underwriter would then attempt to rate an "occurrence" cover of $1,000,000 in excess of $350,000 in the normal manner. Variations of this approach may be used for some other types of more unusual catastrophe coverages.

Formula Rates. Catastrophe excesses have fixed rates perhaps 99% of the time. They are not thought to be conducive to formula rating for two main reasons: lack of loss frequency and lack of a profit backlog. By the nature of the coverage, the contract is not subject to a frequency of losses. That being the case, it is easy to understand why it is not practical to employ a rating formula based upon losses when there are not sufficient losses needed to develop a loss experience. Also, generally a formula approach does not allow the reinsurer a chance to build up enough of a backlog of profits to pay the big loss when it occurs.

In spite of the foregoing, formula-rated catastrophe coverages are used on occasion. Sometimes formulas are devised which merely take into consideration a reinsurer's profits and in a sense force rate reductions in recognition of those profits. A variation of this occurs when "commissions" are allowed as an alternative to a rate reduction. These two practices are sometimes referred to as no-claim bonuses, since the commission (perhaps 20% of the reinsurance premium) is only applicable if there is no loss to the contract for the year in question. Since all of these formula arrangements when taken together appear in such a small percentage of catastrophe excesses, no further examination of various formulas is warranted.

Summary

The property catastrophe reinsurance contract protects an insurance company's policyholder surplus and lessens the exposure of operating results to large fluctuations caused by losses from catastrophic perils. The contract should be carefully designed to be an integral part of an insurance company's comprehensive reinsurance program. The cost of the reinsurance coverage afforded by the contract will depend upon the amount of reinsurance provided, perils reinsured against, the individual company's exposures to the perils, prior catastrophe loss experience of the company, and competitive conditions in the reinsurance market.

The occurrence form of excess-of-loss contract is used extensively and provides indemnification for all loss suffered by the insurance company due to one event (occurrence) over an agreed-upon amount (retention), but not exceeding another agreed-upon amount (limit of liability or limit). The catastrophe potential of hurricanes, tornadoes, earthquakes, floods, fires, and riots is omnipresent to the worldwide insurance industry and is usually reinsured in the commercial reinsurance market.

The well managed insurance company will carefully select its reinsurers to assure continuity of the reinsurance relationship. The reinsurer's primary function is similar to that of a banker in providing a facility for building up funds during catastrophe-free years which may be called upon in catastrophe-loss years. The insurer and reinsurer should strive toward aiding each other's financial strength, so each may play its proper role in society.

A well tailored property catastrophe program will be a suit of armor around an insurer's policyholder surplus.

*   *   *   *   *   *

About the Author of Chapter 8

Robert Skelton Gilliam, Jr., was born on April 16, 1913, in Petersburg, Virginia. He was educated at the Virginia Military Institute, receiving a B.S.

Degree in electrical engineering in 1934. Because of his military background, he entered the Army early in World War II as a first Lieutenant in 1940. He served in Washington, D.C., and in the military government of Korea, being discharged from active duty in 1946 as a lieutenant colonel.

His insurance career began in 1937 with three years of service as an engineer in Virginia with the Southeastern Underwriters Association. In 1940, just before entering military service, he joined Marsh & McLennan in New York, also as an engineer. After the War in 1946, he returned to Marsh & McLennan until 1963, at which time he was a vice president. In that year he became a vice president of Excess & Treaty Management Corporation in New York, becoming its president five years later in 1968. In 1979 he retired as its chairman, but he continues to serve as chairman of Excess & Treaty Holding Corporation and its subsidiary, Excess & Treaty Reinsurance Corporation.

9

The Excess of Loss Treaty in Casualty Insurance

by LeRoy J. Simon*

Reinsuring the casualty lines of business presents both the buyer and the seller with one of the most difficult and challenging problems in the reinsurance business. Primary insurers are quite familiar with the difficulties they have in estimating casualty loss reserves. Many difficult evaluation problems exist when a report of a claim has been received by the company, but in addition many problems are encountered in attempting to establish a reserve for losses which are incurred but not reported (IBNR). A primary insurance company has an easier task of evaluating reserves, because many of the losses it experiences are small and thus simpler to estimate. There is also a relatively high frequency so that there will be a tendency to "hit the averages." A primary company has also availed itself of reinsurance which stops the loss from affecting its figures beyond its retention.

The portion of the business that the primary company reinsures in its excess of loss casualty treaty has a number of fundamental evaluation problems. The frequency of losses is relatively low. The loss severity is high and the layers of loss limit are sufficiently large, so that they often do not serve as an effective limitation. Perhaps the most difficult single problem for reinsurance of casualty lines is to evaluate the treaty at any particular time with respect to its eventual loss development. Since this problem is difficult for the reinsurer, it is similarly difficult for both the

* FCAS, Senior Vice President, Prudential Reinsurance Company, 213 Washington Street, Newark, New Jersey 07101. While the author was the principal draftsman of this chapter, the work includes the combined contributions and efforts of the following Prudential Reinsurance Company personnel: Paul B. Ingrey, Joseph E. Carney, David W. Forrest, Howard N. Nelson, James N. Stanard, and George E. Stoffel. To these individuals the author extends grateful acknowledgement and sincere thanks for their assistance.

primary company (and its broker, if one is involved) and the reinsurer to agree upon an evaluation involving such a high content of unsettled losses and IBNR.

For these and a number of other reasons to be developed in this chapter, casualty lines were the principal contributor to the poor operating experience suffered by professional reinsurers during the mid-1970's. Looking forward, these lines continue to promise the most challenging problems for years to come. When examples in this chapter illustrate a point, the reader should remember that reinsurance is a highly individualistic endeavor and, therefore, is not susceptible to a "cook book" approach with an identical recipe for all. Hence, examples are meant to be unique illustrations and should not be applied in other situations.

Principal Types

A broad range of types of casualty reinsurance is available to a primary company. The principal types, which will be treated in detail, are: a) facultative, including automatic facultative—obligatory or optional, b) quota share, c) working covers, including aggregate working excess, and d) clash, catastrophe excess of loss, or contingency covers, including intermediate excess. The first type involves reinsurance of individual risks, and the other three types are implemented by means of treaties.

FACULTATIVE

Visualize a primary company which has established a normal operating pattern and has certain treaty reinsurance protection. It may be necessary for that company to write a policy which has an unusually large limit of liability in order to properly service its client or its agent. Since such a risk does not conveniently fit within the company's normal operating pattern, it will seek facultative reinsurance to eliminate this extreme peak and bring the net risk position of the company down to a size that fits within its normal operating pattern (see Chapter 5). In contrast to having, say, each of five companies issue separate policies for a fifth of the risk, a single primary company will issue the policy and facultatively reinsure it. In addition to being of service to its client and agent, the primary company gets the advantage of retaining the full portion of the expense element in the premium for the entire risk to help offset its overhead. If, instead, the risk were divided among five primary companies, each of them would receive a smaller dollar amount for expenses but would still have many of the fixed costs which they would have to cover.

The primary company may elect to reinsure on a net excess facultative basis (where its overhead and original agent commission expenses are not reimbursed directly as regards a particular policy) or on a gross excess basis (in which it receives a ceding commission to cover its overhead and agent commission expenses). To illustrate these two bases, consider the following example.

	USE OF GROSS EXCESS FACULTATIVE BASIS	USE OF NET EXCESS FACULTATIVE BASIS
a. Original premium	$10,000	$10,000
b. Original commission and overhead	2,500 (25%)	2,500 (25%)
c. Net dollars available for loss	7,500	7,500
d. Facultative premium for the excess reinsurance	2,000	1,500
e. Less facultative commission	500 (25%)	0
f. Net available for loss (c – d + e)	6,000	6,000
g. Net expense ratio (b – e)/(a – d)	25.0%	29.4%

All other things being equal, the primary company using the net excess facultative basis for cessions will have a lower loss ratio and a higher expense ratio but in the final analysis will have the same number of dollars available for paying losses.

A primary company may coordinate its facultative reinsurance in such a way that it protects the primary company's exposure ceded to its treaty reinsurers. It may do this for a number of reasons. For example, the class of business, although covered by the treaty, may be more hazardous than usual and, therefore, the company wishes to protect the exposure to the treaty. Or facultative reinsurance may be required by the treaty reinsurer, either because of the class of business being written or because a catastrophe cover treaty warrants that limits will not exceed a certain amount. Then, too, it may be financially advantageous to the ceding company, because a facultative cession on a proportional basis will receive a ceding commission while an excess treaty normally would not provide a specific commission allowance. A class or kind of insurance may be specifically excluded by treaty terms, but for the primary company which wishes to write such a piece of business while retaining a prudent amount, facultative reinsurance is the answer. Finally, by placing a risk facultatively, the primary underwriter may be able to establish the price and coverages for the total risk based partially on the facultative reinsurer's expertise rather than relying solely on its own.

Occasionally a treaty reinsurer may be asked, as a "special acceptance," to allow a risk which is otherwise not covered to be included in the treaty. This request is made on an individual basis, and all reinsurers involved in the treaty must agree to its acceptability. The treaty underwriter must analyze the individual risk or consult with its facultative underwriter counterpart to determine its acceptability. Since the rate for the treaty does not contemplate such an extrahazardous risk or higher limit of coverage, a specific additional premium would be charged for the special acceptance. Special acceptances ordinarily have entirely different risk potential characteristics (when compared to the treaty itself) relative to the reinsurance premium charged (being much closer to facultative placements) and should not be subject to profit commissions, retrospective rating or swing plan provisions; but specific negotiations will often alter this rule depending on the circumstances.

If a company develops a rather frequent need for facultative reinsurance in a particular line or class of business, it may be possible to procure a somewhat automatic facultative arrangement whereby the terms and conditions are fairly well fixed in advance. The facultative reinsurance underwriter may still review each case with considerable care and reject some from time to time. When such an arrangement becomes more automatic and trends toward an obligatory arrangement in which the reinsurer does not reject individual risks at all, one approaches a treaty situation.

QUOTA SHARE

There is a general dearth of proportional treaties in casualty lines for several reasons. Quota share casualty treaties are not too common an approach, because it is difficult for the reinsurer and the company a) to strike and maintain a balance between pricing and underwriting, b) to agree upon the degree of risk to be assumed by each, and c) to arrive at a common understanding of the treaty's evaluation at any particular time. For example, if a primary company has a hefty quota share arrangement on casualty business, the inherent problems in the slow development of the true loss experience might lead the company to become over-optimistic or careless. Quota share arrangements are used in special situations involving new lines of business, special risk situations or ventures into new classes for a smaller company. In this way the primary company can rely on the professional reinsurer's expertise, or it may simply have a partner in a risky venture who is willing to rely on the specialized talents of the primary company to make a reasonable return for both of them.

Casualty reinsurance coverages do not use the surplus share concept which is used so often in property lines (see Chapter 6). Theoretically, it would be possible to do so, but it is indigenous to the property business to be rated per $100 of insurance, and that rate is the same for every dollar of insurance. It is fundamental to the liability business, however, that there is one rate for a certain basic level of coverage (basic limits) and another set of rates for excess coverage (in the form of an increased limits table). This latter set of rates charge less per dollar of coverage for each higher amount. Hence, in property reinsurance it is difficult to cite an existing authority for the cost of excess layers, while in liability it is easier to do so by reference to the published excess limits tables.[1] And so the property reinsurer and reinsured find that they can more easily agree upon equitable rates by using surplus share reinsurance. The company seeking liability reinsurance has not been forced to this expedient and has chosen to keep the maximum retention feasible for it under a basic/excess arrangement. Reinsurers are also satisfied with such an arrangement, because it keeps the primary company exposed to the first-loss impact, thus encouraged to better control its underwriting and claims.

Working Excess of Loss

Working level reinsurance treaties—working covers—are broadly descriptive of treaties covering categories of business in which the reinsured writes policies which generally expose the treaty reinsurer to loss. In other words, there is a real expectation of a certain number of losses affecting the treaty each year. Such covers normally have a relatively low attachment point and a relatively small limit of liability for the reinsurer. There is also sufficient volume of business that the normal expected frequency of losses will result in a number of claims against the treaty every year. For instance, a working excess for a large company operating throughout the country might be designed to apply to a single retention level (for example, $250,000) to all losses over a broad spectrum of lines of business (say, automobile liability, general liability, and workers' compensation). By way of contrast, a smaller company might have variations in its net retentions by line of business and by class. Such varied retentions could easily reflect the company's confidence gained from its own underwriting: large retentions are selected in those areas where the company feels its staff is well developed and experienced, while low retentions (as small as $25,000) are used in newer areas until experience is developed.

---

[1] "First loss" tables used in property excess insurance and reinsurance have not been generally accepted, probably because they are not based on a broad enough sampling of statistics.

A basic characteristic of a working excess treaty is that it spreads the loss of the primary company over time and allows profits in the good years to offset losses in the bad years. Working excess covers should provide the reinsurer with a profit over a reasonable period of time. The buyer should give thoughtful consideration to whether it really wants a working excess cover under such an assumption and should make its intentions clear when negotiating with the prospective reinsurer. If the intent is to provide the reinsurer with a profit over a reasonable period of time, then both parties should feel an obligation to ride with the treaty through the ups and downs likely to occur. If the intent is that the treaty be one of pure risk, then either party should be free to leave the agreement at any time. The underwriting and pricing of the cover differs greatly depending upon the intentions of the two parties and whether those intentions are clearly stated at the start.

Working excess covers again focus attention on the most difficult problem in reinsuring casualty lines of business; namely, there are often differences of opinion between the two parties with respect to the profitability of a given treaty. The primary company tends to feel that all losses which might impact the treaty have been reported to the reinsurer and are adequately reserved by the primary company itself. On the other hand, the reinsurer often feels first, that there is a large element of unreported losses and, second, that reported losses are more adequately reserved on the basis of the reinsurer's judgment, which often results in significantly higher reserves than those estimated by the primary company. Attempts to reach a meeting of the minds on these matters of reporting and reserving often test the relationship between the two parties. When a treaty arrangement is terminated, it is often because each party feels that the other is unreasonable in its expectations of the current profitability status of the treaty. In addition to that, of course, there may very well be differences of opinion about the future potential profitability as well.

The company and reinsurer should also arrive at an understanding by which the primary company retention will move upward to keep pace with inflation and help avoid the inexorable increase in excess exposure and the prohibitively expensive reinsurance costs that would otherwise follow. One way to adjust the retention for inflation is through normal renewal negotiations that move the retention upward, thereby keeping the excess exposure relatively constant. Another way is through the formal treaty wording providing for the indexing of the retention via an index clause (to be discussed at the end of the section, "Rating Plans.") Of course, it is always possible to keep the primary company retention fixed and simply allow the cost of the reinsurance to keep increasing. (Some of the realities of such an increasing cost approach are discussed under "Inflation" in the section, "Rating Casualty Treaties.")

A variation of the working excess cover is one which is written on an aggregate basis, whereby the primary company retains its normal retention on each occurrence and additionally retains an aggregate amount of the losses which exceed this retention. The reinsurer then steps in for the excess occurrence losses once the aggregate retention has been exceeded by the accumulated losses. Primary companies seeking this type of cover are reflecting the belief that "a normal number of abnormal losses is normal." Covers of this type are difficult to evaluate and they also alter the reinsurer's cash flow. Such covers nevertheless should produce a lower premium due to the aggregate retention, but a relatively higher loading due to the increased uncertainty of the reinsurer. Primary companies with modest surpluses and no easy access to additional capital often find a total aggregate approach necessary in order to put a firm stop on surplus depletion regardless of its being caused by unusually high loss frequency, or loss severity, or a combination of both. In certain states, laws concerning assessable mutuals make this approach very helpful to the primary company.

CLASH COVERS

The fourth type of casualty reinsurance available to a primary company is in the pure risk area of clash, catastrophe excess of loss, or contingency covers. These three terms are essentially interchangeable and for simplicity the first will be used. In the transition from working covers to clash covers, there exists a continuous gradation of situations in between. One can well imagine that there is sufficient judgment and variation in practice among reinsurers in the two extremes that the situation is even more individualistic in this "in between" area. There can be little help for the reinsurance buyer in this area except that it should select its reinsurer with particular care. If there is a run of ill fortune in this intermediate area, it can be costly to the reinsurer — a few too many claims or an unexpected severity compound quickly, and the reinsurer's premium is usually not very responsive in the short term in this area. Therefore, it is extremely important that the reinsurer have the financial stability and solidity to be able to respond as necessary.

At the opposite end of the spectrum from working covers are the clash covers which are pure risk situations. Clash covers are those treaties which are written on an occurrence basis but are not exposed by any one policy issued by the primary company. Also included would be treaties

which, while exposed by the issued limits, are far removed from anything except a disastrous occurrence — for example, workers' compensation or automobile no-fault covers that are written above a very high
retention. A hallmark of this type of treaty is that it does not increase the
capacity of limit offering capability of the ceding company but instead
gives fundamental protection to the company for the rare event. There
are a number of possible uses for such a cover when it attaches above the
level of any policy limit issued:

a . For workers' compensation which is issued without a policy limit
quoted.

b. For any policy where unlimited medical benefits may be provided or awarded. An example would be the unlimited medical
benefits under automobile insurance policies.

c. For the event in which the company affords automobile liability
coverage for two insureds and one of them borrows the other's
car, resulting in a pyramiding of limits.

d. For a large occurrence producing injuries which may result in
liability against several parties, more than one of whom may be
insured by the company. This situation could involve two or
more contractors for general liability and workers' compensation,
or different insureds for automobile liability and products liability, or insureds for general liability and automobile separately.
Consider also an earthquake resulting in multiple workers' compensation losses from different insureds, or a conflagration producing any combination of fire legal liability, general liability, or
workers' compensation losses. Further possibilities are any insureds for whom the company affords liquor law liability (even
incidental) and automobile liability, or for whom the company
affords automobile or general liability and workers' compensation coverages. The combinations are almost limitless and often
the event that is never visualized is the one which involves a
clash cover.

e. For a limit on the company's maximum loss per occurrence,
should it be held liable for a judgment in excess of its policy limit
offered.

f. For unexpected excesses above the company's treaty protection.
For example, if the company's normal treaty coverage includes
loss adjustment expenses as part of the loss total, it is possible that
extensive loss adjustment expenses combined with an adverse

verdict for the full policy limits may exceed the company's treaty protection.

g. For treaty inadequacy due to no-fault coverage legislated in other states. For example, if the company has agreed to accept a state's no-fault automobile coverage for its insureds while they are driving in that particular state, the resulting exposure could be substantial. If the company has no direct business in that state, its normal treaty reinsurance could be grossly inadequate.

In one sense, there are two broad categories of treaty reinsurance: those that are pure risk-bearing treaties, and those that are designed to be cost-plus over time. It is perhaps redundant to say that there should be a clear understanding between the parties that the pure risk-bearing contracts are risk-bearing. Normally, one expects a premium to be paid and no losses will happen to most risk-bearing contracts. In those rare instances where a loss does occur, there should be no thought of the reinsured "paying its own way" over a reasonable period of time. If no claim occurs, there should be no expectation of a price decrease. The successful reinsurance underwriter in this type of reinsurance is one who builds a sufficient volume of this business to have a good judgmental basis upon which to establish premiums for each individual submission.

A reinsurer must be particularly aware of the fact that risk-bearing contracts can become working excesses if it is not careful. The primary company can grow to a level where the unusual policy of yesterday becomes the norm of today. This transition can also happen if the benefit levels through legislation or court action or inflation change the unusual or rare event of yesterday into today's mode of operation.

Among the special underwriting considerations for pure risk treaties are:

a. What are the maximum policy limits warranted by the insured? These limits are to be less than the attachment point of the cover.

b. What is the density of coverage which may create the possibility of two insureds clashing? For example, does the company insure 1 in 1,000 cars in a given city, or 1 in 10?

c. The underwriter must be particularly alert to the laws of the states in which the company has significant exposure with respect to no-fault benefits, workers' compensation benefits, and the climate as regards excess judgments or punitive damages.

d. The variety of lines of business which the insurer provides will influence the number of opportunities for potential clashes of coverage.

e. If workers' compensation is involved, the classes of risk written by the company will have a significant influence.

f. Of increasing importance is the treatment of loss adjustment expenses. Are they apportioned to layers of underlying reinsurance according to the loss payment, or are they added to the loss payment to create a final "ultimate net loss" which is then subject to the risk-bearing protection? As defense costs rise into six-digit figures, this treatment becomes significant.

Rating Casualty Treaties

The rating of casualty treaties is an inexact science and has almost as many techniques as there are underwriters. Before getting into rating specifics, it is necessary to define the concept of "balance" for a treaty as the measure of premium developed under the treaty in relation to the loss limit provided. Now, consider two polar opposites of philosophy: 1) each individual treaty should seek to obtain a high degree of balance over each annual term, and 2) a "right rate" is charged for each situation with no care about balance per se, and a collection of unbalanced situations is thought of as a book of business which has its own balance. To illustrate, suppose a carefully developed premium for a given company for a relatively high excess cover produces a premium equal to 40% of the limit provided; a second company which is one-tenth the size of the first would develop a premium equal to only 4% of the limit under the same terms and conditions. Under 2) above, the risk is every bit as acceptable as the larger company with its better balance; under 1), it would not be. Each philosophy has its place — the primary company should check its reinsurer's philosophy and see if it fits with the company's operation.

PRICING FACTORS

The pricing of a casualty reinsurance treaty must contain the same basic elements of cost that any insurance coverage must contain:

a. An amount to cover losses. For a reinsurer there is an element of normal expected losses, an element for the abnormal but nevertheless foreseeable losses, an element for catastrophe losses which occur rarely but do occur, and an element for "free cover" which could also be described as the totally unforeseeable loss.

b. An amount to cover expense. This amount includes ceding commission to the primary company, acquisition (or marketing) costs of either the reinsurer or a broker, and the operating expenses of the reinsurer.

c. A profit for the owners of the reinsurer.

Before discussing various rating plans themselves, the factors which must be involved in order to arrive at adequate rates in each of the areas above will be considered.

The Expense Allowance. The simplest factor to consider is the expense allowance. The reinsurer must provide a sufficient element in the rate to cover its own expenses. Ceding commissions vary depending primarily on the type of business written. For example, surety classes still carry reinsurance commission allowances of about 40%. Such allowances reflect the traditionally high original agent commissions of the company, and manual excess rated covers may have high reinsurance commissions built in to cover loss adjustment expenses as well as agent commissions and company operating costs. But most "rare event" covers will provide no commission allowance at all. Acquisition costs of the reinsurer vary depending upon its marketing mechanism — direct marketing through salaried account executives, or indirect marketing through a reinsurance intermediary. While the intermediary's costs are recorded as commission for Annual Statement purposes, the costs of account executives are classified as salaries, travel, etc.

The Profit Margin. The next factor to consider is the profit margin. While the underwriting profit might range anywhere from 5% to 20% of the final premium as a hoped-for target, the history of reinsurers in the casualty treaty area in recent years has not been encouraging. The potential for investment income to the reinsurer is an important consideration. On a typical casualty excess treaty, this can be worth an additional 10% to 25% of the premium. Depending on the ceding company and reinsurer's management philosophy about underwriting profit versus bottom-line profit and the tax position of each company, it could be advantageous for both parties to include a higher underwriting profit margin in the treaty but allow the ceding company to retain and invest a portion of the reinsurance premium as "funds held." In the final analysis, however, a successful underwriter (either primary or reinsurance) must aim to produce an underwriting profit in order to survive over the long run.

As in making any investment decision, a risk taker (in this case, the reinsurer) would expect a larger return on a more risky investment than on a safer one. An exact definition of what "more risky" means is hard to give, but one concept that is often applied here is that an investment expected to gain or lose a larger amount of money is more risky than one which would yield an almost guaranteed return. This concept applies to reinsurance pricing in several ways. First of all, a contract with a large reinsurance limit would require a larger profit percentage than a small limit. Also, a higher retention for a ceding company (which will eliminate more of its usual losses) requires a higher profit percentage for the reinsurer — although, because of the correspondingly lower reinsurance premium associated with higher retention, the total dollar margin would usually be lower than for a lower retention. Finally, the less sure the reinsurer feels about its ability to correctly estimate the expected losses, the more risky the treaty appears and, therefore, the larger percentage profit loading it will need. As a practical extension of this, the more credible and detailed data that the ceding company can provide to the reinsurer, the lower the profit margin the reinsurer should require.

A related feature influencing the profit margin is the risk position of the reinsurer. If it underwrites very large lines of reinsurance for its own account and thus subjects its surplus to the potential of fairly wide swings, it should seek a larger profit for this risk position. More than off-setting this, however, should be a lower expense ratio because a) there is less effort involved per dollar of premium in placing the primary company's treaty, and b) the multiple layers of retrocessionaires and their profit elements are eliminated. The primary company should be cognizant of the reinsurer's true risk position. For example, how much does the reinsurer retrocede? Who are its retrocessionaires? What is their stability? How much "friction in the system" is it paying for as the second reinsurer finds protection from a third reinsurer, and so on?

The Loss Element. The most difficult factor to evaluate is the loss element of the price. The reinsurer must make its "best guess" in establishing the average ultimate value of reinsurance claims occurring during the contract year. An "average" is used because consideration must be given to the possibility of catastrophes either in the form of a single large event or in the form of an unexpected burst of frequency of more normal sized losses. If a catastrophe is expected once every ten years, the best guess would be that there will be no catastrophe next year. However, on the average, one would have 10% of a catastrophe. This "best guess" is often referred to as the expected value of the losses, or more commonly "expected loss cost." The estimate of expected loss cost will, of course, be heavily influenced by the company's past data, because such statistics represent the type of losses usually experienced by the risks the company covered. However, one must be careful because some unusual types of losses might not be properly represented in the data. To take this into account, the reinsurer will normally add provision for "free cover" to its statistical estimate of expected "normal" losses.

However, if a truly unusual catastrophe is present in the data, it should not be assumed that it will repeat itself year after year, and therefore should be partially discounted.

The company's known loss experience is deceptively enticing as a base for evaluating the treaty's price. Unfortunately, the experience of past years cannot be used as a good estimate of the future expected loss cost without making adjustments to reflect for two extremely important factors. 1.) All the losses that will ultimately be settled for these past years are not accurately known yet. This is the issue of loss development and IBNR. 2.) Even if all losses for these years have been reported and are exactly known, it must be recognized that a loss occurring in 1975 (and settled in 1979, for example) would on the average, cost substantially more if it had occurred in the 1979 contract year (and was settled in 1983). This is the issue of social and economic inflation.

IBNR and Loss Development. The "long tail" on casualty business is a well-known problem for the entire insurance industry. Consider all the accidents occurring during 1973. The total dollar losses (paid plus outstanding) for these accidents, as they are known at the end of each subsequent year, increase year by year before finally leveling off when all cases are closed. This increase will also happen with the number of known claims (open and closed). Exhibit 1, based on the actual experience of a primary company during 1962-73, shows this phenomemon quite clearly. For example, at the end of the third year,[2]

- 80% of the claims ("events" on the graph) have been reported to the primary company and fully 20% are still to come in the future;

- only 35% of the eventual loss pay-out is registered on the financial records of the company in the form of paid loss or known reserves; and

- a mere 4% of the eventual loss pay-out has actually been paid and thus represents a firm figure with no room for argument (unless some subrogation possibility exists).

Two things cause this lag in information. First, *loss development*, which is the tendency for the reserves on open claims to fluctuate either upwards or downwards. And second, *incurred but not reported* (IBNR) claims, which are claims that occurred during the year in question but have not yet been reported. A common way to analyze data for this long-tail effect is to organize it as in Exhibit 2. Here each separate "acci-

---

[2]While the principal discussion in this section is based on the Accident Year concept, the graph is of Policy Year data. This is not of significance in its use as an illustration of the lag.

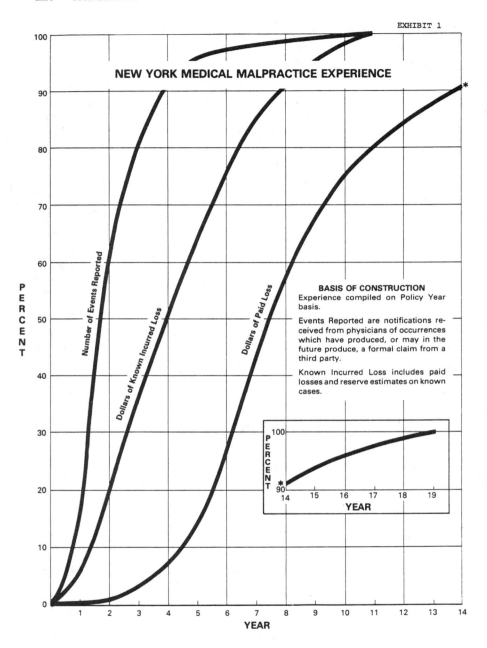

EXHIBIT 1

NEW YORK MEDICAL MALPRACTICE EXPERIENCE

BASIS OF CONSTRUCTION
Experience compiled on Policy Year basis.

Events Reported are notifications received from physicians of occurrences which have produced, or may in the future produce, a formal claim from a third party.

Known Incurred Loss includes paid losses and reserve estimates on known cases.

dent year" is shown, with the known losses one year later, two years later, etc. If the assumption is accepted that the past pattern of reserve changes and claim reporting will continue (which is often not a totally valid assumption), the ratios of loss reported at each point in time can be developed. These ratios are called age-to-age factors and are shown in Exhibit 3. Using these, one can fill in the unknown squares and project at what amount the most recent accident years will ultimately close out. There are two particular cautions with regard to working these factors. 1) Do not assume that the earliest accident year is necessarily fully developed (in this example one should consider adding a factor for further development beyond 96 months). 2) The assumption of stable patterns over a long period of time is rarely valid, since systems, procedures, policies and personnel change and may affect the pattern, hence thoughtful adjustments must be made for these factors.

If a company were to compare its "loss development triangle" for all losses for a given line with a loss development triangle of losses excess of a fixed (working level) retention, it would almost certainly see that the excess loss development was much more severe. There are several reasons for this difference. First of all, in certain lines, large cases are often reported late or else develop as surprises from small reserves. For example, a doctor may use a commonly accepted treatment technique on a pregnant woman under a legal aura in which "the doctor can do no wrong." The child upon reaching a certain age, and under a legal aura of "if the damage is great it must have been negligence," sues for damages. The defense cost will be significant and, of course, there may be a major award as well. Secondly, a treaty written with an aggregate retention can easily be deceptive. There may be no suspicion that the primary company will use up the aggregate until years later when a run of "ill fortune" results in a large number of modest sized adverse court decisions plus a few very large losses. Suddenly, the reinsurer has a loss under the treaty and it comes as a total surprise. Many other reasons and illustrations could be cited, but these should suffice to make the point.

One attempt that primary companies have made to shorten the long tail on reporting losses is to issue policies on a "claims-made" basis. One cannot help but speculate on the effect if a company's reinsurance were on a similar basis and the only claims which were validly within the treaty year of coverage were those which had been reported to the reinsurer and on which the company had reserved fully up to its retention.

Even if it were not for these late reported and late-to-develop losses, the leveraged effect of a fixed retention would cause excess loss development to be more severe. What is meant by a leveraged effect can be illustrated by an example. In Exhibit 4 there are eight reserved claims. Assume that each claim will finally settle for 10 % more than its current reserve. Overall, this final effect will show an adverse loss development

EXHIBIT 2

Paid and Outstanding Losses
(in thousands)

Accident Year	12 mos	24 mos	DEVELOPED 36 mos	THROUGH 48 mos	60 mos	72 mos	84 mos	96 mos
1967	$ 2606	$ 5079	$ 5778	$ 7293	$ 7900	$ 8226	$ 8165	$ 8375
1968	3176	6021	7176	7391	7310	8317	8810	
1969	4512	7733	9827	10819	12562	13377		
1970	4645	7625	9931	10572	11416			
1971	5010	7528	9283	11187				
1972	5980	9502	13005					
1973	6411	10541						
1974	7431							

EXHIBIT 3

Age-to-Age Factors

Accident Year	12 to 24 mos	24 to 36 mos	36 to 48 mos	48 to 60 mos	60 to 72 mos	72 to 84 mos	84 to 96 mos
1967	1.949	1.138	1.262	1.083	1.041	.993	1.026
1968	1.896	1.192	1.030	.989	1.138	1.059	
1969	1.714	1.271	1.101	1.161	1.065		
1970	1.642	1.302	1.065	1.080			
1971	1.503	1.233	1.205				
1972	1.589	1.369					
1973	1.644						
Mean	1.705	1.251	1.133	1.078	1.081	1.026	1.026

of 10%. However, excess of the first $25,000 retention, one sees that the loss development is 40%. The exact relationship between the overall result and the excess loss development depends on the distribution of claim sizes. However, on the average, the excess will always be considerably more than the overall loss development figure. This example also illustrates that development on known losses to the primary company can become IBNR to the reinsurer in the situations where a small case reserve suddenly develops to an amount over the retention and is then reported to the reinsurer. For this reason, claims-made policies may have certain desirable effects for the primary company but will still have significant IBNR potential for the reinsurer.

EXHIBIT 4

The Effect of Loss Development on Excess Claims

Reserve	Reserve Amount Excess of $25,000	Closing Amount (10% Higher)	Closing Amount Excess of $25,000
$10,000	$ —0—	$11,000	$ —0—
10,000	—0—	11,000	—0—
15,000	—0—	16,500	—0—
20,000	—0—	22,000	—0—
24,000	—0—	26,400	1,400
30,000	5,000	33,000	8,000
35,000	10,000	38,500	13,500
40,000	15,000	44,000	19,000
TOTAL	$30,000		$41,900

Since $\frac{41,900}{30,000} = 1.40$, there is a 40% loss development on excess claims.

Severe excess IBNR can occur even if the overall reserve is correct, in other words, if there is no adverse loss development. Consider twelve similar claims that the company is contesting. The company feels that it will be able to settle two thirds of these claims for $10,000 each, but that the other one third of the claims will each close for the total policy limit, which is $50,000. If each of these claims is reserved for $25,000 originally, after closing there will be a 7% "savings" on the total reserve. However, excess of a $35,000 retention, there will now be four claims totaling $60,000 when prior to that there were no reserves excess of the retention. Workers' compensation reserves set at discounted values will cause the same effect as in the two previous examples, since the payments on them "rub off." Therefore, reinsurers normally insist on cases trended to ultimate rather than considering the present value of the benefits due in the future. These effects make the examination of only known excess loss experience misleading, which causes many disagreements between a primary company and its reinsurer.

One final note. Schedule P from the Annual Statement is prepared in accident year format and can be used to analyze a company's net loss development. However, because the schedule shows only experience net of reinsurance, it is relatively useless from the point of view of a reinsurer which is trying to estimate the development that might occur on excess claims. With respect to IBNR and loss development, one must try to use every talent and expertise available, spend any amount of time necessary, employ whatever manpower and computer resources are required, and then be prepared for the inevitable—because the chances are, "you ain't seen nothin' yet."

Inflation. The second major adjustment that must be made to loss data is trending—to reflect economic and social inflation. Economic inflation refers to the fact that medical care and other things that insurers purchase to settle claims rise in price (and substantially faster, it appears, than the Consumer Price Index), plus the legislated link to inflation which ties some workers' compensation annuity benefits in a number of states to an index. Social inflation refers to increased jury awards, increased liberal treatment of claims by workers' compensation boards, legislated increases in benefit levels (in some cases retroactively), and new concepts of tort and negligence that emerge to increase insurance losses. To recognize the effects of economic and social inflation, the claims in our data must be adjusted to reflect what each of the same claims would have been worth if it had happened in the proposed contract year.

Inflation's effect on the excess reinsurer has received much discussion in recent years. As in loss development, inflation has a severe leveraged effect on a fixed excess retention. Consider the following examples contained in a report[3] issued by the Reinsurance Association of America (RAA) in 1974:

> Before considering inflation's impact on aggregate numbers, consider an individual case reserved today at $75,000. The primary carrier's retention is $50,000 and, therefore, the loss is split $50,000 to the primary carrier and $25,000 to the reinsurer. Assuming an average annual inflation rate of + 8.0%, the identical claim occurring three years hence will cost $75,000 × $(1.08)^3$ or $94,480. The primary carrier's ultimate costs will still be $50,000 while the reinsurer's excess loss cost increases from $25,000 to $44,480, an annual increase of + 21.2%. The difference between the + 21.2% and + 8.0% annual rates is referred to as the "leveraged" effect of inflation which must be borne by the excess carrier.

> The excess carrier is, in fact, subject to two forces, increased claim cost and increased claim frequency. This double-barrelled effect of inflation is illustrated in the following example.

> An insurance exposure is expected to generate annually,

---

[3] "Memorandum to Member Companies," May 7, 1974. Reinsurance Association of America, 1025 Connecticut Avenue, N.W., Washington, D.C. 20036. pp. 7-10.

on the average, ten claims excess of $35,000 in today's dollar value. Assume it will take three years for the claims to be settled (a very conservative assumption). The excess reinsurer's attachment point is $50,000 and its pure loss costs, given no inflation, would be:

Claim	Excess Loss Cost
$ 35,000	—0—
37,000	—0—
39,000	—0—
42,000	—0—
45,000	—0—
48,000	—0—
51,000	$ 1,000
57,000	7,000
70,000	20,000
102,000	52,000
	$80,000

Excess Loss Cost = 4 claims totalling $80,000

Given an annual inflation rate of +8.7% or +28.4% over a three-year settlement period, the ultimate expected excess loss cost would now be:

Claim	Ultimate Value (Claim × 1.284)	Excess Loss Cost
$ 35,000	$ 44,940	$ —0—
37,000	47,508	—0—
39,000	50,076	76
42,000	53,928	3,928
45,000	57,780	7,780
48,000	61,632	11,632
51,000	65,484	15,484
57,000	73,188	23,188
70,000	89,880	38,880
102,000	130,968	80,968
		$182,936

Excess Loss Cost = 8 claims totalling $182,936

In the above example, an +8.7% annual increase in inflation

produces an *annual* increase in total excess cost of 31.7 % ($\sqrt[3]{182,936/80,000} - 1$) which includes a dramatic increase in the number of claims brought into the excess area. An independent actuarial study[4] on this subject produced the following theoretical results using actual claim distributions:

Annual Rate of Inflation	Retention	Annual Inflation Rate For Primary Writer	Annual Leveraged Inflation Rate Writer
+ 8.6 %	$10,000	+ 7.3 %	+ 18.0 %
	25,000	+ 8.0 %	+ 23.0 %
	50,000	+ 8.4 %	+ 29.6 %
+ 20.8 %	$10,000	+ 17.2 %	+ 45.9 %
	25,000	+ 19.1 %	+ 59.7 %
	50,000	+ 20.1 %	+ 78.4 %

These examples taken from the RAA report assume that inflation has a similar across-the-board effect of raising all sizes of claims equally. Yet it is an unresolved but important question whether its true impact is relatively greater on severe claims than on smaller ones. Also note that, while the examples dwell on liability-type claims and inflation, legislated increases in workers' compensation benefit levels have an effect similar to inflation. The reinsurer must be careful to fully reflect such law changes in the data.

This unequal sharing of inflation between the primary company and the reinsurer is the reason reinsurance rates must increase each year for a contract with a fixed retention, even though the primary company is getting rate increases on its business which reflect inflation. The point is that the rate increases for the primary company increase the volume of its premium, but its liability is decreased to the extent the inflation pushes more of its risks beyond its retention limits into the reinsurer's liability. To that extent, then, the reinsurer receives more risk than the reinsured, hence the reinsurance rate must increase more than the primary's increase. For example, say that a company's subject premiums increase by 20 % in a given year. Further assume that 10 % of this increase was due to additional exposures and the other 10 % was due to a rate increase. Of

[4] Lewis H. Roberts, "The Impact of Inflation on Reinsurance Costs," *Best's Review, Property / Liability Insurance Edition*, March, 1973, pp. 14-18.

that rate increase, assume that 8% reflects one year's additional severity inflation whereas 2% was due to other factors. Therefore, the reinsurer would be getting 8% more premium strictly for inflation even if it kept its reinsurance rate the same. The RAA report demonstrates that an 8% overall inflation rate could represent a 25% per year inflation in excess claims cost. The reinsurer would then need a 17% increase in the reinsurance *rate* in addition to the 8% increase in the subject premium to have adequate funds to meet its 25% higher expected claim cost.

One answer to the above problem would be for the primary company to increase its retention each year to keep up with the increase in claims cost. (Note that this is not the same thing as the index clause, which is another response to this problem. The index clause will be discussed later.) It can be seen from the RAA report and the analysis following that leaving a retention fixed in an inflationary environment is, in effect, decreasing the real level of risk[5] the company retains. However, primary company underwriters resist moving up too much, because they do not enjoy the thought of having to explain large losses to the company's board of directors.

One thing to notice in working through an example of adjusting past claims is that the data should include historical claims that were settled for considerably less than the retention level being priced. Trend and loss development can easily push these claims over the new retention level. Starting only with claims excess of the new retention would woefully understate the potential claims in that layer.

These concepts of developing and trending past losses to reflect current conditions are the same as those used by primary companies in preparing their own rates. One question that often arises is, If fully adequate loss development factors (that reflect inflation) are applied and then trend factors are applied on top, isn't there a doubling up? The answer is, No. If the inflationary and claims development environment expected in the future is the same as that which occurred in the past, then applying both trend and development factors separately does *not* cause double counting. To see this, consider the example in Exhibit 5 of one claim, a broken leg, that occurred in 1975 and will close in 1981. This claim is reserved for $40,000 at June, 1978. From past development patterns, it is observed that this company's total claim dollars for a given accident year grows on the average an additional 10% from 42 months to ultimate (note that 6/78 is 42 months from the beginning of the 1975 accident

---

[5] The premium the company retains will also be reduced under these circumstances because more will be paid for reinsurance.

year). While we have no guarantee that this individual claim will grow 10%, the observed growth must come from somewhere, so in this case assume that it comes evenly over all claims. This 10% growth partially reflects inflation that will occur between 6/78 and the closing of this claim in 1981. Applying 10% loss development gives the prediction that, on the average, this claim will ultimately close for $44,000. Recall that by trending and developing, we are trying to estimate what a similar loss would ultimately cost if it occurred in the proposed contract year (1979). In other words, if a broken leg similar to that which occurred in 1975 occurred in 1979, for how much would it ultimately close? In Exhibit 5 this new accident is called the hypothetical claim. If the actual claim will close in 1981 for $44,000, then the hypothetical claim which happened four years later will close four years later in 1985, and it should close for $44,000 *times four years' trend.* The inflation in the loss development factor reflects the growth on the average in this claim between 6/78 and 1981, and the trend indicates the increased costs expected for an accident closing in 1985 versus 1981—there is no overlap![6] Of course, if it is believed that future inflation and development patterns will be different from past patterns, adjustments must be made to the factors to reflect such beliefs.

Now that all past year losses have been placed on current cost levels, compare these losses to the past subject premiums that were collected. However, now the premiums must be adjusted to reflect what they would have been if they had been collected during the proposed reinsurance contract year (under the new, presumably higher, rates), instead of what was actually collected in the past. This adjustment is called "putting the premiums on current rate level." To make the adjustment, one must determine what effect the rate increases had on the earned premium each year. Note that it is not simply a matter of applying each year's rate increase percentage because those numbers apply to written premium. The techniques for doing this become somewhat involved and need not concern us here.[7]

A shortcut to trending each loss to current levels and adjusting all past premiums (but not a shortcut around the loss development procedure) is to trend the proposed retention downward at the inflation rate. When this trending is done, instead of saying what premium and past losses would be if they had occurred during the proposed contract year

---

[6] For a technical treatment of this subject see "Trend and Loss Development Factors," Charles F. Cook, *Proceedings* of the Casualty Actuarial Society, Volume LVII, pp. 1-14.

[7] The interested reader may refer to "Rate Revision Adjustment Factors," LeRoy J. Simon, *Proceedings* of the Casualty Actuarial Society, Volume XLV, pp. 196-213.

under the terms of the proposed contract, one calculates the retention in each of the past years that would be equivalent to the retention in the proposed new contract.

EXHIBIT 5

Loss Development and Trend
Independence Illustration

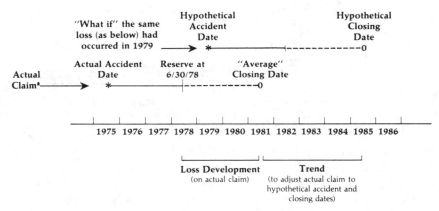

An alternative pricing technique that is becoming more popular is that of finding a smooth probability distribution curve that fits the loss distribution by size, as in Exhibit 6. Either the raw loss data must be adjusted to reflect trend and development before the curve is fitted, or the curve must be adjusted for these factors after it has been fitted. This is a very popular technique in the medical malpractice line because of the availability of a closed claim study by the National Association of Insurance Commissioners which gives a distribution of loss by size. Insurance Services Office is also exploring the use of this technique to set increased limits factors.[8]

In addition to using loss experience to rate a working cover, the reinsurer should determine how much premium the ceding company is collecting for the layer of liability in this area, based on the increased limits factors that the ceding company is using. In fact, this is a method often

---

[8] See the following articles, "Estimating Pure Premiums by Layer—an Approach," Robert J. Finger, *Proceedings* of the Casualty Actuarial Society, Volume LXIII, pp. 34-52. "Credibility of 10/20 Experience as Compared with 5/10 Experience," Lewis H. Roberts, PCAS, XLVI, pp. 235-250. "On the Theory of Increased Limits and Excess of Loss Pricing," Robert S. Miccolis, PCAS, LXIV, to be published.

EXHIBIT 6

Loss Distribution by Size

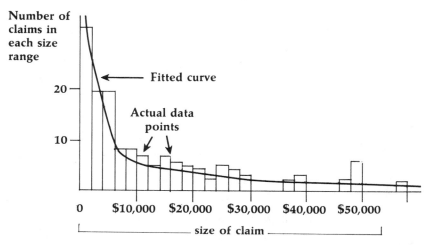

used to price an excess treaty, especially in cases where there is not credible data to calculate a rate based on experience. In this approach, one collects premium less ceding commission to cover the reinsurer's expenses. (See, for example, the coded excess approach described in the "Rating Plans" section.)

Judgment must be used constantly to develop a truly "best guess" of expected loss cost. Because so many projections and areas of judgment are involved, one of the real risks in a working cover is that the reinsurer and the primary company will disagree about the projection factors. What the reinsurer has to worry about is the very real possibility that this disagreement will cause the primary company to cancel the treaty, going elsewhere for better terms and that the reinsurer's more pessimistic projections of the loss development and IBNR ultimately turn out to be correct, and leave the former reinsurer in a substantial loss position.

RATING PLANS

There is a wide variety of rating plans which can be employed with respect to casualty excess reinsurance. The rating freedom enjoyed by reinsurers and their primary company clients permits a tailoring of the situations to meet the needs and desires of the primary company. Flexibility and imagination should be the hallmark of the progressive reinsurance underwriter, and the variety of companies in the marketplace enables the primary company to find the kind of rating plan in which it has a particular interest. If a buyer does not have a preconceived idea of the type of rating plan desired, he would be well advised to test different markets to get some idea on how such a plan might be constructed. Let's consider some of the rating plans popularly in use.

Fixed Premiums. A fixed (dollar) premium is quoted by a reinsurer and is paid in advance or in installments, the price presumably varying with the timing of payment. This fixed premium is the most straightforward method of payment but lacks flexibility to meet changing conditions—it cannot grow as the portfolio protected grows and must, therefore, be reconsidered each anniversary. The method is primarily used for covers of a catastrophe nature where past experience is of little or no guide to the premium which should be charged. It is also used occasionally for new portfolios where the reinsurer requires a minimum premium to put the business on its books and the rate quoted is no guide as to how the business will develop. In such situations this minimum premium is only a temporary expedient, and a more flexible rating basis should be applied as soon as feasible. In practice (some would say, "in unsound practice"), one finds the fixed premium system is occasionally used for large insurers where the portfolio of liability business is too complex to respond to detailed rating analysis. Here the ceding insurer generally presumes that it will pay back its own losses over time and, therefore, in a working excess situation, the fixed premium will be adjusted in the future as necessary.

Rate per Unit. When a fixed premium is not suitable, a "rate per unit" is used to try to reflect changes in the exposure to the reinsurer. The change in the premium income of the primary company is in many cases a measure of this changing exposure and, therefore, is a convenient yardstick on which to adjust the reinsurance premium. As an exception, one may find an excess of loss rate tied to the total sum insured, or perhaps more exceptionally, employer's liability cover rated on total wages declared under the original insurance policies.

If the premium income of the primary company is to be used as the base against which the rate is applied, it must be carefully defined and fully agreed to by both parties. In a typical case it will be the original premium income related to that part of the primary company's business which is protected by the treaty. This means the gross premiums, after eliminating premiums on risks which are excluded from the treaty and also after deducting premium paid for reinsurance inuring to the benefit of the treaty. This does not mean to exclude premiums on risks which, merely because of their size, do not expose the treaty—although this is a matter of individual discussion and negotiation. Generally speaking, deductions are not made from the gross premiums thus arrived at for commissions, taxes and other amounts which the primary company has to meet out of its gross premium income. Technically, the claims experience should be related to earned premiums, and that premium used for adjustment purposes. The earned premium basis eliminates the distortions which would occur if the written premium is taken and the portfolio is either growing or declining. Whether one is to use an earned or a written basis, it must be clearly defined in the reinsurance contract along with all other elements that make up the base of "subject" premium. Protection for loss occurrences under the contract must, in the event of termination, follow the earning of the premium. If the premium base is earned premium, coverage would be on a "losses occurring" basis, and losses happening after the termination would not be covered. Such "runoff" protection could be purchased, of course, at an additional negotiated premium.

Fixed Rate Basis. Within the "rate per unit" type of treaties, let's first consider a fixed rate basis. The reinsurer, having considered all the facts, quotes a *rate* of premium which is firm for the duration of the contract. The contract can be continuous, subject to cancellation with suitable notice or for a fixed period, usually of twelve months. Because of the effects of inflation, changes in social structures and habits, changes in legislation and so forth, reinsurers tend to review contracts at least every twelve months in order that the rate can be reevaluated and the treaty terminated if necessary. While reinsurers wish to maintain continuity of market in these changing times, it is not possible in most cases to offer frozen terms. The fixed rate is used for all types of excess of loss covers, but is normally the only one suitable for catastrophe layers. Normally the final amount produced by application of the rate to the final, actual exposure base will not be known until some time after the close of the period involved when the actual premium, as opposed to the estimated premium, is known. Therefore, it is normal to provide for a deposit premium to be paid at inception based on a percentage of the estimated premium for the policy period. The percentage varies but is normally in the region of 75%-85%.

Manual Excess. The manual excess method of pricing reinsurance, whether it be at low levels or at relatively high levels, calls for the calculation of the excess premium which is produced through the rating manuals and increased limits tables for the particular layer of reinsurance being purchased. An allowance is agreed upon for overhead and commission costs, and the primary company pays the resulting manual excess premium for its reinsurance. This method puts the reinsurer in a position of pricing the reinsurance based upon the exposure to loss. (This will be later contrasted with pricing based primarily on experience.) The manual excess method is often used with small companies or lines of business which do not produce a lot of volume, although it may be used as a starting point for an experience based pricing system as well. To use the manual excess method, the reinsurer must have a fair degree of confidence in the basic manual rate and the increased limits table being used and must set the ceding commission to be fair to both parties. The ceding commission should be designed to cover operating costs of the primary company.[9] In theory at least, the reinsurer should profit from loss experience more favorable than the manual excess calculation implies, and one would not expect to have profit commissions or experience rating play a part in the pricing of a manual excess cover unless the full ceding commission were not allowed to begin with or there is some other contract feature that affects the pricing. In a competitive market with a relatively easy entry, many shades of variation exist and no rules go unbroken.

Coded Excess. A variation on the manual excess method or a refinement of the fixed rate basis (depending upon how one approaches it) is "coded excess." This is a form of rating used on excesses which are exposed on a per policy basis, and the protection is given on a per policy basis. The original portfolio will be analyzed into bands by size of sum insured. The reinsurer will state the percentage of the original premium it requires for each band of sum insured, and the total reinsurance premium will be the sum of the reinsurance premiums for each band. New business is then coded into the band in which it falls, and the reinsurance premium is thus determined for it. This is similar to the fixed rate basis but is refined by fixing the rate for each band rather than for the entire cover.

Advance Deposit Premium. The advance deposit premium (ADP) system is more suited to property reinsurance, although it is occasionally used on casualty business in spite of the difficulties inherent in delayed development and evaluation. ADP is a rating scheme that is open ended. The reinsurer quotes a rate which is then split between a claims fund and a reinsurance premium. The claims fund is usually held by the reinsurer and used to pay the treaty claims. This fund is built up over a period of years, and in the event that it exceeds a stated maximum figure, the rate

---

[9] Particular care must be exercised if allocated loss adjustment expenses are to be shared in proportion to the losses paid by the two parties, because current Insurance Services Office ratemaking procedure assumes that all such expense is paid by the basic limits policy; therefore, there is no provision for it in the increased limits factors.

payable in the following year would be reduced to the stated reinsurance premium. The rate will remain at that level until such time as the fund drops below the stated maximum, at which time the rate reverts to the full rate, i.e., reinsurance premium plus claims fund. The contract is continuous, subject to an annual cancellation clause. Should the reinsured cancel the contract after the first or second year, it would only receive a refund of one third or two thirds, respectively, of the claims fund. If the contract has run for three or more years, in the event of cancellation, 100% of the claims fund is refunded after all claims are settled. The quoted rate for such an arrangement would contemplate the potential return of the claims fund and would be significantly higher than a similar treaty without this feature. Generally speaking, the higher the rate, the lower the reinsurer's risk and the lower the reinsurance premium portion of the rate quoted.

In the event that the reinsurer can foresee a possible adverse trend, a fixed rate may be pitched deliberately higher than the expected loss calculation (and normal profit margin) would indicate and a profit commission offered to allow for the possibility that the expected trend may not develop. The unwary reinsurer will not set the rate high and thus will not have enough total funds with which to pay for those cases where the experience does turn adverse.

Swing Rating (Experience or Retrospective). Another technique which allows the final costs to the primary company to vary with actual experience is swing rating, also referred to as experience[10] or retrospective rating. This technique is a rating formula by which the reinsured pays a provisional premium to its reinsurer. This premium is adjusted, based on actual developed experience and subject to a minimum and a maximum rate. This experience rating period normally encompasses three years and contains a loss loading factor which generally would be 100/80ths or 100/75ths, designed to cover expenses, profit, and the risk that the actual experience will exceed the maximum more often than falling short of the minimum. Generally speaking, the higher the maximum rate (compared with "normally" expected losses), the lower the load factor. An alternative method for the reinsurer to cover expenses, profit, and risk is a flat fee expressed as a percentage of subject premium. In this way, the reinsurer's margin does not depend upon the actual loss experience (as long as it is within the maximum and minimum). The percentage loadings to

---

[10] Actually a misnomer since "experience rating" has a well accepted meaning in the primary insurance business involving the use of past experience to fix a rate to be used prospectively.

losses would make sense if the reinsurer's expenses were proportional to the losses; however, this is not really the case.

IBNR and loss development again become an important issue in retrospective rating plans. At the end of the three-year rating period, the known losses would normally be quite a bit less than the ultimate amount of losses occurring in those years. Remember that at the end of the three-year period the latest year of experience is only twelve months mature. To handle this immaturity, the retrospective premium adjustment calculated at the end of the period is considered provisional and is updated at the end of the following year, still, however, only including accidents occurring during the first three years. Provisional adjustments are usually made for several more years until the original three-year period can be considered closed. If this system is used without modification, what will usually happen is that the first provisional adjustment will show very favorable experience (because not all losses are known yet) and, therefore, will indicate that premiums should be returned to the ceding company. As the subsequent adjustments are made, each will show worse experience and will indicate that additional premium will be due from the primary company to the reinsurer. To avoid this fluctuation, predetermined IBNR factors, usually expressed as a percentage of provisional premium, are added to the first few provisional adjustments. One other common provision is for deficit and credit carryforwards, which means that if the minimum is not attained or the maximum is exceeded during one three-year rating period, the shortfall or excess is added to or subtracted from the losses during the next three-year rating period.

Index Clause. A contract provision that was developed in Europe as a means of combatting the difficult reinsurance problems raised by inflation is the index clause. This technique calls for the primary company's retention to be determined at the time the loss is paid by multiplying the retention at the time the loss occurred by the percentage growth in an agreed index. In practices, this technique leads to a more equitable sharing of the inflation (as reflected by the index) between the primary company and the reinsurer. The purpose of the clause is sometimes stated in the contract wording as being "the intent of the parties that the company's retention and the excess carrier's limit of liability will retain their relatively monetary values which exist at the date of commencement of this agreement." The index itself can be anything on which the two parties agree. Three popular ones are the Consumer Price Index, the "Medical Care Service" component of the Consumer Price Index, and the "Hourly Earnings Index" from "Monthly Labor Review." The contract retention is usually calculated either quarterly or annually. The index clause is not a panacea for the problems of inflation in excess casualty reinsurance, because factors not reflected in the index are naturally not reflected in the indexed retention.

From the reinsurer's point of view, the advantage of the index clause is that it is not so dangerously exposed to an increase in the inflation rate. This fact can become an advantage to the primary company as well, because the reinsurer does not have to be as conservative in its allowance in the premium for future inflation. In other words, whenever a risk is shifted to a reinsurer under a working excess cover, it will charge expected loss cost plus a profit loading (based on riskiness). If by using an index clause the primary company decides to retain part of the risk of future inflation, it not only avoids paying the reinsurer a charge for the expected future loss due to inflation under the contract but also the reinsurer's risk charge associated with this future uncertainty. Another advantage to the primary company of keeping the relatively monetary value of the retention the same over time is that it prevents inflation from continuously moving the primary company's net retention in real dollars downward. In other words, the primary company is following a more consistent reinsurance strategy—and (everything else being equal) can expect a more stable reinsurance rate. While reinsurance prices for indexed covers are much lower than otherwise, primary companies resist them because they are unable to fix their retention firmly on any particular pending claim (since the retention depends upon the time the claim is settled and the value of the index at that time). The expected adverse net development from this cause should be reflected in the company's IBNR reserve.[11]

Adjust Indemnity Losses. Another technique, this one designed to confront some of the problems of social inflation, is used on workers' compensation to adjust indemnity losses. These losses are revalued, if necessary, to include within the reinsurance treaty only benefits to the extent of current law level at the date of accident. Additional benefits granted retroactively or prospectively are excluded from consideration under the reinsurance treaty.

Evaluating the Casualty Excess Reinsurer and Reinsured

A casualty reinsurance treaty is expected to be a long-term commitment on the part of both parties and must be entered into only after joint

---

[11] A detailed and excellent treatment of this clause is available in "Nonproportional Reinsurance and the Index Clause," Ronald E. Ferguson, *Proceedings* of the Casualty Actuarial Society, Volume LXI, pp. 141-164.

consideration and negotiation. What should each party look for when considering this close working partnership? The primary company must look for a reinsurer that is professionally established and of known reputation and financial solidity. To do otherwise in a casualty reinsurance situation invites the possibility of serious disappointment in the future. In selecting its reinsurer, perhaps the primary company should follow the advice that it would give to one of its insureds in selecting its insurer. In addition, there are a number of special services which the primary company may expect from its reinsurer in the casualty field. These services bring the experience and expertise of the reinsurer's staff to bear on particular problems and help the two partners in achieving better results under the reinsurance treaty.

One of the most valuable services is the expertise that the reinsurer brings in the claims area. This service begins with a claim audit conducted before the reinsurer agrees to underwrite the treaty. The audit assists in evaluating the ability of the primary company to handle claims in the particular area to be covered by the treaty and gives the primary company an evaluation of its strength and weakness in the claims area. It continues with the review of individual claims submitted to the reinsurer during the life of the treaty. Since the reinsurer's claim people only see large and unusual cases, it is natural that they can be of considerable help to the primary company by providing advice and counsel. In those cases where the reinsurer may have the significant position on a particular claim and the primary company may lack a special expertise, the reinsurer may assume the dominant position in carrying the claim through to completion. Such a situation would develop through the cooperation of both parties.

Periodically throughout the life of the casualty reinsurance treaty, the reinsurer's claim people will audit the primary company's claim operation. This is particularly helpful to the reinsurer in evaluating the renewal terms of treaties and evaluating the desirability of continuing on the contract. However, the primary company also benefits greatly from these audits since it receives the advantage of an outside view of its procedures and performance. Since this can be done by the reinsurer's claim people who have similarly reviewed other companies, it can add valuable information to the claim manager's arsenal. A vital part of any such audit is a thorough discussion of the results with senior management of the primary company in order to make the results as valuable as possible to all concerned.

Another service the reinsurer may provide is to make available an actuarial critique of the premium rates, loss reserves, and incurred but not reported loss reserves of the primary company. Here again, the broad overview of the industry as seen by a reinsurer is particularly valuable in providing a background against which the primary company can measure its performance.

As the primary company's expertise varies in different areas, so will the need for the special abilities the reinsurer possesses, such as underwriting knowledge and experience. Since the reinsurer generally operates in the broad spectrum of the insurance market, it develops a considerable knowledge of both the usual and the unusual that is going on. This information can be brought to bear with respect to underwriting, pricing, and various controls and procedures that can be helpful to the primary company. The reinsurer may pick up trends in various states (perhaps where the primary company is not operating) which will eventually affect the company's operations. The reinsurer would also be alert to legal developments which could give rise to new exposures or could limit troublesome situations in the future. Further, it can be of specific assistance in introducing or suggesting means of coordinating other disciplines within the primary company, such as financial planning.

The reinsurer looks for a wide variety of features in the companies with which it deals: its financial condition, its underwriting team, the claims organization, but above all the company management. The special long-term nature of the casualty reinsurance business dictates that particular care must be given to evaluating the top management of the primary company and to investigating its motivation for buying reinsurance. Once coverage is bound by the reinsurer, it is literally in the hands of the primary company for a considerable time into the future even if the treaty is cancelled subsequently. Because of the difficulty in measuring the true loss experience as it develops, the reinsurer's commitment will be for a long period of time even if it does not initially think of it being that way. The reinsurer must have complete trust and faith in the management and in its integrity to conduct business in the way indicated. To help assure that things are on the right track, reinsurers conduct underwriting audits of their primary companies to improve the rapport and also to serve as a means of cutting off problems before they really become serious. One must keep in mind that it is not unusual for the reinsurer to have a liability under the treaty that is a significant multiple of that retained by the primary company.

The primary company underwriting team is the front line, on which the reinsurer must rely to perform its job properly and in accordance with the understood intentions of the parties. Therefore, communications between the top management and its underwriters must be clear, concise and authoritative. When the company operates on a branch office system, there must exist proper controls in the home office to ascertain the degree to which it is able to have its underwriting policy carried out in the field.

The ability of the primary company underwriters to handle the type of business for which it is seeking reinsurance must also be evaluated. At one extreme, it may be going into a new line of business with untested personnel. At the other extreme, it may be expert in the field and want to substantially increase its capacity to handle any risk which comes along. Each situation must be separately evaluated and approached in a different manner.

All too often the operation of the primary company's claims department is erroneously overlooked. One of the principal products which the reinsurer offers is the capacity that it extends to the primary company. The primary company claim department is the one that pays out losses and, therefore, uses that capacity in the manner that most directly affects the reinsurer. Since the claims personnel spend the reinsurer's money, their ability and experience are most important to the reinsurer. Equally important is the proper reserving of cases in a prompt and adequate manner and notification of significant losses to the reinsurer. In the casualty business particularly, it is important that effective procedures are in place to assure the prompt and adequate reporting of losses to the reinsurer. The claims handling itself is also of great importance, since it is well known that improperly handled small claims turn into large claims; and, therefore, losses which should not impact the reinsurer become serious matters for it. For these reasons, many reinsurers underwrite the claim department of the primary company as thoroughly as they underwrite the company's underwriting department and its top management. This review and evaluation of reserve integrity, technical proficiency, control of allocated loss expense, and timely monitoring of loss reserves can be of inestimable value to the claims department management team.

While there are many common sense attributes that one might look for in a claim department, there are also a number of philosophical features that should be evaluated. Does the company settle fairly and promptly, does it settle cases at any cost to get them off the books, or does it deny every claim possible and allow the courts to decide whether or not it pays? Is it alert to the varying judicial climates in different jurisdictions? How has the evolving punitive damage problem affected the operation and settlement efforts of the claim department? What are the controls and procedures with respect to subrogation? Does the company have a claim specialist for each major line or class of business? Does it have house counsel and, if so, what experience and expertise does it have?

For information on the financial condition of a company, a reinsurer can readily obtain a capsule presentation from an annual publication, *Best's Insurance Reports, Property-Casualty* (A.M. Best Company, Oldwick, New Jersey 08858). Financial data for the last five years are presented, and a narrative gives information about the company management, investments, and operations. In addition, rating values are assigned by Best's for the financial condition and for the size of the assets of the company. Of particular interest to the reinsurer is the ownership and control of the company. Is it a true insurance underwriter and risk taker, or a vehicle for financial operations, or just where does its motivation lie?

The reinsurer should also be interested in developing its own assessment of the financial condition of the company through examining a number of aspects. For example, the ratio of written premium to surplus will provide an indication of the ability of the company to withstand deterioration of its loss and expense experience in the event of adversity. The ratio of loss reserves to surplus will measure its ability to withstand an error in evaluation of its potential liabilities. Similarly, the structure of the asset holdings can be examined to evaluate the degree of risk introduced by holdings of common stock and the extent to which the company assets are dependent upon receivables rather than investable funds.

Other features in evaluating the primary company would include its ownership. For example, if it is owned by another corporation, the credit worthiness of the parent must be of considerable importance. The future ability of the insurance company to honor its commitments will be inextricably dependent upon the parent's ability to allow it to do so. While state insurance department regulation may protect the public from suffering certain types of losses at the hands of unscrupulous individuals, such protection is not readily available to help the reinsurer. Another important feature is the growth pattern of the primary company over the last few years. It is also of importance to know where the growth has occurred—in areas where the company has previously established an expertise, or in new ventures and experiments. Finally, the financial condition of the company is very dependent upon its loss reserve position and the evaluation of its known and its incurred but not reported losses. Tests of reserve adequacy can be obtained from special actuarial studies that the company might provide, from the company's Annual Statement, or from the Early Warning Tests of the National Association of Insurance Commissioners.

There are many underlying reasons for seeking reinsurance, and the primary company must be willing to make its best presentation of its philosophical background for seeking reinsurance cover. Some may view reinsurance as a leveling device which will take the peaks and the valleys out of the primary company's experience but will pay the reinsurer a profit over a reasonable period of time. Others may view reinsurance as a means of "grossing up" their lines, thus providing a very substantial market and earning a credit for their expenses. Some companies may carefully purchase facultative reinsurance for the primary purpose of protecting their reinsurance treaties, and thus are judiciously trying to produce a profit for the treaty in the same way they are trying to produce a profit for themselves. There may not be a right philosophy or a wrong philosophy in these areas, but the two partners would do well to have a clear understanding of the ground rules under which they are operating.

A wide variety of additional factors is studied by the reinsurer in considering a particular treaty. These would include a) the distribution of business by class, limits and geographic location; b) the type of rating structure being used—published manual rates, extensive modification of rates by experience and schedule rating, and pure judgment rating; c) standard, deviated or independent rates; d) the company's experience with loss development; e) significant changes in the book of business over the past several years; f) expansion or withdrawal from certain territories, classes or lines; g) carefully selecting terms or conditions for a proposed treaty to avoid the need to reveal adverse loss experience of the past; and finally, h) changes in the laws or court decisions or whether there is any pending legislation that might affect this particular book of business.

Punitive and Extra-Contractual Damages

Aside from those "normal" losses ordinarily contemplated by any reinsurance arrangement, two special types of losses have appeared in recent years: punitive damages and extra-contractual damages. Punitive damages are awarded by a court to a plaintiff (in addition to any compensatory damages applicable) as punishment for the defendant's wrongful acts which the court finds to be aggravated, intentional, willful or wanton in nature. Most states permit the awarding of punitive damages and provide varying standards by which culpability is judged, ranging from gross negligence to intentional and malicious conduct. In all those states, however, the defendant's punishment, rather than the plaintiff's compensation, is the motive for awarding such damages.

For insurance purposes, a distinction should be made between those punitive damages which have been awarded against the insured and those against the insurer or reinsured. There are several states which by statute or case law prohibit the insurer from providing coverage for punitive damages, because it is against public policy for an insurer to indemnify in cases where punishment is the purpose of the award. In other words, if the insurer indemnifies for the punitive damages, there is no punishment and no deterrent. Generally, primary policies do not exclude punitive damages and, thus, in the vast majority of states where coverage is not prohibited by public policy, the insurer will indemnify for such awards up to the limits of the policy. In such cases, in the absence of an exclusion of punitive damages in the reinsurance treaty, the reinsurer will respond for its share of the award. Exclusion of these punitive damages in the reinsurance contract is unusual.

For reinsurers, the real conflict arises in those cases where the insured or some third party is awarded punitive damages against the insurer or reinsured. Usually, the liability arises from the handling of a claim or defense of a lawsuit against an insured. However, there are many cases where underwriting errors or engineering and inspection errors are the basis for the award of punitive damages. Any area of the primary company's operations presents, in today's climate, a risk of exposure to liability and a punitive damage award.

There are at least three schools of thought on the question of the reinsurer's responsibility for a punitive damage award against its reinsured. Some reinsurers take the position, which is not without merit, that the reinsurance contract should not indemnify for punitive damages, because they do not arise from the insured risk. Rather, punitive damages are awarded because of the activities of the primary insurer, which are more properly covered by some form of errors and omission coverage. The other extreme is taken by many primary insurers, their position being that the reinsurer has traditionally agreed in its contract to "follow the fortunes" of the insurer and should thus share in this liability exposure. An intermediate position is that the reinsurer should indemnify for punitive damages in those cases where the reinsurer was given the opportunity to counsel with the primary company and to participate in the decision-making process which led to the award of damages.

These three approaches to punitive damage awards raise another issue, the question of extra-contractual damages in general. Extra-contractual awards are made by a court because of an insurer's liability to the insured for negligence or bad faith. The awards against the insurer in excess of policy limits may be due to liability for negligence or bad faith, and be compensatory rather than punitive. While the nature of the damages awarded may differ, the issues between the insurer and reinsurer are the same. The current thinking among a number of leading reinsurance underwriters is toward including coverage in the reinsurance treaty for such punitive and extra-contractual awards, spelling out those situations in which the reinsurance treaty would respond, the specific percentage of the award for which the treaty would respond, and including a specific premium charge for this coverage. In a freely competitive reinsurance market there will, of course, be many approaches to the solution of the punitive damage and extracontractual obligations problems.

Summary

Casualty excess of loss treaty reinsurance is one of the most difficult and challenging areas in which the reinsurer and the primary company strive to reach a mutually satisfactory arrangement. The United States is unique in having a legal and social climate which makes predictions of future losses in the casualty area nearly impossible. However the valuation is done, the two parties in reinsurance have maximum competitive freedom in reaching suitable terms and conditions. The buyer is protected by a free marketplace, while the seller is free to make a reasonable profit because "he only has to be right."

A broad range of types of casualty reinsurance is available to a primary company: facultative, quota share, working cover, and catastrophe. The first may be written on a gross or net basis to protect the primary company's exposure ceded to its treaty reinsurers. As to quota share, there are a limited number of proportional treaties in casualty lines because of difficulties in maintaining a balance between pricing and underwriting. Working excess of loss treaties usually have a low attachment point and are used when there is a real expectation of a certain number of losses affecting the treaty each year; accordingly, they also have a relatively small limit of liability for the reinsurer. In the transition from working covers to the pure risk area of catastrophe covers, there is a continuous gradation of situations in between. A hallmark of the clash (catastrophe) cover is fundamental protection to the primary company for the rare event.

The rating of casualty treaties is inexact and has almost as many techniques as underwriters. However rated, the pricing of casualty reinsurance must contain the same basic elements of cost which apply to any insurance: an amount to cover losses, an amount to cover expenses, and a profit for the owners of the reinsurer. The most difficult factor to evaluate is the loss element, for the reinsurer must make its "best guess" in identifying the average ultimate value of claims, past and future. Perhaps the crux of the difficulty lies in valuing future losses, both late reported losses and late-to-develop losses, all of which are affected by economic and social inflation. Important developments in trending losses, however, have been helpful.

There is a wide variety of rating plans which can be employed in casualty excess reinsurance. Some plans require a fixed premium but others provide for a rate per unit—on a fixed rate basis, on a manual excess basis, or by coded excess. Additionally, there are advance deposit premium plans, swing rating plans (including experience or retrospective), index clauses, and adjustments for indemnity losses.

Aside from those "normal" losses ordinarily contemplated by an reinsurance arrangement, two special types of losses have appeared in recent years: punitive damages and extra-contractual damages. While the nature of the damages awarded may differ, the issues between the insurer and reinsurer are the same and will present a challenging problem for years to come.

Reinsurance managers who are basically "gamblers," who prefer to concentrate on cash flow rather than sound underwriting, or who are undercapitalized and overextended will ultimately fall by the wayside. Those reinsurers which are financially sound, staffed by adequately trained people, and oriented toward providing a solid operation over the long run will grow, prosper, and provide a valuable service to the primary insurance industry.

* * * * * *

About the Author of Chapter 9

LeRoy J. Simon was born in St. Paul, Minnesota, on November 19, 1924. During World War II he served from 1943 to 1946 as a navigator in the South Pacific. Following military service, he continued his college studies at the University of Minnesota, receiving the B.S. Degree in 1948 and the Master of Arts Degree in statistics the following year. In 1954 he became a Fellow in the Casualty Actuarial Society.

His insurance career started with a summer job at Northwestern National Life Insurance Company while he was a student. In 1949 he was employed as statistician for the Mutual Service Casualty Insurance Company in St. Paul, becoming its casualty actuary during the next eight years. In 1957 he joined the Insurance Company of North America as assistant actuary, becoming actuary for the company during his eight years of service there. In 1965 he became the first general manager of the National Insurance Actuarial and Statistical Association, and six years later was appointed vice president of the Prudential Property and Casualty Insurance Company. In June, 1973, he became senior vice president of his current employer, Prudential Reinsurance Company, where he is responsible for all underwriting operations.

In addition to his employment contributions, Mr. Simon has written and spoken extensively on insurance, research, and actuarial matters in this country and internationally. He is a member of the American Academy of Actuaries and the International Actuarial Association, of which he presently heads the U.S. delegation on its Conseil de Direction. He was a charter member of the Society of Insurance Research and served as its president in 1973. He served on the board of directors of the Casualty Actuarial Society and was its president for the 1971-72 year. For many years he has served on the faculty of the Reinsurance Seminar and the NAIC Commissioner Seminar, both conducted by The College of Insurance.

10

Special Covers and Classes

by E.J.W. Lovett*
E. Ray Fosse**
Albert W. Davis***

Special Covers

In the great majority of cases the reinsurance contract takes its origin directly from the original contract concluded by the original insurer. It is logical, therefore, to find wordings, articles and clauses in such contracts which not only confirm this origin but effectively link and limit the liability of the reinsurer under the reinsurance contract to no more than that of the insurer under the original insurance contract. There is an abundance of phrases employed, such as "terms and conditions as original," "to pay as may be paid under the original insurance," and "to follow the fortunes of the ceding company," among others.

Types of Special Covers

As already described elsewhere in this book, there is a wide variety of different ways of effecting reinsurance. These may differ widely also in their effect and effectiveness in protecting a ceding company. However, the objective in each case is, in principle, the same, namely that following the occurrence of an insured loss, the insurer which issued the

* The SPECIAL COVERS section of this chapter was written by E. J. W. Lovett, Managing Director, Alexander Howden Insurance Brokers Ltd., 22, Billiter Street, London EC3M 2SA, England.
** The REINSURING CROP-HAIL INSURANCE section of this chapter was written by E. Ray Fosse, Executive Secretary, Crop-Hail Insurance Actuarial Association, 209 West Jackson Boulevard, Chicago, Illinois 60606.
*** The REINSURING SURETY and REINSURING FINANCIAL GUARANTEES AND FIDELITY INSURANCE sections of this chapter were written by Albert W. Davis, CPCU, Vice President in charge of the Bond Department, North American Reinsurance Corporation, 100 East 46 Street, New York, New York 10017.

insurance may recover a part of that loss from a reinsurer. It is the type of reinsurance contract that predetermines the amount or proportion of the loss that the reinsurer is required to pay. There is, however, a group of reinsurance arrangements which is unique in that it relates to what might be termed the "housekeeping" of insurance. Such arrangements may be referred to as "special covers." In practice a variety of terms and names may be encountered, but it is important to bear in mind that they do not represent some esoteric or magically new form of reinsurance. In fact, they originate in a somewhat special area of operation of an insurer or reinsurer. These special covers can usually be identified as relating to one or another of the following areas:

1. Errors of judgment or control by the reinsured in conducting its normal insurance business.

2. Financial loss incurred by an insurer or reinsurer, secondary to but arising out of the occurrence of a normal insurance loss.

3. Additional costs incurred by an insurer to minimize the subsequent effects on it following and arising out of the occurrence of a normal loss. Such costs may be termed a "tertiary" loss.

4. Optimization of the results of reinsurance arrangements.

Before considering these areas in detail, it is essential to make a point of fundamental importance. While it is always possible to consider any form of reinsurance contract on a theoretical basis, there are certain essential considerations which will limit what can be arranged in practical terms. The main limitation is whether any reinsurance market exists at all for the proposition in question; secondly, if there is a market, whether it is sufficient for the placement required; thirdly, whether the contractual terms agreeable to the parties are economically worthwhile for the reinsured. Terms and conditions that may be satisfactory for the reinsurer (and thus to establish a market) may not be so for the reinsured, and vice versa. This is obviously true in general reinsurance practice but it also applies when considering special covers.

The available market for the placement of special covers is in many cases substantially smaller than the market for "normal" reinsurance contracts. This, in practice, may be offset by the fact that the amount of cover being sought is likewise restricted. It is obvious that placement of a cover of $50,000 is always easier to complete than $50,000,000, whatever the nature of the contract, assuming that any market exists at all.

ERRORS OF JUDGMENT OR CONTROL

In broad terms an insurer arranges its overall reinsurance program on the basis of various criteria, such as the market requirements for gross underwriting limits or its own need to restrict exposures to certain net limits per risk, per event, or per time period. If all assessments made were correct, then a normal gross loss experience might reasonably be expected to give rise to a normal net loss experience. However, unexpected contingencies, errors of judgment, or errors of control in handling and operating a portfolio of business can in themselves give rise to an abnormal net loss experience. This is notwithstanding the fact that the gross loss experience might be deemed to be normal, and the reinsurance arrangements in force adequate for the reinsured's normal needs.

Firstly, an example of error judgment may be useful. A reinsurance program — consisting of proportional as well as excess of loss contracts — may be designed to leave a reinsured with a net loss on any one risk not exceeding whatever sum it considers itself able to support in financial and underwriting terms. The assessment of such a net loss, especially in the property branch, is frequently based on the probable maximum loss on one risk. Whether the exposure is expressed in such terms as "probable maximum loss" or "amount subject," the fact remains that human judgment is applied in moving from the sum insured to a lower figure which the reinsured may reasonably and safely retain net for its own account. It happens with regrettable frequency that such assessments are inaccurate, and often extraordinarily so. There are many cases on record where assessment of the probable maximum loss was as low as 10% of the sum insured, when the loss that eventually occurred destroyed 100% of the property. It is in the case of large risks, too, that greatest pressure is exerted on insurers to underwrite large lines and thus to assess the probable maximum loss at the lowest possible figure. Consequently, when an error of judgment does occur, the effects can be serious.

The effect of an error of judgment in accurately assessing the probable maximum loss on any particular risk falls both on a reinsured and its reinsurers. In the case of the latter, the reinsurer may recover its reinsurance loss for any abnormal loss so arising, either within the year of account (e.g., by affecting the profit commission payable) or at renewal in the renewal terms. For the reinsured, however, the abnormal loss experience might prove to have serious effects on its finances. One of the most common approaches in mitigating this is to effect excess of loss reinsurance on a "per risk" basis. While per risk excess reinsurance is a normal component of many reinsurance programs, there may be special reasons for taking out additional and more specific per risk protection for judgment errors. In such cases, the deductible is fixed at the level of (or somewhat above) the normal probable maximum loss amount fixed by the reinsured as its normal maximum retention. The amount of cover required would be calculated as a function of the minimum percentage of probable maximum loss assessed by the reinsured. For example, some companies employ a minimum of 20%, together with the maximum exposure that is likely to arise in practice. The rating of such covers is based on a number of factors, such as past experience, potential exposure, and the type of portfolio in question.

Turning now to errors of control, there are various instances in which these may occur. Two examples may be cited, one from fire insurance and the other from casualty. Both cases illustrate how an insurer can acquire an accumulated liability in excess of its underwriting limits, the adverse effect of which can be minimized by arranging special reinsurance facilities.

Overlining. When an insurer sets underwriting limits for its operations in a particular class of business, it is possible for those limits to be exceeded when business is underwritten through different agencies and/or branches of the company. Until controlled properly, such overlapping would produce a combined net exposure in excess of the established underwriting limits. In fire insurance, "overlining" is the term used to describe such excess of net exposures. It should be possible to eliminate such excesses by rigid control over the way in which the business is written: placing restrictions on underwriting limits, and arranging facultative reinsurance as soon as the overlining is discovered. In practical terms, however, it is difficult to make such control completely effective. Indeed, it may not be practicable or economical to take steps that are fully effective.

Whether additional reinsurance protection is required for the above case depends largely on existing reinsurance. If existing reinsurance contains a warranty for the control of underwriting limits, then the effects of any overlining would fall on the reinsured. To protect the reinsured against such effects would require special reinsurance, either on an excess of loss basis or on a special facultative/obligatory basis. Alternatively, if the underwriting limits were not enforced by a warranty, then the effect of any inadvertent overlining would fall on any reinsurers. In practice, it is likely that the problem of overlining would be assessed and dealt with as between the reinsured and the reinsurers. They would consider the normal reinsurance program in effect — in light of actual results, of potential exposure, and of the degree of effective control displayed by the reinsured over its operations.

Accumulation of Liability. In casualty insurance, underwriting limits can be exceeded by the accumulation of liability illustrated by travel accident policies. The unexpected accumulations arise when such policies are granted by different agencies or branch offices to different people who coincidentally travel on the same aircraft. While control of such accumulations is practically impossible to achieve, the loss can be protected by reinsurance, traditionally by excess of loss reinsurance on a "per-event" basis. Such covers frequently include not only personal travel accident insurances but also any personal accident insurances written on individual life or group schemes, as well as lives covered under life policies issued by the insurer.

It is possible to envisage other areas of abnormal loss to a reinsurer from errors of control, of omissions, and the like. But in arranging additional or special reinsurance protection, there is a limit to what is economic and reasonably worthwhile. All such areas are concerned with abnormal loss experience arising from errors or omissions of the insurer but where the gross loss experience may be considered to be "normal." Whether special protection is to be sought to minimize the abnormal loss depends on the probability of the event's occurring, coupled with the scale of the effect of it. If the probability is high but the scale is small, then little action would seem necessary. If the probability is low but the scale is high, then special steps would seem essential. If both the probability and the scale were high, then it is necessary to examine the whole reinsurance program, rather than merely take special steps to plug a gap that in these circumstances would seem to be fundamental and not merely a weakness in the overall reinsurance program.

SECONDARY LOSS

As already discussed, the occurrence of a loss under a policy or policies issued by an insurer may give rise to recoveries from its reinsurers which still leave it with a net retained loss. That loss may or may not be aggravated by the insurer's own errors or omissions, and the aggravation itself may or may not be reduced by the operation of a special cover. In practice this net retained loss to the reinsured may be further increased as a direct consequence of additional costs or expenses. Such a "secondary loss" may be defined as the additional costs or expenses (including loss of revenue) that the insurer is obliged to incur or suffer following the occurrence of an insured loss and following a recovery from its reinsurers.

Reinstatement Premium. A secondary loss is illustrated by the operation of certain types of excess of loss property contracts. When a loss occurs which causes a recovery from excess of loss reinsurers, the reinsured is required to pay to reinsurers an additional premium to reinstate the cover diminished by the loss recovery. This "reinstatement premium" is an additional charge on the reinsured directly consequent upon the occurrence of the loss and is additional to that proportion of the original loss which the reinsured has to bear. In general, such additional premium bears a proportion to the amount recovered from reinsurers and not to the net amount retained by the reinsured. In the distant past when amounts of cover, premium volumes and rates for excess of loss contracts were more modest than they are today, such reinstatement premiums were of modest dimensions. In some cases it was not unknown for reinstatement to be free, without any additional premium required. Nowadays, however, the situation is materially different: the initial reinsurance premium payable for property catastrophe covers is substantial, and the method of calculating the reinstatement premium is designed to assist reinsurers to recoup their losses rather than to ease the position of the reinsured. Reinstatement premiums may thus represent a heavy burden on a reinsured which already had to bear its proportion of the original loss.

Additional charges such as reinstatement premiums relate simply and directly to the occurrence of an insured loss. Accordingly, liability to pay any reinstatement premium is itself reinsurable, and contracts to reimburse the reinsured for reinstatement premium payments have become quite normal practice. Since the amount at risk is modest in comparison with the limit of liability under the original contract to which the additional premium relates, there should be little difficulty in finding a market for the protection. Similarly, since the cover for the reinstatement premium has characteristics similar to those under the original excess of loss contract, the terms and conditions are often closely similar.

Where the original excess of loss contract provides for more than one reinstatement, it is clear again that further protection may be obtained to cover the liability for further reinstatement premiums. The terms and conditions for a second or further reinstatement premium would clearly depend on the terms and conditions of the original contract, but taking account of the fact that the second reinstatement premium cover could only be called upon to pay in the event the first reinstatement premium cover is exhausted.

Collecting Commission. Another example of additional costs falling on a reinsured following a loss can be found in the marine market. Here it is not uncommon in facultative hull business for brokers to charge the reinsured a collecting commission on the amount of the claim collected from reinsurers. In such circumstances the reinsured may reinsure that collecting commission as part of the hull facultative reinsurance and thus with the same reinsurers which accepted the hull risk.

Reduced Reimbursement. The concept of secondary loss affecting an insurer can be extended into many other different aspects of insurance and reinsurance operation. For example, it is not unknown for reinsurers to agree to return a predetermined part of the reinsurance premium subject to there being no loss under the contract. In other words, the net premium of the reinsurance to the reinsured would be augmented by the occurrence of a loss. Such increase in cost can be looked upon as a contingent expense arising from an insured loss and in principle can be considered for protection under a special cover. The amount of cover would naturally be relatively modest, and the terms would be related to the terms of the original contract. A somewhat parallel example is to be encountered in certain proportional treaties where the calculation of the profit commission represents a specially high proportion of the reimbursement of costs to the reinsured. It is not unknown for a reinsured to reinsure under a special cover the profit commission in such treaties. Here again the essential factors of reinsurance are met: that the loss relates to an original insured loss or losses and that as a result the reinsured suffers a contingent loss, either through incurring additional expense or through suffering a reduced reimbursement from reinsurers.

Increased Rates. Another example is to be seen in certain excess of loss contracts where the rating is based on burning or claims cost and provides that, if the claims recovered from reinsurers exceed a certain figure, the reinsured is required to pay an increased rate. This increase is usually proportional to the aggravation in claims cost, up to a predetermined maximum. Again, such increased cost arises directly out of insured and reinsured losses and as such are, in principle, capable of forming the object of a special cover. In general, it must be repeated that whether such cover is available and whether the terms are attractive or even economical will depend on market availability at the time.

There are those in the markets who argue that a reinsured should not be entitled to reinsure additional costs in every case, in particular citing the example of reinsuring the profit commission under proportional treaties. Perhaps there are cases where the arrangement of a special cover could be against general market interests and not in accordance with strict reinsurance principles. Some care must be necessary but the availability of any market for the cover will decide whether or not placement is effected.

To summarize, any reinsured will have a legitimate insurable interest in respect of any additional costs or any reduction of revenue which arise directly from the occurrence of an original insured loss or losses. Such insurable interest may be made the object of a special cover. The examples given are not exhaustive and others will occur from time to time, especially arising out of changes that develop in the way that reinsurance is handled.

TERTIARY LOSS

The primary loss to a reinsured is that which is suffered directly from the occurrence of an original insured loss, after normal reinsurance recoveries and after taking account of any aggravation by virtue of errors or omission, whether or not such errors are in turn the subject of special reinsurance. The secondary loss is the further extra expense or loss or revenue that must be borne by the reinsured and which arises directly from the occurrence of an insured loss. What further loss, then, can indirectly be incurred by the reinsured? Tertiary loss is defined as any further additional cost which the reinsured may choose to incur after an insured loss under an original contract. Although a tertiary loss is still further removed from the original loss than is the secondary loss, nevertheless the tertiary area is one in which judgment can be exercised by prudent management to save expense and mitigate long-term effects from heavy losses. While primary and secondary losses are involuntary to the reinsured, tertiary losses are incurred voluntarily.

Take again the example of excess of loss property catastrophe contracts. It is common nowadays for such contracts to have clauses restricting the number of reinstatements and establishing the cost of those reinstatements. Regardless of such terms for reinstatement, it is perfectly clear that should a loss exhaust the first amount of cover, after reinstatement thereof the reinsured is left in a worse position than previously. If the contract specified only one reinstatement, then after the first total loss the reinsured is left with cover for only one further total loss; if provision is for two reinstatements, then the reinsured is left with only two amounts of cover. The reinsured is then, at least potentially, more exposed than before. Two choices remain open: either to wait for a further loss to happen and then decide whether fresh cover is needed, or to seek additional cover at once before further losses occur.

The question of arranging for further additional reinstatements, either under the existing excess of loss contract or by an entirely separate contract, and the advisability of either course of action will depend on a number of factors: the length of time still to run to the expiry of the main contract, and the anticipated exposure to further loss, among others.

Nevertheless, should a further substantial loss occur, any additional cover then for further reinstatements is likely to be more expensive than before the occurrence of such further losses. The choice is simple:

1) whether to take cover right away which may be cheaper now than later but which also may ultimately be unnecessary, or

2) to wait and see, either saving the cost of the cover if not required or paying a great deal more after the additional cover becomes essential.

Prudence tends to favour the early taking out of cover rather than a philosophy of wait and see.

It is such attempts, voluntarily made, to avoid an increase of costs or to minimize the longer term effects of losses on reinsurance costs that may be termed the area of tertiary loss. Inevitably, anticipation and applied judgment are involved, and the loss or additional expense are at best contingent. One other factor needs to be borne in mind: the insurance portfolio of the reinsured and its own particular reinsurance program cannot be taken in isolation. The discussion centers on large losses that affect reinsurers seriously; undoubtedly such losses will also affect other insurers and in turn their reinsurers. Accordingly, whole markets are likely to be affected, with the result that the terms and conditions and availability of additional cover may ultimately be influenced less by the results of any one reinsured's own contracts than by the overall pattern of losses. Prudent action by a reinsured is thus based on an appraisal not only of the further results under its own portfolio of business but also of the general trend affecting the similar portfolio of other insurers.

To summarize, tertiary loss arises from insured losses causing an insurer to decide voluntarily to arrange special covers or additional protection, with the object of minimizing the ultimate additional cost to itself. Such covers are by their nature transitory to meet the special circumstances arising out of specific events rather than being normal contracts that continue from year to year.

OPTIMIZATION

The straightforward reinsurance of reinsurance business accepted by a reinsurer and passed on by it in the form of a retrocession can be considered as normal reinsurance business and in no way a form of special cover. However, when the retrocession is effected on a special or selective basis, then perhaps it is right to consider it as coming within the scope of special covers, especially when the object of effecting the retrocession is to optimize the results for the reinsurer.

Selective reinsurance of part of a risk or part of a portfolio, for reasons other than ordinary reinsurance practice, may be considered to be a form of special cover. An example is selecting from a portfolio its worst hazard, e.g., earthquake from a fire portfolio, or substandard lives from a life portfolio. Such selective reinsurance may be effected when the original reinsurance was accepted or subsequently in the light of information received that the risk was inferior to that initially envisaged. It may also be effected when the reinsurer changes its underwriting policy and affects the retention of business already on the books, or in the light of a change of external circumstances affecting the portfolio reinsured. Similarly in certain markets it is not unknown for excess of loss reinsurers to reinsure part of their acceptance on a contract, either on a first loss or on a second loss basis, and sometimes on both, achieving a retrocession perhaps at a net cost less than the original acceptance and thus giving a guaranteed underwriting profit. Whether this retroceding is strictly in accordance with the traditional principles of reinsurance is open to question, but it may be sound commercially.

Another example of optimization is often encountered in proportional treaties, particularly where they are used as a basis for reciprocal exchanges. The volume of such exchanges is frequently based on the relative profitability of the proportional treaties. Thus, a drop in the profitability of an insurer's treaty can bring about either a corresponding drop in the volume of business earned on a reciprocal basis or its complete loss. The insurer thus wishes to optimize the results of its proportional treaty, and especially protect it from the effects of abnormal loss experience. It is not uncommon therefore to effect excess of loss reinsurance, to protect only the reinsurers on the proportional treaty on a per event basis (sometimes cover is sought on a stop loss basis). This will minimize the effect of individual large losses or loss events on the profitability of the treaty and thus help to preserve the amount and quality of the reciprocity received. It is not unusual for the cost of such protection to be charged to the proportional reinsurers. Not infrequently the latter object to this charge since they feel no need for the excess protection, the cost of which merely reduces the profit they receive under the contract. In some cases the cost of the excess protection is borne by the reinsured and not passed on to reinsurers. Such excess of loss cover can be very effective, especially in localized and highly unbalanced portfolios.

While it would seem perfectly legitimate to arrange special covers to optimize either a risk or the whole portfolio of business underwritten by a reinsurer, by selective reinsurance in one manner or another, there would appear to be some forms of protection that strike at the roots of the long established rule of practice that proportional reinsurers follow the fortunes of the reinsured. Nevertheless a reinsurer has a right, and perhaps a technical and commercial responsibility, to examine its portfolio of risks and seek to take whatever action it deems appropriate by way of retrocession to optimize its results. It is neither unknown nor common for an insurer, when placing a reinsurance, to require a warranty that no retrocession whatsoever is effected by the reinsurer without prior approval of the reinsured.

Other Possibilities

The world of reinsurance is never static. It is undoubtedly true to say that new types of special arrangements or special covers, however they may be called, are coming into existence every day. Indeed, generally the term "special cover" can reasonably be applied to any reinsurance that is not of a relatively standardized or commonplace nature. Furthermore, thanks to the fact that the reinsurance business operates relatively free from regulation, permitting the reinsurance contract to be established on almost any basis that may be agreed between the parties, the possibilities for special cover are limitless. Inevitably, therefore, special covers not touched upon here will be devised with considerable skill, for special circumstances always demand special treatment.

Take, for example, the decision of an insurer to close down part or all of its insurance operations. To close its books at the earliest possible date, it would be extremely beneficial to reinsure the run-off of the portfolio of policies still in force when active operations are terminated. This reinsurance could also apply to the losses outstanding at that date, that is to say, a reinsurance of the reserve for outstanding losses. A somewhat similar arrangement is to be seen in the closure, by reinsuring forward, of the accounts of Lloyd's Underwriters after the closure of the third year of each year of account.

Exceptional circumstances can also arise outside the control of a reinsured which have the effect of increasing its liability beyond the limitations of the policy wording. Extra contractual obligations relating to the levying against the reinsured of punitive damages are one example. Another example is derived from excess judgments where the settlement to the original insured goes beyond the policy limits. Such obligations and judgments may be made the subject of special covers.

Summary

Special covers are something more than a mere predetermined apportionment of an original loss between a reinsured and its reinsurers.

Any additional or contingent losses, any additional expenses or costs, or any reduction of revenue or income that may be incurred by a reinsured arising directly or indirectly out of insured losses may be the subject matter of some form of special cover in reinsurance or retrocession. Likewise, the latter may form the basis of some program for the optimization of results under business accepted. In particular, all such covers follow the basic principles of reinsurance. In practice, they vary with and are essentially dependent on the particular circumstances of the particular situation.

The subject of special covers is specialized, requiring the attention of experts, and is rarely static. Just as economic and trade demands have their varying influence on how insurance is handled, so too does the requirement for special covers alter and develop in the light of changes in reinsurance practice.

*   *   *   *   *   *

About the Author of Special Covers

E. J. W. Lovett was born in London on January 2, 1923 and was educated at Westminster School and Trinity College Cambridge. He served in the Royal Signals during and after World War II, being discharged from the army in 1947 as a captain.

In that year, he joined the treaty department of Sterling Offices Limited, an established firm of reinsurance brokers, and travelled extensively for the company. He became an Associate of the Chartered Insurance Institute and has lectured on reinsurance at the College of Insurance in Great Britain.

He was managing director of Sterling Offices when it was acquired by Alexander Howden in 1974. In 1976, Howden integrated its United Kingdom broking operatings, including Sterling Offices Ltd., into a single company, Alexander Howden Insurance Brokers Limited, of which he was appointed a managing director. His special interests are corporate planning and developments in computer operations in the field of reinsurance.

Reinsuring Crop-Hail Insurance

by E. Ray Fosse*

Crop-Hail Insurance

INSURING CROP HAZARDS

The hazard of hail, or vulnerability to hail damage, varies from crop to crop and by stage of vegetative growth as to any given crop. At one extreme, severe hail damage can be sustained on some crops, at given stages of growth, without any identifiable reduction in yield. To illustrate, much of the winter wheat crop is systematically grazed extensively in the early stages of spring growth. Leaves of a corn plant no more than twelve to eighteen inches in height may be removed with little or no effect on yield, simply because those early leaves constitute such a small portion of the total "factory" from which the grain is produced. The other extreme is best illustrated with tree fruit, the grade and value of which can be affected by even very light hail. Since the leaf of tobacco is the product of the plant, any loss of its leaf area is a direct reduction in the amount of product.

Damaging hail may be manifested in three general categories. The plants may be totally destroyed, a good example of which is just-emerged soybean or cotton plants; or, damage may be only to the extent of removing leaves (defoliation) or destroying portions of plants. Finally, the product or fruit of the plant may be affected directly, causing either total destruction or disposition beyond reach of the harvestor, or a reduction in the grade or quality of the product (tree fruit).

The extent or amount of loss from hail is expressed as a percent

* Executive Secretary, Crop-Hail Insurance Actuarial Association, 209 West Jackson Boulevard, Chicago, Illinois 60606.

reduction in yield of the product. (In the case of fruit or vegetables, loss may be more of grade reduction than of reduction in tonnage.) The amount payable is obtained by taking such percent (less any applicable excess or deductible provision) of the amount of insurance. Thus, there is a 100 % coinsurance feature inherent in the hail insurance policy.

"Crop-hail" is the term commonly used as an abbreviation for insurance on growing crops against direct loss from damage caused by hail. For some crops, primarily tobacco, loss caused by wind is a covered peril when wind is simultaneously accompanied by hail which causes loss of 5 % or more. Loss by fire is also covered in standard hail policies, in most states for an indivisible premium. Kansas, Washington, and Oregon require that fire coverage be optional, but most hail policies in those states are nevertheless written with such coverage.

Insurance on a crop is placed by the acre. Up to the reasonably expected value of the crop per acre is specified in the application, which serves as the declaration page of the policy. Generally, except in the midwest states, the hail policy is subject to a 5 % minimum loss provision. This requires that no loss is payable unless the ascertained loss per acre is 5 % or more; when the loss equals or exceeds 5 %, the whole loss is paid. (This is often referred to as the "franchise clause.")

The policy may be written subject to a variety of optional provisions for self-retention. In crop-hail parlance these provisions are called "excess over loss" or XS forms. XS forms of coverage are elected mostly in the higher rated areas; however, even in many of those areas the majority of the business is written for full coverage. A commonly used form providing 10 % self-retention is the XS10IP, which is different if not unique in the insurance business. The "IP" (increasing payment) form provides two unusual features. One is that once the ascertained loss is 70 % of the crop, the self-retention provision begins to disappear for higher percentages of loss, up to 80 %, until finally 100 % of the loss can be paid out. The other unusual feature requires, for losses above 80 % of the crop, the payment of more than the loss (up to the face amount). Also, once a loss exceeds 10 % of the crop during the policy period, the self-retention does not apply to any subsequent losses during that period, and the gross ascertained percent of such subsequent losses is then paid without any reduction. For example, a loss of 11 % on one occurrence followed by another loss of an identical amount during the same policy period would require the insurance payment of 1 % for the first loss and 11 % for the subsequent loss.

The precise language from the XS10IP form itself follows:

EXCESS OVER 10% LOSS—INCREASING PAYMENT PROVISION—(Symbol: XS10IP)

This Company shall have no liability, and the insured shall not make claim for loss to any acre of the insured crop until the ascertained percentage of loss occasioned by perils insured against exceeds 10% thereof. The amount then payable on any loss or losses shall be determined by the percentage of loss per acre which is in excess of such 10%; except that whenever the ascertained percentage of loss exceeds 70%, the percent of loss payable as obtained above shall be increased an additional 1% for each percent the ascertained percentage of loss exceeds 70%. In no event shall the total payment per acre exceed the amount of insurance applying.

To illustrate the operation of the XS10IP provision, if the loss is 65%, the award is 65% less 10%, or 55%. For a loss in excess of 70%, the self-retention of 10% is decreased one percentage point for each percentage point the loss exceeds 70%, up to 80%. For a loss in excess of 80%, the self-retention becomes an increasing payment feature: the insurance payment is increased one percentage point for each percentage point the loss exceeds 80%. For example, if the ascertained loss is 85%, the award is 90%, which compensates the crop owner for 5% more than the measured crop loss. The additional 5% is for extra expense of harvesting a severely damaged crop. The following illustrates the operation of the XS10IP provision.

If the ascertained percent of hail loss is:	The insurance award is:
5%	0
10%	0
11%	1%

(For any loss over 10% of the crop, and up to 70%, deduct 10% of the loss to arrive at the insurance award.)

70%	60%
71%	62%
72%	64%
73%	66%
74%	68%
75%	70%
76%	72%
77%	74%
78%	76%
79%	78%
80%	80%
81%	82%

If the ascertained percent of hail loss is:	The insurance award is:
82%	84%
83%	86%
84%	88%
85%	90%
86%	92%
87%	94%
88%	96%
89%	98%
90% to 100%	100%

The scope of hail insurance activity in the U.S. is, in a word, universal. Hail insurance is written in the forty-eight contiguous states on about 200 crops by about 200 companies. These companies vary in size and capacity from the giant multiple-line company to single-state insurers and local mutuals. While all U.S. crop-hail writings amount to only about 2/3 of 1% of the total property and casualty insurance premiums, and for most companies would not exceed 3 to 5% of their premium writings, some few companies write nothing but hail. Of the 200 or more companies (out of 1400 property and casualty companies in the U.S.), perhaps 80% of the premiums are written by 50 companies (or groups of companies under common ownership and/or management). The largest single writer in the U.S. has about 8 to 9% of the business, operating in only eight midwest states. In short, there is vigorous competition.

Some 80% of crop-hail insurance is concentrated in twelve states and about 90% in nineteen states. More than 90% of the liability currently assumed annually is on five major crops: corn and maize, cereal grain crops, soybeans, tobacco, and cotton, in that order. For the period 1948-78 paid losses have averaged about 60% of earned premiums.

In 1978 an estimated 600,000 hail policies were written, with an average policy premium of $606. Annually, about 20% of the policies in force incur a paid claim. Also, about 20% of claims reported (filed) are not paid, because either no actually measurable loss was sustained or else the ascertained amount of loss fell below either the minimum or deductible, according to policy type. In some areas, 3 to 5% of policies normally incur two or more losses in the same season. Exhibits 1 and 2 show distribution of the U.S. hail business by state and crop.

There are financial aspects of the hail insurance business unlike those in other property and casualty lines, and a reinsurer can ignore these only at great costs. Historically, the time for paying premium was

EXHIBIT 1
Industry Crop-Hail Results
1978

State	Rank by Premium Income	1978 Premiums	1978 Losses	1978 Loss Ratio	1977 Premiums	1977 Loss Ratio
Alabama	32	149 520	41 019	27 43	209 790	59 53
Arizona	18	3 873 870	511 640	13 21	3 852 501	25 50
Arkansas	24	2 393 753	1 986 383	82 98	2 749 924	37 22
California	31	416 830	155 989	37 42	728 089	1 07
Colorado	21	3 452 476	2 397 513	69 44	3 850 865	76 88
Connecticut	38	41 970	450	1 07	105 082	13 06
Delaware	44	3 201			2 802	
Florida	30	848 867	418 946	49 35	886 901	60 62
Georgia	19	3 701 262	2 439 609	65 91	3 730 799	78 74
Idaho	15	5 212 166	3 782 765	72 58	4 858 784	52 01
Illinois	2	47 307 623	29 969 306	63 35	48 264 804	45 68
Indiana	11	8 443 994	1 902 986	22 54	7 958 265	60 81
Iowa	1	61 659 071	69 935 235	113 42	60 018 792	61 16
Kansas	6	18 287 882	9 478 466	51 83	19 150 521	67 20
Kentucky	13	6 980 040	4 308 444	61 73	7 842 561	80 14
Louisiana	45	2 388			9 299	18 52
Maine	46	1 878			2 974	27 64
Maryland	35	62 506	8 347	13 35	79 756	3 74
Massachusetts	42	7 324			8 842	14 22
Michigan	27	1 906 416	292 929	15 37	1 884 480	33 10
Minnesota	4	28 791 516	29 423 585	102 20	27 041 612	58 51
Mississippi	33	111 462	24 599	22 07	149 790	34 66
Missouri	12	7 642 033	5 754 427	75 30	8 479 408	68 57
Montana	9	13 070 916	17 192 616	131 53	9 373 737	31 59
Nebraska	3	30 922 032	24 926 194	80 61	29 066 167	84 43
Nevada	36	53 873	7 350	13 64	6 481	
New Hampshire		0	—	—	448	
New Jersey	43	3 460			13 260	75 41
New Mexico	25	2 183 335	3 656 660	167 48	2 262 319	53 14
New York	37	44 671	43 114	96 51	42 629	66
North Carolina	7	17 748 695	7 226 061	40 71	14 350 514	91 54
North Dakota	5	28 744 532	11 895 351	41 38	21 067 246	111 95
Ohio	22	3 206 815	476 778	14 87	3 150 209	51 31
Oklahoma	17	4 491 261	1 175 505	26 17	5 356 506	29 39
Oregon	28	1 370 524	534 085	38 97	693 307	62 87
Pennsylvania	39	34 145	8 352	24 46	39 077	34 93
Rhode Island	47	350			1 350	
South Carolina	16	4 584 865	1 579 100	34 44	4 516 173	73 98
South Dakota	10	10 204 554	9 351 845	91 64	8 429 269	66 83
Tennessee	26	1 956 672	1 203 193	61 49	2 173 342	76 91
Texas	8	16 077 313	10 964 389	68 20	24 603 369	45 90
Utah	34	72 572	7 544	10 40	32 950	69 41
Vermont	41	9 158	8 190	89 43	11 080	
Virginia	23	2 839 536	2 227 371	78 44	2 939 147	72 46
Washington	20	3 697 591	1 528 630	41 34	2 299 918	41 33
West Virginia	40	11 833			6 191	
Wisconsin	14	5 836 003	2 296 211	39 35	5 628 193	83 40
Wyoming	29	1 319 099	874 159	66 27	1 033 740	184 16
TOTAL		$349 781 853	$260 015 336	74.34	$338 963 263	63.99

Premiums and losses not available for inclusion in 1978 report have been estimated as less than 1% of total.

1978 CHIAA 306Y

EXHIBIT 2
United States

All Crops			Crop			
All Losses			All Forms Except CNP* and MPCI*			1977

Crop	Liability (000)	Earned Premiums (000)	Paid Losses (000)	Loss Ratio Pct.	Ave. Rate	Loss Cost
001 Wheat	869 994	45 600	27 499	60	5 24	3 16
002 Barley	196 796	8 971	7 928	88	4 56	4 03
003 Rye	2 618	137	118	86	5 23	4 52
004 Oats	108 678	4 790	3 651	76	4 41	3 36
005 Flax	16 406	785	895	114	4 78	5 46
006 Corn Grain	2 272 248	56 003	29 271	52	2 46	1 29
007 Corn Ensilage	537	26	23	91	4 78	4 34
008 Buckwheat	214	13	11	87	6 08	5 29
010 Soybeans	1 115 889	38 402	24 377	63	3 44	2 18
013 Popcorn	4 887	194	121	63	3 96	2 48
014 Sweet Corn	8 269	187	46	24	2 26	55
015 Rice	32 398	409	116	28	1 26	36
016 Emher	27	2	5	289	5 96	17 25
018 Other Sorghum	716	21	53	257	2 91	7 47
019 Milo Maize	93 073	2 740	1 343	49	2 94	1 44
023 Sunflowers	68 892	3 890	4 397	113	5 65	6 38
024 Alfalfa Hay	1 583	57	29	51	3 57	1 83
025 Clover Hay	31	1	**	43	2 25	96
028 Cotton	465 661	19 276	8 912	46	4 14	1 91
029 Cotton LSTP	17 372	740	143	19	4 26	82
030 Tobacco A	92 952	5 826	3 938	68	6 27	4 24
031 Tobacco B	1 956	45			2 31	
032 Tobacco C	136 369	7 532	6 044	80	5 52	4 43
033 Tobacco D	405 972	15 427	12 798	83	3 80	3 15
034 Tobacco E	6 630	290	199	69	4 37	3 00
035 Tobacco F	7 243	662	467	71	9 13	6 44
036 Tobacco G	2	**	1	525	5 73	30 05
040 Apples	16 154	765	1 016	133	4 74	6 29
041 Peaches	3 660	244	278	114	6 67	7 59
042 Pears	1 786	76	132	175	4 24	7 42
043 Cherries	655	23	20	87	3 58	3 13
044 Plums	2 551	148	58	39	5 82	2 25
045 Apricots	60	3		2	4 45	07
046 Oranges	24				1 00	
049 Pecans	43	1			3 00	
050 Grapes	567	23	5	24	3 98	95
052 Strawberries	239	12	2	20	5 03	1 02
053 Cranberries	17	1			4 24	
054 Blueberries	70	2			3 35	
060 Peas Seed	17 005	598	171	29	3 52	1 01
061 Peas GPC	4 903	225	141	63	4 59	2 88
062 Beans Seed	22 611	971	690	71	4 29	3 05
063 Beans GPC	1 751	58	6	11	3 29	35
065 Peanuts	1 366	46	2	4	3 39	13
066 Potatoes	63 994	1 274	648	51	1 99	1 01
067 Onions	2 715	125	54	43	4 60	1 99
068 Beets	9				1 99	
069 Carrots	618	9	2	22	1 52	33
071 Sugar Beets	4 616	229	180	79	4 97	3 90
072 Watermelons	2 320	116	82	71	5 01	3 54
073 Cantaloupes	705	70	38	54	9 94	5 34
074 Cucumbers	442	23	18	79	5 30	4 18
075 Squash	47	3		13	6 54	84
076 Pumpkins	86	6		4	6 95	28
077 Tomatoes	7 860	381	329	86	4 85	4 19

EXHIBIT 2 (Continued)

Crop	Liability (000)	Earned Premiums (000)	Paid Losses (000)	Loss Ratio Pct.	Ave. Rate	Loss Cost
078 Tomato Plants	105	6			6 01	
079 Peppers	4 462	159	27	17	3 56	61
081 Eggplant	485	18	4	25	3 66	91
082 Cabbage	1 137	39	22	56	3 45	1 93
083 Lettuce	368	12			3 31	
084 Spinach	75	3			4 59	
086 Mustard	1 680	154	182	118	9 19	10 82
101 Hay	894	29		1	3 24	03
103 Wht sml grn mix	3 301	92	8	9	2 78	24
104 Millet	1 264	93	63	68	7 37	4 99
111 Clover Seed	85	3			3 43	
163 Sweet Potatoes	13				2 16	
167 Onion Seed	615	16	6	39	2 52	98
176 Wheatgrass Seed	302	33			10 76	
177 Mint	3 151	31	1	2	1 00	02
178 Bromegrass Seed	47	3			7 18	
179 Lentils	5 862	125	7	6	2 14	12
183 Safflower Seed	281	24	13	54	8 49	4 61
184 Vetch	3	**			6 63	
186 Rapeseed	474	17	4	26	3 57	93
203 Meadow Fesc Sd	18	1			4 68	
211 Alfalfa Seed	2 650	68	11	16	2 55	41
252 Timothy Seed	433	16	1	9	3 78	33
259 Bluegrass Seed	345	9			2 73	
260 Canarygrass Sd	1 392	46	10	21	3 27	70
297 Sweetclover Sd	91	4	1	29	4 16	1 21
306 Chili Peppers	1 627	144	81	56	8 85	4 99
308 Kidneybeans Dry	1 015	29	6	19	2 84	54
327 Nectarines	1 097	52			4 75	
361 Tomatoes Stake	259	15			5 64	
362 Tomatoes Gpfm	10 162	640	452	71	6 30	4 45
363 Tomatoes Pr Can	47	2	6	380	3 52	13 40
364 Apples GY	1 398	45	95	209	3 24	6 77
370 Tomatoes G P	41	2			6 00	
370 Tomatoes F M	39	1			3 58	
374 Potatoes—Red	57	3	1	53	4 66	2 48
375 Potatoes—White	4 164	350	192	55	8 40	4 61
394 Tobacco J	406	9			2 20	
404 Triticale	517	36	18	51	6 93	3 52
405 Wild Rice	330	17			5 18	
406 Austrian Peas	849	65	29	44	7 66	3 37
407 Apples—Wind	529	19	2	10	3 55	34
408 Apples-Gy-Wind	20	1			3 00	
421 Tomato one harv	23	1			3 50	
440 Dwarf Apples	39	2			5 34	
997 Blanket	64 241	1 137	656	58	1 77	1 02
998 Special Crops	367	12	10	91	3 15	2 86
999 Unknown	3 058	111	57	52	3 64	1 87
Total for States	6 204 105[1]	221 152[2]	138 222	63	3 56	2 23

These data, both countrywide and for each state, are published annually by Crop-Hail Insurance Actuarial Association. Cumulative experience by crop, policy form, and state are also published annually.

* Cotton named perils and multiple peril crop insurance.
[1] Estimated industry liability more than $10 billion.
[2] Only about 80% of the industry business is reported to CHIAA; of that, not all is included in published data because of some reporting relationships. However, analyses indicate these data are fully representative of industry experience.

extended to harvest time, at least for a majority of the policies. This made total sense, at least in the days before a "cash economy" on the farm. The industry has largely held onto this practice, often as an element of competition. In recent years, however, it has become fairly common to extend discounts for cash-with-the-application. The most common allowance is 5% but there are some for 10%. The significance of the discount-for-cash practice is that rates for crop-hail insurance are made on the presumption of collections in due course, with no loading for extensions of credit.

Secondly, the seasonal nature of the business inheres a reverse cash flow, even without extending time for collection. The business is put on the books in a relatively short period. Spring and early Summer are the seasons of high hail frequency, and thus disbursement for claims payments begins concurrently with issuance of policies and in advance of even normal property-casualty collections. Earnings from investment of unearned premium and loss reserves are negligible because of the time frame within which hail insurance begins and ends each season. Gain from underwriting is essentially the only source of earnings from hail insurance.

Finally, price competition has become a hazardous way of life in the hail insurance business. Part of the reason is that agriculture is a "static" industry, in terms of units of potential sales. Indeed, the number of farms continues to decrease; and with increased size, there may be some increased tendency to self-insure. In any event, while premium volume has increased dramatically during the years 1974-79, policy count has increased only moderately. There is thus keen competition for shares of a market which, unlike automobiles and homes, is not increasing in size.

There is room for rational price competition in crop-hail insurance. The range of verifiable expense factors is such that some degree of rate variation can be justified with expense differentials. One danger lies in the potential for miscalculating loss cost, for which there is no lack of proven data. The really serious threat is to hail operations with expense factors at the upper end of the range: a rate cut taken by even a small segment of the industry almost forces all to the same reduced rate level, if a market position is to be maintained.

Rating Crop-Hail Insurance

Crop-Hail Insurance Actuarial Association (CHIAA) is the only national statistical and rating organization for hail insurance. It receives experience from writers of about 80% of the U.S. hail business. Currently, it records more than one million detail items of data annually and about one quarter million summary records, from members, subscribers and statistical reporters. (The latter make and file their own rates but they have entered into a reciprocal data exchange with the Association.) The statistical plan, and the 100% coinsurance policy, lend to hail insurance rate-making the capacity for "loss cost" method of rating, in that exposure (liability) is specific to each loss and is recorded. The method first determines the loss cost, the ratio of losses paid to the liability applying, and then with known ratio of expense and profit to premiums, calculates rate by dividing the loss cost by the anticipated (target) loss ratio.[1] To illustrate, assume that for a given rate area liability is $10,000, losses are $100, and that expense and profit factor is 40%:

Loss Cost	= $100 ÷ $10,000 = .01
	X $100 = $1.00.
Anticipated Loss Ratio	= 100% — 40% = 60%
Calculated Rate	= $1.00 ÷ 0.60 = $1.67

UNDERWRITING CROP-HAIL INSURANCE

Without adding to the lexicon of "underwriting" definitions, crop-hail underwriting is different. Consideration of the individual policy risk is scarcely more than a clerical function. The unit of evaluation or analysis in crop-hail underwriting is geographical area, usually a township or a group of townships (county). The element of concern is not quality of risk but the amount of liability; the primary objective in underwriting is balanced distribution of probable loss, and the means of achievement is *distribution of liability* by geographical areas. Another major difference is that the underwriting task, as well as overall reinsurance arrangement, precedes inception of the submission-issuance period.

At first thought, one might take balanced distribution to suggest equal distribution. The uninitiated have been known to hypothesize that if the rate is correct for every rate area, then one should expect to realize the anticipated loss ratio by accepting liability of any amount from any or all areas. Such an expectation, were it realistic, would lend a considerable convenience to crop-hail underwriting. But, fortunately, hail does not occur in the same place(s) each season or in the same amounts each time at a given location.

Such a simplistic view omits the critical element of probability of occurrence (frequency) and intensity of hail. There is ample evidence that hail is a random kind of event, although the probabilities are that greater

---

[1] Since crop-hail insurance rating is so important, it is suggested that the reader see "Crop-Hail Insurance Statistics, 1978," available at no charge from CHIAA, for additional information.

loss frequency and intensity can be expected in some areas than in others. The aim of underwriting, then, is to equalize or spread *loss*, rather than liability *per se*. Since rate, a function of loss cost, is the most reliable indicator of that variation in loss probability, the procedure is to apportion exposure to loss (liability) by rate level, permitting greater retention of liability at lower rate levels and progressively less as rate increases. For the purpose of an organized approach to this procedure, line schemes are developed by the underwriters. While the underlying principle of line schemes has common subscribership, and all of them are similar in general design, the schemes nevertheless vary from company to company. The following is one approach used to establish a line scheme for crop-hail underwriting.

a. Postulate either the given (limited) or anticipated state premium volume. (1 below)

b. Postulate the maximum percentage of state premium which is acceptable as a single storm exposure (in property, MPL). (2 below)

c. Define the hazard unit to which that exposure applies. (3 below)

d. Apportion to the underwriting unit. (4 below)

e. Graduate by base rate level. (5 and 6 below)

EXAMPLE:

1) Assume state premiums of $600,000

2) Assume 75 % thereof as single storm exposure net $450,000

3) Consider nine townships as the hazard unit, since it is the basic rating unit and within such an area the path of most storms may be described. In a state having counties of relatively uniform size, the county could be used, e.g., Iowa.

4) $450.000/9 = the low limit for township underwriting unit at the highest rate level . . . . $ 50,000

5) Decide the multiple of the low level which is comfortable for the high level: the rate range for most states is such that 5 levels ought to be sufficient, therefore 4-5 times $50,000 could be a guide. $250,000

6) Assume a base rate range from $3.00 to $15.00, a spread of $12.00 from low to high. Assuming five levels, $12.00 ÷ 5 = about $2.50 in rate interval per level limit. Thus, the limits for base rate areas are:

$ 3.00—$ 5.00 . . . .$250,000.
$ 5.50—$ 8.00 . . . .$200,000.
$ 8.50—$10.50 . . . .$150,000.
$11.00—$13.00 . . . .$100,000.
over $13.00 . . . .$ 50,000.

Having established the line scheme objectives, hail managers may endeavor to realize the distribution objectives in various ways.

a. By aggressively planned and implemented marketing strategies, business can be attracted from most or all areas.

b. Restrictions on acceptance may be applied to areas from which an "overflow" of business develops.

c. Arrangements can be negotiated for participation in the writings of other primary writers in areas where a company is not entered or has no agency plant.

d. Similar arrangements can be negotiated for others to participate in the direct writings of a company which has a general overflow in an area or state.

e. It is not uncommon for a company to employ pricing tactics as part of its general marketing strategy for achieving distribution of business.

While the above may be good strategies in theory, most of them are limited by the general competitive nature of the hail insurance business and the apparently unlimited capacity of both primary and reinsurance underwriters. (Insatiable appetite may be a better term for it.) For example, historically, companies were not reluctant to serve notice to agents of limits per acre or limits per agency. In recent years, however, they rarely refuse to take all that is offered.

Today, the typical underwriter relies primarily upon the use of treaty reinsurance to control the distribution of liability. Originally, however, crop-hail reinsurance began with facultative exchange between the primary underwriters themselves. It was simply that one underwriter had more business in a given area than was desired. The other underwriter desired more business than had been written, so the two exchanged business. This kind of interchange gave way to the use of treaty surplus arrangements with the professional reinsurers. It is not uncommon for a company to negotiate up to three lines in excess of the line scheme net retention. Thus, it will be seen that a line scheme is the key to not only distribution objectives but also to the use of reinsurance as the major tool in achieving those objectives.

Reinsurance Applications to Crop-Hail Insurance

PROPORTIONAL REINSURANCE

Quota Share Treaties. The principal uses of pro rata forms of reinsurance in crop-hail operations are quota share and surplus share treaties. Quota share is used for capacity of not only individual companies but also for pools, particularly general agencies, and management and joint underwriting ventures. Commonly these entities obtain the use of one or more policy-issuing companies and perhaps "silent participant" primary writers; the balance of capacity needs are met with a quota share participation of the professional reinsurer. However, some companies are either obliged to use, or as a matter of prudence elect to use, quota share for managing premium-to-surplus ratio problems. As an example, a company created to serve an organization membership may be obligated to accept more than it judges to be a prudent exposure for a limited territory of operations (e.g., a single state company).

For quota share contracts, there must first be a meeting of minds on percentage participation of the source of business. Prudence may suggest that risk of the reinsurer will not exceed that retained by the reinsured and that the assumed portion will cut across all locations, crops and forms written. A second important matter is the rate level at which the business is written. It is not the purpose of reinsurance to finance an inadequate rate; any departure from rates which are demonstrably required to pay losses and expense and return expected gain must be taken into account in terms of the reinsurance agreement. Finally, the ceding commission to be granted must be determined. As has been pointed out, crop-hail insurance practice is afflicted with reverse cash flow. Year-end accounting is common to quota share contracts, which means the reinsurer also will enjoy *no income from investment* of current premium income.

Commonly, the reinsurer shares loss adjustment expense in the same proportion as assumed losses. Ceding commission must recognize all other expense—acquisition, overhead, taxes, and fees. The allowance in the rate for such expenses varies by rate level; the intelligent reinsurer must be informed as to both the allowance in rate and the actual costs incurred by the operation in which the quota share participates. And, if the rate level is significantly deficient, then allowances for such deficiency can be made by adjusting ceding commission.

Surplus Treaties. In recent years the use of surplus treaties has become quite common in hail insurance. Their function is primarily the distribution of liability and location capacity. They also indirectly afford stability as to overall results for any given year. In simplifying the handling of facultative exchange, the use of treaties has transferred to reinsurers a considerable share of the hail insurance premium generated by the primary underwriters on essentially quota share terms. The following procedures are typical of those used in the business:

1) The primary writer decides an intended net retention of liability per location, in terms of a general line scheme, as the net "line."

2) The reinsurer agrees to assume, pro rata from each location, the liability in excess of the net retained amount, not to exceed the retained amount (one net line). This is a "first surplus line" example.

3) If more than the net retained amount one line is to be ceded, the primary writer may negotiate a second surplus treaty or even a third.

4) However, if only infrequently there is needed additional capacity beyond that provided by the first, or first and second line surplus treaty(ies), the primary writer may resort to case location facultative cession. But a third line surplus treaty is not unheard of.

5) Ceding commission is negotiated either as an average for all location sources or variable according to location sources. Rate varies by location, as does the portion of rate available for rate components other than losses.

In contracts for both quota share and surplus reinsurance there may be a "profit-sharing" feature. Although arrangements vary, generally such sharing begins only above some substantial margin over break-even, and care is taken that deficits are carried forward to be absorbed by the reinsured.

NON-PROPORTIONAL REINSURANCE

Excess or stop-loss reinsurance is perhaps the most commonly used form of non-proportional reinsurance in crop-hail. Because of the nature of crop-hail, only the *aggregate* excess is used (instead of occurrence or risk.) The purpose is essentially protection against catastrophe; however, some writers negotiate contracts with terms which more nearly suggest working covers in the interest not only of catastrophe protection but also of quite stable or consistent annual net experience. Most of the hail business is written by major multiple line companies whose surplus could bear severe crop-hail experience. But even these companies prefer to devote little of their disposable surplus to crop-hail and thus resort to aggregate excess of loss covers specific to the crop-hail line.

Cut-in (or attachment) and limit terms describing the reinsurer's liability vary considerably, according to the felt needs of the primary writers. As an example, a contract might provide for 90% of the loss in excess of 70% loss ratio, with a limit of $1,000,000. For most primary hail companies a 70% loss ratio will produce not more than 110% combined ratio; for an occasional specialty hail company, as low as 102-105% combined. In this example, the reinsurer would pay its limit at a loss ratio of 81.11% on $10,000,000 gross premium operation: 81.11% of $10,000,000 = $8,111,111 losses; 70% loss ratio = $7,000,000 for excess of $1,111,111, of which 90% = $1,000,000. For larger operations the covers may be negotiated by layers and with two or more participants.

The rating of excess contracts in crop-hail can be interesting but the mechanics are straightforward. The following information is necessary: a) territory of operation, b) industry experience for the area (minimum ten years), c) reinsured's experience for the area (minimum ten years), d) reinsured's distribution of business relative to industry, and e) rate level used by the reinsured *vs* the statistically indicated rate.

Based on U.S. industry experience, loss ratios exceeding 70% are relatively infrequent. However, for some states they occur with distressing frequency. For any given year there is an amazing variation in loss ratios among individual companies, either countrywide or for a single state. The following table will illustrate:

For 1948-78:	U.S.	Iilinois	Texas	Montana
Number years loss ratio greater than 70%	6	7	12	8
Top ten writers 1977:				
Range of loss ratio	56-71	16-57	29-54	14-42
Average loss ratio	64	38	49	32

There may be other special purpose reinsurance covers, providing variations on quota share, surplus lines and excess, but these are the forms of general application to crop-hail. Very little use of reinsurance is made directly for purposes of finance, but that purpose may be served indirectly when a reinsurer agrees to an advance on ceded losses when extreme experience occurs early or in midseason (and before premiums are collected).

The objectives of underwriting reinsurance of crop-hail business are similar to the distribution of risk objectives of the primary underwriter. There are substantial benefits to specialization in hail reinsurance: a) A book of business from various operational and geographical sources enhances potential for success (even survival). b) The specialist will accumulate the knowledge necessary for becoming a market for various sources. c) Hail operations require a substantial degree of continuity for planning and for success.

All-Risk Crop Insurance

As of 1979, all-risk crop insurance is not an operational concern for either primary or reinsurance underwriters. However, there are indications that industry could enter into joint venture programs with the federal government, pursuant to administration objectives of greater farmer participation in shared cost insurance as alternative to a hodge-podge of costly government disaster relief programs. If such programs come about, the professional reinsurers will be faced with both a new need and an opportunity. The following, then, is a forward look.

Proposals for industry involvement envision that the Federal Crop Insurance Corporation (FCIC) would provide for industry all-risk customers the same federal premium subsidy as may be available for FCIC customers. An aggregate excess of loss cover would be provided by FCIC at some cut-in point not much greater than a combined ratio of 100%, sufficient to put private companies "safely" at risk (and to warrant a profit potential). Most companies would require additional reinsurance of the extent to which they are at risk.

The principal difference in underwriting problems between crop-hail and all-risk crop insurance is the potential for *large area* catastrophe resulting from drought, flooding, and excessive heat. This potential is in great contrast to the scope of the usual hail storm or accumulation of storms. And with all-risk, the individual risk *must be underwritten*, in contrast to crop-hail for which underwriting is mainly controlling distribution of liability.

Rate adequacy is always important; but in all-risk crop insurance, the basis of which is guarantee of yield, care must be taken that the specific yield guaranteed bears an acceptable relationship to "normal" yield. Otherwise, not just fortuity but also normal variation is insured against, which becomes not insurance but rather a social program. Also, the rating and pricing problem for both primary and reinsurance underwriters is ever so much more difficult than for crop-hail because there is no reliable statistical base. Presumably, therefore, reinsurers will assume all-risk business only in connection with crop-hail insurance and in relatively modest proportions to crop-hail.

Summary

Crop-hail insurance premiums of $350 million for more than $10 billion of liability are written annually in the U.S. by about 200 companies. While coverage is offered in all areas and for all crops, the activity is concentrated in nineteen states and on five major crop classes of corn and maize, cereal grains, soybeans, tobacco, and cotton.

Rating of crop-hail insurance is accomplished by the loss cost method, using all-time liability, premiums, and losses collected specific to crop and policy form within township location. The key to underwriting crop-hail insurance is distribution of liability. A location line scheme is the basic tool for not only the primary underwriter but also for determinations of proportional cessions of reinsurance, of which the most commonly used forms are quota share and surplus. Aggregate excess of loss is the most generally used form of non-proportional reinsurance.

*   *   *   *   *   *

About the Author of Reinsuring Crop-Hail Insurance

E. Ray Fosse was born and reared on a Williamson County, Southern Illinois, farm. A 1940 graduate of the University of Illinois in agricultural education, he was a teacher of vocational agriculture before and following World War II. During the War, he was a pilot of light bomber aircraft in the European Theater of Operations and was discharged in 1945 as a lieutenant colonel in the U.S. Air Force.

In 1952 he entered the insurance field as Illinois-Indiana farm and hail special agent for National Fire Insurance Company, a member of the CNA group. He became assistant secretary and manager of farm and hail operations. He is a past president of both the National Crop Insurance Association (NCIA) and the Crop-Hail Insurance Actuarial Association (CHIAA). He has been manager and executive secretary of CHIAA since 1968.

Reinsuring Surety

by Albert W. Davis*

Of the total number of insurance companies operating in the United States, approximately fifty write most of the surety business. These fifty share an annual premium volume of slightly in excess of $800 million, perhaps 1% of the total premium volume in this country (1978 anticipated figures). And approximately ten reinsurers then participate in one fourth of the $800 million, or $200 million. Because of the limited number of insurance companies engaged in writing surety (both ceding companies and reinsurers), and because there is a high concentration of risks shared among those companies, the importance of reinsurance is magnified. It is safe to say that today no company writing surety business operates without at least one automatic treaty with a reinsurer.

Any insurance company writing surety business must employ a staff of specialists who concentrate solely on this line because of its underwriting complexity and difficulty in settling claims, which are generally infrequent and severe. Because of the complexity of the line, reinsurers tend to follow the ceding company's practice of employing specialists. It is a true saying that the surety reinsurance underwriter could easily step into an underwriter's shoes at the primary level without missing an underwriting note. Conversely, a ceding company underwriter would have little difficulty in acclimating himself to reinsurance underwriting techniques. It becomes essential, therefore, for the student as well as the professional surety reinsurer to have a firm grasp and understanding of the differences between surety and insurance, the

* CPCU, Vice President in charge of the Bond Department, North American Reinsurance Corporation, 100 East 46 Street, New York, New York 10017.

methods of reinsuring surety, the primary marketplace, the underwriting problems of surety, and its claim handling procedures.

Differences Between Surety and Insurance

Suretyship exists whenever one party agrees to guarantee that another party will faithfully perform an obligation; should the obligation go uncompleted, there exists a promise to indemnify or pay a stated sum. The party which must perform the obligation is referred to in surety nomenclature as the principal; the party who guarantees performance is the surety; and the third party to whom the guarantee is given by the surety and for whom the principal will perform is referred to as the obligee. Generally, speaking, the agreement to perform between the principal and obligee must be in writing, and the agreement by the surety to guarantee performance, which is commonly called a surety bond, must also be in writing. More specifically, the Statute of Frauds mandates that promises to answer for the debt of another must be in writing. The surety bond is such a promise.

No single line of insurance differs so markedly from its brethren than the surety line. There are many experts who believe that surety is more akin to the granting of credit by a bank than the insuring of risks by the philosophy of the law of large numbers. Several of the basic differences are:

1. The principal is primarily responsible in surety. Basically, any insurance policy agrees to indemnify up to a specified amount against loss from specified events such as fire or burglary. The surety bond, on the other hand, agrees to indemnify the obligee (not the principal who has purchased the bond), should the principal fail to comply with the terms of the contract undertaken. The amount of the loss, the degree of damages, can only be fixed *after* failure to perform. The bond amount serves only as the maximum liability for which the surety would be liable.

2. The surety premium charge contemplates no losses. Historically, surety rates have been promulgated on the basis of loss-free experience. In theory, at least, the premium charge consists of two distinct factors, a credit factor and an expense factor for the surety, which represents the expense in handling the business. This, of course, differs from insurance where the intent is to create a premium fund from which losses will be paid.

3. There is no reliance on the law of large numbers in surety. Underwriting surety is an individual matter, with no attempt at broad

class distinctions. However, like insurance, class distinctions are accounted for in the premium rates.

4. Generally, there is no cancellation clause in a surety bond. Rarely will a surety be given the option of cancelling a bond once it is issued. This applies even to the discovery of fraud on the part of the principal or the non-payment of premiums. The reason for non-cancellation is the third party involved who is the primary beneficiary of the surety bond. It is only fair that the third party should not be penalized because of differences between the principal and the surety. There are rare exceptions, especially in license and permit bonds, where the obligee will allow the cancellation clause. It is also to be noted that there is no fixed date for a surety bond to expire. Completion of the obligation will terminate a bond. Again, there are exceptions in license and permit bonds whose terms run for the duration of the license or annual permit.

5. The bond wording will generally be determined by the obligee, not the surety company. Additionally, the amount of the bond and the third party beneficiaries are all dictated by the obligee. In insurance, of course, the contract is always authored by the company.

Classes of Surety Bonds

Approximately 70% of all revenue generated in the surety industry emanates from one class of bond, the contract bond, which guarantees that a specific construction project will be completed properly by the contractor. The other classes of surety bonds are commonly called miscellaneous surety and include the following: court fiduciary bonds, judicial bonds, license and permit bonds, public official bonds, and bonds in favor of the United States Government (official, immigrant, excise, and custom bonds).

Down through the years, the miscellaneous surety bonds have been, on an industry average, extremely profitable to the surety writers. This fact, coupled with the fact that most of these bond amounts are relatively small, place the surety company in a position where reinsurance is not needed. On the other hand, the reinsurers feel that this type of business helps support the capacity that is required for contract bonds. In all negotiating sessions between ceding company and reinsurer concerning the surety treaty, a pertinent negotiating point is the inclusion or exclusion of miscellaneous surety.

EVOLUTION OF SURETYSHIP

The need for and the growth of miscellaneous surety have been dependent upon local laws and customs as well as the increasing complexity of the laws promulgated by the federal government. The growth of contract bond premiums, on the other hand, has been tied directly to the growth of the United States construction industry and the amount of tax money the federal and state governments budget for public work programs. In this way the premium growth of the surety line is tied directly to the health of the United States economy.

While the first surety company to begin operation was the Fidelity and Deposit Company of New York, which began writing fidelity in 1880 and the following year began writing miscellaneous surety bonds, the first originator of contract bond underwriting was the American Surety Company of New York, which was organized in 1884. Two present day giants of the surety industry, the Fidelity and Deposit Company of Maryland and the United States Fidelity and Guaranty Company, began operations in 1890 and 1896, respectively. Indeed, between the period of 1894 and 1898, at least twenty-five new surety companies were formed to take advantage of a newly enacted federal law, the Heard Act (1894), which for the first time in the United States required a contract surety bond guarantee for all construction projects which were funded by the United States Government. The Heard Act is thus credited with fathering the surety industry.

As with most young industries, this period which saw the birth of the 20th Century was highlighted by fierce competition among the new companies together with abuses. This led to the formation of the Surety Association of America in 1908. Among its goals were the standardization of rates to be charged by its member companies and the inclusion for membership into its ranks of all qualified surety companies. To this date, the Surety Association of America continues to be the major voice of the surety industry in rate making and legislative matters.

CO-SURETYSHIP

Co-surety is a procedure whereby two or more companies jointly and directly participate in the execution of a bond. Because of the great number of large construction projects which must be bonded, together with the federal government's requirement that no surety company should issue a bond for more than 10 % of its policyholder surplus, co-surety is common in today's marketplace. On large bonds it is customary for the ceding company to ask its reinsurers to participate as co-surety. It is also not unusual to have a company ask its facultative reinsurers for co-surety participation.

Traditionally, each co-surety will limit its liability to a specified amount in the bond they execute. The aggregate of the amounts for which the companies will commit themselves will equal the total amount of a bond required. In the event of a loss involving co-suretyship, each company will be obligated to pay its pro rata share of the loss. However, should one of the co-sureties become insolvent before the loss occurs, the remaining solvent companies are obligated to pay the entire loss subject to: 1) no individual co-surety will pay more than its dollar commitment; and 2) all the co-sureties will be required to pay only the aggregate of their commitments.

Almost all of the contract bonds furnished today are in reality two bonds, a performance bond and a payment bond. While the performance bond directly affects the owner, the payment bond is intended to benefit third parties such as subcontractors, suppliers of materials, and laborers working on the bonded project. Generally, the payment bond guarantees to these third parties that if collection proceedings are instituted within ninety days from the date of the last furnishing of materials or labor, they will be paid. This guarantee of payment often results in lower prices quoted on bonded construction projects, since the supplier should have no collection difficulties.

The practice of separate performance and payment bonds can be traced back to the enactment of the Miller Act by the federal government in 1935. While this Act pertained only to United States Government construction projects, the requirements and procedures established by the Act were gradually adopted by most of the states and by most of the municipalities in the United States. It is estimated that the majority of the public construction projects underway today, regardless of whether they are federal, state, or local, would adhere to the procedures outlined by the Miller Act.

Marketing Surety

SPECIALISTS

Surety is a highly sophisticated line and the marketing of this line is done, for the most part, by specialists: independent insurance agents who concentrate on contractor accounts. These agents even have their own trade association, The National Association of Surety Bond Producers, whose executive offices are located in Washington, D.C. Additionally, the surety specialization is carried one step further in the company ranks. Any significant writer of surety has a separate department to handle this business, staffed by individuals specifically trained in this line who concentrate their entire time on surety production and underwriting.

Some surety companies will receive from 50% to 75% of all their writings from specialist surety bond producers. Other companies, equally successful, try to maintain a ratio between business received from these specialists and business written by their other agency plant. Their reasoning is that business generated by specialists may sometimes be too sophisticated and too difficult to handle. (However, it can safely be said that no statistical data is available supporting the view that the loss ratio is affected by the type of producer with which a company deals).

THE EXPENSE RATIO

This degree of separation and specialization in surety has one measurable effect, a heavy expense factor. This is one of the few lines in the insurance portfolio where the expense ratio is expected to continually exceed the loss ratio. The high expense factor is particularly important to the reinsurer, which will be asked to share the costs of the ceding company. Many knowledgeable reinsurance people feel that one of the drawbacks to reinsuring surety is the extremely high reinsurance commission factor that must be paid the ceding companies by the reinsurer. This, in turn, leaves few dollars of premium to pay losses. Data compiled by A.M. Best & Company[1] show expenses for the industry at the end of 1976 as follows:

Agency Commission & Brokerage	28.3%
Other Production	9.8%
General	13.8%
Taxes, Licenses, & Fees	4.0%
Loss Adjustment	7.5%
Total	63.4%

In determining what reinsurance commission to pay its client companies, the reinsurer must take into account the fact that the size of surety bonds written by a company directly affects the expense ratio, especially the agency commission ratio. Under the current premium rating plans in use, the percentage of agency commission paid on a bond decreases as the amount of the bond increases. Thus, a company that normally writes larger contractors will have a lower agency commission ratio than a company whose portfolio consists primarily of smaller or medium-sized contractor accounts.

---

[1] *Best's Aggregates and Averages, Property-Casualty,* 38th edition (A.M. Best Company, Oldwick, New Jersey 08858), 1977.

Additionally, the type of treaty executed between reinsurer and ceding company should have a bearing on the reinsurance commission allowed the client. Quota share treaties have historically carried a higher scale of commission. This is only fair since the ceding company should be reinsuring a stated fixed percentage of every bond it writes. Under this arrangement the reinsurer should also be prepared to accept a percentage of the overall expenses of its client. A surplus share treaty does not promise this equality and the commission, therefore, would normally be lower. Here, it is customary for the reinsurer to state in the treaty that "a commission of 12 ½ %, including premium tax over the company's commission to the agent, will be paid subject to a maximum of 42 ½ %." The reader is cautioned that this is only a rule of thumb.

Functions of Surety Reinsurance

CAPACITY

To attract and retain business, the surety reinsurer must be able to provide three basic functions: capacity, stabilization of underwriter results, and financing. With the sophistication of modern construction projects and with the continuing impact of inflation on construction costs, it is not unusual to see a construction project in the category of $50,000,000 and above. Underwriting prudence dictates that no surety company keep that much risk on its own books. Thus, providing the capacity to issue a single bond for these amounts and the ability to spread risk are the most important functions of surety reinsurance.

STABILIZATION

The volatility of the surety line is caused in part by four items: 1) the fact that there are usually several bonded construction projects affected by default at any given time; 2) the large amounts of cash that must be quickly expended by the surety company in order to help cure the default and meet the company's legal obligations; 3) the time lag affecting salvage recoveries back to the surety; and 4) economic factors that tend to affect claim settlement procedures. For example, it is more costly to settle contractor defaults in a rapidly rising inflationary period than otherwise.

Because of these factors, it is not unusual for even the largest surety writer to see a fluctuation of up to thirty points in its loss ratio in the surety line for any one given year. Obviously, such fluctuations are unacceptable to both the top management of an insurance company, whose desire is to demonstrate stability, and also to the stockholders who are not particularly pleased with seeing earning affected by one line of business. Thus, the surety reinsurer must be willing to stabilize a company's results by offering a treaty that in the bad years will absorb significant losses. Most knowledgeable reinsurance people feel that a surety treaty should be allowed to mature for at least three years before judging profitability. Adverse experience in one year only indicates that the reinsurer is performing its function as a stabilizing influence. Conversely, a healthy profit picture to the reinsurer over a twelve-month period may mean that the reinsurer is either recovering the losses of a previous period; or by mutual consent, storing up loss dollars for future losses (for example, in a new treaty).

FINANCING

The financing facility provided by the surety reinsurer takes two forms: 1) the sharing of the financial burden caused by the unearned premium and loss reserves; and 2) because of the high degree of expense involved in surety, the reinsurer through commission allowance agrees to participate in the cost of doing business as a surety writer.

Methods of Reinsuring Surety

SURPLUS SHARE

The most common type of reinsurance treaty has always been the surplus share arrangement. Under this program the surety company decides what percentage of each bond it wishes to keep for its own net account before reinsurance begins. It could range anywhere from $100,000 or less, up to $5,000,000 or $10,000,000. Over this selected amount, the reinsurers will share on a proportionate basis with the surety company. The hazard in this type of treaty to the reinsurer will lie in the makeup of the company's contractor portfolio. If only large losses occur, then the major portion will fall to the reinsurers. This could be compounded when the same company has a large number of smaller contractors with little loss development, and requiring small bonds that fall beneath the retention level. In effect, the reinsurer would be receiving an insufficient amount of premium from the entire portfolio to cover the high risk losses. Conversely, if the ceding company decides on a large retention and most of its losses, as a result, fall within the company's net retention, the experience of the ceding company will be far worse than the reinsurer.

One can readily see that under the surplus share arrangement, the reinsurer and the company, in a given year, could have significantly different results from the same book of business. In the mid 1970's this type of program has caused the reinsurers most of their underwriting problems, because results have not tracked with their client companies.

QUOTA SHARE

The second type of common treaty is the quota share program, which can be described as a fixed percentage sharing of liability, premium, and losses between the ceding company and the reinsurers from the first dollar of cover. Under such an arrangement, the ceding company and the reinsurers agree on their pro rata percentages, and this schedule does not vary all the way up to the treaty maximum. The concept of quota share was traditionally designed for smaller companies, companies entering the surety business, or companies which wished to expand into territories where they had not been previously. However, during the decline of the stock market in 1975 and with the continuing variances in the Dow Jones Average, this type of program has been increasingly used to offset pressure on a company's policyholder surplus. How? Because the program improves a company's cash flow position through: 1) the reinsurance commission paid to the company by the reinsurer (tracking with the company's overhead which includes producer's commission), and 2) the reinsurer's agreement to share proportionately in the unearned premium reserve and the loss reserves of the company in every premium dollar.

The basic advantage to the reinsurer in this kind of program is the exact tracking of underwriting results between the reinsurer and the ceding company. However, there are disadvantages. It is expensive to administer since every item written must be accounted for unless both parties agree to "bulk" all items. More importantly, a quota share on a bad book of surety business may give the reinsurer worse results than a surplus share program in the same book.

EXCESS OF LOSS

The third general type of program is the excess of loss cover. Whereas the other two programs discussed always deal with a distribution of risk through a pro rata division of premiums, the excess of loss program concerns itself strictly with losses. Under this type of arrangement, the surety company agrees to assume a given amount of each loss (its retention), and the reinsurer then assumes either the entire loss or a stated percentage of each loss which exceeds the retention level.

One should remember that a contract bond loss differs from other lines of insurance in that a series of construction projects, all with varying claim costs, are involved. There is no practical way to provide excess of loss on each project. Thus, the surety excess of loss treaty will apply on a per contractor basis and will, thus, include all claims outstanding against the individual contractor. Additionally, it is possible for the reinsurer under this type of agreement to place limits on the amount of work a contractor can undertake and be eligible for an excess of loss cover. For example, the reinsurance treaty might specify that the cover applies to a contractor as long as he maintains a work program of less than $10,000,000.

In reinsurance techniques, each program must be customized for the ceding company. Additionally, it is not unusual to have a program incorporate more than one of these treaties. For example, one could easily have a quota share treaty which would allow the reinsurer and the ceding company to track its results identically, and on top of that, place a surplus share which would be designed primarily for capacity. Another type of program could be arranged entailing a high net retention by the ceding surety company. Additionally, the company would then purchase an excess of loss arrangement underneath the surplus cover to protect its own net retention, thereby reducing its exposure.

Underwriting Surety

OBJECTIVE: A BALANCED PORTFOLIO

The reinsurance underwriter's primary task is to constantly monitor its company's share of the surety marketplace as well as its individual reinsurance percentage of a given company's business. In both cases the objective is to avoid overconcentration by a sufficient spread of risk. For example, business from any marketplace consists of a combination of high quality risks, average risks, and poor risks. A reinsurer's management must define which of these segments, or combination of segments, should be solicited. Eternal vigilance is also the watchword on an individual ceding company's portfolio. No matter how high the quality of risks underwritten, the volatility of the surety line will generate a severe loss at some given point in time. While the loss is unavoidable, the percentage of loss assumed from any company can be regulated by the reinsurer. Thus, unlike other lines of reinsurance where the aim is to increase market penetration, the marketing thrust of the surety reinsurer is aimed at retaining only its desired percentage of the market.

In addition, the reinsurance underwriter is constantly aware of the fact that the volume of surety premium and the degree of risk are dependent on the construction programs undertaken throughout the United

States. In turn, construction activity is greatly dependent on the economic policy of the federal and state governments regarding public works. The rate of inflation, which directly influences construction costs and the cost of borrowing money from banks, affects construction programs accordingly. For example, a contractor undertakes a project by submitting a bid which is based on certain cost factors at the time the construction project begins. A subsequent and sudden inflationary spiral will increase these costs. At the same time, the original price cannot be changed after the bid. If the inflation rate is pronounced, the job becomes unprofitable. Too many unprofitable jobs lead to bankruptcy. The most frustrating thing to the professional reinsurer is that these items are totally out of the control of the surety underwriter, and yet they play an active part in arriving at an underwriting decision.

Ideally, the reinsurance underwriter should strive for a mixture in its portfolio of large surety companies and smaller companies. The larger companies tend to attract the bigger and thus heavier exposures while other companies usually cater to the moderate-sized contractors. Additionally, the underwriter should then balance its portfolio by adding regional companies whose marketing operation is restricted to several states in an adjoining area. Lastly, if the underwriter were clairvoyant, it would then concentrate its marketing activities in those regions of the country which were undergoing an expanding economic boom, and it would shun or cancel those companies whose business was concentrated in economically depressed areas.

UNCOMPLETED WORK DETERMINES LOSS POTENTIAL

It would indeed be a simple underwriting affair if every contractor bonded by surety were allowed to undertake one construction project at a time, and only after its completion be allowed to begin another project. However, in the reality of the marketplace, this is impractical. A contractor, depending on its size, will have anywhere from three to fifty projects underway at various times during the course of one year. The surety underwriter is faced with committing itself to bonding each of those projects when they begin. Underwriting of a contractor is thus centered on determining the contractor's ability to undertake a volume of construction work and, based on that determination, qualifying it for a line of credit. Surety underwriters are not clairvoyant, and the analysis of a firm's current financial statement and work program must be weighed against the future pitfalls of inflation, oscillating bank interest rates, and other economic factors.

Establishing a Contractor's Line of Credit. A credit line is established by setting a single bond maximum and an aggregate work program limit. For example, a surety will agree to allow a contractor to bid any single job of $5,000,000 subject to a total uncompleted work program of $15,000,000 (stated as $5,000,000/$15,000,000). If there is a single factor that segregates good surety underwriting from mediocrity, it is the procedure established to monitor a contractor's line of credit. Mediocrity will call for a schedule of uncompleted work by the contractor at selected time intervals. The underwriter will then evaluate the amount uncompleted in relation to the line of credit. The underwriter may also decide to segregate projects which are bonded from the non-bonded work program.

Good underwriting, on the other hand, while insisting on the same schedule of uncompleted work will insist that one of the schedules coincide with the exact date of the fiscal year end of the contract. This develops a meaningful comparison from year to year. The underwriter will also ask that the contractor furnish estimated costs to complete each project and the profit potential of each. By comparing previous schedules, the underwriter notes whether a job is on target as to profitability during its various stages of completion. Several unprofitable jobs are red flags to the underwriter, and steps can be taken long before the financial damage is stated on next year's balance sheet. Additionally, by securing data concurrent with the financial statement, the underwriter observes whether any "overbillings" might appear to inflate the financial condition of the contractor.

A reinsurer and ceding company's exposure to loss is directly related to the line of credit established for an account. An excessive line of credit allows a contractor to bid on work that either it is technically unqualified to handle, or lacks the financial or manpower resources to handle. Thus, its ability to complete the work is weakened. A surety company that grants excessive lines of credit or uses them for competitive reasons to lure contractors into its portfolio is ultimately going to incur severe losses, and its reinsurers who have failed to identify this permissiveness will likewise suffer.

Uncompleted Work and MPL. Can a surety and its reinsurers identify the maximum probable loss from a contractor's uncompleted work program? The answer is, No! And why not? Because of the varied factors that make up the work program, such as the class of contractor involved, the payment obligations, the geographic area, and the quality of claim handling available.

The Class of Contractor. The heavy engineering contractor completing a highway is an entirely different risk from a developer completing a condominium project in a resort area. The former has substantial assets invested in machinery and equipment. Generally, it uses its own work force. Conversely, the condominium developer is characterized as a contractor who relies on others to perform the work, and who is highly leveraged. Historically, the highway contractor would cost its surety substantially less should a default occur.

Payment Obligations. The majority of the losses paid by a surety are for unpaid bills rather than costs to complete a project. Thus, the severity of a loss depends on the contractor as a business manager. In other words, how current was the contractor in meeting its payment obligations?

Geographic Area. The location of a defaulted contractor's projects makes a good deal of difference to a surety. The cost to complete a project in the Virgin Islands differs from that of a project in Austin, Texas. Such factors as supply logistics, availability of labor, and contractors willing to complete the project — all will affect ultimate costs. Additionally, areas that provide construction work twelve months a year have lower completion costs than geographic areas in which winter months deter construction.

Quality of Claim Handling. The most underrated factor in surety is the invaluable knowledge of experienced claim people because delay increases claim costs. Surety claims demand immediate responses, together with expertise. A surety company possessing a good claim department, therefore, can save loss dollars by knowing what to do and how to do it.

Conditions Of The Treaty

The individual underwriting techniques in evaluating contract surety do not differ much between ceding and reinsurance underwriters. However, there are two distinct and highly important factors for the reinsurance underwriter to consider before granting a surety reinsurance treaty to any company. These are the terms and conditions of the treaty, and the underwriting philosophy or management characteristics of the primary company which include its staffing, hiring, and salary requirements.

Equal Terms. In most pro rata surety treaties, the ceding company in its desire to create capacity elects to have more than one reinsurer participate. It is not unusual to have three or four reinsurers sharing one treaty. Currently, one large surety writer has six reinsurers, and several large writers employ four or five. In the majority of cases, the treaty terms are exactly alike, including the commission paid, so that no one participant gains an advantage over fellow reinsurers. Also, since the treaties are pro rata, the pricing factor is not important since all companies will share in a proportion of what the primary writer charges for its bonds.

However, there is one situation where treaty terms may vary among reinsurers. The best example is a company with two reinsurers for several years deciding to realign its treaty by inviting two more reinsurers to participate because of its adverse results. It would be common practice to have the older reinsurers receive more favorable terms by way of lower reinsurance commission or additional miscellaneous surety business, which would have the ultimate effect of serving as a payback to them.

Jointly, reinsurers are mostly concerned about the capacity they afford a client company. Emphasis is always placed on the relationship between that capacity and the company's net retention. As a rule of thumb, where there are one or two reinsurers, a ratio of three units of capacity to one unit of retention is desirable. On those treaties that employ more reinsurers, the reinsurance underwriter will generally try to keep its individual participation limited to the amount that the primary writer retains for its own account, a one-to-one ratio. Thus, if four reinsurers were employed in a treaty, the reinsurance underwriters would jointly try to maintain the treaty at a four-line basis or a ratio of five-to-one.

Miscellaneous Surety. The miscellaneous surety line which normally averages about one third of a company's total surety portfolio, is becoming increasingly important. In treaty negotiations, the reinsurer will generally insist on including the less hazardous of miscellaneous business lines in the contract treaty to support the capacity afforded for the more hazardous contract bond line. Accordingly, the inclusion of miscellaneous surety becomes dependent on the historical profitability or unprofitability of the existing treaty.

Miscellaneous surety can also be used either as a vehicle of funneling additional revenue into the treaty or as a means of paying back the reinsurer for past unprofitability. For example, the company with a large book of contractors in need of much capacity may decide to grant the reinsurers a separate quota share treaty on its miscellaneous book, the income from the quota share treaty offsetting the hazards of the contractor treaty. Another example is the creation of an excess of loss treaty for miscellaneous surety; the premium rate for such treaty would function as a payback for prior deficiencies and as revenue to compensate for the contract bond treaty. In summary, it becomes apparent that a company with a substantial miscellaneous book is in a better position to attract reinsurers than one which writes predominately contract surety business.

Overlines. Practically every surety treaty provides for special acceptances or overlines. This practice is used for individual contractor accounts whose principals may desire to bid on construction projects that are larger than the capacity afforded automatically by the treaty. In these cases, the ceding company will ask the reinsurance underwriter, either in writing or by telephone communication, to grant additional capacity for the specific project. In this situation the reinsurance underwriter should ask for the same information and evaluate the case on the same basis as would any ceding company underwriter. Financial information, construction projects underway, and similar factors are all reviewed. Some reinsurers will agree to accept this data verbally because of their long-term association and/or confidence in their client's ability, and because of time pressures. Other reinsurance underwriters require a written presentation. While most companies tend to accept these overlines, a few reinsurers feel that such additional capacity should be offered facultatively to companies not participating in the treaty. One of the questions a ceding company should ask its reinsurer is its attitude toward special acceptances, since a negative disposition may impose added expense and time on the underwriting staff in preparing facultative offerings.

Commission. The commission terms and the profit-sharing terms, if any, are of interest to both parties, because they affect the cost of the reinsurance. Generally speaking, surety treaties that call for a flat commission will provide for a 40% commission, plus 2½% for premium taxes, for a total of 42½%. Profit-sharing terms, if any, would take the form of either a sliding scale commission or a stated percentage of contingent commission.

A sliding scale commission is one which varies inversely with the loss ratio under the treaty. The scale generally ranges from a minimum commission of 35% to a maximum of 50%. A provisional commission of 40%, equal to the normal flat commission, will generally be paid, subject to adjustment at annual intervals in accordance with the terms of the sliding scale.

In a treaty with a contingent commission, the contract will contain a formula for the calculation of profits under the treaty and provide for a stated percentage of these profits to be paid to the ceding company as additional commission. Here, too, calculations are normally made annually.

There is a growing feeling in the reinsurance community that profit-sharing arrangements should either be eliminated entirely or computed on a three-year cycle basis to correspond with what is now considered to be a normal construction project cycle.

CHARACTERISTICS OF THE CEDING COMPANY

Regardless of how favorable the treaty terms are to the reinsurer, unless the ceding company's contractor portfolio is satisfactory, there is no way the reinsurer can produce a profit over the long run. Hence, the evaluation of a ceding company's surety portfolio, together with an evaluation of the efficiency and technical knowledge of the company underwriters, are the most important underwriting criteria on which a reinsurer relies.

Financial File Review. An underwriting evaluation of the ceding company's portfolio is generally done by the reinsurer before the consummation of a new treaty. On established accounts, the evaluation is done on the average of once every three years. However, a deteriorating loss ratio or a specific request from the client company for counsel could lead to more frequent reviews. During its review, the reinsurer will scan the company's underwriting files in the home office. Surety underwriters generally keep separate files by contractor account which contain all financial data and other pertinent underwriting data. Individual bond files identifying specific bonds are generally ignored by the reinsurer. The number of accounts reviewed will depend on the volume of business generated by the company and should always include accounts from all sections of the United States where business is underwritten. The review should answer the following questions. Are proper underwriting techniques being used both at the branch office and the home office level? Is there proper communication between field and home office, or are home office guidelines generally ignored by the field forces? Do the company underwriters seem to be bending to pressures exerted by the company's marketing force, or are they writing surety business under pressure because of other lines of insurance?

Production Plans. The production plans of the company should be reviewed, both as to long-term objectives and the percentages of growth over the previous three to five years. Are certain sections of the country producing the majority of income for the company? Is the company deriving its income from a select group of agents?

Claim Department. Claim department procedures should be reviewed and the establishment of reserves analyzed, since the accuracy of a ceding company's claim reserves is critical to the reinsurer. Initial reserves are extremely difficult to establish accurately. Additionally, the surety industry does not have any incentive to set realistic reserves. The premium charge is not affected in any way by reserving, since theoretically losses have no influence on ratemaking. This is contrary to most lines of insurance where the pricing of the product is based on past experience. Lastly, the surety line produces a significant time lag between the first indications of a potential loss and the actual demand for payment from either the property owner (obligee) or a disgruntled subcontractor. All these factors have led to different reserving practices currently in the surety industry. The reinsurer must constantly monitor each of its clients in order to evaluate its loss potential.

Staffing. The reinsurer should review the company's hiring and training programs. The salary ranges should be analyzed and compared with the industry averages. The adequacy of the staff of the bond department in relationship to the volume produced is also evaluated by the reinsurer, since people are the cornerstone of the surety business. Regardless of the underwriting techniques utilized and regardless of the reinsurance terms and capacity afforded, a company that is understaffed will eventually have underwriting problems.

Surety Claim Handling

SEVERITY

The most important characteristic of contract bond underwriting is the extreme dollar severity of loss that occurs when a contractor is unable to complete its bonded projects. Initial claim handling may take several months and involve hundreds of hours to complete. The potential exposure and ultimate loss to the surety and its reinsurers are difficult to calculate at the outset when estimates are made for the purpose of reserving. The amount to reserve becomes a matter of determining four categories of exposure: 1) estimated costs to complete the projects as defined by the original contract and any change orders agreed to by the parties; 2) tabulation and the verification of all outstanding obligations due subcontractors, material men, and laborers who performed or furnished material on the projects; 3) a "guesstimate" of the impact of inflation on estimated completion costs; and 4) the cost of additional equipment, unpaid taxes, and other miscellaneous items. Consideration must also be given to the cost of guaranteeing bank loans and the handling of the ongoing payroll and overhead.

PROCEDURES

From the beginning of its investigation and audit, a surety claim department is focusing on the upcoming choices or options which are available. Four of these options are: 1) The obligee will undertake to complete the projects and pay all bonded obligations due. Thereafter, it will request the surety for reimbursement of all costs incurred for performance and/or payment obligations in excess of the contract balances. This method may be the simplest of surety claim handling choices; however, it might be very expensive. Generally, this option is not exercised by the surety, but it might be considered if the contractor and the principal are in a hopeless legal argument or there are hopeless financial difficulties. 2) The surety will attempt to obtain bids from other contractors to complete the remaining performance obligations. In this case the obligee must accept the new contractor. The cost to complete the performance obligations, in excess of the remaining contract balance, would be the responsibility of the surety. The total of the performance and payment cost would then be the surety's exposure and final loss. 3) The third option for the surety and the defaulted contractor would be to enter into a financing arrangement which would allow the original contractor to complete the projects under the supervision of the surety. Such an arrangement might encompass a number of methods to generate sufficient cash flow and improve the contractor's financial position. For example, a surety might consider advancing surety funds or guaranteeing a bank loan. 4) Fourthly, the surety would work out a compromise settlement on its performance obligation and "buy back" its bond. In this case the surety would still have its bonded payment obligations to pay out.

It is to be emphasized that each contractor default carries its own unique characteristics and problems. Each option involves legal rights which must be observed by the surety. The surety claim department generally reviews each option carefully, then determines the best option to reduce its exposure, yet faithfully perform its obligations. Generally speaking, it is usually less expensive for the surety to keep the original contractor on the projects. The second option might be considered if a defaulted contractor has either irreparable financial difficulties or has had a performance totally unacceptable to the obligee. A claim department might also be more inclined to select the second option if the bonded projects are in their early stages of completion or if bankruptcy has been filed by the contractor.

Effect On Reinsurers

One can readily see that the claim procedure chosen may have a significant impact on the reinsurer. The first option offers simplicity and is easy to administer. Option two's main advantage is that the cost to complete can be reasonably determined by obtaining bids from new contractors. The additional costs above the original contract then becomes the claim amount on the performance obligation. The disadvantage of

the second option is the extra time needed for the new contractor to ac-
climate itself with the project. This extra time requirement generally
makes for an unhappy owner and may create additional lawsuits because
of the delay.

The third option of financing a contractor has the greatest exposure
to escalating claim costs, since there is generally no definite ceiling on the
costs. Under such an arrangement, the surety agrees to simply finance
the contractor to complete the projects. If the original cost estimates were
inaccurate, of if a sudden inflationary spiral affects the cost of materials
and supplies, the amount of the claim will escalate. However, the
greatest dilemma lies in the fact that once a surety agrees to finance, it
makes itself vulnerable to paying more than the bond limit requirement,
since the surety becomes committed to complete, regardless of the cost.
In effect, this third option provides that the surety and the reinsurer agree
to an open-end performance bond. It is because of such a provision that
every surety treaty will call for a joint decision between the company
and reinsurer before the financing of a defaulted contractor can be undertaken. The fourth alternative must be considered by the surety, since it
stops or sets the total claim amount. It allows the obligee to quickly complete the project. However, it is definitely the least attractive option for
the surety.

SALVAGE

An established principle of law that arises when a surety bond is executed is one of indemnification, which requires the principal under the
bond to reimburse the surety for any payments made by the surety
under the bond obligations. The principle of subrogation also grants the
surety reimbursement. In surety, the primary obligation is always from
the principal to the obligee, with the surety acting as a guarantor. Any
reasonable payment made by the surety, therefore, allows the surety to
be subrogated to the rights of the obligee against the principal, with the
right to enforce the obligation either in the name of the obligee, or in its
own name as surety.

Generally, a surety would not be liable under its surety bonds for
more than the principal's liability. Under this premise it is an essential
condition that the principal must be found liable before the surety can
become liable. However, there are special circumstances where this
would not apply. An example of this latter category would be punitive
damages assessed against the surety for negligent claim handling.

From this legal principle of indemnification flows the right to
salvage. The surety's basic definition of salvage is "assets recovered by
the surety in reimbursement for claims it has paid." Salvage could be in

the form of assets that the principal or indemnitors may hold, or monetary funds owed the principal by the obligee. An example of the former would be the equity value of the equipment that a contractor may own. An example of the latter might be the monies owed the contractor by the obligee, but not yet paid, or contract balances left to be paid upon completion of the project, sometimes called retainage.

The degree of salvage recovery in surety is extremely high, more than in any other line of insurance. However, recovery is usually eighteen to thirty months after the original claim notice or default. This time lag is the main reason for the adverse influence of surety losses on overall insurance company results — the loss having a negative impact in one year, and the salvage recovery having a positive effect on operating results one or two years later. These traumatic swings between profitability and loss occur sooner or later with every writer or surety and are one of the major reasons that companies need and depend on reinsurers. It is also one of the main reasons why many experienced surety executives feel that customary twelve-month operating results for the surety line are misleading. They point out that the profitability of the line must be judged over a longer period of time, either three or five years, to take into account the cycles of loss and salvage.

Government Regulation of Surety Business

There is no direct federal control over the rates and premiums charged by surety companies. As with all lines of insurance, most direct control has been left up to the individual states. All surety companies and surety reinsurers must be licensed by the state insurance department of each state in which they conduct business. Regulation extends to forms and rates used by surety companies, with varying degrees of control exercised by individual states. Since most surety companies also write other lines of insurance, it is not surprising that the degree of state regulation is often greater for insurance lines than for surety lines. For example, insurance lines require more policy forms than surety lines, are a greater threat to insolvency historically, and yield more premium volume (and premium taxes).

The major regulation carried out by the United States Government is through its so-called "Treasury List," a schedule published annually in July. That list shows those surety companies that have the U.S. Department of Treasury approval to issue surety bonds on federal construction projects or to act as reinsurers of such bonds. The importance of qualifying for the Treasury List should not be underrated, because most municipalities and local governments will not accept bonds without first verifying that the surety company is approved by the U.S. Treasury.

Surety companies seeking to write bonds on federal construction projects may apply to the Treasury Department for inclusion on the list of approved sureties. The application requires information on a company's individual charter and articles of incorporation, its state insurance department licenses, its officers, any holders of more than 5% of stock in the company, and its financial condition and methods of operation. Included in the Treasury List is the maximum single bond limit that the surety will be allowed to write. The limit is calculated as 10% of the approved policyholder surplus of the company as determined by the Treasury Department.

Summary

Suretyship exists whenever one party agrees to guarantee that another party will faithfully perform an obligation: should the obligation go uncompleted, there exists a promise to indemnify or pay a stated sum.

No single line of insurance differs so markedly from its brethren than the surety line. There are many experts who believe that surety is more akin to the granting of credit by a bank than the insuring of risks by the philosophy of law of large numbers. Several of the basic differences are: 1) The principal is primarily responsible in surety. 2) The surety premium charged contemplates no losses. 3) There is no reliance on the law of large numbers in surety. Underwriting surety is done on an individual basis without any attempt at broad class distinctions. 4) Generally, there is no cancellation clause in a surety bond. 5) The bond wording will generally be determined by the obligee, not the surety company. Approximately 70% of all revenue generated in the surety industry emanates from one class of bond, the contract bond, which guarantees that a specific construction project will be completed properly by the contractor.

Co-surety is a procedure whereby two or more companies jointly and directly participate in the execution of a bond. Because of the great number of large construction projects which must be bonded, together with the federal government's requirement that no surety company should issue a bond for more than 10% of its policyholder surplus, co-surety is common in today's marketplace. On large bonds it is customary for the ceding company to ask its reinsurers to participate as co-surety.

Surety is a highly sophisticated line marketed by specialists: independent insurance agents who concentrate on contractor accounts. Any significant writer of surety has a separate department to handle this business, staffed by individuals specifically trained in this line who concentrate their entire time on surety production and underwriting.

This degree of separation and specialization in surety has one measurable effect, a heavy expense factor. This is one of the few lines in the insurance portfolio where the expense ratio is expected to continually exceed the loss ratio. Many knowledgeable reinsurance people feel that one of the drawbacks to reinsuring surety is the extremely high reinsurance commission factor that must be paid the ceding companies by the reinsurer. In determining what reinsurance commission to pay its client companies, the reinsurer must take into account that the size of surety bonds directly affects the expense ratio. Thus, a company that normally writes larger contractors will have a lower agency commission ratio than a company whose portfolio consists primarily of smaller or medium-sized contractor accounts.

To attract and retain business, the surety reinsurer must be able to provide three basic functions: capacity, stabilization of underwriter results, and financing. In reinsurance techniques, each program must be customized for the ceding company. Additionally, it is not unusual to have a surety reinsurance program combine quota or surplus share with excess of loss.

The reinsurance underwriter's primary task is to constantly monitor its company's share of the surety marketplace and its individual reinsurance percentage of a given company's business. In both cases the objective is to avoid overconcentration by securing a suffecient spread of risk. Underwriting of a contractor is centered on determining the contractor's ability to undertake a volume of construction work and, based on the determination, qualifying it for a line of credit. The analysis of a firm's current financial statement and work program must be weighed against the future pitfalls of inflation, oscillating bank interest rates, and other economic factors.

A reinsurer's and ceding company's exposures to loss are directly related to the line of credit established for an account. Can a surety and its reinsurers identify the maximum probable loss from a contractor's uncompleted work program? The answer is, No! And why not? Because of the varied factors that make up the work program, such as the class of contractor involved, the payment obligations, the geographic area, and the quality of claim handling available.

There are two distinct and highly important factors for the reinsurance underwriter to consider before granting a surety reinsurance treaty to any company. These are the terms and conditions of the treaty, and the underwriting philosophy or management characteristics of the primary company which includes its staffing, hiring, and salary requirements.

The most important characteristic of contract bond underwriting is the extreme dollar severity of loss that occurs when a default arises and the contractor is unable to complete its bonded projects. From the beginning of its investigation and audit, a surety claim department is focusing on the upcoming choices or options which are available. Four of these options are:

1) The obligee will undertake to complete the projects and pay all bonded obligations due. Thereafter it will request the surety for reimbursement of all costs incurred.

2) The surety will attempt to obtain bids from other contractors to complete the remaining performance obligations.

3) The surety and the defaulted contractor would enter into a financing arrangement, which would allow the original contractor to complete the projects under the supervision of the surety.

4) Fourthly, the surety would work out a compromise settlement on its performance obligation and "buy back" its bond.

The surety's basic definition of salvage is "assets recovered by the surety in reimbursement for claims it has paid." The degree of salvage recovery in surety is extremely high, more than in any other line of insurance.

There is no direct federal control over the rates and premiums charged by surety companies. As with all lines of insurance, most direct control has been left up to the individual states. The major regulation carried out by the United States Government is through its so-called "Treasury List."

Reinsuring Financial Guarantees and Fidelity Insurance

by Albert W. Davis*

When the term financial guarantee is used in reinsurance nomenclature, the observer is alerted to a hazardous or undesirable line. Accordingly, most reinsurance treaties automatically exclude such a line with the standard phrase, ". . . .business excluded — financial guarantee." Yet, very few treaties ever define the term itself.

All of the insurance lines discussed in this chapter — surety, credit, municipal bonds, mortgage insurance — could be considered financial guarantees if one were to rely on the strict definition as "the insuring of another party's ability or obligation to pay a debt or complete a contractual obligation." For example, contract surety guarantees that a construction project will be completed at the agreed price and that the subcontractors and suppliers for the project will be paid. Credit insurance guarantees that the seller of a product will be paid should the buyer or debtor become insolvent and not pay the bill. Municipal bond insurance tells an investor that the interest due on its bond is guaranteed and that the principal will be paid when due. Mortgage insurance guarantees to the lending institution that the mortgage payments will be paid by the insurer if the individual homeowner cannot make the monthly payments. However, to lump these four lines under the same category would be a grave mistake. Surety and credit are written and reinsured throughout the world. On the other hand, munipical bond and mortgage insurance, having only entered the marketplace in the 1970s, have encountered the traditional problems but are still considered by some as attractive products.

* CPCU, Vice President in charge of the Bond Department, North American Reinsurance Corporation, 100 East 46 Street, New York, New York 10017.

The volatility and insurability of these four lines greatly depend on the salvage and subrogation potential available to the insurer and its reinsurers. Thus viewed, the underwriter will place the highest degree of risk on a case where it is asked to make an outright promise to pay a sum of money directly to a third party — a true financial guarantee. The appeal bond in surety is perhaps the best example. There the individual who wishes to take a court case to a higher level (after having lost the first round) must post a surety bond that in essence provides that, should the individual lose again, the surety will pay upon demand the original damages and costs.

More important is the fact that the profitability of each of these lines is greatly dependent on changes in economic conditions affecting debtors' ability to repay their obligations. Each line also offers significant catastrophic potential due to rising claims which could develop as the economy plunges from recession toward depression. At the same time, rising claims affect the financial strength of the reinsurer. Even moderate stock market declines cause a shrinkage of policyholder surplus. If the insurer and its reinsurers have not been prudent in the handling of these lines, they could face the dreaded threat of huge losses at a time when they are least able to absorb them.

The reinsurer who wishes to achieve continual success in any of these lines must:

1) Possess an intimate knowledge of the product it reinsures. Such an underwriter must know as much as (or preferably more) than the reinsured about the marketing, underwriting, and claim handling of the line.

2) Insist that the exposure be handled equally by the reinsured and the reinsurer. In other words, the reinsurer cannot permit the catastrophe potential to be entirely transferred to it from the ceding company. Thus, the quota share treaty, for all the traditional reasons, becomes the most effective method of reinsuring these lines. While not advocating that quota share treaty be the exclusive mechanism for reinsuring these lines, nevertheless every reinsurance program should be partially quota shared to insure equal tracking of results between reinsured and reinsurer.

Mortgage Insurance

BACKGROUND

Mortgage insurance is not a new phenomenon; its beginnings can be traced from the last century. By the 1920's this type of insurance was widespread, especially in New York. The newly emerging surety companies of that era were particularly active, having easily adopted mortgage insurance to fit their other lines which also guaranteed financial performance.

There are, however, significant differences between mortgage insurance now and insurance as it was issued in the pre-depression days. In the 1920's, there was little if any regulation of the industry by either government or banks. The size of reserve funds carried by insurance companies bore no relation to potential claims, and these funds often were used to purchase additional mortgages. In an effort to increase premium writings, many companies at that time insured anything: unimproved land, nonamortized mortgages, overappraised properties, and unfinished buildings among others. In addition, 100% guarantees were given for the face amount of a mortgage.

In 1929, as the beginnings of the depression were being felt, some of these properties began to go into default. In an effort to survive, mortgage insurers espoused the novel idea of forming subsidiary companies that would purchase these loans before they could be formally declared in default. It was hoped that these subsidiaries, after giving a 100% new mortgage to the parent insurer, would be able to remain liquid enough to pay the insurance premiums and interest. The logic behind this reasoning was that times were bound to improve and that the properties held by these companies would then increase in value, enabling the subsidiaries to sell the properties at a profit. However, things did not get better, and the end result was a wave of losses which caused wholesale failures of the parent companies. Indeed, several of the larger insurance companies operating today were on the brink of bankruptcy then because of their extensive writings of mortgage insurance.

Ultimately the results were so horrendous that by 1932 every state had legislated from existence all types of mortgage insurance. The memory of these failures lingered for a long time. It was not until 1957 that Wisconsin became the first state to allow mortgage insurance again within its boundaries. In July, 1973, New York became the 50th and last state to allow insurance of this type to be sold.

WHAT IS MORTGAGE GUARANTEE INSURANCE?

Mortgage insurance protects the lending institution or mortgagee against the peril that the individual borrower or mortgagor will fail to make the required periodic financial payments resulting in a default on the loan. The maximum amount of insurance on each mortgage is limited to 20% or 25% of the total mortgage loan, and indemnity extends solely to the lending institution. Mortgage insurance does not protect physical property, nor does it involve payment of a loan in case the borrower dies (which is the death payment commonly provided by credit life insurance).

Many compare mortgage insurance with suretyship because both lines involve three parties to a contract: an *insurance company* guaranteeing the performance of the *principal* for the benefit of a *third party*. In mortgage insurance this third party would be the mortgagee, and the performance would be the monetary payments required by the terms of the mortgage. Furthermore, the underwriting of both lines involves analysis of financial information. However, one striking difference should be noted. In mortgage insurance, there is no recourse or subrogation by the insurer against the borrower beyond the property which was used as security for the mortgage loan. This seems only equitable since the borrower receives no benefit from the insurance once a default occurs.

Prior to the creation in 1957 of the first private mortgage insurance company, Mortgage Guaranty Insurance Corporation (MGIC), insurance was available only through two government agencies: the Federal Housing Authority (FHA) since 1934, and the Veterans Administration (VA) since 1944. As the popularity of this government insurance grew through the late 1940's and early 1950's, the ability of the government to render effective service diminished considerably. Also, the adherence of the government to a non-flexible interest rate on the mortgages it protected proved unattractive to investors when the mortgage market was tight. MGIC's founders geared their company's marketing directly to offset these factors and attempted to offer a striking alternative to the federal government's program.

Comparison of Government and Private Insurance. There are several differences between insurance by FHA and that offered by private insurance companies.

1) The private mortgage insurers emphasize speed in service. Generally, same-day service is given to the lending institution in underwriting an application. Government insurance generally takes weeks for approval.

2) Unlike the FHA, private insurers do not insure the full face amount of mortgage loans. Maximum insurance is written to either 20% or 25% of the loan amount.

3) FHA insurance generally remains in force for the full life of the mortgage, which is generally twenty-five or thirty years. Private insurance can be purchased either annually or in multiple years for periods up through fifteen years. The term of private insurance lasts on the average the first seven years of the mortgage.

4) The FHA commonly insures large tracts of development land. Regulatory restrictions imposed by the Federal Home Loan Mortgage Corporation limit a private insurer to a maximum of 10% of its policyholder surplus in any specific tract of land or area which is separated by one half mile or less.

5) The FHA imposes a ceiling on the interest rate to be charged on a mortgage loan insured by it. Private insurance on the other hand has no such restrictions. The market plus individual state regulations dictate what interest can be charged. It is interesting to note that statistics accumulated at the end of 1972 showed that in a relatively short period of fifteen years, the private mortgage insurance premium volume had reached a point where it exceeded the combined premium for the FHA and VA programs.

Definitions. The mortgage insurance industry, like others, has its particular nomenclature. Some of the terms are widely used and deserved to be understood by the student of reinsurance.

1) *PMI* — the private mortgage insurance company. In most of the trade literature, this is the title used when referring to the insurer.

2) *Loan-to-Value Ratio* — the most important ratio in mortgage insurance. This determines the eligibility, the premium rate for insurance, and the interest rate charged on the mortgage. It also determines the mortgage's liquidity in the secondary market. The ratio is determined by dividing the amount of the mortgage loan either by the appraised value or the selling price of the mortgaged property — whichever is lower.

3) *Freddie Mac* — the nickname for the Federal Home Loan Mortgage Corporation. This is a federally funded agency created in 1970 by the Emergency Home Finance Act, Title III. It is the regulatory authority over mortgage guarantee companies as well as the savings and loan industry. In addition, it serves a vital function in the secondary market in the purchasing of mortgages.

4) *Fannie Mae* — the nickname for the Federal National Mortgage Association. A quasi-governmental agency, its stock is also available to the public and is actively traded on the stock exchanges. FNMA was created by Congress to purchase VA and FHA mortgages and today has a vital function in the secondary mortgage market.

How Is Private Mortgage Insurance Administered?

Underwriting. With minor exceptions, insurance is available only to lending institutions which are regulated and supervised by federal or state authorities — savings banks, commercial banks, savings and loan lenders,and mortgage bankers. These lending institutions, by law, must have adequate appraisal facilities and proven ability to service any mortgage loan they initiate. The experience of these organizations makes it possible for the insurance companies to write mortgage guarantee insurance without pre-inspecting or pre-appraising each piece of property submitted for insurance, thereby providing rapid service in underwriting at a substantial savings in overhead expense since a staff of engineers and appraisers is not needed.

The first step in the insurance process is for a lending institution to become approved by the mortgage insurer. (This approval can be equated to the appointment of an agent by a property and casualty company). A great deal of emphasis is placed by the insurer on the capability and integrity of the financial institution. It is the bank which eliminates loans having excessive risk. Furthermore, the bank's ability to service mortgages should prevent most delinquencies from becoming defaults.

The major underwriting emphasis in mortgage insurance is on examining the qualifications of the lending institution. It is only after a satisfactory analysis has been made by the insurer that a master insurance policy is issued, setting forth the terms and conditions of the insurance. However, this master policy does not obligate the lender to secure insurance from that particular company issuing it, nor does it obligate the company to issue insurance on a particular loan. Indeed, it is common for the lender to have contracts with two or three mortgage insurers and to distribute the business among them. The master policy outlines the procedures, rights, and duties of the parties when a borrower fails to make the required payments. The master policy cannot be assigned.

The individual policy of mortgage insurance is issued after title closing. At the closing, the insurance premium is paid by the individual to the lender, who in turn notifies the mortgage insurer that the premium has been collected. This notification triggers the execution of the policy, and it is mailed directly to the lender. The individual policy can be assigned and is renewable at the option of the lender.

Reinsurance. Mortgage insurers operate under a dual regulatory system. Each state insurance department imposes its own restrictions, some of which exist in other states. Additionally, the federal government through the Federal Home Loan Mortgage Corporation insists that its requirements be met. Accordingly, the private mortgage insurance company operates under two important restraints:

1) Total insurance risk or exposure outstanding for the company cannot exceed twenty-five times its policyholder surplus. This exposure

is measured by adding the amount of insurance on each mortgage, with each mortgage loan being subject to a maximum of 20-to-25 % insurance.

2) Total insurance in force for the company in any one standard metropolitan statistical area (SMSA) is limited to no more than 20 % of the company's total writings. The amount of insurance in force is defined as the sum of all the individual mortgage loans that are insured. The term SMSA was created by the United States Department of Commerce, which determines its boundaries and specifications.

Because of these restraints, the major problem facing mortgage insurers is capacity. Therefore, any reinsurance program must be geared toward offsetting the pressure that new business places on policyholder surplus. As a result, quota share reinsurance or surplus aid reinsurance appear to be the most attractive program to a mortgage insurer.

An interesting phenomenon in underwriting mortgage insurance is that in times of "tight money," when there are more mortgage applicants competing for available money, underwriting tends to be stricter. During such times the lending institutions are concerned less about mortgage declinations since they have enough applicants. But the issue is reversed in "loose money" times when the underwriters feel more pressure is exerted to acquire mortgage loans by lending institution which have fewer applicants.

Claims. The master policy issued to the lending institution requires the lender to notify the insurer when a mortgage is four months delinquent in payment. In some states the requirement is two months. From a practical standpoint, and depending on the efficiency of the lending institution, these notices will normally contain a list of mortgages that are 30, 60, 90, and 120 days delinquent. At a certain point, depending on the state insurance law, the lending institution makes a decision to file an official claim with the insurer.

When a claim notice is received, the private mortgage insurer has two options available. In the first instance, it requires the lending institution to acquire title to the property either through a foreclosure sale or through a voluntary conveyance of title to the bank. The bank in turn conveys the title of the property to the insurer. When this is done, the insurer becomes obligated to pay the amount equal to the principal and interest accrued during the loan, plus allowable expenses involved in the foreclosure. Because of these additional expenses, especially on property in a badly declining area, it is possible that the entire default could exceed 100 % of the value of the mortgage.

The other option for the insurer, and the one most frequently used, is not to take title to the property but rather to pay its maximum of 20 % (for an 80 % mortgage) or 25 % (for a 75 % mortgage). Exercise of this second option has several advantages for the insurer. It effectively puts a maximum on the amount of liability that the insurer has on each mortgage it insures. At the same time, by leaving title of the property with the lending institution, the option relieves the insurer of the expense in handling the property and arranging for its sale.

The Marketplace. The private mortgage insurance business gives the appearance of a highly concentrated industry. Approximately fifteen companies specialize in this insurance with the largest four writers dominating the marketplace. However, the industry also competes actively with the United States Government's FHA and VA insurance. In turn, both the private sector and the government compete with the lending institutions, which rely on their own ability to evaluate the risk inherent in mortgage lending. In other words, the bank can choose not to insure its mortgage, retaining the risk in its own account in a form of non-insurance.

The greatest common denominator between the three areas is the loan-to-value ratio of the loan. Currently, the best estimate is that government insurance has a virtual monopoly on mortgage loans with a ratio of 95 % or more of the value of the property. On loans when the ratio is between 90 % and 95 % of the property value, the government and the private mortgage insurers equally share the market. On the majority of loans under the 90 % ratio, it appears from the available data that self-insurance (or non-insurance) by the lending institution is most used.

Credit Insurance

The essential lubricant for the wheels of economic development in any individual country has been credit. Indeed, the history of economic development can be traced in the history of credit — the loan of money, or the time given for the payment of goods or services sold on trust. Credit must be extended and the appropriate risks must be incurred at every stage of the long and complicated economic cycle from production through distribution and finally consumption.

Credit insurance is designed to protect merchants and manufacturers against financial losses arising from the insolvency or protracted default of buyers to whom goods have been sold and delivered, or for whom work has been done or services rendered, on normal credit terms. Within this definition are contained the three basic principles of credit insurance: 1) Credit insurance covers credit risks at all stages of manufacturing and distribution, other than the final sale to the general public. Thus, while it covers trade obligations, it does not cover consumer credit. 2) It does not guarantee payment of a debt at the due date. It indemnifies only following the insolvency or protracted default of a buyer. 3) It does not cover the whole of a risk; the insured merchant is always required to retain an uninsured portion for its own account. This guarantees that the insurance does not become a substitute for the merchant's prudent selection of customers and vigorous pursuit of slow payers.

Underwriting

Domestic Credit. The essential risk in credit insurance can be divided into two categories, domestic and foreign. Transactions where the seller of the goods and the buyer are located within the boundaries of the same country are referred to as domestic credit. Here, the underwriter is faced with evaluating the commercial risk, with a decision made on the ability of the untimate buyer to pay for the goods delivered.

While the premium generated in the course of one year from export credit insurance is almost impossible to compute, it is estimated that the annual worldwide premium generated from domestic credit insurance was approximately $500,000,000 in 1977. Only a small segment of this would be generated within the United States.

The type of policies issued in domestic credit insurance varies according to the law and customs within individual countries. However, the insurance contract is designed to cover either a single transaction or a continuing business relationship. In a single transaction the policy is issued to cover an individual contract of sale. The insurance is taken out when the contract is negotiated, and the risk begins when the goods are delivered or the work started. Coverage ends when payment for the goods or services is made. It is obvious that the execution of insurance for a series of single contracts can be time consuming and expensive and that this coverage is only suitable when transactions are substantial and require individual treatment. An example would be the sale of large pieces of construction equipment. Preferred alternatives include the issuance of a policy called the Specific Account Policy, which will insure a series of transactions with one or more named buyers over a period of twelve months. Another alternative is the Whole Turnover Policy, designed to cover the entire spectrum of business transactions by the seller over the policy period.

The Whole Turnover Policy is by far the more popular policy because of its convenience. Before providing this coverage, and because of the need to determine the appropriate premium, the insurance company generally secures from the seller of the goods to be insured full information concerning past experience of bad debts, plus a list of the company's principal buyers with indications of the credit limits allowed to each. Additionally, the underwriters of the company relying on their own information sources will underwrite these buyers. The insurance company reserves the right to either exclude from coverage any specific buyer or reduce the amounts of credit it is willing to insure.

Many sellers will have a disproportionate number of buyers who buy infrequently and whose credit limit is very small. Rather than subject the insurance company and the insured to prequalifying these individual risks, the policy may contain a discretionary limit. This limit enables the insured to grant a stipulated amount of credit to small buyers without justifying it to the insurance company. However, if an individual transaction were to exceed this discretionary limit, the insurance company would have to be notified. Lastly, policies can be extended to cover goods before they are delivered to the buyer. An example of this would be specially manufactured items which, in the event of an insolvency on the part of the buyer, could not be resold without a substantial loss to the seller.

Export Credit.

Legal Factors. As the economies of many nations throughout the world develop, their desire to export goods increases, and their reliance on credit and credit insurance gains more acceptance. The basic objectives of credit insurance are as applicable in the United States and Great Britain as they are in Japan and Australia. However, the laws throughout the world differ and the legal definitions of insolvency, default, and the legal wording of individual insurance policies will differ among countries. Additionally, the procedures of meeting claims in different countries must be related to local legislation and local currencies.

Economic Factors. Commercial credit insurance is always tied to the economic well being of a specific country and the type of goods being exported. In the latter category, every credit insurer keeps a close analysis of the goods it is insuring. For example, the amounts of insurance on foodstuffs, or textiles and clothing, or timber are all carefully analyzed. The underwriter is concerned that during the course of any decade one of these products will be in scarce supply and the other in overabundance; these two factors add or subtract from their salability. The more salable a product, the less likely it will cause a credit insurance claim. Additionally, the economic cycle of recession and prosperity has a direct relationship to the number of insolvencies in any given country. The underwriter's anticipation that downswings in the economic cycles are likely becomes extremely important to the credit underwriter. Thus, credit insurance is tied to swings in the economy of a nation more closely than any other line of insurance.

In many ways credit insurance is a luxury insurance, because in order for it to exist and grow, it must cater to a well established market which is governed by a well established credit system. This is the main reason why it is exceptionally difficult to maintain an adequate volume of credit insurance in underdeveloped countries. It is for this reason that the predominant bulk of premiums generated from credit insurance are developed in Europe, an area of the world that has for centuries dominated world trade.

Political Factors. In export credit insurance, the underwriting becomes more difficult because of the lack of complete information that can be developed on the buyer. The primary trade association for all credit insurers is the International Credit Insurance Association (ICIA), founded in 1928 and now headquartered in Zurich, Switzerland. However, the main risk derives not from lack of information but rather from political and monetary factors.

The inability of perfectly solvent buyers to pay for goods may come about because of political reasons within the country or from political movements, such as the blocking of local currency deposits, exchange controls, or embargoes on external payments to foreign countries. Added to such causes is the risk of devaluation of the local currency, or even confiscation of property. The catastrophe potential of such risks is simply too great for private insurers to handle, which has been recognized ever since the close of World War I. Thus, export insurance, unlike its brethren in the domestic field, has in the Twentieth Century become a marriage of convenience between private insurers and the government. This type of cooperation can take several forms. In some countries, including the United States, the normal commercial insurance risk is covered by local companies, and the political risks are insured by a government agency. For example, the Foreign Credit Insurance Association (FCIA) and the Export-Import Bank of the United States (EXIM) have been providing United States exporters with credit insurance since 1961. FCIA insures the commercial risk, while EXIM insures the political risk. The Bank also provides FCIA with several excess of loss reinsurance treaties on commercial losses. Furthermore, it is interesting to note that although these two agencies appear as joint insurers under the credit insurance contract, the exporter only has to deal with FCIA. In some countries the entire risk, including the political aspect, is underwritten by local companies and the government will act as a reinsurer. In still other countries, specialized companies are created which are jointly financed and jointly managed by the federal government and private enterprise.

REINSURANCE

All reinsurance treaties in credit tend to be almost exlusively proportional and more specifically quota share. It is customary under a quota share arrangement to assign different reinsurance categories according to the size and classification of the debtors.

A surplus share is also used. However, it is more burdensome from an administrative point of view. As in the quota share, the attachment of liability and premium will be done on a predetermined basis and on the basis of the fluctuating outstanding credits.

Credit reinsurers prefer to avoid excess of loss treaties on this line. The only exception would be the rare occasion where substantial premiums are generated by a proportional business. In these situations, strict adherence is made to a ceiling on aggregate liability. In this way, an accumulation of losses through catastrophe will be avoided.

Insuring Municipal Bonds

The concept of insuring municipal bonds was born in the early 1970's. The then radical concept of revenue sharing by the federal government, coupled with pressure from environmentalists and others for pollution control enforcement, compelled many municipalities to begin large construction projects. Additionally, shifts in population mandated new public buildings for the newcomers. The only way to finance these ambitious undertakings was to issue municipal bonds for raising the necessary revenue. Today, approximately 20,000 municipalities have issued bonds to the public. The basic premises behind this type of insurance, then, are twofold: 1) The interest savings to the municipalities will substantially offset the premium costs of insurance and financing charges. Why? Since many of the municipalities had not previously engaged in large construction projects, their credit ratings were questioned by potential investors. Insurance was created to absorb such risks and enhance the attractiveness of municipal bonds to a wider range of investors. With the guarantee of bond principal (and interest), investor risk was reduced, and municipalities could benefit through reduced interest cost. 2) The additional security offered to investors through insurance will allow smaller municipalities with good credit ratings the opportunity to compete in the marketplace on an equal footing with larger, more prominent municipalities.

Presently, two organizations provide insurance coverage for new issues of municipal bonds, a company and an association of four companies. The MGIC Indemnity Corporation is a wholly owned subsidiary of MGIC Investment Corporation, the parent of several companies specializing in long-term financial guarantees. The Investment Corporation is publicly owned and listed on the New York Stock Exchange. While the Indemnity Corporation insures individual municipal bond issues, it also offers insurance on municipal bond funds and portfolios of municipal bonds held by individuals, banks, insurance companies, or trust departments. The association of companies, Municipal Bond Insurance Association, was founded in 1974 and has concentrated its efforts on the guaranteeing of new municipal bonds. The Association is not an insurer itself but rather is a pool of four insurers which participate in the individual policies issued by the Association.

Municipal bond insurance applies to the principal and interest payments as they become due, not on an accelerated basis. Typically interest payments are scheduled to be paid every six months over the term of the bond, which can range from ten to twenty-five years. Thus, the insurance protects and guarantees each payment and is automatically paid if the municipality responsible for payment fails to honor its obligations.

The insurance provided is both irrevocable and unconditional. The statement of insurance which is attached to the bond becomes part of the basic security and accompanies the bond in all future sales. Because of this feature, the entire premium charge for insurance is collected at the beginning of the policy term when the bonds are delivered to the purchasers.

UNDERWRITING

Generally, underwriters will attempt to restrict coverage either to general obligation bond issues or to basic utility obligations such as water, sewer, and electric services. The service fees generated by such utilities are governed by law or contract, and the fee should provide full revenue coverage of operations, maintenance, and debt service on the bonds. Within these guidelines, the underwriters will generally put a maximum dollar limit on the debt service (the total of principal and interest to be paid on the bonds) that they will insure over a short period of time (such as two years). Additionally, there will also be a maximum debt service amount, regardless of the time period involved.

Since the taxing power of municipalities is important, the underwriter will generally have a minimum population limit. For example, a municipality with less than 10,000 people might not be considered. Additionally, the underwriters will attempt to avoid a geographic and economic concentration of insurance, much in the same way as a fire underwriter will avoid a concentration of insurance in any particular area. The underwriter will look for an unqualified legal opinion that the bonds are free of any litigation that would affect their validity. There also should be no right of the bondholders to accelerate payment in the event of default.

What is a typical insured bond issue? In 1976, according to the Municipal Bond Insurance Association,[1] such an issue was a $4,000,000 general obligation of a medium-sized town. The insurance premium ranged from $35,000 to $80,000. According to the Association the average life of an insured issue would be approximately fifteen years. In 1976 around 70% of all bond issues insured by this organization were general obligation types.

To be insurable by the MGIC Indemnity Corporation, at least 75% of the bonds in a portfolio must be rated BBB/Baa or better; up to 25% of the portfolio bonds may be non-rated or be industrial aid/pollution control bonds. All portfolio bonds to be insured must be approved by the insurer as to their insurability, but all of the bonds in a portfolio need not be insured.[2] A holder may insure any part of its municipal bond holdings as long as the portfolio for which insurance is applied meets the minimum size, quality, and diversification requirements of the company.

GOVERNMENT REGULATION

Because it was recognized that insurance of municipal bonds differs from other forms of guarantees, New York State on July 8, 1971, promulgated Regulation No. 61 which governs insurance of this type. This regulation consisted of a number of provisions which can be summarized as:

1) Municipal bond insurance is classified as surety and, in consequence, an IBNR (incurred but not reported) loss reserve computed at the rate of 5% of premiums in force must be carried.

2) A formula is utilized to determine exposure and capacity. This ruling states that no insurer shall have outstanding a cumulative net liability, under policies in force, in an amount which exceeds twenty-five times the sum of a company's capital and surplus, plus a contingency reserve, plus 50% of the unearned premium reserve. The term

---

[1] Municipal Bond Insurance Association, 34 South Broadway, White Plains, New York 10601, 1976 Annual Report, p. 3.

[2] "MGIC Indemnity Corporation," undated pamphlet from its parent corporation, MGIC Investment Corporation, P.O. Box 756, Milwaukee, Wisconsin 53201, p. 2.

"cumulative net liability" shall mean 25 % of the insured unpaid principal and insured unpaid interest covered by policies in force insuring municipal bonds. Thus, for the purpose of determining capacity, exposure is considered to be 25 % of that debt service, and adjusted policyholder surplus is multiplied by twenty-five to arrive at a company's total permitted exposure.

REINSURANCE

The underwriting problems and opportunities facing a ceding company and a reinsurer in this line of business are vastly different for each other. For the ceding company wishing reinsurance, the main objective of a program would be spread of risk. Because of the extreme concentration in the limited number of companies participating in this coverage, every insurer of municipal bonds would as a matter of prudence wish to cede a specific percentage of its writings. Additionally, a ceding company may feel that it is insuring too much in a given geographic area. It can reach this judgment based solely on the amount of municipal bond issues emanating from a particular section of the country. However, that decision may also be forced on the company because of a heavy concentration of property and casualty writings in the same area. Insuring against the perils of fire and windstorm in an area may be actuarially sound, but when one adds the hazards of economic failure, overconcentration becomes an acute concern to the underwriter. A third area of overconcentration to the ceding company can be found in its investment portfolio. Most insurance companies carry large amounts of municipal bonds. For example, at the end of 1977, insurance companies held $45.7 billion worth of bonds from state and local municipalities.[3] Holding a group of municipal bonds from a geographic area, while also insuring their issuers' creditworthiness, can become too much exposure even for the largest of multiple line writers.

The Quota Share Treaty. The best type of reinsurance program appears to be the quota share approach, since the desired objective of the ceding company is spread of risk. For an individual issue, the reinsurance cover would apply to the gross liability based on the par amount of the bonds issued. An example of such a cover follows:

Par Amount for Single Issue Gross		Par Amount For Single Issue Obligatory Quota Share		
0	- $ 7,500,000	10 %	- Max of $	750,000
$ 7,500,000	- $20,000,000	20 %	- Max of $	4,000,000
$20,000,000	- $30,000,000	33 1/3 %	- Max of $10,000,000	
$30,000,000	- $50,000,000	50 %	- Max of $25,000,000	

While such a treaty would take care of the normal requirements of an insurer, it does not eliminate the problem of concentration in any geographic area that could occur after the treaty has been consummated. Thus, an additional treaty or a separate section to the existing treaty could be put together which would apply specifically to this problem. In this case, either a quota share or a surplus share could be arranged which will specifically cede to the reinsurer new business from that geographic area. Since the danger of overconcentration is the problem here, the treaty could call for a minimum of 50% cessions to the reinsurers of new issues. While the ceding company would probably prefer this section to be on an automatic basis, it is doubtful that any reinsurer would consent to such a proposal.

Special Acceptances. To cope with overconcentration, the procedure of "special acceptances" is used. This procedure will allow the reinsurer to underwrite any new issue in the concentrated area and evaluate its own investment portfolio. Additionally, the reinsurer would probably insist on a maximum dollar limit per issue. Such a reinsurance section could be worded as follows:

At those times when the aggregate liability in force for any specified geographic region exceeds the company's guidelines, the company may reinsure:

1. Up to a maximum of 50% of the cumulative in-force liability for that specific geographic area.
2. Up to 90% of any new bond issue on a political subdivision in this geographic area. The limit under this section should not exceed $25 million, par amount for any one bond issue, and will include any amount ceded under the normal obligatory cover schedule.

Reinsurance Underwriting. The underwriting problem facing the reinsurer is indeed unique. It is being asked to assume business whose exposure to loss has a term running from fifteen to thirty, or even forty, years. This longevity certainly increases the degree of risk. It has been argued that no one is clairvoyant enough to foresee fifteen to twenty years into the future. Natural disasters such as flood and earthquake could destroy a municipality. Additionally, the economic depression to a community caused by the shutdown or bankruptcy of a major industry that supports a good percentage of the population would certainly affect tax collections. Lastly, financial mismanagement of a municipality by a political party too long in power, once thought to be impossible, has in recent years become a reality.

---

[3] "Municipal Bond Sales," *Journal of Commerce,* May 18, 1978.

Proponents of municipal bond insurance caution that, on the surface, the degree of risk appears great. However, several factors turn the long-term danger into a positive rather than a negative factor. One positive factor is that insurance only covers principal and interest payments on bonds as they become due under the original schedule of payment. For instance, legal debt service payments on $10,000,000 of principal and interest spread over twenty years would be $500,000 principal per year, or only 5% of the total. The exposure from the bond principal would be limited to this 5% as it came due. Since it may be assumed that a municipality in financial difficulties would eventually receive federal or state help, it is likely that the obligation of insurance would only be for a temporary period of time.

Another favorable aspect of the long-term spreading of risks is that the risk-reward ratio becomes more favorable with time. This improvement is due to the premium being fully collectible at the beginning of the insurance term and only taxable to the insurer as it is earned. Most of the premium is thus available for investment purposes during much of the protection period. Additionally, since 50% of the earned premium goes into the special contingency reserve, which receives special tax benefits, the reserve structure of a company is not depleted by taxes in good years; rather, the reserve is allowed to build up over time in relationship to the insurer's total exposure.

The contingency reserve is an additional reserve established for the protection of policyholders against the effect of excessive losses which might occur during a severe economic cycle. New York's Regulation 61 requires that the contingency reserve:

....shall consist of allocations of sums representing fifty percent of the earned premiums on policies insuring municipal bonds. Allocations to such reserve made during each calendar year shall be maintained for a period of at least 240 months, except that withdrawals may be made by the company in any year in which the actual paid losses on the said type of policy exceed thirty-five percent of the earned premiums thereon, but no such releases shall be made without the prior written approval of the Superintendent.[4]

On one issue all parties may agree. There exists the unanswerable question, In light of the newness of municipal bond insurance and the scarcity of satisfactory statistics or actuarial tables, what guarantee is there that the current premium charged will be adequate to pay future losses? Only time will verify or refute the judgment of the municipal bond insurers.

---

[4]   Regulation 61, New York State Insurance Department, July 8, 1971.

Fidelity Insurance

The number of insurance companies writing a significant portion of the fidelity line of business is extremely limited. The four largest writers of fidelity insurance dominate over 40% of the entire market, while the fifteen largest writers account for over 80% of the premium volume. The entire insurance market within the United States produces an annual fidelity volume of approximately $350,000,000 (estimated 1978 figures).

Coverage

The fidelity policy protects an employer against loss from fraudulent or dishonest acts committed by its employees, whether acting alone or in collusion with others. The employer is protected whether the employee wrongfully abstracts money, merchandise, or any other property belonging to the employer for which the employer is legally liable. While the peril insured seems clear enough (fraud or dishonesty by the employee), the definition requires that two criteria be present before a claim will be honored. First, the employee must intend to cause a loss to the employer. Secondly, the employee must intend that either the employee or someone known to the employee receive a financial benefit outside the normal course of employment. Thus, the intent of the individual to do harm and to profit from the deed must be present. To illustrate, the throwing of packages from a company delivery truck at random rather than delivering them would not be covered, because the culprit would not benefit financially from the act. Additionally, the policy of fidelity specifically excludes three types of losses.

1) Loss of potential or consequential income from the fidelity act. For example, the theft of bonds would cause future loss of coupon payments to the insured. While the value of the bond is reimbursable, the loss of future coupon payments is not.

2) All damages of any type where the insured is held legally liable (except direct compensatory damages arising from the loss). This exclusion specifically refers to any punitive or exemplary damages assessed against the insured by reason of tortious or dishonest acts or conduct of an employee involving a third party.

3) All costs, fees and other expenses incurred by the insured in establishing the existence of or amount of a loss. Here, as in No. 1, the intent is to exclude a specific type of consequential loss.

Main Classes

Fidelity bonds can be written either on a specific individual or on a specific employment position. Groups of individuals or positions can also be bonded through a schedule bond. However, the vast majority of fidelity policies are written on a blanket basis covering all employees of a business. Most of these blanket fidelity bonds are sold as packages and include several burglary coverages collectively known as "crime insurance." These package policies are specifically aimed at two distinct types of business enterprise: 1) the financial institutions of the United States such as commercial banks, stock brokers, credit unions; and 2) commercial concerns such as manufacturers, service industries, and contractors. The premium income for the industry is almost evenly divided in fidelity between these two types of business risks.

Commercial. The underwriting results from commercial fidelity business over the last decade have been consistently profitable. As a result, almost all insurance companies are willing to provide this coverage either as part of the special multi-peril package policies or as individual policies from their own bond departments. The only significant underwriting limitation that many of these companies would impose would be on the size bond that they underwrite, for example preferring to limit their maximum bond to $1,000,000.

Financial Institution. However, the financial institution business has proven extremely volatile and fraught with underwriting dangers. Blanket bonds for financial institutions are package policies tailored for the requirements of the individual bank. For example, the insurance protection needed by a commercial bank will in many cases differ from that needed by a savings bank, simply because the exposures are different. However, in all cases these package policies will cover the following: 1) fraud and dishonesty of all employees at the bank; 2) burglary and robbery coverage both on and off the premises while property is being conveyed by bank messengers. 3) Also, there are separate agreements for forgery protection, counterfeit currency protection, and extortion and kidnapping coverage.

CLAIMS

Because the coverage required is very broad and because the amounts of liability required are large, the insurer of financial institutions assumes the severity of risk from such incidents as: 1) external attacks by criminals through robbery, larceny and burglary; 2) external attacks by criminals who take hostages or threaten violence to individuals; 3) internal attacks through fraud and embezzlement — the so-called white collar crimes; and 4) the misuse of electronic data processing equipment to circumvent existing control systems.

Over the last decade, by far the largest single cause of loss to insurance companies has been embezzlement. Statistically speaking, the greatest number of embezzlements occur in the larger institutions which have many branch offices. The most common source is the loan department where fraudulent accounts are created by a loan officer, usually working with an outside conspirator. Loans are processed for non-existent borrowers and then the conspirator collects the monies.

The greatest hazard facing fidelity insurers and reinsurers today, in the opinion of many experts, is the vulnerability of modern electronic data processing systems to abuse. Most financial institutions and large corporations have individualized EDP systems. However, these systems consist of one or more large computers and banks of stored data, usually accessible through telephone circuits from individual terminals. With a little knowledge and dedication, an employee at one terminal can read, alter, or delete data or tamper with the sophisticated programs that manipulate this data.

Electronic and magnetic data have now replaced information that previously was kept in record books. Many of today's corporate assets are no longer represented by stocks and bonds or gold bars located in the vault, but rather by simple magnetic wiggles on a disk.

. . . .Gold bars in vaults, notations in a ledger, or for that matter, written reports from a corporate research project are immutable and immovable things compared to magnetic wiggles, which can be read, altered, or destroyed at the touch of a teletypewriter key. For criminal purposes, funds can be fraudulently credited to an account, a bank balance can be programmed never to be overdrawn, or the record of ownership of very large sums of money can be altered.[5]

The peril of burglary or robbery to the insurer is limited either to the amount of money immediately available to the thief or the amount of money it can carry away. The loan officer in a bank can generally embezzle only within the confines of the lending authority. However, the magnitude of a loss to an insured from altered computer data knows no limit and indeed staggers the imagination.

REINSURANCE UNDERWRITING CONCERNS

Before a reinsurance underwriter decides to enter into a fidelity treaty, it must make an analysis of three distinct factors: 1) the severity potential of the portfolio it is being asked to reinsure; 2) the percentage of financial institution business making up the portfolio; and 3) the

[5] Tom Alexander, "Waiting for the Great Computer Rip-Off," *Fortune Magazine*, July, 1974, pp. 143-150.

percentage of the market that its potential client dominates.

Severity. Fidelity losses are infrequent but they are severe. It is a rare fidelity loss that is a clean, well defined act. Generally, the fraud or embezzlement has taken place over several months or years. Obviously, the longer the loss goes undetected, the greater the potential for severity. Additionally, the amount of the loss is always in question primarily because of complicated financial transactions. Because of this complexity, a separate audit is generally required of the insured's books, a time consuming measure. The end result to both the ceding company and the reinsurer is a constant upgrading of the initial reserve as the auditors uncover more and more of the defalcation.

The world is indeed getting smaller. Most of the large corporations and financial institutions have offices around the world. Almost all of these corporations insist on fidelity coverage for U.S. employees as well as foreign based employees. As these companies expand into different countries, controls and audits exercised by the home office grow weaker, making the opportunity for fraud and embezzlement more attractive, and also harder to detect. Adding to this problem is the fact that claim investigation and claim payments in foreign countries are extremely difficult.

It was not too long ago that most corporations were satisfied with fidelity coverage in amounts of $1,000,000 or less. Similarly, financial institutions did not consider coverage in any great amounts to be a requirement. However, in today's marketplace it is not unusual for a medium-sized corporation to seek $10,000,000 worth of fidelity coverage and for financial institutions to seek up to $50,000,000 of coverage.

Commercial fidelity bonds are issued either in commercial blanket covers or blanket position bond covers. The former type of bond covers all officers and employees collectively. In the event of a loss, regardless of how many employees are involved, the aggregate amount collectible is the bond penalty. However, the blanket position bond in the event of a collusive loss will apply the bond penalty to each identifiable employee involved in the loss. Thus, for example, a $50,000 blanket position bond would fully protect a firm if four bonded individuals collectively embezzled $200,000. An unsuspecting underwriter who merely assumed that $50,000 is its maximum possible loss could be rudely awakened and its reinsurer equally shocked by such an event.

Financial Institution Business. The second area of concern to a reinsurer is the percentage of financial institution business contained in the portfolio it is being asked to reinsure. Because of the higher limits and greater perils insured against, the financial institution policy presents a severe hazard to the reinsurer.

Part of the severity problem in fidelity is the fact that many of the coverages issued to banks are required by law. Thus, the maximum possible loss to the reinsurer is the statutory minimum. For example, in commercial banks no loan can exceed 10% of a bank's surplus position. The amount of coverage required is also equal to that 10%.

Probably the greatest factor in severity losses is the historical precedent whereby all financial institution bonds are written on a discovery basis. Thus, the fidelity carrier is obligated to indemnify losses that occur during its term and also to cover losses that occurred since the inception of the financial institution's business, but which were not discovered until the present policy term.

An additional pitfall to the reinsurer lies in the fact that most of the non-dominant writers of fidelity will include this minor line in their commercial lines for reinsurance purposes. If the reinsurer has not done its homework, it could find that a line of business producing $50,000 to $100,000 in premium can include one or two financial institutions.

REINSURANCE METHODS

There is no single definitive method of efficiently reinsuring fidelity. The best treaty is the one that adequately protects the ceding company from its exposure to severity and which, at the same time, grants to the reinsurer enough premium base to make the assumption of risk attractive.

Excess of Loss. In companies with a minor participation in the line, the tendency is to include fidelity exposure in casualty treaties. Thus, most of this type of fidelity is reinsured on an excess of loss basis. In the absence of financial institution business, and because most of this type of fidelity business will be associated with package policies (which include property and casualty covers), this inclusion with the commercial lines seems the best approach.

A reinsurer will generally opt for an excess of loss program for those companies which write a meaningful volume of fidelity business and which will include a good percentage of financial institution business. The main criteria in determining such a program would be a significant premium volume to the reinsurer to compensate for the capacity afforded. Like casualty, the usual procedure in excess of loss is to have a working layer immediately over the company's net retention, followed by significantly larger layers of excess coverage. While there is no ironclad rule as to premium, it is generally assumed that any writer having in excess of $5,000,000 in fidelity premiums would be better off with an excess of loss program.

Facultative. Because of the increasing demand for large limits of liability, particularly in the financial institution area, facultative placement of excess layers is common in today's reinsurance marketplace.

Pro Rata. Most fidelity books do not lend themselves to excess covers, because the subject premium is too small. To compensate for this, the reinsurer will generally opt for a pro rata treaty on all but the largest writers of fidelity business. This pro rata type of cover has several advantages with a smaller book, the most important being that the premium charge is a proportionate share of what the ceding company charges.

Summary

Three of the insurance lines discussed in this chapter — credit, municipal bond insurance, and mortgage insurance — could collectively be considered financial guarantees. As a group they present certain common hazards to the reinsurer. Their profitability is dependent on changes in economic conditions which affect a debtor's ability to repay its obligation. Salvage potential affects the volatility of the line. And lastly, each offers a significant catastrophe potential. The fourth and last line discussed, fidelity, is not a financial guarantee and is immune from the catastrophe exposure. However, results are also dependent on economic conditions and salvage recovery.

Mortgage insurance protects the lending institution or mortgagee against the peril that the individual borrower or mortgagor will fail to make the required periodic financial payments, resulting in a default on the loan. The maximum amount of insurance on each mortgage is limited to 20% of the total mortgage loan, and indemnity extends solely to the lending institution. Insurance is available only to lending institutions which are regulated and supervised by federal or state authorities. The major underwriting emphasis in mortgage insurance is on examining the qualifications of the lending institution.

Credit insurance is designed to protect merchants and manufacturers against financial losses arising from the insolvency or protracted default of buyers to whom goods have been sold and delivered, or for whom work has been done or services rendered on normal credit terms. The essential risk in credit insurance can be divided into two categories, domestic and foreign. Transactions where the seller of the goods and the buyer are located within the boundaries of the same country are referred to as domestic credit. Foreign credit involves a buyer and seller in different countries. Underwriting must take into consideration legal, economic, and political factors as well as the traditional financial ability of the risk.

Municipal bond insurance applies to the principal and interest payments as they become due, not on an accelerated basis. Typically, interest payment is scheduled to be paid every six months over the term of the bond, which can range from ten to twenty-five years. Thus, the insurance protects and guarantees each payment and is automatically paid if the municipality fails to honor its obligations. The basic premises behind insuring municipal bonds are twofold: 1) The interest savings to the municipalities will substantially offset the premium costs of insurance and financing charges. 2) The additional security offered to investors through insurance will allow smaller municipalities with good credit ratings the opportunity to compete in the marketplace on an equal footing with larger, more prominent municipalities.

The fidelity policy protects an employer against loss from fradulent or dishonest acts committed by the employees, whether acting alone or in collusion with others. The vast number of fidelity policies are written on a blanket basis covering all employees of a business. Most of these blanket fidelity bonds are sold as packages and include several burglary coverages collectively known as "crime insurance."

Over the last decade, by far the largest single cause of fidelity loss to insurance companies has been embezzlement. The great hazard facing fidelity insurers and reinsurers today, in the opinion of many experts, is the vulnerability of modern electronic data processing systems to abuse. Before a reinsurance underwriter decides to enter into a fidelity treaty, it must make an analysis of three distinct factors: 1) the severity potential of the portfolio it is being asked to reinsure; 2) the percentage of financial institution business making up the portfolio; and 3) the percentage of the market that its potential client dominates.

*   *   *   *   *   *

About the Author of REINSURING SURETY and REINSURING FINANCIAL GUARANTEES AND FIDELITY INSURANCE

Albert William Davis was born on June 30, 1938, in New York City. Educated at Manhattan College, he received the B. A. Degree in economics in 1961. He received the professional designation of Chartered Property Casualty Underwriter in 1965.

After graduating from college, his insurance career began with The Aetna

Casualty and Surety Company in New York. He worked for twelve years in its bond department from 1961 to 1973, becoming manager of its White Plains, New York, office. In 1973 he joined his current employer, North American Reinsurance Corporation. Currently he is vice president in charge of the bond department. He has written several articles on suretyship for national publications.

11

The Reinsurance Market
The Assuming Reinsurer

by John L. Baringer*

The previous chapters in this book have given the reader an introduction to the nature and purposes of reinsurance and have described the various forms of reinsurance available. This chapter will now deal with the "market" — where a ceding company might obtain reinsurance, the relationships between reinsurer and reinsured, and the responsibilities of the various parties in maintaining that relationship. Included will be a description of the types of assuming reinsurers which function in the worldwide market, the methods used by reinsurer and reinsured in contacting each other, and criteria used by ceding companies in choosing a reinsurer.

The Assuming Reinsurer

To understand the reinsurance marketplace, the reader should first recognize the various components which form that market. There are four types of reinsurers, regardless of the particular markets in which they may function: a) the professional reinsurer; b) reinsurance assuming departments of primary insurers; c) certain underwriting organizations, pools, and associations; and d) Lloyd's of London.

The "professional" reinsurer is a term used in the business to describe a company or corporate entity which devotes its entire effort to the assumption of risk through reinsurance of others, as opposed to the assumption of insurance as its main thrust. In other words, the sole

* Chairman, Rochdale Insurance Company, 99 John Street, New York, New York 10038.

business of a professional reinsurer is reinsurance. Generally speaking, the professional reinsurer is equipped to provide reinsurance for nearly all lines of property and liability business and has expertise in most all forms of reinsurance, i.e., excess of loss and pro rata, and facultative and treaty. The term "professional" is not, however, intended to imply that such companies have more expertise than other kinds of reinsurers, although some may differ with this opinion. In any event, the professional reinsurer is an important segment of the marketplace and accounts for the largest sector of the business.

The reinsurance assuming departments of primary insurers are no less "professional" than the so-called professional reinsurers. Each department is a unit of a larger entity which assumes primary insurance risks as well as reinsurance risks. For the most part, the established reinsurance assuming departments of primary insurance companies are structured along the lines of the professional reinsurers. The departments have reinsurance underwriting specialists, reinsurance loss specialists, and are equipped to write the business in much the same manner as the company which specializes only in reinsurance. However, all reinsurers are not structured the same way insofar as staff is concerned. Some reinsurers place more emphasis on actuarial services, while others lean more heavily on loss analysis or some other facet of reinsurance technology. A complete list of such reinsurers is not available, since the Annual Statement required by state insurance departments permits the amalgamation of a primary insurer's reinsurance assumed statistics with its direct insurance statistics for purposes of determining the insurer's solvency. However, it would be fair to say that most all primary insurers participate in the reinsurance business in one way or another, and as many as one hundred write a substantial volume.

The third type of reinsurer — the category of underwriting organizations, pools, and associations — is similar to professional reinsurers in handling reinsurance only. The third type differs, however, from the first two categories in that the management which provides the underwriting and loss handling expertise for organization members is generally independent of the companies which actually assume the risk. Companies participating in such organizations are usually primary insurers and may or may not maintain separate reinsurance departments within their own operations. Syndicate type clauses may be used to bind the reinsurance contracts and treaties written by the group. Such clauses provide that each participating company is identified with a specific share of the business, each for its own part and not one for the other. Management is compensated by the member companies through an underwriting fee, which is usually designed to cover expenses plus a profit-sharing contingent commission to provide incentive for quality underwriting.

Although last on the list of reinsurer types, Lloyd's of London is far from least. It differs greatly from the other three types, however, in the entity used to assume risk. In Lloyd's the risk takers consist of private individuals who assume insurance and reinsurance risks against their personal estates. In the other three types of reinsurers, however, risks are assumed by corporate entities. At the time of this writing, there are over 11,500 private individuals (or names) assuming risks through Lloyd's. Underwriting syndicates, each representing as few as 30 or as many as 700 individuals, have been formed within the Lloyd's community to organize the members into an orderly market. These syndicates are under the direct management of a "managing underwriter" and his staff who set syndicate policy, provide all the underwriting, loss handling, and accounting services for the names they represent, and are responsible for reporting results and distributing any profits. There are more than 300 such syndicates at Lloyd's, certain of which are specialists in specific kinds of business. The terms of the business placed at Lloyd's are set by the specialists who write only a portion of a given risk for their groups, with the balance of the risk being accepted by other syndicates who agree to follow the lead of the specialist.

Enabling legislation was passed in New York in June of 1978 to establish a market mechanism for the U.S. comparable to Lloyd's of London. The New York Insurance Exchange is scheduled to commence in 1979 as a central insurance market comprised of individual underwriting members to accept reinsurance and direct business for risks located outside the U.S. It will also write direct insurance on certain high-premium, specialized, or unusual domestic risks. The Exchange's original title, New York Reinsurance Exchange, was changed when it became apparent that under certain conditions direct business would be written as well as reinsurance. Another part of the same legislation established a "free trade zone" in which licensed insurers may write corporate risks producing a premium of $100,000 or more and certain other risks under a minimum of regulation.

The Market

The preceding categories are the kinds of reinsurance companies or markets from a structural point of view, i.e., corporate or Lloyd's. Similar types of reinsurers exist throughout the world, and the market available to the ceding U.S. insurance company is broad indeed. With the exception of the United States, the licensing status of a reinsurer in other countries is not a major problem; a reinsurer is typically licensed to act throughout a country instead of only in part of it. But in the U.S., where insurance is regulated by the various states rather than by a federal or central authority, the problems of licensed vs. unlicensed reinsurance are substantial. Since few reinsurers are licensed in all fifty states, the market should therefore be subcategorized as follows: a) the domestic reinsurance market; b) the alien reinsurance market; and c) the Lloyd's and London company market.

A domestic reinsurer in any given state is a reinsurance company or assuming reinsurer organized under the laws of that state, known as its state of domicile. When licensed in other states also, that reinsurer becomes in those states a "foreign reinsurer." An "alien reinsurer" is from a country outside the United States. However, since the rules and regulations of the individual states differ, it is necessary to futher subdivide reinsurers into authorized and unauthorized, or licensed and unlicensed. Within the U.S., there are approximately fifteen states which require a reinsurer to be licensed there (and thus to be "authorized") in order for a ceding company domiciled in that state to take credit in its Annual Statement for reserves (loss and unearned premiums) on business it has ceded to its reinsurers.[1] Nearly all of the United States reinsurers, whether professionals or departments or associations, have licenses in at least the key states to permit the credit to be granted their reinsureds. Suffice it to say, most of the reinsurances emanating from U.S. insurance companies, where substantial unearned premium reserves and loss reserves are involved, are written by authorized domestic reinsurers. Unauthorized reinsurers are involved when larger capacity is needed and in those reinsurances where balance sheet credits are not a major problem for ceding companies. (The accounting problems of authorized vs. unauthorized reinsurance are discussed later in Chapter 21.)

The alien reinsurance market plays a somewhat lesser role than the domestic market in reinsuring U.S. insurers, but it is nevertheless significant. Many of the larger professional reinsurers of the alien market abroad have established U.S. branch offices or wholly owned U.S. subsidiary companies. Some of the better known examples are the Swiss Re's ownership of the North American Re, and the ownership of the Christiania General by Storebrand Insurance Company of Oslo, Nor-

---

[1] However, as of November 22, 1977, one state changed its regulations. The New York State Insurance Department relaxed its "full compliance" requirements with solvency standards of unlicensed reinsurers by substituting "substantial compliance" requirements by amending its Regulation 20, the arguments against which are still under review by the Department.

way. However, Societe Commerciale de Reassurance (S.C.O.R.) of Paris has a branch office here, as do several other government owned reinsurers. There is a vast market of other alien reinsurers available to the U.S. ceding insurer as well. Companies in the private sector such as Copenhagen Re of Denmark, Norwich Union of England, Folksam of Sweden, as well as government owned companies as Instituto de Resseguros do Brazil (I.R.B.), the Indian Reinsurance Corporation, Central Re of Taiwan, Korean Re — to name a few — have played a significant role in helping to solve the capacity problems of the U.S. insurance and reinsurance industry. While most of the business these government owned reinsurers accept from other countries is obtained through reciprocal agreements, they nevertheless provide a substantial source of capacity to the world market. While not too well known in the U.S., the I.R.B. of Brazil is one of the ten largest reinsurers in the world, its 1977 volume of business exceeding $1 billion worldwide.

The Lloyd's and London company market is perhaps the largest reinsurance market situated in one location in the world. This market has evolved over many years due to the international concept of Lloyd's itself and the onetime vastness of the British Empire. Because of its syndicated nature, Lloyd's is the equivalent of several hundred separate insurance and reinsurance companies of small-to-medium size doing business under one roof. It therefore has become a center for worldwide insurance and reinsurance, attracting other companies to establish underwriting offices in the area surrounding it in London. While most of these companies are British owned, many are from other foreign markets — Japan, Europe, and South America. London is the only city in the world where such a tremendous amount of underwriting capacity exists at one location. Even the reinsurance markets of the communist world are represented in the London company market, e.g., the Black Sea and Baltic General Insurance Company, Ltd., which is owned by Ingosstrakh.

Methods of Entering the Market

The Direct Market

There are two methods a reinsurer may use to obtain its business: the direct (nonbrokerage) market, and the brokerage market. Although the differences in approach to the acquisition and servicing of reinsurance accounts are significant, the benefits derived from each by the ceding insurer are essentially the same.

Direct markets are those reinsurance companies which operate through their own salaried sales force and have a staff capable of providing all the services needed to perform an all-around reinsurance business. Such staff positions will include actuaries, underwriters, statisticians, and loss specialists as well as sales personnel. Generally speaking, these direct reinsurers prefer to handle an entire account rather than only a portion of the business involved. In the past they also have specialized more in the writing of third party liability business (although property risks form a substantial portion of their business). All of these companies offer reinsurance on a full multiple line basis and provide substantial capacity to their reinsureds through retrocession facilities. Through retrocession agreements, they share their largest exposures with other insurance and reinsurance companies in the U.S. and abroad. Were it not for these retrocession facilities, their capacity to absorb large risks and whole accounts would be limited to the amounts they could retain for their net account only.

THE BROKERAGE MARKET

The brokerage markets, as distinct from direct markets, are those reinsurance companies which obtain all or most of their business through reinsurance brokers who represent the ceding company in the purchase of its reinsurance. As a general rule, the brokerage markets are inclined to write only portions of a single account, retaining most of their business net with only a limited reliance on retrocessions. The main thrust of the sales efforts of the brokerage markets is that of keeping a solid rapport with the many reinsurance brokers. While some brokerage markets are known as "followers," most prefer to have a strong influence in the development of terms and conditions, and therefore maintain a staff of competent underwriting, accounting, and loss handling specialists.

The function of the reinsurance broker is to act as a go-between in arranging reinsurance terms and conditions between the ceding insurer and the brokerage market. The broker works for the ceding company by presenting the reinsured's business to the market and arguing the reinsured's point of view, thereby establishing acceptable terms and conditions to both parties. The broker also acts as a conduit through which communications between the reinsured and the reinsurer are passed, including the payment of premiums by the reinsured to the reinsurer and the collection of losses for the reinsured from the reinsurer.

The custom of the market has been to view the broker as the ceding company's agent in all respects except for the collection of premiums, although a recent decision in New Jersey[2] has upset this line of thinking.

---

[2] In re Pritchard & Baird, Inc., 3/1/79, U.S.D.C., D.N.J., B-75-3202 (U.S. Court House, Newark, New Jersey).

The court ruled that the broker is the agent of the ceding company in all respects, stating that monies in the hands of the broker are the property of its principal, the ceding company, and that monies paid by the reinsurer to the broker had, in fact, been paid to the reinsured but that payments by the ceding company to its broker did not constitute receipt by the reinsurer. This ruling may be appealed to a higher court, but at the time of this writing no other ruling is available. Nevertheless, the customary practice of the industry has been for the reinsurance broker to collect the premiums from the reinsured and remit them to the reinsurer, and to collect loss payments from the reinsurer and remit them to the reinsured. This collection responsibility places the broker in a fiduciary capacity and carries with it the obligation to handle funds forthrightly and expeditiously. While there have been occasional instances of brokers not carrying out this duty properly, the brokerage community as a whole has recognized its responsibility and acted accordingly.

Traditionally, the reinsurance broker has performed its functions without much regulation by state insurance departments, although this picture is changing. New York now requires reinsurance brokers to be licensed, and it is generally felt that some other states will follow the pattern set by New York. The broker of insurance (as distinct from reinsurance) has been required by New York law for some time to maintain its accounts in fiduciary manner. That law is also specific in that premium payments by an insured to the broker constitute payment to the insurer (Sec. 121). While this fiduciary requirement is specific as it pertains to insurance brokers, many believe the same understanding pertains to reinsurance brokers. If so, this would place the reinsurance broker in the position of being the agent of the reinsured in all matters, except for collecting premiums, where by tradition the broker is the agent of the reinsurer.

In addition to these fiduciary functions, the broker must have a broad knowledge of the entire market and its current thinking, a thorough knowledge of the various types of reinsurance available, a complete understanding of the insurance company's underwriting and accounting problems, and the capability of drafting appropriate treaty and contract wordings. The broker is, in all respects, a representative of the reinsured, with the responsibility of advising the reinsured on the type and terms of the reinsurance being sought and the quality of the markets available. The reinsurance broker must not only be in a position to give quick and efficient service in the arrangement of facultative reinsurances on large or special risks but above all must be able to obtain prompt claim settlements.

Compensation for the services rendered by the reinsurance broker comes from the reinsurance market in the form of brokerage commission on the premiums paid by the reinsured to its reinsurer. The rate of brokerage commission varies from as little as one half of one percent to as much as ten percent of the premiums involved, depending upon the type of reinsurance and the amount of premiums. This cost to the brokerage market is offset by the fact that reinsurers using brokers can operate without an extensive sales organization and branch office network, compared to direct market reinsurers which must develop and service their own business. Each segment of the market has its own advantages, and the choice is up to the reinsured.

It should be recognized that the reinsurance broker is not responsible for the failure of either party to make appropriate payments caused by insolvency of either. If the broker has knowledge of an impending insolvency of either party, it has a moral obligation to so advise the other party and assist in taking whatever steps are necessary to protect the interest of each. The broker also has an obligation to exercise due diligence in recommending reinsurance companies to participate in the ceding company's program, but the final choice of markets rests with the reinsured.

ETHICS OF THE MARKETPLACE

The ethics of the business call for certain relationships to exist between the reinsured, the broker, and the reinsurer. While most brokers prefer that the reinsured and reinsurer know each other personally for better understanding of each other's point of view, visits between reinsurer and reinsured should involve the broker at all times. Only in this way can the broker effectively perform its function as intermediary and avoid any misunderstandings.

The ethics of the market also preclude the reinsurer from discussing the business of the reinsured with any broker other than the one designated by the reinsured. Generally, the broker's authority to discuss a particular contract or treaty with a reinsurer is given through the medium of a "broker of record letter," and it is most important that the reinsurer clearly understand the broker's authority before negotiations commence. However, more than one broker can be used on the same business by joint action or allocation of specific markets; furthermore, separate brokers might be used on separate reinsurances between reinsured and reinsurer.

Another point of ethics in the marketplace develops when a reinsurer has cancelled a piece of business written through a broker. In such a case, the reinsurer should avoid any direct resolicitation of the business involved. Furthermore, a reinsurer should avoid using the broker's introduction as a means of soliciting on a direct basis other business from a current reinsured. Most of these points will probably seem obvious to the reader, but it is quite surprising how often they are overlooked.

Although the broker functions mainly as the intermediary between the reinsured and the broker-oriented market, there are instances where the capacity of that market is insufficient to meet the needs of the reinsured. In these instances, the broker may elect to bring one or several of the non-broker markets into the picture in order to complete the coverage. There are also situations where the reinsured wishes to have a portion of the business written by the direct market, with the broker placing its share in the broker market. The two markets can work well together and generally respect each other's interests.

Funk and Wagnalls, in their *New "Standard" Dictionary of the English Language*, 1959, define the word "gentleman" as:

1. A well-bred and honorable man; in common usage, a respectable and well-behaved man; as ladies and gentlemen (the usual form of address in public assemblies).

2. A man of the higher class or of gentle extraction; in England, one above yeoman.

3. The body-servant of a man of rank; a valet; as a gentleman's gentleman.

Reinsurance has been known as a gentleman's business, and it should be apparent that the term is rather appropriate. While we may or may not be of "gentle extraction," we should be well-bred and honorable and, further, servants of the reinsured. And if we happen to be ladies in the reinsurance business, we strive for the same high standards of respectable and honorable behaviour.

Choosing a Reinsurer

CRITERIA IN SELECTION

The choice of one reinsurer or a group of reinsurers over others is difficult to make. To choose the most appropriate market involves many considerations, some of which are obvious while others are more esoteric in nature. Some of the more obvious factors are:

a) **Financial Stability.** Does the prospective reinsurer have sufficient resources to meet its obligations when large losses occur? An adequate appearing balance sheet is not necessarily the only criterion. Most reinsurers have retrocession facilities to protect them against disaster losses, and it is well for the reinsured to have some knowledge of the financial quality of the retrocessionaires as well as the reinsurer signing the agreement.

b) **Continuity.** Does the prospective reinsurer have a record of long-range relationships with reinsureds, evidencing its willingness to continue providing vital services following poor operational results of its reinsureds? This factor is often overlooked by buyers of reinsurance who sometimes have a tendency to think only of the short-range picture.

c) **Flexibility.** Does the prospective reinsurer have an open mind to new approaches in solving problems? Reinsurance is not a predesigned product which can be mass produced through standard policy forms. Rather, it is a custom-made product which requires imagination and considerable expertise in determining the most appropriate form of system to use in solving the problems at hand. The reinsurer with an open mind will weigh all the information at hand and design an overall program capable of meeting the specific needs of the reinsured with the least amount of effort and expense.

d) **Service.** Is the prospective reinsurer capable of providing the services desired? Sufficient staff should be available to assist the reinsured in evaluating its needs as they relate to large risk exposures, concentrations of risks, and other similar underwriting problems. The reinsurer should also be able to assist in solving accounting and cash flow problems and should provide prompt and equitable loss adjustments. When needed, the reinsurer should be capable of assisting the primary insurer in the evaluation of loss reserves and of providing expert assistance in the defense of certain large and difficult third party claims.

e) **Confidentiality.** Does the prospective reinsurer maintain a confidential relationship with the reinsured? While rates and policy forms are not secret after they are filed, and financial results and statements are published regularly, the thinking and future plans of any company are of a strict confidential nature and should not be treated lightly. The reinsurer must, however, be given complete details of such plans in order to give appropriate weight to the way in which changes in a company's plan of operation, proposed rate structures, or new lines of business will affect the reinsurance program.

METHODS OF ACQUIRING REINSURANCE

Brokerage: The Intermediary. Choosing a reinsurer is difficult for the management of any ceding company. It is particularly difficult to decide whether to use the brokerage market or the direct market or a combination of both. There are advantages and disadvantages to any one of the three options, although most reinsureds will agree that a combination of both markets offers the greatest chance of obtaining the desired results. Some of the advantages of dealing with the brokerage market are:

a) The ceding company has the benefit of the thinking from several reinsurers rather than just one or two, since brokerage market reinsurers are more inclined to take small to medium shares in a given contract. The business is, therefore, subject to the critique of several underwriters.

b) With several reinsurers participating in a particular reinsurance contract or treaty, the ceding company can expect more long-range continuity in the event of adverse results at any point in time. While some of the participating reinsurers may wish to revise terms or discontinue their participation, it is more than likely that a substantial portion of the participants may be content to continue at existing terms if they can be satisfied that proper corrective measures have been taken by the reinsured to prevent the adverse conditions from continuing. In such event, only part of the program would need replacing.

c) The brokerage market offers greater capacity for the handling of large exposures such as occur under catastrophe reinsurances covering windstorms, earthquakes, etc.

d) As reinsurances placed in the brokerage market are usually participated in by several reinsurers, this segment of the marketplace is usually inclined to take a more flexible attitude toward new approaches to a problem or toward new concepts of reinsuring the unusual.

e) Assuming the reinsured has chosen a knowledgeable broker to handle its business, the reinsured has the advantage of a well-qualified reinsurance staff working in its interests to see that the terms and conditions of the reinsurance concerned are appropriate to the exposures. In the long run, this should save the ceding company's management much of the time and effort which goes into negotiating such a program. Moreover, it is important for the reinsured to understand that the broker is the reinsured's representative in any such negotiations, not the representative of the reinsurer.

On the other side of the coin, there are some disadvantages to the use of the brokerage market. Some of these are:

a) Some minor accounting complications occur when preparing Annual Statements which require the listing of business in force with various reinsurers. If the brokerage market is used, the list will usually be quite substantial.

b) Not all brokerage market reinsurers are licensed in the key states, and many of the overseas markets are not licensed in any of the various states of the U.S. This may require extra work at year end to make an accurate appraisal of outstanding losses in order to obtain cash advances or letters of credit to cover the reinsurer's share of unpaid claims. Where needed, these advances or letters of credit on unpaid claims must be in the hands of the reinsured on or before December 31, or else the ceding company will be unable to take credit in its Statement for recoverables on such unpaid claims. In the event of substantial losses occurring late in the year, severe penalties to surplus can develop.

c) Since several reinsurers are usually involved in any one reinsured loss, it usually takes the broker several days to collect cash loss payments from the market. Unless the broker is willing to advance loss payments to the reinsured on behalf of the reinsurers, loss recoveries might well be delayed a week or so over the time it takes to recover a loss from a direct reinsurer.

d) In many cases the reinsured does not have a first-hand acquaintance with the underwriters involved in setting the terms of the reinsurance. This can lead to an impersonal relationship which might be to the disadvantage of the two parties.

The Direct Market. For the most part, one might say that an advantage of the brokerage market would be a disadvantage when dealing with the direct market, and vice versa. This is not necessarily true in all instances, however. Some of the advantages of the direct market are as follows:

a) The ceding company deals with fewer companies, which simplifies accounting procedures to some extent.

b) The direct reinsurance market is usually prepared to provide reinsurance on all lines of business. If an "account approach" is taken, the adverse results of one line of business at any given time may be offset by profit on other lines. In such cases, the reinsurer is generally willing to ride a succession of deficits pending the outcome of corrective measures. In many cases, the brokerage markets are more specialized, and the results of a given line of business will have to stand alone.

c) The direct reinsurer is usually closer to the reinsured and may be less disturbed by temporary setbacks in the results.

d) The direct reinsurer is usually licensed in all the key states and, more often than not, nearly all states. This avoids the necessity of letters of credit or cash advances at year end.

e) In the case of large losses, the reinsured may receive cash payments several days earlier than from a brokerage market, thus easing its cash flow problems.

On the other hand, there are some problems which can develop in a direct market relationship.

a) The reinsured and the reinsurer may be in an adversary relationship as buyer-and-seller, with differing financial outcomes as objectives. Unless the reinsured is knowledgeable on the subject of reinsurance, it may not be getting general market terms.

b) The direct reinsurer may be reluctant to share the more sought-after segments of the reinsured's account with others, leaving only the high risk portion to others—which can work to the disadvantage of the reinsured.

c) In the event of a dispute or misunderstanding, the reinsured must represent its own interests without the expertise of a knowledgeable broker.

d) The top executives of the reinsured company will doubtless spend more time in reviewing and negotiating reinsurance terms and conditions than if the brokerage market is used. Such time may well be spent solving other problems.

As one can see, there are things to be said for both segments of the market, and there are probably as many other thoughts on the pros and cons of one side over the other as there are people in the reinsurance business. The above thoughts are therefore not definitive. In the end, the final choice of one reinsurance market over another will be based upon the terms being offered, tempered by judgment. The lowest terms are not necessarily the best terms when all things are considered.

OBTAINING QUOTATIONS

If the ceding company wants to do a complete and thorough analysis of its reinsurance needs and obtain competitive quotations for its program, there are several steps which should be taken well in advance of the date on which the program is to become effective. These steps are:

a) Develop a complete analysis of past reinsurance results on a treaty-by-treaty basis for at least the prior five years. Specific information should then be developed showing:

1) A list of large gross losses categorized by size and showing

for each the date of loss, location and name of insured, reinsurance recoveries if any, line of business, and type of risk. If third party losses are involved, the list should also include the development of reserves by date.

2) Premium exhibits showing gross and net premiums by line and by state on a year-by-year basis.

3) A profile of risk exposures by size. In the case of property risks, this profile should show the number of risks in various size categories. For third party business, premium figures on an excess limits basis should also be developed by various rate combinations.

4) Outlines of underwriting practices, listing types of risks which are on the company's prohibited list and those which are written on a limited basis.

5) Exhibits showing gross and net underwriting results on a line-by-line basis.

6) Corrective measures in problem areas, as well as any planned changes in future underwriting philosophy.

7) If pro rata treaties are involved, the actual results on an earned-to-incurred basis by years.

8) Growth estimates for the near future.

All of the above information should be presented and discussed thoroughly with the prospective broker or direct reinsurers.

b) If the company wishes to have the advice and counsel of more than one broker, the company should ask the brokers involved to refrain from contacting any markets until a choice of brokers has been made. The initial discussions with the brokers should be of a nonspecific nature, seeking ideas and suggestions only. The company should then decide which broker offers the best service and has the best suggestions and give that broker the freedom to contact all markets available for quotations.

c) On its own, the company should contact several of the direct reinsurers, giving them all the same information and asking that they submit quotations. It is important that all reinsurers be asked to quote on the same limits and conditions as otherwise the comparison of terms will not be meaningful.

d) Having received quotations from several direct reinsurers and from the brokerage market, the company can then compare the results. The broker should have quotes from several strong markets such as Lloyd's of London, the larger U.S. companies, and perhaps some foreign markets.

The final decision should be based on several factors which will include among other things the cost of the proposal, the financial status of the parties, the market expertise, reputation, and services offered by the reinsurer, and the general terms of the contract. It is important to see the proposed contract wordings or the detailed outlines of a treaty to be certain that all parties fully understand the terms. It is also important for the reinsured to understand that more than one person approaching the reinsurance market on its behalf can create serious problems in the negotiations. If the company feels compelled to use more than one broker, it should then give each broker certain reinsurance markets to approach, or ask that they approach the markets jointly.

After The Choice Is Made

The Honorable Engagement and Disputes. Reinsurance is considered an honorable engagement between two sophisticated parties, primarily because the transactions by their nature must be based upon trust and confidence between the reinsured and the reinsurer. In nearly all instances the reports of premiums flowing from the reinsured to the reinsurer are based upon bulk figures with virtually no information on the individual risks involved. The initial information on which the reinsurer bases its judgment, either for ratemaking purposes or for purposes of determining reinsurance commission rates to be paid on pro rata treaty accounts, is supplied by the reinsured and accepted by the reinsurer in good faith. Without this bond of trust between the two parties, the industry could not function. For this reason, nearly all reinsurance contracts contain an arbitration clause. That clause specifically states that the contract or agreement is not to be treated merely as a legal document but rather as an honorable engagement, and that any disputes or disagreements are to be settled by arbitration, the results of which are to be binding on both parties. The purpose of this clause is to prevent either party from placing a meaning on technical phraseology of the agreement which was not the real intent of the agreement. It, therefore, becomes apparent that a full disclosure of the facts and a complete understanding of the intentions of both parties during negotiations is vital to the development of a sound relationship between reinsured and reinsurer.

Terminations. The failure of either party to act in good faith may give the other party cause for termination of the agreement. Under normal conditions, reinsurances are only terminated because of one or more of the following reasons:

a) Continuing adverse results, in which case the reinsurer will wish to terminate the agreement or renegotiate the terms and conditions of the agreement.

b) Better than average results, in which case the reinsured may wish to terminate or renegotiate.

c) Changes in the ceding company's growth pattern or underwriting philosophy, which might cause the reinsurer to become concerned about the exposures under the agreement.

d) Changes in the financial conditions of either party, which might cause one party to become concerned about the ability of the other party to meet its obligations under the agreement.

Reinsurances are written either on a specific term basis or on a continuous basis. In the first instance, the agreement is intended to run only for its term, expiring at the end thereof with no continuing liability. Upon such expiration, a new agreement is negotiated if needed. Continuous contracts or agreements, on the other hand, have no stated expiration dates but provide for termination at specific future dates by either party giving appropriate notice of its intent to cancel.

Under normal circumstances reinsureds and reinsurers follow the procedures for termination as expressed in the contract wording. There are, however, situations which can cause either party to terminate for cause at any given time. Two examples of these situations are: the reinsurer might terminate on short notice for non-payment of premium by the reinsured; or either party may wish to terminate for breach of warranty or violation of contract conditions. Some reinsurers may list specific reasons for permitting interim cancellation — such as war, impairment of the ceding company's capital, or a change in ownership control of the ceding company. Such special terminations by either party might be done *ab initio* in the event of non-payment of premium or similar circumstances. In any event, cancellation for cause is an action which rarely takes place because of the traditions of good faith which have become the standard of the industry.

Multiple Reinsurers

Previously in this chapter mention was made of the possibility of more than one reinsurer participating in the same reinsurance agreement. This is particularly true of reinsurances placed in the brokerage market. In such circumstances, it is important that all reinsurers receive the same consideration and that uniform treaty wordings be issued. In most cases the terms and conditions of such treaties will be based upon extensive negotiations between the reinsured and two or three substantial reinsurers considered "lead reinsurers." While each reinsurer has reviewed all the information available on the account under consideration and perhaps quoted terms and conditions independently of the others, each has in the end compromised its thinking to develop terms which are acceptable to all. Most reinsurers are unwilling to share in a treaty or contract on terms which are less favorable than those of any other participant; so the end result will be a group of reinsurers all of which share the business on the same basis. It is not unusual for one or two or these reinsurers to assume the position of lead reinsurer, overseeing the approval of the final wording, and being responsible for the general supervision of losses and other duties of a similar nature. This does not mean, however, that the other reinsurers in the business have given up their rights to be involved in the administration of the program or to exercise individually their rights under the contract or treaty involved.

Another important point is that each reinsurer participating in a multiple reinsurer program is responsible only for its own share unless otherwise stated. "Each for his own part and not one for the other" is the wording generally used when such contracts or treaty wordings have been prepared on a syndicated basis (i.e., all reinsurers signing on a single contract wording as opposed to each reinsurer issuing a separate wording for its share).

Summary

The market for reinsurance is international, consisting of four types of reinsurers: companies whose sole business is reinsurance, companies which write insurance direct for the public and also for other insurers through reinsurance assuming departments, certain underwriting organizations (pools and associations), and Lloyd's of London. Though competition is international in scope, the regulatory restraints affecting reinsurers are not, since each country has its own requirements. Indeed, U.S. reinsurers and insurers are often at a competitive disadvantage with the remainder of the world because of varying laws and regulations among the fifty states. It is to counteract such disadvantage that the New York legislature passed in 1978 a law permitting the formation of an "insurance exchange" to compete more effectively worldwide and with fewer government restrictions.

Of the two methods available to a reinsurer to enter the market — direct with its own employees, or through a broker — each method varies considerably in acquiring and servicing business. However, the benefits derived from each by the ceding insurer are essentially the same.

While a reinsurer's employee is usually compensated by salary, a reinsurance broker receives a brokerage commission for services rendered. The rate of brokerage commission varies from as little as one half of one percent to as much as ten percent of the premiums involved, depending on the type of reinsurance being placed and the amount of premiums handled.

Ethics in the reinsurance market are taken seriously by all concerned, and necessarily so. A large portion of all reinsurance transactions are initiated orally between parties, later to be confirmed in writing. The importance of one's integrity in reinsurance can not be overstated.

The choice by a ceding company of a reinsurer, whether direct or through a broker, involves these considerations: the reinsurer's financial stability, its continuity in the business, its flexibility in meeting a ceding company's problems, the service it renders its clients, and its reputation for confidentiality. Both the direct approach and the brokerage approach in securing a reinsurer offer significant advantages and disadvantages to the ceding company, which should appraise them carefully in its selection. There is much to be said for both methods, and many ceding companies accordingly use the services of each in placing their reinsurance.

*   *   *   *   *   *

About the Author of Chapter 11

John L. Baringer was born December 3, 1921, and attended South Bend Central High School in South Bend, Indiana. He did college work at both the University of Notre Dame and Tennessee Technological Institute. During World War II he served in the Air Force as a navigator on a B-17 until October, 1945, when he was discharged as a captain.

His insurance career started as an underwriter with American Mutual Reinsurance Company from 1945 to 1950. From 1950 to 1963 he was a reinsurance account executive with Booth, Potter, Seal & Company and became a partner in the firm during the latter half of his employment. He then became the president of his own firm for a year and a half, Baringer & Company, before it was merged into Willcox, Baringer & Company, Inc., at the close of 1964. A year later he was elected a director of Johnson & Higgins, then the parent of Willcox, Baringer, and he continued as president of Willcox, Baringer until his retirement at the end of 1976. Currently he is chairman of Rochdale Insurance Company, a firm he organized in 1955 for the Co-Operative Insurance Society, Ltd., in Manchester, England, now owned and operated by Duncanson & Holt, Inc. He also serves on the board of directors of United Americas Insurance Company, a reinsurance company organized in 1978 by Duncanson & Holt with the backing of South American and European interests.

12

Planning and Managing a Reinsurance Program

by Richard F. Gilmore*

Two stories came to mind which may indicate the intended scope of this chapter. The first is undoubtedly apocryphal and is told about Abraham Lincoln. When asked if he had an opinion as to the proper length of a man's legs, Lincoln averred that they ought to be long enough to reach from a man's waist to the floor. A reinsurance program should be similarly constructed and as all sets of legs differ, so will all reinsurance programs. A "six-foot" ceding company will look most clumsy lumbering about on a "three-foot" reinsurance program.

The second story, not apocryphal, concerns a large company which increased its retentions dramatically, reasoning that it was extremely well financed (having many millions in surplus) and there was no valid reason for it to reinsure excess of a retention which was only a miniscule percentage of its surplus. Some years later, the same company found a reason: its retention then equalled earnings of 15¢ per share and since setting its retention, the company's focus had changed to the point where it was now considerably more concerned about the effect on its shareholders of a catastrophic loss than about the "logic" of maintaining its retention at a "realistic" percentage of its surplus.

The moral of both stories is identical: there is no such thing as the perfect reinsurance program. Ceding companies are all different and a program that would be ideal for Company A might be a disaster for Company B. Nor do ceding companies remain static. Their business

* President, The Mercantile and General Reinsurance Company of America, 310 Madison Avenue CN 1930, Morristown, New Jersey 07960.

changes and their objectives alter significantly over time. Sometimes the changes are initiated by the company itself and at other times the environment in which the company operates forces alterations in operating philosophy. Just as no corporate plan can be etched in stone, so no reinsurance program can be frozen based on current circumstances.

The reader who hopes to find a formula for the "proper" reinsurance program in this chapter will be disappointed. What will be provided is a comprehensive discussion of the considerations which are essential to construct a reinsurance program to successfully solve a company's reinsurance problems, provided the company's objectives have been properly analyzed and the problems are recognized. The aim here is not to provide specific answers about how a reinsurance program should be constructed and retentions selected, but rather to discuss the questions which should be asked and the analyses which should be conducted in order to arrive at correct decisions.

Planning a Reinsurance Program

Reinsurance programs flow from a set of corporate objectives and should be the result of an examination of the company, its book of business and its goals. Let's look at some of the elements of the company which should be analyzed:

Management: What kinds of people are involved in the management of the company? Who are the stockholders (if any)? How do the top executives think? What kinds of department managers run the day-to-day affairs of the company?

Goals: Is the company in a static position or does it intend to grow significantly during the next "N" years? Are the company's goals simple (e.g., to make an underwriting profit) or are they more complicated (e.g., to grow at a rate in excess of its peer companies and to have a return on shareholder's equity of at least "X" % and to have earnings per share increase at least "Y" % per year)?

Business: Does the company write a soft, predictable book of business or does it take on some difficult risks? Does the company intend to expand into new lines or new territories? Have the results been good or bad? Is the book of business subject to catastrophes or shock losses? If so, how and where?

Financial: How does the company measure up to all of the Early Warning Tests as published by the National Association of Insurance Commissioners (N.A.I.C.)? If additional financing were to be needed, where would the company get it? Does the company expect more than the normal amount of financing from its reinsurers?

We could continue asking questions for a long while, but the direction of our inquiry is undoubtedly clear. Let's examine some of these questions in greater detail.

MANAGEMENT

The classical functions of reinsurance are defined and discussed elsewhere in this volume. The reader may wish to review those purposes and definitions in the context of program design, since a reinsurance program is constructed to fulfill those purposes. However, viewed from management's standpoint, decisions on reinsurance transcend the intellectual and approach the emotional level — a reinsurance program must be designed so that it gives overall comfort to the ceding company. This means that the people in the company must be at ease with the program. It must insulate them from worry. If management is not totally confident that the program provides proper protection, then the program is not the right one for it. If management is almost exclusively interested in preventing wide fluctuations in loss experience, or (to say it differently) if management wants to have loss experience results which are highly predictable, then it will undoubtedly place considerable reinsurance and buy covers over rather low retentions. Of course, the size of the book of business is a factor as well, since predictability or stability of experience are both functions of size. On the other hand, if management's predominant interest is in maximizing its income and retaining as much of its business as possible, it will probably take greater risks, absorb higher retentions and will also recognize that its results could be subject to substantially greater variability.

The absolute decision as to the level of retentions is so dependent upon management attitudes and goals that if one were restricted to the use of a single criterion, this would be the one to select. It is the personality of management which can have such a dramatic effect on the design of a proper reinsurance program for a given company. While one chief executive officer (C.E.O.) might well be able to handle the impact of a large loss on the company's results, another might be totally unable to do so; the same comments apply to division heads with regard to their results. That the reinsurance program must provide comfort to various levels of management is certainly one of the most important considerations in the design of the program.

To over-dramatize the point somewhat, a number of years ago the author worked in a department which wrote, among other strange things, a form of accidental death insurance which was sold at airports to cover in the event of an airplane crash. This business was called "ticket accident" or "TA" business. Since commercial airline crashes are fairly dramatic occurrences, everybody in the company of course knew when a tough loss occurred. The president, among others, would call as soon as a crash was announced and inquire as to the company's liability. An elaborate procedure had been established so that we could tell, sometimes within hours after the crash, what the potential liability was likely to be. The president really wanted to know that our loss would not be any greater than "N," and we always reminded him that our loss could not exceed $500,000, because that was the retention under our first catastrophe (occurrence) excess program. No matter how intelligently our reinsurance program had been constructed, if we had told him that we could take a $1,000,000 loss, he would have been mighty uncomfortable — and nobody likes to see the boss in pain. Nor would it have mattered much, at least at the time, if our purchase of catastrophe coverage in excess of $500,000 had been uneconomic. What he wanted was comfort and he got it.

If the comfort of management is so important, who is it that must be made unapprehensive? If a company has a strong and independent C.E.O., and a board of directors which does not take a great deal of interest in the day-to-day affairs but rather restricts its activities to, say, the investment area, then the opinion of the C.E.O. will perhaps be the only significant one in determining retention levels. But, of course, the decisions would be reviewed and approved by the board of directors or would be within parameters previously established by the board. Conversely, if the company is one which operates on a highly participative basis and tends to come to collective or generally supported decisions, then the opinions of many executives will be needed before a reinsurance program can be designed and overall retention levels determined.

Regardless of the personality of management, in almost all companies, it is the C.E.O. and the senior executives who make the major reinsurance decisions, because the reinsurance program can have such a dramatic impact on the company's results that an improperly designed program could even affect the company's ability to continue in business. The position of the board of directors must always be considered and should undoubtedly be viewed in the context of adverse results. The board will want to be assured that the company's reinsurance program has been established in such a way as to protect the policyholders in the case of a mutual company or the interests of shareholders in the case of a stock company. While it is a subject which is seldom discussed, management must also be certain that its own continuity in office is not affected by a poorly designed program. As management hates surprises, boards like them even less.

It is one thing to design a reinsurance program and select retention levels based on the theoretical probability (or historical pattern) of certain events occurring. It is an entirely different matter to pay the loss or losses after the statistics and history have proved to be unreliable predictors of the future. It is bad policy to regard a reinsurance program as a theoretical solution to problems which probably will not occur; one must instead make the assumption that the worst can occur and devise a program which will perform satisfactorily when things do not go well.

In this context, be wary of approaches which are too "actuarial" in nature. Over the years many companies have suffered as a result of taking too statistical an attitude towards their reinsurance program. Reinsurance considerations should be approached pragmatically, not esoterically. If, for example, the retention level has been set high on the theory that the business is well spread and not really subject to a significant catastrophe loss, it is difficult if not impossible to defend the wisdom of the decision after a large loss occurs. Somebody will have to explain the loss to the board and/or shareholders and/or policyholders and those groups will be interested in the fact that the loss happened, not in the statistical wisdom which proved that it was almost inconceivable.

In this context, as in most reinsurance decisions, cost is one of the most predominant factors. It has often been argued that "sleep at night" covers — those that are purchased at very high levels and are almost solely designed for the comfort of management or at the insistence of some nervous board member — should be priced at very low rates. The argument is that the covers are not really needed because the exposure is not there. There is truth to this approach but reinsurers are cautious about accepting such arguments because they have seen total losses occur on such covers. Two views should probably be taken: 1) covers which really do not present significant exposures should be modestly priced, but 2) management can sometimes get a better idea of the real exposures which may be involved by taking a hard look at a surprisingly high rate quoted on a cover which they do not believe is exposed. An honest evaluation of the quote might change management's mind about the reality of the exposure since the reinsurer's opinion could be more valid than management's. These comments are not intended as an argument for buying over-priced covers, but rather as a suggestion that an outside opinion could represent a more rational analysis of the loss potential.

Department heads, underwriters and branch managers must also be considered. For example, it does no good to design a complex reinsurance program which results in the ceding company having a net retention of $1,000,000 on any one property risk if the manager of the property department is a "basket case" trying to write to a net retention which he or she thinks is too high. Of course, one could always find a new manager for the property department, but the point is undiminished — the department manager must be in sympathy with the reinsurance program and must believe that the reinsurance program satisfies his or her needs. There have been innumerable cases where the people underwriting the book of business have defeated the basic intentions of the reinsurance program by changing their underwriting postures. This change is quite difficult to detect unless one is extremely close to the day-to-day operations of the company or is familiar with the phenomenon and has established control systems to discern changes in underwriting which were not in accord with the company's basic reinsurance philosophy. As an example, it is fairly easy for a branch or home office underwriter to place greater amounts of facultative reinsurance because the underwriter is exercised about the retention levels established by the company's reinsurance program. Sometimes such placements are unconscious actions. The underwriter feels in the stomach (as all underwriters do) that he or she has to retain too much of a given classification of risk. Another thing an underwriter might do is to become ultraconservative on a given type or class of risk. An underwriter can always find a dozen rationalizations for cutting back and obviously in this case may well have defeated management's basic goal, if that goal were, for instance, to retain a greater percentage of the company's gross written premium. The additional facultative cessions could account for more ceded premium than was saved by the increased retention level.

As a slight digression, a few comments with regard to "in-house" reinsurance are probably in order. There are many different forms of in-house reinsurance, ranging from loss limitations on departmental, divisional, or branch office results to the placing of what purport to be "real" reinsurance treaties which might, as an example, underlie the company's catastrophe program and provide protection at a different attachment point for a particular class of business. While such programs can be effectively used by a sophisticated management, they can also cause some strange problems. One can hypothesize a situation where the effective use of in-house covers could make the results of all divisions satisfactory on a "net" basis and leave only the corporation with a loss. To use an uncomplicated example, let's say that a company buys catastrophe property coverage excess of an occurrence loss retention of $1,000,000 but has never had a loss excess of $500,000. Let's further suppose that the personal lines department has expanded over the years and is fairly well spread, except for a substantial concentration in the company's home state. Because the book of personal lines business is not large enough to sustain a $1,000,000 loss, management decides to protect the department against an occurrence loss in excess of $500,000 and writes, by memorandum, a reinsurance "treaty," charging a premium to the department and providing coverage of $500,000 excess of $500,000. If a $1,000,000 loss occurs, the department is "forgiven" the second $500,000 by virtue of a loss "recovery" under the in-house treaty. This action however, does not remove the loss from the company's books and while the department manager is free of the loss, the C.E.O. and perhaps the fellow in charge of in-house reinsurance are stuck with the loss. Obviously, since the ceding company really retains the loss, in-house reinsurance in not reinsurance at all, because there has been no transfer of risk.

It is also extremely difficult to establish initial terms for such covers, since "arms-length" negotiations are impossible under such circumstances. There is no "market" working to establish "proper" terms (whether such terms be right or wrong) at the outset, nor has any "bank" truly been created nor any continuity established with a set of reinsurers. Invariably the terms and conditions of such covers tend to be overly generous to the "cedent department" unless the individuals setting the terms have wide experience in reinsurance and are able to both develop and implement provisions which are comparable to those which would be quoted commercially. If the terms are substandard (in a market sense), then the profits of the operation being protected will be over-stated until losses develop which demand a revision in terms. Here again in-house programs can run into trouble because there is no overall market yardstick for payback and the revisions in terms could be unrealistic, either too favorable or too harsh.

Theoretically, in-house reinsurance can represent a savings to the ceding company, since the profit margin of the reinsurer can be eliminated. However, as is true with insurance, on an overall book basis the largest part of reinsurers' "risk charge" is taken up by losses in excess of the expected values, and their actual net profit margin is considerably less than the theoretical margin built into the rates. (Over the last ten years the reinsurance industry in the U.S. has a "trade ratio" of just under 103%). The formidability of creating terms on a proper basis argues against the adoption of in-house programs except by the most discerning and sophisticated managements which are capable of recognizing the inherent problems.

Some of the apparent benefits of in-house programs should also be analyzed both before and after taxes, since on an after-tax basis the potential benefits seem to be reduced. There is a "time value of money" consideration involved here which should be carefully reasoned. Tax considerations are outside the scope of this chapter, but it is obvious that the tax consequences of any reinsurance program are quite critical, and proper counsel should be sought to ensure that the tax element has been professionally analyzed.

While the point is valid that the reinsurance program must provide comfort for various levels of management (and some personnel who might not be considered management in the normal sense of the term), it can be overdone. We must recognize that not everyone in a given company can agree with every facet of an overall reinsurance program. One of management's jobs, however, is to make certain that as many as possible do agree and that those who were not enthusiastic supporters are not acting counter to the company's objectives.

GOALS

If the company is looking for growth during the next few years, then it must have defined some reasonably explicit areas in which it intends to grow. Let's say, for example, that the company wishes to increase its market share in the commercial multiple peril business. Since this is a highly competitive field, the company will certainly need sufficient capacity to be an effective competitor, perhaps with companies that are many times its size. (Obviously the company must do a lot of other things too, such as strengthen its underwriting and claims departments and develop a marketing plan, in all of which its current or potential reinsurers will be most interested; here, however, we are primarily concerned with the actual reinsurance program). The ultimate decision as to how much capacity the company needs can only be resolved when an analysis of the marketplace has been conducted. However, as part of that decision, it must also be determined that the necessary reinsurance can be purchased at terms which are compatible with the company's overall growth plans. It would be futile to decide that the company needed capacity of $5,000,000 per risk only to find that such capacity could not be found, or that, if corralled, the pro-rata capacity needed could only be found at a ceding commission of 25 % when the ceding company needed 27.5 % to break even, or that the excess capacity required was available only at terms which would leave the company too few dollars to pay the anticipated losses and expenses on its retained portion.

It would also be inadvisable to attempt growth too quickly by trying to obtain capacity which was too great for the contemplated size of the book of business. Such an action will result in treaty facilities which are unbalanced, i.e., the premium for the treaty is not equal to a substantial portion of the limit on the cover. Unbalanced treaties can have a short life span, since one or two large losses will eliminate all possibility of profit for reinsurers, and they will be unwilling to continue offering capacity at affordable terms. Under such circumstances the company can be forced to retrench after expending great effort to expand and could be left with the reputation of an "in-and-outer" in its (direct) marketplace.

If a company were operating in a poor liquidity position and also had a bond portfolio (carried at amortized values in its Annual Statement) which showed values considerably in excess of market, one of its goals must be the conservation of cash. It would be an inopportune time to increase retentions and create a potential demand for cash even if increasing retentions represented a wise course of action for the book of business based on its current favorable results and long-term potential profitability.

If one of the company's main objectives were to increase its earnings per share each year, it could face some difficult trade-off decisions in the design of its reinsurance program. Increased earnings per share are affected by the reinsurance program as follows:

1. The amount of cessions impacts cash flow, since premiums (net of ceding commissions, if any) passed on to reinsurers decrease (potential) investment income.

2. Higher ceded premiums tend to stabilize results, since the exposures ceded to reinsurers under a properly designed program tend to be those which are subject to greater variability.

3. Stabilization of results does not mean, however, that net profits have been retained at the highest possible level. Usually stabilization will result in ceding profits to the reinsurers over the long term.

4. The additional capacity provided by the reinsurance program will always result in a greater direct written premium volume and usually increases the company's net written volume as well, since the company is a more effective competitor in the marketplace. The additional business written because of increased capacity is not all ceded to rein-

surers; substantial amounts are retained in the net account.

The trick in designing the reinsurance program is to balance both the gross and net accounts, using the reinsurance treaties to build a larger and more profitable book while gradually increasing the net retained portion as size and quality increase the stability. This process, properly executed, continually increases earnings per share.

One of the main points to recognize is that the program which currently delivers the lowest net cost to the cedent does not necessarily produce the lowest net cost in the long run. A ceding company must be careful to avoid taking excessive fortuitous profits out of a book of business; these profits tend to be a "lien" against the future results on the book. If results on the ceded portion worsen (which is a high probability if original reinsurance terms have been set to yield the highest possible profit to the cedent), the required revision in terms can have a most drastic effect on the cedent's then current results. The company seeking steady growth is well advised not to mortgage future profits by attempting to maximize current earnings.

There are times that a clear statement of corporate goals will not lead to an equally clear direction for the design of the reinsurance program. There can be objectives which produce potential conflicts, both on direct business and on reinsurance ceded. Whatever the goals of the company, the reinsurance program must be designed to assist in their attainment. Those involved in design and implementation should be well aware of the company's basic objectives and carefully analyze the impact of those objectives on the reinsurance program.

BUSINESS

Complete knowledge of the book of business being protected is essential to the design of the reinsurance program. Reinsurance underwriters are sometimes amazed at the paucity of information presented on covers which they are asked to underwrite and quote. The absence of comprehensive data which is significant to the cover does not benefit the ceding company. Underwriters are usually conservative and when faced with deficient information their impression of the cedent is reduced, and they are forced to make pessimistic assumptions about the book of business. Underwriters are more nervous about unknown exposures than those which they can analyze. Ceding companies should do their homework and have available all of the reasonable information which their reinsurers will need in order to assist in the design of the program and, ultimately, present quotations. In this regard, the cedent's intermediary and/or its reinsurers will be of valuable assistance in requesting specific information and often in aiding in its preparation.

The collection of information necessary to analyze the reinsurance program is not a function performed solely, or perhaps not even principally, for the benefit of reinsurers. The cedent needs the data in order to evaluate the proposals presented by reinsurers and make decisions about the final program. The cedents must be as conversant with the detailed information as the reinsurers, otherwise they cannot rationally interpret reinsurers' suggestions and make necessary modifications. Of course, no one understands the book of business and the basic figures associated with it better than the ceding company, but sometimes the reasoning behind the complicated statistics which reinsurers request is difficult to understand. The ceding company should also be as familiar as possible with the use to which the data will be put by reinsurers, particularly so that it may correct any misunderstandings which could exist and interpret the data properly for its own benefit and that of the reinsurers.

It is difficult to generalize about the information which is necessary to design a reinsurance program and select retention levels, since the requirements are totally dependent upon the lines and classes of business involved, the types of reinsurance treaties being considered, and the history of the reinsurance program. On a general basis, however, it is possible to list and discuss the types of data which might be required. Four exhibits are shown, certain of which apply mainly to pro rata reinsurance while others relate principally to excess reinsurance.

1. *Line Counts (Exhibits 1A, B)*. Show policy counts, limits, and premium exposures by line of business or in summary form, aggregating similar lines of business into general classes. Usually basic divisions between such classes as personal and commercial lines and primary and excess business are maintained. Often the limits issued are charted to demonstrate the distribution graphically, and inferences of reasonable retention levels can be drawn. These studies are also valuable as a guide to assessing the extent to which exposures are balanced to premium income. They are also essential for the calculation of "manual increase" premiums. In certain areas, such as excess casualty business, additional information relative to underlying deductibles or self-insured retentions will also be needed.

The "manual increase" calculation involves an analysis of the premium and limits on third party business, usually by statutory line, in order to determine the actual amount of gross premium which a ceding company is collecting for limits in excess of the deductible on the reinsurance treaty. A manual increase table is used which gives the percentage increases required above the basic premium for each set of increased limits. A simplified example of such a table follows.

Table 1

Bodily Injury Liability Increased Limits
(Factors to increase limits from basic limit of 10/20)

PERSONAL AUTOMOBILE

Limit Per Accident	Limit Per Person:							
	10	25	50	100	150	200	250	300
20	100							
50	123	150	169					
100	152	173	180	189				
150	159	179	192	200	207			
200	165	186	200	205	211	214		
250	170	191	206	211	214	219	221	
300	177	196	211	214	219	223	224	226

If the deductible under the treaty were 50/100, the percentage of premium necessary to provide coverage excess of that figure could be calculated by applying the factors in the table to the actual premiums of the ceding company for the various limits which it issues. For example, if the company had $200,000 of premium for limits of 100/250, the calculation would be as follows:

FACTOR FOR 100/250	211
FACTOR FOR 50/100	180
DIFFERENCE	31
% of 31/211	14.7%

For this block of policies the company would have collected a premium of 2.11 times the basic 10/20 rate. In the aggregate all such policies represented total premiums of $200,000, so that the premium for the excess of 50/100 would be, on a gross basis, 14.7% of $200,000 or $29,400. A similar computation would be made for all sets of limits for all lines of business, taking care to use the proper increased limits table for each line. The total of all the manual increase premiums would then be summed, adjusted by an expense factor to produce a net cost, and the percentage of the total premium which this represented would be determined. This latter figure could then be compared to percentage rates calculated by other methods.

2. *Concentration Studies (Exhibits 2A,B).* Analyze exposures in certain geographical areas, showing accumulations of premiums, liability,

EXHIBIT 1A

UNKNOWN INSURANCE COMPANY

LIMITS PROFILE

BY UNIT COUNT AND PREMIUM DISTRIBUTION

COMMERCIAL AUTOMOBILE B.I.

1976

Occurrence Limit		Premium		Policies	
($)		($)	(%)	(#)	(%)
0 —	100,000	787,317	37.4	96	50.5
100,001 —	150,000	108,599	5.2	2	1.1
150,001 —	200,000	46,159	2.2	5	2.6
200,001 —	250,000	16,011	0.7	3	1.6
250,001 —	300,000	334,987	15.9	40	21.1
300,001 —	400,000	2,200	0.1	1	0.5
400,001 —	500,000	528,298	25.1	16	8.4
500,001 —	1,000,000	282,708	13.4	27	14.2
		2,106,279	100.0	190	100.0

1977

Occurrence Limit		Premium		Policies	
0 —	100,000	2,049,795	18.1	197	18.3
100,001 —	150,000	300,154	2.7	11	1.0
150,001 —	200,000	412,760	3.6	39	3.6
200,001 —	250,000	739,459	6.5	33	3.1
250,001 —	300,000	3,907,361	34.4	606	56.2
300,001 —	400,000	160,694	1.4	16	1.5
400,001 —	500,000	2,536,832	22.4	101	9.4
500,001 —	1,000,000	1,241,619	10.9	74	6.9
		11,348,674	100.0	1,077	100.0

1978

Occurrence Limit		Premium		Policies	
0 —	100,000	4,046,653	16.0	428	21.7
100,001 —	150,000	580,021	2.3	16	0.8
150,001 —	200,000	1,873,011	7.4	120	6.1
200,001 —	250,000	3,152,112	12.5	81	4.1
250,001 —	300,000	10,851,690	43.0	1,205	61.0
300,001 —	400,000	1,348,937	5.4	23	1.2
400,001 —	500,000	2,540,546	10.1	75	3.8
500,001 —	1,000,000	841,170	3.3	27	1.3
		25,234,140	100.0	1,975	100.0

EXHIBIT 1B

A SECOND UNKNOWN INSURANCE COMPANY
Excess and Umbrella Liability Business
(Policy Count; Premium Amount; Unit %/Premium %)
Policy Limits Issued Excess of Various Underlying Limits

Underlying Limits	149,000 or less	150,000 to 249,000	250,000 to 349,000	350,000 to 499,999	500,000 to 999,999	1,000,000 to 1,999,999	2,000,000 to 4,999,999	5,000,000	5,000,000 to 10,000,000	Total
149,000 or less	3 162,000 0.5/0.6	5 490,000 0.9/1.9		10 572,000 1.8/2.3		1 32,500 0.2/0.1			1 385,000 0.2/1.5	20 1,641,500 3.6/6.5
150,000 to 249,999			1 355,000 0.2/1.4	1 150,000 0.2/0.6	2 331,100 0.4/1.3	17 333,200 3.1/1.3				21 1,169,300 3.8/4.6
250,000 to 349,999		7 124,800 1.3/0.5	4 312,100 0.7/1.2	1 115,000 0.2/0.5	35 2,343,700 6.3/9.6		2 53,300 0.4/0.2			49 3,039,900 8.8/12.0
350,000 to 499,999				3 162,100 0.5/0.6						3 162,100 0.5/0.6
500,000 to 999,999	1 69,600 0.2/0.3		3 276,500 0.5/1.1	1 212,500 0.2/0.8	38 2,615,200 6.8/10.4	110 4,458,700 19.7/17.7	40 1,152,900 7.2/4.6	23 1,219,800 4.1/4.8	5 377,000 0.9/1.5	221 10,382,200 39.7/41.1
1,000,000 to 1,999,999		1 26,700 0.2/0.1			2 145,100 0.4/0.6	32 2,494,500 5.7/9.9	36 1,374,900 6.5/5.4	21 1,451,300 3.8/5.7	6 313,600 1.0/1.2	98 5,806,100 17.6/22.9
2,000,000 4,999,999					1 23,800 0.2/0.1	1 60,500 0.2/0.3	13 464,600 2.3/1.8	4 108,100 0.7/0.4		19 657,000 3.4/2.6
5,000,000 to 9,999,999						2 20,700 0.4/0.1	10 148,700 1.8/0.6	12 314,300 2.2/1.2	2 46,900 0.4/0.2	26 530,600 4.7/2.1
Over 10,000,000				1 5,600 0.2/-	1 7,400 0.2/-	2 96,400 0.4/0.4	17 570,300 3.1/-	64 935,900 11.5/2.3	15 239,800 2.7/0.9	100 1,855,400 18.0/7.3
TOTAL	4 231,600 0.7/0.8	13 641,500 2.3/2.5	8 943,600 1.4/3.7	17 1,217,200 3.1/4.8	79 5,557,300 14.2/22.0	165 7,496,500 29.6/30.0	118 3,764,700 21.2/14.8	124 4,029,400 22.3/16.0	29 1,362,300 5.2/5.4	557 25,244,100

EXHIBIT 2A

A THIRD UNKNOWN INSURANCE COMPANY

Florida 12/31/78 State/Territory Inforce Policy Count

Automobile Physical Damage

Definition	(#) Collision and Comprehensive	(#) Comprehensive Only
Miami, Miami Beach, Homestead Area	268	116
Duval County	653	245
Broward County Balance; Fort Lauderdale	431	171
Palm Beach County	6,832	2,119
Orange County	1,642	696
Pinellas County	11,190	3,641
Hillsborough County	2,715	948
Escambia County, Santa Rosa County	426	193
Polk County	1,968	555
Sarasota County	3,442	1.065
Brevard County	1,619	577
Various	618	266
Miami	12,723	3,855
Miami Beach	3,254	945
Dade County South	129	51
Dade County Balance	575	127
Broward County South	4,014	1,307
Broward County North	9,432	3,102
Broward County Balance	7,711	2,525
Manatee County	2,455	676
Charolotte County, Lee County	4,694	1,253
Leon County	258	72
Alachua County, Columbia County, Marion County	1,478	469
Seminole County, Volusia County	4,119	1,484
Citrus County, Hernando County, Pasco County, Sumter County	4,693	1,332
Indian River County, Martin County, St. Lucie County	3,246	902
Collier County, Desoto County, Glades County Hardee County, Hendry County, Highlands County, Okeechobee County, Osceola County	2,713	761
Clay County, Lake County, Levy County, Putnam County, Union County, Walton County, Remainder of State	3,069	971
Flagler County, St. Johns County	485	136
Okloosa County	303	70
Monroe County	1,338	363
Total	98,493	30,993

EXHIBIT 2B
ALABAMA
100% Homeowners Direct Written Premium by County
@ 12/31/78 — 140,685 Dwellings Totalling $23.312.688

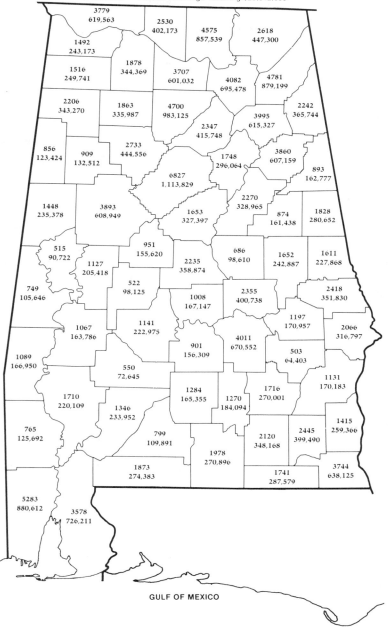

GULF OF MEXICO

policy counts, etc. These exposures are particularly applicable to property business in wind, flood, and earthquake zones. Often, PML considerations or other data which would limit or interpret the raw exposure
are also displayed. The explicit information required is a function of the
classes and types of business which the ceding company writes and the
territories in which it operates. Simple state breakdowns of direct written
premiums by line of business, although they are used for other purposes
as well, can also be included in the general category of concentration
studies.

3. *Experience Figures.* (See Experience History — Property Pro-Rata,
Table 4, page 376). Display historical results on the book of business, for
the classes involved, usually showing written and earned premiums, paid
and outstanding claims, expenses (if applicable) and earned-incurred loss
ratios by year and in summary.

4. *Loss Studies.* Take many forms, some examples being:

A. Loss severity studies (See Experience History — Property
Working Excess, Table 6, page 378) show all losses, often in excess of a
given threshold, ranked by the size of the loss. In this way, mean, me-
dian, and maximum losses can be determined, leading toward conclusions on appropriate retention levels.

B. Accident period studies (see Experience History — Property
Working Excess, Table 5, page 378) compare losses occurring during
given periods, usually annual, with earned premiums during the same
periods and produce "pure" loss cost figures which form the basis for the
rating of many excess reinsurance covers. Such studies normally involve
the calculation of loss costs excess of various deductibles and subject to
various maximum limits. Care must be taken to include loss adjustment
expenses in the data on the same basis as they will be covered under the
(proposed) treaty, i.e., if loss adjustment expenses are not covered, obviously they should not be included in the experience study.

C. Loss development studies (see Experience History —
Casualty Excesses, Table 13, page 392) demonstrate how the losses
which occurred during a given period of time developed subsequently.
These are often combined with accident period studies (B. above). Both
paid and outstanding figures should be presented on an individual claim
basis, and the status of each claim (open or closed) should be noted. The
premium (exposure) base used should accurately reflect the historical exposure of the business but also should not differ from the subject
premium base of the (proposed) treaty, unless any differences have been
considered in the rate calculations. These studies are extremely impor-

tant whenever long-tail business (such as casualty, ocean marine, A&H, etc.) is involved. Accident year/loss development studies should not be restricted to use on excess business, since long-tail pro rata accounts should also be analyzed on this basis in order to present valid statistics.

D. Occurrence/aggregate loss studies (see Experience History — First Catastrophe Excess, Table 10, page 386) show total losses incurred from a given event or aggregate losses over a given time period. In all cases, but particularly on aggregate losses, care must be taken to be certain that data is presented on either a losses "incurred" or losses "occurring" basis, depending on how the treaty is to be written.

"Losses incurred" basis means the traditional accounting figures with which most people are familiar. On this basis earned premiums are equal to written premiums for the period plus the prior unearned premium reserve, if any, less the current unearned premium reserve. Incurred losses are equal to paid losses and loss adjustment expense, if applicable, less the prior outstanding loss reserve, if any, plus the current outstanding loss reserve. In the losses incurred definition, the date of loss and the exposure period are both ignored and only the accounting period is germane, i.e., it is assumed that any premium, written or earned, or any loss, paid or outstanding, which is booked during a given accounting period relates to exposures during that period. This procedure has its foundation in the assumption that the previous unearned premium reserves and the previous outstanding loss reserves were calculated with 100% accuracy, i.e., there was neither a deficiency nor a redundancy in either of these reserves. While this assumption is accepted in the business, it is almost never accurate and is used only as a matter of convenience. There are also occasions under which the assumption would not be accepted, such as in the case of assuming a loss reserve portfolio. While it might be assumed, for the sake of accounting convenience, it would almost always be subject to eventual reconciliation based on the final run-off of the figures and the assuming reinsurer would, in the final accounting, only be liable for losses which occurred during the period it participated on the treaty.

The "losses occurring" basis calculates losses by summing the paid and outstanding values on all losses which occurred (happened) during a given time period, ignoring the date of payment or date of establishment of reserve. This calculation is continued until all losses have been settled, i.e., there are no losses remaining in reserve and there is no possibility of additional losses or, sometimes, an agreement is made to disregard any losses which are incurred beyond a certain time after the close of the period under consideration. The premium side of a losses occurring calculation should be figured on an exposure year (or period) basis but in practice this is often ignored and accounting year (or period) earned premiums substituted. This approach virtually always tends to understate the exposure since a true exposure year earned premium, assuming even modest growth by the company, would be greater than the accounting year (or period) earned premium. From a practical standpoint the use of accounting year subject premium does not ordinarily impact the calculation drastically, since if the higher exposure year premium had been used, the loss cost percentage would have been less and the developed premium about the same. There are times, however, when the failure to use exposure year premiums can cause a substantial distortion in the results, and in certain of these cases true exposure period premiums would be calculated.

This whole subject is complicated and has many consequences in other areas of the business such as rate calculations, contingent commission calculations, run-off provisions in the event of treaty cancellation, and many other areas. A further discussion of the complications of operating on a "losses incurred" or "losses occurring" basis is outside the scope of this chapter, but the student of reinsurance should understand this area and all of its complications clearly, or there will be no possibility of grasping the basic concepts of the reinsurance business. The importance of understanding the difference between "losses incurred" and "losses occurring" and the consequences which flow from the distinction cannot be overemphasized.

E. Claims inflation studies (see Experience History — Property Working Excess, Table 7, page 379) compare mean average values over a period of time indicating the extent to which losses have escalated. These figures can also be compared to policy counts and/or limits exposed to observe changes in severity rates. In this context the word "inflation" is used to connote any escalation in loss figures, not just those caused by economic inflation.

Depending on the size of the book of business, it is common to develop certain of the necessary figures using sampling techniques, but some studies, particularly those involving losses rather than exposures, require that the figures be prepared on a 100% basis.

One area which frequently causes problems is the calculation of losses excess of a given deductible. When such data is to be collected, it is wise to pick a threshold less than that required and to accumulate, and retain, data on a "ground-up" (see discussion below) basis, so that the figures can be massaged at a later date if necessary to provide additional summaries. Particularly when working excess of loss programs are involved — unless the ceding company systematically establishes a method for keeping track of these ground-up losses — it will have to continually dig into historical records to re-develop the information each time it is needed. Many companies fail to maintain information on a comprehensive basis, keeping records only on those losses which penetrate the deductible at a given point in time. If the program is changed in future years (and it almost always is), the company may have to go back to individual loss records to collect data for evaluation or rating of a revised program. A threshold equal to 50% of the deductible of the current program is recommended. It is also wise to keep separate note of the amount of loss adjustment expenses since the handling of loss adjustment expenses under the program can change.

The term "ground-up" is used frequently in the reinsurance business and means the loss, or sum of losses in the case of an occurrence involving more than one loss, from the first dollar, prior to the application of any (reinsurance) deductible. The term is usually amplified by adding, either specifically or as an implication, the phrase "subject to the cover." Thus "ground-up" losses subject to a per risk excess treaty protecting the reinsured's net retention would equal the net loss from the first dollar after reduction of the gross loss by recoveries from other treaties, such as surplus covers, and facultative placements, but before the application of the deductible on the per risk excess cover itself.

Ground-up losses subject to a property catastrophe (occurrence) excess cover would be the sum of all individual losses occurring as a result of a given catastrophic event — after deducting all facultative, surplus, quota share, risk excess and other recoveries intended to "inure to the benefit of" the catastrophe cover, but before the application of the deductible (retention) of the catastrophe excess cover itself. This explanation may be confusing to the student since it requires an understanding of how the various treaties in a program relate to each other. Unfortunately there are no absolute rules which define this relationship, since reinsurance programs are constructed in an infinite variety of ways. Generally, but not always, the following apply:

1. Facultative recoveries are deducted first and inure to the benefit of all treaties.

2. Surplus treaty recoveries come next and inure to the benefit of working (risk) excess treaties.

3. Working (risk) excess recoveries are the final deduction before the individual loss or losses are subject to a catastrophe (occurrence) excess (if applicable).

4. Underlying catastrophe excess recoveries inure to the benefit of the ceding company and not to the benefit of higher catastrophe layers.

5. If a quota share treaty is involved, one must know exactly where it fits since there are essentially no rules relating to its positioning in the program.

6. An aggregate excess of loss contract usually protects the absolute net after all other recoveries have been made.

7. If more than one layer of a given type is involved (e.g., first and second surplus treaties or first and second working excess treaties), the underlying layers inure to the benefit of the cedent, not to the higher layer reinsurers.

The above explanation may obfuscate the student more than it enlightens, but if studied carefully should be of some assistance in understanding the positioning of treaties in a program. Obviously, it is critical to the understanding of any treaty to know the precise relationship which it bears to other treaties within the overall program; otherwise, the specific exposure to a given treaty cannot be ascertained. It is dangerous to make assumptions; if one does not know or understand how a program fits together — ask. There is no embarrassment to seeking clarification because there are no rules. In trying to analyze interrelationships, concentrate on this question: What was the intention of the program with regard to the amount of the ceding company's net retention, either on a per risk (or per policy) or per occurrence basis?

In the case of all data to be accumulated, considerable care must be exercised to determine, in complete detail, the exact information which is desired. Changes in the book of business and the history of the reinsurance ceded in prior years can have a significant impact on the precise information needed and how it should be assembled and displayed. If, for example, a company is contemplating changing from a pro rata to a "working excess" program (see definition below) on its property classes, while at the same time reducing cessions of facultative reinsurance, the premium and loss information to be gathered must be in such a form as to demonstrate what the historical results would have been if the proposed new program had been in force during the past "N" years. Both pro rata and facultative premiums and losses which had been ceded in the past years and which will no longer be ceded must be added back into the net experience in order to produce accurate figures. This procedure is critical to both the design and the rating of the new program.

Similarly, changes in the reinsurance program over the years can influence occurrence losses and such figures must also be presented on an "as-if" basis, since the ground-up losses subject to the occurrence cover will differ from year-to-year, reflecting changes in the pro rata and/or risk excess programs. Here again the ceding company's intermediary and/or reinsurers can be of great assistance and will undoubtedly wish to be involved in the decisions on the data being collected, the methodology used and the form in which it will be presented. The significance of assembling accurate and comprehensive data cannot be stressed too highly, since such data form the foundation of innumerable decisions.

The term "working excess" treaty is used with some abandon in the business and often interchangeably (sometimes in the same sentence) with other terms such as "risk excess," "burning cost excess," "spread loss," and "casualty excess." Working excess is an ill-defined term but it is intended to apply to a cover which is routinely subject to loss from a single policy. Under working excess treaties, a frequency of loss is not unusual but rather is to be expected. (One wag in the business once described a particular property working excess cover, which had awful experience because of both high frequency and severity, as a "slave" excess). Working excess does not necessarily connote any given class of business: it could cover property, casualty, ocean marine, boiler and machinery or any other class or classes of business, although the term seems to be applied with greater frequency in the first party areas. Obviously then, working excess can mean that the cover is exposed to a loss from one risk, as in property classes, or to an occurrence loss resulting from exposure from a single or more than one policy, as in casualty classes. The opposite of a working excess is a catastrophe excess, since the latter is (usually) not exposed to a loss from a single risk or policy and a frequency of loss is not anticipated. Covers which present both per policy and per occurrence exposures are usually called "intermediate excess" covers.

FINANCIAL

An analysis of a ceding company, using the criteria of the NAIC Early Warning Tests, can provide a wealth of information about the company and its basic financial condition. The elements of these tests are covered elsewhere in this volume, and the reader is urged to study some live examples of test data as well as the booklet published by the NAIC entitled, "Using the Early Warning System."[1] There are eleven separate tests involved in the Early Warning System. Not all of them would be

---

[1] Available from the National Association of Insurance Commissioners, 1125 Grand Avenue, Kansas City, Missouri 64106.

germane to a given reinsurance program, and some of them might not be illuminating at all. While our suggestion that readers study the "Early Warning Tests" does not necessarily represent an endorsement of them, they do present a wealth of financial information in a format which is usable.

Of course, the management of any company is fully aware of its own financial situation and any restraints on its operations which this condition may impose. Since a reinsurance program can be of material assistance in the financial area, it is important for a ceding company to be candid with its reinsurers about these considerations. Often providing some form of financial assistance is the most important single objective of the reinsurance program. Reinsurers must be intimately familiar with a company's Convention Blank (Annual Statement) and other reports, public or private, about the company's financial condition, particularly those dealing with reserve adequacy. The "General Interrogatories" Part A, Sections 1, 2 and 3 of the Blank, which deal with reinsurance transactions should also be studied carefully. Many of the questions involved here can have a substantial influence upon the company's financial condition and also bear directly on the construction of the reinsurance program.

Designing A Program For A Typical Company

In order to analyze program design in a definitive context, we are going to make some assumptions about a "typical" company and evaluate its requirements. Since the factors of company management, goals and financial circumstances have already been commented upon, these considerations will be omitted except for occasional references, and the emphasis will be on the book of business of the ceding company. A reasonably complicated portfolio of insurance and a fairly large company have been chosen to illustrate a comprehensive reinsurance program, but some of the more exotic problems which can arise from unusual books of business have been avoided. Some of the information presented here, because it has been necessarily capsulated, may not be totally clear to the inexperienced reader; confusing points should be discussed with an experienced reinsurer. It is not expected that all readers will agree with the conclusions or comments given, since there may be other equally good or better solutions to the problems posed.

ASSUMPTIONS FOR THE TYPICAL COMPANY

1.   The typical insurer chosen for illustration is a stock, agency company

writing in twenty states in the Middlewest, Southwest, Plains, and Rocky Mountain areas.

2. The company's shares are widely held, with the largest blocks not exceeding 10%. The board is evenly split between management members and outside directors representing banking, investment, and local business interests.

3. A direct written premium volume of $100,000,000 is split as follows:

($000 omitted)

Fire	2500
Allied Lines	1000
Homeowners, Farmowners	22500
Commercial Multi-Peril, Special Multi-Peril	20000
Inland Marine	2000
Workers' Compensation	3500
Fidelity	1000
Miscellaneous Liability	11000
Auto Liability	23000
Auto Physical Damage	13500
Total	100000

4. Statutory assets of the company total $180,000,000, with a policy-holder surplus of $45,000,000, an A + Best's rating, and a sound investment portfolio of $150,000,000 consisting of 80% bonds and 20% equities.

5. The company developed an average trade ratio during the last five years of 97.5%.

6. It has sound, experienced management of a basically conservative nature with primary goals of:

   A. An underwriting profit averaging 2.5% or better over a five-year period;

   B. Growth averaging 15% compounded per year over a five-year period, but targeting 30% and 20% for the next two years.

   C. A ratio of net written premiums to statutory surplus not exceeding 2.5-to-1; the current ratio is slightly in excess of 2-to-1 and management wishes to increase their leverage by raising the ratio modestly; and

D. GAAP operating income, before federal income taxes, equal to a return on shareholder's GAAP equity of 20% or greater.

7. The company experienced a compound growth rate of approximately 20% over the last five years, but growth has been at the rate of 30% for the last year and 25% for the year prior, reflecting the company's desire to increase leverage by adding volume. Expansion has been mainly in the commercial lines areas with increases averaging only about 10% on personal lines business. No territorial expansion of significance has occurred during the last five years and none is contemplated. About five years ago the company entered a number of states outside its normal operating territory with adverse results. No new lines of business are anticipated and emphasis will continue on increasing penetration into commercial lines accounts through the company's existing experienced and loyal agency force. The company is not interested in specialty lines classes of business and concentrates on "bread-and-butter" lines. Business is basically located in small and medium-sized towns, suburban and rural areas, and fairly small amounts of business are written in large cities. Rates are deviated approximately 10% on personal and commercial packages, and workers' compensation is written on a participating basis.

8. The company's reinsurance programs have operated satisfactorily in the past, except that its rapid growth in the past two years has created some concentration problems and it recently had a serious wind loss. The company's third-party covers have shown rising losses and reinsurers are seeking significant rate increases. Property pro rata treaty cessions have been fairly substantial, and the company is considering modifying both its existing working excess program and its pro rata treaties to reduce the amount of cessions, potentially cutting its facultative cessions as well by adding additional limits to its pro rata treaty facilities.

CURRENT REINSURANCE PROGRAM FOR THE TYPICAL COMPANY

Property Business. The company's property (first party) reinsurance program covers fire, allied lines, inland marine, auto physical damage, and section 1 of homeowners, farmowners, commercial multi-peril, and special multi-peril business. The company's book of property business was distributed as follows during 1978:

Table 2

($000 omitted)

Line	Direct Written	Net Written	Direct Earned	Net Earned	Ceded Written	Ceded Earned
Fire	2500	2450	2250	2205	50	45
Allied Lines	1000	980	900	882	20	18
Homeowners, Farm-owners, Section 1	14625	14040	13163	12636	585	527
Commercial Multi-peril, Special Multi-peril, Section 1	12000	9924	10800	8886	2076	1914
Inland Marine	2000	1900	1800	1710	100	90
Auto Physical Damage	13500	12690	12150	11421	810	729
Total	45625	41984	41063	37740	3641	3323

The maximum property policy issued is $3,900,000 except that the company will issue up to $5,000,000 on superior risks, ceding the surplus of $3,900,000 on a facultative basis.

First Surplus. A ten-line cover is maintained with a maximum cession of $1,500,000 any one risk on commercial lines business. The minimum retention is $50,000. On personal lines business the minimum retention is $25,000, and only two lines with a maximum cession of $50,000 each line may be ceded to the treaty. The company's line guide calls for net retentions varying between $50,000 and $150,000 on commercial lines business and for specific maximum cession limits on each risk, depending on policy type, construction, level of fire protection, occupancy, location of risk, and other factors. The company defines a risk as comprising "all values within four walls and under one roof." The cedent does not consider PML, as such, but rather it is built into its line guide. The commission terms are a provisional commission of 35%, subject to adjustment as follows:

If the loss ratio is:	The commission is:
65% or greater	the minimum of 32.5%
less than 65% but not less than 55%	32.5% plus 1/2 of the difference between 65% and the loss ratio
less than 55% but not less than 45%	37.5% plus 3/4 of the difference between 55% and the loss ratio
45% or less	the maximum of 45%

In reinsurance parlance this adjustment is called a "sliding-scale" commission formula and would be described as "a provisional commission of 35% at 60% loss ratio sliding down on a 1/2-for-1 basis to a minimum of 32.5% at 65% or greater and sliding up on a 1/2-for-1 basis to 37.5% at 55% and up further on a 3/4-for-1 basis to a maximum of 45% at 45% or less."

Second Surplus. A fifteen-line cover provides a maximum cession of $2,250,000, except for personal lines business where the maximum cession is two lines totalling $100,000. Ceding commission is a flat 30% with an annual profit commission of 33 1/3% after reinsurer's expenses of 5%. The profit commission formula calls for unlimited carryforward of any deficit created by the loss ratio being in excess of 65%, i.e., with a ceding commission of 30% and an agreed reinsurer's margin of 5% for expenses and profit, a loss ratio in excess of 65% would not entitle the ceding company to any profit commission, but the excess of 65% would eat into the reinsurers' margin. The deficit carryforward provision allows reinsurers to recapture any part of their margin lost in past years before paying profit commissions on the results of future years.

The two surplus covers are used on an almost parallel basis with a heavy percentage of cessions being made across both treaties, i.e., the company does not use the entire capacity of the first surplus before ceding to the second, rather it tries to "feed" both treaties a reasonably equal share of most risks.

Working (Risk) Excess. A single cover is maintained which protects the company's maximum net retention of $150,000, with a limit of $100,000 excess of $50,000 any one risk. There is an occurrence limitation in the program which provides for a maximum recovery of $400,000 any one event. The current rate is 2.5% of "gross net earned premium income" (GNEPI). GNEPI is equal to the gross earned premiums, less cancellations and refunds, on the lines subject to the treaty, less the ceded earned premiums for any covers which "inure to the benefit of" the cover in question. Thus in calculating the GNEPI for the working excess program, the ceding company's gross earned premiums would be reduced by the ceded earned premiums for the surplus treaties and facultative cessions, because these reduce the exposure to reinsurers under the working excess treaty. The GNEPI for the catastrophe excess would be the same as that for the working excess cover, except that it would be further reduced by the ceded earned premium on the working excess since it also reduces exposure to the catastrophe cover. Rates could also be based on "gross net written premium income"

(GNWPI). Both GNEPI and GNWPI (as well as any other more exotic subject premium bases) are generically referred to as "subject matter premium income" (SMPI). SMPI is a lazy term, fairly commonly used but not truly definitive, since it does not reveal whether subject premiums are written or earned. The use of the SMPI term can cause considerable confusion and should be avoided. GNEPI is the most common base, since it more closely approximates true changes in actual exposure over a period of time. GNWPI is most frequently used on a new or rapidly expanding book of business, since the earned premiums on such a book tend to lag behind the written and may, in these circumstances, understate the actual exposure. It could be argued that "in force" premiums would be the best measure of actual exposure but such a base is not frequently used except in the case of smaller companies, usually mutuals, where the amount of "insurance in force" (not premium) is used with some regularity.

Castastrophe Covers. Four layers of coverage provide a total of $10,500,000 excess of a first loss retention of $1,500,000 in any one occurrence. The covers are arranged as follows:

1ST Layer: 90% of $1,500,000 Excess of $1,500,000

2ND Layer: 90% of $3,000,000 Excess of $3,000,000

3RD Layer: 95% of $3,000,000 Excess of $6,000,000

4TH Layer: 95% of $3,000,000 Excess of $9,000,000

The current aggregate rate for all layers is 1.1% GNEPI, split as follows:

FIRST LAYER — .35%
SECOND LAYER — .35%
THIRD LAYER — .24%
FOURTH LAYER — .16%

The rates shown above would ordinarily be expressed on a ¢% basis. Thus, .35% would be shown as 35¢%. This is simply reinsurance jargon or shorthand but after one is familiar with this usage, somehow 15¢% seems clearer and more definitive than .15%, probably because it is easier to miss the decimal point that it is the "¢" sign.

Reinstatement provisions allow one reinstatement on all covers at pro rata as to time and amount.

The company had a severe windstorm loss in 1978, producing ground-up losses of approximately $7,000,000. This loss was a considerable shock to the company and its reinsurers. While they were aware of the rising volume and increasing concentration, they did not believe that a tornado loss could impact their portfolio to this extent.

The company carries no other property reinsurance except for facultative cessions.

Casualty Business. The company's casualty (third party) reinsurance program covers workers' compensation, fidelity, miscellaneous liability, auto liability, and section 2 of homeowners, farmowners, commercial multi-peril and special multi-peril business.

The company's book of casualty business was distributed as follows during 1978.

Table 3

($000 omitted)

Line	Direct Written	Net Written	Direct Earned	Net Earned	Ceded Written	Ceded Earned
Homeowners, Farm-owners, Section 2	7875	7245	7088	6521	630	567
Commercial Multi-peril, Special Multi-peril, Section 2	8000	7360	7200	6624	640	576
Workers' Compensation	3500	3220	3150	2898	280	252
Fidelity	1000	920	900	828	80	72
Miscellaneous Liability	11000	10120	9900	9108	880	792
Auto Liability	23000	21160	20700	19044	1840	1656
Total	54375	50025	48938	45023	4350	3915

The maximum casualty policy limit issued is $1,000,000 except in occasional cases where the company issues higher limits and uses excess facultative reinsurance to reduce the maximum policy exposure to $1,000,000.

The company maintains excess of loss coverage to protect it in excess of an occurrence retention of $50,000 up to a maximum limit of $5,000,000. Reinstatement is unlimited and free.

The layers are arranged as follows:

1ST Layer: 100% of $100,000 Excess of $50,000/Occurrence

2ND Layer: 100% of $850,000 Excess of $150,000/Occurrence

3RD Layer: 100% of $4,000,000 Excess of $1,000,000/Occurrence

The third layer cover is strictly a "clash" cover since it is not exposed on a policy limits basis. It would take the involvement of two or more original insureds in the same loss occurrence to invade this cover. The current aggregate cost for all layers is 6.9% GNEPI, split as follows:

FIRST LAYER — 5.00%
SECOND LAYER — 1.55%
THIRD LAYER — 35¢%

The company maintains no other casualty reinsurance except facultative.

EXPERIENCE HISTORY FOR THE TYPICAL COMPANY

Property (First Party) Business. *Pro Rata Program.* The company's first and second surplus treaties have been running well: they have earned substantial increases in the sliding-scale commission on the first surplus and significant profit commissions on the second surplus, except during the last year, when wind losses caused problems. An experience recap is as follows.

Table 4

($000 omitted)

Year	1ST SURPLUS					2ND SURPLUS				
	Earn Prem	Inc. Loss	Comm %	L/R E.P.	Comb %	Earn Prem	Inc. Loss	Comm %	L/R E.P.	Comb %
1974	433	243	37.0	56.1	93.1	314	149	35.8	47.5	83.3
1975	497	288	36.1	57.9	94.0	361	199	33.3	55.1	88.4
1976	572	252	45.0	44.1	89.1	415	187	36.6	45.1	81.7
1977	715	390	37.9	54.5	92.4	519	260	35.0	50.1	85.1
1978	930	655	32.5	70.4	102.9	675	506	30.0	75.0	105.0
Total	3147	1828	37.1	58.1	95.2	2284	1301	33.7	57.0	90.7

The commission percentages have been calculated by adding the percentage payable on the ceded written premiums to either a) the additional percentage payable on ceded earned premiums on the first surplus, or b) the profit commission percentage on ceded earned premiums on the second surplus. This approach is somewhat unorthodox, but the author believes that it presents a more accurate picture of the results. The approach normally taken would be to add the dollars of ceding commission paid on written premiums to the dollars of additional commission payable because of the sliding scale adjustment, or profit commission, and divide the result by the written premium in order to calculate a commission percentage. This method, while used frequently, disregards the fact that the sliding scale adjustment is based on earned premium and that, presuming continuing experience similar to that producing the sliding scale adjustment, additional adjustments will be paid in the future on the currently unearned premiums. The "normal" approach tends to understate the commission ratio. The method used here is similar to the way in which "trade ratios" are calculated — the items which are a function of written premiums, e.g., commissions on ceded written premiums, use written premiums as the base when the ratio is calculated, and the items which are a function of earned premiums, e.g., incurred losses and profit commissions, use earned premiums as a base. The percentages thus developed are then simply added together.

Wind losses resulting from the $7,000,000 catastrophe were $190,000 for the first surplus and $202,000 for the second. Obviously in the absence of wind, the results for both treaties would have been exceptionally good. Wind losses are included in other years as well, but no aggregation from a single event was substantial.

The commission terms on both of these covers have been improved over the years, and the actual terms in force during a given year have been ignored. In other words, the commission terms are on an "as if" basis, reflecting the 1978 treaty year provisions. While other significant modifications have also been made to the program, no attempt has been made to compensate for differences in retentions, cessions limits, or underwriting policy as reflected in the company's line guide.

The use of "as if" figures in Table 4 and in other tables to follow (unless otherwise noted) does not present the true experience of reinsurers. The actual results must also be evaluated since the real profit or loss of reinsurers is quite significant in analyzing the overall reinsurance program. The way in which the participations of various reinsurers in the program is structured is also important. If, for example, the property program is running profitably and the casualty program at a loss, reinsurers on the casualty side cannot consider property profits as an offset unless they participate, on a somewhat equal basis, in both programs. The same comments apply with regard to participations across various parts of the property or casualty program. If the property catastrophe program is in trouble while the pro rata property program is profitable, reinsurers must participate in both parts of the program in order to consider combining the results of the various parts and viewing their profit or loss on an overall basis. Considerable thought should be given to the question of allocation of shares in the various treaties, and it is usually unwise to award substantial shares in profitable treaties to reinsurers who do not participate in the less attractive or potentially more dangerous treaties. It is to the ceding company's advantage to take particular care in making the allocation of shares in the various treaties involved; this set of decisions can have a significant impact on the program in the future. The company should approach the question by analyzing participations in the context of the greatest potential advantage to them in the event that certain parts of the program develop adversely. If this procedure is followed, reinsurers which participate on an across-the-board basis will often give consideration to profit on one part of the program when evaluating losses on another part.

Working (Risk) Excess Program. The working excess of our typical company has also shown favorable results. Again, changes in the terms have been ignored and results are shown on an "as if" basis; "premium developed" is based on the current rate of 2.5%. An experience summary follows.

Table 5

($000 omitted)

Year	GNEPI	Excess Losses Incurred	Pure Loss Cost %	Premium Developed	Loss Ratio
1974	18211	296	1.63	455	65.1
1975	20943	419	2.00	524	80.0
1976	24084	452	1.88	602	75.1
1977	30105	527	1.75	753	70.0
1978	39137	985	2.52	978	100.7
Total	132480	2679	2.02	3312	80.9

The individual losses to the cover for the various years, shown as the actual loss to the cover (i.e., 100% of the loss excess of $50,000, after deducting recoveries, if any, from facultative and both of the surplus treaties), were as follows:

Table 6

1978	1977	1976	1975	1974
100000	100000	65000	71215	41634
*100000	85220	57215	66427	36411
*100000	64307	48750	46318	29980
74329	52670	31200	37850	27500
*69220	41666	24681	29000	26200
57204	35248	24325	26482	19814
56300	31400	21675	21640	17620
52000	27421	17000	18210	15555
42600	16310	16250	15382	13650
35900	13528	15708	12640	11150
34306	11120	14362	11629	10604

(continued on next page)

Table 6 (continued)

1978	1977	1976	1975	1974
31333	10615	13827	10431	9875
29750	9800	12400	10250	8200
27500	9750	11659	9676	7469
21674	8250	11500	8490	6248
19420	7108	10659	7300	4340
17780	2587	9400	4319	3286
15631		8767	3669	3108
14600		7800	3402	1640
13250		7428	2100	889
12879		6809	1946	827
11450		5222	624	
11607		4318		
10599		3069		
8600		2976		
7231				
5618				
4219				
985000	527000	452000	419000	296000

The "*" denotes wind losses incurred in the catastrophe loss, totalling $269,220. Wind losses are included in other years as well, but no single event produced sufficient losses to highlight. It is assumed for purposes of analysis that all claims are closed. In actual practice some of these claims, although usually not a large percentage, would remain open, particularly on the latest accident year. The foregoing analysis would almost always be done on a class basis with components for personal and commercial lines business summing to the totals shown in the exhibit. Distinguishing between these broad classes is important in order to make projections of anticipated future results based on the scheduled growth of each class in coming years. If the mix of business in the portfolio has changed, the results of this exhibit will most likely reflect the differences in exposures by line of business.

An analysis of loss severity indicates the following:

Table 7

	1978	1977	1976	1975	1974
Total	985000	527000	452000	419000	296000
Number	28	17	25	22	21
Average	35179	31000	18080	19045	14095

While the experience has been quite satisfactory over this period, there has been a significant increase in the severity of the claims against the working excess during the last two years reflecting the shift in the company's book of business away from personal lines and toward commercial business with higher retained limits exposing the per risk excess. Additionally, the impact of inflation has caused the issuance of higher limits on many commercial insurance policies, and the company has an excellent "insurance-to-value" program which automatically increases personal lines policies to meet rising property values. A comparison of the policy limit studies for the last five years reflects the increases in limits which have occurred. The comparison does not indicate a significant increase in the relative severity of losses when compared to the limit profiles over the years, except in 1978 when a major windstorm was responsible for a number of maximum risk losses which, of course, impacted the severity.

Catastrophe Program. For the sake of brevity, the entire history of the catastrophe program is not shown here, but a summary of the covers in force over the last ten years is as follows:

Table 8

(\$000 and company's participation omitted)

Layer	Amounts			Year(s)
1ST	500	Excess	500	69-73
"	750	"	750	74-75
"	1000	"	1000	76-77
"	1500	"	1500	78
2ND	1000	"	1000	69-73
"	1500	"	1500	74-75
"	2000	"	2000	76-77
"	3000	"	3000	78
3RD	1000	"	2000	69-73
"	1500	"	3000	74-75
"	2000	"	4000	76-77
"	3000	"	6000	78
4TH	1000	"	3000	72-73
"	1500	"	4500	74-75
"	2000	"	6000	76-77
"	3000	"	9000	78
5TH	2000	"	8000	77 (ONLY)

A study of this exhibit will reveal how additional limits were added periodically and how these additions impacted underlying layers and caused reconstruction of the program. It would be an interesting exercise for the reader to analyze these changes, on a year-by-year basis, and try to determine the logic behind the various alterations which were made each time limits were added to the program.

The development of the company's retention and the 100% limits of the company's total catastrophe program as a percentage of the GNEPI have been as follows.

Table 9

($000 omitted)

Year	GNEPI	Retention	%	Limit	%
1969	11025	500	4.54	2500	22.7
1970	12127	500	4.12	2500	20.6
1971	13340	500	3.75	2500	18.7
1972	14674	500	3.41	3500	23.9
1973	16140	500	3.10	3500	21.7
1974	17756	750	4.22	5250	29.6
1975	20419	750	3.67	5250	25.7
1976	23482	1000	4.26	7000	29.8
1977	29353	1000	3.41	9000	30.7
1978	38159	1500	3.93	10500	29.9

A number of things are evident from this display:

1. The pattern of increase in the absolute level of both the retention and the limits of these covers seems to be smooth and rational, but a closer examination of the percentage figures indicates that the amount of reinsurance which the company has purchased and the retention levels are not really consistent over the years. The retention ranges between 3.10% and 4.54% of GNEPI, a variation of about 46%, while the limits range between 18.7% and 30.7%, a variation of about 64%. It must be remembered that there are many considerations involved in the decision to select given limit and retention values, and that the exposed volume of business does not necessarily represent the true catastrophe potential. Certainly the degree of concentration by geographical territory is the most significant, but the specific types of business are also germane. If, for example, an increase in the company's auto physical damage premiums occurred because the company had decided to write a "few" mobile home parks, this decision would represent an entirely different exposure than if the same increase came from writing additional homeowners business in an area where the company had no existing concentrations. The point is that an analysis of exposures must be in sufficient depth to discover the true potential of catastrophic losses; sometimes surface comparisons can lead one

astray. All of these considerations are pertinent to both the establishment of retention levels and the maximum limits which the company should buy.

2.   The company's current occurrence retention represents 3.3% of its current statutory surplus of $45,000,000. Depending on a company's size and other factors, retentions expressed as a percentage of surplus can vary tremendously. There are large companies whose retentions are less than .5% of surplus and small companies whose retentions are 5% of surplus. When expressed as a loss ratio percentage, a total loss to all layers of cover, including the company's co-participation would produce an additional 5.96 points based on its 1978 net earned property premium of $37,740,000. In the absence of any change in the catastrophe program for 1979, a loss of 4.59 points would result, based on an anticipated increase in volume of 30% to approximately $49 million. When viewed in this light, these figures are substantial and could turn a reasonably good year into one with quite a bad result. A total loss would also require the payment of reinstatement premiums of $300,000-$400,000 if the loss occurred during the Spring tornado season. While it may not be totally logical to assess the value of a total loss to all layers, it is a fairly rational assumption that the cedent would not have purchased the higher layers of cover if a total loss were out of the question. A further analysis of this sort could be made based on presumptions that less than a total loss occurred. The probability is that almost all losses would be less than the total limit of the covers, but use of the "worst possible" result can be valuable to the company.

When attempting to analyze the setting of retentions as functions of surplus, premium income, or loss ratio, it should be remembered that there is almost always a linkage between these items on a corporate basis (and usually on a departmental basis). This interrelationship can vary by company but on a general or industry basis the following relationships apply.

a.   Based on the widely accepted 2-to-1 ratio of net written premiums to statutory surplus, the retention as a percentage of surplus would be twice the percentage of premium, e.g., a retention of 5% of surplus would equal 2.5% of net written premium.

b.   Based on the average industry loss ratio over the last five years of 73.5% (disregarding the less than 4% difference between net written and net earned premiums), a retention of 2.5% of net written premium would translate to approximately 3.4 loss ratio points. In summary, on an industry average basis: 5 % of surplus = 2.5 % net written premiums = 3.4 loss ratio points. Again, these relationships do not necessarily apply to an individual company or department, but there is a natural relationship between the three elements. These relationships would also change as one looked at a particular class of business, since the average loss ratio would be different and any given company's loss ratio and premium-to-surplus ratio would most likely not be the same as the industry rates.

On a general basis, large companies tend to set retentions as a percentage of corporate or departmental premium income (which obviously infers a relationship with loss points as well). These companies are less concerned about the possibility of ruin because of their (usually) favorable surplus position. It should also be noted that equating retentions to premium income can also be translated, almost directly, into earnings per share. Smaller companies because of their (presumably) less healthy surplus must be concerned about the possibility of economic ruin and consequently tend to relate retentions to surplus. Each management must analyze its specific financial condition, its objectives and its own personality in order to decide on the proper criteria to be used in establishing retention levels. Notwithstanding the general relationship between surplus, premium income, and loss ratio points, it is a worthy exercise to analyze retentions as a function of all three criteria. It should, however, be remembered that as a company increases in size, the sheer magnitude of its surplus should be recognized and that it undoubtedly can afford to set retentions as an increasingly greater percentage of surplus. If this theory were adopted, it would distort the interrelationship between surplus, premium, and loss ratio points.

This latter point may be somewhat contentious, since it infers that there need not be a constant relationship between surplus and premium volume (and most authorities do not recognize size as a component of the premium-to-surplus ratio). The author is dealing here with pragmatic considerations relating to the establishment of retention levels; in these circumstances one is not analyzing the theoretical solvency of a company and must recognize that the raw magnitude of surplus is a more important factor than the ratio. There is a conflict here because, while larger companies could set retentions as a higher percentage of their surplus, they usually do not, because they are more concerned with earnings per share and/or departmental results. Larger companies tend to have more departmentalized or divisionalized operations while smaller companies tend to think in terms of total corporate results. Conflicts and anomalies in setting retentions are common because each company is different and has its own specific set of criteria.

3.   Notwithstanding an increase in 1978 of $500,000 (50%), the value of the deductible will deteriorate in 1979 due to the anticipated increase in volume, particularly when this increase is also viewed as adding to the concentrations in the portfolio. While the retention is not as low as it has been on occasion, the first layer is exposed to a relatively minor wind loss. Recognizing that the company has heavy exposure in the "tornado belt," the frequency of wind losses to this first layer, as currently constructed, could well make its purchase uneconomic. Prior to 1978, however, the company had never had a windstorm loss in excess of its occurrence retention, and since substantial premiums had been paid, there was a reasonable "bank" on the first layer and some "bank" on the second layer. The third and fourth layers were purchased at quite favorable terms, and no significant funding of those covers has been accomplished. The company's reinsurers presumably have been aware of the increasing volume of business and the potential for severe occurrence losses as a result of the concentrations in the portfolio. It can be safely assumed that the reinsurers would have preferred more healthy increases in the retention level, but maintained the current program because of the company's good experience.

Having mentioned the subject of "banks," a digression is in order since this is a widely debated concept. From a ceding company's viewpoint, the premiums which it pays for catastrophe reinsurance are being banked against future losses. There is little doubt that reinsurers, almost universally, agree that some part of the money paid, in reality, should be credited to the account of the ceding company. There are, however, dissenters to this consensus who argue that each year's premium belongs entirely to the reinsurers, since they have taken a very significant risk and are entitled to the full profit if the loss does not occur. They argue that catastrophe business is really rated on a "pooled" basis: that all premiums are put into a pot to pay losses over a given period of time and that no single ceding company is entitled to a "refund" out of that pot. While there is truth to this argument also, the real debate is less on the theory of the bank than it is on what part of the premium paid on each layer of coverage can be said to have been credited to the ceding company and what portion is reinsurer's margin. There is no firm answer to this question, but certainly there is general agreement among reinsurers that low layer covers, which carry heavy premiums, should be subject to what amounts to "experience rating" and that after subtracting reinsurer's expenses and a profit margin, the ceding company is entitled to recover the balance as loss payments, improvements in terms, or, in some cases, refunds of the premiums paid. The last seldom if ever occurs unless a refund provision has been built into the contract originally.

There is further agreement that in no event can the bank be considered to equal the entire premium paid; the absolute maximum share would be in the area of 75% on low layers and the percentage will decrease as the level of the layer increases. On very high layers the concept of a bank virtually disappears, with the entire premium considered to be a risk charge. The bank theory is most commonly debated in terms of "paying back" a large loss. The amount of premium to be considered as having been funded against future losses is an important element in determining how much of the loss should be paid back, over what period of years, and how other continuation terms of the cover should be affected.

4.   There is a danger in relating retention levels on each class of business to corporate surplus. There is no guarantee that each line of business, or at least more than one line of business, could not sustain a catastrophe loss during a given year. If a company maintained a high occurrence loss retention on its property business and also on, say, boiler and machinery business, the impact on surplus could be double the amount anticipated, unless this possibility had been considered in setting the retention levels on each class of business. There is also, of course, the possibility of more than one catastrophe loss occurring in any year on a given class of business. One solution to this problem is to make an estimated allocation of corporate surplus to each major line of business or each major department and then analyze retentions in terms of this smaller amount. No in-depth study has been made but for our typical company a reasonable allocation of surplus to the property department might be a figure of between 30-35% of the total surplus, since the property written premiums represent about 45% of the total and it can be argued that it takes more dollars of surplus to support casualty business than property. (The author recognizes that some authorities in the business have stated that one dollar of surplus can support more dollars of casualty business than property business. But it is believed that in today's marketplace, and presuming the existence of adequate property catastrophe reinsurance, property business is more stable and predictable than casualty business and therefore requires less surplus). This allocation approach would produce a figure of approximately $15,000,000 (using 33 1/3% of $45,000,000), and in this light the current occurrence retention on property business is about 10% of the allocated surplus. Using instead a rule-of-thumb ratio of

2.5-to-1 for property business would produce a surplus allocation of about $17,000,000 and a percentage deductible of about 8.8%.

5. When retentions and limits are established, one of the main criteria is the projected volume for the coming year. This volume is not easy to establish with accuracy, particularly when a company is in a growth posture. Volume projections can easily be overestimated, based on the enthusiasm of the marketing department rather than on rational evaluation. It is prudent to keep estimates on the low side rather than to predict rapid growth and, consequently, set limit and retention levels which may prove erroneous relative to the actual increases achieved. Premium estimates can also affect other considerations, such as minimum and deposit premiums on catastrophe and working excess programs, so that these estimates should be looked at from all aspects before they are finalized.

6. The purchase of additional layers of catastrophe protection (and other types of reinsurance as well) is, among other things, a factor of the conditions which exist in the reinsurance market at the time. Sometimes additional covers or higher limits than are essential are purchased because they are available at attractive terms. In this way protection which will become essential in the near future is "reserved" at a time when terms are favorable. On other occasions quotations and conditions are stiffer, and less than a truly comfortable limit may be purchased.

A summary of the experience of the catastrophe layers follows:

Table 10

First Catastrophe Excess

($000 omitted)

Year	Cover			GNEPI	Rate	Premium	Payback*	Losses
1969	90%	500 X	500	11025	27¢%	30	15.0	—
1970		"		12127	27¢%	33	13.6	—
1971		"		13340	27¢%	36	12.5	—
1972		"		14674	25¢%	37	12.2	—
1973		"		16140	25¢%	40	11.0	—
1974	90%	750 X	750	17756	29¢%	52	13.0	—
1975		"		20419	29¢%	59	11.4	—
1976	90%	1000 X	1000	23482	32¢%	75	12.0	—
1977		"		29353	32¢%	94	9.6	—
1978	90%	1500 X	1500	38159	35¢%	135	10.0	1350
Total						517		1350

* See discussion of payback below.

It is obvious that the experience on the above cover is quite adverse and that neither reinsurers nor the ceding company really anticipated that a $7,000,000 ground-up loss was likely. We have already discussed the problems which led to this condition. Renewal negotiations on this cover will be interesting.

The use of the term "payback" in the above exhibit is in a different context than previously discussed under "bank." In this instance the term means the number of years it would take to collect a premium equal to the actual limit of the cover after considering the cedent's co-participation (if any). In the case of the 1978 first layer, the limit is 90% of 1500, or 1350: and if the premium is 135, it is said that the payback is ten years. Reinsurance underwriters in the U.S. tend to use payback as a term while London underwriters use the term, "rate on line." The terms are really synonymous, with payback being the arithmetic reciprocal of rate on line. Some underwriters also use the term "amortization period" in place of payback. Whatever the term, it is often abused but certainly is one of the most popular ways of stating and calculating rates, not only on catastrophe covers but on other reinsurance treaties as well.

The essence of the payback concept is that the reinsurer is thinking in terms of how often the loss to be protected could occur. In viewing a catastrophe cover, particularly one which does not have any loss experience, the underwriter thinks of the question, "If I reinsured this company perpetually, how often would I expect, either in a single occurrence or in the aggregate, to pay out the total limit of the contract?" Payback is a fairly useless concept in a vacuum, but reinsurance underwriters learn by experience the general level of paybacks which the market requires for certain types of exposures. They then use payback on a comparative basis to relate the exposure on the treaty being rated against the market yardsticks with which they are familiar. The use of the payback concept by an experienced underwriter can be a highly sophisticated tool, but it can also be dangerous in the hands of a neophyte who does not have the market experience to be able to make valid analyses of the exposure and comparisons with other similar accounts and exposures over a period of many years in the business.

The main problem with paybacks is that there is a propensity for them to become easy "formulas" for rating. As such, they tend to fall into patterns which disregard the true exposure under the treaty. For example, the rates for similar first layer catastrophe covers for companies of a given size, particularly when there is no loss experience, tend to be consistent. This stereotyped approach to rating produces many anomalies, because the exposures presented by companies of a given size can be dramatically different. The factors of class and type of business, geographical area of operation, and the degree of concentration in the portfolio are only a few of the elements which can require different rates for treaties which may look similar on the surface. Payback, as one item in the underwriter's toolbox, can be used effectively, but it is only a single implement and cannot be used as a simplistic replacement for in-depth analyses of exposures and other, more complex, rating techniques.

The experience on the company's second catastrophe excess cover shows a premium of approximately $500,000 paid over the last ten years, and a total loss of 90% of $3,000,000, being $2,700,000, for a loss ratio of about 550%. The third layer has had premiums of a little over $300,000, and the 1978 loss was 95% of $1,000,000, being $950,000, for a loss ratio of about 317%. The premium for the fourth layer has been approximately $220,000 and it is loss free. The fifth layer was in force only during 1977 and the reinsurers on that layer, which were mostly those participating on other layers as well, took up participations in either the new third or new fourth layers in 1978.

Casualty (Third Party) Excesses. The experience on the company's casualty program appears excellent, but since this is a "long-tail" account, it is essential to analyze it in depth in order to discern the most probable eventual result. Determining ultimate results on third-party excess business is a most difficult task, requiring all of the skills of both the company and its reinsurers, and is the subject of considerable discussion and potential disagreement between the parties to the treaty.

First Casualty Excess. A summary of the results of the first layer cover follows. The losses shown are 100% of the excess of $50,000 and the developed premium is at the current rate of 5% GNEPI.

Table 11

($000 omitted)

Year	GNEPI	Excess Losses Incurred	Pure Loss Cost %	Premium Developed	Loss Ratio
1974	22539	975	4.326	1127	86.5
1975	25920	1166	4.498	1296	90.0
1976	29808	750	2.516	1490	50.3
1977	37260	725	1.946	1863	38.9
1978	48438	650	1.342	2422	26.8
Total	163965	4266	2.602	8198	52.0

It is interesting to note the increasing loss ratios from 1978 back to 1974. While there could be many potential causes, this pattern is typical of long-tail business. As losses develop and mature, the experience of the older years tends to deteriorate. The individual losses, both closed and pending, included in each year are shown below (loss adjustment expenses are included in the ultimate net loss before application of the deductible).

Table 12

($000 omitted)

Losses Occurring Basis

1978	1977	1976	1975	1974
100	100	100	100	100
80 C	72 C	87	100 C	100 C
62	59 C	75 C	100 C	83 C
51	57	62	94	78
42	45	55	76	69 C
37	40	50 C	70	57 C
37	38 C	42 C	61 C	49 C
35 C	35	37	52 C	47 C
31	35	37 C	51 C	36 C
28	35 C	31 C	50	35
27 C	29	28	47	34 C
21	27	27	47	28 C
21	25 C	25 C	32 C	27
17 C	25	20	30	25
17 C	24	17	27	21 C
12	16 C	17 C	27	19 C
10 C	15	15 C	27 C	17 C
10	15 C	12 C	25	17 C
8 C	11 C	8 C	22	15 C
4 C	8	5 C	19 C	15
	7 C		15	15 C
	7 C		15 C	13 C
			14 C	12 C
			13 C	12 C
			12 C	10
			11 C	8 C
			10	7 C
			10 C	7 C
			7 C	7 C
			7 C	5 C
			7 C	5 C
			5 C	2 C
			5 C	
			5 C	
――	――	――		――
650	725	750	1166	975
8 Closed	10 Closed	11 Closed	20 Closed	25 Closed
12 Open	12 Open	9 Open	13 Open	7 Open
20 Total	22 Total	20 Total	33 Total	32 Total

Table 12 (continued)

1978	1977	1976	1975	1974
		($000 not omitted)		
Mean Average Closed Claim:				
24750	28500	28818	27650	27650
Mean Average Open Claim:				
37666	36666	48111	47154	41429
Mean Average Claim:				
32500	32955	37500	35333	30469

While the average claim values are interesting statistics, great caution must be exercised in their interpretation. These figures are not at all comparable to the similar figures presented on the property working excess. This is an undeveloped set of numbers, and because of the fact that many years will be required before the ultimate experience is known, such figures as these are subject to considerable misinterpretation. Some cautious observations, however, can be made.

1.   The average closed claim value seems to be remaining constant and has actually decreased modestly during the last three years. It would be quite improper to conclude from this apparent "fact" that there was no indication of an upward trend in severity. In long-tail business the tendency is for the less significant claims to be first to close. The corollary is true also — the tougher claims, which will eventually be the ones with the largest settlements, tend to stay open for a long time. Sometimes the uninitiated tend to believe that reserve salvages (i.e., aggregate settlement values on closed claims are less than aggregate reserves) prove that the reserves were adequately established. Nothing could be further from the truth: reserve values tend to be established on an average basis and unless very significant salvages are realized on closed claims, the probability is that the remaining reserves are deficient rather than adequate. Actuaries use techniques of determining average claim values on losses closed during a given year or years, regardless of the actual date of loss, and then calculate a trend line on the average values of these closed claims to establish the expected future values. These future values are then combined with frequency values, which are also trended, in order to produce total expected claim aggregates for future years. These techniques, however, usually require a considerably greater volume of claims than is available in most excess treaties and are more applicable to first dollar losses than they are when a deductible of any significance is involved.

It should also be recognized that "excess" claims are involved here and not claims from the "ground up." Certain axioms which apply to overall reserves from the first dollar are totally inapplicable to excess losses, and those involved in casualty excess reinsurance, either as cedent or reinsurer, should be aware of these distinctions. The advice is to be extremely suspect of surface conclusions and to always remember that there is a great difference between excess and first dollar losses in the long-tail field and that there is little comparison between the conclusions which can be drawn from studying excess first party claims and those which flow from an analysis of excess third party claims.

2.   The average open claim values for the various years would seem to indicate a decreasing trend, but again this would be an erroneous inference. Two phenomena are at work here, the first being that by no means all of the excess claims for these years have emerged; the second is that the reserve values tend to increase as the outstanding losses mature. This means that, in all probability, by the time the ultimate experience for all of these accident years is determined, there will be considerably more claims in the more recent years and the values of all open claims will escalate. Approached pessimistically, one can extrapolate a significant increase in both the frequency and severity of losses in the newer years, particularly 1978 and 1977. Empirically these average claim values are telling the skilled observer that the ultimate losses in these years will confirm an expected increase, resulting from the additional exposures, higher limits, and the greater emphasis on commercial lines business, and also caused by deteriorating environmental factors.

3.   The loss frequency in 1975 is probably more indicative of the eventual relative frequency in the less mature years. An analysis of frequency in 1974 and 1975 compared to the limit profile would reveal a more realistic indication of the ultimate frequency which might be expected in the more current years. As policy limits increase, one should also expect an increase in severity; both frequency and severity will be influenced by the environment.

While there is a reasonable number of claims included in this data, caution must always be observed by recognizing that any conclusions may be affected by the statistical reliability of the data. Reinsurers often perform a number of statistical analyses knowing that the figures are not really reliable. Since they frequently have little data with which to work, they do not have much choice. After the analysis is completed they either use it totally, partially, or throw it out altogether, depending on how much reliability they place on the data. Often the exercise proves valuable even though the result may be discarded.

An accident year analysis and a "triangulation" of this data will serve to confirm or deny some of the implications made by the study of average claims information. Following is a summary of the subject earned premium exposure (on an accounting, not an exposure year basis) and a summary of the loss development pattern on the casualty excess claims:

Table 13
($000 omitted)
Losses Occurring Basis

Acc Year	GNEPI	Losses Incurred During					
		N	N + 1	N + 2	N + 3	N + 4	Total
1974	22539	320	207	211	130	107	975
1975	25920	233	233	239	461		1166
1976	29808	140	287	323			750
1977	37260	392	333				725
1978	48438	650					650
Total	163965	1735	1060	773	591	107	4266
Pure Loss Cost (% of GNEPI)		1.058	.918	.988	1.220	.475	4.659

It is easy to see why this analysis is called a "triangulation." The losses shown are the incremental losses developed during each period, i.e., the losses are not the aggregate developed as of the end of each period but rather the increases incurred which emerged during each successive year. The "N" period is the accident year itself, while "N + 1" is the second development year for each accident year, i.e., 1975 calendar year in respect of 1974 accident year, 1976 calendar year in respect of 1975 accident year, and so forth. The "pure" (not loaded for expenses or risk charge) loss costs are calculated by dividing the incremental incurred losses during each period by the amount of earned premium during the same period, i.e., all accident years have developed for at least one year, so the loss cost for "N" is equal to the total losses for that period divided by the total premium (1735 divided by 163965). Similarly, the "N + 1" loss cost is equal to the losses (1060) divided by the earned premium for the years which have developed to at least N + 1, i.e., 1974-1977, earned = 115527. Since only two years (1974-1975) have developed to N + 3, the calculation for that period is the losses divided by the premium for 1974-1975 only (591 divided by 48459).

Triangulation is not a perfect technique — all it can do is predict how the losses would develop in future years if the pattern of prior years were followed precisely. Obviously all conditions in the future will not be identical to the past, so the technique is deficient. Since, however, conditions over the last 5-10 years have tended to deteriorate and it is not really expected that they will ameliorate in the near future, many experienced reinsurers have considerable confidence in triangulation approaches. They believe that future conditions will be at least as adverse as those experienced in the past, so that the triangulation will not tend to overstate the results to be expected in future years. While it is not always true, the results produced by triangulation will tend to indicate the minimum rates necessary to sustain the cover in the future. There are numerous other forms of triangulation in addition to the example produced here. Since this procedure is fairly complicated and technical, additional detailed discussion is beyond the scope of this chapter. Those interested in learning more about the subject should consult experienced reinsurers who use it continually, not only for the purpose of calculating rates but also to establish their own "incurred but not reported" (IBNR) loss reserves and to project their own results on a class of business and corporately.

The final result, acknowledging the potential deficiencies in the technique, indicates that the minimum rate necessary to cover the losses (only) to be expected in the future would be 4.66% of GNEPI. This rate presumes that there will be no additional loss development beyond $N+4$, which is most improbable. It is more likely that further losses will emerge and that the minimum rate should be increased by adding increments for the years $N+5$, $N+6$, etc., until the ultimate loss cost is determined. This result can often be accomplished by plotting the development factors and extrapolating the development curve. In this case such a curve would be difficult since the pattern is somewhat erratic, but there are other statistical techniques which can be applied to smooth out the curve and estimate the additional points. Such techniques would result in adding between .50% and 1.00% to the rate. There are also extrapolation factors which have been developed through the study of large blocks of casualty excess claims; such factors could be used to advance the development beyond $N+4$.

If the information were available, one could also gather the necessary data for years prior to 1974 and add it to the calculation. While additional development can be helpful, when data become too old they tend to be distorted by the tremendous changes which have occurred in the environment and the book of business over the years and are therefore less reliable. This ceding company's portfolio has changed so much that figures earlier than 1974 would be virtually useless, and even the figures prior to 1976 are somewhat suspect.

Additional useful information can be gleaned from the triangulation. The figures shown on the diagonal represent the developments which were incurred during a given calendar year; the sum of all incremental incurred losses during a given year for all accident years must always equal the total incurred losses during the calendar year. Thus the last figures in each column, when summed, equal the total development during calendar year 1978. These figures can also be compared to similar figures for the prior year(s). In this procedure accident year 1978 must be omitted from the comparison between calendar years 1978 and 1977, since 1978 has only developed for one year. The total development for all other accident years during calendar year 1978 was equal to the final figure in each column, or an aggregate of 1224. For the preceding calendar year (1977), the total for the four accident years involved (1974-1977) was 1048. This comparison is quite startling since it indicates that there was greater development in calendar year 1978 than in calendar year 1977 for accident years 1974-1977, which varied in age from one year to four years. Ordinarily the development in each accident year reduces from one calendar year to the next, particularly when the deductible is relatively low. If the losses incurred during a given calendar year on a given accident year or years increase by a margin greater than the increase in the prior calendar year, it is patent that the prior reserves were quite deficient.

Such developments usually indicate that a ceding company has reevaluated its reserves and probably its techniques for establishing them; the impact of such an endeavor falls into one calendar year. If true, this action could distort the developmental pattern since the current accident year figures (1978) may not be comparable to the "N" developments for prior years. In this instance the company did hire a new claims manager in early 1978 who was more experienced in the settlement of commercial liability losses, and the manager's review of the pending claim portfolio caused significant increases in many reserves.

In addition to the loss studies, an excess limits premium should be calculated by studying the limit profile on the various classes of business. Through this study the gross premiums which have been charged for limits in excess of the deductible on the first excess cover can be determined. The gross figures would be reduced by a factor to recognize expenses, and the net figure can then be compared with the rates developed by the experience and triangulation studies to develop final anticipated rates on the existing covers. All of these figures can also be massaged to develop rates for alternative covers which the ceding company wishes to consider.

Second Casualty Excess. The second layer casualty excess cover has also experienced some losses, but there have been no claims against the third layer. An experience summary for the second layer follows.

Table 14

Year	GNEPI	Excess Incurred Losses	Pure Loss Cost %	Premium* Developed	Loss Ratio
1974	22539	—	—	349	—
1975	25920	50	.193	402	12.4
1976	29808	550	1.845	462	119.0
1977	37260	350	.939	578	60.6
1978	48438	350	.723	751	46.6
Total	163965	1300	.793	2542	51.1

*at the current rate of 1.55%

All of the losses indicated are still outstanding. These figures are also presented on an "as if" basis. A triangulation of this data might also be performed but since there are only six claims involved on the second excess, it would not be too revealing.

Since the losses to the second layer are totally immature, it is difficult to come to any conclusions about this cover, except that the loss reserves against the cover at this time are quite substantial. While reinsurers will probably be quite nervous about the ultimate results, they may well be willing to continue at current terms, because the ceding company has already indicated its willingness to adjust terms to realistic levels by virtue of agreeing to major rate increases in each of the last two years when all of the indicated losses emerged.

Third Casualty Excess. The third layer cover is loss free and since the GNEPI figures for this layer are identical, the total premium can be calculated by applying the rate to the aggregate GNEPI. The rate has not changed during the last five years.

Aggregate GNEPI = 163965   Rate of 35¢% = 574

Since there are no losses to the cover, the loss ratio is zero and there is no developed loss cost.

On both the second and third casualty excess layers, the study of the line count exhibits and the calculation of the excess limits premiums will be central to the decision as to the adequacy of the rates on these covers.

While the validity of the approach can be argued, reinsurers will frequently assume that the experience on the second layer will tend to follow the experience on the first layer. They will be prone to rate the second layer cover on a relative basis to the first unless other factors lead them in a different direction. It should be noted that this approach would not apply to the third layer because of its "clash" nature.

Before proceeding to the conclusions on the renewal of the cedent's reinsurance program for 1979, the general subject of "gross line" versus "net line" underwriting must be considered. Is it advisable to approach ceded treaty reinsurance as having been passed on to another (re)insurer and therefore no longer the responsibility of the ceding company? Some ceding companies take this approach and regard treaty cessions as being similar to facultative cessions. The theory on facultative business is that the reinsurer has had the opportunity to underwrite and, frequently, to rate the business and consequently has accepted the risk in the same fashion as the primary company. In many cases the facultative underwriter has in fact set the terms on the original policy, which condition usually does not exist in treaty reinsurance. Rather, the reinsurer relies upon the skill of the cedent to set proper terms on the primary business. In fact, there are few other commercial agreements under which one party places its fate so completely in the hands of the other party. Many reinsurance treaties are designed to permit deliberate adverse selection against the reinsurer, e.g., property surplus treates, and few, if any, treaties contain sufficient limiting provisions to prohibit a ceding company from dramatically changing the content of the book of business to the detriment of the reinsurers.

In the short run, reinsurance can improve results for the ceding company on a bad book of business, but no amount of loss recoveries from the reinsurers can change the basic quality of the portfolio and even the most loyal reinsurers will eventually tire of losing money. Can a company move its reinsurance from market to market, continuing to produce adverse results and not eventually run out of market? Unfortunately, the answer is yes, depending on the size of the company. A small or even medium-sized company can pursue this philosophy for quite a few years, and if there is ample capacity in the reinsurance market, the cedent may not have to correct its gross results for a considerable period. Larger companies will find it much more difficult to disregard the results of their reinsurers because they will run out of market fairly quickly. Depending on the conditions which exist in the reinsurance marketplace, the reception given a company, which has "shopped" its reinsurance program regularly can be quite different. In soft market times new reinsurers may be anxious to write the program, but if the market is tight, it could be a struggle for the company to find new reinsurers.

Most professionals in the insurance business accept as axiomatic that they must underwrite on a gross line basis. The quality of their portfolio is best stated by analyzing the gross results (except for facultative cessions). All of their marketing and underwriting plans are designed to produce a quality book, and if the results are adverse it is the primary carrier's task to alter its marketing and underwriting strategies to produce profitable business. This is not to say that there are no occasions under which the cedent loses its responsibility for the results produced on ceded treaty business. In many circumstances where unbalanced portfolios are involved, the reinsurers are fully cognizant of the fact that the business is of a volatile nature and that the ceding company probably does not collect enough premiums over a period of many years to pay back a loss if it does occur. In these instances, both parties know that the reinsurer must suffer the outcome whatever transpires. This subject must be, and usually is, approached on a rational basis. Depending on the size and nature of the business involved as well as the type of treaty, the ceding company must accept some, or a large, degree of responsibility for the eventual result. The company must make the necessary revisions in its primary book of business and/or in the terms of the reinsurance cessions to do its best to see that its reinsurers come out in an ultimately favorable position.

Sometimes it appears that a company is ceding too much reinsurance. Because of the "leverage" effect, the impact of large amounts of ceded reinsurance on the net retained portfolio can be quite sensational. A good broker friend of mine likes to tell the story about one of his clients who had recently purchased a substantial book of business and assumed a large portfolio of unearned premiums at the yearend. The impact of this assumption could have reduced the company's surplus substantially, and in order to obviate some of the impact, the company had immediately purchased a 50% quota share treaty on the assumed portfolio. The broker asked the president of the company what the ceding commission had been on the quota share cover. Having been told that it was 40%, he responded by telling the president that he now knew that a 20% commission had been paid to purchase the portfolio. My broker friend had surmised, correctly, that if the president had been able to cede off 50% of the portfolio at twice the ceding commission that he had paid for it, then the impact on his surplus would have been zero. In this particular case the ceding commission of 40% was fully justified because of the company's unique abilities to manage the specialty class of business involved and the fact that it had purchased the portfolio at a bargain price. There are many examples of similar situations, almost all of them free from opprobrium.

Occasionally, however, so much reinsurance is ceded that the originating company becomes insulated from the results of the business. If a company has a book of business which it acquires at a total cost, including all expenses, of, say, 30% and then cedes 90% of the business at a ceding commission of 40%, the gain of 10% on 90% of the business is leveraged against the 10% net retained volume and the expense ratio becomes negative. An example will make this effect clear.

	Gross	Ceded	Net
Premium	1000	900	100
Expenses	300	360	-60
Net	700	540	160

As can be seen, the ceding company had made a profit of 60 on the retained portion remaining on its books and therefore might have little interest in the outcome on the business. It could tolerate a loss ratio of 130% and still net 30 on the transaction. Reinsurers, on the other hand, will lose money whenever the loss ratio exceeds 60% even without considering their own expenses.

If cession percentages are high, the margin over expenses does not have to be great to produce a leveraged effect. Ceding companies can use this phenomenon to benefit their balance sheets by improving their surplus positions, and there is nothing improper about doing so as long as they maintain sufficient interest in the business to be concerned about the results.

Conclusions on Renewal and Revision of the Reinsurance Program

PROPERTY PROGRAM

First and Second Surplus. Because of the company's desire to increase its commercial package business, it needs additional capacity in its surplus facilities. The company believes, based on its own and industrywide results, that increasing its commercial package business will be of substantial assistance in attaining its goal of an average 2.5% underwriting profit. In addition, its studies indicate that increased cash flow, particularly from the third party elements of these programs, will assist in attaining its goal of 20% GAAP return on investment. The company has conducted a profitability analysis on every major class of business and sees no better alternatives which would allow it to attain these two major goals. The entering of new classes, such as malpractice or excess liability lines, was viewed as too dangerous from an underwriting standpoint in comparison to the company's underwriting skills.

With current ceded written premiums of approximately $1,800,000 and with an anticipated increase of approximately 50% in its commercial business, together with higher limit cessions to both of the treaties for the coming year and the recapture of approximately $300,000 in facultative cessions, the anticipated premium to be ceded to both the first and second surpluses is estimated to total about $3,000,000. While this amount will not produce a truly balanced situation, reinsurers will undoubtedly agree to increase the capacity of the two treaties to $4,750,000. The balance on the treaties wll improve in future years as direct and ceded volume increases. This increased capacity together with the company's retention of $250,000 on superior risks will allow it to issue a total limit of $5,000,000. One way to revise the program would be as follows.

First Surplus: Change the cover to a nine-line treaty with a minimum retention of $50,000, a maximum net line of $250,000, and a maximum cession limit of $2,250,000. There would still be a minimum retention of $25,000 and a maximum cession of two lines of $50,000 each on personal lines business.

Second Surplus: Change the cover to a ten-line treaty with a maximum cession limit of $2,500,000, retaining the current provision of two lines and a maximum cession of $50,000 per line on personal lines.

The combination of the two treaties will now give the company capacity to write a maximum policy of $5,000,000 on commercial business, and it will use facultative for those occasions where additional limit is required. This structure will give the cedent a substantial increase in capacity, $1,100,000 more than the current limits of $3,900,000. It would be anticipated that the 1978 facultative cessions of approximately $500,000 written premium, all on commercial business, would be reduced to about $200,000 for 1979. The company made its estimates by sampling its facultative cessions during the year and by calculating the amount which would not be ceded, based on the higher cession limits to be available under the revised surplus treaties. The company also made a marketing study which gave it an indication of the distribution of business, by policy limit, which it might expect based on its new line guide. The study formed the basis of its estimated ceded for 1979. Maintaining its current retention of $25,000-$50,000 on personal lines will increase the premium volume ceded to the treaties and will also reduce the company's concentrations in certain areas, relieving some of the potential exposure to the catastrophe excess contracts protecting its net retentions. These changes will require a major revision in the company's line guide to now reflect maximum retentions varying between $25,000 on personal lines business and up to $250,000 on the highest quality commercial policies. Because of the overall favorable results on these treaties and the company's conservative underwriting approach, reinsurers will be inclined to go along with some imbalance in the treaties and also to continue the current favorable ceding commission terms.

Working (Risk) Excess. With a new maximum retention of $250,000 the risk excess cover also needs revision. In view of the company's increasing volume, it can well afford to increase the retention on the first risk excess and this will assist in accomplishing one of its goals of reducing ceded premium, at least on a percentage basis. One way to revise the working excess program would be to increase the retention to $100,000 and the limit to $150,000, with the occurrence limit also being increased to $600,000. (This occurrence limit would continue the formula on the current treaty, being equal to four total losses.) The occurrence limitation probably wil not impact the cedent significantly, since losses from a given occurrence which would not be recoverable because of the limitation will fall to the catastrophe covers, presuming that the cedent's retention would be taken up by other losses and further that the occurrence loss did not go through the top of the catastrophe program. Obviously catastrophe reinsurers will be interested in this limitation, and it could affect the rates on the catastrophe covers.

An examination of the individual claims under the working excess (as described earlier under "Experience History") will demonstrate that an increase in the deductible from $50,000 to $100,000 will remove a large percentage of the losses from this cover, and a recalculation of the pure loss cost on an "as if" basis will undoubtedly mean a substantial saving on the rate. A recalculation of the rate on this cover is quite complicated since it will involve analyzing both the losses and the GNEPI to determine the results which would have occurred if the revised line guide had been in force during the last five years. Some of the considerations involved in this calculation become quite subjective and a full reevaluation of prior losses is sometimes omitted. Instead, a simple reconstruction of the prior experience is done, disregarding the anticipated changes in the cessions to the surplus treaties (due to revisions in the line guide), and judgment is used to modify the indicated values. Even this exercise is not simple and will require input from the company to estimate the changes in exposure. The company's market survey will be of considerable assistance in making this evaluation.

In the case of our typical company, an analysis of prior experience for the period 1974-1978, reconstructing actual losses only, would indicate a pure loss cost of approximately 74¢% (the reader will have to accept this figure on faith). Reinsurers will have little confidence in this estimate because of the very significant changes which have occurred in the book of business, particularly during the last two years. To demonstrate this change, the estimated pure loss cost for 1978 (only) for the new cover is about 1 ¼ %. This estimate does not include any additional pure premium for the anticipated change in the mix of business, i.e., a higher percentage of larger risks which will be protected under the new risk excess cover. The experience reconstruction considers only how the actual losses would have changed because of the alteration in the terms of the surplus treaties and of the risk excess itself; it does not attempt to evaluate the change in the mix of the portfolio because of increased emphasis on the commercial lines business nor the other changes in the cedent's line guide.

Based on the prior experience and their estimates of the increased exposure, reinsurers will want a rate of at least 1.5 % for the new cover, and the company will probably find this rate hard to swallow. This potential disagreement is frequently handled by using an experience rating approach. In this instance a three-year retrospective rating plan might be an ideal solution. Reinsurers will trade a flat rate of, say, 1.5 %, for a formula rate of, say, a minimum of 50¢ %, a maximum of 2 % and a provisional of 1%. Considerable bargaining can be involved in the establishment of final rates for the retrospectively rated plan, since "trade-offs" of a lower minimum for a higher maximum rate, and vice-versa, are often made. The actual rate would be determined by the realized results under the treaty over the next three-year period as a whole. The actual losses would be loaded by a factor, usually 100/75, and applied against the GNEPI for the period under adjustment to determine the rate and premium. An example, using hypothetical future experience, is shown below.

Table 15

Year	Estimated GNEPI	Actual Losses	Loaded @ 100/75	Developed Rate	Actual Premium
1979	49000	450	600	1.224	600
1980	66000	900	1200	N/A	1200
79-80	115000	1350	1800	1.565	1800
1981	81000	1800	2400	N/A	2120
79-81	196000	3150	4200	2.143*	3920*

*the maximum rate of 2% applies

Note that the amount shown in the "actual premium" column is the accumulative amount as of the end of the period. The premium payable during each year is the aggregate premium due less the amount previously paid. In practice, the provisional rate of 1% would be payable each year and it would be adjusted based on the calculation shown above. The rate is calculated on the basis of the aggregate loaded losses divided by the aggregate GNEPI; each year does not stand on its own. This example demonstrates the effect of the maximum rate, since the experience would dictate a rate of 2.143% but the maximum rate payable is 2%. If the experience had indicated a rate of less than 50¢%, the minimum would have applied. Reinsurer's loss ratio in this example is 80.3%, again showing the effect of the maximum rate, since the loss ratio would always be 75% unless either the maximum or the minimum applied. It happens quite frequently that the maximum rate does apply. This particular example, and it is only one of an infinite number of possibilities, indicates that reinsurers would have lost money at a flat rate of 1.5% since their premium would have been 2940 against 3150 in actual losses.

Catastrophe Program. The property catastrophe program needs revision because of the increased retentions under the surplus and risk excess programs and also because of the increased concentrations as reflected by the large catastrophe loss in 1978. With a 50% anticipated increase in commercial business, 15% in personal lines, and considering the changes in retentions, the estimated GNEPI for the catastrophe covers for the coming year is about $48,500,000 [1978 earned premium, plus a 50% increase on commercial lines, 15% on personal lines, less about $3,000,000 ceded to the surplus covers, less approximately $500,000 ceded to the working (risk) excess]. With this increase the company also needs additional catastrophe limit. Various alternatives are possible and can be charted as follows.

Table 16

($000 omitted)

GNEPI	Retention (1st Layer)	Percentage of GNEPI	Limit (All Layers)	Percentage of GNEPI
48500	1500	3.09	10500	21.6
"	1750	3.61	12000	24.7
"	2000	4.12	13500	27.8
"	2250	4.64	13500	27.8
"	2250	4.64	15000	30.9
"	2500	5.15	15000	30.9
"	2500	5.15	16000	33.0

The possibilities are really endless but these probably reflect the major ones which should be considered. There will be considerable negotiation between the cedent and reinsurers on both the establishment of the deductible level and the total amount of cover which is necessary for the company's comfort. Reinsurers will probably want to see the retention at $2,500,000, but this may be too great a step during one year. Obviously, cost will be one of the most important criteria for the final decision. With a $7,000,000 tornado loss in 1978, it would be quite possible that the same storm would produce losses in the area of $10,000,000 if it were replicated in 1979. Also the changes in the surplus, working excess, and possibly facultative programs will cause an increase in the net ground-up loss which would have been subject to the catastrophe excess treaties. The loss to these covers will have to be reconstituted on an "as if" basis.

A more severe loss, or one which hit another part of the company's territory, could produce even higher losses. One possibility is that a compromise will be reached on the retention level, setting it at $2,250,000. The company undoubtedly will not be satisfied with less than $15,000,000 of total cover. A careful analysis of the additional concentration expected from the increased volume of business will be helpful to the company in making its final decision on the total limit required. It is patent that the price of the company's catastrophe program will increase substantially in 1979, but determining the final price is not an easy matter since it involves the elements of "paying-back" (amortizing) the past loss plus rating the cover on a "going-forward" basis. As previously discussed, some part of this loss has already been banked. Deducting reinsurer's cost of 20-25 %, the aggregate net premium paid for the first layer cover over the last ten years was approximately $400,000, and since the total loss was $1,350,000, it can be said that the amount to be amortized as a component of the total future price is $950,000. Presuming that the parties agree that $950,000 is the proper amount (and there could be some give and take), the important question remains: Over what period should this agreed amount be repaid?

The discussion of the term over which the loss should be repaid will start with reinsurers suggesting a payback period of about five years, and the company countering with a term of about ten years. The subsequent negotiations will most likely be conducted in good faith with the reinsurers recognizing that the company is under no obligation to repay the loss. The company's reaction to this first difficult loss in many years will set the tone for future negotiations, and it will certainly be critical in reaffirming continuity with its reinsurers. The reinsurers know that the company could simply say that it would not pay back any part of the loss since reinsurers had taken the risk and had charged what they thought was a proper premium. In the final analysis, if reinsurers were not reasonable, the company could seek new markets and existing reinsurers would have no payback at all. Nor is the payback negotiation independent of the continuing terms of the contract. If the payback is less than satisfactory to reinsurers, this condition will be reflected in the rates for continuation of the cover on a going-forward basis. If the payback portion is generous to reinsurers, this condition will also reflect in the continuing terms, since reinsurers will have great confidence in the ceding company's willingness to adjust the program as experience warrants. The whole negotiation, ideally, is approached as a mutual problem which must be solved rationally. It is normal that the amortization on the first layer will be the fastest and amortization on the higher layers will be over a greater period. Any payback will only benefit continuing reinsurers — any reinsurers who decide to withdraw from the covers would not receive their share of the payback, and any reinsurers who withdraw in the future would ordinarily lose any future amount which had not already been paid. While the payback will be calculated on the basis of the all-time deficit on the various layers, i.e., the condition which all reinsurers would be in if they had been on the program with identical shares over, say, the last ten-year period, it should be recognized that in most circumstances every reinsurer's position is quite different since it may have been on the program for differing shares and for shorter periods. When covers are in a payback status, it is difficult to change the construction of the layers, since this could complicate the payback terms immensely.

The terms for the cover going forward must also be realistic, based on the exposures which exist today and the experience on the covers. This is necessary because there can always be another loss to the program. With these comments as a background, the most probable term for the first layer amortization is seven years, representing a compromise between the reinsurer's original request of five years and the cedent's original suggestion of ten years. The final agreement of seven years will undoubtedly satisfy reinsurers, since it will be viewed as a significant and fairly expensive improvement in the cedent's original offer. The amortization periods for the second and third layers would most probably be ten years each. A period of greater than ten years is simply too long and, rather than extend the period beyond ten years, it would be more likely that some part of the loss on the higher layer covers would be totally "forgiven" and the balance amortized over the ten years. In this case because the loss to the third layer was not a total loss, it makes sense to maintain the amortization period at ten years. Since the parties have agreed to a deduction of about 25% from the last ten years' premium in order to arrive at the net loss on the first layer cover, this establishes a pattern for the higher layers and, as previously discussed, the deduction for these layers will be greater than for the first layer. It is probable that the parties will agree to use a factor of 65% for the second layer and 60% for the third layer. On this basis the net loss to the covers would be $962,000 for the first, $2,375,000 for the second, and $770,000 for the third. With amortization periods of seven years on the first and ten on the second and third, the annual amounts to pay back the loss would be $137,000, $237,500 and $77,000 respectively, or a total of $451,500. If we assume that the company agrees to a first layer retention of $2,500,000, we can present a recap of the amortization of the loss and the probable continuing terms for the various layers of the new program. It is also assumed that the company will settle on total catastrophe protection of $15,500,000. The layering and rates would be as follows.

Table 17

(rounded to nearest $1000)

Layer	Cover	Amortization Premium	Continuing Payback Years	Continuing Premium	Total Premium
1st	90% 1500 XS 2500	137	4	338	475
2nd	90% 3000 XS 4000	238	7	386	624
3rd	95% 3000 XS 7000	77	10	285	362
4th	95% 4000 XS 10000	—	17	224	224
5th	95% 4000 XS 14000	—	26	146	146
Total	15000 XS 2500	452	10.5	1379	1831

The entire catastrophe program for the coming year will cost the ceding company a total of $1,831,000, being a combination of the amortization of the loss and the continuing premium for the covers going forward. It may seem that the revised rates on these covers are quite high, particularly on the first and second layers. An analysis of the pure loss cost on the first layer indicates that a rate of 69¢% is the historical cost. This is derived from the fact that the revised cover would still be a total loss in the 1978 occurrence which would produce a loss of $1,350,000 and the total GNEPI for the last ten years is approximately $196 million (1350/196000 = 69¢%). This rate loaded to produce a 75% loss ratio would indicate a gross rate of about 92¢%. On the estimated GNEPI of $48.5 million for 1979, this rate would produce a premium of about $446,000. Since the company is paying a total premium of $475,000, including the amortization of the prior loss, it can be seen that the continuation terms are really quite reasonable for the ceding company. It can be argued that the pure loss cost for the catastrophe cover should not be calculated by using the loss dollars divided by the subject premium base for the entire ten-year period. If a shorter period were used, obviously this would increase the pure loss cost. The reader can calculate his or her own loss cost for the second and third layer covers and come to his or her own conclusions.

It is probable that these rates would have been higher than those agreed if there had not been a long-term relationship with the ceding company and if the company had not agreed to what reinsurers regarded as a reasonable payback of the loss. There are other, more conservative, approaches to the rating of these catastrophe layers which would indicate rates higher than those to which the parties agreed. These approaches, while valid, would probably price the first and second layers out of the market. Reinsurers are counting on the excellent relationship which has been built with this company over many years. The future of these covers will depend on the future experience, and both the cedent and the reinsurers are now well aware that substantial catastrophe exposures exist and that the covers could take a stiff loss at any time.

In view of the company's agreement to increase the retention to $2,500,000, there is an additional alternative which could be attractive to it: add an aggregate cover protecting the company's net retention. This cover would most likely be written for a limit of 95 % of $2,000,000 excess of $2,500,000 in respect of wind, hail, or flood losses for occurrences which were regarded as catastrophes by the Insurance Services Office and received an ISO catastrophe number. The cover would protect the company for the "band" of losses betweeen zero and $2,500,000 per occurrence. Obviously then, it would take a minimum of two such occurrences to invade the cover, since any loss over $2,500,000 would be covered by the catastrophe program (unless it went through the top of the fifth layer). If, for example, the company sustained an occurrence loss of $5,000,000, the excess of $2,500,000 would be recovered from the first castastrophe cover. The retention of $2,500,000 would exhaust the retention under the aggregate cover, and any subsequent occurrence loss, as defined, would be recoverable from the aggregate cover. Thus, in the event of two occurrence losses in the same (treaty) year, the company's retention would be reduced from $5,000,000 (2 x $2,500,000) to $3,000,000 ($2,500,000 from the first loss and $2,500,000 less the $2,000,000 recovery from the aggregate cover on the second loss.) The price for a cover of this type would be about $200,000, a ten-year rate.

While such covers are written to protect the "band" from the "ground-up" to the retention level on the first catastrophe layer, it is also common to impose a deductible on such covers. The deductible is sometimes on a straight basis and sometimes on what is called a "franchise" basis. An example of a straight deductible would be a cover which protected the "band" of loss between $250,000 and $2,500,000 and under which the maximum from any single loss which could be counted towards satisfaction of the aggregate deductible would be $2,250,000. If a franchise were used, the same cover would protect the entire loss as long as it exceeded the franchise of $250,000, and in this case the maximum from any single loss would be $2,500,000. While such franchise deductibles are fairly common, they do present something of a moral hazard since an occurrence loss which approaches the franchise amount does not count until the deductible is exceeded, but then counts from the ground-up. A tendency to "stretch" such a loss could exist. Reinsurers normally are not too concerned about such potential moral hazards, depending on the reputation of the ceding company. There are companies, however, for whom reinsurers would not write such a cover.

CASUALTY PROGRAM

The company estimates an increase of about 30% on its total casualty book in 1979. Because of the severe loss development which has occurred during the last year or so, an increase in the retention level on the first layer cover is probably wise. This will keep the cost of the cover at a rational level and is also in conformity with the company's goal of reducing reinsurance cessions. The most likely change would be to increase the deductible from $50,000 to $100,000 and retain the existing limit of $100,000. This would keep the "working" level cover in balance, and the second layer could then be correspondingly modified to $800,000 excess of $200,000. The third layer cover would remain at $4,000,000 excess of $1,000,000 and would continue as a "clash" cover, since the maximum casualty policy limit will stay at $1,000,000.

Considerable massaging of the loss development figures will be necessary to arrive at final conclusions on the proper rate level for the new covers. It should be remembered that the loss development pattern for a cover of $100,000 excess of $100,000 will not be the same as for the cover of $100,000 excess of $50,000. Since the deductible has been raised, the "tail" on the cover will tend to be extended, not in absolute dollars but in a relative development sense. The pure loss cost on the new cover will be reduced from the 2.602% GNEPI for the old cover to 0.641. A portion of the losses which had previously fallen to the second layer cover will now be protected by the first layer as a result of the increase in the attachment point and maintenance of the limit at $100,000. The components of the new loss cost are: a) 0.458 % for limits of $50,000 excess of $100,000 which, when compared to the old cost of 2.602 %, represents the value of the increased deductible, and b) 0.183 %, which is the cost for limits of $50,000 excess of $150,000 (or the losses which were previously covered under the second excess and now fall to the first excess.) Since the old triangulation indicated that the 2.602 % pure loss cost would develop to, say, 5.5 % (4.66 % plus .50 % to 1.00 %) or about 2.1 times, one approach would be to say that the development on the new layer would be at least as great. In practice a new triangulation would be done, and it would indicate a projected ultimate pure loss cost of 1.60 % (which the reader will also have to accept on faith). As would be expected this figure shows a development of greater than 2.1 times.

The pure loss cost for a new second layer of $800,000 excess $200,000 would be 0.610 %, a reduction from the prior cost (0.793 %) of 0.183 %, corresponding directly to the losses "transferred" to the first layer. All of the figures cited are undeveloped pure loss costs and do not represent rates for these covers. They indicate the relative, not the absolute, values of the different covers.

This reconstruction of the various layers of the casualty program can cause some problems in terms of the existing reinsurers, depending on how many of them have lines on both the existing first and second layers. It would not be sound practice to reduce the limits on the first layer by the amount of the increase in retention since this would force out some reinsurers who, it would appear, will lose money on the cover over the last five years as the losses mature, presuming that the ultimate loss projections prove to be valid. An alternative would be to increase the limit on the first layer by an amount which would remove most of the losses from the second layer and allow current second layer reinsurers a participation in the new first layer. In this case, the alternative is not particularly effective since the losses to the current second layer are small in number but with a fairly high severity. Total losses to the existing second layer stand at $1,300,000 and, evaluated at 12/31/78, were as follows.

Table 18

ACCIDENT YEAR (DATE OF LOSS)	CURRENT OUTSTANDING LOSS RESERVE*
1978	$350,000
1977	250,000

(continued on next page)

Table 18 (continued)

ACCIDENT YEAR (DATE OF LOSS)	CURRENT OUTSTANDING LOSS RESERVE*
1977	100,000
1976	300,000
1976	250,000
1975	50,000
TOTAL	$1,300,000

*excess of the current deductible of $150,000

It would take an increase in limit of $100,000 or more to have an impact on the loss cost, and if that limit were added to a new first layer, the cover would become $150,000 excess of the new retention of $100,000. While this cover would be slightly unbalanced, it is an alternative which should be carefully considered by the company. The pure loss cost for the layer of $150,000 excess of $100,000 would be 0.793%, but the cost of a second layer of $750,000 excess of $250,000 would be reduced by an identical amount to 0.457%. Obviously, the pure loss cost of these layers will total to the same figure however they are structured, but the structuring is important in terms of getting the most rational set of terms for the covers. Some reinsurance underwriters are comfortable with certain layers of cover and others prefer different layers. Designing the layers so that they accommodate to the preferences of the market-place can often make a substantial difference in the final rates and terms which can be negotiated. This would be particularly true if the second layer cover could be reconstructed so that it would have been loss-free on an all-time basis, since some casualty excess reinsurers will price loss-free covers at fairly low rates. In this instance such an alternative approach would be impractical since the second layer would have to be written with a deductible of $500,000 (the highest loss currently in reserve), and the probability is large that the currently reserved losses could finally settle for values in excess of the reserves. Even if the second layer were written excess of this deductible, the first layer cover would then be $400,000 excess of $100,000, which would be a very unbalanced working layer.

The reinsurers on the revised first layer, presuming it to be $100,000 excess of $100,000, will be looking for a rate in excess of 2%, based on their conviction that the indicated pure loss cost is about 1.6%, as indicated earlier. They will also be nervous about the future development of losses, even excess of the higher retention, and will probably want to inject some kind of a formula rating approach which would give them greater protection against rapidly escalating losses. A formula which called for a provisional premium rate of 2%, with a minimum of 1.0% and a maximum of 4%, would probably be appropriate, with the final rate being determined on the basis of the ultimate experience on the next three years taken as a whole, using the same approach described under the property working (risk) excess above. This approach would not give the company a guaranteed rate during this period, but it would give them the opportunity of paying less for their reinsurance if the experience were good, because the minimum rate is less than one half of the probable flat rate.

If the first layer were written for $100,000 excess $100,000, then the second layer would become $800,000 excess $200,000. The loss development pattern for this layer is extremely adverse, since all of the current losses were reported during the last two years and heavy reserve increases were made during 1978. It is quite probable that the rate of 1.55% on the current second layer will prove deficient. With the increase in the deductible of $50,000 (and a corresponding decrease of $50,000 in the limit), reinsurers may be willing to continue the 1.55% rate for the revised layer. They really would prefer a rate of about 2%, and it will be difficult for reinsurers to decide whether to seek the increase now or to rely upon the company's already indicated good faith and wait to see how the experience will develop during the coming year. In all likelihood, reinsurers will conclude that they will stick with the current rate on the revised cover, since the increase in the deductible is of considerable value to them, and they will seek the company's general agreement to a revision in the rate at the next renewal if the experience indicates the need for a change.

As an alternative approach on the first casualty excess layer, if the company finally decided (after many hours of discussion with its intermediary and reinsurers) that this layer should be $150,000 excess of $100,000, then this layer would have the same limits and deductible as those of the property working excess cover. The company could consider a combined cover which would protect all classes of business. While this type of cover is used by some ceding companies, it often causes significant problems because it mixes both long and short-tail business with totally different loss development profiles.

At very high deductible levels and for quite large companies, property and casualty exposures are combined into what are called "global excess" covers, and such covers are logical since they do provide the company with consistent amounts of protection against catastrophe losses whether the loss be caused by a property or casualty peril. Since these global covers are usually rated principally on the property exposures, which present the greatest probability of loss, the very high limits of casualty protection are included at fairly minimal cost. On lower layer covers where a frequency of loss can be expected from both property and casualty exposures, there are no savings to be expected from combining the perils. Rather, it is possible that the reinsurance costs on the property portfolio could be adversely affected if poor results ultimately emerged on the casualty portion. Since both books of business are included in the same subject premium base for the combined treaty, the property business (even if profitable by itself) might have to assist in "paying back" the losses on the casualty portion. It is at this point that combined property and casualty programs often fall apart, since it is not rational for the property book to shoulder a long-term burden of high rates because of casualty losses. (As an interesting aside, consider the intramural debate which would occur between the managers of the property and casualty departments if this circumstance came to pass, as it has with a number of companies.) Nor is there any benefit to the ceding company in having consistent limits and deductibles on both classes. In the case of the ceding company which we are examining, it is true that it may have come to the conclusion that the limits and retentions on the first layer working excesses for both property and casualty could be the same. This is mostly a coincidence and the deliberations and considerations which went into making these decisions were quite different, even though some of the financial elements were not dissimilar because of the reasonably comparable size of the books of business.

When property and casualty perils are included in the same low-lying layers, the results tend to become confused and the covers are extremely difficult to evaluate. The more quickly developing property losses are analyzed against a subject premium base which includes third party premiums. Since the casualty losses take longer to develop, the loss cost for the working excess program is distorted and depressed. While it might appear that this result could inure to the benefit of the ceding company by keeping the rates on the program lower than they should probably be, in the end it can only cause problems for the ceding company by deferring the apparent cost of excess third party losses and misleading the company into thinking that the book of third party business is in better condition than, in fact, it is. If the company sees good gross results and net figures which are consistently profitable because of reinsurance costs which are too low, it could easily embark upon an expansion program resulting in considerable effort and expense to produce a book of losing business. The ceding company could very well defer necessary underwriting actions on the primary level which were essential to continued profitability of the portfolio. After the losses on a combined property and casualty excess fully mature and the real loss cost is known with greater reliability, the company will have to recognize that problems exist on its book of business. By that time many years have elapsed and the company could well be left with a book of unprofitable business which will take a number of years to repair. While reinsurers who were on the cover during the years when it was underrated will still be liable for the losses which occurred during that period, a revision in terms will be necessary going forward. During the time that it takes the ceding company to repair the basic book of business, the cost will be retained by them, either in terms of higher retentions, increased rates on the working excess, or, more probably, both.

It is much better for the ceding company to have a continuing reasonable cost for its reinsurance than to have costs which are too low for a period of time and which must be increased dramatically to compensate for the years when they were depressed. Deficient reinsurance costs, particularly on long-tail business, if they exist for a number of years, could literally lead to insolvency; this factor has contributed to insolvencies in the past. A sophisticated, mature management is aware that it is in a better position to make proper decisions on management of its portfolio if it knows the accurate results than if it is deluded by reinsurance costs which do not measure up to reality. Unfortunately, it is less sophisticated managements which are sometimes convinced that property and casualty exposures can be combined at the lower levels, and it takes many years for them to find out that the advice they received was not good counsel. Once such programs get into trouble, it is also difficult to unwind them because significant changes in terms may well be required which may not be possible for the ceding company to make. Also a single set of reinsurers would have been involved, and if the program is split into parts again, it is not always easy to satisfy the old reinsurers with participations in the new program.

It is always difficult to make drastic revisions in a reinsurance program which has fallen on hard times. It is much wiser and more advantageous for the cedent and the reinsurers, in concert, to put their best efforts into designing the program on a sound basis throughout its life and avoid the necessity of taking heroic steps to repair problems which could undoubtedly have been avoided if greater care had been taken in the design and rating of the program originally.

One of the worst problems to solve occurs when a ceding company has been operating with a property working excess program, only to find that it must go back to a pro rata program. Great consideration should be given to changing from pro rata to working excess because, while an excess program can be attractive from the standpoints of administration, retaining premium volume, and apparent cost, it can be a nightmare regression to recreate pro rata facilities if the company were premature in its decision and the excess program proves unworkable. The entire book of business must be reunderwritten and specific cessions made to surplus treaties. Additionally, there is no recent experience upon which to build a set of terms for the new covers, and it is difficult if not totally impossible to create "as if" experience. Surplus reinsurance treaties give ceding companies many advantages which either are not present or else have diminished importance when working excess covers are used. Among these advantages are:

1. **Stabilization of Results.** Surplus treaties accept the peak exposures and remove the unbalanced portion of the business from the portfolio. The result is a more balanced net retained book and more stable and predictable results. Surplus cessions also reduce the concentrations in the portfolio thus lessening the catastrophic exposure to the net book.

2. **Predictability of Cost.** While ceding commission terms, including profit commissions, do change because of varying results under surplus treaties, the variances are relatively minor as a percentage of ceded premiums. The cost of a surplus treaty is almost totally predictable and highly stable.

3. **Surplus Relief.** Because the ceding commissions payable under a surplus treaty allow the company to recover all of its original costs, any drain on statutory surplus from ceded premiums is eliminated. Unearned premium reserves on the ceded portion are carried by reinsurers and they take the statutory penalty. Usually ceding commissions are set at levels excess of actual expenses, so that the company actually realizes a statutory profit and decreases its statutory expense ratio. Surplus cessions also reduce net written premiums and allow a ceding company to maintain a satisfactory ratio of net written to surplus.

4. **Reservation of Business for Future Growth.** Business ceded to a surplus treaty can always be recaptured, gradually or abruptly, with or without a portfolio transfer. As the net retained book grows, the terms of a surplus treaty can be altered so that additional stable, profitable segments of business previously ceded can be retained. Business emanating from new territories or new lines or sublines can be ceded and later recaptured as it seasons.

All of these points argue against abrupt and drastic changes away from surplus treaties; they do not argue against the judicious use of working excess covers as part of an overall program. The most sagacious advice a ceding company can receive on this subject is to be circumspect about the decision, and be as certain as possible that it is ready to move from pro rata into working excess covers on its property portfolio.

Overall Considerations

The question of financial security is of paramount importance to a company in selecting reinsurers to participate in the formation of the program and equally important for all of the reinsurers which will eventually take up shares. The ceding company must be absolutely certain that its reinsurers are financially sound, so that they will still be around when it comes time to pay the inevitable losses under the program. Obviously, this is particularly relevant when long-tail business is involved but the question of continuity of reinsurers makes financial security almost as significant on business which produces claims more quickly. Continuity is critical to the cedent since it will be making an investment in its reinsurers which may not pay off for many years in the future. This is true whether the business involved is property, casualty, or any other line. If, for financial reasons or otherwise, the reinsurers no longer exist when it comes time to collect on the cedent's investment, the ceding company loses.

The reputation and financial condition of a potential reinsurer are very material, but the ceding company's analysis should not stop there; the ceding company should also attempt to evaluate the reinsurer's experience and ability. If the reinsurer is not extremely knowledgeable on the underwriting side of its business, it is possible that its own results may be so adverse that it cannot long remain in business. The ability of a reinsurer to produce a profit on its portfolio is just as important to its continued existence as it is for a primary company. Ceding companies should recognize that the success or failure of a reinsurer is totally dependent upon its underwriting skills, not just on the particular cedent's program but on the reinsurer's entire book of business. The reinsurer's overall abilities are important to every cedent with which it does business; if the reinsurer is unsuccessful it does not matter whether the ceding company's program contributed to the loss or not, the results are the same and could still impact the cedent, particularly one which has ceded nothing but excellent business.

The ceding company should also take great care in determining who is performing the underwriting on behalf on the reinsurer and where the reinsurer is located. Reinsurance companies which put the responsibility for their underwriting in the hands of others (who could be more interested in the fees received for underwriting than in the final results on the book of business produced) could have adverse results and consequently be forced to withdraw the underwriting authority which had been granted. This situation has occurred many times in the reinsurance market and is not a theoretical problem. These statements are not intended as a blanket indictment of all underwriting agencies or pools. Some of these organizations are among the leaders in the business; others are not necessarily as sound.

Reinsurers which enter the market on an experimental basis can also be cause for concern. Particularly when market conditions in the reinsurance business are soft, many companies enter the market on a test basis and will make an eventual decision as to how long they stay on the basis of the results which they achieve. Since soft market conditions are not conducive to profitable results, these companies sometimes withdraw after experiencing adversity.

All of these considerations and more must be appraised by the ceding company when deciding on its reinsurers. Since many cedents are not sufficiently experienced in the reinsurance business to make such evaluations, they frequently rely upon their reinsurance intermediaries for guidance. Reinsurance brokers maintain a constant surveillance of all companies operating in the reinsurance market and know the abilities of each reinsurer. Consequently, intermediaries are able to make intelligent recommendations about the reinsurers which a ceding company should consider. The ceding company should be careful to point out to its intermediary any particular points which concern it about financial security and potential continuity of reinsurers. As for direct reinsurers which do not operate through intermediaries, their reputations and abilities can be checked by asking their client ceding companies and by studying their results.

The question of rates and terms is always important in any reinsurance program. The ceding company needs no advice to seek the most favorable terms which it can obtain from reliable reinsurers. There are, however, many reasons why a ceding company should be wary of reinsurance terms which appear unusually favorable. Reinsurers, particularly if they are not experienced enough to be able to create realistic terms, only have to live with the results for the period during which they participate on the covers. The ceding company must live with its book of business until it can change the results, and it must suffer the consequences of any ill-conceived programs long after the reinsurers which may have recommended the program have passed on.

Only a few of the possible alternatives for our typical company have been considered. There are numerous other approaches to solving their problems, and there are some additional questions which should be asked.

1. With essentially unlimited exposures on workers' compensation occurrence losses, should the company consider buying additional limits on its casualty excess program?

2. Would it be wise to consider adding casualty exposures to the higher layers of property catastrophe cover as one possible solution to the above question?

3. Is $5,000,000 capacity on commercial property risks really enough for the company to serve as an effective competitor in that field?

The best approach in designing the proper reinsurance program for any company is for it to do business with experienced and realistic parties in the reinsurance market: reinsurers and intermediaries which are professionals in the business and which can distinguish rationality from wishful thinking.

He who wishes to cede or assume reinsurance successfully must be, with the anonymous sage, "One who has the just average faculties we call 'commonsense'; a man of strong affinity for facts, who makes up his decision on what he has seen. He is thoroughly persuaded of the truths of arithmetic. There is always a reason, in the man, for his good or bad fortune. Men talk as if there were some magic about this, and believe in magic, in all parts of life. He knows that all goes by the old road, pound for pound, cent for cent—for every effect a perfect cause—and that good luck is another name for tenacity of purpose."

Summary

Reinsurance programs are designed to reflect the ceding company's basic objectives. To design a program properly, a number of elements must be analyzed: 1) the personality and capabilities of management, 2) the company's growth, profitability and other major goals, 3) the company's book of business, and 4) the company's financial condition.

The personality and style of management will influence the retention levels and amounts of reinsurance needed in order to provide the proper degree of comfort for the company. Growth plans, possible entry into new lines or territories, and profitability goals impact the design of the program. Whatever the goals of the company, the reinsurance program must be constructed to assist in their attainment. Complete knowledge of the book of business is essential for correct statistical information about the portfolio. An analysis of Early Warning Tests and other financial data is necessary to determine the cedent's needs and its basic financial condition.

Throughout the chapter, numerous definitions of reinsurance terms were given and many comments were included about the way ceding companies and reinsurers think about practical aspects of reinsurance treaties.

To analyze program design, a typical company was constructed and its management, goals, book of business, and financial condition analyzed in detail. The cedent's current reinsurance program was presented as well as the full history of the program, including changes over the years and experience figures, and these were explored in detail. This exposition gave insight into the concepts of program design, the terms and conditions involved in typical treaties, and showed the effect which the experience results have on modifications to the program. A discussion of the renewal of the cedent's program, including the give and take necessary to compromise the views of cedent and reinsurers, presented valuable information on the negotiation process.

*   *   *   *   *   *

About the Author of Chapter 12

Richard F. Gilmore was born in Detroit on January 17, 1932. After graduating from the Detroit public schools, he attended the University of Michigan.

His 25-year career with the Continental Casualty Company began in 1950 as an accounting clerk in its Chicago office. From 1951 to 1963 he worked in accident and health insurance, first in the agency-underwriting department and later becoming superintendent of the company's guaranteed renewable division. In 1963 he was moved to the reinsurance division where he became an assistant vice president. A few years later he was appointed general manager of CNA's Canadian operations in Toronto for three years. While in Toronto he was also president of CNA Assurance Company, president-elect of the Canadian Association of Accident and Sickness Insurance, and director of the Better Business Bureau of Canada. Following Toronto he returned to Chicago in 1974 as senior vice president and director of international operations for CNA. He left the company in 1975 to organize a Montana company specializing in the manufacture and distribution of handcrafted gift products. He returned to the reinsurance business in 1976 when he was appointed president and chief executive officer of The Mercantile and General Reinsurance Company of America.

In addition to his leadership in reinsurance, he is a frequent contributor to insurance publications. He is a popular speaker before many groups, including the Reinsurance Seminar of The College of Insurance. His interests outside insurance are many and varied: back-packing, skiing, playing bridge and an electronic organ, and fishing. He boasts only somewhat facetiously that he is "the greatest trout fisherman in North America."

13

How Reinsurance is Marketed

by W. J. Gilmartin*

This chapter will describe the two distribution systems used in marketing reinsurance: selling reinsurance direct from the reinsurer or through a reinsurance intermediary. It will examine the legal status of salespersons in each and discuss the comparative merits of each system. In most respects, this chapter will be a survey of the advantages claimed by each system rather than a resolution of those claims, because in most cases the contending claims cannot be tested analytically. Therefore, the reader wanting a clear-cut answer to the question — Which is best for me? — may be disappointed. As is often the case when two systems flourish side by side, there is no categorical answer. Even so, the concerned reinsurance buyer should be enlightened from the arguments claimed by the champions of each system, and it is hoped that a useful purpose may be served by compiling such claims and counterclaims.

Distribution Systems Compared

PRIMARY INSURANCE

Both the primary insurance business and the reinsurance business are a part of the total insuring process. One might expect their distribution methods to be similar, and this is the case. In the primary sector, there are four distribution methods: independent agents, including brokers; exclusive agents; salaried salespersons; and consultants.

Independent Agents. Independent agents are independent contractors who serve their clients' insurance needs by representing a wide variety of companies operating within the American Agency System. For example,

* Senior Vice President, CNA Insurance, CNA Plaza, Chicago, Illinois 60685

the typical agent may regularly represent from six to ten insurers, which authorize the execution of policy forms kept in each agent's office. The first allegiance of such agents is to their customers, the insured, whose policy expiration records are owned by the agents. Accordingly, independent agents are free to seek out the best product in the best market available within the system for their customers. A broker is also an independent contractor and is similar to an independent agent except in the matter of binding authority. Such authority is usually lacking since the broker is not regularly contracted by an insurer in representing it, because the broker's function is to represent the insured. Both agents and brokers are paid a commission by the insurance company with whom they place their customers' insurance. Whether agent or broker, however, each stresses the independence of its role in serving its clients, since the insurers represented cannot direct the work of either as their employees.

Exclusive Agents. Exclusive agents contract to represent one company only, hence the term, "exclusive." They usually have binding authority and are paid a commission by that company to serve as its legal agent. Policy expiration records of insureds are owned by the company, since the policyholders are the customers of the insurer, not the agent. Though exclusive agents are not employees in the sense that their work can be directed, in effect the insurer can exercise influence because of the exclusive nature of their relationship.

Salaried Salespersons. Salaried sales personnel are employees of the insurance company they represent. As such, their work is directed and they are paid a salary for their services. Since they are employees of their insurance company, they are obviously legal agents of that company and are so licensed by state insurance departments. The principal differences between exclusive agents and salaried salespersons are in the methods of compensation and degrees of control exercised by the insurer over their sales functions.

Consultants. In primary insurance, consultants are paid a fee by the insured to design, place, and supervise an insurance program for the insured. In all but exceptional circumstances, consultants are legal agents of the insured.

REINSURANCE

While the primary sector has four distribution methods, the reinsurance sector has only three, only the first two of which are significant in volume of reinsurance produced: reinsurance intermediaries (sometimes called reinsurance brokers), account executives, and consultants.

Reinsurance Intermediaries. Intermediaries or brokers in reinsurance are the counterparts of independent agents in the primary sector. The intermediary is an independent contractor who is free to place a client's reinsurance with any reinsurer dealing with intermediaries. Though most reinsurers accept business through intermediaries, a few do not (just as some primary insurers do not accept business through independent agents). The intermediary will seek out the best terms in the best markets available, which markets or companies are collectively known as the "brokerage market." Even though intermediaries are paid a commission by the reinsurers with which they place their clients' reinsurance protection, intermediaries nevertheless view themselves as representatives of the ceding companies for which they act.

Account Executives. Account executives are employees of the reinsurance companies they represent. They are paid a salary for their production and underwriting efforts and are the legal agents of the companies which employ them. These reinsurance companies are called "direct writing reinsurers," since they typically do not accept business through intermediaries.

Consultants. Consultants are paid a fee by a ceding company to design, place, and supervise the reinsurance program of that ceding company. In all but the most exceptional circumstances, a consultant is the legal agent of the ceding company.

The reader may have noticed the absence in the reinsurance sector of a counterpart of one of the primary insurance salespersons, the exclusive agent. In the reinsurance business, sales personnel are either independent contractors paid by commission or salaried staff; that is, no salespersons solicit on a commission basis for one company alone.

Functions Of Reinsurance Sales Personnel

The Intermediary

The reinsurance intermediary visits prospective clients to identify their reinsurance problems and to make recommendations. Once the recommendations are acceptable in principle, the intermediary will negotiate on behalf of the ceding company with brokerage companies to obtain the coverage. If terms are agreed upon and coverage attaches, the intermediary will prepare contracts to document the arrangement. The contracts are normally first presented to the ceding company for approval and then to the reinsurers for their approval.

Although some contract wordings are fairly standardized, reinsurance agreements can involve certain points which require negotiation and the intermediary will represent the ceding company in such negotiations. The intermediary will also receive and transmit correspondence and accounting documents between the ceding company and its reinsurers. Premiums will normally be paid to the intermediary for transmittal to reinsurers. In the event of a claim, the intermediary will present the loss report to reinsurers and collect funds on the client's behalf; should a difference of opinion arise, the intermediary will represent the ceding company in the resolution of those claim differences. Reinsurance terms are normally reviewed by both the ceding company and reinsurers at least once a year, and the intermediary will represent the ceding company in renewal negotiations in the same manner as in the original placement.

THE ACCOUNT EXECUTIVE

Salaried account executives, whose principals are direct writing reinsurers or direct writers, are salespersons in the same sense as intermediaries. They visit clients to identify their reinsurance problems and make recommendations in collaboration with the staff of the reinsurer. If the terms and conditions of a program recommended are acceptable, the necessary contract wordings are prepared for the approval of the ceding company. If negotiation is required over some language in the contract, the negotiation will be direct between the two parties, with the account executive as the contact point. All correspondence, accounting documents, and funds will be transmitted direct between the ceding company and the direct writing reinsurer. All matters involving claims will be dealt with direct between the two parties, including the resolution of any differences which may arise.

THE CONSULTANT

Consultants in reinsurance solicit business in much the same fashion as intermediaries, performing essentially the same functions for their clients as intermediaries. The principal difference is in the method of compensation: the consultant is paid a fee by the ceding company, while the intermediary is paid a commission by the reinsurer. Consulting arrangements account for such a small portion of reinsurance placed in the U.S. market that we shall limit the remainder of this chapter to intermediaries and salaried account executives.

Legalities in the Marketing Process

AGENCY

Whether a reinsurance intermediary is the legal agent of the ceding company, the reinsurer, neither of them, or both of them — at different points in the reinsurance relationship — can become an issue of importance. Although the intermediary views the ceding company as its client in the placement of risk, i.e., the party whose interest is paramount in substantive negotiations, it does not necessarily follow that the reinsurance intermediary is the legal agent of the ceding company. In the initial placement of a risk as well as in matters involving transmission of funds, attachment of coverage, full disclosure of material facts, and interpretation of contract language, the specific circumstances of each transaction would be considered individually to determine whether an agency relationship exists. In the absence of specific provisions in the reinsurance contract, determination would be made in accordance with the general body of law governing the relationship between principal and agent, as well as the customs and practices in the reinsurance field.

A recent case in the U.S. District Court of the District of New Jersey, specifically involved the legal status of a reinsurance intermediary in both the transmission of funds and the transmission of information. In this case,[1] the court held that the reinsurance intermediary, Pritchard & Baird, was the agent of the ceding company for transmission of funds. While one might agree with the outcome of this case, one might nevertheless disagree with the reasoning process by which the court arrived at its decision. The court held that the intermediary was the agent of the ceding company, because the essential element of an agency relationship existed, namely control. The court found that the ceding company controlled the intermediary in the sense that among other things the ceding company could accept or reject prospective reinsurers, the terms, conditions, commissions, and limits of the treaty and that the intermediary presented the treaty to potential reinsurers on a take-it-or-leave-it basis. The court took the view that because the intermediary could not act on behalf of the ceding company, the intermediary was controlled by the ceding company and therefore was its agent. By the same reasoning process, the court could have held the precise opposite: that the intermediary was the agent of the reinsurers since the intermediary had to clear terms, conditions, commissions, and limits with reinsurers as well as with the ceding company. The intermediary was controlled by reinsurers in much the same sense as by the ceding company. In the view of many, the fact that the intermediary could not act on behalf of the ceding company should have suggested to the court that the intermediary was *not* an agent of the ceding company. By the same reasoning, the court could have held that the intermediary was not an agent of either.

The court further reasoned that the intermediary was the agent of

---

[1]Pritchard & Baird, Inc., et al., v. Midland Insurance Co., et al., B-75-3202, (D. N.J., Mar. 1, 1979).

the ceding company because the reinsurers relied on the intermediary's apparent authority to collect money on behalf of the ceding company. In point of fact, in this as in most reinsurance relationships, both parties rely on the apparent authority of the intermediary to collect funds on behalf of the other, but on this count the court declined to infer a dual agency relationship. We do not suggest that only a dual agency finding would be a proper one. Rather, we suggest that the line of reasoning used by the court might not be suitable to a finding of anything but dual agency.

Presumably, the Pritchard & Baird case will be appealed. If the U.S. Court of Appeals for the Third Circuit affirms the decision of the lower court, this case may be regarded as a substantial precedent, but only if the Court of Appeals does not limit its ruling to the particular facts. Otherwise, when another court is asked to resolve a dispute involving the legal status of a reinsurance intermediary, it is possible that such a court would disregard the Pritchard & Baird case above. The court might reason on its own from parallels in the primary sector, or even refer to English precedents. But one would hesitate to predict how a court would settle the question, particularly if the issue is complicated by collateral matters.

TRANSMISSION OF FUNDS

Let us consider the following questions which could arise in the absence of contractual or statutory provisions. All of the questions underscore the need for careful preparation of the reinsurance contract to reflect the intent of the parties. Is the reinsurance intermediary the agent of the ceding company for receipt of funds? That is, if the ceding company pays reinsurance premiums to the reinsurance intermediary, is it constructive receipt by the reinsurer? And, is payment of claims by the reinsurer to the reinsurance intermediary constructive receipt by the ceding company?

Largely as a result of the Pritchard & Baird case, a clause is now widely used in reinsurance treaties to eliminate all doubt and make specific the responsibility of the parties. With such a clause, termed the "intermediary clause," the reinsurer assumes any credit risk involved in the transmission of reinsurance funds. A frequently used clause reads as follows:

_____ is hereby recognized as the intermediary negotiating this contract. All communications (including but not limited to notices, statements, premiums, return premiums, commissions, taxes, losses, loss adjustment expenses, salvages, and loss settlements) relating thereto shall be transmitted to the ceding com-

pany or the reinsurers through _____. Payments
by the ceding company to the Intermediary shall be deemed to constitute payment to the reinsurers. Payments by the reinsurers to the
Intermediary shall be deemed to constitute payment to the ceding
company only to the extent that such payments are actually received by the ceding company.

As of this writing, the Examiners Handbook of the National Association
of Insurance Commissioners states:

Credit will not be granted to a ceding company for reinsurance effected on or after January 1, 1979, which by its terms require
payments to an intermediary unless the reinsurance agreement includes a provision whereby the reinsurer assumes all credit risks of
the intermediary related to payments to the intermediary.

TRANSMISSION OF INFORMATION

Attachment of Coverage. If a reinsurance company puts an important
condition on the attachment of liability (such as an exclusion of a particular class of business), and that condition is not reported to the ceding
company by the intermediary, and a serious loss occurs on the excluded
class before the misunderstanding is discovered, is the loss covered?

Full Disclosure of Material Information. Let us assume that: a) a ceding
company discloses material information to the reinsurance intermediary
but that information is not passed on to the reinsurer, and b) the reinsurer
asserts that knowledge of this information would have altered its decision to reinsure the business on which a serious loss occurred, and c) the
court agrees that the information is material. Is the intermediary the
agent of the ceding company, or the reinsurer, or neither? Put in simpler
terms, is disclosure to the reinsurance intermediary disclosure to the reinsurer?

Interpretation of Contract Wordings. Let us suppose a reinsurance intermediary, without consultation with reinsurers, interprets an exclusion
in a reinsurance contract for a ceding company. Let us further suppose
the ceding company acts on the interpretation but the reinsurers take a
different position in defense of a subsequent claim. For whom was the
reinsurance intermediary the legal agent, if any, in interpreting the contract wording?

In each of the situations above, the ceding company would look to
the reinsurer if the intermediary's action is correct. If the action were not
correct, the ceding company must look to its intermediary for relief from
any negligence involved.

Misunderstandings can occur whether a ceding company is dealing direct or through intermediaries. Nevertheless, direct writing reinsurers maintain that the intermediary is another party through whom discussions must pass and that this use of a third party increases the possibility of misunderstanding. On the other hand, intermediaries maintain that their representation has been known to resolve a misunderstanding in the ceding company's favor, because of the weight of the intermediary's overall account with the brokerage markets involved.

It might be noted in passing that when problems of the sort mentioned above have arisen in the past, too often they have involved a ceding company acting as a mere front, with the primary agent arranging the bulk of the coverage as reinsurance, and where the agent has conducted many of the important negotiations without the intimate involvement of the fronting company. Truth to say, fronting, which is too often viewed as easy money, can be dangerous. Not only is there a solvency risk and the possibility of a gap in coverage but, in addition, the fronting company could conceivably be assessed punitive damages for mishandling claims on fronted business, which reinsurers might view as outside the pale of their coverage. Or, the fronting company could encounter regulatory problems in withdrawing from the fronted class of business should its reinsurance support cease.

Cost Comparisons

An important consideration in the comparison of distribution systems is the matter of cost. In the long run, no system will survive which cannot justify its costs, for costs are the measure of benefits provided. If the benefits are valued by the users of a system, its costs will be willingly incurred. If not, an alternative will be used.

Most ceding companies view reinsurance as a cost of doing business. They recognize that much of the reinsurance obtained through treaties tends to be experience-rated in the long term, which means that they largely determine their own costs from their underwriting results. Exceptions are short-term facultative placements and certain transfers of pure catastrophe risk. Over the long term with treaties, a ceding company will probably be asked to pay aggregate reinsurance premiums equal to claim recoveries, plus reinsurers' expenses and plus a reasonable profit. In buying reinsurance, then, costs are important in both short-term and long-term comparisons.

Direct writing reinsurers contend that the cost of their reinsurance protection will be lower in the long run than the cost of brokerage market companies. They cite these reasons: their solicitation expenses are lower since the salaries of their account executives are "realistic," claim recoveries under either style of operation will be equal, and there is the tendency to experience-rate reinsurance treaties regardless of the method used in creating them. And, if an American company's treaty is placed by an intermediary in London or elsewhere abroad, there will be an additional brokerage commission paid to the foreign intermediary. Brokerage rates for domestic treaty business tend to range from 1% of premiums earned on pro rata treaties, to 5% of premiums earned on working excess of loss treaties,[2] to 10% of premiums earned on catastrophe excess of loss treaties. Brokerage commissions on reinstatement premiums are at 50% of the normal rate. If foreign brokerage services are involved, the above rates may become 2% to 2½% on pro rata treaties, 10% on working excess treaties, and 15% on catastrophe treaties. Brokerage commission rates for facultative placements vary widely, but the most common are 2½% on pro rata and 10% on excess of loss.

The brokerage market counters the above contentions with arguments of their own: solicitation expenses may or may not be greater for intermediaries, depending on how they are compared; claim recoveries under either style of operation are not necessarily equal because the services of the intermediary can improve the ceding company's position; and the interests of the ceding company are better served by having its needs met by a broader segment of the market through the intermediary than any one direct writer can provide.

Ideally, one would hope for a clear definition of distribution costs to permit comparisons to be made. With a definition, statistics could then be collected which might settle the issue conclusively enough to say to a reinsurance buyer, "The weight of evidence suggests that it will (or will not) cost you more to deal with a reinsurance intermediary than to deal with a direct writing reinsurer." Sad to say, however, it appears that any such data are likely to have internal contradictions, as we shall presently see. Also, it appears that we shall be frustrated in any attempt to prove conclusively, at least to the satisfaction of a disinterested observer, that the cost of dealing through intermediaries is, or is not, more expensive than dealing with direct writing reinsurers. Two examples will be given to illustrate the difficulty: financial reporting practices, and mix of business.

DIFFERENCES IN REPORTING PRACTICES

Brokerage companies' cost of sales, i.e., intermediary commissions, are included with all other commissions, including ceding commissions,

---

[2]Lower brokerage rates may be negotiated based on a lower loading factor.

in their published financial statements. Direct writing reinsurers, on the other hand, include most of their cost of sales in their general expenses, since their salespersons are salaried. Any comparison of general expenses, therefore, which does not include intermediary commissions would be incomplete: brokerage companies would be shown as operating at a fraction of the cost of direct writing reinsurers. To the contrary, any comparison of selling expenses which does not include the costs of salaried personnel is equally incomplete: direct writing companies would be shown as selling services at a fraction of the cost of brokerage companies.

Our problem, then, begins with the definition of costs. If by costs one means the cost of sales, possibly direct writers do have lower costs, but the vital statistic for a reinsurance buyer is not cost of sales alone. Rather, it is the reinsurer's margin — the margin in the reinsurance price for all expenses of the reinsurer. Such margin consists of cost of sales, general expenses, and profit. It is this margin that is going to determine the reinsurance cost. To illustrate, if each of two reinsurers operating differently earns a total margin of 5% over and above claims, the breakdown of that margin may be as follows:

	Direct Writing Reinsurer	Brokerage Company
Cost of Sales	1/2 %	2%
General expenses	1-1/2	1/2
Profit	3	2-1/2
Total margin	5%	5%

From the ceding company's point of view, the cost of doing business with each reinsurer is identical, 5%. So it is true that in the long run lower costs of sales tend to be reflected in lower margins, but only if two additional conditions hold true: general expenses are roughly similar, and profit margins are roughly similar.

While brokerage companies pay intermediary commissions which direct writing reinsurers do not, there is some indication that the general expenses of brokerage companies are significantly below those of direct writing reinsurers, because reinsurance intermediaries perform many of the functions that are performed by the home office staff of direct writers. Brokerage companies contend that, as compared to direct writing reinsurers, there is a trade-off between cost of sales and general expenses. But even were this not the case, brokerage companies assert they would have no alternative but to reduce their profit margins below those of direct writers to avoid structuring themselves out of a competitive parity.

Theoretically, this hurdle of incomplete comparison could be overcome if unpublished intermediary commissions were available. When intermediary commissions were combined with the general expenses of brokerage companies, the combined total could then be compared with those of direct writing reinsurers. However, in gathering such data, one should analyze and compare not just cost of sales and general expenses for direct writers and brokerage companies but also their total margins (cost of sales, general expenses, and profit margins). Now, if the combined total of all three categories were higher for one group than the other, one could engage in all sorts of conjectures in reaching for cause-and-effect: competitive parity is lacking among the two groups, or one group is more efficient at sales and service than the other, or one group is more aggressive than the other, and so on. And if the cost of sales is important to a reinsurance buyer when choosing one of the distribution systems, one might even expect the variation in total margins to be reflected in a higher growth rate for the group with lower overall margins. But a further difficulty lies ahead which compounds the problem of comparison.

DIFFERENCES IN MIX OF BUSINESS

There is a considerable difference between the expense levels and profit margins of pro rata and excess of loss reinsurance, because of stability or the lack of it. The expense ratio involved in soliciting and administering excess of loss business is many times that of pro rata business. And the margin of profit (or loss) on excess of loss business is subject to wide fluctuations: excess of loss rewards are greater, but so are the penalties. The expenses and profit margins on pro rata business tend to be more stable; accordingly, they tend to be a much smaller percentage of premium than for excess business.

Given this difference in expenses and profit margins among types of reinsurance, and given the fact that the mix of business is not at all consistent within the members of each group, let alone for the two group as a whole, we have a potential anomaly. One sector of the market can operate at lower margins on each element of the portfolio, but show higher margins in the aggregate. To illustrate:

Pro Rata Business	Group A	Group B
Ceded premiums earned	$1,000,000,000	$700,000,000
Reinsurers' margins thereon	15,000,000 (1-1/2%)	7,000,000 (1%)
Excess of Loss Business		
Ceded premiums earned	$200,000,000	$500,000,000
Reinsurers' margins thereon	30,000,000 (15%)	50,000,000 (10%)
Total Business		
Ceded premiums earned	$1,200,000,000	$1,200,000,000
Reinsurers' margins thereon	45,000,000 (3.75%)	57,000,000 (4.75%)

Ironically, because direct writers may have a higher proportion of their portfolio in excess business, a raw comparison without regard to mix might well show them with higher, not lower, costs. Obviously, the mix of business can influence comparative results, so we should try to analyze excess of loss and pro rata business separately. Unfortunately, no such data exist as reinsurers are not required to divide their published results between excess of loss and pro rata business; and even if they were, we would still encounter a further problem.

The all important statistic, margin, which includes profit (or loss) will also be influenced by the period of time chosen for any comparison. If one were to choose the ten-year period, 1967 through 1976, a period when many direct writers were experiencing problems with their large book of casualty excess of loss reinsurance business and surety reinsurance, one would see them operating at negative margins. However, this negative result would not be the case for many brokerage companies during that period because of their different mix of business. But if one chooses the prior ten-year period, 1957 through 1966, which includes the worst insured loss in history, Hurricane Betsy, much of the brokerage market with its large book of property catastrophe business would be operating at negative margins for that period. Again, this negative result would not be the case for many direct writing reinsurers during that period because of their different mix of business.

Given the difficulty in comparing costs, what can we say about the last test we have set, the relative growth rates? All data available suggest that each distribution segment is flourishing. If there is anything inferred from growth rates, the brokerage market has been growing at a significantly faster rate than direct writers here in the United States during a recent ten-year period: 377% v. 200%, according to the figures below. But a word of caution is in order. Some indeterminant portion of the growth of U.S. brokerage markets has been at the expense of other brokerage markets abroad and does not represent a real movement of business from one camp in the U.S. to the other. Moreover, some brokerage markets work both sides of the street, so that some volume of direct business is included in the premium base of brokerage markets. In spite of such distortions, the brokerage growth rate has been impressive. Here are the estimated comparative data for the beginning and ending years of the preceding ten-year period available at this writing:

Year	Net Written Premiums U.S. Dir. Writ. Reins.	Net Written Premiums U.S. Brokerage Market	Net Written Premiums U.S. Reinsurers Combined
1967[3]	$ 501,000,000	$ 583,000,000	$ 1,084,000,000
1976[4]	1,504,000,000	2,784,000,000	4,288,000,000
Growth Rate	200%	377%	296%

While these statistics tend to contradict some of the claims of direct writing reinsurers, the contradiction is too inferential to be conclusive. In fact, conclusive statistics are lacking either way on all counts. Lacking conclusive statistics, there is an inclination on the part of some buyers to accept the contention of direct writing reinsurers that it is more expensive to deal through intermediaries. These buyers are inclined to feel that because an intermediary can earn such large dollar amounts on some treaties, then in the absence of proof to the contrary, the expense of dealing through intermediaries must be higher than dealing direct. Indeed, it appears that the large dollar account which generates substantial dollar commission amounts is the Achilles Heel of the intermediary fraternity in the debate over costs.

Other Comparisons

REPRESENTATION

It may appear that while buyers tend to give direct writers the benefit of the doubt on the question of expenses, they tend to give intermediaries the benefit of the doubt on the question of representation. Just what, then, are the pros and cons of having an intermediary's representation in the marketplace?

Fundamental Allegiance. Intermediaries maintain that their fundamental allegiance is to the reinsured, whereas the representative of the direct writing company is fundamentally concerned with the welfare of that company and the support of its position. Intermediaries claim that each direct writer has its own preference when it comes to structuring treaty programs, and that account executives may tailor their recommendations to conform to such preferences which may not always be in the ceding company's best interests. The direct writing reinsurers counterclaim that intermediaries sometimes make recommendations with the largest commission in mind, not the client's best interests.

Direct Contact. Direct writers feel that contact between the ceding company and the reinsurer builds the best and warmest long-term relationship. Many intermediaries for their part say that contact between their client and its reinsurers is not discouraged, but there are some negotiations best conducted through the buffer of an intermediary, one to whom both parties can speak frankly without the sometimes obscuring necessity of face-to-face diplomacy.

---

[3] J. A. Munro, "Annual Analysis of the United States Reinsurance Market," *The National Underwriter,* December 6, 1968, Part 2, pp. 24 and 25.

[4] John R. Zech, "Annual Analysis of the United States Reinsurance Market," *The National Underwriter,* December 9, 1977, Part 2, pp. 24, 25 and 28.

Canvassing the Entire Market. Intermediaries contend that their function is to canvass the entire market and obtain the best plans and the best price available. The ceding company usually does not know all of the markets, nor does it choose to spend the time to touch all these bases.

Averaging of Results. Direct writing reinsurers aim to write all of a ceding company's account, or most of it. They maintain that this gives the ceding company the benefit of averaging the profitable and unprofitable portions of their reinsurance program. Intermediaries, they say, tend to place different elements of a reinsurance program separately, and thereby lose the benefit of averaging. In reply, intermediaries point out that it is a simple matter to arrange a "bouquet" of treaties in which all reinsurers participate across-the-board, but this arrangement rarely produces the lowest cost. They further point out that there are some exposures which by their catastrophic and unbalanced nature should not be averaged against the whole reinsurance program of a ceding company. They assert also that direct writers sometimes leave difficult portions of a program to be taken care of elsewhere and assume only the good business, which actually may be needed to put the best overall program together.

Contract Wordings. Intermediaries contend they can prepare or negotiate more liberal contract wordings than direct writers in providing their clients with maximum protection in borderline cases. Here it must be admitted that reinsurance contracts (although somewhat standardized) can be rather technical, the full implications of which are not always clear except to specialists in contract language. Nevertheless, too much should not be made of this point in favor of intermediaries, since any direct writer which may pass off restrictive language on its clients can expect to receive its competitive due.

Renewal Terms. Intermediaries maintain that they regularly initiate improvements in contract terms at renewal time, whereas direct writers tend only to respond to such initiative and accompanying persuasion, and the client may not be aware that the time to apply pressure is at hand because of general market conditions. Accordingly, intermediaries as representatives of the ceding company see themselves as being more alive to opportunities to improve terms, while viewing direct writing reinsurers as being more defensive about improvements in terms. Here, it must be recognized that conditions do exist for a different sense of initiative and even a different inclination.

Claims. Intermediaries will negotiate with reinsurers on behalf of their clients if a controversy over claims should arise. This function is perhaps the most sensitive of all issues, since there is always the danger of imputing something less than the utmost good faith to direct writing reinsurers in the settlement of claims. Such an inference would be baseless. Nevertheless, there are claims on which a valid difference of opinion can exist, and intermediaries suggest that in such cases their clients are well served by having an intermediary with its persuasiveness in their corner. Direct writers for their part dismiss the suggestion that a client would need partisan representation in the settlement of bona fide claims.

Eliminating the Need for a Reinsurance Department. Intermediaries suggest that their representation may reduce the ceding company's expense of maintaining its own outgoing reinsurance department. The point has possible value to small ceding companies which cannot afford to employ their own specialists and which choose the services of intermediaries for such assistance.

In all of the above assertions, the reader can appreciate the opposing viewpoints. The direct writers do not see the ceding companies as needing the partisan representation of an intermediary. Instead, they maintain that intermediaries only create "noise in the channel" and unnecessary expense. To the direct writer, reinsurance problems are not so complicated and ceding company executives are incapable of representing their company with effectiveness worthy of their business success.

SYNDICATION

It is customary for intermediaries to syndicate their placements, i.e., to split an offering among many reinsurers. In this fashion, business tends to be disseminated widely through the brokerage market in small, easily absorbed portions. Syndication permits brokerage markets to enjoy the spread which comes from a wide sharing of reinsurance business, and this sharing has undoubtedly contributed to the huge capacity and diversity of the brokerage market. Because of this technique, many reinsurers have been able to enter the reinsurance business without having to underwrite an unbalanced portfolio, and without having to buy or burn their way in. However, syndication is not without associated problems, such as those having to do with security and continuity.

Security. Neither of the competing factions has a monopoly on financial security. There are large and financially sound reinsurers among direct writing reinsurers and brokerage markets alike. Ceding companies need never lack for sound security, whether dealing direct or with the brokerage market. Nevertheless, the syndication of business by reinsurance intermediaries tends to bring into play companies which do not compare in financial solidity with the large direct writing reinsurers.

Direct writers are quick to compare their financial prowess with that of the smaller brokerage companies, particularly those non-admitted companies, which sometimes appear at "the bottom-of-the-slip." Since financial failure of a reinsurer is ultimately the risk of the ceding company, not the intermediary, there can be cause for concern if the security used by intermediaries is in any way open to question. Responsible reinsurance intermediaries are aware of this problem and maintain surveillance committees to approve the brokerage markets they use. The record of responsible intermediaries has been exceptional, but it still must be admitted that some of the smaller, less well known reinsurance markets do not have the appeal among ceding companies to equal that of the large direct writing reinsurers. Furthermore, it is simpler for the ceding company to appraise the net worth of one large direct writing reinsurer as contrasted with a long list of brokerage companies, some of which are not readily known.

Continuity. A primary purpose of reinsurance is to protect ceding companies against large, random losses which upset the best laid plans of actuaries and underwriters. The lot of reinsurers is to take on those exposures which are less predictable. But reinsurers are not prophets and they are every bit as fallible as others when it comes to forecasting the timing and the impact of these large, random losses. The comforting certainty that goes with spread and the law of averages, the foundation and cornerstone of the primary business, is simply not part of the reinsurance scene for reinsurers. Instead, reinsurers must deal with precisely those elements of uncertainty which frustrate and derange the primary insurance mechanism.

The reinsurer must look elsewhere for its stability, and it does so through its financial strength and the use of time in its treaty relationships. The real role of most treaty reinsurance programs is not to spread the losses of the unfortunate few among the fortunate many. In point of fact, during a major natural disaster, it is sometimes the few who are claim-free, not the many. Treaty reinsurers often view their role as spreading losses over time, over the premium-paying years, especially if their catastrophe reinsurance is priced in contemplation that a payback will take place. Amortization of catastrophe losses may strike many as a contradiction in terms; and reinsurers might like to agree. However, reinsurers have to accept the world as they find it, not as they would like it. The fact is that ceding companies with good experience want that good experience recognized, whether caused by low hazard classes, low hazard territories, or sheer good fortune. They are unwilling to have the poor experience of competitors spread back to them, so there remains no place to spread such losses except back to those who produce them. Bowing to reality, then, many reinsurers experience-rate many of their treaties. Ceding companies recognize the practice even if they do not always agree with it.

Given some form of experience rating as a fact of life, continuity then becomes an important feature of a reinsurance relationship, one of distinct value to the ceding company. A long-standing relationship between the parties in reinsurance allows the reinsurers to accumulate funds against an impending catastrophe.

Ceding companies, on the other hand, have the comfort of knowing they are building an "experience credit" which will act as a buffer against any drastic change in cost when disaster strikes. Just as important, both parties build a mutual confidence of value to each and which comes only from a successful long-term association. Moreover, continuity also facilitates the resolution of differences which may arise, because long-term partners tend to bend. The saying in the business is "continuity is the coin of the realm."

Direct writing reinsurers contend that the syndication of business sometimes results in a loss of continuity, of which the ceding company is not even aware. They point out that it is not unusual for companies down the slip to come and go, or for percentages of participation to change without attracting the notice of the ceding company; and these changes represent a partial loss of continuity. Direct writers, which generally write the whole of a treaty, point out that the continuity from a 100% participation is out front for all to see. In their defense, intermediaries contend that the experience of the whole market over the life of a treaty will govern negotiations, not the experience of short-term participants. Intermediaries further note that when renewal negotiations with a direct writing reinsurer fail, 100% of the continuity is lost. On the other hand, the loss of part of a market on a cover intermediaries place does not disrupt continuity as totally.

Intermediaries further contend that even when a treaty arrangement ceases and the more difficult run-off begins, they maintain influence with those brokerage markets because of their other continuing dealings with them. Contrariwise, the ceding company in a changing treaty arrangement with its direct writer is no longer a client of that reinsurer and may have no further influence with it. Direct writing reinsurers for their part counter with the observation that intermediaries sometimes use markets which drop in and out of the business quickly and whose attitude may be inflexible when it comes to the run-off of their liability.

SERVICES

Direct writing reinsurers contend that they provide more sophisticated underwriting, accounting, and claims services than are available from brokerage market companies. However, brokerage market companies say there is little demand for such services; and when there is, they can provide them readily. In fact, some brokerage market companies which are also primary writers provide a full range of services up to and including the running of a captive insurance company.

What, then, should a reinsurance buyer make of this cut-and-thrust? That the two systems are at each other's throats? Hardly. A close order review of the issues may leave the impression that there is competitive warfare between the two distribution systems, but this is not so. In fact, in some cases the two systems share an account and the ceding company is well served by the full capacity of both systems. Should, then, the reinsurance buyer conclude that there is an abundance of vigorous and healthy competition between the two? Indeed. And that the reliance on price alone in buying reinsurance can mislead? By all means. An unknown sage expressed it well years ago:

> It's unwise to pay too much,
>   But it's worse to pay too little.
> When you pay too much,
>   You lose a little money — and that is all.
>
> When you pay too little,
>   You sometimes lose everything,
> Because the thing you bought was incapable
>   Of doing the thing it was bought to do.
>
> The common law of business balance
>   Prohibits paying a little
> And getting a lot —
>   It can't be done.
>
> If you deal with the lowest bidder,
>   It is well to add something for the risk you run:
> And if you do that,
>   You will have enough to pay for something better.

Summary

There are three methods of distribution in reinsurance: the intermediary, which is the counterpart of the independent agent or broker in the primary sector of the insurance business; the account executive for direct writing reinsurers, which is the counterpart of salaried salespersons in the primary sector; and the consultant, which is the counterpart of consultants in the primary sector. The reinsurance intermediary is paid a commission by the reinsurer but may be the legal agent of either the ceding company or the reinsurer, depending upon the circumstances. The account executive is the employee and therefore the legal agent of the direct writing reinsurer. The consultant is paid a fee by the ceding company and is normally the legal agent of the ceding company. This chapter concentrates more on the first two methods, since consulting arrangements account for such a small portion of reinsurance placed in the U.S.

There are certain legalities in the marketing process which are important to all parties concerned. Whether a reinsurance intermediary is the legal agent of the ceding company, or of the reinsurer, or of neither of them, or both of them, can become an issue of importance in the initial placement of a risk, the transmission of funds, the attachment of coverage, the full disclosure of material facts, and the interpretation of contract language. In the absence of specific provisions in the reinsurance contract, determination of the question of legal agency would be made in accordance with the general body of law governing the relationship between principal and agent, as well as the customs and practices in the reinsurance field. The recent Pritchard & Baird case specifically involved the legal status of a reinsurance intermediary in both the transmission of funds and the transmission of information. In this case, the court held that the intermediary was the agent of the ceding company.

An important consideration in the comparison of distribution systems is the matter of cost. In the long run, no system will survive which cannot justify its costs, for costs are the measure of benefits provided. Unfortunately, however, no objective comparison of costs between direct writing reinsurers and brokerage reinsurers is possible because of differences in their financial reporting practices and their mix of business. While the reported cost of sales may be less for direct writing reinsurers than for brokerage companies, the reported general expenses of brokerage companies appear to be significantly lower than for direct writers. When the total reinsurance margin for each system is considered (including cost of sales, general expenses, and profit margins), the two systems would not appear to be significantly different. All available data suggest that each system is flourishing.

It may appear that buyers tend to give direct writers the benefit of the doubt on the question of expenses, but they also tend to give intermediaries the benefit of the doubt on the question of representation. On this point, intermediaries maintain that their fundamental allegiance is to the reinsured while the account executive is fundamentally concerned with the direct writer's position, the direct writers counterclaim that intermediaries sometimes make recommendations with commissions as their incentives rather than the interests of the ceding company. Pros and cons can be offered on other competitive aspects of the distribution methods: which system primarily serves the ceding company's best interests, whether the entire market needs to be canvassed in serving the capacity needs of the ceding company, which system produces contract wordings and renewal terms more favorable to the ceding company, whether one system is superior in handling claims if controversies should arise, and which system provides the ceding company with greater continuity and financial security. The contest between the two opposing systems will continue, for such is the competitive system.

*   *   *   *   *   *

About the Author of Chapter 13

W. J. Gilmartin was born in Philadelphia on January 15, 1927, and was educated in the Radnor, Pennsylvania, public schools. Upon graduation during World War II, he entered the U.S. Air Force where he served in 1945 and 1946. After military service, he majored in insurance at the Wharton School of Finance at the University of Pennsylvania, receiving the B.S. Degree in 1950.

His insurance career began after college as a student actuary in the accident and health department of CNA in June, 1950. Four years later he joined CNA's newly formed division for assumed reinsurance and was named superintendent shortly thereafter. He became vice president in 1966 and senior vice president in charge of reinsurance (ceded and assumed) in 1978. His responsibilities also extended over CNA's international operations, professional liability, pools and associations, and excess and surplus lines. In addition to his responsibilities with CNA in the United States, he also serves as Director of CNA Reinsurance of London, Ltd.

14

Underwriting the Reinsured

by Dr. Laszlo K. Gonye*

There are in general three situations in which the reinsurer under-writes the reinsured. First, is when the reinsurer is considering entering into a new reinsurance relationship. Second, the reinsurer underwrites the reinsured when the reinsurer is called upon to structure desired coverage or to expand the dimensions of an existing relationship. In this case, the reinsurer is acting much like a consultant, for example, when the reinsurer is asked to consider increasing existing covers or to under-write new ones. Third, the reinsurer underwrites the reinsured continual-ly as part of the normal review process on existing business. Once a rela-tionship has been established, the underwriting process is a continuous activity.

How does the reinsurer go about this activity? Before getting into this, it might be useful to establish a few ground rules that will put the discussion which follows into perspective. The concepts discussed on underwriting the reinsured are valid for both treaty and facultative rein-surance, but the emphasis here is on domestic treaty underwriting. This is not to minimize the importance of facultative reinsurance, but the analysis of facultative business is weighted heavily towards individual

* President, Skandia America Reinsurance Company, 280 Park Avenue, New York, New York 10017. The author acknowledges the significant contributions of his co-author, F. Eugene Duffee, Vice Presi-dent of Skandia America, and his Skandia America colleagues, James F. Dowd, Vice President, General Counsel and Corporate Secretary, John B. Laadt, Assistant Secretary, and Robert H. Alex-ander, Financial Analyst.

risk characteristics. In treaty reinsurance the emphasis is placed first and foremost on evaluating the caliber of the reinsured. The reinsurance underwriter is called upon to consider all of those factors relevant to whether it is in the best interests of both parties to establish or maintain a reinsurance relationship. An important factor in this analysis is the quality of the specific type or types of business under consideration. Because of the nature of treaty reinsurance, however, the underwriter does not consider, except in a general way, individual risks.

This chapter will not attempt to offer insights or instructions as to how specific types of treaties are underwritten. The author is attempting, rather, to develop a general analytical framework that can be used in the evaluation of any kind of treaty. Other chapters will discuss the details of different types of treaty coverages. And the discussion applies only to the lines of insurance underwritten by property/casualty insurance companies. Reinsurance of the life business involves different underwriting criteria.

In underwriting the reinsured, the reinsurer considers three major dimensions of the reinsurance risk. First, the reinsured is evaluated as a business entity to determine if it will be mutually beneficial to establish a reinsurance relationship. This general evaluation has two aspects. The first is a qualitative inquiry into the honesty, integrity, and reputation of the reinsured. The second is a quantitative evaluation of the reinsured's financial well being. Following this, the underwriter evaluates the specific proposal or existing program. Finally, an evaluation is made of the social, economic, and political environment which will affect the reinsurance relationship and specific covers involved.

The Essential Risk

Most leading reinsurers place great emphasis on evaluating the character and integrity of the reinsured. To them the essential risk to be underwritten is the living business enterprise. The most important questions are: "What do I know about the company — its history, its reason for being, its reputation and its experience?" "Does it have capable and stable management?" "Does the company have good people?" "Are they professional?" To deal with people of honesty, integrity, character, and proven ability in any area of commercial endeavor is important, but there are certain characteristics of reinsurance that make these generalities particularly significant:

— There is a partnershiplike relationship between the parties.

— Dealings between the reinsurer and reinsured must be performed with utmost good faith.

— The reinsurance relationship hopefully will be long-term.

— Over the term of the relationship, both parties must profit.

The reinsurer must begin with the realization that it is dependent on the reinsured for the quality of the business being offered and for its profitability. The partnership characteristic quite simply means that, within the parameters of the agreement, the two parties share good and bad insurance outcomes in that the reinsurer is obligated to accept all of the risks (and perhaps more) of the reinsured subject to the treaty. The reinsurer, in a treaty relationship, cannot reunderwrite each transaction, for it is not in a position to see the individual risks that are ceded.

Even if the historical experience of the business forming the subject matter of the treaty or related treaties has been excellent, there is the ever present possibility that the conditions and reasons upon which the reinsurance was accepted may change. In recent years this has become an increasingly serious consideration. Underwriting philosophies and management may change. The geographical and class emphasis may change. Basic underlying conditions that affect the profitability of various lines of insurance and reinsurance may change. Classes of business that were once considered excellent or at least underwritable have become difficult and sometimes uninsurable. The experiences from products liability, various professional liability covers, and workers' compensation are well known examples of lines that have been significantly affected by current social, economic, and political trends. Insurance products are priced and sold today but underwriters may not know what the true costs to produce these products will be for many years to come. Thus, a major problem for the reinsurer is the time lag on reinsurance experience. The treaty establishes a relationship with the reinsured that involves human judgment, integrity and skills relating to the reinsured's:

— general administrative capabilities,

— underwriting decision making,

— ability to collect and compile meaningful statistics for the reinsured's and the reinsurer's benefit, and

— prudent use of the reinsurance facility, including a willingness to represent and protect the interests of the reinsurer.

This last point is a manifestation of what is known as "utmost good faith." It means that the reinsurer must treat the reinsured fairly and honestly, and conversely, the reinsured must accord the reinsurer the same treatment. It means that each party is convinced that the other is doing, and will continue to do, the right thing. It means that both parties, in their relations with each other, will seek and maintain a philosophical meeting of the minds as to the intent and nature of the cover. To many, this is the most important consideration, because even with the most precisely drawn reinsurance agreement it is not possible to put into the language of the contract every dimension of basic intent and understanding. In a viable and growing relationship with the reinsured, there are many areas where judgmental considerations or errors by either side can be accommodated or overcome by philosophically compatible parties working together towards a common goal. Thus, good faith means a commitment to maintaining a good working relationship and communication.

Unless otherwise agreed when a reinsurance relationship is established, both parties contemplate that it will be of a long-term nature. In most cases its success or failure cannot be judged in short time segments such as one or three years, as is prevalent in direct risk underwriting. The reasons are largely practical. The two parties enter into a relationship in which the reinsurer expects to profit from following the underwriting skills and business judgment of the reinsured and from which the reinsured benefits by services offered to it by the reinsurer. Neither party can reap the true benefit of what is offered by the other on a short-term basis because of the volume of business involved and the relatively long-term nature of the underwriting cycles.

There is no definable cycle for property catastrophe covers. Overall experience in this area is a matter of chance, and there has not been, at the time of this writing, a major catastrophe for many years. The success of a property catastrophe cover cannot be judged on a short-term basis. There are, on the other hand, economic cycles for most other lines of property/casualty coverages which also cannot be easily predicted but which last several years. The timing of these cycles differs by line of business, and it differs for insurers and for reinsurers. When the upside and downside timing of these cycles are combined, no matter how fine the analysis, the reinsurance underwriter is thinking in terms of several years and cannot evaluate the success or failure of the relationship in any lesser period of time. The reinsurance professional projects its evaluation into the future, through more than one cycle, as far ahead as is possible. This commitment to establish and maintain long-term relationships with client companies is crucial to the reinsurer's image in the marketplace. Reinsurers who maintain a relationship through decades are those that show true character.

Obviously, the reinsurance relationship must also be profitable to the reinsurer in the long term. Thus, a major objective of the evaluation is to determine that any deficit which the reinsurance treaty might produce during one or more years will fall within the premium to be produced over some reasonable time period.

THE CREDIT THEOREM

A reinsurance treaty may in some respects be equated to an extension of credit. The reader might reasonably suppose that the essential nature of a reinsurance treaty is transfer of risk and/or sharing of business — so much premium and loss for the account of the reinsurer, so much for the cedent. But that is merely the flesh of the relationship. Its life force is a promise founded on philosophical compatibility to perform the mutual obligations assumed by the two parties, many of the obligations being unstated, during a term of indeterminate length.

To correctly understand the reasons for and the kind of appraisal made by the reinsurer of a company which has requested reinsurance coverage, the reader should recall the essence of the insurance mechanism. Insurance is the key to the modern economic world. No structure would be erected which involves the capital of other than the owner; no wheel or gear would turn in a factory; no truck, vessel or aircraft would transport goods — without the existence of guarantees to replace destroyed property, especially that property mortgaged to a creditor, or guarantees to indemnify any person injured in consequence of the activities of the builder, the building owner, the factory operator, or the truck driver. Credit is extended by financial institutions in reliance on evidence that the loan collateral is protected by insurance, so that the collateral can be replaced in the event of its destruction and hence will continue to support the ability of the borrower to repay the loan. The function of the insurer is to make it possible for business as well as personal activities to continue in a normal manner without being disrupted by accidents and other foreseeable but unintended events. The essential function of insurance is not simply to pay the fire damage or the workers' compensation benefit or the court judgment, but rather to provide for continuation: the promise that if any event insured against should occur, the insurance will be present to restore the financial condition to its status before the event. Personal and commercial activities can then continue upon the reliance that this underlying security of the insurance promise does exist. Sale of insurance depends upon confidence that the insurer will perform its promise. The role of the reinsurer is to assist the insurer to do its job, that is, to put its capital resources, expertise and business reputation behind the promises which the insurer issues.

The analogy to credit is imperfect. If the reinsurer pays funds in excess of premium received, the reinsured does not incur a legally enforceable obligation to repay the credit plus interest. Although the reinsurer does pay a contractual obligation, the obligation to repay is incurred upon trust, mutual dependence, and sharing of good and bad fortune (the subject of the transaction being unpredictable events).

In what sense is it correct to say that the reinsured is using the reinsurer's capital? This question must be answered within the framework of statutory insurance accounting and the models of industry norms used to examine the fiscal health of companies. The reinsurer extends its capital to the reinsured in five ways: assuming unearned premium reserve liability, assuming loss reserve liability, assuming prepaid acquisition cost liability, assuming transfer of risk, and, extending its good name to the reinsured.

1.   The reinsurer assumes the unearned premium liability on the portion of the reinsured's gross unearned premium reserve represented by the liability ceded to the reinsurer. The reinsured states its liabilities on a net basis — after deducting liability ceded to the reinsurer.[1] Since there is a limit upon the multiple which the reinsured's net liabilities can bear to its policyholder surplus, the reinsurer enables the reinsured to write more business than its own resources can carry. Premium (and unearned premium liability) written for the account of the reinsurer is not charged against the reinsured's surplus. The gross premium writing of many companies is twice their net writing, and in some cases much greater. If the gross business achieves a profit greater than the profit retained by the reinsurer on the portion ceded to the reinsurer, the company keeps the balance of profit on the business produced by virtue of the reinsurance capacity: this "leverages" the ceding company's surplus by earning profit on a larger volume of business than it could earn on the smaller volume permitted by its surplus.

2.   The reinsurer assumes the loss reserve liability on the portion of the reinsured's gross claims represented by the liability ceded to the reinsurer. (This transaction might produce a profit on the reinsured's books.)

3.   The reinsurer assumes liability for prepaid acquisition costs on the written (and unearned) premiums ceded to the reinsurer. This is the most important element of the use of the reinsurer's capital. Statutory accounting principles do not permit a company to take prepaid expenses in-

---

[1] This basis is permitted when the state where the reinsured is domiciled permits credit for reinsurance ceded to the reinsurer.

to its equity. The company must set up the 100% reserve for unearned premiums, disregarding the probability that if the policy should be cancelled and the company should have to return that unearned premium to its policyholder, the company would be able to recapture any commission previously paid to agents or brokers, and state premium taxes paid, when the premium was originally received for the full policy term. Therefore, in the company's assets the company only carries the remainder of the original premium after deducting prepaid acquisition costs, for example, 25%. The shortage — 25% of the unearned premium — is deducted from surplus, because the cash asset is only 75% of the liability. By reinsuring this unearned premium liability, the company recaptures the missing commission and tax portion of the premium dollar from the reinsurer: the company records a cession to the reinsurer of 100% of unearned premiums but pays in cash only the balance after deducting the compensating commission allowed by the reinsurer. That commission is often more than the company's actual out-of-pocket expenses.

The company might record a transfer of $1,000,000 of unearned premiums to the reinsurer, for which the company had received cash of $750,000, but then reduce its assets by only $650,000, picking up an extra $100,000 if the reinsurer allows 35% commission on the cession. This difference is reimbursement of the underwriting and administrative costs incurred by the company to put the business on its books, and is also an advance recognition by the reinsurer of the profit margin in the business which the reinsurer ultimately expects to return to the reinsured, but which is instead allowed at the inception of the transfer of liabilities. The extra $100,000, together with the prepaid expenses of $250,000, is immediately added to the company's surplus. The transaction appears on the books of the representative parties as shown in Exhibit 1.

4.   The reinsurer gives the reinsured an opportunity to consume the reinsurer's funds by collecting claims from the reinsurer in excess of net premiums paid to the reinsurer. This is a direct transfer of funds to the reinsured from the surplus of the reinsurer. Most of this text is concerned with that transfer, commonly called transfer of risk. Why do we, in the chapter, call this "an extension of credit"? The reinsurer issues a contract to the reinsured with either a fixed term or with a cancellation option. During the term of the contract, the reinsured has the theoretical opportunity to call upon an unlimited amount of the reinsurer's assets by presenting claims for reimbursement of losses. But, in fact, that opportunity is limited: it is limited to the losses arising from insured events

which actually occur[2] during the reinsurance contract term, and is further limited by two other factors:

a) The restrictions in the reinsurance contract upon loss recoverable per event. Most reinsurance contracts, however, have no contractual limit upon the aggregate amount of claims which the reinsured can recover from the reinsurer as respects events which occur during the term of the contract.

b) The premium adjustment terms of some reinsurance contracts, whereby the reinsured compensates the reinsurer for losses in excess of initial premium, by return of some of the commission previously allowed by the reinsurer or by payment of additional premium to the reinsurer.

The practical limit upon the extension of capital to the insurer is the reinsurer's judgment of what the aggregate amount of reinsurance claims can possibly be, which is critical to its decision whether to grant reinsurance. This is the point of most underwriting appraisals. From the point of view of the reinsurer's management, the reinsurance treaty represents an extension of capital of a certain amount — unstated, perhaps, but nevertheless real in its intended limit — which the reinsurer hopes will be repaid within a reasonable period of time after it is drawn upon; but which the reinsured has no legally enforceable obligation to pay. The reinsured's motive to assume an implicit, silent obligation to repay is to inspire the reinsurer's confidence in the risk, to preserve continuity with the present reinsurer or, if that fails, to gain such a reputation for integrity that succeeding reinsurers will be eager to enter the field of risk.

EXHIBIT 1

Transfer of Unearned Premiums at 35% Commission

BOOKS OF REINSURED

ASSETS		LIABILITIES	
BEFORE TRANSFER:			
Cash	750,000	Unearned premium (U.P.)	3,000,000
Other assets	15,250,000	Other liabilities	11,000,000
		Surplus	2,000,000
TOTAL	$16,000,000	TOTAL	$16,000,000
U.P./Surplus = 150%		(25% Equity U.P. = $750,000)	

---

[2] Under a claims-made policy form, the insurer (hence the reinsurer) is only liable for accidents on which a claim is made during the policy term. Another exception to the rule that the reinsurer is only liable for events which occur during the reinsurance contract term is aggregate loss under a policy whose term does not fall fully within the reinsurance contract term, unless the aggregate loss is pro rated over the term of the reinsurance contract.

BOOKS OF REINSURED

ASSETS	LIABILITIES

TRANSFER:

The reinsured pays $650,000 cash and cedes U.P. $1,000,000.

AFTER TRANSFER:

Cash........................	100,000	Unearned premium	2,000,000
Other assets	15,250,000	Other liabilities	11,000,000
		Surplus....................	2,350,000
TOTAL	$15,350,000	TOTAL	$15,350,000

U.P./Surplus = 85.1%

(25% Equity U.P. = $500,000:
Equity Decrease of $250,000)

Surplus increase $350,000 = 17.5% Surplus aid

The reinsured sets up no contingent liability in the Annual Statement for return of the $350,000 surplus aid if the reinsurance should be cancelled, as it would if the reinsured borrowed the sum from a bank rather than a reinsurer. The contingency is stated in the Annual Statement: General Interrogatories — Part A, Question 31 — Ceded Reinsurance Report.

BOOKS OF REINSURER

ASSETS	LIABILITIES

BEFORE TRANSFER:

Cash	1,300,000	Unearned premium (U.P.).....	50,000,000
Other assets	248,700,000	Other liabilities	150,000,000
		Surplus...................	50,000,000
TOTAL	$250,000,000	TOTAL	$250,000,000

TRANSFER:

The reinsurer receives $650,000 cash and assumes $1,000,000 U.P.

AFTER TRANSFER:

Cash	1,950,000	Unearned premium	51,000,000
Other assets	248,700,000	Other liabilities........................	150,000,000
		Surplus	49,650,000
TOTAL	$250,650,000	TOTAL	$250,650,000

The limit of the capital extension is as much a factor of the reinsured's ability to repay as it is of the reinsurer's ability to continue at risk, taking the chance that more losses will come before the initial ones have been matched with premium. That limit is reached when the reinsurer serves cancellation notice because losses incurred exceed the sum of premium paid in the past and which conceivably could be paid in the future. That limit is in the mind of the reinsurer when accepting the transfer of risk. The question is asked, "How much of my available resources may I in good conscience commit under the circumstances?" The responsible reinsurance underwriter does not knowingly accept a treaty which presents the possibility of committing resources to exceed the bounds of reasonable expectation of repayment.

Cancellation for reasons of irretrievable deficit is an admission of failure by the two parties to achieve the original purpose of the reinsurance transaction. Sometimes the reason for this failure is outside of the control of either party, or is due simply to unanticipated or catastrophic events beyond the expectation of the parties negotiating the treaty, or more tragically an unrealistic appraisal by the reinsurer of what the reinsurance treaty should be expected to achieve. For example, a small company desired to compete with larger carriers for certain heavy commercial business as its main reason for being. A reinsurer gave the company an amount of capacity which was many times the premium the company could develop. In a few years, the reinsurer compared the capacity with the premium, then cancelled. Another reinsurer gave it a whirl, then likewise cancelled because the treaty was unsound; and the company closed its doors.

5.   The reinsurer lends its good name to the reinsured. The reinsurer's image in the marketplace is one of its most important assets, since the quality of its image affects the quality of the clients it attracts. An important element of its image is its reputation for continuity and stability, earned by reason of fair, reliable performance; and this element is, in part, dependent upon the quality of its clients, their soundness, stability, fairness, reliability. If a reinsurance relationship should have a long life, the reinsurer gains much credit, however well or ill-deserved; but if the relationship should be brief, or troubled by litigation, coverage disputes or financial difficulites of the reinsured, no one but the principals know the reason, yet the reinsurer's image is prejudiced no matter how innocent it might be.

The reinsurer wants its clients to be proud to name it as their reinsurer just as the primary insurer wants its clients to reflect credit upon it. Secondly, the reinsurer lends its credibility to the reinsured. When agents, bankers, security analysts, and buyers evaluate a company, it is not unusual for the security behind the company's policy to be considered, including the security of the company's reinsurance, asking, "Will the company be able in the future to offer its present gross capacity?" "Will the company be able to stay in business?"

In no real sense is the reinsurer the guarantor of the company's solvency; however, analysts tend to feel that the reinsurer has scrutinized the company carefully, with the professional knowledge and experience which only the reinsurer has, and many also feel that the reinsurer has given the company its seal of approval. Aware of this attitude, often the reinsurer is reluctant to withdraw its support from a reinsured, not merely for the consequences which will be discussed later but because of the damaging effect such action might have on the reinsurer's image in the marketplace of all potential reinsureds. The reinsurer's motive in extending credit sometimes beyond the point of no return can thus be seen to be partly a selfish one. This fact of involvement of the reinsurer's reputation with that of the company sometimes explains the gradual and seemingly hesitant way a reinsurer disengages itself from a reinsured, and "loses" the reinsured's account to competition.

THE LIVING BUSINESS ENTERPRISE

Appraisal of the reinsured has subtle and subjective aspects. Of course, no one wants to do business with a person lacking integrity or competence, even one in possession of a profitable book of business. Reinsurers have learned to regret headlong decisions made solely upon "underwriting" considerations which indicate that the offered business should produce a profit, without examining first the source. The living business enterprise is the essential "risk" underwritten by the treaty reinsurer, for the following three reasons:

1. **The Treaty.** The treaty establishes a general field or mode of operation which people have to apply on a day-to-day, case-by-case basis. Human judgment, integrity, and skill are required to make all of the decisions needed, such as:

a) determine what risk will be insured, at what price, under what conditions;

b) determine what part, if any, of that risk shall be ceded to the reinsurer; whether facultative reinsurance should be purchased to protect the treaty reinsurer; compute the ceded premium; process payment;

c) record a potential claim; decide coverage; investigate liability; estimate its value, notify the reinsurer; consult with the reinsurer concerning proper reserve; defend and/or settle in cooperation with the reinsurer; and

d)   decide what statistics should be compiled so that the reinsured understands what business has been written and can sensibly report it to the reinsurer.

Remember, a reinsurance treaty seldom consists of an identical sharing of policies issued by the company, and seldom consists of a single flat percentage of all of the policies of the company, or of all policies in a line of business. Usually the treaty has a special definition of risks eligible for cession, certain exclusions, and a special definition of what loss or portion of loss to which the reinsurance applies. It sets a broadly drawn framework within which the reinsured has freedom to decide what exposure to cede to the reinsurer.

While the reinsurance treaty encapsules an agreement made between individuals, the persons may change, and the reinsurance may continue, because the contracting entity is a corporation and because the relationship has grown to extend to other individuals within the company. The person acting for the reinsured wants to know and be compatible with a particular broker or reinsurance underwriter; many reinsurance treaties are cancelled when the personnel of the reinsured or reinsurer change. When a long-standing reinsurance relationship is achieved, intercompany contacts at many levels occur — management, claims, underwriting, investment, actuarial and data processing — each level contributing to mutual good will and common philosophy. This kind of relationship will have the effect of reducing the impact of the loss of one individual on the relationship.

Reinsurance treaties are framed broadly. The opportunity for "error" or subversive interpretation exists. As a corrective device, the reinsurer has the contractual right to audit the reinsured's books and does from time to time examine the cession and loss records. It would be impractical, however, for the reinsurer to undertake to examine the source documents and the underwriting files in sufficient depth to ascertain that every cession, every payment, and every claim is correct. Nevertheless, errors are rare and routinely are retroactively corrected as soon as discovered.

Our industry is so well characterized by honesty, unquestionable integrity and fair dealing that the typical reinsurance underwriter operates with a sense of security. If the underwriter were overly conscious of vulnerability, it would be difficult to write an appreciable volume of business. Hence, the underwriter normally assumes the business risk which initial appraisal indicates to be limited as respects the character of the personnel of the insurer. The underwriter focuses instead mainly upon the objective record of their competence.

The main body of this text lays emphasis upon the dependence of the reinsured upon its reinsurer for capacity, financing of reserves, surplus aid, averaging of losses, and catastrophe protection. Yet when the reinsurer considers whether to offer reinsurance, it is done with an understanding of dependence upon the reinsured for the business involved and for any profit on that business. The actual experience of the reinsurer on the business ceded, with few exceptions, will reflect the care taken by the personnel of the ceding company to guard the interests of the reinsurer. Under the "good faith" reinsurance relationship, the ceding company is expected:

a) to use the reinsurance facility prudently from the point of view of the reinsurer, not necessarily from the point of view of the reinsured;

b) to refrain from using the full capacity of the treaty in cases of volatile or unpredictable exposures; and, of course,

c) to devote as much energy to the defense of claims whereon the reinsurer's exposure is much greater than the reinsured's as it devotes to claims well within its retention. Therefore, the most important question in the mind of the reinsurer when appraising the reinsured is: What is the attitude of this company toward its reinsurers? How does the company observe its responsibilities toward its reinsurer?

2. Potential Inability to Perform. The reinsured might become unable to perform its "good faith" obligations under the reinsurance treaty. Some of the reasons for this failure might be:

a) Incompetence of its personnel. Some reinsurance treaties are negotiated only with the chief executive officer, without checking the personnel who will actually implement and use the treaty. Failure to acquaint oneself with them is a mistake.

b) Insolvency or financial impairment. The reinsurer must examine the fiscal health of the reinsured to project the period of time the reinsured can be expected to remain solvent, to be in control of its own affairs, to continue to produce profitable business, and to continue to settle claims responsibly.

c) Sale or merger of the reinsured, resulting in material changes of the party reinsured and termination of the reinsurance relationship.

d) Cession by the reinsured of its retention. This eliminates its risk handling incentive and makes the reinsurer the primary carrier.

e) Loss of key personnel to competitors or by death or disability. The reinsurer should consider the depth of personnel, and whether the entire enterprise is dependent upon the intellect and energy of one or two persons whose absence will cause the insurer to deteriorate or die.

3. Possible Changes in the Business Reinsured. The nature of the business reinsured might change fundamentally from that which produced the historical record which is the basis of the treaty under consideration. Such changes may include:

a) Changes in law or judicial interpretation of statutes which increase the liability of the company under its policies or create new insurable risks which were not contemplated when the treaty was written, thus changing the underwriting risk which the reinsurer had originally assumed. Examples of this kind of change: the imposition of unlimited medical benefits on "no fault" automobile policies, indexing of workers' compensation benefits, pension legislation creating fiduciary liability for administration of retirement benefits, claim practices acts mandating time requirements in loss payments, and the extension or liberal interpretation of statutes of limitations on time to bring suit.

b) Acquisition of a block of business significantly different from the business in force at the date the treaty took effect which would be subject to cession unless specifically excluded.

c) Loss of a block of business, perhaps due to competition or loss of an agency plant or insolvency of an agent or a change in law — which eliminates the need for the kind of insurance written previously.

d) The occurrence of claims far more numerous or larger in amount than those which had historically occurred.

This third set of reasons involves looking at the market, the universe in which the company is operating, to foresee changes which might overtake the prospective reinsured and hence could seriously damage the prospect of profit under the proposed treaty. Sometimes the client company has knowledge of impending action, recognizes trends, has observed adverse court decisions in its territory, or knows of insurance department rulings which will change its accounting of profit and loss or change its ability to non-renew or produce certain business. The reinsurance underwriter is thus not simply looking at the reinsured but the entire environment in which it operates.

THE ENVIRONMENT

The reinsurer must be well informed about current social, economic, and political trends. The underwriting of the reinsured cannot be separated from the environment in which they both exist. Insurance is such a reflection of what is going on in society that the success of both parties is, to a great extent, an indication of how they have responded to trends and developments prevalent in society. For the reinsurer this manifests itself in several ways. First, its underwriting is, to a certain extent, a matter of intelligent and informed selection of those reinsureds who know what's going on and how to operate successfully in society. The reinsurer, of course, must also know what's going on to make this kind of evaluation. In addition, the reinsurer sets its own underwriting programs: which covers to offer and which to avoid, what layers to play in and what prices to charge. Such decisions reflect, in so many instances, the reinsurer's ideas of current social trends and how these will be projected into the future. Finally, there is a service function that goes beyond the basic reinsurance functions outlined in the beginning. Reinsureds look increasingly to their reinsurers for assistance and advice in the underwriting of specific types of coverages and in the development of underwriting and claims programs. In this regard, a well informed reinsurer will be able to provide a much higher quality of service than one which is not.

CONTINUITY

Underlying the reinsurer's appraisal of the prospective reinsured is the concern with continuity, the crux of the credit theorem. The treaty underwriter will agree to accept an unknown quantity of risks over an unknown period of time. The main purpose of the appraisal is to satisfy the underwriter that any deficit which the reinsurance treaty might produce during one year, and during a series of four or five years, will fall within the premium to be produced over a reasonable period of time. If that period of time must be especially long, the reinsurer must be especially careful. The reinsurer is mainly considering four elements — dollar amount, time, expectation of payback, and the character of the reinsured as a factor in this expectation — in language such as the following:

> . . . the ultimate amount of dollars (potential deficit) to be extended to the account of the reinsured, and

> . . . the period of time over which losses and premiums will develop, and

> . . . the period of time contemplated for payback of any deficit — if any payback can reasonably be expected at all — and

. . . the character of the reinsured as a strong contributing factor in the expectation of payback.

Let us imagine that a product liability treaty is being contemplated in 1980 to be effective in 1981 to pay up to $1 million excess of $1 million each loss against an annual premium of $2 million. Three such losses (adjusted to current monetary values) have occurred in the three years 1976-1978; none are known in 1979 on the business to be covered by the treaty; the premium will cover six losses in three years, but the loss record has no statistical credibility. The musing of the underwriter might run as follows:

"How many losses of $1 million each can this treaty give me each year? If four losses occur in the first year, will I ever be made whole? When? Could four recur in the second and third years, too? If four losses occur in the first year, when will I know — investigation and litigation of a case takes five years — not until I have run four years of exposure? If reported losses total $4 million for the first year, can I get at least $4 million premium for the second year? What is the ability of the company to increase the present premium? Can the company increase its primary rate, or must it find the money elsewhere within its portfolio? Is there a collateral source, another treaty now ceded to me or to others, with a proven profit record which could be used to offset a deficit on this treaty? If I should be forced to ask for $4 million premium for the second year after I already have $4 million of losses, will the company continue the cover at an uneconomic price until the frequency of loss returns to normal and I am whole, or will the company look for another reinsurer who did not pay the losses? If no other reinsurer should volunteer, would the company discontinue this class and let everyone swallow their losses? How important is this facility to the company — is it vital to its overall operations? Does it generate earnings on other classes, which might subsidize a deficit on this class? Am I being asked to carry a risk without benefit of all of the premium produced by reason of this risk? What is my payback security?"

The reinsurance underwriter should not unrealistically think that one can look outside the funds produced by the individual treaty in question for ultimate recoupment of any deficit which might incur. Many reinsured companies sincerely assure their reinsurer that "we will pay our own losses," suggesting either that losses sustained by the reinsurer under the treaty will not be the full responsibility of the reinsurer which receives the premium for those losses or that any profit earned by the reinsurer is a gift. If the premium were negotiated without the benefit of credible historical record, or if the reinsurer granted the cover as an accommodation to the account of the reinsured, a feeling of responsibility for the welfare of the reinsurer is quite natural. However, the reinsurer and the reinsured should carefully avoid entry into a situation where no true transfer of risk is contemplated by the parties or by the terms of the contract. If the reinsurance contract should specify that the full amount of any deficit incurred by the reinsurer shall be matched by premium or return commission, the efficacy of the contract may be called into question and credit for ceding the reinsurance might be disallowed in the Annual Statement of the reinsured by regulatory authorities. The reinsurer merely has a legitimate right to expect that the reinsured will give it every reasonable opportunity to be made whole out of the specific business reinsured, by continuation, at terms perhaps more costly than the initial terms but affordable by the reinsured; and to make adjustments in underwriting conditions which loss experience shows to be necessary from the point of view of both parties.

Before accepting a treaty, the reinsurance underwriter has a duty to question whether any annual deficit, in a reasonably foreseeable amount, will be offset with premium in subsequent years. The underwriter should ask whether the reinsured:

> . . . is able to fund a deficit, because the reinsured will be in business during the future years required to amortize the deficit and the reinsured has a bank of profit to use for this purpose or has the ability to increase the original premium base; and

> . . . is willing to fund the deficit, if the price of doing so is acceptable. The price might be unacceptable if the means to achieve that end are these — to reduce the reinsured producers' commissions to a point not acceptable to the producers; to increase primary rates to a non-competitive level; to exclude risks essential to the saleability of the product; to withdraw from certain lines of business or states; to penalize policyholders for late reporting of claims; or to sever certain employees or agents.

The task of the reinsurer is to set its expectation of a payback at a realistic level so that continuity of the reinsurance relationship can be achieved.

Measuring the Fiscal Health of the Prospective Reinsured

INFORMATION GATHERING: THE SOURCES

Obtaining accurate information about the reinsured is essential. A resourceful and imaginative treaty underwriter will have little difficulty in this area, because there are many ways to go about it and many places to look. Sources of information that should always be considered would include the following:

1. The New Submission. This information will be obtained directly from the reinsured or through its intermediary. It should contain a brief description and history of the company, the resumes of its top officers and underwriters, a summary of the most important aspects of the proposed contract, and underwriting information relating to the proposal. The contract summary will usually be presented in duplicate as an acceptance slip. If the reinsurer accepts the proposal, the slip will be signed and dollar or percent participation noted.

2. Direct Contact with the Reinsured. Direct writing reinsurers (those which do not deal through intermediaries) will always have direct contact with their client companies on new submissions. Reinsurers accepting business through intermediaries may not. They may have to rely on the intermediary for whatever additional information is needed. This might be the case, for example, where the reinsurer accepts a small share in a property catastrophe cover. In most cases, however, the reinsurer will want to meet and get to know the reinsured. This will be arranged through visits made with the intermediary. The contact may cover three areas: a) There will be a general meeting during which the reinsurance underwriter endeavors to learn as much as possible about the company, its underwriting philosophy, its officers, underwriters and claims personnel. b) Sometimes the reinsurer will wish to conduct an underwriting audit, where the underwriting administration of the specific business offered is examined in minute detail. c) A pre-quote claims audit will usually be made when the business offered is casualty or workers' compensation. Such an audit is done because of the volatility of those lines and because of their long-tail and IBNR loss development characteristics. The quality of claims handling and reserving practices is paramount in these lines and is examined in great detail. Exhibit 2 illustrates the type of information to be sought.

EXHIBIT 2

Pre-Quote Claim Review

General Outline of Information to be Sought By Casualty Claim Auditor

l.   Analysis of claim reports. Taking a random sample of fifty closed files:—

  a) What is the lapse of time from the incident to the first report to the company? Seek explanation concerning those cases where the first report is more than thirty days after the incident. For example, 1) claim is first brought against a local retailer of the product manufactured by our insured in a different state; or 2) a contractor breaks a water main and the resulting water damage to foundations and abutting structures is hidden below ground for a long period of time.

b) What is the lapse of time between first report to the company and first report to the reinsurer? Discover the reasons for any unusual delay in cases where a report to the reinsurer is not simply precautionary because the reserve is below the reinsurance attachment point.

(Comment: Postponement of notice of claims, in order to avoid upsetting a reinsurance treaty which might otherwise appear to be running well, has rarely occurred.)

2. Initial investigation of claims.

a) The promptness of initial investigation.

b) The quality of the initial investigation, within the first fifteen days after the claim report. For example, who was assigned to investigate, and what instructions were given? Were the right questions asked by the investigator? Was the coverage promptly analyzed? Were witnesses found? Were copies of police reports and hospital reports obtained, et cetera? Were adequate background data obtained concerning the claimant? Are reports and comments dated? Are files in good order?

3. Quality and promptness of follow-up of claims.

Were the right questions investigated, such as: Which of several parties were actually at fault? What is the identity of the manufacturer of any item of equipment which caused injury? Are there subrogation possibilities, et cetera?

4. Quality of attorneys assigned to cases.

5. Quality of loss settlements.

a) Does the company make settlement offers promptly for cases involving clear liability by the insured?

b) Were the offers realistic?

c) How were settlement offers by the claimant handled?

d) When the claimant makes first contact with the company, does the company maintain control, or does it push the claimant to an attorney?

e) Is there a pattern of resisting all cases?

f) Are settlements made upon adequate information concerning insurance coverage, injuries, and company defenses?

g) Are settlements fair, and in line with injury and damage?

6. Excess judgments.

a) Does the company know how to protect itself against a judgment excess of policy limits?

b) Has the company ever defended a suit by its insured for a loss in excess of policy limits? If so, how well did it handle the problem?

7. Quality of loss reserves. Prepare a loss development worksheet showing the development of losses excess of 70% of the proposed reinsurance excess point, showing the incurred (paid plus O/S) loss at each December 31 following occurrence up to settlement. Take a large enough sample to reveal the pattern of time required to settlement.

Analyze the company's attitude toward loss reserves: Do they show a pattern of reaching ultimate reserve in steps? Or does the company attempt to set up the entire ultimate reserve at the earliest date indicated by facts? Does management "manage" the loss reserves, or "budget" them? Does the company adjust their reserves up or down as soon as new facts appear? Do loss reserves include a reserve for defense and allocated loss adjustment expenses? Are the reserves realistic at the present time? Do they include an allowance for future inflation above present values to expected date of settlement?

This claim reserve analysis should be made separately for each major line of casualty business — auto, workers' compensation, M & C, malpractice, products, et cetera.

8. Competence of claim staff, considering the work load.

9. Attitude of the company's claim officers and management toward the reinsurer. Aside from prompt reporting of reinsurer's loss potentials, does the company have a proper attitude of defending the reinsurer's interest? Shall we trust these people to play with our money?

3. The NAIC Annual Statement and Early Warning Tests.* The Annual Statement is a standardized financial reporting format adopted by the National Association of Insurance Commissioners. It contains a detailed analysis of the reinsured's financial operations as of December 31 for each calendar year. A copy should be obtained from the reinsured whenever an evaluation is being made, for it is the single most important source of financial information available.

The Early Warning Tests attempt to identify "priority" companies which need closer monitoring by state insurance departments. Test ratios for all licensed companies are compared with the performance of companies which have become insolvent in the past, with the objective of predicting insolvency one year in advance as respects 96% of companies which became insolvent, and three years in advance as respects 82% of companies which became insolvent. Data used for the tests are obtained from each company's Annual Statement, and the results are given to each filing company by the NAIC in March or April of each year.

4. Best's Publications. The information developed, assembled and

---

* At the NAIC's December, 1978, meeting in Las Vegas, the Early Warning Testing System was redesignated "Insurance Regulatory Information System" (IRIS). Hence, wherever the term Early Warning Test appears in this and other chapters, it refers to one or more of the eleven tests that are now part of IRIS.

published by the A. M. Best Company[3] on the property-casualty insurance industry and companies within the industry is truly remarkable
and is required reading for any reinsurance underwriter who is
evaluating a company on which Best's reports. The specific publications
that should be consulted include:

Best's **Insurance Reports.** This annual volume contains comprehensive
reports on the financial position, history, and transactions of over 1500
insurance companies and branch offices of foreign companies operating
in the United States and Canada. The Reports include stock companies,
approximately 300 prominent mutual property-casualty companies, exchanges, and American "Lloyds" organizations. For most companies the
Reports include policyholder's ratings which indicates Best's opinion of
the comparative position of each company or association measured by
industry standards. These ratings focus on competent underwriting, cost
control, adequate reserves, net resources, and soundness of investment.
Ratings are A + and A (Excellent), B + (Very Good), B (Good), C +
(Fairly Good), and C (Fair).

The Reports also include financial size categories which are determined by the surplus to policyholders, conditional or technical reserves,
plus equities in the unearned premium reserves, or less indicated shortages. These financial strength measurement categories range from
I — $250,000 or less, to XV — $100,000,000 or more. Other items included are: a) loss, premium and admitted asset information on approximately 2,000 mutuals, b) information on state funds and associations,
and c) a listing of retired companies and associations.

Best's **Key Rating Guide.** This booklet summarizes the five-year
operating and financial data contained in Best's Insurance Reports.

Best's **Aggregates and Averages.** This volume includes statistical
data for the property/casualty insurance industry and is supplemented by
specially prepared tabulations and aggregates. Statistical information is
broken down in a number of useful ways that permit the user to compare
the statistical profile of an individual company to the entire industry or to
groupings of similar companies. Also included is by-line underwriting experience for every major line of insurance on an individual company
basis broken down by company type, e.g., stock, mutual, Lloyds, or reciprocal exchange.

Best's **Review — Property/Casualty.** This is Best's monthly magazine. Appearing on the last few pages of each issue are the following sections: reports on companies, executive changes, retirements, new direc-

---

[3] A. M. Best Company, Inc., Ambest Road, Oldwick, New Jersey, 08858.

tors, company developments, and an index of insurance companies reported on. These sections should be used in conjunction with Best's Insurance Reports to keep abreast of changes throughout the year.

Best's **Executive Data Service.** This reference book reports on
industry-wide experience by state, for each of the major lines of prop-
erty/casualty business and for companies or groups writing a significant
premium volume.

5. The Facultative Reinsurance Department. The reinsurer's own
facultative reinsurance department can be an extremely valuable source
of information because of the closeness of facultative underwriters to the
marketplace on a day-to-day basis.

6. Inquiries within the Marketplace. Sometimes the reinsured will offer references — people or companies that have had dealings with the
reinsured and who may assist the underwriter in the process of evaluation. These can include former and present reinsurers, banking and credit
references, and individuals familiar with the reinsured and members of
its staff.

7. Public Records. If the insurer's securities are publicly traded, the
underwriter can develop a tremendous amount of useful information by
obtaining its proxy statement, 10K, 10Q, and 8Q reports filed with the
Securities and Exchange Commission. If the company has recently gone
public, or is about to go, the underwriter can obtain the SEC registration
statement and the prospectus. Finally, if the company is new or recently
formed, the underwriter can obtain the company's application for a
charter, the certificate of authority, the company's by-laws, and the
biographical affidavits filed with the state insurance departments. In addition to these documents, the underwriter might request a copy of
whatever feasibility study may have been prepared in connection with
the formation of the company.

8. The Investment Department. Analytical reports on the reinsured
may be available to the reinsurer's investment department from stock
brokerage firms and other securities dealers.

9. Argus F. C. & S. Chart. This chart is published annually by the National Underwriter Company[4] and presents financial and operating
results of approximately 1,400 property and casualty insurers. This
source is somewhat similar to *Best's Key Rating Guide,* but without any
ratings.

10. The Insurance Periodical Index and the Business Periodical Index.
References to articles in trade and general business periodicals may be

---

[4] The National Underwriter Company, 420 East Fourth Street, Cincinnati, Ohio 45202.

found in these volumes.[5] The Insurance Periodical Index is a particularly useful reference because it covers forty-seven insurance periodicals from the United States, Canada, and United Kingdom.

11. Who's Who In Insurance. This reference from The Weekly Underwriter[6] contains biographical data on important people in the industry, such as date of birth, home and business address, education, and professional career.

Red, Yellow and Green Flags: Interpreting The Facts

The underwriter appraises the fiscal health of a prospective reinsured to a depth appropriate for the type of cover and the degree of involvement contemplated. However, the results of some types of reinsurance covers depend little upon the long-term fortunes of the reinsured but rather are outside its control or influence, rendering intensive fiscal analysis unnecessary. Example: a property catastrophe cover for which a premium is set by the reinsurer upon a base which is relatively unaffected by the operating soundness of the reinsured, and from which losses will be relatively unaffected by the fiscal health of the reinsured during the term of the cover.

At the other extreme, where the fiscal health of the reinsured is essential, reinsurance ties the fortunes of the reinsurer inescapably to the long-term fortunes of the insurer. An example is a quota share or working excess on long-tail business, such as workers' compensation and products liability. In that case, the reinsurer depends upon the ability of the insurer to perform all of its obligations during the period which will expire before the reinsurer can appraise the reinsurance results. This performance will extend at least until the final settlement of all claims which arise out of that initial period of the underwriter's commitment. In the case of workers' compensation policies, the period to settle losses runs from ten to forty-five years; in the case of products liability, the period runs from eight to fifteen years. Therefore, in the case of long-tail business, reduction of the reinsurer's line to a minor percentage participation does not protect the reinsurer against the effects of nonperformance by the reinsured; it only reduces the dollar amount of the damage to the reinsurer. If the reinsurer writes several treaties which have adverse long-tail development, it will find that a little poison taken frequently makes it just as sick as one large dose.

---

[5] The Insurance Periodical Index is published by the Special Libraries Association. For further information contact Chief Librarian, College of Insurance Library, 123 William Street, New York, N.Y. 10038. The Business Periodical Index is published by the H. W. Wilson Company, 950 University Ave., Bronx, N.Y. 10452.

[6] The Underwriter Printing and Publishing Co., 50 East Palisade Ave., Englewood, N.J. 07631.

Safe Period Needed to Complete Reinsurance Obligations

BUSINESS:	Property	Property	Casualty Short-Tail	Casualty Long-Tail*
COVER:	XS Catastrophe	Pro Rata & Risk X/L	Pro Rata & X/L	Pro Rata & X/L
PERIOD:	2 years	3-5 years	6-7 years	Over 8 years

*   Generally speaking, the higher the attachment point of the reinsurance on casualty business, the longer is the period of time to reach utimate settlement of losses. A low working layer on workers' compensation business has a shorter tail than an upper layer, because losses exhaust the limit sooner and end the reinsurer's involvement.

Both skill and judgment are required when interpreting the facts, as two illustrations will show. For example, if one should correlate the qualification of a prospective reinsured to survive the required safe period for the cover requested with the company's policyholders' rating by the A. M. Best Company, it is suggested that a reasonable correlation would be a period that over eight years requires an A + rating and three to five years requires at least a C + rating. Obviously, by this standard, the reinsurer would be cautious and not enter into relationships with companies lacking a Best's rating. An individual insurer may not have such a rating for any of several reasons: because of its small size, or because it furnished information too late for use by Best's, or because the company disputes Best's judgement, or because it has been in business for fewer than five years, or because its rating granted earlier has been omitted for some reason not related to the reinsurer's interest. Such caution and unwillingness to reinsure, however, would deny reinsurance to many otherwise worthy companies, would restrict the reinsurer's profit opportunities, and would not permit the reinsurer to play its traditional role in the development of small and new carriers for which reinsurance may be vital. Hence this correlation is useful only in those cases where the reinsurer's involvement is nominal or the company is large and well established, or where the rating is "Excellent." In cases where the required safe period extends beyond two years and the company is either not rated by Best's or the rating is less than "Excellent," the underwriter must make an independent appraisal. Even when the Best's rating is "Excellent," the underwriter must look at the most current annual and quarterly statements, because significant changes in the company's status could have occurred subsequent to the date of the Best's report.[7]

---

[7] It is suggested that the reader refer to Herbert Denenberg's article: "Is A-Plus Really a Passing Grade?" which appeared in *Best's Review, Property-Liability Edition*, December, 1969; and to Robert A. Bailey's article: "Best's Ratings and Insurer Insolvency" which appeared in *Best's Review, Property-Liability Edition*, September, 1974.

Another illustration requiring the use of judgment in inter the facts is the NAIC Early Warning Tests given the filing company in March or April each year. If the underwriter seeks guidance from such tests, there may be little help in appraising a recently formed company, or a company operating in a single state, as well as others critically in need of appraisal before reinsurance is offered. About 600 smaller companies, mainly county mutuals, are omitted from the NAIC testing program, including some recently formed malpractice insurers.

The NAIC testing program operates on a voluntary basis and involves the application of test formulas to Annual Statement figures. These test formulas are based on overall industry usual ranges of performance, rather than on normative standards differentiated for age and size of insurer and nature of business written. Their purpose is simple and limited: they are designed to pinpoint a present fiscal crisis rather than to project long-term prospects of the company. Although the NAIC tests have evolved since 1971, they are still in an early stage of development.

Reacting to the less than universal acceptance of the NAIC tests, in 1978 the American Insurance Association developed five test refinements using discriminant analysis techniques. The data base used by the AIA comprises 300 Annual Statement data items covering four or five years from two groups: 1) fifty insolvent or "troubled" companies, and 2) fifty solvent companies whose size and underwriting mix are comparable to the insolvent group. It is hoped that an improved base will ultimately yield a reliable set of predictability tests. Meanwhile, the reinsurance underwriter depends upon his or her intelligence, insight, and specific case information.

The Effects of the Reinsured's Insolvency upon the Reinsurer. A precisely drawn reinsurance treaty which covers a carefully delineated portfolio might produce a profitable result for the reinsurer in spite of financial difficulty of the reinsured. If the reinsurer decides to proceed with a company having a low probability of survival through the "safe period," the reinsurer should be prepared to face the consequences. If the reinsured becomes insolvent shortly after termination of the reinsurance agreement, even if the treaty results appear to be not unprofitable prior to that date, the consequences may be painful and can include:

1. Key personnel may depart. As the company approaches insolvency, its good personnel may be inclined in their own self interest to leave the company, reducing thereafter the quality of risks written and the quality of loss settlements.

2. The agency plant may disappear. The premium volume needed

to produce the necessary reinsurance premium will diminish, rendering the reinsurance rate inadequate.

3. The production of business will be slowed or stopped. As agents and brokers learn of the company's difficulty and lose confidence in it, they may stop the flow of good business or offer marginal risks. More importantly, they may withhold payment of balances due the company as a protective measure for their clients.

4. Statistics may deteriorate and be late in submission. This deterioration will reduce the reinsurer's knowledge of the situation and frustrate its controls. The situation may even appear deceivingly better than it is. Losses reported later may be reserved in lesser amounts as the company fights to maintain a decent appearance.

5. The reinsurer may experience professional embarrassment with damage to its image and good name.

6. There will be a heavy expenditure of executive time, resulting in lost opportunity to handle other business. This expense might be measured in several millions of dollars of lost business.

7. After insolvency, the construction of the reinsurance contract in a litigious atmosphere may not comport to the intent of the original parties.

8. After the company is declared insolvent or placed in conservatorship, the reinsurer might find that its liability is materially enlarged above the limits defined in the reinsurance treaty. The following factors will determine the outcome of this question:

a) Whether the reinsurer achieved the cutoff of liability for development of losses after the termination of the treaty, or whether the reinsurer remains liable on open and unrecorded losses.

b) Whether the premium or commission adjustment balances due the reinsurer at the date of insolvency will be recoverable.

c) Whether losses are settled after insolvency of the company in an amount greater than what would have been settled if they had been handled diligently by the management with whom the treaty was originally negotiated.

d) Whether losses that would have been excluded from the reinsurance contract are determined by the liquidator to be covered, perhaps because the contract wording is found to be imprecise or silent on critical questions, or because the exclusion was a "good faith" understanding between the reinsured and the reinsurer which does not bind the liquidator.

e) Whether the regulator of the ceding insurer's domiciliary state takes a position, contrary to the established practice in the industry, on the reinsurer's right to set off balances due the liquidator.

f) Whether the provisions of the various insurance guaranty acts invoked by the insolvency create additional problems. Though the recently developed case law in this area clearly upholds the position that reinsurance proceeds are payable to the domiciliary liquidator and not to affected guaranty associations, the expense of relitigating this question in a jurisdiction which has not clearly adopted this position may be a factor.

g) Whether there exist cut-through or reinsurance assumption endorsements.

h) Whether the claim handling mechanism employed by the liquidator is competent and efficient enough to resolve claims promptly and economically, or whether it permits claims to degenerate to the detriment of the reinsurer.

i) Whether the ability of the reinsurer to respond to serious claims is effective, in contrast to its more traditional oversight role.

Checking for Creditworthy Characteristics. What are the desirable characteristics affecting the credit status of a prospective reinsured? Expressed differently, what does the reinsurance underwriter look for in measuring the fiscal health of a prospective reinsured? In addition to appraising the ownership of the reinsured, there are five other important criteria: 1) adequate and verifiable policyholder surplus; 2) an operating profitability stemming from competent underwriting and sound rates; 3) adequate loss reserves reflecting sound reserving practices; 4) conservative investment practices; and 5) responsible, creative, energetic, and competent personnel.

If the prospective reinsured has written a significant volume of business during the last three years, the reinsurer can appraise the first four characteristics by examining the two most recent Annual Statements, paying particular attention to the Insurance Expense Exhibit (filed separately by April 1). If the appraisal is being made mid-year, the most recent quarterly balance sheet and profit and loss statement should also be examined. The third characteristic requires a claim audit. To appraise the people involved in the enterprise, direct conversation is essential, conducted either by the professional intermediary if one is employed or by the reinsurer.

If the prospective reinsured has been in business for less than three years or is in the process of formation, the appraisal is based upon such items as a) an SEC Registration Statement or a prospectus designed to attract investors; b) a feasibility study prepared by an actuary, projecting the market, competition, possible results, and justifying the proposed rate levels; c) the claim history of the business the company proposes to write; d) the company's application for a charter and certificate of authority; e) the company bylaws; and f) the track record and resumes of the operating personnel, available from biographical affidavits filed by the organizers with the insurance department of the domiciliary state. The main questions center on capitalization, whether funds are deposited in cash or other liquid assets; the soundness of the plan of operation; the loss controls; underwriting controls; and quality, experience, and integrity of the promoters and executives. The reinsurer may seek help with the investigation from its banker or legal counsel or a credit-reporting agency.

A sixth area of inquiry, important to all five considerations, is the ownership of the company — its directors and principal stockholders. In the case of a mutual company, who are its directors, or the persons who hold a management contract or who control a large block of policyholders? And in the case of a reciprocal exchange, who is the attorney-in-fact? These persons and their business affiliations must be assessed for conflicting motivations which may be regarded as strengths or weaknesses in the context of a reinsurance relationship.

ADEQUACY OF SURPLUS. As to the first criterion, how high is up? The reinsurer must decide, however, and measures a prospective reinsured's surplus against demands which might be made upon it:

a) Against the reinsured's net retained policy limits. Except for the surety line where special circumstances may exist, one could question the prudent judgment of an insurer which commits more than 2% of its surplus on a single risk. Of course, a property risk might be subject to probable maximum loss ("PML") or maximum foreseeable loss ("MFL") evaluation, and an insurer might write 5% of its surplus on an 80-story, fire-resistive office tower in the belief that no loss could exceed 40% of that amount. The question before the reinsurer is simply: Is the company's judgment prudent in the light of possible losses on its book of business?

b) Against catastrophe loss exposure, the accumulation of loss on many risks because of one event. While the economics of the marketplace often determine this exposure to surplus, one would not expect a carrier willingly to expose its surplus to a catastrophe loss greater than 5%. The ratio of this loss retention is an index of the conservatism of management, and of how attractive the reinsured is to reinsurers.

c) Against a potential operating and investment deficit, amounting to the portion of surplus which could be consumed by two consecutive underwriting year deficits. If it is felt that surplus could be reduced by 25% as the result of ultimate operating deficit on premiums written in the current year, and by an additional 25% on the premium to be written during the succeeding year, the surplus is inadequate for the demands upon it.

The function of surplus is to serve as a buffer of last resort in protecting the life of the company. As such, surplus is a "bank account" to pay the amount by which claims, operating expenses, and investment losses exceed earned premiums: to cover a deficit for two, three, or more years successively. The potential for deficit (if it exists) lies in the premiums written by the personnel of the company. Hence, the potential depends on the classes and quality of risks written, the rate level, and the volume of premium in force and on stream.

The measurement of margin required for an expected or possible two-year operating deficit on net premiums written, against current surplus, produces the "rule" that surplus should not be less than one third to one half of premiums written (i.e., premiums written should not be more than three to two times surplus). Why two years for the operating deficit? Because that is the minimum time needed to reverse the causes already in progress toward the deficit, even if the company's management acts immediately to do so. The relationship is illustrated below:

Premium Written	Operating Deficit	%	Current Surplus	Two-Year Deficit	Future Surplus	Surplus Decrease
10,000,000	500,000	05%	4,000,000	1,000,000	3,000,000	25%
10,000,000	1,000,000	10%	4,000,000	2,000,000	2,000,000	50%
10,000,000	1,500,000	15%	4,000,000	3,000,000	1,000,000	75%
10,000,000	2,000,000	20%	4,000,000	4,000,000	none	100%

Thus, a company with a premium-to-surplus ratio of 2.5 can absorb a two-year operating deficit of 10% of premium written before the red flag falls, before the game is over, before the coach and players are fired. If the premiums written-to-surplus ratio were 2:1, or $5,000,000 current surplus in the above case, the company could absorb a deficit of 12 ½ %

over two years before it lost 50 % of its surplus. Annual written premiums rather than the fraction earned in a single year are used in this analysis, because such figures focus on the *ultimate* development of losses arising from the written premiums three to fifteen years after the policies have expired and the written premiums are earned.

To comment on the other criteria, we look to the Annual Statement for useful data. Although preparation of the Annual Statement is prescribed by detailed instructions from the NAIC, the Statement is unaudited before submission to an insurance department. Honestly held but inaccurate interpretations or assumptions based on necessarily incomplete information may have the effect of overvaluing assets and undervaluing liabilities. A detailed analysis of the data reported in the Annual Statement is a highly technical and time-consuming task which is best performed by experts. The reinsurance underwriter can check certain items, however, to see whether the true situation is better or worse than it appears. One must consider in support of the utility of the Annual Statement that, though it is not required to be audited, it is, nevertheless, the subject of rigorous examination by state insurance authorities in the testing of assets and liabilities.

The Testing of Assets. To the knowledgeable student, the Statement is replete with detail and clues for various financial tests such as those applied to an insurer's assets. Using the 1978 blank, the following illustrates what can be discovered beneath the surface figures when penetrating questions are raised.

Cash. While cash is shown on Line 6 of Page 2, Schedule N later in the Statement identifies the banks holding the cash deposits. A substantial deposit could be in a bank suspended or declared insolvent after the Statement date. Officers, directors, or major stockholders might own a major bank depository, raising questions about security. A single deposit might represent too large a proportion of surplus. Deposits in foreign banks should be noted, ascertaining the stability of the country, its exchange controls, and the reputation of the bank.

Bonds. Bonds are shown on Line 1 of Page 2 and are usually carried at amortized value, which valuation method assumes they will be held to maturity. But severe cash drain could force their sale. What is the difference between amortized value and market value shown in the Summary of Schedule D? Subtract this difference from surplus and then test the ratio to premiums written again. Check current market value of bonds of a single issuer aggregating over 3 % of surplus, in case a large holding dropped drastically in value since the Statement date, e.g., Penn

Central bonds carried in the 1969 Statement of a company at $5 million were worth $200,000 nine months later. The $4,800,000 difference equalled 8% of the company's surplus as of 12/31/69.

Schedule D may show bonds or debentures of affiliates. If such affiliates should become insolvent, what would be the effect on this company? Non-insurance enterprises may rightfully augment their assets with non-tangible items such as patents, or might hold land or other difficult-to-appraise items which would not be admitted assets for insurers in the statutory accounting scheme. The Special Deposit Schedule shows bonds deposited by statute with insurance departments. These special funds may not be used to pay losses in the ordinary course of business and, hence, should be deducted from liquid assets of a company with thin surplus.

Stocks. Stocks (Line 2 of Page 2) are volatile assets and can cause wide swings in surplus. Are any stock issues owned unusual, or are any in excess of 10% of the company's surplus?

Check Part 6 of Schedule D for any affiliates or subsidiaries which may write a volume of insurance with the effect of pyramiding the parent's surplus. Proper appraisal of surplus requires that all insurance affiliates be consolidated into the parent carrier. Recent developments affecting intercorporate holdings will be found in SEC 10K and 10Q filings, prospectuses and stockholder reports.

Exhibit 1 — Analysis of Assets, shows the nonadmitted asset of excess of book value (cost) over market value (Statement). The company's surplus will increase in the future if this loss of value is recovered. This item may explain a decrease in current surplus (see Part 1A — "Capital Gains and Losses").

Loans, Real Estate, and Agents Balances. On Line 3 of Page 2 is an unusual asset, mortgage loans. Is any loan over 5% of surplus? Are any loans to officers or directors or "interested parties"? (See Schedule B). Line 4 of that page shows real estate whose valuation may be subjective. For some items, a market may be non-existent. (See Schedule A.) Check the basis of valuation — recent appraisal less depreciation versus cost? A sharp change might be a red flag. Line 5 of that page lists collateral loans, which are highly unusual if more than nominal. Is there a substantial loan to an officer or director or interested third party? (See Schedule C.)

Line 8 of Page 2 shows a critical item, agents balances, which may exceed the company's surplus. If 10% is uncollectible, how much will surplus be cut? Such balances are "good" assets (admissible) until they are over ninety days due. If the company's reinsurers are sound, it is sensible to measure agents balances against surplus after deducting ceded reinsurance balances payable net of ceding commission (Page 3 — Line 18), though the company is fully responsible for payment of premiums due reinsurers, regardless of whether agents balances are collected from agents. The industry norm, reflected in NAIC Early Warning Test 8, is that agents balances should be less than 40% of surplus, usually 30% for stock companies and 21% for mutuals.

Compare the prior year ratio of agents balances to gross direct premiums written (Part 2 C, Col. 1, Page 8) with current year balances to see whether collections are accelerating or decreasing. Are agents losing confidence? Claims and expenses cannot be paid from uncollected balances; balances withheld by agents cannot be invested. If the company is owned or controlled by a managing general agent, the balances may be earning interest for the agent rather than the company. A company having a retrospective commission plan with an agent may have to write off a large sum of return commissions due if the agent becomes insolvent or defaults. See Exhibit 2, agents balances over three months due (a nonadmitted asset), for any change from the prior year.

Reinsurance. Deduct from assets any reinsurance premiums (Line 9 and 11 of Page 2) held by, or loss recoveries due from, reinsurers which became insolvent after the Statement date unless the company has cash withheld or an irrevocable letter of credit for the unpaid loss. See Schedule F — Part 1A and Part 2. Carriers who "front" are especially vulnerable to nonrecoverable loss funds.

Testing of Liabilities. The loss reserves shown in Col. 5 of Part 3A of the Underwriting and Investment Exhibit (Page 10) are broken down by accident year in Schedules O & P, which show the changes or "development" of values from prior Statements to the current Statement. To determine whether the reserves are understated or overstated is an impossible task without a comprehensive claim audit; but the Statement does give a valuable overview.

Schedule O (Loss Reserves). Schedule O — Part 1 — deals with the lines of business whose claims are usually settled within two years (accident and health, fidelity, surety, and physical damage other than Homeowners, commercial multi-peril, marine, aircraft, boiler and machinery), and shows the difference between: 1) the reserves shown in the Statement at date of accident, and 2) the payment of those losses in the current year, plus the remaining reserve in the current Statement, including IBNR. Theoretically, the difference should be zero if the reserves set up originally were accurate. If 2) exceeds 1) by a substantial percent, as respects the reserves for unpaid losses two years prior to the current year (Col. 19) because the reserves were short two years prior, then that shortage (Col. 19 divided by Col. 17) should be added to the current reserves on the assumption that the current reserves may be short by the same percent. Accident and health is the line most likely to produce reserve shortages when business recession encourages claimants to extend their periods of disability beyond the period that the insurer considered necessary in estimating the needed reserve.

Schedule P (Loss Reserves). Schedule P shows development of third party and compensation losses and recasts prior year Statement results to show what those results would have been if the company had used loss data known subsequently. If the loss and loss expense ratio of previous accident years shows a pattern of development in Part 2, that change might be added to or subtracted from the current accident year's loss ratio to indicate the probable development of this accident year five years hence. The current surplus might also be adjusted by multiplying the change factor by premiums earned and adding to or subtracting the product from surplus. Example: 1978 Annual Statement of Company A and Company B, both actual cases.

COMPANY A

Auto Liability 1974 Accident Year Losses incurred

at 1974 Stmt	at 1975 Stmt	at 1976 Stmt	at 1977 Stmt	at 1978 Stmt
63 %	78 %	82 %	92 %	102 %

Auto Liability 1975 Accident Year Losses Incurred

	81 %	101 %	112 %	122 %

Comment: Since 1974 losses increased from 63 % to 102 % in four development years, or thirty-nine points, and since 1975 losses increased from 81 % to 122 % in only three development years, or forty-one points, perhaps forty points should be added to the current accident year losses to estimate that year's development.

COMPANY B

Auto Liability 1974 Accident year Losses Incurred

at 1974 Stmt	at 1975 Stmt	at 1976 Stmt	at 1977 Stmt	At 1978 Stmt
80 %	79 %	81.5 %	79 %	77 %

Auto Liability 1975 Accident Year Losses Incurred

	82 %	83 %	80 %	79 %

Comment: Because 1974 did not significantly change by development during the next four years, and because 1975 losses showed a similar pattern, perhaps three points could be subtracted from the current accident year losses to estimate that year's development.

Changes in loss ratio between accident years may be due to changes in loss retention under reinsurance treaties or changes in primary rate level. Changes in loss ratio of a given accident year as it develops over five to ten years is probably due to inflation and internal forces reflecting personnel, such as consistent failure to admit the true value of claims or consistent overreserving.

Part 3 of Schedule P shows the loss development as respects paid and unpaid claims separately. It shows the portion of paid and unpaid claims on each individual accident year of business, at each year of development. The current year plus six prior years are compared to show the outstanding and paid loss ratios after one year of development; the six prior years are shown after two years of development; the five prior years are shown after three years of development, etc. — each accident year being compared with the "actual" result as developed to the current year, not as originally shown in the Statement for the accident year. One expects the ratios to be consistent at each stage in development, e.g., all third-year figures should be similar. Marked differences in development year ratios reveal changes in the company's willingness or ability to pay losses quickly. For example, if both the 1975 and 1976 accident years produced an 80% loss ratio in the 1978 Statement after three years' development, but Lines 7 and 8 of Schedule P — Part 3B show:

	Acc Yr 75	Acc Yr 76
Line 7 paid losses	35%	20%
Line 8 unpaid losses	45%	60%

then a significant change has occurred in the company's loss settlement practices. Perhaps payments are being avoided to decrease cash outflow. Schedule P shows dramatically the difference in time to develop to payment between short-tail auto liability and CMP versus long-tail malpractice, workers' compensation, and products liability, whose unpaid loss ratios remain a large portion of the total loss ratios after five years of development. A high proportion of unpaid losses after five years of development is a yellow flag; stop and look before proceeding. The high proportion may be acceptable in lines such as workers' compensation but unacceptable if the preponderance of a company's business is in other lines.

Schedule P — Part 1F — shows the breakdown of IBNR applicable to individual accident years for auto and general liability, malpractice, workers' compensation, products liability,[8] and miscellaneous Schedule P classes such as CMP. The grand total of IBNR on all accident years is shown on Page 10 — Underwriting and Investment Exhibit — Part 3A, Cols. 4A and 4B. It is necessary to study five consecutive Annual Statements to see the pattern of IBNR as a percent of current year earned premium, one year prior, two years prior, etc. Certainly, the IBNR amount should reflect change in premium volume. A reduction of IBNR as a percent of current year earned premium, compared to the percent used in the prior year for the same line of business, will wave a flag the color of which may only be determined by further inquiry into the individual characteristics of the company's growth rate and mix of business.

The trend of loss development in Part 2 should be the same as the trend in IBNR in Part 1F. The company has the opportunity to take down "profit" by reducing the current IBNR on previous accident years by an amount greater than the nonappearance of IBNR losses — that is, new cases first reported in the current year, shown as "one year development of IBNR losses" which are paid or first reserved in the current year on accidents in prior years shown on Part 1F, not including changes in reserves on losses first reported in prior Statements (which are included in developments in Parts 2 and 3). The company also has an opportunity to book a "loss" of income by increasing the current IBNR on previous accident years by an amount greater than the appearance of IBNR losses.

The total development or net change of all cases plus IBNR reserves, both new reserves and changes in prior reserves, is found in Part 2 by subtracting the current Statement year total for a given accident year from the adjoining figure for the prior Statement year (1977 incurred losses reported in 1978 Statement minus 1977 incurred losses in 1977 Statement). If one compares this figure with the Part 1F "development" of IBNR only on new cases first set up in 1978 on 1977 accidents, one then sees the amount of development due solely to changes in values during 1978 on losses reported during the accident year 1977. See NAIC Early Warning Tests 9 and 10.

A further clue as to adequacy of reported Schedule P loss reserves is found on Part 1, Col. 8 — "number of claims outstanding." If the number of open cases per million of earned premiums (Col. 2) does not reduce coherently with passage of time (e.g., current year claims at 125 per million dollars of earned premiums; one-year prior claims 24% of cur-

---

[8] First appearing as a supplement to the 1979 Annual Statement.

rent year open case rate equals thirty per million E.P.; claims dated two years prior 9% of current year open cases at eleven per million E.P.; three-year prior claims at five per million E.P., etc.) — then the current loss reserves may be a bomb with a delayed fuse, since the longer claims remain open, the larger they tend to grow. The company may have a high proportion of claims in suit, subject to the vagaries of our legal system. Speed in disposing of claims is as much an index of good claim management as is the sometimes more time-consuming vigorous defense of the claims. The company should achieve a fine balance between early recognition and disposition of meritorious claims versus zealous defense of inflated or fraudulent claims.

The *average value* per claim also indicates the safety versus vulnerability of the total loss reserves. Divide the sum of "losses unpaid" (Col. 9) and "loss expense unpaid" (Col. 10) by the number of outstanding claims (Col. 8), then compare it with the premiums earned during the accident year (Col. 2). If the average value of claims aged more than two years is high (over 20¢ per $100 earned premiums on the line of business), then a deficiency in only a few cases (e.g., a court judgment four times the reserve) could have a severe impact on the adequacy of the total loss reserve.[9] If the average value per claim is low (10¢ per $100 of earned premiums), then the total reserve is relatively safe from future difference between reserve and settled loss amount. If 10% were added to the average claim value of all cases, and this amount is multiplied by the number of outstanding cases, the product should not exceed 10% of the company's surplus if the surplus is adequate.

Contingent Commissions. The reserve for contingent commission (Line 3 of Page 3) is the net difference between commissions owed by the company to its producers (or return commission due reinsurers) and return commission owed to the company (or additional commission due from reinsurers). Distortions are hard to discover without examining original accounts. If the reserve exceeds 3% of earned premiums (Page 4, Line 1), the expense ratio is volatile; the company may be operating with managing general agents whose business may not be stable. The reserve does not include rate adjustment on excess of loss reinsurance ceded.

Borrowed Money. The item, borrowed money (Line 8 of Page 3), represents an extraordinary item in an insurance carrier's Statement, and an explanation should be sought from the company. Borrowing by an upstream holding company is not shown.

---

[9] Potential deficiency is limited by the attachment point of reinsurance. Schedule P shows losses net of reinsurance. Gross losses are not displayed after Page 10.

Unearned Premium Reserve. The amount of unearned premiums (Line 10 of Page 3) is normally an item taken at face value. But the figure could understate or overstate the demand on surplus in some cases. Examples:

— If the company writes a seasonal business such as growing crops, the unearned premium at the peak of the season is high but non-existent at the end. Such a company's surplus should be considered when the unearned is at its peak.

— The method used to compute the reserve could slow down the rate of earning (sum of the digits) and inflate the unearned over the semi-monthly fractional basis.

— Quarterly or other short-term method of billing premium can speed up the rate of earning, can reduce unearned premiums, and can improve surplus.

Penalties for Unauthorized Reinsurance. The amount by which unearned premiums ceded and losses recoverable from unauthorized reinsurers exceed funds held by the company, shown as a liability on Line 15 of Page 3, may be restored to surplus if the reinsurers shown in Schedule F, Part 2, are creditworthy.

Excess of Statutory Reserves Over Statement Reserves. (Line 16 of Page 3) is an unusual reserve, applicable to current plus two prior accident year loss ratios on auto liability, general liability, malpractice, and compensation. The reserve is equal to the difference between the Statement loss ratios and the greater of the lowest loss ratio developed on the five years prior to the most recent three years, adjusting the most recent three years to a minimum of 60% (65% on compensation), but not above 75% (80% on compensation). This prevents understatement of current IBNR below the historical loss development. This penalty may be due to writing high deductible policies which produce loss ratios less than the minimum. If, in fact, the company's loss reserves pass scrutiny, the penalty may be considered as an addition to surplus.

ADJUSTMENTS TO SURPLUS. The import of the above is that Annual Statement figures cannot be taken at face value. Areas in the Statement were selected for comment to stress the fragility of surplus. The strength of the insurance mechanism should not be overlooked, however: chiefly, the fact that time can work to the advantage of the carrier which enjoys an interval between the date of the obligation to pay and the payment date. For example, before cash must be disbursed from what may be inadequate reserves, additional cash will flow into an ongoing organization, giving time to make corrections before the consequences of prior errors must be met.

Further, the funds derived from policyholders, held as unearned premium and loss reserves, are invested on a conservative basis stipulated by state law and regulation. One can reasonably hope that investment income on these reserves will achieve its primary and necessary function: to offset the effect of economic inflation upon loss reserve valuations. It is a difficult if not impossible task to adjust each long-term claim reserve for annual changes in costs of medical care, consumer goods, and other items which determine ultimate claim values. If those items are increasing at a rate per annum roughly equivalent to inflation, the investment income on claim reserves should, at the minimum, match that increment. Of course, the quality of the portfolio investments and their inherent volatility characteristics are an indispensable element in this equation. Any margin available for payment of dividends to policyholders or stockholders exists only after this requirement is satisfied. Unfortunately, investments of reserve funds sometimes produce a loss, draining surplus rather than augmenting it.

The following adjustments to surplus are not necessarily reflected in the Annual Statement but should also be considered:

1) The sum of adjustments required by the above analysis, such as recent appreciation or depreciation of securities; uncollectible reinsurance recoveries or agents balances; shortage or redundancy of loss reserves; audit premiums due on workers' compensation policies, etc.

2) The equity in unearned premium reserves. If the company should reinsure (or sell) its portfolio of in-force policies or run it off to expiration, it will recapture from the reserve (which was set at 100% of the original premiums) part or all of the expenses incurred to acquire those premiums and part or all of the profit margin contained in them. This equity, an increment to surplus, can be calculated in several ways. We shall discuss only two:

a) Actual underwriting expenses incurred, limited to 100% minus the loss and loss expense ratio. The underwriting expenses in total from Line 4 on Page 4 (or Col. 2 of Part 4, Page 11), can be divided by net premiums written (Col. 4, Part C, Page 8), and the quotient is the underwriting expense ratio. The equity might be considered to be that ratio multiplied by the unearned premium reserve.

However, not all of the prepaid expenses are certain of recapture by sale or run-off. The conservative practice used in the NAIC Early Warning Test No. 6 is to compute equity at 50% of the sum of the following items detailed in the Underwriting and Investment Exhibit, Part 4, Col. 2: total underwriting expenses, Line 22, plus net commission and brokerage, Line 2f, plus taxes, licenses and fees, Line 18e (the latter two items being counted twice). One can take equity simply at the sum of commissions and taxes disbursed (Lines 2f plus 18e), giving no credit for overhead expenses.

b) Gross margin: 100% minus average loss and loss expense ratio to earned premiums, multiplied by unearned premiums. Method a) considers earned-incurred loss ratio solely as a ceiling upon credit for prepaid expenses, allowing nothing for profit margin. Method b) includes the profit margin demonstrated by results. One approach is to use the average of five years' losses and loss expenses, plus a 10% loading, divided by five years' earned premiums, taking losses from Lines 2 and 3 on Page 4 of the Statement. This merges the results of all prior accident years which affect the current year's result. The writer feels that the average of the three most recent accident years as developed in Schedules O and P is more significant. Part 3 of Schedule O and Part 1 of Schedule P display these loss ratios nicely. Still more refined methods compute the equity on each separate line of business, depending on its profitability shown in the Insurance Expense Exhibit filed by April 1 of each year.

PROJECTION OF SURPLUS. One can estimate the surplus to be displayed one year subsequent to the current Statement by applying the two-year operating ratio to the projected earned premiums, deducting 100%, then adding the result (if a profit) or deducting the result (if a deficit) from the current surplus, as adjusted in the preceding analysis (disregarding equity). The two-year operating ratio is the sum of:

1) current plus prior year losses and loss adjustment expenses, plus dividends to policyholders, divided by premiums earned;

2) current plus prior year underwriting expenses, divided by net premiums written; and

3) current plus prior year net investment income earned, divided by net premium earned.

This estimate assumes that the future premium income will be similar to the current income. The projection combines NAIC Early Warning Tests 4 and 5.

Other Elements of Fiscal Health. *1. Methods Used to Compute IBNR.* If a substantial and long-term reinsurance commitment is being contemplated, the underwriter should discuss with management its methods used to compute IBNR. The premise of IBNR formulas is that losses emerge evenly in time out of the unearned premium reservoir to reach the ultimate amount. The danger is that the formula will anticipate earnings, perhaps fictitious earnings. Some carriers subtract recorded losses from either i) the original net premium (gross less acquisition costs), or ii) the "permissible" or expected ultimate loss ratio. The balance is posted as IBNR. Such a method fallaciously assumes that the company's rates will produce the intended loss ratio. Problems arise when ultimate recorded losses exceed the expected losses, reducing the IBNR balance to zero (or even a negative figure).

Let us accept the premise that, during the normal course of loss development, behind recorded losses stand unrecorded losses. The IBNR formula should change constantly to reflect the actual level of losses being recorded. Each year of development of prior accident years should trigger an updating of the formula used to estimate the development of the current accident year. Each increment of recorded losses changes the estimate of ultimate losses, e.g., if 1975 recorded losses as of 12/31/78 were 12% greater than the 1975 recorded losses as of 12/31/77, probably 1976 losses will also grow by 12% over their 1978 recorded amounts when recorded at 12/31/79, after the same period of development, if the same causes are at work. IBNR reserve should anticipate this change.

Each insurer develops a pattern of loss development peculiar to its own business, territory and personnel. Let us say auto liability written by the insurer under examination shows a seven-year pattern of development, expressing in column (1) below the cumulative recorded losses (paid plus outstanding) as a percentage of the amount incurred in the seventh year of development. The IBNR is then 100% minus the recorded percent, divided by the recorded percent. The ultimate losses shown in column (2), and IBNR in column (3), are expressed as a percent of *recorded losses.*

(1) Recorded Losses - Cumulative	(2) Ultimate Losses	(3) IBNR
During accident year: 40% ultimate	100/40 = 250. %	60/40 = 150%
At end 1st dev. year: 60% ultimate	100/60 = 166.7%	40/60 = 67%
At end 2nd dev. year: 75% ultimate	100/75 = 133.3%	25/75 = 33%
At end 3rd dev. year: 86% ultimate	100/86 = 116.3 %	14/86 = 16%

Relying on its own pattern, updated for changes in kinds of risks written in the intervening years regardless of "expected" loss ratio, the insurer would estimate the ultimate losses in the accident year two years prior to the current year by multiplying the cumulative recorded losses of that year by 1.333. The insurer would set an IBNR equal to the difference between the ultimate and recorded losses, being 33% of recorded and 25 % of projected ultimate losses. This method is completely responsive to current conditions and is self-adjusting because the development pattern is restated annually.

It should be kept in mind that recent change in loss reserving practice, perhaps due to financial pressure on management or change in claim department personnel, is not discoverable from prior loss development. If prior case loss reserves were accurate while current ones are not, application of loss development factors derived from the previous pattern to current year losses will not produce accurate current year ultimate losses. Tests of adequacy of Schedule P loss reserves (such as NAIC Tests No. 9 and 10) only measure reserves aged four to five years. The function of IBNR — to convert partial incurred amounts to those ultimately to be recorded — is achieved only if case reserves are accurate. The bias in the claim department to approach the ultimate amount in steps or to anticipate the worst at the earliest date of evidence is best discovered by the claim audit procedure.

If time permits, the reinsurer can ask the broker or client to prepare an exhibit of losses by line of business, incurred in each of the past accident years as recorded (excluding IBNR) at the end of each calendar year of development (e.g., 1974 workers' compensation losses as of 12/31/74, 12/31/75, 12/31/76, etc.) until development ceases. This will show the percent of ultimate losses recorded as the accident years progress to settlement.

But we can also make a crude estimate of the loss development pattern from six consecutive Annual Statements. Subtract the IBNR losses shown in Cols. 2-6 of Schedule P - Part 1F, set up in each Statement as respects each active year, from the incurred loss totals shown in Part 2 for the same Statement year. For example, in the 1978 Statement, from 1978 incurred loss Col. 7, subtract the sum of IBNR amounts from Part 1F for the accident year 1973; next, deduct the IBNR on accident year 1974, etc. Repeat this process with each of the six Statements until all IBNR figures included in Part 2 totals have been purged. Then losses recorded in accident year 1973 can be divided into the recorded amount of 1973 losses as shown in the 1978 Statement, etc. Assume the figure recorded in the fifth year of development (1978) for auto liability is at least 96 % of ultimate. The ratio of 1973 recorded losses during the first development year is 1973 recorded losses recorded at 12/31/74 divided by the amount recorded at 12/31/78; the second, third, and fourth development ratios to "ultimate" are computed in like manner. One can then compare the IBNR projected from these development ratios with the IBNR used by the insurer.

2. Underwriting Leverage. a) Subsidiaries as financial leverage. Statutory accounting practice permits insurers to treat as an admitted asset any subsidiary insurer they may own, carried at statutory book value (excluding equity in unearned premiums). Each carrier can expand premium volume on its own net worth, although the same surplus is used twice or as many times as the number of subsidiaries riding on the same surplus. Whereas increased premium volume is expected to produce increased underwriting stability, allowing the insurer to absorb larger dollar-sized losses as a smaller percent of premium volume — when the volume is leveraged on thin capital, a flaw anywhere in the pyramid may trigger a collapse. So, the group may be weaker than one subsidiary.[10]

If an insolvent insurer is a subsidiary of a solvent parent, the uninitiated might think that debts of the subsidiary can be recovered from the parent. But the same "corporate veil" that shields the individual shareholders from liability for a corporation's debts also protects the parent company shareholder from the debts of an insolvent subsidiary. The insurance company parent may be subject to regulatory influence, however.

b) Dangers of leverage. The ratio of premium writings to surplus is "underwriting leverage."[11] Writings generate claims, thence are transformed into loss reserves at 100 % of premiums written minus expenses and profit. Loss reserves grow with time since they are fed by social and economic inflation and the necessary lag time to develop facts. Therefore, loss reserves *cumulate* without any change in claim count per million dollars of premium or even change in policy limits written, to become in aggregate several times larger than the policyholder surplus which was the initial limiting measure of the premium volume which started the flow of cash into reserves.

Whatever target regulatory authorities set on premium writings as a multiple of surplus is the leverage factor available to management. Let us say the limit for our carrier is a multiple of three. (If surplus is cloned into four parts, the parent's surplus plus the surplus of three subsidiaries each having surplus equal to one-half the surplus of the parent, the multiple is higher: 2.5 x 3.) Assume management desires to maximize the cash flow into its organization and views each surplus dollar as a license to triple that dollar. Surplus funds are the insurer's own funds. Loss reserves

---

[10] The value of a subsidiary can also be understated. e.g., a property/casualty carrier might carry as an asset only the statutory surplus of a solid life subsidiary having a much higher market value.

[11] This concept was developed by Leandro S. Galban, Jr., now vice president and senior insurance analyst of Donaldson, Lufkin & Jenrette, New York, N.Y., in an address entitled "Leverage and Capital in the Property and Liability Business," delivered October 2, 1977, at the annual meeting of The National Association of Casualty and Surety Executives.

are policyholder funds: the leverage effect is that the insurer uses the policyholder funds, when transformed into investment-earning loss reserves, to transform one surplus dollar into three loss reserve dollars. But this leverage can work against management as easily as it can work for management if the losses grow (without protection of a stop-loss excess of aggregate reinsurance cover) faster than investment income plus earned premium minus the claim payout rate.

The accumulation of loss reserves to become several times greater than policyholder surplus derives from the holding of a portion of each year's premium income in the investment portfolio for a number of years from initial reserve until claim payment. The longer the "tail" of the business, the longer is this period. We illustrate below the cumulative loss reserves on a mature book of casualty losses when the claim payout rate runs ten years. Though the industry norm as reflected in NAIC Early Warning Test No. 2 is that a growth rate of 33 % is not unusual, all other factors being sound, we illustrate a 20 % [12] compound rate of growth on premium writings. Assume a 2 % profit factor, 28 % expense factor, leaving 70 % available for claims; then funds held in reserves from prior-year writings cumulate as follows:

(Current surplus: $43 million; surplus eight years prior: $10 million)

Underwriting Year	P. Writings at 20% Growth	Permissible Loss at 70%	Current Yr. Payments	Cumulative Payments	Balance in Reserves
8 Yr. Prior	$ 30 Million	$ 21.0 Million	02 %	99 %	01 %	210,000
7 Yr. Prior	36 Million	25.2 Million	04 %	97 %	03 %	756,000
6 Yr. Prior	43 Million	30.0 Million	12 %	93 %	07 %	2,107,000
5 Yr. Prior	52 Million	36.4 Million	16 %	81 %	19 %	6,916,000
4 Yr. Prior	62 Million	43.4 Million	22 %	65 %	35 %	15,190,000
3 Yr. Prior	75 Million	52.5 Million	20 %	43 %	57 %	29,925,000
2 Yr. Prior	90 Million	63.0 Million	16 %	23 %	77 %	48,510,000
1 Yr. Prior	108 Million	75.6 Million	05 %	07 %	93 %	70,308,000
Current Year	129 Million	90.3 Million	02 %	02 %	98 %	88,494,000
						$262,416,000

The loss reserves at the current year, derived from nine years of writings, are 203 % of current writings and 610 % of current surplus as regards policyholders. How big is the margin for error? A 10 % deficiency in reserves would reduce surplus to $16.7 million, mandating a maximum net premium volume of $50 million next year if the deficiency is discovered now. What investment income did loss reserves produce?

---

[12] If 20 % growth rate includes 8 % monetary appreciation in constant dollars, the $30 million initial premium translates to $55.5 million and the $10 million initial surplus translates to $18.5 million. The real growth rate is 12 %.

3. Rate Level. Inadequate primary rates are the largest single cause of deficits incurred by insurers and their reinsurers. While only one filed rate may be available for a risk in a given classification, the rate may be high or low for the individual risk. The job of the underwriter is to select the risk for which the available rate is adequate and decline all others; or make a special filing for the risk; or request the insured to consent to a higher rate; or apply a deductible or self-insured retention or participation in loss; or redefine the basis of valuation of insured property or definition of persons insured, etc. Each company operates in a different environment, ranging from full rating freedom to none. The company may be locked into a dividend or rate discount scheme which might have been derived from prior operations which differ from the present situation. The reinsurance underwriter must look into these questions and determine how the company's rates and underwriting modifications compare with competitors writing the same risks at a profit.

The rating environment determines the turn-around time: how soon the profitability of the business can be changed by changing rates. In some states, thanks to bureaucratic delay and political sensitivity, the ability to rapidly adjust rates for personal lines is restricted. Rate flexibility on commercial lines is limited by forces of competition: to hold good business, the company can charge no more than others do for average business. Within the constriction of competition, the secret to success is the primary underwriter's ability to find the above average risk in the class which is not underrated for its characteristics. Those reinsurance underwriters most recently from the ranks of primary insurers often provide valuable insights into the standard books of property and casualty business, particularly in personal lines or small commercial business.

A reinsurer having a facultative reinsurance or a primary insurance facility has an advantage which can be used to evaluate commercial rates. Facultative or primary underwriters can examine a sample of the company's policies to compare the rates with the rates charged by others who write the same kind of risk in the same territory.

The reinsurer may be able to influence the primary carrier's rate level, or may not. Suggestions, such as different increased limit tables, territorial variations, loss control procedures determining rate credits or debits, may be welcome, or not. These matters concern the underwriting of the reinsurance cover offered to the carrier, discussed in other chapters. Except for experimental classes developed in full partnership with the reinsurer, the reinsured has full responsibility for its rates. Only after detailed probing, when the reinsurer is satisfied that the primary rate level is adequate, should the reinsurance cover be offered.

4. *Diversification.* Fiscal health is enhanced when all the eggs are not in one basket. The reinsurer prefers to find that the reinsured has several diverse books of business which do not depend upon the same fortunes. The opportunities for profit and loss should be balanced. For example, a company devoted exclusively to property insurance in a hurricane area or to one product line may not have a healthy future. If the business depends upon the resourcefulness and integrity of one managing general agent, that agent should be the proper target of the fiscal analysis; but public information in that case is scarce.

On the other hand, the carrier which either spreads its resources too thin in trying to write all lines, or spreads out into a larger territory than its underwriting personnel can deal with effectively, gets into trouble quicker than the carrier which specializes in one product line and concentrates on its own backyard. The danger is that the carrier will push into new territory before it is ready with people, funds and know-how.

5. *Depth of Staff.* The quality of an insurer's staff is important, particularly in the claim department. A carrier suffers indigestion when work flow backs up because production is ahead of underwriting and claim handling. Then policy dailies and claims get lost in a bottom drawer. One check is the new claim count compared with the count two years prior, and the number of personnel at both dates. A healthy company is not buried under unprocessed paper, but is busy. The workload status can only be known by a personal visit.

6. *Credibility of Results.* The volume written by the carrier may be too small to produce credible results, or current underwriting programs may be too recently developed to assess. The reinsurer's underwriting problem is to determine whether the statistical results displayed to it represent the same business to be written under the proposed reinsurance cover. The carrier being examined may not be the same as the carrier which produced the results displayed.

7. *Policy Terms.* The turn-around time depends upon the period that policies must remain in force at the same rates. Auto vendors' single interest policies can run for five years at the rate prevailing when the auto was financed by the bank. Allowing for the depreciation of the amount of insurance as the auto ages, and considering the ratio between loan balance and the owner's equity, is the current rate adequate? The Annual Statement, Part 2B (Page 8) displays the split between short-term and long-term policies. The shorter the policy terms, the better the company's control of its near-future results. (If the proposed treaty requires the reinsurer to run off the portfolio at termination of the treaty, long policy terms require the reinsurer to forecast results accurately.)

8. Effects of Previous and Existing Reinsurance. The reinsurance underwriter cannot focus its attention solely upon the business to be written in the future under the reinsurance contemplated. The terms of previous reinsurance may affect the health of the carrier and of any new insurance being contemplated.

—Prior reinsurance may be subject to an annual aggregate deductible which grows with subject premiums. Has the carrier reserved for this deductible? Loss retention may be indexed. Are the extra retentions reserved, or will they be paid out of surplus?

—Prior reinsurance may be subject to an annual aggregate limit. Are some claims not recoverable from reinsurers, or will they be paid out of surplus?

—Prior reinsurance may be adjustable with reinsurer's losses. Is this adjustment reserved, or will it be paid out of surplus?

—A general quota share treaty may require that all reinsurance protection inures to the benefit of the quota share reinsurer. The contemplated reinsurance, therefore, applies to a larger gross line than developed in the company's net retained history. Were the statistics prepared on that basis?

—Cancellation of existing reinsurance may require return of advance commission, which will reduce the company's present surplus.

—Cancellation terms of existing reinsurance might provide that the in-force portfolio will not be returned by the prior reinsurer (for transfer to a new reinsurer) until all losses have been run off or until the premium has been adjusted. The company might owe the portfolio to the new reinsurer but have no funds to pay.

Will The Marriage Be Happy?

Often grounds for divorce were evident to an objective observer before the marriage, and should have been recognized by the parties before they contracted to live together. A reinsurer's realistic appraisal of how happy the proposed marriage might be should include the following considerations:

1. Support. Does the prospect have, in fact, the premium volume promised and needed to support the capacity requested? Many proposals have been based on wildly optimistic production goals.

2. Reasonable Capacity Requirements. Will the treaty capacity requested strain the reinsurer's resources? Will the client escalate its demands for capacity soon after the reinsurance commences? Knowing the size of risks in the field in which the reinsured wants to write, the reinsurer should be able to forecast whether the capacity initially contemplated will be sufficient to penetrate the market and to satisfy the client's need to compete. If the reinsurer should extend its capacity beyond the level it can prudently afford, at especially good terms in the desire to capture the insurer's entire account or acquire "control" or a degree of dominance which might assist the reinsurer to obtain adjustments for experience and/or sweep in collateral business, it might be unpleasantly surprised to find itself reduced to a minor role in the future when the stakes of the game escalate out of its reach.

3. Balance. Does the proposed cover have a good ratio between limit of cover and annual premium net of acquisition costs? While this may be an inappropriate consideration for a catastrophe cover, it is a useful rule of thumb to be employed in other areas. Balance is an aspect of the first two considerations. This concept is elaborated elsewhere in this text, considering the ability of the cover's premium to absorb losses.

Balance within kinds of exposures is equally important. An ancillary class of business, representing a small portion of the subject business, should not be capable of producing losses greater than the profit potential on the entire account. If the reinsured wishes to venture into North Sea drilling rigs and asks the reinsurer to follow, certainly the experience should be combined with the main book of business for rating purposes if the accommodation is truly linked to the main book of business.

4. Competitive Vulnerability. Does the prospect have a sufficient share of the market to be able to influence rates and terms and quality of risks written?

5. Fair Dealing. What is the prospect's record of negotiation for equitable terms? What is its concept of the "good faith" obligations of the reinsured to the reinsurer? Is the reinsured open minded to the reinsurer's point of view? Will it willingly adjust terms to results?

6. Need for the Cover. Is it an essential part of the prospect's underwriting facility?

7. Profit Record. Have both the prospect and its reinsurers made a profit on the business under discussion?

8. Information Output and Access. Does the prospect have good information about its risks in-force, classifications written by policy limit, premium size, coverage, source, location, etc., and quality appraisals? Will the prospect disclose this information in a continuous process of communication to enable the reinsurer to forecast the future objectively?

Are channels of communication open so the two parties can try to solve problems cooperatively?

This question is not meant to categorize as unworthy those carriers which do not communicate beyond the data required to be reported in the treaty. It is simply raised as a point to consider when forecasting the happiness of the reinsurance relationship. Many reinsureds do not take advantage of help the reinsurer would like to offer if asked, or do not let the reinsurer know that help is needed until the results speak for themselves. The attitude of most reinsurers is: let me understand what you are doing, and I will try to give an intelligent contribution. Some carriers prefer to limit the reinsurer's access to information, and in periods of prosperity this policy does not hurt the relationship; but the reinsured which has kept the reinsurer informed will find that such a policy produces great benefits in time of trouble.

9. Claim Handling Capability. If the treaty covers a special risk outside of the cedent's normal business, has a firm of claim specialists been mutually agreed upon?

10. Accounting Promptness and Accuracy.

11. Prompt Payment of Balances.

12. Trends. Is the company moving forward or falling back? What is the five-year progress of surplus, premiums, net income?

13. Morale. Is the staff happy or just doing a job? How long has the current staff been on the scene? Is it coming, staying, or going? Are the departments talking to each other, helping each other?

Those reinsurers which operate through brokers upon a fractional, "following" participation may not be as concerned with the above questions as those which assume responsibility for the entire relationship. The focus of the former may be on one year's result at a time, feeling less of an obligation to preserve continuity if the annual results are not satisfactory, while the reinsurer which undertakes all or a leading share of the reinsurance risk must have wide side-vision. A first class professional reinsurance intermediary can be expected to screen potential clients, to avoid representing unsound or untrustworthy carriers, and to act as a buffer between the reinsurer and those carriers whose needs the reinsurer is unable or unwilling to service.

The Problem of Responsibility

The reinsurer should be cautious about entering a situation of mutual dependency, where the size of the assumed account can have a critical effect upon the reinsurer's overall results and where the size or exclusivity of the account ceded to the reinsurer can have a critical effect upon the cedent's overall results if the reinsurance should be cancelled or drastically altered. Many reinsurers decline 100% account assumptions to avoid the responsibility they entail. When the reinsurer shares a treaty or a part of an account segmented into several treaties with many reinsurers, it maintains an independent flexibility. On the other hand, if the reinsurer allows one account to dominate its portfolio, it becomes a captive to the account's fortunes. Afraid to lose the account, the reinsurer may adopt a weak or passive negotiating posture, may fail to insist upon corrective action or may become blind to situations needing correction, and may even lose objectivity and realistic judgment. Conversely, if the reinsured is dominated by one reinsurer, the consequences can be equally unhealthy because options and points of view become limited.

Whether operating singly or collectively, the reinsurers have responsibility to act responsibly:

—not to give an undeserved or unearned subsidy, which will temporarily inflate and overstate the reinsured's profit;

—not to give the reinsured leverage beyond its ability to use it economically; and

—not to capriciously extend capacity upon which the reinsured becomes dependent.

If a reinsurer elects to enter into a new reinsurance relationship, the reinsurer hopes to find a compatibility, not necessarily in an emotional sense, but in honest recognition of mutual dependence. And, in a warm spirit of candor, it expects that both parties will cooperate beyond the letter of the written contract to accommodate the interests of each other. Although the reinsurer is selling a service for a profit, it knows that the two parties are joined by self-interest and it is the best interest of each to seek a fair balancing of advantages which the reinsurance relationship should bring to both if they do their job well.

Summary

The reinsurer evaluates the reinsured when it has been submitted a treaty for consideration, when it is called upon to advise the reinsured as to the structuring of desired coverage, when changes in existing treaties are requested, and as a part of its normal anniversary review process. The essential risk to be underwritten is the character, integrity, and ability of the reinsured.

The analysis follows from the nature of reinsurance: dealings between reinsurer and reinsured must be characterized by utmost good faith. The relationship in most cases will be long-term. Both reinsurer and reinsured must profit from the relationship.

Reinsurance can be compared to the extension of a line of credit. Although the reinsured is not legally obligated to repay the reinsurer, there is a moral obligation to do so that is based upon trust, mutual confidence, and the sharing of good and bad fortunes. In addition, the reinsurer extends credit to the reinsured in other ways: by assuming the reinsured's unearned premium reserves and loss reserves, by assuming liability for prepaid acquisition costs, and by lending its good name to the reinsured.

In evaluating the reinsured's creditworthiness, the reinsurer must be satisfied that any deficit produced by a treaty will be covered by premiums over a reasonable time period. If the period is particularly long, the reinsurer must be particularly careful. There are four elements to this consideration: time, potential deficit, expectation of payback, and the willingness and ability of the reinsured to cover a potential deficit. The reinsurer must determine a minimum "safe period" for the reinsured to remain fiscally healthy so that the reinsured is able to complete all of its reinsurance obligations. The safe period will depend upon the nature of the treaty.

What specific creditworthy characteristics should the reinsurer require? These should include: adequate and verifiable surplus, operating profitablity, adequate loss reserves, conservative investment practices, responsible, creative and energetic personnel, and owners free of conflicting motivations. Adequacy of surplus must be measured against the potential demand that might be made thereon: net policy limits, catastrophe loss exposures, and potential operating and investment deficits. In appraising this, the reinsurer should carefully review the assets and liabilities section of the reinsured's NAIC Annual Statement to determine that assets and liabilities are not understated or overstated. Adjustments to surplus that are not reflected in the review of the Annual Statement should also be considered, the most important being the equity in the unearned premium reserve.

The above will give the reinsurer an immediate perspective of the reinsured's fiscal health. Other considerations that will allow a projection of fiscal health two or more years into the future are: methods used by the reinsured to compute IBNR loss reserves, underwriting leverage, rate levels, diversification, depth of staff, credibility of results, policy terms, and the effects of previous and existing reinsurance.

The reinsurer must make an overall appraisal as to whether
surance relationship will be, or will continue to be, successful. ...
this, the reinsurer might ask the following:

—Is there enough premium available to support the treaty's capacity?

—Are capacity requirements reasonable?

—Is there a proper balance between the treaty's net annual premiums
and the requested capacity?

—Is the reinsured vulnerable to unusual or unforeseen competitive
pressures?

—Will the relationship be one of fair dealings?

—Is there a legitimate need for the treaty?

—Has the reinsured made a profit for itself and its reinsurers, and will
this continue?

—Does the reinsured have good information about its risks and is it
available to the reinsurer?

Lastly, in a reinsurance relationship, the reinsurer seeks compatibility
in the sense of there being an honest recognition of mutual dependence
based on a spirit of candor. It expects that both parties will operate
beyond the letter of the written agreement. In the end, the reinsurer
knows that it is in the best interest of both parties to seek a fair balancing
of advantages if each is to do its job well.

*   *   *   *   *   *

About the Author of Chapter 14

*A native of Budapest, Hungary, Laszlo K. Gonye was born in February,
1922. He was educated at St. Benedict College, receiving his baccalaureate
degree in arts and sciences in 1941. The ensuing year he was awarded the
M.A. degree in jurisprudence by P. Pazmany University. Following this, he
completed his doctoral work at P. Pazmany University and received a Ph.D. in
political science. His early career included various assignments for the
Hungarian Foreign Trade Board and as a commercial diplomat in Vienna in
the late 1940's.*

*After coming to the United States, Dr. Gonye worked on his master's
degree in economics at Northwestern University, Evanston, Illinois, which he
completed in 1960. That year he embarked on his insurance career starting
with the Allstate Insurance Companies in their corporate planning unit. He
subsequently assisted in the formation of Allstate's reinsurance department
where he served as assistant manager for six years. In 1966, he joined North*

American Reinsurance Corporation, a Swiss Re group affiliate, as group vice president in charge of management information and analysis. In late 1969, he became associated with Skandia Group in New York as North American Zone chief executive officer and U.S. manager of Skandia's U.S. Branch. He presided over the domestication of Skandia's U.S. Branch in 1974 and now serves as president of Skandia America Reinsurance Corporation and Hudson Insurance Company. In 1977, Dr. Gonye became president of Skandia Corporation, the holding company for Skandia's North American operations, and is similarly identified with Skandia Advisory Service Corporation (organized in 1978), and American-European Reinsurance Corporation (formed in early 1979). In February, 1979, the board of directors of Skandia Insurance Company, Ltd., Stockholm, Sweden, named him a deputy managing director of the parent organization in addition to his North American duties. Dr. Gonye was elected chairman of the Reinsurance Association of America for 1978-1979 following service as vice chairman the preceding year and as secretary-treasurer for two years prior.

15

Administration and Maintenance
of Business in Force

by James D. Koehnen*

Relationships Among the Parties

When a reinsurance relationship is established, the parties to the contract expect to achieve many objectives in addition to indemnification of losses. Most important are the continuing exchange of significant information and provision of services. The value of such a close and continuous relationship is highly beneficial to both parties. The reinsured looks to the reinsurer for advice and help in underwriting its business, in handling its claims, in writing new lines of business, in spotting trends and pitfalls, and in a host of other problem areas where the reinsurer's facilities are extensive and immediately available. The reinsurer expects to share all significant developments experienced by the reinsured, including prompt and accurate reporting of premiums and losses. This chapter will describe the service relationship in terms of the administration and maintenance of business in force, the principal agent of which is the account executive. Additionally discussed will be the difficulties which lead to and can result from the breakdown of the relationship.

THE ACCOUNT EXECUTIVE

Producer, accountant, claimsman, negotiator, underwriter, actuary, educator, statistician, consultant — the account executive is all of these to the reinsured, to some degree, at one time or another. Although he or she may not be a specialist in all of these functions, there must be sufficient knowledge in each area to satisfactorily counsel the reinsured client.

---

*President, American Re-Insurance Company, One Liberty Plaza, New York, New York 10006.

This is true whether the account executive represents a reinsurance company or a reinsurance brokerage firm. Indeed, the responsibility is great, and his or her efficiency probably can be measured by a simple test of wisdom: to know what one knows, to know what one does not know, and to know the difference between the two. As the information required by the reinsured becomes more detailed, the account executive must seek assistance elsewhere — either within the company being represented, or if functioning in the brokerage market, from one of the participating reinsurers.

The situations in which the account executive can be useful to the reinsured are many and varied. For example, a slight change in the law may greatly change the experience on business flowing into a treaty, requiring intimate knowledge of treaty terms and the likely ramifications of the new law. Reinsurance underwriters, actuaries or attorneys may have to be contacted to interpret and quantify the impact, so that the account executive can discuss the subject knowledgeably with the reinsured. Reinsurers have a good overview of insurance industry problems, because they deal with many different insurers and have membership in trade associations. Solutions to problems achieved in one area of business can be shared with the reinsureds in another. When the reinsured contemplates writing a new class of business, the account executive can offer valuable advice in reviewing and analyzing marketing strategy. For all practical purposes, the account executive is the "reinsurance company" to the reinsured company, conveying to the reinsured the philosophies and ideas of its management. The executive must establish a relationship of mutual trust and understanding, with strong emphasis on the principle of "utmost good faith." Services rendered should look toward a long-term relationship; any other basis will not provide opportunity for adaptation of the contract to suit the business experience and practices of the reinsured.

When the account executive performs for a reinsurance broker, the function is somewhat different, although responsibility remains for all matters pertaining to the reinsured client. In such a role the account executive is responsible to two parties — the ceding insurance company and the reinsurance company. Success is measured by the excellence of performance as an intermediary between the two parties. It is the executive's responsibility to bring them together, help resolve any differences, and complete a mutually satisfactory contract.

A proper reinsurance relationship resembles a partnership — working together for a common good. It requires constant communication between both parties and adjustments, if necessary, to the ongoing reinsurance program. The responsibility for making the "partnership" work must be shared — both the reinsured and its representatives and the reinsurer and the account executive must contribute equally. While personal relationships will develop in any business endeavor, it is important that a reinsurance arrangement should not be consummated or maintained solely for that reason. The reinsured company should periodically evaluate the counsel and assistance provided, and the account executive must make certain that its services are consistently of the highest quality.

In keeping with that high quality, all parties in the reinsurance relationship must strive in every way possible to avoid any conflict of interest. Because information exchanged between the parties is of a confidential nature — financial, underwriting, and claims — the potential for a conflict of interest is ever present.

The elements that create a conflict appear with less frequency between two reinsurance companies, or between two reinsurance brokers, or even between a reinsurance company and a reinsurance broker. In such situations, the parties normally are competing for a primary insurance company's business or, as a result of sharing an account, are working together for the joint benefit of the primary company.

The most frequent difficulty arises in the claims area, when two or more direct writing reinsured companies report the same claim to their same reinsurer. The situation can be further aggravated when the reinsurer is a "lead" reinsurer[1] rather than a "following" reinsurer.[2] The moment the reinsurer becomes aware that a claim has been reported by two different reinsureds, there is an immediate obligation to handle each company's file on a confidential basis as if it were the only reported claim for that particular loss. Due to both legal and technical complications, most reinsurance companies promptly advise their reinsureds of the conflict of interest and request that they receive only that information which the reinsureds wish to forward voluntarily. Despite such precautions, however, the reinsurer still must reserve its files adequately and sometimes report the matter to its own reinsurer. To properly evaluate the situation, the reinsurer must review two or more files each time additional information is received, fully realizing that new information on one file may affect the other and that only one of the reinsureds may be privy to the information.

The matter becomes further complicated if the reinsureds have different retentions, such as $25,000 and $500,000, where there is an

---

[1] The reinsurer which initiates and/or controls an account.

[2] The reinsurer which participates in an account either by invitation of the lead reinsurer or the reinsured.

overall cover of $1,000,000. If the final, adjudicated loss is $200,000, against both reinsureds equally, the reinsurer will obviously pay a great deal more than if the company with the $500,000 retention paid it all in a prior, pre-trial settlement. The reinsurer must proceed with extreme caution. It is entirely possible that the company with the $500,000 retention should pay the loss, obviating any payment by the reinsurer, but any such solution must be developed from irrefutable facts and the reinsurer is obliged to take infinite care and to remain scrupulously fair and impartial throughout the negotiations.

When dealing with claims, the variations of conflict of interest are many and diverse. For example, two reinsureds can work to the disadvantage of one reinsurer; one reinsured may favor its current reinsurer over a cancelled reinsurer; a reinsurance broker may bring pressure to bear in behalf of one reinsurer over another; or even a reinsurer may be tempted to favor a long-standing client over a new one. In practice, however, few conflicts are permitted to occur because of reinsurers' strict adherence to impartiality, and to dedicated conformance to the practice of utmost good faith.

THE REINSURER AS ADVISER AND CONSULTANT

It is the function of the reinsurer to provide technical insurance expertise and managerial services that will ably assist the reinsured in the efficient operation of its business. The services might be grouped under four general classifications — underwriting and actuarial, claims and rehabilitation, systems and procedures, and financial.

Underwriting, Including Actuarial. When the opportunity arises for a reinsurer to design a reinsurance program for a prospective reinsured or to evaluate and revise an existing program, the reinsurer can truly act as a consultant. The reinsured's objectives, for the immediate and distant future, should be identified by reviewing its current book of business and evaluating the responsiveness and cost of its present reinsurance program. Its management should be asked to outline carefully what is expected from the ongoing program. Armed with the necessary underwriting and financial information, the reinsurer can then design a reinsurance plan and, after review and discussion, provide a detailed reinsurance program that responds accurately to the needs and expectations of the reinsured.

In constructing a reinsurance program, particular care should be taken in establishing the reinsured's net retention, on both excess of loss and pro rata treaties. Each reinsured must decide how much business it wishes to retain net, based on its particular circumstances. Unfortunately, there is no master formula by which a reinsured can automatically compute the net retention, on a particular class or book of business, that will necessarily prove to be 100% satisfactory. A misjudgment may be made at any time. Therefore, after a reinsurance program has been put in force, the reinsurer must repeatedly update the figures and its analysis to make certain that the reinsurance program continues to be responsive to the reinsured's needs.

There are four situations that routinely require the reinsurer's advice, as well as the ultimate revision of any in-force reinsurance program: a) inflation, b) changes in size or financial strength of the reinsured, c) new coverages or greatly modified existing coverages imposed on the reinsured by statute, and d) expansions of the reinsured's operations into areas where it has had little, if any, prior experience.

a) *Inflation.* Both economic and social inflation have been increasing insured values and the average cost of claims, thus disrupting the originally intended proportioning of risk and premium for many contracts. While equity between the reinsurer and reinsured is maintained on quota share and surplus share contracts, excess of loss and catastrophe covers might no longer generate reinsurance premiums in line with anticipated reinsurance costs, because of the leveraged effect of inflation on losses under such covers.[3] In periods of inflation, fairly frequent revisions might be required simply to maintain the proper balance of premium and loss under reinsurance contracts.

b) *Financial Strength.* If the size and financial strength of the reinsured is growing in proportion to the increasing monetary values of claims brought on by inflation, the reinsurer will typically try to increase the dollar net retention of the reinsured under surplus share, excess of loss, and catastrophe covers. This increase maintains the relative strength of the reinsured's existing protection and keeps it from ceding ever growing amounts of premium to the reinsurer. However, unequal inflation by line might call for different treatment of the components of a multiple line contract, as currently is the case with legal changes impacting workers' compensation, but not liability. As such components diverge, it might be desirable to establish separate retentions or even separate contracts. However, if the reinsured is having financial difficulty, it might not be wise or feasible to adopt either separate retentions or separate contracts. Either approach necessitates retaining increased amounts of potential liability, which means that an entirely different and more supportive

---

[3]See in-depth discussion of inflation in Chapters 7 and 9.

plan would probably be needed. With or without inflation, as the reinsured grows and becomes stronger financially, periodic review and analysis is necessary to determine just how much it can comfortably afford to retain net. Thought may eventually have to be given to the replacement of share reinsurance by less supportive excess coverages.

c) *New Coverages.* When new coverages are required by statute, it normally takes a period of time before there is a reliable indication of their loss experience. In such circumstances, the reinsured has obvious and immediate need of protection, and the reinsurer is usually able to work out an insurance or financial plan that meets this requirement. Because the reinsurer is, in some respects, both banker and insurer rather than just insurer, there are a great variety of solutions available to solve the reinsured's problems.

d) *Untried Business Lines.* A new line of business frequently creates new problems for the reinsured, some of which may not be recognized at first. Perhaps a separate and more flexible treaty should be established temporarily, until the new line has stabilized, rather than expose a smoothly operating existing treaty to potential disruption. Often, the reinsurer has had experience in the new line and can advise the reinsured not only on the best reinsurance approach to use but also on pitfalls to be avoided in the line itself. Frequently, the reinsurance designed will provide start-up financial support.

Claims, Including Rehabilitation. The reinsurer can be of substantial assistance to the reinsured in the claims area, especially on large claims, since a reinsurer works with a great diversity of such incidents. These claims are larger in size, more complex, and involve more serious injuries than those customarily confronting many reinsureds. Having dealt with such cases over a period of many years, the reinsurer can be expected to have developed an expertise in properly evaluating them, in establishing adequate reserves, and in helping to bring these claims to a successful conclusion.

Frequently a reinsured incurs a loss in a geographical area in which it does not normally operate. This is a situation in which the reinsurer can again lend valuable assistance. A reinsurer deals with losses all over the United States on a daily basis, and the names of outstanding adjusters and law firms are maintained on a current basis. Such information can save the reinsured much time, money, and unnecessary effort.

Cooperation between claim departments of the reinsured and the reinsurer is of utmost importance. If the reinsurance program is to function properly, claims must be reported promptly and accurately, so that a proper evaluation may be made and an adequate reserve established. Reinsureds are regularly expected to report to reinsurers claims that potentially may exceed the reinsured's retention on the basis of liability. In addition, many reinsurers now strongly urge reinsureds to immediately report all claims involving the following type losses, irrespective of liability: fatalities, paraplegics and quadriplegics, serious burns, serious brain injuries, or amputation of any extremity. The potential for loss in such cases is tremendous, and the degree of difficulty in properly evaluating that potential is vastly more complex. By virtue of repeated exposure, the reinsurer should be able to give valuable advice on liability and coverage, as well as on the care and cost of serious injury cases.

The larger the physical disability case, the more important is the rehabilitation effort. Massive injury cases often cause complete disruption and frequently permanent impairment of an individual's mental and physical well-being. The path to recovery can be long, arduous, emotionally difficult, and enormously expensive. Specialized, expert care made immediately available can make recovery more probable, improve the chances of return to a useful life, and save hundreds of thousands of dollars. Successful rehabilitation is more likely to occur if the reinsured notifies the reinsurer promptly, so they can work together to achieve their common goal.

Although rehabilitation services vary among reinsurers, medical references and first-hand medical data are frequently contributed through a staff rehabilitation expert. That expert will have a knowledge of hospitals, doctors, and rehabilitation centers, developed from extensive personal experience. When working with a reinsured who has few, if any, employees knowledgeable in this area, such a person can also be invaluable as to services rendered. As an example, an employee of the reinsured can be trained to provide the constant supervision that is required to bring a massive injury case under control quickly, ensuring the greatest chance of recovery possible. Finely tuned claims handling, intelligently administered and operated on the basis of mutual trust and cooperation, can achieve remarkable results.

Systems and Procedures. The accounting, auditing, and data processing departments of the reinsurer can provide valuable guidance to the reinsured company in establishing procedures and controls for compiling and evaluating information that goes well beyond the minimum requirements of the reinsurance arrangements. Of particular significance might be counsel about the types of data processing hardware appropriate to the needs of a growing insurer, and guidance in the implementation of a new data processing system. Also beneficial is advice about the establishment of internal checks and controls that naturally arises out of the accounting and auditing functions of the reinsurer. Proper implementation of systems and procedures will allow for easy and inexpensive adaptations made necessary by changing conditions.

Financial Services. The financial services provided by the reinsurer also may transcend the usual support inherent in reinsurance contracts. The investment department is able to counsel the reinsured, particularly the small reinsured company, concerning market trends and investment alternatives. Additionally, because of the nature of reinsurance, the management of the reinsurer is able to provide intelligent and impartial advice relative to competition and the methods of combating it. Close contact with rating bodies, legislative bureaus, governmental officials and agencies enables reinsurer personnel to give advice in those areas as well.

Knowledge in all these areas can be conveyed in several ways, among which is personal contact between the reinsurer's representative and its counterpart in a reinsured company. Groups can be reached through a lecture, where topics are presented by reinsurance specialists to those interested in the particular specialty. The lecture approach is widely used and effective in industry gatherings where there is a concentration of interested parties. The format can range from speeches with question-and-answer periods to classroom or "round table" discussions with the reinsurance representative often acting as discussion leader. A reinsurer can be helpful in presenting a seminar, perhaps annually, to interested clients in three or four convenient geographical areas, such as New York, Chicago, Atlanta, and San Francisco. The program would typically be divided into several parts to include: fundamentals of reinsurance, property reinsurance, casualty reinsurance, contract language, accounting, and current and future changes anticipated that affect reinsurance. Topics must be prepared with infinite care, and the discussion leader should be an individual of senior position, highly respected in the field. Such seminars are often well received and well worth the effort and study required for their presentation.

Reinsurance Auditing

The Underwriting Audit

Reinsurance treaties contain specific articles defining coverage extended and exclusions, so that the types of business that can be ceded under the treaties are clearly outlined. The underwriting audit augments those articles by enabling the reinsurer to determine if the treaty provisions are being observed. Such an audit also reveals whether there are any substantial changes in underwriting policy, such as the issuance of larger policy limits than permitted, or expansion into new classes of risk not previously written. The audit also examines ceded reinsurance premiums from regular treaty business for errors in overpayment or underpayment, as well as premiums on acceptances of risks which are special exceptions to exclusions under the reinsurance treaty.

When conducting an audit, the reinsurer should look carefully at the type of business being written, the quality of the risks accepted, and the geographic location of those risks. It should also obtain a policy profile of the business in force, which divides a company's policies by class and limits of coverage. Such a study will indicate the primary company's underwriting philosophy and housekeeping. For example, files not in order and information not available when needed for proper risk evaluation may reveal that more attention is needed to improve the quality level of underwriting personnel and the controls exercised over them.

The underwriting audit is a versatile tool useful to both reinsurer and reinsured. For example, an audit of an unprofitable property surplus agreement will reveal to both parties whether bad underwriting by the reinsured company or merely bad luck is responsible. Any corrective action can then be custom designed in light of the facts, since numbers alone cannot give a complete and fair picture of the cause.

The results of a reinsurance audit should be shared with the reinsured company to provide it with an outsider's opinion of its business. Since reinsurers see a diverse spread of business and can compare the underwriting approaches used by many companies, their comments can be of assistance, particularly to small or medium size regional companies.

The Claims Audit

The claims audit by the reinsurer is the review of claim case information from the files of the reinsured company. It is normally accomplished periodically as a cooperative project between the parties, but the reinsurer's right to conduct the audit as a safeguard is usually provided for in the treaty. While the audit is functionally a first line of defense by the reinsurer against misuse of the treaty, it can assume the nature of a service call or goodwill visit. The experienced account executive recognizes the periodic claim audit as affording a singular customer relations opportunity representing a service bridge with the reinsured company over which the benefits flow in both directions. While providing the reinsurer with necessary information, the audit is a check-and-balance for the treatyholder's own claim operation, and thus is welcomed as a valuable service. Although claim audits cover the entire spectrum of business written, the following comments refer primarily to the cases of most serious concern — excess claims.

Purposes. The audit serves three purposes for the reinsurer: technical, treaty, and collateral. The technical purpose is to document the essentials of all active claim cases and selectively share in shaping their outcome. The treaty purpose is the immediate corporate objective: to use the technical input from the audit to test the treaty for current profitability and for permanence. The remote corporate purpose relates to collateral albeit important matters of inter-company relations and maximum service to the treatyholder over the long run.

Technical. The technical purposes of the audit are accomplished via the following steps. 1. First, the applicability of coverage is confirmed or questioned for each case, as to both policy and the reinsurance contract. 2. Then, independent judgment is made by the auditor concerning the degree of any incurred liability under either the policy contract or the reinsurance contract, or both, on the basis of all information contained in the central claim file of the reinsured company. 3. The reinsured company's prospectus for preparation, litigation, settlement, or further investigation of given cases is examined and, if necessary, discussed with the company. 4. The quality, currency and completeness of pertinent investigational field data, as well as the acceptability of defense counsel's analysis based thereon, are appraised. 5. The reliability and reasonableness of the ceded reserve per case are critically examined and refined if necessary in the light of current information.[4] 6. The company's estimate of reserves not yet thought to involve the reinsurer on an excess basis, but above a selected key retention level, is reviewed, and probably additional claims are uncovered. 7. An incurred-but-not-reported (IBNR) study may reveal initial reporting failures by the reinsured to notify the reinsurer promptly of critical case developments, and the claims auditor may seek the counsel of the reinsured's claims manager on the cause and remedy of such problems. 8. Lastly, the claims auditor will offer to assist the reinsured in various other technical ways: the selection of local defense counsel, medical witnesses, or specialized medical facilities; the choice of optimal trial venue; the supplying of any new relevant case law; and guidance on possible vulnerability to an excess judgment or a

---

[4] At this juncture, individual case evaluation and "pricing," in concert with readily accessible on-premises personnel of the reinsured, may save valuable time and effort later on in the life cycle of a given claim file. Early resolution of uncertainties or disagreement, as to the proper excess reserve to be carried, is a necessity for the preservation of a sound and mutually profitable treaty relationship.

punitive damage verdict, against which special protective measures may be indicated.

Treaty. After the above technical studies and reviews are made, a final compilation of case reserves is agreed upon in the field with the reinsured and the reinsurer's claims auditor. The result places in the hands of the account executive the critical data necessary for determining the expected ultimate loss cost of the treaty, with a revised rate possible in reflecting the updated loss development. When the technical input from the audit is used to test the treaty for current profitability and for permanence, the treaty purpose of the claims audit is fulfilled.

Collateral. The technical performance of the reinsured in handling and disposing of its claims is one of the leading indices of general corporate expectations and is so regarded by the professional reinsurer. Invaluable insights are gained by the observant auditor during the study of the reinsured's field supervision and the quality of its work product. These insights are useful to the account executive and the underwriting committee in evaluating a long-range business relationship with the reinsured.

Procedures. The scheduling of the audit is not determined primarily by the technical purposes of the reinsurer's claim department, but rather by the dynamics of the treaty contract. For example, the provisions of the contract covering renewal and termination impose performance dates upon the reinsurer's claim department, as do the provisions for the settlement of retrospective or profit-sharing arrangements. The timing of the audits is, therefore, best determined through close liaison between the auditor and the account executive, the latter being familiar with treaty servicing needs and being responsible for deadline requirements.

Care must be taken to give adequate notice to the reinsured, so that it may prepare the subject files for the auditor's use. In spite of advance preparation, however, some interruption in the normal home office routine of a reinsured is to be anticipated in the hosting of an audit. This interruption is especially likely for those accounts having a sizable inventory of excess claim cases and where the audit requires a significant period of time for completion.

Reinsurer Preparations. In arranging for the audit there are certain preparations by the reinsurer which must be made to insure the success of the undertaking. The auditor must be entirely conversant with the special terms of the reinsurance contract. A quick reference digest of the principal provisions of the contract, pertinent to the claims function, should be prepared for use on location. At an appropriate date, well in advance of the appointed audit, a list of outstanding, reported claim cases should be provided to the reinsured so that the files will be available upon the auditor's arrival.

Simultaneously with the above, the reinsured should be asked to furnish a detailed statistical listing of outstanding cases which have not yet been reported to the reinsurer, but which may represent additional reinsurance exposures. The culling of these cases from the reinsured's general case inventory is possible through the arbitrary selection by the reinsurer of a key case reserve level, pegged to a percentage of the retention, over which all subject claims so reserved must be examined. For example, if a treaty covered the portion of claims greater than $100,000, the reinsurer might request a listing of all claims the reinsured valued at $50,000 or more from the ground up.

The bane of the reinsurer and a problem that requires constant attention is the failure of the reinsured to report claims of which it has knowledge that are likely to involve the reinsurer, the so-called incurred-but-not-reported claims (IBNR). Though some of the reinsurer's IBNR claims are also unreported to the reinsured, this is not typically the situation. The root cause in most instances is a combination of contributory failures on the part of the reinsured's claim supervisory staff, including the under-reserving of claims, and a neglect of the basic treaty obligation to share not only the losses but also the right to involvement in the reserving and in the defense of the claims. Each audit provides a fresh opportunity for the reinsurer to initiate, or renew, the perpetual appeal for faithful performance by the reinsured company of the reporting obligation.

Methods of File Review. There are two methods of individual file review available to the auditor. One is total reliance upon a cover-to-cover review of the reinsured's file. The other is reliance upon interrogation of the responsible supervisor and/or claim manager. In practice there is no substitute for thorough file review; total reliance upon any other source of information is professionally obsolete. In some circumstances the claim file by itself fails to fully provide the necessary answers to basic technical questions, and thus some consultation and interrogation are needed. In others, where unusual handling problems may arise, a discreet mix of the two methods proves most effective.

In the interest of saving time the auditor might be tempted to "read from the top down" and relinquish the opportunity to arrive at an independent appraisal of questions of liability and of appropriate reserve value. In general this temptation is better resisted, although through experience the auditor can learn to discriminate effectively between sources of opinion which are reliable and those less reliable.

The desirability of independent review and appraisal on the part of the auditor cannot be emphasized too strongly. Such independence will be the basis of conviction and authority when consulting with the reinsured's claim personnel on questions of case reserve differences. As far as possible it is the auditor's obligation to reconcile such differences and generate reserve figures both on individual cases and in the aggregate, which the reinsurer's account executive will find supportable when entering rate discussions with the reinsured. The auditor's results and the credibility of the consequent accounting turn less upon one's natural talents for persuasion than upon the accuracy with which one has read the individual claim files during audit.

At the close of the audit, its overall results (insofar as they are known at that juncture) as well as the auditor's observations and suggestions relating to the availability and sufficiency of factual case data are customarily discussed between auditor and claim manager. This discussion not only consolidates common efforts towards common goals but also commits both parties to the recognition of any weak areas in operational as well as technical procedures, shown in relief by the audit.

The auditor's final function is to summarize, in simple and brief form, a list of the dollar figures which represent modification of the outstanding gross incurred loss reserves, in addition to the newly discovered IBNR reserves, confirmed and updated by the audit, and found to be chargeable against the losses assumed by the reinsurer. From this summary, the account executive can derive the net change in the loss account of the concerned treaty. He or she should include, under separate exhibit, the IBNR notices for the creation of new departmental claim files with excess reserves, and mention any new or chronic problems of substance discerned during the audit, but not admitting of resolution on the auditor's own initiative.

Potential Problems

The nature of treaty reinsurance is such that its value to the reinsured and to the reinsurer is only proven on a long-term basis. For this reason the reinsurer considers cancellation of an existing treaty only as a last resort, after failure at all other means of obtaining a reasonably satisfactory solution to the problems at hand. When the reinsured company shares this view, either in the maintenance of a valued relationship or in an effort to cultivate one, the probability of negotiation and compromise is greatly enhanced.

The market for property and casualty reinsurance is quite obviously limited to companies writing these lines of insurance — approximately 1,300 domestic companies in the United States. As many as one hundred reinsurers seek their business, and there are numerous reinsurance brokers actively engaged in the same pursuit. Competition is keen and it behooves the reinsurer to pay particular attention to its existing book of business.

It is true that the current reinsurer, because of its relationship with the reinsured, has the advantageous position; but imaginative and aggressive competition (or uninformed competition) can overcome this advantage. Price competition is particularly hard to deal with by the present reinsurer, since it has all of the information necessary to properly price the cover. The prospective new reinsurer either has a conviction that the program will work at a lower price or is attempting to buy its way into the account. Concessions other than price may also be made to acquire particularly desirable accounts.

The best way for the present reinsurer to defeat its competition is to maintain a good relationship with its reinsured, keep abreast of current trends in the industry, and share its information with the reinsured. Also, the experience under the contract should not be allowed to deteriorate to such an extent that a drastic rate adjustment becomes necessary. Frequent minor increases can be more easily negotiated than an infrequent extreme change.

PRICING ISSUES

The vast majority of cancellations occur through an irreconcilable difference of opinion over the cost of the reinsurance. On excess of loss reinsurance, this disagreement usually concerns the premium charged; on share reinsurance it is the commission returned. And the casualty side of the business inevitably presents the more nettlesome problems because of its "long-tail" nature — policies in which ultimate liability cannot be determined until many years after expiration. The cause of disagreement on third party liability, automobile no-fault, and workers' compensation is the valuation of specific case reserves and the IBNR. On quick settling business, however, the cause of disagreements is often the contradiction that while recent poor experience of the reinsured represents a trend to the reinsurer, it appears as only a statistical aberration to the reinsured.

The long-term nature of casualty business brings forth many legitimate issues for resolution if any agreement on rate is to be reached. These issues begin with differences between reinsured and reinsurer claim departments on individual case reserves and the philosophies underlying them. Both parties try to use the pattern of known losses to statistically predict the final results for any period of accident years. Unfortunately, several IBNR methodologies might be employed, predicated upon differing assumptions about the short and long term rates of change observed in past statistics, and they can and do produce widely divergent results.

Interposed on top of these traditional sore points in excess of loss reinsurance negotiations is the recently perceived necessity of bringing past losses and premiums to present value by means of applying inflation factors to the experience of prior years. Reinsurers have had the problem of educating their reinsured companies on the value of such inflated numbers as a basis for current pricing not unlike that which rating bureaus may have initially faced with regulators when first filing rate revisions using historical data similarly adjusted. The excess of loss reinsurer, however, is more acutely aware of the leveraged impact of economic and social inflation on serious cases; it understands that an accident involving the same set of circumstances has more loss potential today than if it occurred one or more years ago. Past accidents must be viewed at today's cost levels. Such an analysis projects severity and frequency of losses into an excess layer by assuming a recurrence of similar types of losses in the future.

An index clause providing for the upward adjustment of retentions relative to inflation can be used, especially in a negotiation where differences on reserving are wide. In effect, the index clause apportions the cost of inflation between reinsured and reinsurer. However, some reinsureds object to indexing because it takes the certainty out of the reinsurance recoverable on outstanding losses, thus impacting Schedule P development in the Annual Statement. If the reinsured is not willing to pay the price for reinsurance without an index clause or will not consider the clause going forward into the future to mitigate costs, then the reinsurer must make a determination whether to cancel the contract.

Non-Pricing Issues

A number of serious non-price issues exist which can threaten the maintenance of long-term treaty relationships. These involve the very dynamics of the insurance business which cause both intended and unintended changes in the reinsured company's book of business and bring greater pressures to bear on the treaty reinsurance facility. Some issues relate to changes in policy coverage, while others pertain to rating formulas and changes in company growth or management.

In recent years the courts have often broadened the extent of coverage beyond that which was originally contemplated under the policy, and hence under the reinsurance treaty. This broadening is a part of the social inflation affecting all insurers and can lead to a situation where the reinsurer insists on amending the treaty to specifically exclude a certain coverage. If the reinsured will not accept the exclusion, cancellation can result. For example, medical malpractice insurance went from what appeared to be high profitability to being nearly unwritable in a very short period of time, thereby creating serious problems for the companies writing that line and for their reinsurers. Since it was classified as Other Liability in the Annual Statement prior to 1975, it was included under excess of loss treaties covering liability business. If the reinsured continued to write medical malpractice insurance on a primary basis, the reinsurer had a problem in determining the best method of providing the reinsurance. If the reinsurer felt it was necessary to insert an exclusion in the basic treaty and provide a separate facility for medical malpractice reinsurance, and if negotiations on the matter were not successful, the unfortunate final outcome was cancellation of the treaty. Another example of social inflation was the passage of unlimited medical provisions under no-fault automobile financial responsibility laws in a few states. This situation added a new dimension to both underwriting and pricing of covers exposed to this development.

The very wording of the primary policy itself has become a point of serious contention. Opposite interpretations of the basic coverage provided have led to an attempt to clarify the intent of the current wording.

On the rating side, formulas which do not respond quickly enough to the ever-accelerating changes in loss patterns need to be discarded and more responsive ones adopted. For example, prospective formulas using unadjusted data on casualty business or calendar year contingents for long-tail business are out of phase with the inflationary times. Agreement is not always reached on the change desired by one party or the other.

The overall growth of the reinsured or its desire to introduce new product lines or expand geographically can serve to introduce fundamental differences which must be recognized, adapted to, and negotiated. Further, in this situation the reinsurer, through its overview of the market and underwriting experience or through published data from rating bureaus or trade publications, may have information that will help with a reinsured's marketing plans.

Another important continuing consideration for the reinsurer is the overall financial position of the reinsured, although it is much less likely to be a cause of treaty cancellation than the underwriting reasons already described. The company's Annual Statement provides a convenient starting point for any such overall evaluation. Additionally, other monitors can be established through early warning tests or state insurance audit reports on a company's financial condition.

In the event the reinsurer finds a situation has deteriorated to the point where corrective action (i.e., increased rates or adjustments in loss reserving practices, for example) would be ineffective, it must seriously consider more drastic alternatives. If the ceding company's policyholder surplus is impaired, time can be bought by providing a quota share arrangement whereby the reinsured can obtain the needed policyholder surplus relief. However, such assistance would not be offered unless the reinsurer believes that the condition is such that nothing more than a boost in surplus, provided by a quota share treaty, is required. For example, unrealistic claim reserving practices are not cured by policyholder surplus relief; rather, such practices can exacerbate the problem over a period of time.

When the reinsurer is becoming overly exposed by providing services to the reinsured covering certain extracontractual losses (mortgage guarantee and other cut-through endorsements) or is endangering its reputation in the insurance and financial fraternities by becoming party to potentially improper fronting arrangements, it may opt to sever relations with the reinsured company, especially one in danger of insolvency.

It has been recognized that the relationship between the reinsurer and the reinsured company is close to that of a partnership, requiring good communications and a fundamental meeting of minds. Should the reinsured company merge with another insurer or be taken over by another company, the management of the "partner" may be changed. In such a case, the risk to the reinsurer is also changed. Many reinsurance contracts provide that, should there be a change in management of the reinsured company, the reinsurance contract is automatically cancelled. If the reinsurance contract does not so provide, the termination clauses can be evoked by the reinsurer and the treaty is cancelled nevertheless; but the time interval then required frequently runs to the end of the following quarter or even the following year.

State insurance departments often object to such cancellation provisions. Since the merged or acquired company is without reinsurance momentarily, its policyholders and claimants understandably have a temporary reduction in the financial strength behind their insurance protection. Also, if the merged or acquired company is verging on bankruptcy, removal of reinsurance can be the fatal blow. Such objections can frequently be overcome by providing in the reinsurance contract for cancellation in the event of a change in management, except in the case of liquidation, rehabilitation, or conservatorship.

Direct Access and Insolvency

DIRECT ACCESS BY ORIGINAL INSURED OR MORTGAGEE

Does the policyholder insured have any right to payment of a claim by the reinsurer? No. There is no privity of contract between the reinsurer and the original insured, since a reinsurance contract is between the reinsured company and the reinsurer. The original insured, not being a party to the contract, has no rights thereunder.[5]

However, if a policyholder is not satisfied with the financial stability of its insurance company, the policyholder may ask that provision be made with the company's reinsurer so that in the event of insolvency of the insurance company, any part of a loss covered by reinsurance be paid directly to the policyholder. Such protection can be accomplished through a "cut-through endorsement." The "cut-through endorsement" is so named because it provides that the reinsurance claim payment "cuts through" the usual route of payment from reinsured company-to-policyholder and then reinsurer-to-reinsured company, substituting instead the payment route of reinsurer-to-policyholder. The effect is to revise the route of payment only, and there is no increased risk to the reinsurer. There is, however, additional work involved and, unless the policyholder has a large interest or there is substantial premium involved, the reinsurers are reluctant to issue such endorsements. Also, reinsurers are reticent about direct involvement with policyholders.

If a mortgagee is not satisfied with the financial stability of the insurance company from which the mortgagor, the property owner, has secured property insurance, the mortgagee may require a "guarantee endorsement," sometimes called a "mortgagee endorsement." This endorsement is a form of cut-through endorsement which revises the route of payment of the mortgagee's interest in any claim payable under the policy in the event of insolvency of the insurance company. However, what distinguishes the guarantee endorsement from a cut-through endorsement is that the guarantee endorsement will often go beyond the limits of the reinsurance payable by the reinsurer to the reinsured company, and actually provide that the reinsurer be responsible for paying

---

[5]*Fontenot* vs. *Marquette Cas. Co.* 247 So. 2d 572 (1971) citing *Insurance Law* and *Practice* Sec. 7694; 46 C.J.S. *Insurance* Sec. 1232; 44 Am. Jur. 2nd *Insurance* Sec. 1867 Olson, "Reinsurers' Liability to the Insolvent Reinsured." 41 Notre Dame L. 13 (1965).

the full insurance protection provided by the reinsured company to the mortgagee in the event of insolvency of the reinsured company. Since a loss payable by the reinsurer to a mortgagee may go beyond the reinsurance which would be payable to a reinsured company, the reinsurer may be assuming an additional risk in such endorsements. For this reason a fee or additional premium may be charged for each such endorsement issued.

Guarantee endorsements providing for more than the reinsurance are restricted by some state laws to insurance for physical damage to property and payment thereon to mortgagees or other loss payees. Endorsements are attached to the original policy and the reinsurance contract is amended accordingly to provide for issuing these endorsements. The users of either a cut-through endorsement or a guarantee endorsement should examine the contract wording carefully.

Lack of confidence by the mortgagee in a particular insurer may not reflect the mortgagee's adverse concern over the company's financial strength so much as the company's inability to secure a satisfactory financial rating from the insurance industry's financial rating organization, A.M. Best Company. Insurance companies with less than five years of operating experience are routinely excluded from Best ratings, regardless of their financial strength. For such young companies that are financially sound, the availability of a "mortgagee endorsement," by whatever name, is a distinct advantage in improving the marketability of their policies on mortgaged property.

In spite of the supposed lack of privity of contract, direct access to reinsurance proceeds by the original insured can occur through another route in the case of insolvency (bankruptcy) of the insurance company. Reinsurers, operating under the assumed principle that the original insured has no access to reinsurance proceeds, sometimes unintentionally create a direct action for reinsurance proceeds by the original insured. The classic case is the insolvent ceding company with "follow-the-fortunes" language used in its reinsurance contract. Follow-the-fortunes language means just that: the reinsurer will follow the fortunes or be placed in the position of the ceding company. Courts have held on occasion that when this language is in a reinsurance contract and the insurer becomes insolvent, the reinsurer is placed in the position of an insurer and the reinsurance is then payable to the original insured.[6]

Another case where the original insured has access to the reinsurance proceeds occurs when an insurance company wishes to retire

[6]First National Bank of Kansas vs. Higgins, 357 SW 2nd. 139 (1962).

from a line of business. The company can do this by reinsuring 100% of its issued and outstanding policies. This type of reinsurance, known as "bulk reinsurance," usually requires regulatory approval.[7] By assuming 100% reinsurance of the original insurance company's policies, the reinsurer steps into the shoes of the original insurer and is liable to the original insureds as if it were the company originally issuing the policies.

INSOLVENCY AND REINSURANCE

Reinsurance contracts, in general, are contracts of indemnity and not of liability. This means that the reinsurer owes nothing to the reinsured company until such time as the reinsured company pays a claim. Under this principle, if the reinsured company becomes insolvent (bankrupt), the reinsurer owes only that portion of a claim that is actually paid in the insolvency proceeding.[8] For example, in a 50% quota share treaty, if a claim is allowed by the liquidator to a claimant but only 20% of the claim is actually paid by the liquidator because of inadequate funds, the reinsurer contractually owes to the liquidator only 10% of the total allowed claim. However, insurance statutes or regulations will not allow credit for reinsurance ceded unless the reinsurance contract provides that the reinsurance will be payable to the liquidator or the statutory successor of the insolvent company, without diminution because of the insolvency. Under this provision, called the "insolvency clause," the reinsurer in the example cited above owes the full 50% of the allowed claim and not just 10% or one-half of what is actually paid.[9]

When a reinsured company is placed in liquidation (declared bankrupt), the state insurance commissioner is usually appointed liquidator of the company and stands in the place of it.[10] The relation between the reinsurer and the liquidator is, therefore, similar to that between the reinsurer and the reinsured company: the reinsurer should work closely with the liquidator, and vice-versa. Also, it should be remembered that the insolvency or bankruptcy of a reinsured company does not automatically relieve the reinsurer of any of its future responsibilities at that time under the reinsured contract. At company insolvency, the reinsurance contract will usually be cancelled on a "cut-off" basis, meaning the reinsurer is not liable for claims occurring subsequent to the cancellation date. Of course, the reinsurer would return an unearned premium portfolio at the same time.

---

[7] Sec. 77 N.Y. Insurance Law.

[8] *Fidelity & Deposit Co.* vs. *Pink,* 302 U.S. 224 (1937).

[9] Sec. 77 New York Insurance Law.

[10] Sec. 510 et seq. New York Insurance Law.

Recently, there has been a new "party" added to liquidation proceedings: guaranty funds. Such funds, required by almost all states, were created by statute, and receive monies from assessments on all licensed companies writing certain property and casualty lines to pay the debts of any insolvent insurance company in each state.[11] Some funds are funded with pre-assessments before insolvencies occur; others are post-assessment funds. Often these funds, looking for monies from which to be reimbursed once they have paid outstanding claims, attempt to gain access to reinsurance proceeds. As reinsurance contracts are presently constructed, and particulary as modified by the insolvency clause, the guaranty funds have no contractual right to reinsurance proceeds: the reinsurer's relationship is with the liquidator of the insolvent company, and with no one else!

Reinsurance contracts as well as insurance laws and regulations provide that reinsurance proceeds are part of the general funds of the insolvent reinsured company, for the benefit of all creditors, not for the benefit of any particular creditor or any class of creditors. Guaranty funds are a class of creditor, or a particular creditor, and have no preferential rights to reinsurance proceeds. When either a guaranty fund or an original insured, unprotected by a cut-through or guarantee endorsement, attempts to obtain reinsurance proceeds during the course of an insolvency, the liquidator generally sides with the reinsurer. It is the liquidator's duty to marshall all of the assets of the insolvent reinsured company for the benefit of all creditors.[12]

When reinsurance contracts are negotiated through a reinsurance broker or intermediary, the possible insolvency of the broker must be considered. The relationship between the reinsurer and the reinsured company, after the broker's insolvency, is governed by the reinsurance contract, particularly the "intermediary clause" in the contract. That clause appoints the broker and usually provides the manner in which payment between reinsured company and reinsurer is to be made. Additionally, the clause should clearly state either of two provisions: that payment to the broker is payment to the reinsured or reinsurer, or that payment to the broker is not payment to the reinsured or reinsurer, until the money is actually received by either party. The important reason for this is rather apparent, since the provision will determine which party loses at the broker's insolvency. Unless the intermediary clause is carefully

---

[11] Article 14.2 California Insurance Law, Sec. 1063 et seq.

[12] Sec. 510 et seq. New York Insurance Law. See, however, Sec. 1063.2 California Insurance Law and similar laws wherein creditor priority is assigned to the guaranty fund.

worded, the paying party may have to pay again.[13] Recently, the Examiner's Handbook of the National Association of Insurance Commissioners has been amended to provide that no credit for reinsurance should be allowed the ceding company when payment to an intermediary is involved, unless the reinsurer is responsible for the failure of the intermediary to pass on payment to the ceding company or reinsurer. This would appear to discount the importance of equity in the business relationship.

Summary

Looking back, we see that the reinsurer has many roles to play if it is to be an effective partner in a reinsurance contract. The provision of indemnification of losses is only a small part of the potential worth of reinsurance, though some reinsureds, particularly those dealing through brokers, may only be seeking this aspect of reinsurance.

Principally, the ideal reinsurer is a trusted adviser and consultant, providing the benefit of its underwriting, actuarial, and claims handling experience to the reinsured. It must keep current with technological, economic, social, and legal changes taking place to be sure that both it and its client can adapt in a timely manner to the financial implications. In reacting to changes in the environment or changes within the reinsured, the reinsurer must be willing to be financially supportive in an informed manner, thus taking on the roles of either banker or insurer. Further supportive functions of the reinsurer may include the provision of accounting, data processing, auditing and investment advice.

The reinsurance partnership must involve a two-way flow of information and be mutually beneficial financially. To this end, the claims and underwriting audit assist the reinsurer in addition to the reinsured, though these audits should only be a supplement to information flowing by means of the normal reporting disciplines. From such information the reinsurer is able to maintain a pricing and underwriting structure responsive to its financial exposures, and the reinsured is able to receive the benefit of an outsider's opinion of its operation.

If substantive problems arise with respect to the underwriting or reserving practices of the reinsured in the eyes of the reinsurer, or if a major difference in opinion about the proper cost of the reinsurance cannot be resolved, the reinsurer may have to make the difficult decision to

---

[13] For examples of the many problems that can arise when a reinsurance broker or intermediary becomes insolvent, see the many proceedings involving the bankruptcy of Pritchard & Baird, New Jersey reinsurance intermediaries. (U.S. DC, District of N.J., No. B-75-3202)

terminate the reinsurance relationship. Financial problems on the part of the reinsured might also force this action, though the reinsurer would typically come to the aid of a company with sound management that could be expected to work its way out of temporary difficulties.

In the event a reinsured becomes insolvent, its reinsurer may find itself obligated to pay the reinsurance directly to an insured of the insolvent company, since the reinsurer may have created a contract of liability because of careless contract wording. Or the reinsurer may have provided cut-through endorsements which would cover payments of the reinsurance to insureds. Both of these actions require the reinsurer to pay the insured directly to the extent of the reinsurance loss. If the reinsurer has provided a guarantee endorsement to a mortgagee, which is a form of cut-through endorsement, it may be responsible to pay the full insured loss to the extent of the mortgagee's interest in excess of any reinsurance payable. When insolvency clauses are involved, as required by state regulations, the situation becomes increasingly more confusing and potentially more expensive.

* * * * * *

About the Author of Chapter 15

James D. Koehnen was born in Chaska, Minnesota, on October 27, 1920. He was educated at Seattle University, receiving the B.S. Degree in Commercial Science in 1950. During World War II he was in the Air Corps for three years.

His insurance career began with five years of service as a state insurance examiner with the Washington Insurance Department from 1948 to 1953. From 1953 to 1962 he was a reinsurance broker in Seattle with Frank Burns, Inc., becoming a vice president. In 1962 he joined the Safeco Insurance Group for three years before moving from Seattle to San Francisco. There in 1965 he was appointed vice president of his current employer, American Re-Insurance Company, and was in charge of its West Coast office. In 1972 he became executive vice president, in 1973 president, and in 1975 chief executive officer.

16

The Reinsurance Entity

by James F. Dowd*

All that has gone before in this book dealt with reinsurance as a product. We shall now look at the nature of the entity offering the product, first at the outside or organizational shell of the entity, and later at the internal organization of people into departments and functions.

Types of Reinsurance Entities

The business of reinsurance is not so generically unique or distinguishable from insurance as to commend the universal adoption of any particular form of business enterprise. Reinsurers are, after all, entities of all kinds which are participating in the business of insurance but which have chosen to substantially limit their activities to the assumption of risk from other insurers. This would include, of course, the reinsurance department of primary insurance companies. In order to be able to deal with this subject with a degree of comprehension compatible with utility, we must first establish parameters to insure that we are addressing those types of entities most common to the reinsurance industry. As the subject of analysis, we shall limit our scope to the United States reinsurance market and to organizations operating as "professional" reinsurers which are representative of the organizational forms reinsurers have elected. Perhaps the word "elected" may denote misleadingly too deliberate an

* Mr. Dowd is a member of the New York Bar and is Vice President, General Counsel and Corporate Secretary of Skandia Group, 280 Park Avenue, New York, New York 10017. Acknowledgement is given to the substantial contributions of T. Darrington Semple, Jr., Resident Counsel and Secretary of American Re-Insurance Company and Edmond F. Rondepierre, Senior Vice President, General Counsel and Secretary of General Reinsurance Corporation, who were the principal reviewers of this chapter.

activity, since many of the forms of entities presently employed by rein-surers are the product more of evolution than purposeful organizational planning. The establishment of parameters is a practical consideration which, while restricting the scope of analysis, will increase the depth with which the more familiar organizational forms may be treated. The organizations chosen for analysis represent a cross section of almost every organizational form encountered in the insurance business, with the most notable exception being the reciprocal exchange. Included are both stock and mutual insurers, U.S. branches of alien insurers, and a class which the industry refers to generally as "pools." A pool, in the con-text used here, is a conduit for risk assumption with the ultimate liability residing in the individual companies which are members of the pool.

A determinant of form and therefore adjunct to its discussion is ownership, and the subject group includes public companies, privately owned, wholly owned subsidiaries, mutually owned companies and what might be described as joint ventures.

It is not surprising to note that the preponderance of reinsurers are stock companies, which enjoy all of the attributes of corporations rang-ing from limitation of owners' liability to the ability to raise additional capital through the issuance of additional shares. It is elementary to note that the corporation organized to engage in the reinsurance business is subject for reasons grounded in concepts of policyholder security to con-siderably more legal strictures and limitations than the normal business corporation. Insurance companies, in general, and reinsurers as a sub-group are subject, in varying degrees of specificity, to the insurance laws of the fifty states, the District of Columbia, Puerto Rico, and the Virgin Islands.

Government regulation of the insurance industry exists principally to protect the general public against the insolvency of insurers and to make certain that insurers, in their dealings with the public, conduct their business ethically and competently. Thus, unlike general business cor-porations, insurance companies are permitted to do business in a state only after satisfying requirements that reasonably ensure their ability to honor all potential obligations. Reinsurers, however, do not deal directly with the general public and, therefore, the regulatory impulse to protect the public should not be triggered by reinsurance transactions. Neverthe-less, most states perceive as their obligation some supervision of rein-surers in order to provide yet another safeguard for the interests of policyholders whose risks are ultimately reinsured. It is this motivation to assess and assure the security afforded by reinsurance which prompts legislatures and regulators to impose restrictions on reinsurers similar to those imposed on primary insurers.

A state usually will regulate reinsurance by placing limitations on the financial operations of the primary insurance companies which might cede business to reinsurers. This usually means that a ceding insurer will not be permitted to take credit as an asset or as a deduction from liabilities for any reinsurance that is ceded to reinsurers not meeting the state's qualifications. The regulation of reinsurers will be treated elsewhere in this text, but some brief reference to it in this chapter is appropriate since it is one of the factors which shape organizational form.

An example of an individual state's activity directed specifically at reinsurers may be found in Regulation 20 promulgated by the Insurance Department of the State of New York. New York State has traditionally enjoyed a reputation as a bastion of financial certainty in matters of reinsurance. On November 22, 1977, the New York Insurance Department issued a controversial amendment to its Regulation 20 which dramatically changed the standards for the acceptability of reinsurers. It is now possible for insurers domiciled in New York to obtain partial credit, under certain circumstances, for business ceded to some reinsurers not licensed or approved by the Insurance Department of the State of New York. While this change was heralded by promises of increased market capacity, it nevertheless increases the potential of insolvency. By providing less than comparable standards of solvency for the certification of non-admitted reinsurers, New York's Regulation 20 has given them the same status as admitted reinsurers. The New York Insurance Department has, in substance, relegated to the ceding companies its power to determine basic questions of reinsurers' solvency, accepting in return a simple certification.

Most states apply to reinsurers substantially the same criteria required of primary insurers. For example, in most states reinsurers must meet the same requirements as domestic primary insurance companies for minimum amounts of paid-in capital and surplus. There are, in addition, many other regulated areas shared by both primary insurers and reinsurers. A reinsurer, like a primary company, is subject to restrictions on investments and to financial reporting requirements. Also, like primary insurance companies, reinsurers must also submit to periodic examinations by state authorities.

Reinsurers are presently free from the regulatory arm of the states in certain significant areas. For reasons which are associated with the recognition of economic realities and the distinction of the reinsurer's role, the reinsurer is either not required to participate or to participate only as a nominal member in the various social schemes such as guaranty associations, assigned risk programs, FAIR plans, or wind pools. The inclusion of reinsurers in such programs would, in addition to imposing administrative burdens, have the effect of doubling the impact on the same premium dollar as it flows through the primary company to the reinsurer.

The equality in bargaining power and expertise which exists between the reinsurer and its client enables the reinsurer to be free from rate and form filing requirements. All business dealings, therefore, are performed on a level which presumes equality of expertise and within a professional context of the utmost good faith. Both the buyer and seller in reinsurance negotiations are knowledgeable and commercially sophisticated.

The absence of much of the regulation affecting primary companies has an impact on the structures and organizational forms which have evolved and been assumed by reinsurance entities. In the first place, reinsurers generally require far fewer personnel than primary companies. This is attributable in part to the pyramidal structure of the insurance industry which places the heaviest personnel burden on primary insurers to conduct their individual contacts with millions of insureds. The marketing of the insurance product to the public, the handling of claims, and the administration of these activities require great numbers of people. The reinsurer on the other hand is relieved of this personnel intensity by virtue of the aggregation which occurs during the upward motion of insurance risk bearing within the pyramid. A good rule of thumb suggests that reinsurers employ one person per million dollars of premium income, a ratio which even the most efficient primary insurer could never hope to approach. These ratios will vary widely dependent upon various factors, perhaps the most significant of which is the degree to which a reinsurer is involved in accepting risks facultatively.

Classes of Reinsurance Entities in the U.S.

PROFESSIONAL REINSURERS

In the United States there are basically three classes of entities which engage in the reinsurance business: professional reinsurers, reinsurance departments of primary companies, and various groupings or syndications of insurers which for the sake of convenience will be referred to here as reinsurance pools. This chapter will confine its focus to the role of the professional reinsurer. A professional reinsurer, although likely empowered by its charter and license to operate as a primary insurance company, chooses to engage almost exclusively in reinsurance and writes little or no insurance on a direct basis.

REINSURANCE DEPARTMENTS OF PRIMARY COMPANIES

Reinsurance as noted above is not limited to professional reinsurers. There are a great many primary companies which also engage in the reinsurance business. In fact, in recent years there has been a dramatic increase in the number of primary carriers which have established separate departments exclusively to write reinsurance business. These reinsurance departments of primary insurers are in competition with professional reinsurers, and they usually employ the same *modus operandi* and organizational functions as the professional reinsurers. References to this "departmental reinsurer" will be made where helpful throughout this chapter.

The professional reinsurer differs in some respects from the departmental reinsurer. Though it is a point subject to some debate, it has been suggested that the professional reinsurer is more clearly able to assure confidentiality in a business where information is an asset and competition is strong. The argument continues that in dealing with a professional reinsurer the ceding company knows that all information related to it about its activities will be held in strictest confidence. In contrast, a primary company may be loath to convey ideas and proposals about new products or rate innovations to the reinsurance department of a competing primary insurer. The implication of this is not that it is impossible to construct house rules within a departmental reinsurer which would make the disclosure and employment of such information to other departments unlikely. Rather, the implication lies in the perception of the buyer of reinsurance when presented with an alternative which may appear more palatable. The acceptability of confidentiality as a tenet of professional reinsurers only is belied by the success which has been met by the reinsurance departments of several primary insurers.

The other and perhaps more concrete reason why the professional reinsurer might seem a more attractive entity for accepting reinsurance than the reinsurance department of a primary insurance company is technical expertise. The sole enterprise of the professional reinsurer is reinsurance, and it is constantly engaged in gathering intelligence about the workings of various insurance markets. While professional reinsurers cannot claim to have a monopoly on technical reinsurance expertise, the principal dedication to reinsurance by a company would suggest an amalgamation of the various disciplines necessary for such expertise to be nurtured.

POOLS

The third major type of reinsurance entity is that which is described above as the reinsurance pool. Such organizations are usually of two types. One is a special purpose pool or syndicate organized to provide for its members reinsurance protection and management on certain types of risk. Some examples of these pool-type entities are in lines which are highly specialized, high-risk or call for greater capacity than individual underwriters care to provide. The other type of reinsurance pool is formed for the purpose of writing the more traditional lines of reinsurance. These organizations provide insurers of divergent interests an opportunity to participate in the reinsurance business through competent, experienced reinsurance management. The motivation for participating in such an arrangement may be as divergent as the makeup of their membership. For some members of such a pool, it may be their only access to the reinsurance market. For others it may be an opportunity to participate in a different book of reinsurance risks to balance those being written in their own company. It is for many smaller primary insurers a chance to participate in the reinsurance business under competent and proven management without incurring the expenses attendant with entry into the reinsurance business on their own. One of the significant professional reinsurers presents a variation on the reinsurance pool theme with a mutual reinsurance company in the position of manager and various insurers acting as retrocessionaires of the reinsurer.

Recently there have been created a number of companies which, while differing in form, may be said to be similar in many respects to the pooling arrangements described above. These companies are joint ventures through which a number of generally non-U.S. primary carriers join together to form a new U.S. corporate entity to engage in the business of reinsurance under the management of a U.S. professional reinsurer. This joint venture is usually undertaken in order to provide a foothold in the U.S. reinsurance market for companies which have few other alternative means through which to enter this market. These organizations, most newly formed or in formation at this writing, are the product of a strong desire among foreign insurers, particularly European and Japanese insurers, to participate in the largest insurance market in the world. They choose to enter as reinsurers because of the comparative ease of formation, as compared to a primary insurer, which permits premium writings to begin more quickly. They choose to enter under the management of existing U.S. reinsurers, because they recognize the peculiarities of the U.S. market and are aware of the dangers which await the uninitiated. There is some further compulsion to management arrangements which arises from an extreme shortage of individuals possessing reinsurance experience and the difficulty of dislodging from their present employment those who are experienced and who have a demonstrated record of success. No small factor in the thinking of the shareholding participants is the opportunity to educate themselves for some acceptable time period as a prelude to their own independent entry in the U.S. The U.S. companies which are the prime movers in these arrangements see in them an opportunity to produce management fee income which will help to stabilize underwriting results. The U.S. organizers are also motivated by considerations of maintaining an orderly reinsurance market which may become difficult with the introduction of numerous new entities.

Forms of Reinsurance Entities

THE STOCK COMPANY

The major share of the U.S. reinsurance market is held by the professional reinsurers. The organizational form of the professional reinsurer varies. It could be a stock company, a mutual company, or a U.S. branch of an alien company. An examination of the largest professional reinsurers reveals that the vast majority are stock corporations. The advantages of organizing a corporation are the same for a reinsurer as they would be for any business enterprise. A corporation has available to it the most convenient method of raising capital through the issuance of its shares and provides its owners with a limitation of their liability to the amount invested in the corporation. This "corporate veil" and governance by a shareholder selected board of directors are the principal characteristics distinguishing corporations from other forms of business enterprises such as a partnership or individual proprietorship. A corporation may be either publicly owned, with its shares traded on an exchange and subject to federal securities laws, or a private or closely held company where stock ownership is in the hands of a single entity or a small number of people. In the larger publicly held reinsurance companies the board of directors elected by the shareholders is specifically charged with the management of the affairs of a corporation and it, in turn, delegates responsibility for day-to-day management to the officers. A number of the professional reinsurers which are in corporate form are not owned by individual shareholders but rather are the wholly owned subsidiaries of other corporations. These other corporations may be insurance entities, holding companies, or companies not necessarily related to the insurance industry.

The motivation for the formation by a primary insurer of a wholly owned reinsurance subsidiary might be the problems previously discussed which a primary carrier encounters when competing against professional reinsurers for reinsurance business. By establishing a wholly owned but separate entity which engages exclusively in reinsurance, the parent primary insurer can somewhat eliminate some of the competitive disadvantages. The subsidiary is a professional reinsurer and, although wholly owned by a primary company (perhaps even by a primary company which is a competitor with the ceding company), there is nevertheless sufficient isolation of operations, management, and expertise to provide prospective ceding companies with a greater sense of confidentiality and technical prowess.

A number of U.S. professional reinsurers are wholly owned subsidiaries of alien insurers which may not do any insurance business in the United States. Many of these subsidiary professional reinsurers were incorporated as U.S. stock companies (i.e., domesticated) only after having first entered the U.S. reinsurance market as U.S. branches of the alien insurer, a popular entry approach in the early part of this century. The U.S. branch as an organizational form will be discussed later in greater detail.

The Mutual Company

The mutual form of organization is also available to reinsurers although it is infrequently chosen. The only major reinsurer which has the mutual form is organized as the syndication of the reinsurance interests of mutual primary companies. One of its main attributes is the large proportion of the business assumed which is retroceded to the members of the syndication. The reason for the unpopularity of the mutual form for reinsurers has to do with the difficulty of applying the "mutual" ownership concept to a reinsurance business. A mutual insurer is theoretically owned by its policyholders, and this format can only be applied cumbersomely to a reinsurer by equating a reinsurance transaction to the issuance of a primary policy.

U.S. Branches of Alien Insurers

Some special attention should be devoted to the entry of alien insurers into the U.S. reinsurance market. In the last decade the reinsurance business has grown into a profitable enterprise. In addition, as with the primary insurance market, premium volume increased and the availability of risk-bearing capacity became a problem. It thus became quite attractive for many alien insurers attracted by this capital shortage to do a reinsurance business.

One traditional means of entry for an alien insurer is through the establishment of a U.S. branch. A U.S. branch as an entity in New York is a creature of the Insurance Law of the State of New York. A United States branch is defined in the New York Insurance Law as "the business unit through which business is transacted within the United States by an alien insurer, or the assets and liabilities of such insurer within the United States pertaining to such business or the management powers pertaining to such business and to such assets and liabilities. . . ." This definition, together with the other statutory provisions which relate to a U.S. branch, has the effect of creating a hybrid entity distinguishable by according to it some of the attributes usually attributed to the corporation as a whole. The end result is an entity, entirely the creature of statute, which has no counterpart in any other industry with the possible exception of banking.

The United States branch must maintain separate assets and surplus which must be sufficient to meet the obligations it assumes. The assets are physically placed in trust under the supervision of the Superintendent of Insurance. New York law requires a U.S. branch of an alien insurer to keep in trust, under the control of the New York Superintendent of Insurance, the amount necessary to secure the claims of all policyholders and creditors of the alien insurer in the United States. Also, a U.S. branch is limited in the amount it may invest in the stock of other insurance corporations. This limitation is arrived at by reference to the amount maintained in the U.S. branch's "trusteed surplus," as opposed to the policyholder surplus used to arrive at such an investment limitation for domestic insurers. A U.S. branch is required to be capitalized much in the same way as if it were a separate corporation with assets localized and segregated from those of its parent. The U.S. branch is also subject to many of the insurance law organizational requirements.

Whether an alien insurer maintains a U.S. branch or domesticates a stock company in the United States to engage solely in reinsurance is not always a mutually exclusive choice. Some insurers and reinsurers are operating in the U.S. reinsurance market through both a U.S. branch and a wholly owned corporate subsidiary.

THE NEW YORK INSURANCE EXCHANGE

An entirely new form of entity is the New York Insurance Exchange, still in its infancy at this writing. The Exchange was created by legislation in New York State enacted on July 20, 1978, and will consist of underwriting syndicates organized to provide a centralized market facility for writing three types of business: reinsurance of all kinds, primary insurance on risks located entirely outside the United States, and primary insurance on risks which have been submitted to and rejected by the also newly created New York Free Trade Zone. Besides certain New York State tax advantages accorded members, the Exchange hopes to provide a new reinsurance market which will compete for business often conceded to the London market. The authors of the Exchange concept predict that it will introduce new capital to the insurance and reinsurance industry and stimulate employment in New York State.

The organizational model for the Exchange is Lloyd's of London. There will be four classes of membership in the Exchange: underwriting and broker members who would have voting rights, and associate brokers and subscribers without voting rights. The operation of the Exchange will take place at a physical location in New York and will consist of the brokers bringing business to the floor of the Exchange where the underwriting syndicates will compete for it. The ownership of the underwriting syndicates will consist of investors which may be subsidiaries of insurance and reinsurance companies, brokers or individuals. The enabling legislation limits broker ownership of any single underwriting syndicate to less than 20%.

The syndicates which will comprise the underwriting elements of the Exchange may assume any one of a number of legal forms, including partnership, joint venture, corporation, or individual proprietorship. While it is too early to predict which organizational format will be most widely used, the limited partnership form is most widely discussed. The principal characteristic of a partnership is that each of the partners assumes jointly and severally all of the liabilities of the partnership. In a limited partnership, however, each of the limited partners is liable only for its investment in the partnership and thereby limits its personal liability. General partners in a limited partnership continue to have unlimited liability.

The Growing Role of the General Counsel

We are daily being reminded in hundreds of ways, large and small, that the world around us is growing more complex. The reinsurance industry is part of that world, and to some is one of its more difficult to understand facets. It is a business traditionally noted for its reliance on personal relationships and one which takes pride in its honorable undertakings entered into with a minimum of formality. This is a tradition which its adherents are finding increasingly difficult to perpetuate for reasons which touch on economic, sociological, and legal considerations. As a result of the accelerated development of the reinsurance industry, the appearance of yet untested new entrants and the development of new forms of coverage, it has become necessary in recent years to instill a greater degree of formality in the relationship between the reinsurer and its ceding companies. Combined, these factors must be added to a full quotient of increased governmental regulatory surveillance to gain an appreciation of why this industry which formerly prided itself on the relative absence of lawyers is increasingly turning to them in recent years. This is, of course, not a phenomenon unique to reinsurance. All sectors of the economy find themselves similarly turning to the legal profession for assistance in dealing with the seemingly endless streams of laws and regulations being enacted or adopted annually. The insurance industry, already heavily regulated, fares worse than most in this regard.

Historically, reinsurers have been perceived to be freer from regulatory constraints than primary insurance companies dealing with the public. The most often proffered explanation for this is that reinsurers are presumed to be dealing with knowledgeable buyers in the person of other insurance companies which may be expected to competently protect their own interests. This presumed equality of relationship, when coupled with the freedom from rate and form regulation which reinsurers enjoy, has traditionally led the management of reinsurers to conclude that the balance of problems confronting them (which could be characterized as "legal" problems) could most economically be handled through the occasional employment of outside legal counsel. It has in recent years become apparent, however, that the economics associated with the outside counsel relationships and the difficulty in obtaining such counsel versed or educable in the special problems of this industry argue strongly in favor of some staff legal representation. While this movement is not yet universal, it is expanding and is being reinforced by additions to existing legal department staffs.

The scope of the responsibilities of those individuals bearing the title of general or resident counsel naturally varies from company to company. A typical job description would indicate that the counsel is the chief legal officer of the company, reporting most frequently to the chief executive officer. The range of specific duties would include general corporate work, and where appropriate, securities law and shareholder relations, mergers and acquisitions, insurance regulatory work and governmental liaison, litigation, some reinsurance claims involvement, contract drafting, employee relations including the employee benefit program, investment compliance with insurance regulation, real estate transactions, and taxation, both state and local. The reinsurance company counsel may have only a single client, but the counsel's practice is certainly diverse.

In addition to having skills generally associated with a competent professional, it is important that the counsel possess an understanding of and keen interest in the business of reinsurance. It is only through close identification with the business aspects of reinsurance that the counsel may truly perform effectively in the service of the client whose cause is espoused. The counsel is expected to be at one and the same time an artful and effective advocate of the client's position, and also an objective insider identifying areas which require legal attention. As a result of professional standing, the counsel has an obligation defined by the code of professional responsibility which binds the counsel and which may be equated to that obligation assumed by the certified public accountant and the actuary, among other professionals. It is in this context that the counsel must establish personally and for the legal department being directed an "honest broker" role, balancing the needs of the corporate employer and the dictates of the environment in which it operates.

It is important as a measure of effectiveness to determine if the counsel is thought to be assistive and supportive of the company's mission, or rather a formalistic obstructionist whose negative response disinclines fellow employees from inviting participation or seeking advice. The strategic position occupied by the counsel within the company would involve participation in almost all questions of substance which confront a business organization. The counsel's confidence must be inviolate, and the ability to speak freely should be a significant contribution to any discussion.

When we address the specific areas of a general counsel's responsibility, we see that they are largely defined by the type of entity, the nature of the industry, and degree to which the entity is subject to various kinds of regulation, both insurance and non-insurance. Foremost of these factors is the nature of the industry. The insurance industry, of which reinsurance is merely a part, is, as noted above, a regulated industry. It is an industry which is primarily regulated by the states, with ever-increasing doses of federal intervention. As a result of a strong public policy grounded in the protection of the insurance buying public, it is unlawful to engage in the business of insurance without first having received the consent of the state. Since this legal requirement results in the regulation of insurance companies, and since reinsurers are insurers which elect to limit their activities to reinsurance, reinsurers are also subject to extensive regulation.

Reinsurers are subject to regulation in the following areas of activity: organization and licensing, capital and surplus requirements, deposit requirement, periodic financial examination, filing of financial statements, restrictions on investments, transactions between members of affiliated groups, dividend payments, mergers and acquisitions, solvency margins, and liquidation or rehabilitation. While there is freedom from rate and form regulation, it is essential that the reinsurer be informed about rate and form filing requirements because of the interest it shares in the outcome of these filings.

The general counsel of a reinsurer will spend a large amount of time on insurance regulatory activities. This time will be divided among the following: insuring compliance with existing laws and regulations, keeping a finger on the pulse of developing areas of legislative and regulatory interest, and maintaining an ongoing liaison with state and federal insurance regulatory officials. Pending, proposed, and newly passed legislation must be reviewed to determine its potential for impacting on the business of the client. This assures the reinsurance general counsel of a continually replenished supply of reading material and the opportunity to exercise literary dexterity by producing a continual flow of written and oral communication advising the management and operating functions of action necessary to insure compliance. Trade associations and business and professional publications are tools used by this professional, and the synthesis and discussion forums they provide are invaluable in making the task manageable.

The time devoted to general corporate legal work will differ markedly from company to company. Those reinsurers whose stock is publicly traded must continually comply with the dictates of the Securities and Exchange Commission or comparable state laws and insurance regulations, and must perforce allocate a considerable amount of time to this activity. Reinsurers which are more insular in a corporate group may find themselves relieved of all but those vestiges of corporate legal work necessarily required to maintain their corporate form. The vitality and participation of the company's board of directors, the frequency with which it meets and its committee structure will also have an impact on the time allocated to general corporate legal work.

The relationship between the legal and claims departments of a reinsurer is subject to variation within the reinsurance community. The extremes may run from little or no contact to instances in which the claim department reports directly to or works frequently with the general counsel. It is important to remember in this context that the claim department of a reinsurer differs markedly in perspective and orientation from the claim department of a primary insurer. The claim department of a primary insurer is principally dedicated to the negotiation and settlement of losses or the defense of claims made by or against its insureds with whom it has a direct contractual relationship. The function of a reinsurance claim department is to monitor losses ceded to it and to conduct periodic audits of the claim departments of its ceding companies. As a result of this slightly increased distance between insureds and claimants and the reinsurer, and the lack of privity of contract between the original insured and the reinsurer, there are ordinarily fewer instances in which reinsurance claim department activities require the attention of the company's general counsel. There are the following significant events in the claims area, however, which should command attention:

1. Any questions of coverage or any declination of coverage by the reinsurer to the ceding company;

2. Any contract controversy which suggests that a demand for arbitration may be indicated;

3. Situations in which the reinsurer is placed in the position of having a possible conflict of interest as a result of having differing interests in the outcome of adversary claims in the same litigation;

4. Any instance in which a claim is made or threatened, or a legal proceeding is commenced, directly against the reinsurer;

5. When the solvency of a ceding company is questionable, or when a ceding company is declared insolvent, placed in liquidation, rehabilitation or conservatorship;

6. When the defense of any claim is tendered to the reinsurer; and

7. When a state guaranty fund claims the proceeds of a reinsurance contract.

There has grown up within the insurance industry a distinction between the general counsel's office and other lawyers within insurance companies whose efforts are directed at claims or other more specialized activities. The general counsel must be expected to bridge that gap and be in a position to provide direction in all areas involving the use of lawyers acting in their professional capacity within a company. As the chief legal executive, the counsel must be the principal architect of the company's legal relationships with all who come in contact with that company, whether they be consumers, stockholders, employees, adversaries, providers of services or other lawyers.

This latter point leads to an extremely important area of activity of the general counsel: the use and supervision of outside lawyers to perform legal work. A discussion of this facet cannot begin without some allusion to the earlier cited economic considerations involved in the creation of the in-house counsel position. It can generally be said that one of the inherent objectives of a house counsel program is to reduce the expense of hiring law firms to represent a company with respect to various of its activites. This objective is not, however, always easily managed. It has frequently been observed that the presence of house counsel will often result in an increase of problem recognition with a sometimes concomitant increase in outside legal fees to assist in their solution. This is usually a short-term impact and is somewhat offset by the economic efficiency of having available house counsel familiar with the type of business, the inner workings of the company, and the personalities involved which can bring these attributes to bear in the resolution of problems.

The use of outside counsel is often recommended by the type question involved and the degree of expertise generally associated with various areas of the law. Generally, for example, it would not be economically feasible for house counsel to devote significant amounts of time to resolving questions in areas of great legal specialty, such as patent and trademark law. It is advisable and usually more expedient in these instances to bring the problem to the specialist rather than attempt to develop a specialty to deal with an infrequently confronted problem.

It is important when using outside counsel, however, that house counsel, in areas where it is competent to do so, determine basic direction and inject expertise into the resolution of the problem. It is not sufficient that the problem be referred to outside counsel with instructions to report upon conclusion. Capable counsel will appreciate direction and assistance and will be motivated to perform more effectively when sensing a genuine interest and receiving the supportive participation of house counsel. It is after all the general counsel who has the responsibility for the outcome and the task, either pleasant or otherwise, of reporting that outcome to management and the board of directors. This is sufficient impetus to induce regular consultation with outside counsel and to require full exposition of legal positions and proposals. If the problem referred to outside counsel is one which involves reinsurance, the house counsel should anticipate and encourage some well-grounded educational sessions in the rubrics, terminology, and customs of the business as a prelude to any other activity. Outside counsel who is well versed by an inside counterpart will generally prove to be more effective and will have to spend less time in education at the expense of the reinsurer.

Aside from working with outside counsel, the balance of the general counsel's time will be devoted to:

1. The legal aspects of employee relations, including the design, maintenance and compliance requirements of the reinsurer's employee benefit program.

2. The drafting and review of contracts, primarily reinsurance contracts but also other agreements which the company may enter.

3. The review and negotiation of leases and contracts in connection with making office premises available for the company's use.

4. Advice to the investment department with regard to the investment restrictions in the insurance laws and considerations involved in private placement investments offered to the employer.

5. Considerations associated with diversification or expansion which may involve mergers, acquisitions, the formation of new entities, and other structural changes.

6. A familiarity and active involvement in the company's tax activities, including planning and the conduct of tax audits.

Though the above list is lengthy, it will expand in proportion to the general counsel's contribution to the well-being of the company.

The Reinsurance Person

A composite picture of the reinsurance person would have to be multi-dimensional. There is no instant identification of a stylized individual embodying a composite of attributes associated with this industry within an industry. Probably the most distinguishable creatures in the public's perception of reinsurance are the account executives on the company side of the business and the reinsurance brokers on the intermediary side. These individuals, charged largely with responsibility for producing new business and nurturing existing relationships, represent generally an interesting admixture of articulate salespersons and knowledgeable technicians. Reinsurance is a business which requires a firm grounding in the principles which underlie primary insurance. To this elemental attribute must be added a reasonable financial acumen and an understanding of the accounting and statistical whirl which is a large part of insurance and reinsurance. It would be impossible for a reinsurance person to discuss a specific proposal for reinsurance intelligently without a good understanding of the implications of such proposal on the financial statements of both the primary insurer and the reinsurer.

The reinsurance person's perspective must include insurance as a whole, since that is the potential market for the product of reinsurance. There must be a sufficiently well-developed information system available to provide the person with current impressions of trends within the insurance industry and the impact on the industry of outside forces from political, economic, legal, social, and technical developments, shaping the environment in which the industry must operate. Sensitivity to nuances affecting market changes is an almost universal characteristic of this person. The reinsurer should be seen as having an overview of the industry, which demands objectivity in discerning opportunities. A quick grasp of technical detail and the ability to acquire, within a short time, a degree of expertise in areas of complexity serve the reinsurer well in analyzing new proposals. These abilities must be supplemented by the ability to effectively communicate both in writing and orally.

By and large, the reinsurance person is a "people" person in an industry where personal relationships and the development of mutual confidence and trust are most important assets. The ability to make accurate judgments about individuals will be tested often, and the perfection of this skill is a valuable tool. An entrepreneurial flair will be fed by the regular flow of opportunities to be identified and transformed into profitable relationships. The international orientation of the business and the spread of potential business in the U.S. will make the reinsurance person generally a well-travelled individual, providing a firsthand opportunity to assess local developments and their effects on business. Travel also provides opportunity to widen the circle of industry relationships and will feed the intelligence network important to early identification of problems and opportunities.

A look deeper into the recesses of a reinsurance company would reveal an internal structure not significantly different from a primary insurer in nomenclature, but with significant differences in function. One will find accounting, investment, claims, marketing, and administration departments which differ in some ways from such departments in primary insurers. As the orientation of the reinsurance company differs overall from a primary insurer's, so must its operational areas differ. The disciplines which guide these areas and the need for the reinsurer to respond to the same regulatory framework as the primary insurer increase the areas of commonality between the two.

The underwriting department of a reinsurer will significantly differ from a primary insurer. This could be the subject of extensive treatment elsewhere, since the marketing and underwriting philosophies of each reinsurer differ. Reinsurance companies may operate either as direct writers, producing their own business by dealing directly with primary insurers, or as brokerage market reinsurers looking to the reinsurance brokerage community to produce the business opportunities which are submitted for underwriting consideration. This difference in approach can produce a vast difference in the personnel needs and internal structure.

Further intrinsic distinctions are created by the mix of the company's business between treaty and facultative reinsurance. A reinsurance treaty is a contract which may cut across one or more lines of business and involve a single contractual relationship between the reinsurer and a primary company, by which the reinsurer assumes interests in a great many of the policies issued by the primary insurer. The description of treaty relationships is treated elsewhere in this text, but for the purpose of discussing internal structure such relationships are characterized by the aggregation of many primary insurance policies by class of business and not by individual attention to each risk reinsured. This business format suggests the possibility of relatively large premium volume to the reinsurer from a single contractual relationship. Facultative reinsurance by contrast involves the reinsurer in the individual risk selection and underwriting process, and the likely concomitant of both a decrease in premium volume from individual transactions and a larger volume of transactions which require a greater number of reinsurance company personnel. Though recruitment practices differ with the reinsurance industry, the great majority of people involved in reinsurance underwriting are products of the primary insurance companies. Those persons bring with them that firm grounding in insurance principles achieved in the primary business. They are encouraged through exposure and training programs of reinsurers, both formal and informal, to add to their repertoire of skills the overview and diversity associated with the role of the reinsurer in the risk-bearing chain.

Summary

Reinsurers are perhaps best described in terms which relate them to primary insurers and measure their distinguishing features and many areas of commonality. Rather than measure their differences, we have attempted to describe the characteristics of the professional reinsurer. The two principal determinants of the form of reinsurers in general are their mission and the regulatory environment in which they operate.

One of the actors on the stage of an increasing number of reinsurance companies is its house counsel. In pursuing a professional role, the counsel is concerned with both mission and environment. Charged with serious responsibilities in each of these areas, there is increasing recognition of the importance of the contribution being made.

The reinsurance person, apart from counsel, will generally be mission-oriented. An amalgamation of that person's skills, though unlikely to describe any particular individual, presents an interesting bouquet.

*   *   *   *   *   *

About the Author of Chapter 16

James F. Dowd was born in New York City on August 21, 1941, and spent his formative years in Peekskill, New York. His secondary schooling at Archbishop Stepinac High School in White Plains, New York, was completed in 1958. He served in the United States Marine Corps from 1959 to 1963 and received a B.A. Degree in political science from C.W. Post College of Long Island University in 1965. Mr Dowd received his Juris Doctor Degree from St. John's University School of Law in June, 1968, and was shortly thereafter admitted to the New York Bar.

His insurance career began in 1971 with Skandia Group where he currently is Vice President, General Counsel and Corporate Secretary of Skandia Corporation, Skandia's U.S. holding company. He holds similar titles in Skandia America Reinsurance Corporation, Hudson Insurance Company, and Skandia Advisory Service Corporation. He serves as a director of Skandia Corporation, Hudson Insurance Company, Skandia Advisory Service Corporation, Hudson Underwriting Limited, and Hudson Reinsurance Company Limited.

He is a member of the American Bar Association and is Chairman-Elect of its Committee on the Public Regulation of Insurance. He is also a member of the New York State Bar Association and the Association of the Bar of the City of New York. In addition, he is a member of the Federation of Insurance Counsel and is the 1979 Chairman of the Legal Committee of the Reinsurance Association of America.

17

Underwriting Income

by Guy K. Patterson*

Much has been said about the purpose and methods of reinsurance, but it must be clearly understood that the primary objective of the reinsurer as a business concern is to make money. One of the key business distinctions between the reinsurer and the primary insurer is the greater potential return on the initial capital invested in a reinsurance concern than on that invested in a primary insurance company. In recent years it has not been surprising to see property/casualty and even life companies establishing reinsurance operations of their own. This stems from the comparatively low costs involved in producing a significant volume of reinsurance business in a short period of time, as opposed to the cost of setting up or acquiring a distribution network to produce primary business. Ideally, over time, this cost advantage enables the reinsurer to direct a higher proportion of its funds to invested assets and thereby provide an attractive profit in relation to its capital base. Recognition of the profit potential of a reinsurance company thus requires an understanding of not only how the business is conducted, but also how the money generated from reinsurance underwriting is managed. The purpose of this chapter is to explore the basis on which underwriting income is measured, and how the varying aspects of measurement are applied in the decision-making process of the reinsurer.

At the outset, it is important to establish that although underwriting income is the product of the principal business of the reinsurer, the production of underwriting income involves many considerations. The

* Chairman, INA Reinsurance Company, 2 INA Plaza, Philadelphia, Pennsylvania 19101. With acknowledgement for advice and assistance to T. J. Strenk, President; Lawrence S. Davis, Assistant Secretary; Paul R. Flack, Actuary; and George H. Roberts, Assistant Secretary.

management of a reinsurance company must satisfy its own information needs as to the progress of each component of the business, and uses underwriting income, along with related measurement criteria, as the basis for making decisions on underwriting and investment policy. Additionally, the management must satisfy reporting requirements of state and federal regulatory authorities, which determine the way underwriting income should be expressed in the context of prescribed reporting formats. This in turn is the basis for evaluating the company's operations in relation to insurance or financial community standards. The reinsurer must therefore recognize and identify its management objectives in terms of generating underwriting income, and make use of appropriate measurement techniques to quantify those objectives.

Measurements

The standard measurement of underwriting income — premiums earned less losses and expenses incurred — portrays one aspect of the business activity of a reinsurer over a period of time. The methods of deriving underwriting income and the contribution of underwriting income to the overall profitability of the enterprise also represent key aspects of the measurement process. From a reporting point of view this process involves the transition from statutory to GAAP accounting, income statement to balance sheet accounting, and underwriting income to operating income.

STATUTORY VS. GAAP

Methods of accounting for underwriting profit or loss within a given period vary according to the reporting requirements imposed upon the reinsurance company, which are only slightly different from those applying to primary insurance companies. Specific guidelines are prescribed by the National Association of Insurance Commissioners (NAIC) for recording underwriting income on the NAIC Annual Statement (*statutory basis*), and by the American Institute of Certified Public Accountants (AICPA) for recording underwriting income in a company's annual report to shareholders under "generally accepted accounting principles" (*GAAP basis*). The GAAP basis also is required for reporting to the Securities and Exchange Commission. These methods are distinguished by the NAIC's concern for the solvency of a company, and concern by the AICPA for the development of a company's earnings (according to the "going-concern" concept). Without dwelling on the full scope of accounting practices, the difference between the statutory and the GAAP method of determining underwriting income is primarily in the identification and timing of expenses incurred within the reporting period. An explanation of the elements in the measurement formula will show how each method is applied.

The amount of *premium earned* on an income statement is dependent on the calculation of the "unearned" portion of the net premiums written (assumed premiums, less reinsurance or retrocessions, and less return premiums). Usually, precision gives way to expediency as an averaging method is used to account for unearned premiums at the end of a period. Although the unearned premium reserve (UPR) is a balance sheet liability, the change in this reserve from one period to the next becomes a factor in the derivation of premiums earned for the income statement. The formula for determining premiums earned for a given period is to take the net premiums written, plus the unearned premium reserve at the end of the prior period, less the unearned premium reserve at the end of the current period (as Exhibit 1 below illustrates).

The practice of determining *losses (claims) incurred* within a given period can also vary, depending on the methods used to establish a reserve for outstanding losses. Since the time and amount of payment are frequently unknown when a loss is reported, this reserve is established against eventual payment. For some lines of business, such as liability or workers' compensation, minimum reserve levels are prescribed under statutory reporting. Also included in this reserve is a provision for losses which have been incurred but not reported (IBNR) as of the end of the reporting period. The outstanding loss reserve is a balance sheet liability, but the change in this reserve from one period to the next is an element in determining losses incurred on the income statement. Losses incurred represent outstanding loss reserves at the end of the period, less the loss reserves at the end of the prior period, added to losses paid (less recoveries) during the period (as shown in Exhibit 1).

Thus, during a given period of time the formula for producing underwriting income includes some premiums which had previously been received, and some losses which are not yet paid, but it does portray as nearly as possible a company's revenues and losses derived from underwriting operations during that period. A simplified measure of this activity can be taken by dividing the losses by the premiums. The ratio of incurred losses to earned premiums (*loss ratio*) is a standard measure-

Exhibit 1

Measurement of Underwriting Income

($ omitted)

		Statutory	GAAP
Net Premiums Written		120	120
UPR end of prior period	47		
UPR end of current period	−55		
Change in UPR	− 8		
Premiums Earned		112	112
Loss reserves end of current period	155		
Loss reserves end of prior period	−130		
Change in loss reserves	25		
Paid losses	55		
	80		
Losses Incurred		80	80
Acquisition Expenses	30		
Deferred Acquisition Expenses (25 %* of change in UPR)	− 2		
	28		
Expenses Incurred		30	28
Total Losses & Expenses Incurred		110	108
UNDERWRITING INCOME		2	4

(Premiums Earned less Losses
and Expenses Incurred)

Loss Ratio	$\left(\dfrac{\text{Losses Incurred}}{\text{Premiums Earned}} \right)$	=	71.4%
*Expense Ratio	$\left(\dfrac{\text{Expenses Incurred}}{\text{Premiums Written}} \right)$	=	25.0%
Trade Ratio			96.4%

* As a simplified GAAP calculation, the expense ratio (25%) is applied to the change in UPR (8) to produce the amount of acquisition expenses to be deferred (2).

ment of relative loss performance for property and casualty insurers and reinsurers alike.

As stated previously, the treatment of *expenses incurred* is the key difference between the statutory and the GAAP measurement of underwriting income. Although a company may not fully "earn" the premiums received in a given period, it has actually paid expenses to acquire those premiums in the form of commissions, brokerage fees, as well as its own overhead costs for such items as salaries, furniture, and office space. Under *statutory* accounting procedures, acquisition expenses are considered incurred during the period in which they are spent. In determining a valid measure of expenses relative to premiums for the reporting period, statutory expenses are divided by the net premiums written (rather than earned) to produce an *expense ratio.*

On a *GAAP* basis, acquisition expenses are deemed to be incurred only when the corresponding premium has been earned, and are therefore deferred to the extent that the premiums are unearned. The simplest, though not always precise, method of calculating deferred acquisition costs is to apply the expense ratio to the change in UPR (see Exhibit 1). For a reinsurer to match the expenses against the UPR accurately, this calculation should be applied on a contract-by-contract basis in order to reflect the wide differences in both acquisition costs and premium reserves between excess of loss and pro rata accounts, and even among pro rata accounts themselves. Although an average expense factor, the expense ratio, can be obtained on the basis of total written premiums, it is not likely to correspond consistently to the varying levels of premiums unearned from one contract to another.

Trade Ratio

Through the basic underwriting income formula, the management of a reinsurer can measure the underwriting activity on a contract, product line, departmental or companywide basis, and can appraise the relative performance of each component of the business by calculating the loss and expense ratios. The combination of the loss and expense ratios, the *trade ratio* (or combined ratio), is an overall yardstick of how the business has been managed. Although it is a common form of measurement, when viewed by itself the trade ratio is often misconstrued as a measure of income. In Exhibit 1, the trade ratio produced from the hypothetical numbers is obviously not an indication of the statutory "profit margin." To take this one step further, by applying a loss ratio of 66.4 % to the same premiums earned and an expense ratio of 30 % to the same premiums written, a trade ratio of 96.4 % would again be produced but the statutory underwriting income would be different. The trade ratio is thus not an absolute measurement, but rather the combination of two separate measurements of loss and expense in relation to the business undertaken in the reporting period.

UNDERWRITING VS. OPERATING INCOME

The measurement of underwriting income may be a portrayal of the predominant business activity of a reinsurer, but it is only a contributing factor in the measurement of the company's overall *operating income,* which is the sum of underwriting income and net investment income. Although the subject of investment income is developed fully in the next chapter, it is important to identify the interrelationship between underwriting and investment income in the process and application of measuring underwriting income.

Both underwriting and investment income are dependent upon the amount of reserves established for unearned premiums and outstanding losses. As described earlier, the premium reserves and the loss reserves are balance sheet items used in the determination of underwriting income. The reinsurer earns most of its investment income from the investment of funds (representing balance sheet assets) "set aside" for these reserves. Therefore, the size and composition of the reserves not only determine underwriting income, they also determine investment income, and hence influence a company's investment policy.

In theory, the unearned premium reserve and the outstanding loss reserve represent the premiums to be refunded and losses to be paid out if a company were to cease doing business. In practice, since reinsurers intend to stay in business, the level of these reserves can provide a measure of a company's capacity to produce adequate underwriting and investment income from the business it assumes on an on-going basis. In this respect, the reserve for outstanding losses is the most critical factor: it is the largest fund maintained by the company, and is also the most susceptible to major changes in the form of large losses. As a general rule, the management of a reinsurer should be more concerned with the adequacy of loss reserves than with underwriting profitability. Although the establishment of adequate reserves might result in a reduction of underwriting income, it might at the same time enhance the income derived from the investment of those funds.

A word of caution is necessary, however. The consistent production of profits from investment depends in large part upon the stability of underwriting results, and the ability of underwriting activity to provide a stream of cash to invested assets. Measurement of cash flow differs from that of underwriting income in that it involves a calculation of premiums *received* minus losses and expenses *paid*. The potential profit advantage of the reinsurer discussed in the opening paragraph of this chapter will become jeopardized if spiraling losses and expenses reduce the net amount of cash flow available for investment. (The subject of cash flow is discussed further in ensuing sections of this chapter.)

Adequacy of Return

RETURN ON EQUITY

Return on equity is one of the traditional criteria used in business to evaluate a company's performance and to compare alternative investment opportunities. This is determined by dividing the overall after-tax net income of a given company by its average capital and surplus (i.e., policyholder surplus) within a reporting period. For both insurance and reinsurance companies the "return" portion of this calculation is divided into three basic elements: underwriting results, investment income, and capital gains or losses.

An historical analysis would show that of the above three elements the primary factor contributing to the overall return on equity for the U.S. property/casualty industry has been investment income. The contribution of underwriting results (statutory or GAAP) to overall industry return on equity has been negligible in recent years, suggesting that insurance companies are seeking at best to break even on underwriting, and are relying on investment income as their primary source of return. (This conclusion ignores, of course, the impact of state regulatory bodies in establishing insurance rates, among other things.)

Taken further, such an analysis would show a particularly high proportion of investment income in the overall return of reinsurance companies. In relation to a primary company with comparable volume and a similar book of business, the cash flow and investment income of a reinsurance company will be better, since not only will its direct costs tend to be lower but the amount of time between the establishment of loss reserves and payment of losses will also be greater. (Of course, the amount and duration of reserves held by a reinsurance company will vary depending on the type of contract, but a certain amount of time will elapse between payment by the primary company and payment by the reinsurer of any given loss. A greater advantage exists for both pro rata and excess of loss contracts, where the reinsurer generally participates in larger risks which take longer to settle. Also, the advantage is particularly evident for types of "long-tail" casualty business such as workers' compensation or disability coverages, where losses are paid out gradually over a long period of time and the reinsurer's share under excess contracts falls at the tail end of the loss payments.)

The temptation to overemphasize the role of investment income, therefore, can be strong for reinsurers. However, in most circumstances, incorporation of investment income considerations into the underwriting decision and rating formula can be a dangerous practice. The long-term success of the reinsurer relies upon its ability to evaluate risks; the prudent underwriter will put aside the consideration of investment income and will establish rates and terms designed to produce an overall underwriting profit. The consideration of long-term underwriting profitability is critically important when one looks at the capital position of the industry in relation to increasing demands for reinsurance capacity. Investment income alone will be insufficient to strengthen surplus and sustain an acceptable return on equity.

What, then, is involved in determining an acceptable margin of underwriting profit? Two of the principal reasons an insurer might purchase reinsurance are protection against catastrophe and stability of results. When reinsurers perform these services via excess of loss reinsurance for the primary industry, they simultaneously expose themselves to the same problem. In fact, reinsurance companies are potentially subject to higher volatility in their underwriting results due to the inherent nature of excess of loss reinsurance. (Of course, certain steps are taken by the reinsurer to mitigate this volatility through its own reinsurance protection, a good "mix" of business, etc.) Accordingly, the reinsurer should contemplate an underwriting profit margin somewhat higher than its primary counterpart, and establish rates accordingly in order to compensate for this higher degree of risk. This higher margin might seem reasonable and appear to be a philosophy easily implemented in view of the relative lack of influence from insurance regulatory bodies over reinsurers. However, the following realities of the reinsurance market make it difficult to obtain adequate underwriting profit margins:

Competition. The competitive activity among established reinsurers is increased further by the formation of new reinsurance companies, departments, or branch offices by domestic and foreign insurers. In order to establish themselves as a market, these newcomers are often willing to accept business at inadequate terms, thus exerting a downward force on the overall rating structure of the reinsurance market.

Inflation. The continuing high rate of both economic inflation and "social inflation" (i.e., the effects of liberal public and judicial attitudes towards awards and settlements occurring from litigation) affects all sectors of the insurance industry. But to the reinsurer the impact of inflation, without corresponding adjustments to retention levels or rates on excess reinsurance, is magnified. This leveraged effect of inflation on reinsurers is best demonstrated with a brief example.

A $5,000,000 excess of loss contract is written with a ceding company retention of $200,000 per occurrence. Over a period of five years the contract terms remain unchanged, but the rate of inflation averages 7% per year. Three losses occur in the first year, and the same three losses occur in the fifth year.

First Year: Loss	Ceding Company Share	Reinsurer Share
1. $150,000	$150,000	—
2. 200,000	200,000	—
3. 350,000	200,000	$150,000
$700,000	$550,000	$150,000

Fifth Year: Loss	Ceding Company Share	Reinsurer Share
1. $197,000	$197,000	—
2. 262,000	200,000	$ 62,000
3. 459,000	200,000	$259,000
$918,000	$597,000	$321,000

The amount of the three losses, subject to a 7% rate of annual inflation, increases by a total of 31% from year one to year five. The reinsurer's share of the losses above the $200,000 retention increases by 114% from year one to year five.

To summarize the question of adequacy, reinsurers have a slight advantage over primary companies with regard to generating investment income, given the general loss payout pattern for a multi-line reinsurer versus that of a primary insurance company. However, the reinsurer should avoid the temptation to pursue this advantage at the expense of sound underwriting standards. Rather, the reinsurer should price its product to compensate for an inherently higher degree of risk being assumed. Only then can a reinsurance company attain long-term returns on capital attractive enough to compete with other industries. Unfortunately, competitive and economic factors do not always support pricing of reinsurance at a level sufficient to compensate for this higher degree of volatility. The determination of an acceptable profit margin therefore can not be expressed in terms of a textbook formula, and frequently the adequacy of return on underwriting can only be determined in retrospect.

PREMIUM-TO-SURPLUS RATIO

The previous discussion has centered around the importance of the reinsurer's maintaining an attractive overall return on equity, and the importance of the contribution of underwriting income toward that end. At this point another measure of the insurance company as a business concern should be touched upon, namely the premium-to-surplus ratio, which is a general measure of solvency. Without belaboring the pro's and con's of this particular gauge, underlying this measure is the assumption that a sound insurance company should maintain a reasonable relationship between its net written premium volume and its statutory (policyholder) surplus. (This concept relates to the concern for solvency by the NAIC, mentioned earlier in this chapter, and hence the statutory surplus is regarded as a "guarantee fund" of the company if it goes out of business.) To fall within the measurement criteria of the NAIC, an insurance company should maintain a premium-to-surplus ratio no greater than 3-to-1, i.e., write no more than $3 in premium per $1 of surplus. Due to the level of risks assumed, it is understandable that the reinsurance industry has consistently maintained an aggregate ratio which is slightly lower than that of the primary industry.

The relevance of this ratio to our discussions rests upon the influence that underwriting income can have on a reinsurer's statutory surplus. As a component of operating income which becomes (after taxes) part of the surplus account, underwriting profit or loss obviously has an ultimate impact on a company's surplus and on its premium-to-surplus ratio. The amount of this profit or loss can thus enhance or diminish a reinsurer's strength and desirability as a reinsurance market.

Without intending to ignore the role that investment income plays in strengthening surplus, the ability of the reinsurer to generate an underwriting profit is becoming more and more critical. In spite of the increasing competition within the reinsurance market, requirements for reinsurance will continue to grow. As a supplement to other sources of capital, internal financing of the industry through underwriting profits is essential if reinsurers are to continue to meet the requirements of the primary insurance market.

Relating Risk to Underwriting Return

A BASIC FORMULA

The Risk Assumed. Obviously, a reinsurer must relate the risk it assumes in a given transaction to the return or margin of profit it anticipates from that transaction. We shall not attempt to develop a complete formula to equate this relationship; many of the factors are in the realm of pure underwriting judgment, and few are susceptible to meaningful actuarial determination.

Some illustrations of the problems of a strict scientific approach are probably pertinent. First, assume two property surplus treaties with essentially identical characteristics — with similarities in premium volumes, maximum and average size risk cessions, geography, expense factors and recent loss histories — and with the only significant variant being a difference in exposure resulting from a portfolio more prone to disaster. An example of this would be a"difference in conditions" (DIC) content of less than five percent in one treaty and over forty percent in the other treaty. Under these circumstances we almost surely have a difference in risk, but one which is difficult to quantify. Another example is two catastrophe covers which are alike in retention, limit, subject premium and state distribution. Both apply essentially to personal lines, but one reinsured company produces its business through a conventional agency plant, and the other through mortgage lending sources. In a hurricane-prone area the risk may be similar, but in tornado territory the possible spot concentrations of the second company are a real difference in risk to a reinsurer.

Thus the first element in our formula, the risk assumed, is difficult to calibrate even in acceptances which are similar. We also find a wide range of covers which command wildly different expected profit margins in the market. Two extremes are illustrated. It has not been unusual to see surplus relief treaties (described in Chapter 6) of more or less guaranteed profit nature carry apparent margins in sliding scale commissions of one or two percent (trade ratio of 98-99%). In deference to currently developing regulatory requirements demanding a transfer of risk, these treaties should be classified as "limited risk treaties." (A general trend of regulation is to render the true "guaranteed profit" treaty extinct.) On the other hand, there are high level excess covers where on any individual cover the reinsurance underwriter does not really expect a loss, but instead considers the cover part of a "book" (a number of similar covers) which is expected to produce an overall, long-term loss ratio in the range of 40-50%. In both of these examples, little actual likelihood of loss has been transferred, yet it seems that the relative profit margin is far greater in the latter case. If we allow perhaps 15% for expenses on the excess covers, at least 35¢ remains out of every premium dollar — versus less than 2¢ in the surplus relief.

Credibility. We have now introduced a new factor into the formula relating risk to return, i.e., credibility, or predictability of result. Again, two extremes are useful as illustrations. On a limited risk type of treaty, if we can obtain accurate results for perhaps five prior years on the subject business, and can also make reasonable actuarial adjustments for inflation, exposure changes, and any other pertinent variables, then we can probably both gauge and limit the chance of loss and, of equal significance, the amount of loss. On a premium of several million dollars, the maximum expected error could easily be less than 10%. In a relatively few years the underwriting will be proven.

At the other extreme is a high level catastrophe excess "book." Take, for example, property covers rated "1% or less on line" (premium divided by limit) — or, to express it in the American market fashion, 100 years or more payback or amortization (limit divided by premium) — where several million dollars of premium generate an aggregate of several hundred million dollars of liability, and we may never know for certain if the underwriter were right or just lucky. The retained profit will, in the aggregate, not have covered the consequences of the super hurricane, the modern day San Francisco earthquake, or whatever. The underwriter is operating at the distant end of the credibility scale as far as any statistical support for the assumptions is concerned; the incentive is possibly a great underwriting result, and hopefully a zero loss ratio.

Credibility differences between these two extremes also influence the predictability of the cash flow generated by the business and therefore the resulting investment income. On a given annual written premium volume, the limited risk treaty will have a very predictable rate of earning the UPR, and probably a reasonably predictable payout rate for outstanding losses. Thus the benefits to the reinsurer, if it is holding the reserves, are quite measurable. On an equal premium volume of high excess business, the rate of earning the premium is also very predictable, and because of lower acquisition costs the actual cash available to the reinsurer for investment may be greater. In fact, if looked at as an isolated transaction, not related to the reinsurer's taxes, dividends, etc., the net premium might be available for investment for one hundred years or more, but, it also might be available for considerably less than one year. If the "100 year" catastrophe occurs early and involves a large portion of the book, a huge negative cash flow is generated. For this reason, few reinsurers give any thought to investment income when setting terms for high excesses — while such income may be the major consideration for the "limited risk treaty."

Between the extremes of the predictable limited risk, quota share treaty and the high level excess cover (alias "sleep-easy cover" — referring, of course, to the state of mind of the buyer and not the underwriter), lies the bulk of the reinsurance transactions which are made today: pro rata contracts involving substantial or total transfer of risk, and working excess contracts and levels of catastrophe covers which expect penetration at fairly frequent intervals. It is not the purpose of this chapter to expound on reinsurance rating theories or enumerate all the known rating and self-rating devices, but a few more illustrations will be offered which relate profit margin to risk.

A first surplus treaty with an annual ceded premium of $6 million to a maximum risk cession of $2 million (excellent balance) will obviously command a lesser anticipated underwriting margin than a second surplus of a million ceded premium and $5 million capacity. To bring the difference into sharper focus, a total loss represents 33-1/3 points of loss ratio on the first treaty and 500 points on the second. Even if the quality of business ceded and the adequacy of the primary rating are the same for both, the reinsurer runs a far greater risk on the second surplus over a relatively short period of five to ten years. Only in the long run, if other factors could be held constant, would the element of risk (the departure from 100% credibility) under each treaty theoretically approach equality.

Another relationship of risk to profit margin exists in self-rating plans of the nature of spread loss and swing plans. The greater the spread between the maximum rate or premium and the expected losses or "burning costs," the less the risk (or chance of an underwriting loss) to the reinsurer. The underwriting margin, along with provision for expenses, for this type of rating is a component of the loss loading factor, usually expressed as a fraction with a value greater than unity, i.e., 100/75ths, 100/80ths, etc. (which means the reinsurer is charging the reinsured 133%, 125%, etc., of the burning cost, which represents the loss portion of the rate). If we had established a loading of 100/70ths for a particular cover with a given maximum rate, a negotiation to increase the maximum rate might be expected to lead to a lower loading factor, say 100/75ths. Similarly, in a contingent fund or banking plan, a higher overall rate allows a lesser reinsurance charge: for example, a shift from an 80-20 program (80% of the premium to the fund — 20% to reinsurance charge, expenses, etc.) to an 85-15 split.

A final example should prove the point without belaboring it unnecessarily. Given excess loss experience during the rating period of a working excess of:

10 losses between $100,000 and $200,000,
4 losses between $200,000 and $300,000,
2 losses between $300,000 and $500,000, and
1 loss in excess of $1,000,000,

if a fixed rate were being developed for alternate cover limits of $500,000 or $1,000,000, the use of the same loss loading applied to the respective burning costs would not be sound. The credibility of the experience for the upper $500,000 of cover is much less than for the lower, and a higher expected *margin* of profit is appropriate to the larger limit.

Stability. In previous paragraphs we have touched upon time periods relating to credibility, or perhaps even more appropriately, predictability of result. But does the reinsurer have all the necessary time to see the final hoped for result or to make appropriate corrections? Only with a stable account. Compared with this final factor in our formula, the others seem the essence of simplicity to quantify.

Some factors which affect the stability of an account are: personalities, ability to pay (profit or loss position), management ethics, management philosophies, changes in management, obligations to stockholders. Yet, most reinsurance underwriters attempt to make an objective evaluation of this quality and let it influence their decisions. Don't they all "sharpen their pencil" for the account they expect to persist with them through good times and bad? What else is "sharpening the pencil" than accepting a lesser expected profit margin for a given reinsurance transfer of risk, in this case in the expectancy of being able to correct deficiencies after they appear? Despite constantly increasing competition for the reinsurance premium dollar and increasing cost pressure on ceding company management, there remain many ceding companies of all sizes which feel that their reputation for stability is a valuable asset.

Our basic formula relating risk to return is now established. Whatever target a reinsurer has selected for overall or average return, to attain it the underwriting of the average risk must seek the average return. Adjustments for above or below average credibility and stability, while keeping the target in sight, are the real tests for underwriting skill.

Having looked in some detail at the profit element in a single reinsurance transaction, we must progress to the various ways a reinsurer may group its acceptance to analyze the relative profit return.

THE ACCOUNT CONCEPT

The account concept is important to both reinsurers and reinsureds. For example, this concept would most certainly apply to a reinsured account that has three profitable contracts with a reinsurer and is resisting an improvement in terms on a fourth which has had a nominal loss. Another hypothetical case with accounts for similar Companies A and B will illustrate the fallacy of simply adding the underwriting results. The table represents the underwriting result for a ten-year period of each treaty.

	Account	
	A	**B**
First Surplus	+ 1,500,000	0
Risk Excess	+ 500,000	+ 500,000
First Catastrophe	+ 250,000	+ 1,750,000
	+ 2,250,000	+ 2,250,000

Both seem to be desirable accounts, as well they may be, but if each of the companies carries fairly similar terms on the respective treaties, the accounts are quite different. If the first catastrophe covers are rated at 5% on line, or a twenty-year payback, Company A seems to have literally weathered a storm, whereas Company B has some clouds on its horizon. When B's catastrophe inevitably hits, the reinsurer's prospective profits for the next ten years will be nominal, if any. At the next renewal, A might be anticipating renewal "as expiring" or even with some improvement in terms, while B might be faced with a commission reduction on its surplus treaty.

The point here is that the grouping of dissimilar coverages, with substantially different risk elements, is not a satisfactory way to measure or equate profit, even over extended time periods. It is difficult to deny that an account showing a profit balance has an advantage over one showing a loss, under any circumstances, but the underwriter who is too lazy to make a judgment analysis of the profit vs. risk components of the whole account deserves his or her ultimate fate.

However, reinsurers do group and track results of similar covers for management control and to develop underwriting policy. In so doing a reinsurer may find, for instance, that its five-year experience on property risk excess business is ten points better than its corresponding experience on property surplus treaties. This may or may not be acceptable to the reinsurer, depending on such factors as relative catastrophe exposure, net accumulated cash flow, or simply a change in point difference from a comparable prior period. The analysis of these covers in relation to one another enables management to determine whether or not such a difference in results is cause for corrective strategy.

Facultative reinsurance is different in almost every respect. Except for the relatively new "buffer layer" concept in casualty or the comparatively rare pro rata facultative of primary coverages of very large risks, the facultative underwriter does not expect to have a loss when accepting an individual risk. Having the opportunity to underwrite the risk, not a privilege normally enjoyed by a treaty underwriter, the facultative underwriter does not expect sympathy from the reinsured if there is a loss. The direct control of coverage and pricing of each and every risk is the envy of the treaty underwriter, but to counterbalance this is the fact that the facultative underwriter only sees risks that a direct underwriter had decided were problems. Many times, if not most often, the underwriter alone or in combination with other facultative underwriters has a much larger share of the exposure than the direct company. Credibility and stability are low on such facultative business and the risk element is frequently high, demanding a superior underwriting result as a target.

Reserves and Cash Flow

Loss and loss adjustment expense reserving involves the current financial evaluation of costs associated with losses which may or may not have been reported. These reserves must be estimated. They cannot precisely be determined in advance. It is therefore vital that proper actuarial and statistical techniques be employed, for without reliable reserve estimates an accurate evaluation of the financial condition of an insurer cannot be accomplished. The point is equally appropriate for a segment of an insurer's business being evaluated for reinsurance.

The ultimate loss reserve for a group of losses is the amount that must be paid in the future to settle all such losses that have occurred during some particular accounting period. This ultimate loss reserve can only be known when all claims in the group have finally been settled. Prior to that time, the value of the total loss reserve must be estimated. For a specific group of claims, the insurer's estimate of the total loss reserve will likely change from one valuation date to another.

A division is usually required between claims which are known and have been recorded on the insurer's accounts and claims which have been incurred but not reported (IBNR). The IBNR reserve is generally defined as consisting of two components. The first of these elements is the "true" IBNR: the provision for those claims whose existence is completely unknown to the company at the date of valuation. This provision reflects the predicted delay in reporting losses to the company and varies with characteristics of the claims being considered. The second component consists of the further development on the reserve for known claims, which includes a provision required for reopened claims.

As loss reserving is fundamentally concerned with the estimation of ultimate loss costs on unpaid claims, an understanding of the trends and changes affecting the settlement of such claims is a prerequisite to the application of proper reserving methods. Generally, claims are homogeneously grouped with consideration of comparable claim experience patterns, settlement patterns, or size of loss distributions. Such a grouping of data must have a proper degree of credibility, i.e., should be large enough to be statistically reliable. The reserving techniques applied to this data can then vary, and the selection of the most appropriate method of reserving estimation is usually the responsibility of an actuary. A competent actuary will ordinarily examine the indications of more than one method before arriving at an evaluation of an insurer's reserve liability. Detailed discussions of the technology and applicability of loss reserving practices is beyond the scope of this chapter. However, it should be kept in mind that the ultimate loss cost will one day be known. The reserving techniques will therefore, in the fullness of time, be measured by the tests of hindsight.

Reinsurance contracts generate cash flow for the reinsurer in as many ways as there are types and variations of reinsurance contracts and terms. Generally, premiums are paid to the reinsurer less any contractual commission allowances and brokerage. The net premium and loss reserves are then held by the reinsurer until the premiums are earned and until the ceding company settles the claims and submits accounts for reimbursement. On rare occasions these funds are withheld by the ceding company, and a combination of interest rate and underwriting terms is negotiated to compensate the reinsurer for investment income otherwise generated by such funds (a common practice outside the U.S. and Canada). Incoming and outgoing premium and loss portfolios obviously have a major effect on the cash flow and the resulting investment income.

To measure cash flow for a specific type of reinsurance, it is useful to construct a model account. A model with simplified assumptions is developed in Exhibit 2 for the purpose of demonstrating the magnitude of cash flow for this particular type of reinsurance account, as shown in Exhibit 3. The model assumes a casualty excess of loss contract in force for the calendar year 1977 with less than desirable underwriting results. Losses covered are those with an accident date during calendar year '77, and the reinsurer is liable for its share of the ultimate losses incurred on such claims. Other specific assumptions are as follows:

1. The annual premium is $1,000,000 payable in four equal quarterly installments.

2. Each installment is received and deposited by the reinsurer in the quarter following.

3. Brokerage is 5%.

4. The account will produce an operating (trade) ratio of 115% and an underwriting loss of $150,000 before administration expenses of 2.9% (shown below).

5. At the end of the fourth quarter, the account is fully and properly reserved.

6. The loss pay-out distribution covers an eight-year period. The distribution was derived from casualty excess of loss experience recorded by a major U.S. reinsurer.

Exhibit 3 demonstrates the estimation of cash available each quarter for investment. A 6% annual rate of return is calculated compounded quarterly, and a present value of such investment income is determined at the end of the contract year.

In summary, the model account produces the following experience:

	Income	% to Premium Earned
Underwriting (Exhibit 2, column 10)	$(150,000)	(15.0)%
Investment (Exhibit 3, column 10)	200,768	20.1%
Gross Result	50,768	5.1%
Administration Expense	(29,000)	2.9%
Net Result	$ 21,768	2.2%

Exhibit 2

Reinsurance Model — Casualty Excess of Loss Contract
(Losses to be Run Off)

Cal. Year (1)	Rein- surer Quarter (2)	Ceding Co. Quarter (3)	Premiums Written & Earned (4)	5% Expense Allowance (5)	Begin- ning OSLR* (6)	Losses Paid (7)	Ending OSLR* (8)	Losses Incurred (9)	Statutory Result (10)	Operating Ratio (11)
1977	1				0	0	0	0	0	.0
1977	2	1	250,000	12,500	0	0	0	0	237,500	5.0
1977	3	2	250,000	12,500	0	0	150,000	150,000	87,500	65.0
1977	4	3	250,000	12,500	150,000	0	650,000	500,000	−262,500	205.0
1978	1	(1977)4	250,000	12,500	650,000	0	1,100,000	450,000	−212,500	185.0
			1,000,000	50,000	0	0	1,100,000	1,100,000	−150,000	115.0
1978	2				1,100,000	53,900	1,046,100	0	0	
1978	3				1,046,100	53,900	992,200	0	0	
1978	4				992,200	53,900	938,300	0	0	
1979	1				938,300	50,875	887,425	0	0	
1979	2				887,425	50,875	836,550	0	0	
1979	3				836,550	50,875	785,675	0	0	
1979	4				785,675	50,875	734,800	0	0	
1980	1				734,800	49,500	685,300	0	0	
1980	2				685,300	49,500	635,800	0	0	
1980	3				635,800	49,500	586,300	0	0	
1980	4				586,300	49,500	536,800	0	0	
1981	1				536,800	32,725	504,075	0	0	
1981	2				504,075	32,725	471,350	0	0	
1981	3				471,350	32,725	438,625	0	0	
1981	4				438,625	32,725	405,900	0	0	
1982	1				405,900	39,600	366,300	0	0	
1982	2				366,300	39,600	326,700	0	0	
1982	3				326,700	39,600	287,100	0	0	
1982	4				287,100	39,600	247,500	0	0	
1983	1				247,500	32,450	215,050	0	0	
1983	2				215,050	32,450	182,600	0	0	
1983	3				182,600	32,450	150,150	0	0	
1983	4				150,150	32,450	117,700	0	0	
1984	1				117,700	29,425	88,275	0	0	
1984	2				88,275	29,425	58,850	0	0	
1984	3				58,850	29,425	29,425	0	0	
1984	4				29,425	29,425	0	0	0	
			1,000,000	50,000	0	1,100,000	0	1,100,000	−150,000	115.0

* Outstanding loss reserves.

Exhibit 3

Reinsurance Model — Casualty Excess of Loss Contract
(Cash Flow & Investment Income)

Cal. Year (1)	Rein-surer Quarter (2)	Ceding Co. Quarter (3)	Change in Cash Position During Quarter* (4)	Average Change (4) × .5 (5)	Cash Position at Beginning of Quarter (6)	Average Cash Position (5) + (6) (7)	Investment Inc. for Quarter (7) × .015 (8)	Cumulative Investment Income (9)	Present Value of Investment Income (10)	Cumulative Present Value (11)
1977	1		0	0	0	0	0	0	0	0
1977	2	1	237,500	118,750	0	118,750	1,781	1,781	1,781	1,781
1977	3	2	237,500	118,750	239,281	358,031	5,370	7,151	5,370	7,151
1977	4	3	237,500	118,750	482,151	600,901	9,014	16,165	9,014	16,165
1978	1 (1977)4		237,500	118,750	728,665	847,415	12,711	28,876	12,711	28,876
			950,000					28,876	28,876	28,876	28,876
1978	2		−53,900	−26,949	978,876	951,927	14,279	43,155	14,068	42,944
1978	3		−53,900	−26,949	939,255	912,306	13,685	56,840	13,284	56,228
1978	4		−53,900	−26,949	899,040	872.091	13,081	69,921	12,510	68,738
1979	1		−50,875	−25,437	858,221	832,784	12,492	82,413	11,770	80,508
1979	2		−50,875	−25,437	819,838	794,401	11,916	94,329	11,061	91,569
1979	3		−50,675	−25,437	780,879	755,442	11,332	105,661	10,364	101,933
1979	4		−50,875	−25,437	741,336	715,899	10,738	116,399	9,675	111,608
1980	1		−49,500	−24,749	701,199	676,450	10,147	126,546	9,008	120,616
1980	2		−49,500	−24,749	661,846	637,097	9,556	136,102	8,358	128,974
1980	3		−49,500	−24,749	621,902	597,153	8,957	145,059	7,718	136,692
1980	4		−49,500	−24,749	581,359	556,610	8,349	153,400	7,088	143,780
1981	1		−32,725	−16,362	540,208	523,846	7,858	161,266	6,572	150,352
1981	2		−32,725	−16,362	515,341	498,979	7,485	168,751	6,168	156,520
1981	3		−32,725	−16,362	490,101	473,739	7,106	175,857	5,769	162,289
1981	4		−32,725	−16,362	464,482	448,120	6,722	182,579	5,377	167,666
1982	1		−39,600	−19,799	438,479	418,680	6,280	188,859	4,949	172,615
1982	2		−39,600	−19,799	405,159	385,360	5,780	194,639	4,488	177,103
1982	3		−39,600	−19,799	371,339	351,540	5,273	199,912	4,033	181,136
1982	4		−39,600	−19,799	377,012	317,213	4,758	204,670	3,586	184,722
1983	1		−32,450	−16,224	302,170	285,946	4,289	208,959	3,184	187,906
1983	2		−32,450	−16,224	274,009	257,785	3,867	212,826	2,829	190,735
1983	3		−32,450	−16,224	245,426	229,202	3,438	216,264	2,478	193,213
1983	4		−32,450	−16,224	216,414	200,190	3,003	219,267	2,132	195,345
1984	1		−29,425	−14,712	186,967	172,255	2,584	221,851	1,808	197,153
1984	2		−29,425	−14,712	160,126	145,414	2,181	224,032	1,503	198,656
1984	3		−29,425	−14,712	132,882	118,170	1,773	225,805	1,204	199,860
1984	4		−29,425	−14,712	105,230	90,518	1,358	227,163	908	200,768
			−150,000					227,163	227,163	200,768	200,768

*Excludes Investment Income

A Reinsurance Portfolio

Within the long-range objectives of the reinsurer, the ultimate concern is underwriting income and cash flow for investment. From time to time, a given line of business may offer unusual reinsurance profit opportunities and tempt a reinsurer to concentrate its efforts on this line for maximum profit. This successful result will almost certainly be short-lived, since the impact of competitive and economic factors on underwriting margins will eventually have a dampening effect on experience. Often the underwriting cycle includes an extended period of loss.

The reinsurer mitigates this adverse experience across lines of business through balance: a mix of business, while not necessarily constant (to the contrary, the availability of various kinds of business at acceptable terms and short-term profit opportunities should not be totally ignored), which enables the reinsurer to ride out catastrophes, underwriting down cycles, accelerated inflation, and other similar events without encountering dangerous financial strain.

A cynical definition of a balanced portfolio is one which never misses a loss. Despite the ominous implication, this might not be an unrealistic goal for a reinsurer, if its share of every loss relates properly to its volume and financial strength. If it were to ensure that it never missed a loss, a reinsurer would have to:

1) have optimum geographic spread;
2) reinsure all lines and classes of business;
3) accept business from a large number of ceding companies, and
4) underwrite all kinds of reinsurance contracts, treaty and facultative, pro rata and excess, per risk and catastrophe.

Does it sound so bad when expressed that way? Within practical bounds, this is the profile of the world's largest and most successful reinsurers.

The reinsurer's talents for production and selection are the principal tools to build the balance, but the reinsurance demands of the ceding companies cannot be ignored and often militate against balance. Therefore, other tools are needed in the form of the reinsurer's retrocessional facilities. For example, earthquake-prone countries tend to produce extremes of earthquake exposure to reinsurers. A retrocessional catastrophe cover can improve the balance of a reinsurer's portfolio, but because of a restricted market for such covers the protection may not be adequate or may be prohibitive as to cost for a satisfactory level of cover. A pro rata retrocessional facility, placed in small units around the world with reinsurers and insurers alike has tremendous potential value. It reduces even a major local disaster to manageable pieces and distributes the pieces throughout the world economy. The same principle applies generally within the U.S. market, whereby the regional or local insurer can well afford to assume small portions of exposure peculiar to other regions of the country, and can probably profit from it, in return for part of the exposure which it cedes.

Through the process of retrocession, the reinsurer substantially augments its function as a risk bearer for the insurance industry by acting as a conduit for redistribution of exposure, not incidentally augmenting its income through overriding commissions. In the world market the reciprocity thus provided may be essential to obtain other profitable business, and the danger of retroceding poor business or frequent underwriting losses to one's own customers is obvious. The effective use of retrocessions is therefore a key element in the stability and profitability of the reinsurer over time, and the reinsurer's underwriting skills are as vital to the success of this type of arrangement as they are to the net retained portfolio.

Summary

Underwriting income affects virtually all facets of an insurance or reinsurance company's operations — from underwriting decisions to reporting and regulation.

As a standard portrayal of the predominant business activity of a reinsurance company, underwriting income represents the net premiums earned minus the losses and expenses incurred. This all-too-simple formula is comprised of underlying calculations to determine each of its components. It is affected by the establishment of premium and loss reserves, and the respective influence of these reserves on premiums earned and losses incurred. Also, while the statutory reporting formula required by state insurance commissioners treats expenses as incurred when spent, the generally accepted accounting principles treat most expenses as incurred only as premiums are earned.

Although underwriting income is measurable in slightly different ways for different purposes, it is just one component of a company's total earnings. In fact, most of the actual profits of a reinsurer are usually derived from investment income. This can be deceptive, however, since chronic underwriting losses will erode a reinsurer's surplus and its ability to generate funds for investment, and thereby will diminish its capacity to provide a market for client companies. The key to achieving consistent earnings is to seek an optimal underwriting margin on the risk assumed.

The concept of relating a given risk to its anticipated underwriting margin, or return, is not always measurable by strict formula. Frequently, the evaluation of each risk and its ultimate potential for loss is almost purely judgmental. However, once a reinsurer has established a target for overall or average return, the underwriting of a given risk involves making adjustments for credibility — or predictability of result — and for the stability of the account with an aim toward the average return. These adjustments are not always calculable, since for certain types of risk, such as a high level excess cover, the credibility is almost nil. Where credibility and/or stability are low, the element of risk is frequently high, and it is appropriate to expect a higher margin of profit in order to aim for the targeted overall return.

The treatment of the various elements which either comprise or affect underwriting income can be shown in a model reinsurance account, which stresses the impact of two important considerations: the establishment of loss reserves and the development of cash flow. The model in Exhibits 2 and 3 is worth studying carefully, since it pulls together much of the chapter text in terms of actual figures.

Finally, no reinsurance company relies on one account, or one type of risk, and the ultimate reflection of underwriting income is in the company's entire portfolio. The successful portfolio mix is designed to assume a fairly wide spectrum of exposures to mitigate adverse loss experience in any particular area, and hence to ensure the stability of underwriting results necessary for long-term growth and profitability.

*   *   *   *   *   *

About the Author of Chapter 17

Guy K. Patterson heads both the international and the reinsurance operations of INA Corporation. Mr. Patterson's entire insurance career has been with INA. A native of Harrisburg, Illinois, and a graduate of the University of Illinois, he joined the Chicago Office of Insurance Company of North America, a major subsidiary of INA Corporation, in 1948. For the following sixteen years, he was active in INA's field operations, advancing to management positions in the company's Birmingham, Richmond, and Baltimore offices. In 1964 he was transferred to INA's headquarters in Philadelphia as manager of ceded reinsurance. He was elected assistant secretary of Insurance Company of North America in 1966, secretary in 1967, and assistant vice president in 1968.

INA Reinsurance Company was formed in April 1971 as an expansion of INA's reinsurance department. Mr. Patterson was elected a vice president of the new company. He advanced to senior vice president and in January, 1975, was appointed president and chief executive officer. He was elected chairman and chief executive officer in 1978. In 1977, he was elected to the additional office of president, chairman, and chief executive officer of INA International Corporation, responsible for all INA's insurance and reinsurance activities in over 145 countries around the world.

18

Investment Income

by Stanley Taben*

Overall Investment Responsibilities

ORGANIZATION

There are two sources of income in any insurance operation — underwriting and investment. While the primary purpose of an insurer is to take risks through underwriting, the insurer also takes risks in its investment function. From the time premiums are received until losses and expenses are paid, many correct decisions must be made if the insurer is to preserve the funds entrusted to it for future obligations. In that respect, the role of the chief investment officer is not unlike that of the chief underwriting officer. Both work with large numbers in striving for stability. Both expect to produce profitable results for the firm. And the success of both is dependent on certain internal variables within the firm and certain external variables outside the firm.

Internally, the underwriting officer is concerned with skills in selecting risk which are properly priced and which are not unduly concentrated — by location, by line, or by retention. The investment officer is concerned with skills in selecting securities and other assets which are fairly valued and which are not unduly concentrated — by industry, by debt or ownership, or by proportions appropriate to the insurer's underwriting "mix." Externally, the underwriting officer must cope with such forces as competition from other insurers, government regulation, infla-

* President, SwissRe Advisers, Inc., 100 East 46th Street, New York, New York 10017.

tion, and vagaries of the weather which can produce catastrophes. The investment officer must also face competition from other investors, government regulation, inflation, and vagaries of the financial world which produce changes in interest rates and security valuations. The chief contribution made by successful investment management within an insurer is to provide an essential cushion against any periodic under-writing losses which may occur, even when underwriting efficiency is at its peak. This involves a steady, reliable flow of investment income, pru-dent investment of loss reserves, and investment of shareholders' equity in a manner designed to keep pace with inflation.

The investment officer is not without help in making decisions. A financial or similarly designated committee of the board of directors of a reinsurer is generally charged with responsibility for management of in-vested assets. The actual investment management of the reinsurer's assets on a day-to-day basis is the responsibility of the senior financial officer of the company, acting under authority granted by the board of directors to the finance committee and in accordance with the overall investment policies established by the finance committee. This committee is usually composed of both inside and outside directors of the company, the inside directors to include the chief executive officer and possibly one or more senior officers of the company. The outside members are appointed for their economic, financial, or investment expertise. The finance commit-tee generally meets monthly to consider the prevailing economic and in-vestment environment and set investment policy. This policy is stated in broad terms and is based on the reinsurer's own tax situation, liquidity position, and other individual needs as well as financial conditions in the market.

INVESTMENT ALTERNATIVES

Broad investment policy involves 1) the allocation of invested assets among various classes of investments such as bonds, common stocks, and preferred stocks; 2) the allocation of fixed-income assets between taxable and tax-exempt bonds; 3) carefully determining the average maturity of the bond portfolio; and other broad policy matters. In addition, the finance committee would likely establish a particular investment pro-gram in terms of security purchases and sales for the period until the next monthly meeting, as well as formally approve all security transactions completed since the last meeting. The finance committee also considers any other matters relevant to the company's invested assets and financial condition and reports regularly to the full board of directors on the status of the reinsurer's invested assets.

Historically, responsible investment management has been a steady contributor to the reinsurer's total operating results, because investment income grows from the cash flow of premium income and from the increasing investible assets of a reinsurer experiencing financial growth. On the other hand, underwriting income is uncertain because of the frequency and severity of losses. At any time, investment income is of primary importance to a reinsurer, because it is the major source of its operating profit. Exhibit 1 summarizes the underwriting and investment income for the two largest United States reinsurers (whose stock is widely held) over the eleven-year period, 1967-1977. The figures shown are before applicable income taxes.

For the reinsurers shown, their steady growth of investment income over eleven years was not interrupted by underwriting losses, since their invested assets were increasing despite their underwriting losses. This divergence of results is possible with an increase in annual premium volume over years, because many underwriting losses do not result in immediate payment, especially liability claims. Yet the rising premium volume increases cash flow, income, and assets in the meantime. For example, when an underwriting loss is acknowledged by a ceding company (or "incurred"), the reinsurer does not ordinarily pay out any cash. Some losses, however, (such as the hull portion of an aircraft loss) are paid within twenty-four hours of the event. The normal lag in payment of a liability claim requiring litigation is due to the delay between the time of a loss and the agreement of the parties in a damage suit to the amount of the claim. This delay can be a matter of years. For those liability claims not requiring litigation, the delay is much less. Thus, even after a loss has been incurred, the reinsurer retains for a while as an asset the estimated amount to be paid as a liability, i.e., the loss reserve, and the assets behind this loss reserve continue to earn income. In a growing company with rising premium volume, then, the loss reserves steadily increase — absent other causal factors — and the assets behind the reserves also increase. And to the extent a reinsurer realizes an operating profit, its shareholders' equity also increases, further increasing the base on which investment income can be earned.

While the basic business of reinsurance is underwriting, with the reinsurer striving to garner an underwriting profit, it is clear that the bulk of the operating profit is derived from investments. The outlook for continuing growth in premium volume seems favorable. But underwriting prospects are not as sanguine and only modest profits are likely to be achieved. Thus, it seems inevitable that the investment phase of the reinsurer's business will gain increasing importance in the future.

EXHIBIT 1

SUMMARY AND COMPARISON OF
UNDERWRITING AND INVESTMENT DATA

(Before Income Taxes, 000 Omitted)

1967-1977

	COMPANY A				COMPANY B			
	Total Assets	Net Premiums Written	Underwriting Income (Loss)	Net Investment Income	Total Assets	Net Premiums Written	Underwriting Income (Loss)	Net Investment Income
1967	$ 257,032	$ 123,745	$ 2,202	$ 7,173	$ 339,598	$ 136,878	$ 413	$ 10,411
1968	279,643	127,098	109	8,173	388,306	158,237	2,611	11,913
1969	303,448	150,489	737	9,508	444,358	191,695	1,851	14,497
1970	340,128	168,810	(1,275)	11,512	546,858	223,998	(855)	18,765
1971	402,988	184,617	6,434	13,757	659,528	252,578	5,246	22,601
1972	471,134	193,009	8,141	16,277	807,015	273,129	2,804	27,136
1973	500,496	199,074	(3,472)	18,400	864,645	297,126	(4,153)	33,737
1974	493,215	229,500	(45,656)	21,332	869,323	331,771	(25,260)	38,224
1975	555,718	263,727	(36,315)	23,890	1,093,655	428,784	(35,949)	44,224
1976	700,901	313,725	(13,912)	32,136	1,370,100	522,238	(5,389)	57,169
1977	816,356	338,150	(623)	40,694	1,595,170	565,669	6,737	71,209

Source: *Best's Insurance Reports, Property-Casualty* (A. M. Best Company, Oldwick, New Jersey 08858), appropriate years.

Traditional Investment Policies

SELECTION

Traditionally, investment policy has been concerned with using cash flow to maximize investment income — with due consideration of the reinsurer's need for liquidity and for stability of asset market value. Investment management, therefore, involves selecting particular securities — fixed income assets as backing for reserve liabilities, common stocks for surplus, and preferred stocks as a hybrid for both surplus and reserves. For the most part, traditional investment strategy can be characterized as one of "buy and hold." Fixed income investments are bought with the idea of holding them to their maturity date. In a similar fashion, common stocks are also bought with a long view of the holding period. For example, once an attractive stock investment is identified, the intention is to "live with the company," so-to-speak, to enjoy the combination of increasing dividends and capital appreciation expected over the longer term.

The reasoning behind the traditional investment approach was that historical changes in interest rates and stock prices were relatively mild. And these changes were expected in the normal course of the business cycle with its regular expansions and contractions. In the case of common stocks, the ups and downs of stock market movements were smoothed out for the investor by "dollar averaging." This technique simply means that systematic purchase of securities was made in equal dollar amounts, regardless of their unit price. Over a long period of time, and as long as the market price rises and falls, the *average cost* of all shares bought will be lower than the *average price* at which the shares are bought, because more shares will have been bought at the lower prices. Additionally, the theory was that a generally rising trend in the long term for the stock market would only be interrupted now and then by limited business recessions. In such a long-term environment the average price at which the stock would be acquired through dollar averaging would be comfortably below some eventual future price, which was expected to be higher.

In the case of fixed income investments, purchase of bonds was also made on a "dollar averaging basis." The rising interest rates which accompanied periods of expanding business provided an opportunity to acquire higher yielding bonds with the substantial cash flow. And this has a beneficial impact on overall investment income. Falling interest rates in subsequent slack business periods were "averaged" with the higher rates over the long term.

The Seventies

The traditional approach to investments was stunned by the traumatic economic events of the mid-1970's. The United States economy suffered a period of double digit inflation, accompanied by a steep recession in the wake of: 1) quadrupling the price of oil by the Organization of Petroleum Exporting Countries (OPEC); 2) major crop shortfalls caused by adverse weather; 3) the bursting of the speculative bubble in real estate, particularly the real estate investment trusts (REITs); and 4) the uncovering of New York City's untenable financial condition and its near bankruptcy. In the financial markets, interest rates soared to double digit levels in both the short and long-term sectors of the market. Peak yields of 12% were reached for short-term prime bank certificates of deposit, as well as the long-term debentures of an "A" rated electric utility company. Aaa telephone debentures yielded 10%. Stock prices plunged, with the popular Dow Jones Industrial Average falling below 600. It is therefore understandable that these circumstances gave rise to a re-examination of the traditional approach to investing the assets of a reinsurer. The basic philosophy of investing in common stocks as the appropriate medium for the shareholders' surplus has been questioned. Moreover, in the case of individual common stock holdings themselves, the "buy-and-hold" approach is also being re-studied. Unfortunately, however, no alternative philosophy has achieved general acceptance by the reinsurance industry.

In the case of fixed income portfolios acquired in earlier periods, the extreme rise in yields of 1974 and 1975 in the wake of double digit inflation brought about a severe depreciation in the value of such bond holdings. A $1,000, 5% bond acquired years before was providing income of $50 annually; but when interest rates in the market rose sharply, that bond declined in value to $760, and the market yield on the bond rose to 8%. The tax-exempt bond market received a further blow from the trauma of New York City and its near bankruptcy, which cast a pall over the entire market for state and local government securities. This depressed bond market occurred simultaneously with severely depressed equity levels, plus negative underwriting results. The combination of events had the effect of sharply reducing statutory surplus for the entire industry. Additionally, if fixed income portfolios were to be shown in Annual Statements at market values (as opposed to amortized values), the industry surplus account would have shrunk further to dangerously low levels. The latter phenomenon was not generally appreciated at the time because of the preoccupation with a declining stock market and its severe impact on the highly visible statutory surplus. Exhibit 2 shows two surpluses for each of the illustrative reinsurers — one computed as required by statute (with bonds at amortized values), and the other shown with the bonds appraised at market value. Fortunately, the conditions were short lived but not unimportant: any insurer forced into liquidation would be valued at such depressed levels, and a major catastrophe could have required reinsurers to liquidate bonds at depressed levels to pay massive claims.

EXHIBIT 2

SUMMARY OF POLICYHOLDER SURPLUS

(000 Omitted)

	COMPANY A		COMPANY B	
	Statutory Surplus	Surplus With Bonds at Market Value*	Statutory Surplus	Surplus With Bonds at Market Value*
1972	$124,613	$131,099	$234,795	$236,292
1973	112,977	110,983	217,444	202,240
1974	53,529	5,397	147,825	45,258
1975	53,856	17,278	208,235	121,600
1976	76,342	84,562	279,624	288,027
1977	108,503	102,613	302,687	330,474

*Includes bond investments of domestic subsidiaries.
Source: Annual reports to shareholders.

THE FUTURE

Looking ahead, the problem of a substantial unrealized depreciation on the bond portfolio can become more troublesome if the size of the bond portfolio increases relative to the size of the surplus account. To the extent that the loss reserves and therefore bond investments increase at a faster rate than the surplus account, the leverage of depreciation of the bond portfolio on the surplus will grow. And this seems to be the prospect. Moreover, the amount of bond investments relative to surplus may be further increased by virtue of the trend of investing less than 100% of surplus in common shares in order to shield the surplus account from the volatility of common stock fluctuations. The alternative investment to common stocks is primarily bonds. For statutory purposes a company's surplus in the Annual Statement is not impacted by depreciation on bonds, unless they are sold at such depreciated levels. However, in terms of market values, the "real" surplus of a company can be as devastated by bond depreciation as by stock market depreciation, though this former reality is hidden by statutory accounting.

Considering the importance of the financial position of the reinsurer to the primary company, and the increasing concern about the bond depreciation problem by the regulatory authorities as well, the reinsurer faces what is relatively a new challenge in the development of investment policy. Statutory accounting notwithstanding, the reinsurer cannot continue to completely ignore the influence of the bond portfolio on true or market value surplus. The potential danger of the leverage of a steadily increasing total of bond investments relative to surplus lies in the resultant impact of any rises in market interest rates. Exhibit 2 also shows the statutory surplus of Company A to have declined (from $124 million to $108 million) while its bond portfolio at amortized value (as shown in Exhibit 3 later in this chapter) more than doubled in size (from $259 million to $625 million). In the case of Company B, statutory surplus increased around 30% over the past six years (from $234 million to $302 million), but the bond portfolio at amortized value (Exhibit 3) increased about 170% (from $405 million to $1,111 million). The leverage inherent in these rates of relative growth can be simply illustrated. In the case of Company B, a 30% depreciation in its 1972 bond portfolio of $405 million would cut its surplus then of $234 million in half, and a 60% depreciation would erase it completely. These magnitudes of depreciation were highly unlikely, since they would have required increase in interest rates on the order of 300 basis points (3.00%) and 600 basis points (6.00%) respectively. With the subsequent substantial increase in the bond portfolios vis-a-vis surplus, much less extreme rises in interest rates today would seriously impact market value surplus.

How can the reinsurer maintain the integrity of the surplus account? There is no simple, sound, safe solution to the problem. A reduction in the equity component in favor of bonds is only superficially satisfactory. In the real world of market value, investment of a portion of surplus in bonds as a means of avoiding potential statutory losses on stocks seems to be an example of getting out the frying pan only to land in the fire. And the problem has not been entirely lost on the regulators of the insurance industry. They have initiated studies on the desirability of valuing bonds at market rather than cost. They have also considered whether there should be for the property-liability business a mandatory securities valuation reserve along the lines presently required of the life insurance industry. To date their conclusions have been in the negative.

Just as the reinsurer exercises judgment in underwriting risk, so may it need to exercise judgment in managing the entire investment portfolio. For example, the size of the equity commitment may have to be enlarged or shrunk in line with the outlook for the stock market in general. The analysis of industries and individual stocks may require judgments on timing of purchases and sales based on the price of shares as well as the fundamental long-term outlook for an industry segment or individual common stock. The time horizon that serves as the backdrop for investment forecasts and policy decisions may be much shorter than has been used historically, because price fluctuations that used to take place in full business cycles a year or more can now occur in a matter of months or even weeks.

In the case of bonds, interest rate forecasts may become the primary basis for fixed-income investment policy. Investment of cash flow may not be automatic on receipt. Cash flow may be employed, along with shifts in the existing portfolio, to accomplish material shortening or lengthening of the average maturity of the bond portfolio in line with the forecast of interest rates. Sector analysis dealing with the spread in yield across various quality gradations as well as various classes of fixed income securities will become more important. Analysis of the yield curve will be required to determine how much risk (in terms of additional length of maturity) should be accepted for an increase in yield based on the outlook for interest rates.

A highly flexible investment management approach geared to an objective of overall return for both stocks and bonds requires a change in investment orientation. The relatively passive "buy-and-hold" policy, traditional in the industry, must be converted to active management based on judgments of future financial markets. Through implementation of such an active policy, the reinsurer can more effectively cope with the forces of a difficult and uncertain future environment.

At year-end 1977, as shown by Exhibit 2, the decline in long-term interest rates had restored the amortized cost/market value relationship on bonds to a healthy condition. It might therefore be argued that the problem no longer exists and that consideration of an alternate investment policy should be dismissed. However, another sharp rise in long-term interest rates could well put the industry back into the same financial bind. That financial condition could worsen, since the growth of the bond account has exceeded and likely will continue to exceed the growth of statutory surplus. This worsening could create problems because of the importance of the reinsurers' financial condition to the primary companies. To protect the interest of the ultimate policyholders, the entire insurance industry must maintain a sound financial condition to support the existing underwriting liabilities and to provide for the increasing need of the public for greater insurance protection. In consideration of the present relationship of policyholder surplus to the assets backing reserve liabilities, and the volatile future economic and financial environment, the traditional investment approach may have to be modified if the industry is to remain financially healthy.

Investing to Protect Reserve Liabilities

MODIFIED OBJECTIVES

In the broadest sense, loss reserves represent the accounting provisions made by the reinsurer for unpaid claims at a particular point in time. Reserves are liabilities, therefore, for which certain assets must be maintained for their eventual payment. While a reserve liability cannot be invested, the assets offsetting the liability can be — hence the often used expression, "investment of reserves." The assets behind these loss reserves of the reinsurer, like the assets behind the premium reserves as well as the policyholder surplus, provide the ceding company with security for the due performance of the reinsurer's obligations. The assets behind loss reserves, then, may be thought of as premium income or other assets maintained for later payment of losses not handled immediately. Such losses may have been reported (referred to as "incurred losses"), or not reported (referred to as "incurred but not reported," or IBNR). Each insurer or reinsurer knows from its own experience that for any given amount of losses it incurs in the former category, a certain amount will materialize in the latter, hence the necessity of a reserve for IBNR. For each category, the amounts of the liabilities are based on the reinsurer's estimate of the size of the eventual payment that will be made.

Both classes of loss reserves are invested in certain approved securities with fixed maturity dates such as bonds, because of the reinsurer's need for both safety of principal and liquidity at any given time to meet its obligations. Mortgages provide safety of principal but not liquidity, hence are little used by the property-liability business. Bonds are used to protect loss reserves even though the precise size of the liabilities and their specific dates of payment are not known when the loss reserves are established. In the case of the IBNR's the estimated liability itself is based solely on the presumption of what has actually happened. However, there is some actuarial basis for calculating IBNR's related to an insurer's experience on the grounds that what was needed in the past will again be needed in the future, relatively speaking. The result of the estimate is sufficiently reliable to equate IBNR's with the "incurred" losses insofar as representing an actual fixed liability is concerned.

In developing an appropriate fixed-income investment policy, the reinsurer faces a challenge. The normal objective in making fixed income investments is to maximize interest income. In the case of the reinsurer, however, this objective must be modified by the need to maintain a degree of ready liquidity and some degree of stability of market value of fixed income assets as well. These requirements are made necessary by the nature of the reinsurer's greater underwriting risk and vulnerability vis-a-vis a primary company. The reinsurer must stand ready to meet unexpected and potentially massive drains on invested assets for loss payments with minimal impact on its surplus. If bonds were sold at a loss, the reinsurer's surplus would be affected adversely. These adverse results can arise from natural catastrophes for which ceding companies rely heavily on their reinsurers. Generally speaking, the normal book of treaty and facultative business of the reinsurer can be characterized as one of low frequency but high severity, with the accompanying general uncertainty and potential for large losses that this can involve.

Factors Influencing Reserve Investment Policy

Liquidity and Stability. The reinsurer obtains liquidity by maintaining an appropriate amount of readily marketable, short-term securities. These are usually United States Treasury or federal agency obligations maturing within five years. In selecting securities for liquidity purposes, the investment manager seeks to minimize the potential loss of principal investment, taking into consideration that a future sale may be necessary at a time when there are generally adverse financial conditions in the bond market. To provide stability, the reinsurer will ordinarily emphasize fixed income securities with a term to maturity of perhaps five to fifteen years rather than longer dated issues with maturities of twenty-five years or more. In addition, medium to higher-grade quality securities are usually stressed in view of the need for ready marketability, again in case sales are required at times of adverse financial conditions in the marketplace.

It is important for the reinsurer to maintain some stability of market value even though for statutory purposes fixed investments are shown on the balance sheet at amortized cost value. By way of background, the rationale for this accounting treatment of bonds is based on the assumption that despite potential declines in market values that would result from a rise in interest rates, the fixed income securities would be held to their stated maturity date and therefore redeemed at par or face value. And under all but the most adverse conditions, it would be unlikely that a reinsurer would need to liquidate securities. However, in the unlikely but nonetheless possible event that bonds need be sold, any loss incurred would be a charge against surplus. The loss of surplus would be measured by the proceeds of the sale relative to the amortized cost of the bonds sold. A lower market value of the bond portfolio would come about as a result of a level of interest rates above that at which the bonds were originally acquired.

The need of the reinsurer to provide a degree of liquidity and market value stability to the fixed-income portfolio will penalize investment income somewhat. Otherwise, the reinsurer could acquire lower quality, long dated, less marketable fixed-income securities which carry higher interest rates and produce a greater income for the reinsurer. Thus, as a matter of broad policy, the reinsurer sacrifices investment income for what might be described as investment flexibility.

As a back-up source of financial liquidity, reinsurers can establish lines of credit with commercial banks for meeting potential massive loss payments from catastrophes such as earthquakes. The bank lines could forestall or prevent the liquidation of securities on short notice at less favorable prices than would otherwise be possible from orderly sales. Moreover, the reinsurer's cash flow could be used to repay a portion of the bank borrowings over a period of time and therefore reduce the actual amount of assets that would otherwise need be sold. This use of cash flow would depend on the size of loss payments, the amount of any borrowing, and the magnitude of cash flow.

Operating Profitability. A final key factor influencing investment policy for reserves is the general level of profitability from operating income, derived from the combination of investment income and underwriting income. This combined operating income (or profit) of the reinsurer is subject to the normal corporate tax rate. Thus, anticipating a profitable year, the reinsurer would ordinarily rely heavily on tax-exempt bonds for investment of loss reserves because of their greater post-tax return vis-a-vis taxable bonds. For example, at the approximately 50% normal corporate tax rate, a 5% tax-exempt bond is equivalent to a 10% taxable issue. On the other hand, if in a particular year underwriting losses placed the reinsurer in a non-taxable position (because the bond portfolio and therefore interest earned was largely tax-exempt), the overall operating loss would be employed to recapture past taxes paid, as permitted by Internal Revenue Service. IRS presently permits going back three years to recoup taxes paid.

In the event a year's operating loss exceeds the taxes paid in the prior three years, the reinsurer has two available options. One is to carry any remaining operating loss forward in the expectation of the subsequent years' operating profit. In this way, the loss could be used to shelter future operating profit against taxes up to the amount of the loss. And under present IRS requirements a particular year's loss may be carried forward a maximum of seven years. A second course of action would involve taking immediate advantage of the loss by maximizing current taxable investment income. This would mean investment of cash flow in taxable bonds to generate taxable income in an amount sufficient to offset the loss. And, depending on the magnitude of the loss, it might also be reasonable for the reinsurer to consider accelerating the accumulation of taxable income by switching a portion of tax-exempt bond holdings into taxable bonds subject, of course, to considerations of capital losses on bond sales and their impact on surplus.

The actual strategy adopted at the time would be a matter of what is most sensible, considering the particular circumstances and outlook for underwriting results. Exhibit 3 shows how the two illustrative United States reinsurers modified their investment strategies in the wake of heavy loss years of the mid-1970's. Notice the division of fixed-income portfolios between taxable and tax-exempt bonds, particularly the increase in taxable bonds as operating results became operating losses.

EXHIBIT 3

SUMMARY OF OPERATING INCOME AND BOND HOLDINGS

(000 Omitted)

COMPANY A

	Operating Income (Loss) (Pre-Tax)	Bond Holdings*		
		Taxable	Tax-Exempt	Total
1972	$ 36,265	$ 19,223	$ 240,307	$ 259,530
1973	(3,395)	17,036	264,634	281,670
1974	(58,329)	47,484	259,864	307,348
1975	2,883	126,172	250,412	376,584
1976	26,956	339,568	178,920	518,488
1977	32,583	339,780	286,202	625,982

COMPANY B

	Operating Income (Loss)	Bond Holdings*		
	(Pre-Tax)	Taxable	Tax-Exempt	Total
1972	$ 55,169	$ 43,643	$ 362,179	$ 405,822
1973	(13,920)	48,219	439,656	487,875
1974	(68,996)	41,049	483,032	524,081
1975	63,322	93,254	581,336	674,590
1976	88,280	152,257	755,308	907,565
1977	48,401	186,198	925,332	1,111,530

*Amortized Values

Source: *Best's Insurance Reports, Property-Casualty* (A.M. Best Company, Oldwick, New Jersey 08858), appropriate years.

In the case of Company B, it would seem that diversion of available cash flow to taxable bonds in 1975 and 1976 was the strategy to generate taxable income sufficient to use up the underwriting losses since tax-exempt bond holdings also increased steadily. On the other hand, the magnitude of Company A's underwriting losses resulted in a reduction of tax-exempt bonds in favor of taxables in 1976. Additionally, Company A may have invested its cash flow in taxable bonds to take full and more prompt advantage of its underwriting losses in 1974 and 1975. Moreover, both companies seem to have resumed heavy purchases of tax-exempt bonds in 1977. The taxable bond holdings showed at year end little change (for Company B), or no change (for Company A), while the tax-exempt bond holdings for both increased substantially.

Investing Stockholder Equity

COMMON STOCKS

The investment of stockholders' equity or policyholder surplus, often referred to as "surplus," has traditionally been in common stocks. This tradition reflected the general belief that common stocks represented the best hedge available to the institutional investor to offset the impact of inflation. Over the past few years, however, the policy of investing the surplus in common stocks has been subjected to re-examination for three principal reasons.

First, and largely based on long-term historical experience, it had been assumed generally that inflation was "good" for common stocks vis-a-vis fixed-income securities. It was reasoned that the overall return from stocks (the combination of capital appreciation and dividends) would be sufficient to at least keep pace with the rate of inflation. The return on equities was expected from increased per-share earnings, which in turn would steadily increase the value of the equity and provide the basis for increased dividend payments as well. As to fixed-income securities on the other hand, it was believed that bond prices would be subject to continuing downward pressure because of rising interest rates from inflation. That was the theory supported by several well regarded studies on stocks and bonds.

Most of those supporting studies were done, however, in the early 1970's before inflation had accelerated. The investment experience of the late 1970's has proven quite disappointing. Both the general indices of stock prices and many of the leading equity shares are at valuation levels little changed from those of a decade ago, despite having been at materially higher levels in the intervening years. Moreover, it is now clear that inflation has negative implications for both stocks and bonds. The acceleration of inflation to double-digit proportions following the 1974 quadrupling of oil prices by OPEC and the continuing inflation rate of around 6% since then have both proven to be as damaging to common stocks as to fixed-income securities. These severe changes have pretty much dispelled the traditional view that inflation was "good" for equities and bad for bonds.

Secondly, the reinsurer is re-examining the policy of investing surplus in common stocks, because it has become increasingly likely that the underwriting cycle now coincides with the economic cycle, with highly adverse consequences for surplus. When the economic outlook turns unfavorable and fears of a business recession increase in the minds of investors generally, there is a downward pressure on common stocks. This, in turn, directly impacts the reinsurer's surplus, because common (and preferred) shares are carried on the balance sheet at market values. Any decline in the market value of common shares results in a comparable decline in the surplus account. This pressure on surplus is accentuated because the unsatisfactory phase of the underwriting cycle now seems to occur at the same time, i.e., along with the general business downturn, with the result that underwriting losses are simultaneously depressing statutory surplus. Thus, the ratio of premiums written to statutory surplus, a key measure of the financial standing and strength of a reinsurer, deteriorates by virtue of general economic as well as underwriting circumstances. And, as a further complication, recent experience has been that not only do both the economic and underwriting cycles coincide, but both have proven to be materially more severe than has been in the case of the past.

Thirdly, at the very time the reinsurer would be struggling with this problem of static or even declining surplus, the primary companies are similarly affected. At such time the primary companies are more likely to look to their reinsurers for surplus relief, because they would be experiencing the same difficulties of pressure on surplus based on economic and underwriting adversity. Thus, the shrinking surplus of the reinsurer lessens its ability to accommodate its ceding companies with surplus relief and take on additional premium volume at the very time when it is most compelling to do so.

In summary, the reinsurer has become decidedly more wary about the traditional policy of using common stocks as the appropriate investment medium for stockholders' equity because of:

- the unsatisfactory "recent" past experience realized on common stocks and the uncertain future outlook,
- the now perceived likelihood that the downturn in the underwriting cycle will occur in concert with the cyclical decline in economic activity and common stock prices, and
- the need to stand ready to provide surplus relief to ceding companies during adverse economic and underwriting cycles.

PREFERRED STOCKS

Preferred shares have also been used, in modest amounts, for investment of the reinsurer's surplus. In the case of preferred shares, the attraction lies in the greater dividend yields vis-a-vis common shares. The yields on preferred shares have traditionally been as much as two to three times that provided by common shares. In fact, the preferred dividend return after appropriate taxes has compared quite favorably with the yield on tax-exempt bonds, which explains why preferred shares were even used sometimes for a portion of loss reserves as well as surplus not placed in common stocks. The post-tax yield of preferred stocks is due to the tax treatment of dividends from all stocks accorded a corporate holder generally. Under IRS Regulations, 85% of cash dividends received by corporate holders of stocks generally are not subject to tax, while the remaining 15% are subject to the approximate 50% tax rate on corporate income. Thus, the effective tax rate on dividends becomes 7½%, and a return of 7% from preferred stock becomes a post-tax return of 6.475% (92½% of 7%).

The disadvantages of preferred shares as investments for either the surplus account or a part of loss reserves are threefold. First, the dividend return is fixed. There is no participation in or benefit derived from any increased earnings of the issuing corporation through an increased rate of dividends or capital appreciation. Second, having a fixed dividend rate, the preferred share price is subject to the same risk of depreciation that occurs on bonds during periods of rising interest rates. This risk of depreciation is accentuated by the absence of a maturity date which, in the case of bonds, tends to stabilize prices somewhat, especially for those with an intermediate term maturity.

In a practical sense, a preferred stock can be thought of as a perpetual bond. However, some preferred stock issues do have sinking funds. This means the corporate issuer is obligated to retire, either through redemption or through purchases in the open market, a specified amount of the preferred shares on a prescribed basis. This sinking fund feature would add some degree of support to the price of the preferred stock in declining markets caused by rising interest rates. The amount of price stability would depend on the size of the sinking fund, i.e., the amount of shares that must be called for retirement or purchased in the open market, and the time period over which the sinking fund operated.

The third disadvantage arises from the statutory requirement that preferred shares be shown on the Annual Statement at market value (along with common shares). This is in contrast to the statutory accounting treatment of bonds which the reinsurer is able to carry at amortized cost value. The decline in the market value of a bond does not pose a problem in the sense of a reduction in statutory surplus. Only if a bond investment is sold at a price below amortized cost would surplus be affected. In such an instance, the difference between the net proceeds of sale and the amortized cost would be charged against surplus. In contrast, a decline in the market value of a preferred stock below its purchase price results in a direct reduction of statutory surplus, since preferred shares are required to be reported at market value. As a practical matter, the change in market value from one valuation date of the balance sheet to another becomes a charge against or credit to statutory surplus, depending on the market value of the stock. This statutory requirement adds an undesirable degree of instability to the surplus account (or reserves) vis-a-vis bonds which, as noted earlier, are permitted to be kept at amortized cost values despite changes in market value.

Finally, in terms of reliability of dividends and safety of principal investment, preferred shares fall between the common shares and bonds of an issuing corporation. Preferred dividends must be paid in full prior to any payment of common dividends, but the payment of interest on debt comes before any preferred dividend payments. And, in the event of corporate bankruptcy, the relationships of the preferred shareholders are senior to that of the common shareholder but subordinate to that of the bondholders.

Exhibit 4 summarizes the investment in common shares and preferred shares of the two illustrative reinsurers relative to their surplus over the past ten years. At least two interesting indications or inferences can be drawn from the exhibit. It seems a fair assumption that at any time the combined total of common shares and preferred shares exceeded the total of surplus, the reinsurer was using preferred shares for investment of some reserves. The combined total exceeded surplus for two of the eleven years for Company A, ten of the eleven years for Company B. The second indication stems from the steady decline in the ratio of common stocks (and preferred stocks) to surplus from 1974 to 1977. That decline would seem to be evidence of a diminishing degree of confidence in equities as an appropriate medium for investing surplus.

EXHIBIT 4

SUMMARY AND COMPARISON OF
STOCK INVESTMENTS TO SURPLUS

COMPANY A

	Statutory Surplus	Common Stocks	Percent of Surplus	Preferred Stocks	Percent of Surplus
	(000)	(000)		(000)	
1967	$ 72,288	$ 51,581	71.4%	$ 949	1.3%
1968	79,075	53,901	68.2	872	1.1
1969	74,230	47,392	63.8	1,468	2.0
1970	72,227	51,641	71.5	7,114	9.8
1971	97,168	73,018	75.1	12,164	12.5
1972	124,613	101,568	81.5	21,833	17.5
1973	112,977	90,831	80.4	19,525	17.3
1974	53,529	57,827	108.0	17,733	33.1
1975	53,856	44,680	83.0	14,864	27.6
1976	76,342	48,928	64.1	None	—
1977	108,503	52,467	48.4	None	—

COMPANY B

	Statutory Surplus	Common Stocks	Percent of Surplus	Preferred Stocks	Percent of Surplus
	(000)	(000)		(000)	
1967	$104,022	$ 94,025	90.4%	$ 14,355	13.8%
1968	123,809	105,361	85.1	15,432	12.5
1969	122,124	107,811	88.3	15,411	12.6
1970	144,492	132,889	92.0	19,348	13.4
1971	183,882	163,507	88.9	26,274	14.3
1972	234,795	222,670	94.8	45,727	19.5
1973	217,444	219,332	100.9	42,467	19.5
1974	147,825	181,618	122.9	34,884	23.6
1975	208,235	235,082	112.9	33,687	16.2
1976	279,624	277,638	99.3	37,053	13.3
1977	302,687	285,250	94.2	28,560	9.4

Source: *Best's Insurance Reports, Property-Casualty* (A.M. Best Company, Oldwick, New Jersey 08858), appropriate years.

Summary

Insurance underwriting involves risk. Management of invested assets also entails risk as it fulfills its three-pronged responsibility of 1) producing a steady reliable flow of investment income, 2) prudently investing loss reserves, and 3) protecting shareholders' equity against erosion from inflation. The job of managing invested assets is assigned to the chief financial officer, who works with the guidance of the finance committee composed of directors of the company responsible to the full board of directors. The more important investment decisions taken include the allocation of assets among various classes of investments (stocks, bonds, preferred stocks, and others), the choice of taxable or tax-exempt bonds, and the average maturity of the bond portfolio.

With strong financial growth over the past decade ... while underwriting profits have been slim ... investment income has become the primary source of operating profit. It has grown steadily along with invested assets despite the volatility of underwriting results and the difficulty of earning more than a very modest underwriting profit. This divergence of investment income and underwriting results is simply a function of the continuing, substantial growth in premium volume along with the normal lag in payment of claims. The prospects for continuing growth of premium volume and therefore cash flow and investment income are favorable. However, the underwriting outlook is less sanguine. Thus it seems inevitable that the investment phase of the reinsurer's business will gain increasing importance in the future.

Prior to the 1974/1975 burst of double digit inflation, investment management entailed the purchase of bonds to support loss reserves while investment of shareholders' equity was kept in common shares. Preferred shares sometimes served as a hybrid investment for both. All investments were made pretty much on a dollar-averaging basis whereby systematic purchases over a period of time evened out the relatively mild ups and downs of interest rates and stock prices brought about by economic expansions and contractions. Both stocks and bonds were bought with a long-term holding period in mind. Bonds were expected to be held until their stated maturity date. Stocks were bought with the intention of "living with the company" so-to-speak for the longer term benefit of rising earnings, dividends, and therefore share prices. Sale of stocks would not likely be contemplated unless there were a fundamental change which altered the long-term outlook.

Stocks rather than bonds were used for investment of surplus, because traditional thinking held that bond prices would be subject to steady erosion because of continuing inflation. However, it was felt that equities would be able to keep pace with inflation through a continuing, if uneven, rise in share prices based on steadily rising earnings and dividends. But the events of 1974/1975 and their traumatic impact on the financial markets ushered in a new environment which changed the idea that inflation was bad for bonds but "good" for common stocks, as well as other earlier ideas about managing invested assets. For example, the traditional "buy-and-hold" investment policy no longer seemed suited to a fast changing and highly volatile economic and financial environment. Internally, meanwhile, the reinsurer's financial condition changed because loss reserves have grown at a rate well above that of the surplus account, thereby increasing the leverage of interest rates on "true" surplus, i.e., surplus with bonds appraised at *market* rather than *statutory* values. This new phenomenon became apparent in the wake of the soaring interest rates and sharply depressed bond prices of 1974, though at the time it received less attention than the collapsing stock market and its direct impact on the highly visible statutory surplus. Looking into the future, concern about bonds represents a new investment risk that the reinsurer may not be able to ignore, despite statutory accounting and the ability to value bonds at amortized cost. Finally, disappointment with the past performance of common shares as an inflation hedge and disillusionment about their future outlook have caused a re-evaluation of the concept of using common shares for surplus investment. Unfortunately, as regards both the internal and external aspects of managing the invested assets, it seems clear that more questions and concerns can be raised than there are satisfactory answers available.

An analysis of the growth and financial condition of two leading reinsurers provides a broad perspective on the industry and helps reveal some of the changes that have taken place over the past decade. By study ing their data we can also make some inferences on how the reinsurers may have shifted their investment policies to cope with both the internal and external forces that were encountered, and perhaps consider what changes in investment approach might be in prospect for the future.

Regulatory authorities as well as ceding companies are scrutinizing the financial condition of reinsurers more closely, especially after the strains of the 1974/1975 period when both underwriting and investment results proved so damaging to the financial health of the industry. The reinsurer's balance sheet is more highly leveraged by virtue of the greater proportion of loss reserves (and therefore bonds) relative to surplus, while the financial markets are considerably more volatile. If the reinsurance industry is to effectively and adequately support the primary companies in providing the insurance coverage needed by the public, the traditional approach to managing investments may have to be importantly modified to meet the new challenges.

* * * * * *

About the Author of Chapter 18

Stanley Taben received his B.A. Degree in psychology from Cornell University in 1954. After two years in the military service as a lieutenant, he began his investment career in New York with major banking institutions.

In 1972 he joined the Swiss Re Group of companies as president and director of SwissRe Advisers, Inc. He also is a director and the chief financial officer for the Group's U.S. operating companies, North American Reinsurance Corporation and its life affiliate, North American Reassurance Company.

19

Budgeting and Controlling Internal Expenses

by William R. Miller*

Administering internal expenses affects all departments of a re-insurer; however, in this chapter little will be said on the budget requirements for the claim and underwriting departments. These departments are basically responsible for controlling losses, acquisition expenses, and generating profitable underwriting. Necessarily, an ample budget is required for these functions to accomplish their basic responsibility. However, budgeting for ancillary services performed by these departments will be discussed. Additionally, the budgeting and monitoring of internal expenses in the tax, investment, accounting, and computer areas will be examined while focusing on the benefits derived from such expenditures.

For all internal expenses there is a direct relationship between the amount of monies budgeted and the benefits received by reinsurers. Such functions as good claim service, development of statistical data, or improving an investment program are all related to the degree that management wishes to perfect these activities through appropriate budgeting.

A large portion of the reinsurance premiums received by reinsurers will be paid out in the form of claim payments and acquisition expenses. Acquisition expenses are closely related to claims since ceding commissions, being a large portion of acquisition costs, are adjusted upward or downward over a period of time in relationship to the amount of loss payments.

---

* CPCU, CLU, President, American Union Insurance Company of New York, American States Plaza, 500 N. Meridian Street, Indianapolis, Indiana 46207.

The reinsurance premium dollar which is left after claim payments and acquisition costs is the gross margin and must cover the reinsurer's internal expenses and leave a net margin, which is the net underwriting gain. Consequently, how well a reinsurer controls its operating expenses for such functions as claim services, underwriting, and computer needs reflects directly on the net underwriting gain it will enjoy. In a period of difficulty, the difference between underwriting profit or underwriting loss will be directly related to the expense controls.

Benefits of Budgeting

In order to budget and establish controls for expenses, it is necessary for reinsurance companies to identify those expenses which are direct and indirect as well as those which are controllable and noncontrollable.

Direct expenses are those incurred directly by a department, function, territory or activity. Indirect expenses are those incurred for the benefit of more than one department, function, territory or activity, and are allocated on some prorated basis to the various functions for which they were made. Controllable expenses are those that the company can influence or regulate to some extent—such as claim adjustment, advertising, survey and underwriting reports, travel, printing, postage, payroll, cable and telex expenses. The noncontrollable expenses are those over which the company has little or no influence, such as taxes, and board and bureau fees. Here the reinsurers have some advantages over primary companies, as some of these expenses are relatively small or may be nonexistent for reinsurers. Expenses such as survey and underwriting reports, board and bureau fees, and advertising will hardly approach the budgeted amount of ceding companies.

The method of handling internal expenses can vary widely among reinsurance companies due to their size and mode of operation. A small broker-oriented reinsurer handling treaties has different accounting requirements and goals than a large direct-writing reinsurer doing both treaty and facultative reinsurance. However, regardless of size, management of every reinsurance company needs a sound accounting system. Moreover, the system must also be flexible enough to handle all types of receipts and disbursements, and be sufficiently automated to assure timely, accurate, and efficient expense data.

Advantages

The budgeting of expenses serves several purposes: 1) controlling expense by function; 2) quantifying productivity; 3) building communication and motivation; and 4) providing material for goal setting. Apart from the statutory requirements for all reinsurers to allocate expenses according to certain uniform classifications, the budgeting of expenses also allows the company to control its expenses by function. Having established a budget, management can then examine the actual expense incurred by function on a quarterly basis to determine whether the function is over or under budget.

As to quantifying productivity, many theorists will argue that any attempt to measure productivity is self-defeating. Nevertheless, it is generally accepted in the business that the processing units of a reinsurance organization can have their input and output measured as a by-product of the internal expense controls. An example is an operating unit which is consistently over budget but behind its schedule in processing. Such a case would force management to monitor the performance of the unit to determine what corrective measures are needed—whether duplication of work should be eliminated, whether streamlining the work load is needed, or whether something else may be required to make the unit operate more efficiently.

It is also important that the development of budgets start from the lowest level of management and move upward. This progression accomplishes better communication between management levels and also creates a motivating influence on the managers involved. The result of having participated in the budget process is a morale boost to the management team.

Lastly, for a reinsurer to set its objectives it needs pertinent expense information to properly budget and control expenses. For example, the company may have met its overall objective of a profit, but remain unaware of the origin of that profit. Thus, does the hail department perform better than the property department or casualty department? Or were the profits made by the facultative operation? It is important for a reinsurer to reach its goals and equally important to know how it was accomplished.

In summary, all the benefits derived from the budgeting of internal expenses are closely related. Communicating with subordinates for input on goal setting results in more enthusiasm, which enhances productivity and creates a desire to operate within realistic budgets.

Influencing Factors

The smaller the reinsurer's staff, the easier it is to budget, monitor costs, and set objectives. The larger staffed reinsurer, and particularly one dealing in facultative reinsurance, will more likely resemble a primary company's operation with more complex budgeting. Branch offices are often used and may be looked upon as profit centers. Hence, any budgeting and cost controls need to be refined for each branch to be sure it is performing properly and meeting its goals.

Another element determining the internal expenses of a reinsurance market is its mix of business. A reinsurer heavily involved in low retention casualty business must allocate more expense to conduct audits by its claim and underwriting departments. Further, a reinsurer dealing in high layer casualty business has less of a need for additional claim staff or underwriters. For markets dealing exclusively in treaty business involving nonhazardous classes, the internal expenses incurred by the reinsurer are still less, since the outside audit work for both claims and underwriting is diminished. For the more difficult types of property lines, additional underwriting and claim supervision will be required. Facultative property and casualty business requires additional expense in the form of clerical help, because each reinsurance transaction must be handled separately.

To some degree expenses are determined on the basis of the company's distribution between alien business from other countries and domestic business from within the United States. In handling alien reinsurance, the accounting problems are compounded because of variances in exchange rates and the withholding of premiums due to the nonadmitted aspects of the reinsurer. Also, more time is required of top management to be sure that its business exists in foreign currencies which are stable, if possible.

Many ancillary services are performed by reinsurers for their clients, such as counseling with respect to policies, forms, rating, claim assistance, marketing, and investments. Since all of these services are either done gratuitously or for no specific compensation, the reinsurer heavily involved in such type of counseling needs to budget accordingly.

Planning: Taxes, Investments, Under-Writing, and Retrocessions

TAXES

Aside from the federal income tax, reinsurers generally are not subject to direct state and local taxes. A majority of state statutes exclude or are silent as respects premium taxes on assumed reinsurance premiums. However, some states do include authorized reinsurance premiums received by reinsurers in computing premium taxes, and a very few states include all reinsurance premiums in their tax base. Indirectly reinsurers do pay their share of state and local taxes, as the ceding commission paid by the reinsurers is to cover the ceding company's acquisition expenses, including an allowance for reimbursement of such items as premium tax, fire marshal tax, firemen's benefit tax, board fees and bureau assessments.

Reinsurers can become involved in retaliatory taxes as most states have enacted retaliatory laws. Basically, retaliation could arise if State "A" taxes its domestic insurers at one tax rate and its foreign insurers (those domiciled in State "B" but doing business in State "A") at a higher tax rate, then State "B" might retaliate and tax its foreign insurers (those domiciled in State "A" and doing business in State "B") at the same higher tax rate.

The retaliatory tax has become a serious problem. Any management team forming a new company must give serious consideration as to the state in which it wants the company domiciled in order to avoid excessive retaliatory taxes. Some established reinsurers are moving their charters to a state with fewer and lower taxes, therefore avoiding any retaliatory taxes imposed by other states. Consequently, taxes are an important part of the budgeted dollars and should not be ignored.

Investments and Underwriting

The management of a reinsurance company will often be involved in the day-to-day investment and underwriting activities, or at least will be closely watching these functions. There is a tradeoff between underwriting profit and investment profit, and good management will monitor this relationship very closely to be sure that profits are maximized.

An explanation for measuring the true underwriting experience of a reinsurer may be helpful. Two operating ratios need to be determined in order to interpret the underwriting results of a reinsurer. One is the ratio of combined losses and loss adjustment expenses incurred to earned premiums, and the other is the ratio of underwriting expenses incurred to written premiums. If the total of the two ratios is under 100%, the difference reflects the approximate profit margin. However, if the total exceeds 100%, an underwriting loss is sustained to the degree indicated.

A conservative reinsurer may establish goals for its combined operating ratio to be in the low 90's and likely assumes less premium to help achieve that purpose. A company of similar size but less conservative in nature will set its combined operating ratio in the high 90's. However, to project the operating ratio in the high 90's can be dangerous for a reinsurer, since its underwriting results thereafter may well exceed 100%. If this unfortunate result happens, one corrective measure is to reduce subsequent premium income in order to bring the ratio below 100%. The obvious result is fewer dollars for the reinsurer to invest, hence the complementary relationship between underwriting and investment.

Another relationship between investment income and underwriting income will depend upon management's objectives and values placed upon leveraging. An example can be taken from a reinsurer attempting to maintain its combined operating ratio under 100%. The reinsurer may be reluctant to reinsure a large unearned premium portfolio if the acquisition cost increases its expense ratio, thus causing the combined operating ratio to exceed 100%. On the other hand, if the reinsurer is less concerned with its combined ratio, it may well assume the large unearned premium portfolio since it will realize additional investment income on the net portfolio assumed. Further, the cash flow from such underwriting program may result in deferred taxation, since taxes are paid on a statutory basis whereby the prepaid expenses in the unearned premium reserve are charged against current income.

The loss portfolios of reinsurers may be outstanding for a number of years, and thus the reinsurer benefits from the interest earned on such reserve funds. For investment benefits, management may decide to write more casualty lines as opposed to property business, since property claims are more quickly settled and the pay-out results in fewer loss reserve funds for the reinsurer to invest. Consequently, there is a trade-off between the mix of business that a reinsurer has, as the casualty lines will historically generate more investment income but also more underwriting losses. Therefore, management must determine the proper percentages of business to be assumed between property and casualty. The volume of both lines of business must be equated with the company's overall capital and surplus position.

Reinsurers need liquidity to meet the needs of their clients for periodic advancement of funds. They are frequently called upon by ceding companies to pay huge sums of money because of such events as natural disasters, large fires, or high jury awards. Generally, these requests from reinsureds for payment of losses occur without warning and, in many cases, before payment is made by a company to the original insured. Thus, the advancement of funds by reinsurers is part of the reinsurance service rendered. Because of this service, primary companies need not necessarily disturb their investment portfolios in order to settle losses. Therefore, one of the basic concerns of a reinsurer in its investment policy is the need for liquidity, either a reasonable amount of short-term investments or securities with a minimum amount of market risk.

Any funds held in excess of a good liquidity position would then be used to invest in high yielding, more permanent-type securities, or even in common equities.

The investment portfolios of a reinsurer are maintained for the two largest liability items, the unearned premium reserve and the outstanding loss reserve. The unearned premium reserve relates directly to the volume of premium being written. Likewise, the loss reserve relates to the same premium income since losses tend to track premium volume. The loss reserve may fluctuate considerably if the reinsurer is heavily involved in property business, since most property losses are paid soon after their occurrence without the need for extended loss reserving. Casualty reserves are more permanent, larger and less fluctuating, since losses being litigated may take years to settle. Also, the unearned premium reserve in recent times has been reduced as reinsureds go to a shorter policy period. In the past, three-year prepaid policies were common and the premium was earned over the full three years of the policy, thus creating large unearned premium reserves. Now, with policies having terms of one year or less, the resulting effect is lower unearned premium reserves.

The type of securities that these reserves are invested in will depend to a large measure on whether the reinsurer is generating underwriting profits. If the reinsurer is developing underwriting gains, it may prefer to have its investment portfolios in tax-exempt bonds so that no additional taxable income is created. If, however, an underwriting loss is anticipated, the reinsurer may wish to move its portfolio into taxable bonds. The taxable bonds will generate roughly two percentage points more in return, and this additional yield can be offset against the underwriting loss. An example is a tax-exempt bond which yields 6% investment income compared with a taxable bond which yields 8%. As long as the taxable income from the bond can be fully offset against underwriting losses, the reinsurer benefits from the higher yield. The reverse is true: if the underwriting is profitable, then the 8% investment income would be reduced to 4% after taxes; in this situation, the reinsurer loses two points of investment by having its portfolio in taxable securities. The relationship between investment and underwriting goals creates controls on premium volume, which affects the expense dollars available for budgeting.

RETROCESSION PROTECTION

A reinsurer "retrocedes" when it cedes all or a part of assumed reinsurance to another reinsurer. In some respects the reinsurer is in essentially the same position as a primary carrier to the extent that reinsurers use retrocessions either as a financing factor or as protection against large exposures to loss. The internal expenses of handling the retrocession program will depend upon its purpose. A catastrophe retrocession which may be infrequently used will be less costly to administer than a program designed to routinely involve retrocessionaires.

Although reinsurers' earnings can and do follow trends with the insurance industry, such earnings differ in stability from those of primary companies. For example, reinsurers are more vulnerable to catastrophe losses and inflation while primary insurers are more affected by changes in premium rates and policy forms. Therefore, a reinsurer's prospects of good earnings from both investment and underwriting need to be protected as much as possible, hence the reason for purchasing retrocessions.

The extent of a reinsurer's retrocession has some bearing on how much cash demand could be made on it at any one time. However, it is generally accepted that reinsurers collect from their retrocessionaires on a paid basis, meaning the reinsurer is reimbursed only after it pays the reinsured. Therefore, the reinsurer cannot expect funds to be advanced to it from its retrocessionaires. However, retrocession protection helps replenish the surplus of the reinsurer and maintains intact much of its investment portfolio. Generally a reinsurer can meet loss payments out of current new business income, except for a major catastrophe or an epidemic of large unrelated losses, in which case it may need to borrow from a financial institution or liquidate some of its securities.

The Promise Of The Computer

Reinsurers' budgets in the past were limited as respects the computer, but recently the budget figures have increased in order to finance development of management reports and studies. Computer programming can be painfully slow and requires a long-term commitment of money and people; however, the results can be quite rewarding.

All reinsurers have a need for the services of a computer because of increased pressures to control costs, to give good service, and to control their share of the market. Limited use of the computer includes sorting, merging, and maintaining basic data for accounting, management, investments, claims, and for some underwriting purposes. More sophisticated systems produce various management reports: pertinent data relative to zone liability for catastrophe exposure, loss development by accident year for each contract, and the storing of experience figures covering many prior years. Also, many schedules and exhibits of the Annual Statement can be handled by the computer such as the balance sheet, income statement, underwriting and investment exhibits, expense exhibit, analysis of assets, and the reconciliation of ledger assets. Additionally, many other accounting procedures are handled by the computer such as maintaining the accounts journal, cash journal and subsidiary ledger.

Management Styles and Uses

Computers are becoming smaller and no longer require special rooms or air conditioning. Equipment can be operated by a limited number of data personnel at lower costs than before, and many standard software programs are available. Consequently, computers are becoming more attractive to small reinsurers and for certain departments or larger reinsurers. Justifying the cost of a computer is obviously an important decision for management, and to reach a proper decision it needs to know exactly what type of hardware and software it wishes to utilize. The basic question thus becomes: What does the reinsurer want from the computer, and what is it willing to spend to get it? Indeed, since most reinsurers have many common traits, many computer programs have the same application for all reinsurers.

Management style of many reinsurers is characterized by heavy reliance upon direct personal contacts, informal communications, and the "feel" for what the business is all about. In many cases a reinsurer is dominated by a single leader or a small group of people, all of whom are highly skilled. Consequently, such leadership may not lend itself to the more structural, formal requirements of day-to-day computer processing. While the informal management in reinsurance companies may be vulnerable to weakness of skills in organization, planning and discipline, nevertheless only with management involvement can a reinsurer's objectives be translated into its computer system. For example, since changing reinsurance needs call for periodic reevaluation, any computer system requires continued updating. As management becomes familiar with existing systems, new sophisticated reporting requirements may be instituted. Continued management involvement with such changes is just as important at the later stages as in the initial stage.

Investments

The investment department of a reinsurance operation must maintain a critical balance between liquidity of investments and long-term securities. To accomplish this delicate relationship, the automation of an investment department can keep an investor current on a daily basis with the mix of securities within the portfolio. Being able to quickly identify those securities with low yields or those which can be offset against one another for capital gains and loss is quite important. Often securities must be "unloaded" in a hurry because of the need for ready cash to pay reinsurance claims. A typical print-out of information on securities will list those purchased and sold by type, showing bonds and commercial paper, their maturing dates, cost, par value, description and yield. For stock purchases the report will show number of shares, description, cost per share, total cost, and yield; and for stock sales the report will show the number of shares, description, sale price, book value, and the profit or loss from each transaction.

Typically a summary report is prepared which shows investments in bonds, stocks (common and preferred), and mortgages. This report will divide the bond portfolio into tax-exempt and taxable bonds. Each bond category is then further divided into tax-exempt state, municipal and revenue bonds, and taxable railroad, utility and industrial bonds. Further, common stocks are listed as financial or industrial, while information on mortgages includes their description.

UNDERWRITING

Since the reinsurance underwriter deals almost entirely in judgment rating and since reinsurers do not file forms, the use of the computer in underwriting has generally been ignored until recently. Pricing of reinsurance contracts by computer has had little application since, generally speaking, no two reinsurance situations have the same exposures. However, it is now being contemplated that certain exposures in catastrophe covers for both property and casualty lines are sufficiently similar to price the "relativity" of such exposures and adjust this rate based on the few contrasting variances. The basic idea here is to take an average company and develop an applicable rate or premium for a typical contract. The company would be average in the sense of its premium distribution, policy profile, lines of business written and underlying reinsurance program. The computer would be programmed for the model company with a typical contract. All prospective reinsureds would then be compared to the model with variations being noted and slight adjustments in the rate being made, either deviating upwards or downwards as the situation dictates. This exercise still leaves a final application for rate-making, which would be the judgment factor applied by the underwriter. Thus, uniformity would exist and the wide swing in pricing by a reinsurer would be eliminated.

LOSSES

There are many management reports that need to be prepared for the reinsurer to operate efficiently. One of the management reports that can be programmed and which is required virtually by all reinsurers is catastrophe zone exposure. Generally, reinsurers will divide the United States into seven catastrophe zones wherein the reinsurer plots all of its catastrophe excess of loss liabilities along with aggregate or stop loss ratio contract exposures as well as the liability under per risk excess covers. Pro rata business will generally be included on a premium distribution basis, then factored by some percentage to have the premium representative of a catastrophe liability exposure. To maintain the above information on a manual basis and to be current is an impossibility, because new contracts and treaties are being added daily and some covers are being non-renewed while others are being cancelled. The zone liabilities, if pro-grammed, would provide the underwriter with zone exposures on a dai-ly basis. Such information would help to control catastrophe exposure and quickly ease the concern for being overconcentrated. Being able to clearly determine the limits of liability by zone would probably generate more capacity, as the underwriter would not need to "guesstimate" the aggregate limits, which probably include a built-in factor for con-servatism.

Another useful report is the experience of catastrophe covers com-pared by loss retentions and limits of liability to subject premiums. For example, experience on contracts having loss retentions equal to 5% of the subject premium and with limits of liability equal to 40% of the same subject premium could be compared with the experience on another group of contracts having retentions and limits equal to 7.5% and 50%, respectively. Armed with such statistics, the reinsurance underwriter can select the most profitable combination of retentions and limits, and deter-mine what pricing changes are needed to improve the results of a given group.

Having the computer allocate losses by accident year and monitor-ing, updating and continuing to develop the experience on such a basis can be rewarding. The accident year statistics have the greatest appli-cation to liability lines although the property lines can also be monitored for late reporting of losses. A poor development on either line simply reflects a poor reserving pattern for the ceding company.

FUTURE POTENTIAL

The buying and selling of facultative reinsurance by computer may not be in the too distant future. A program which might be implemented would involve a group of reinsurers, each with their respective line limits programmed in a central computer system. The line limits would vary according to size of risk, rate, class of protection, type of construction, sprinklered or non-sprinklered, whether mercantile or manufacturing, etc. This information stored in the central computer would now be available to companies wanting to purchase facultative reinsurance through their satellite terminals. A primary company could code in its terminal the amount of facultative coverage it required with a description of the risk to be reinsured, sending this information to the central computer. The central computer would then search through the stored information that it contains to find a reinsurer or reinsurers which would be agreeable to accepting some portion of the risk based on the respective line limits. The computer would then automatically confirm binding coverage to the ceding company and indicate the reinsurer or reinsurers accepting the risk and at what terms. At the same time, a reinsurance certificate would be printed and mailed to the ceding company as final documentation of coverage. In turn, the computer would advise each participating reinsurer of its acceptance, and on a monthly basis would summarize all transactions by giving such Annual Statement information as unearned premium reserves, outstanding losses, and paid losses.

Intervention and Cooperation in Claims

The main purpose of a claim department is to help protect the reinsurer's assets. However, the claim staff can perform other valuable services. Examples would be establishing claim reporting procedures with ceding companies and improving contract language, or incorporating new coverages in contracts such as punitive damage protection for reinsureds. The following will touch on and illustrate some of these services.

Reinsurance agreements in the past were oftentimes loosely worded and did not cover fully all of the procedures relative to intervention and cooperation in claims between the reinsured and the reinsurer. To this degree the contracts were more correctly referred to as gentlemen's agreements. However, in the real world today where a totally legal atmosphere prevails, the reinsurance contracts and treaties are more precise and do provide for both intervention and cooperation between the reinsuring parties.

INTERVENTION

Ordinarily a reinsurer, without formally relying on the provisions of the contract, will set up a line of communication for reports. The reinsurer will arrange, either through intermediaries or in the case of direct writers through executives of the reinsured, for proper claims reporting, claims auditing, and reserve auditing. A typical wording providing for the intervention and association would be as follows: "The reinsurer may, at its own expense, participate with the reinsured in the investigation, adjustment or defense of claims in which, in the judgment of the reinsurer, it is or might become involved." In this spirit, the reinsurer's claimsperson generally agrees to cooperate with the reinsured. The claimsperson is charged with the responsibility of making sure that the reinsured is totally aware of all possible results of a given course of conduct. Further, the association by the reinsurer enables the primary insurer to get another reading on the particular claim problem. However, the reinsurer's representative must not, except under very unusual circumstances, substitute any expertise for that of the primary insurer. For this reason, any reasonable approach to a claim will generally be acceptable to the reinsurer as long as it conforms to good claim practices.

COOPERATION

Further, the reinsurance agreement will provide that the reinsured shall investigate and settle, or defend all claims arising under policies with respect to which the reinsurance is afforded, and that the reinsured will give proper notice to the reinsurer of any event or development which might result in a claim being made against the reinsurer. Some contracts will provide that certain types of injuries are to be automatically reported to the reinsurer regardless of negligence or coverage. Such injuries would involve brain damage, spinal cord injuries, burns and disfigurements, amputations, fatalities, permanent disabilities and personal injuries. In addition, the contract may also provide that claims involving the following circumstances must be reported:

1. Where the total claim reserve, as respects multiple claimants or aggregate claims involving aggregate limits, exceeds 33.33 % (or some other agreed upon percentage) of the loss retention contained in the reinsurance agreement;
2. Coverage disputes between the company and the policyholders or insured;
3. Claims or suits involving a demand or prayer for punitive damages.

The reinsured has an obligation if a right of subrogation or reimbursement should arise out of a loss, a part of which was sustained by the reinsurer, to enforce such right and to prosecute if necessary to protect the reinsurer's interest. In the event recoveries are made on excess of loss contracts, the reinsurer is reimbursed to the extent of its loss less any expense incurred by the primary company. On pro rata reinsurance the expenses involved in the subrogation are deducted from the recoveries, and the reinsured and the reinsurer share in the net recovery according to their respective percentages.

The reinsured will also agree to provide satisfactory evidence of payment of losses against which indemnity is provided by the reinsurance contract. In addition, the reinsured shall on a quarterly basis provide the reinsurer with a report of estimated value for each outstanding claim subject to the reinsurance agreement.

Right of Inspection. A typical provision in reinsurance agreements is that the reinsurer may inspect the records of the primary company. An example of such wording follows: "The reinsurer may inspect the original documents of the reinsured pertaining to the losses recoverable hereunder." This provision permits the reinsurer to make periodic reviews of the company's claim-handling practices. Actually the review may encompass both a claim audit and a reserve audit which differ. A claim audit involves the reviewing of established reserves to see if such reserves are adequate. On the other hand, a reserve audit deals with those losses not yet involving the reinsurer. The purpose of a reserve audit is to analyze whether the reinsured's reserves may ultimately be increased to the point of invading the reinsurance contract. An experienced reinsurance claimsperson reviewing such losses should be able to determine whether there is a conscientious effort on the part of the reinsured to report any case which might reasonably give rise to exposure for the reinsurer.

The auditing provided by a reinsurer is also very beneficial to the primary companies. The review conducted by the reinsurer of the company's claim practices gives the management of the primary company an opportunity to get a "reading" on the caliber of the claim operation, the procedures and reporting techniques, and the general reserving posture. This is a relatively new program for some smaller reinsurers and one which appears to have much impetus.

Excess Judgment Loss. The cooperation between the reinsured and reinsurer on all claim matters is important, particularly on when and how to report losses. Proper communication on a timely basis may eliminate the old problem of excess judgments and a newer problem of punitive damages being assessed against the reinsured.

Most reinsurance contracts deal with excess judgment losses and basically provide coverage on a sharing basis whereby the reinsured participates in such losses. A typical definition of "excess judgment" may read as follows:

> For the purposes of this agreement, "excess judgment loss" shall be damages payable to the reinsured's insured or its assignee as a result of an action brought by the insured or its assignee against the reinsured to recover damages payable to a third party claimant in excess of the reinsured's policy limit as a result of the reinsured's alleged or actual bad faith or negligence in rejecting a settlement within its policy limits or in the preparation of the defense or in the trial of any action against its insured or in the preparation or prosecution of an appeal consequent upon such action. "Excess judgment loss" shall not include any loss suffered by the insured other than the insured's loss to a third party claimant in excess of the reinsured's policy limits.

The above wording spells out that the insured does not benefit from the excess judgment, since all proceeds are passed on to a third party.

Punitive Damage Loss. The question of punitive damages claimed by an insured arises out of a separate action brought by the original insured against the reinsured. Such damages may be defined as money awards granted by courts in excess of compensation to a plaintiff as punishment for a defendant's gross negligence. The handling of punitive damages has not been completely resolved, and presently the reinsurance industry is approaching a punitive damage coverage question on an individual ceding company basis. One means of handling punitive damage losses may be dealt with in the definition of "ultimate net loss," a sample wording of which is:

> "Ultimate net loss" shall not include any amount paid by the reinsured for any punitive, exemplary, consequential or compensatory damages, other than "excess judgment loss," resulting from the action of the insured or assignee or third party claimant against the reinsured arising out of the handling of claims or other matters in its dealings with or on behalf of the reinsured's insureds, unless through written communication the reinsured, in advance of any action, counsels with the reinsurer and the reinsurer concurs, in writing, in the action to be taken by the reinsured.

The above wording clearly states those circumstances wherein the reinsurer will be liable to the reinsured for punitive damage recoveries assessed against the reinsured. It should, however, be noted that the wording as respects both excess judgment loss and punitive damage loss is found in casualty contracts, whereas property reinsurance agreements generally remain silent.

There is a wide range of opinion among reinsureds and reinsurers on whether coverage is afforded for punitive damages under the property reinsurance program. A typical circumstance giving rise to a dispute as respects a property claim settlement would be where a primary company refused to settle a property loss because of suspected arson on the insured's part; because of the refusal to settle promptly, the insured becomes bankrupt. If the reinsured is unable to prove arson against its insured, the insured then brings an action against the reinsured for its failure to settle promptly. Assuming the original insured is successful, the resulting award may include, in addition to the compensable loss, an additional amount for punitive damages because of the reinsured's alleged bad faith.

It can be stated that the reinsurance agreement protecting a portfolio of primary property business should not respond to the punitive damage award, since the reinsurance is not a liability reinsurance contract but rather a first party contract. However, there is a logical argument that the loss should be included under the property contract and payable by the reinsurer, since the reinsured was merely acting on behalf of and for the protection of the reinsurer. It can also be argued that the loss is a liability claim, an action separate and apart from the basic property loss, and therefore the reinsured should look to its general liability policy to make recovery from its casualty reinsurers. This is on the assumption that the general liability policy of the reinsured has been endorsed to provide professional liability coverage. It is therefore apparent that in property reinsurance there can be wide variance of opinion on whether punitive damages should be covered by property reinsurers.

There is no guarantee that a reinsured company can get its reinsurers to provide punitive damage coverage. Reinsurers usually approach the subject of punitive damages on a case-by-case basis, evaluating each case on its own merits. This evaluation is usually based upon classes of business, territories involved, reputation of the company, and the structure of the reinsurance contracts as respects limits and retentions. Fortunately, all reinsurance contracts provide for arbitration in the event there is a difference of opinion between the two parties. The arbitration clause covers differences of opinion so that regardless of the approach taken relative to a given claim or a given group of claims, litigation is not spawned but differences are reconciled at the arbitrator's table.

Summary

The amount of monies a reinsurer wishes to budget for certain functions can produce results which are well worth the dollars spent. However, only so many dollars are available for budgeting and the allocation depends upon management's priorities. One budget area receiving more attention is the reinsurer's electronic data processing unit because of the availability of less expensive computers and software programs. The computer can produce reports which may be used by various departments. An example being that management, along with the claim department, can have reports for monitoring loss developments whereas the same basic information can be used by the accounting department for Annual Statement purposes.

Extra expense budgeted for the claim department to study and improve contract wordings can result in a clearer understanding of the reinsurance terms by both reinsured and reinsurer. The modern reinsurance technicians are prone to be exact and have as few ambiguities as possible in the reinsurance contracts. Consequently, the arbitration table can be avoided.

Planning for taxes, investments, underwriting, and retrocession protection are all related. Profitable underwriting suggests that the investment portfolio be in securities not creating additional taxable income. With unprofitable underwriting the reverse is true — where taxable investment income could be offset against underwriting losses. Retrocession protection stabilizes a reinsurer's investment portfolio by stabilizing its liquidity position.

Computers talking to computers will have many useful applications in the future for reinsurers and reinsureds alike. Those companies taking advantage of the computer will surely have an edge on competition.

In the final analysis the amount of money a reinsurer spends on computers, claim services, management reports, planning for investments and taxes are all important expense dollars. The control of these expenses reflects directly on the profit and success of the reinsurance company. Furthermore, such control also enhances the image of the reinsurer in the marketplace and makes it a viable and respected competitor.

*   *   *   *   *   *

About the Author of Chapter 19

William R. Miller was born in South Whitley, Indiana, on September 16, 1930. In 1952 he graduated from Butler University in Indianapolis, receiving the B.S. Degree in business administration with a major in insurance. He holds both professional designations of Chartered Property Casualty Underwriter (1971) and Chartered Life Underwriter (1973). He has instructed insurance courses in Indianapolis at IU-PUI (Indiana University-Purdue University at Indianapolis).

The first four years of his insurance career were spent as a group service supervisor for the Equitable Life Assurance Society of the United States (1954-1957). He was then associated for six years with two reinsurance intermediaries — as an account executive with Balis & Company of Philadelphia (1958-1960), and as an executive vice president of J. H. Lea & Company of Chicago (1961-1963). In 1964 he joined the American States Group in Indianapolis as a vice president to develop a newly acquired dormant corporation (American Union Insurance Company of New York) into a professional reinsurance operation. In 1968 he was elected a director of American Union, in 1970 executive vice president and general manager, and in 1978 president. Since 1973 he has also served as vice president of the American States Insurance Companies, the corporate parent of American Union.

20

Surplus to Policyholders
The Strength of a Reinsurer

by Marion A. Woodbury*

The policyholder surplus of an individual company is the very foundation of that company's existence. If it has been adequate in the past to withstand various underwriting catastrophes, vagaries of the stock market, or management errors, the company has been able to continue in business. If it has not been adequate, the company has faced the specter of insolvency, or mercifully has been acquired by another company before that specter became a reality, or helped with surplus aid reinsurance if the policyholder surplus problem appeared to the reinsurer to be a temporary problem. The importance of the adequacy of any company's policyholder surplus cannot be overstated.

Just what is policyholder surplus, and why is it so important as a measure of a company's financial strength? For our purposes, policyholder surplus is a term applied to the balance remaining after a company's total liabilities have been deducted from its total assets. It therefore represents the net worth of the company (insurer or reinsurer), and consists of capital stock (if applicable), contributed surplus, earned surplus, plus any contingency funds. As a residual amount, then, policyholder surplus is a financial cushion or buffer protecting the company against the shocks of the marketplace. The larger that cushion relative to a company's liabilities, the stronger the firm.

When a new stock reinsurance company is formed, the founders must not only contribute a specified amount of capital but an additional

---
* President, The Reinsurance Corporation of New York, Chairman of the Board, United Reinsurance Corporation of New York, 99 John Street, New York, New York 10038.

amount of paid-in surplus as well, each amount being determined by the laws of the state in which the company is being licensed. If the company being founded is a mutual organization, it generally must have as much paid-in surplus as is required by a stock company for its capital and paid-in surplus combined. If the individuals forming the company plan for it to be licensed in more than one state, they must also make allowance for the requirements of such other states, with additional considerations for the classes of business to be written in each. While there are minimum surplus requirements, there are no maximum surplus limits when a company is formed.

By law the capital amount must not be invaded by choice during the company's history, so the surplus is designed to protect against the invasion of paid-in capital. If such invasion happens, the company will be subject to state insurance department action, since impaired capital is tantamount to near insolvency.

Aside from legal requirements, adequate surplus is needed by a company for a variety of reasons, including the following: 1) to absorb underwriting losses or operating costs beyond those envisioned in the rate levels used; 2) to absorb declines in the value of the investment portfolio; 3) to allow for adequate loss reserves, and 4) to finance future growth in written premiums. While all of these conditions are not likely to occur at the same time, they did happen simultaneously in 1974 and 1975. For example, the first two conditions acted in concert: industry underwriting losses were $7 billion for the two years, while the Dow Jones Industrial Average slumped severely. At year-end 1972, the DJIA stood at 1,020; two years later it was 600 and did not rise to 852 until the end of 1975. During this turbulent period, an adequate foundation in the form of policyholder surplus was necessary to allow a company to survive.

Moreover, the severity of the financial strain put on the entire property-liability insurance industry becomes even clearer when the impact of those two conditions is realized on the industry's aggregate figures. Without regard to cash flow or other accounting considerations, year-end 1974 policyholder surplus of $20 billion became $12 billion with a 40% decline in the DJIA; policyholder surplus was additionally pressured from part of the $7 billion accumulated underwriting loss for the previous two years. Fortunately, the depreciated stocks were not forced into liquidation at their depressed levels, and underwriting losses declined — both improvements providing the needed relief for enhanced financial strength in the industry. Nevertheless, the simultaneous occurrence of underwriting losses with investment declines points up once again the importance of policyholder surplus as a company's foundation. To show the regained financial strength since 1974-1975, an industry balance sheet for 1976 year-end has been constructed from available data and appears as Exhibit 1.

EXHIBIT 1

Property-Liability Insurance Industry Balance Sheet (Estimated)*

(1976 year-end figures in $ billion, rounded)

ASSETS		LIABILITIES	
Bonds	$ 62.4	Loss Reserves	$ 45.0
Common Stocks	23.6	Unearned Premium	
Preferred Stocks	3.3	Reserves	23.3
Premium Balances	8.4	Other Reserves	9.2
Other	8.1	Total Liabilities	77.5
Mortgages	.3		
Real Estate	1.4	CAPITAL AND SURPLUS	
		Capital Stock	2.2
		Voluntary Reserves	2.0
		Net Surplus	25.8
		Policyholder Surplus	30.0
	$107.5		$107.5

* Sources of individual amounts shown are compiled from Bests's *Aggregates and Averages, Property-Liability*, 1977, and *Argus Chart*, National Underwriter, 1978. Figures exclude 48 reciprocals and 26 Lloyds organizations, which account for approximately 4 % of the totals. Although compiled from the best available sources, the above amounts should be considered estimates.

Amounts shown were collected from 1252 property-liability insurers in 1976, 308 of which were mutual.

However, whether viewed by reinsurance management, a ceding insurer, or a regulator, a property/casualty reinsurance company's policyholder surplus, standing alone, cannot be the full measure of that company's strength or weakness. For that matter, whether the company is a primary writer or a reinsurer, the mere number of dollars in policyholder surplus has little meaning by itself. The policyholder surplus at year-end for two reinsurance companies may be identical, but one company might be financially strong while the other is on the brink of insolvency.

Before attempting to test the role which policyholder surplus plays in measuring the financial strength of a reinsurer, one must first observe two conditions affecting insurance companies: accounting, and government regulation. Insurance accounting procedures are unique, since insureds pay in advance for the promise of protection in the future. Therefore, the traditional accounting rules pertaining to the insurance industry are not the generally accepted accounting principles (GAAP) but rather are determined by state statute and insurance department regulation. For example, under GAAP assets refer to anything of value owned by the company. Under statutory accounting requirements, however, assets are divided into admitted assets and nonadmitted assets. Admitted assets are those recognized by state insurance departments in determining a company's solvency and are prominently listed as "assets" on Page 2 of the Annual Statement. Nonadmitted assets are those not recognized for such purposes and are shown elsewhere in the Annual Statement. The second condition, government regulation, protects the interest of the public when state insurance departments subject all insurers to strict regulation and continuous scrutiny through periodic audit examinations and on-going analyses of required financial statements. Both conditions — accounting procedures and government regulation — produce financial statements which are prepared conservatively.

The Reinsurer's View

The primary desired end result of any stock reinsurance operation is to produce a profit for the investors in the form of dividends and capital gains. In its efforts to achieve this goal, it is essential that management establish policies which will not only satisfy requirements of state insurance departments, but which at the same time will satisfy the expectancies of the policyholders and shareholders.

As indicated earlier, in order to form a new reinsurance company, the interested parties must first comply with the statutory capital (for stock companies) and surplus requirements of all the states in which the company is to be licensed. In addition, further restrictions are placed on the new reinsurer regarding just how the company may invest its capital and surplus funds. Specific requirements are outlined in the insurance laws of each state; for instance, classes of securities and the extent to which the funds may be invested in each class are stated, as well as classifications of what constitutes capital assets and/or admitted or nonadmitted assets. Furthermore, the NAIC requires that its published valuations of securities be used in preparing Annual Statement figures.

After formation, the new company continues to be subject to capital and surplus requirements; however, these are nearly always less than the original requirements. i.e., invasion of surplus (but not capital) is allowed as new business is written. It is with the use of surplus to acquire new business that one of the major differences of insurance accounting laws and regulations becomes important, since they create a problem for management which is not common to other businesses. Under regular accounting rules for other businesses, income affects assets immediately without any need to reserve for future contingencies. In statutory insurance accounting, however, when new business is written the premium income may not affect net admitted assets until earned, i.e., after the policy period for which the payment has been made has expired. When premium income is received, assets are indeed increased, immediately, but liabilities are also increased immediately by a like amount in the unearned premium reserve. Hence, net assets are not affected until the unearned premium becomes earned. However, in the meantime, the expenses and commissions incurred to secure those premiums must be included as a charge against surplus. Consequently, the income and expenses do not track in their effects on the balance sheet. The result of this imbalance is a reduction in the surplus account which management is in the paradoxical position of being dedicated to preserving.

Therefore, as the new company begins to write business, it commences immediately to cut down the size of its policyholder surplus. Since the paid-in capital account cannot be invaded, and since there are limitations on the amount of net premiums which a company may write in relation to its policyholder surplus (explained later in this chapter), the amount of the company's writings must be restricted by the size of its surplus account unless some form of policyholder surplus relief is obtained by a reinsurance arrangement.

But after all the regulatory restrictions have been observed, reinsurance management must still be ever mindful of its one function — protecting its policyholders (the ceding companies) and providing a profit for its investors. With this in mind, it is essential that management be guided by a sound underwriting and investment philosophy. Regardless of the size of the reinsurance company, nothing is more important than a management team that is aware of and guided by a well-planned and well-communicated underwriting guide designed to generate profit, while holding exposure to loss to the lowest point consistent with steady growth. Although some companies may "get by" for a period by concentrating on the cash flow created by loose underwriting in order to finance their investment portfolios, time and again this theory has backfired. We have only to recall the disastrous 1974-75 period for confirmation. Underwriting losses during those two years were coupled with a declining securities market, with the end result that many companies' surplus positions were drained to a near vanishing point.

The Ceding Insurer's View

The primary element in the relationship between the ceding company and the reinsurance company is the sharing of liability in the event of loss. The reinsurer "follows the fortunes" of the ceding company, and the most important concern to the ceding company is that the reinsurer be there when those losses occur. Consequently, using a reinsurer with a strong financial position is more important than the possibility of saving a few reinsurance premium dollars by using a reinsurance market with marginal policyholder surplus. Furthermore, the ceding company should be interested in establishing a long-term relationship which will enable it to build up an equity over the years.

In appraising a reinsurer's financial position, the ceding company will want to consider the reinsurer's liquidity. In fact, liquidity may be of greater importance in measuring the reinsurer's strength than that of the reinsured, for two reasons. On the one hand, the catastrophic loss exposure is more usual for a reinsurer's stock-in-trade than for an insurer. Insurers use reinsurance to reduce or eliminate such exposure, whether from natural catastrophes or unusual claims of large amounts. The reinsurer thus has a normal concentration of potentially large pay-off possibilities. On the other hand, a reinsurer with a few large reinsurance treaties has the possibility of large portfolio premium returns if those treaties are cancelled. In both cases, the ceding company is justified in looking at the reinsurer's liquidity.

Reinsurance organizations are not subject to the same stringent regulations facing ceding companies with regard to the filing of rates and policy forms. For this reason, it is essential that a ceding company scrutinize the financial stability of any reinsurance company with which it plans to place business. The following are important areas of investigation for the ceding company in determining the soundness of a reinsurer's policyholder surplus:

1. The company's rating assigned by A.M. Best & Company, the financial rating organization for the insurance business. Does the rating show financial strength, according to Best's opinion? A rating of A is considered excellent, while C is only fair.

2. The management of the company. Are the managers seasoned reinsurers, and well-experienced in running a strong and healthy operation?

3. The history of the company. Have the operations withstood the test of time? Does the company have a reputation for prompt and equitable loss payments?

4. The company's underwriting philosophy. Is good, sound, underwriting a goal, or does the organization tend to rely on investment income to bail it out?

5. The reinsurer's investment policies. Is the reinsuring company's policyholder surplus stable when viewed from the investment point of view? Since the real worth of an investment portfolio is what it can be sold for in the open market, it is important to know how all the company's investments (particularly those which are non-liquid) are valued on its books.

6. The loss and expense ratios of the reinsurer for the preceding five-year period. If the reinsurer has an unusually high loss ratio, what does it mean? Is it merely a reflection of current trends in the industry, or does it indicate poor underwriting philosophy and standards? Or is the reinsurer's particular mix of business designed to produce a high ratio of claim reserves with a small expense ratio? How do the company's expense ratios over the five-year period for the classes of business involved compare with other reinsurers' ratios?

7. Changes in policyholder surplus. Has there been any significant decrease in the size of the reinsurer's policyholder surplus in the previous year?

8. The ratio of written premiums to policyholder surplus. What is the relationship (ratio) of the reinsurer's net written premiums to its policyholder surplus? The widespread conservative guide for all companies is a maximum ratio of 3-to-1 (covered in more detail later in this chapter). However, industry figures from Exhibit 1 show a ratio of 61-to-30 for 1976, or 2-to-1.

9. The licensing status of the reinsurer. Is the reinsurer an admitted or non-admitted reinsurer? This status is important to the ceding company, since in most states it may only take credit for the reinsurance in its Annual Statement if the reinsurance company is admitted in the state in question. (Otherwise, some form of Letter of Credit or trust deposit arrangement will be necessary.)

10. In the liability area, the company's loss reserve practices. Unlike property business, casualty lines represent essentially deferred liability. Today this deferred liability can continue for a good many years into the future. Hence, the amount of losses incurred and reported by a company must of necessity include a factor for incurred-but-not-reported losses

(IBNR). Although there are many formulas for determining a company's IBNR, it essentially boils down to a matter of judgment based upon experience. A review of the company's loss schedules (particularly O and P) in the Annual Statement will give a hint of the reserving practices of the reinsurance company and will give a strong indication of whether the company has been under-reserving or over-reserving in recent years. It should be noted that if a company has under-reserved, it inevitably becomes necessary to call upon its surplus for the shortage.

11. Increases in premium writings. The shrewd ceding company must also study the reinsurer's premium writing increases over a several-year period. Since, as stated previously, increased premium writings deplete the policyholder surplus, it is incumbent on the ceding company to be certain that the reinsurer's premium writing practices are not overly aggressive.

12. Claims management. How does the reinsurer handle claim payments? Slow payments could be an indication of financial trouble within the company.

13. Retrocessions. What are the reinsurer's own reinsurance (retrocessional) arrangements? Is the company ceding off most of its book of business in an effort to obtain needed surplus relief? How strong financially are the company's retrocessionaires?

14. The ratio of policyholder surplus to unearned premiums. A long-standing guide of financial strength for a company (particularly a property company) has been the ratio of policyholder surplus to the unearned premium reserve. Ideally, this ratio should be 1-to-1. Logically, the larger the policyholder surplus amount compared to the unearned premium reserve (a liability on the balance sheet), the stronger the company. Industry figures from Exhibit 1 show a ratio of 30-to-23.

Most of the information which the ceding company will require for the above analysis of a reinsurer's financial strength will be found in the reinsurance company's Annual Statement. In addition, one of the most helpful tools in assisting the ceding company is *Best's Insurance Reports, Property-Casualty,*[1] which is updated and published annually. This "bible" of the insurance industry gives a separate report for over fifteen hundred companies and branch offices of foreign companies operating in the United States and Canada. It comments on most of the above areas of investigation and includes such items as company history, management, general underwriting policy, and investment policy. It also assigns a com-

---

[1](A.M. Best Company, Oldwick, New Jersey 08858) *78th Annual Edition, 1977*, 1946 + xxvii pp.

parative policyholders' rating ranging from A + and A (Excellent) to C (Fair) for each company.

The Commissioner's View

In addition to the initial capital and surplus requirements already discussed for reinsurance companies, there are continuing financial reports which must be filed throughout the company's life. These reports are thoroughly analyzed by the insurance departments of the states in which the company is licensed. The purposes of such analyses are many — to determine the liquidity and financial stability of the company as of a particular date, to provide some indication of a company's future financial strength, and to ascertain that all aspects of insurance law are being observed in terms of permitted assets and other regulatory matter.

One of the most important requirements for reinsurance companies is the filing of an Annual Statement with the insurance department of each state where the company is doing business. Often referred to as the "Convention Blank" or "Convention Form," the Statement must be filed by March 1 for the preceding calendar year. Unless the reinsurer has been granted a time extension by the insurance department involved, that company may be subjected to a substantial penalty for late filing. This penalty varies from state to state, and it may be as high as $100 per day.

The Convention Form is made up of an identification page, balance sheet, income statement, a statement of changes in financial position, a general interrogatory page, supporting schedules of various items of income and outgo, and a report of premiums and losses for each state in which the report is filed. In addition to the annual requirement of the Form, quarterly financial reports outlining the highlight items of the Annual Statement are now being required in many states as well.

The format for the Annual Statement was created as a uniform blank by the Committee on Blanks of the National Association of Insurance Commissioners (NAIC). Uniformity was recommended to the states, so that companies writing insurance in many states would not be burdened with reports having substantially the same material in different formats for each state. With some exceptions, the uniformity has been followed by state insurance departments.

The NAIC was formed in 1871 as the National Convention of Insurance Commissioners, later changing its name to its present association. A voluntary organization, its membership is made up of the commissioners, superintendents, or directors of insurance from each of the state insurance departments. It maintains headquarters staff in Kansas City, Missouri, and provides a host of administrative, regulatory, and research services to its members. In addition, much of its work is conducted on a committee basis, with each committee responsible for studying and reporting on subjects vital to the public and the insurance industry.

In 1971, a committee of the NAIC developed what is known as the Early Warning System: one set of criteria for life and health insurers, and another for property and liability insurers. The purpose of the latter is to assist insurance departments in identifying property/casualty companies which require particularly close surveillance and to determine the form that surveillance should take. The System is based on eleven tests or audit ratios, plus one management test, which have proven effective in distinguishing between financially troubled and sound companies. The audit ratios are derived from observing the averages produced by statistics of all insurers. For example, by comparing test results for all insurers in a given year with the test results for insurers becoming insolvent during the previous five years, a "usual range" of test results is determined for each of the audit ratios. An insurer showing a wide variation from any of the ratios is then spotlighted as deserving individual checking. The company's departure from a ratio may or may not indicate trouble, but the signal has value to the regulator as a warning.

As the NAIC document describing the System states, however, the System ". . . is not intended to replace in-depth financial analysis or on-site examination of companies. . . . Because these tests are easily subjected to possible misinterpretation and misuse, any valid interpretation of test data must depend to a considerable extent on the judgment of knowledgeable and experienced reviewers."[2] The latter caveat wisely observes the possibility that a given company can fail one or more tests without being in danger, *per se*, of insolvency. As the name of the System indicates, it provides an early warning of conditions which deserve regulatory scrutiny. The report itself admits that "nationwide, about 15 % of the companies tested are expected to receive a priority company designation."[3] With the use of computer technology the NAIC has provided a valuable service to member insurance departments which otherwise would be left to their own devices in detecting signs of financial

---

[2] *Using the Early Warning System: NAIC Regulatory Tests for Property and Liability Insurers* (National Association of Insurance Commissioners, 1125 Grand Avenue, Kansas City, Missouri, 64106), 1977, pp. 33.
[3] *Ibid.*, p. 2.

weakness among licensed insurers. That service is of particular value to insurance departments with limited staff facilities.

Seven of the eleven tests or audit ratios directly involve a ratio which includes policyholder surplus: premium to surplus, surplus aid to surplus, change in surplus, agents' balances to surplus, one-year loss reserve development to surplus, two-year loss reserve development to surplus, and current estimated loss reserve deficiency to surplus. The other four ratios (Tests 2, 4, 5, and 7) involve policyholder surplus indirectly: change in writings, two-year operating ratio, investment yield, and liabilities to liquid assets.

Test 1 is the premium-to-surplus ratio, the net premium written as a percentage of surplus. The higher the company's resultant ratio, the greater is its risk in relation to the surplus available to absorb variations in losses and investment values. The guideline established for this test is up to $3 of net premium written for every $1 of the company's policyholder surplus. According to Exhibit 2, results of Early Warning Tests for 1977, 20% of all companies failed Test 1.

Test 3 is the surplus-aid-to-surplus ratio, the percentage of the company's surplus derived from surplus aid reinsurance. In applying this test, the NAIC is determining whether company management is using surplus aid reinsurance treaties because the company's surplus is inadequate. While the usual range is less than 25%, a company which derives a substantial portion from such surplus aid treaties may be dependent on continued cooperation with its reinsurer to maintain its own financial stability. An additional reason for applying this test is that the surplus aid may improve results on other tests enough to conceal vital areas which would otherwise trigger investigation. Exhibit 2 indicates that at the end of 1977 10% of the companies failed Test 3.

Test 6 is the change-in-surplus ratio, the percentage departure from one year to the next. The change in surplus is considered by the NAIC as an ultimate measure of the improvement or deterioration in a company's financial condition during the year. Obviously, any significant decrease in surplus is regarded as a cause for concern, though the usual range is from a minus 10% to a plus 50%. Ten per cent of the companies failed Test 6 at the end of 1977.

Test 8 is the agents'-balances-to-surplus ratio, the percentage such "accounts receivables" relate to an insurer's surplus. The purpose of this test is to "measure the degree in which solvency depends upon an asset which frequently cannot be realized in the event of liquidation."[4] The

---

[4]*Ibid.*, p. 20.

EXHIBIT 2

APR 26, 1978
ALL COMPANIES

1977 NAIC PROPERTY AND LIABILITY REGULATORY TESTS

KEY ANNUAL STATEMENT INFO ($ THOUSANDS)

PERCENTILES	PREM TO C&S	CHNG IN WRIT	SURP AID/ C&S	2 YR UND RATIO	INV YLD	CHNG IN C&S	LIAB /LIQ ASSET	AGNT BAL/ C&S	1 YR RES DEVL	2 YR RES DEVL	CRNT RES DEFIC	CAPITAL AND SURPLUS	EARNED PREMIUM	TOTAL ASSETS
TEST	1	2	3	4	5	6	7	8	9	10	11			
EQUAL TO OR OVER *	300	33	25	110	9.9	50	105	40	25	25	25			
EQUAL OR UNDER *		-33			4.0	-10								
HIGHEST VALUE	999*	999*	999*	307*	9.9*	999*	999*	999*	999*	999*	999*	2,671,040	4,077,914	6,228,034
99.0	999*	999*	135*	163*	9.9*	999*	247*	207*	211*	999*	248*	362,629	679,072	1,679,541
98.0	735*	999*	81*	146*	8.9	999*	167*	123*	93*	209*	168*	212,520	406,163	862,954
97.0	609*	999*	60*	137*	8.2	999*	145*	107*	76*	131*	124*	125,340	304,819	532,964
95.0	432*	999*	40*	123*	7.5	134*	128*	77*	45*	88*	69*	78,434	175,743	368,142
92.5	392*	174*	26*	117*	7.1	75*	114*	63*	30*	58*	45*	53,564	129,492	212,908
90.0	359*	110*	19	113*	6.8	49	108*	53*	23	43*	33*	40,159	80,365	140,418
85.0	320*	67*	12	108	6.5	35	101	43*	15	27*	20	24,498	46,030	78,567
80.0	288	48*	8	105	6.3	28	95	36	9	18	12	15,260	29,384	54,870
75.0	262	37*	5	103	6.1	24	92	31	6	11	8	11,233	20,490	37,399
50.0	160	18	0	98	5.4	11	74	12	0	0	0	3,502	4,582	8,799
25.0	48	2	0	93	4.7	3	40	0	-2	-2	-5	1,104	585	2,327
20.0	28	0	0	91	4.4	1	28	0	-3	-4	-8	821	236	1,786
15.0	12	0	0	88	4.2	-1	18	0	-6	-8	-13	605	65	1,236
10.0	0	-5	0	84	3.9*	-5	8	0	-10	-13	-22	377	0	677
7.5	0	-12	0	81	3.6*	-8	3	0	-13	-17	-31	300	0	484
5.0	0	-23	0	74	3.1*	-13*	2	0	-18	-26	-51	208	0	312
3.0	0	-42*	0	62	2.5*	-21*	1	0	-30	-46	-75	109	0	176
2.0	0	-50*	0	56	1.6*	-29*	0	0	-42	-74	-99	64	0	122
1.0	0	-98*	0	44	0.6*	-47*	0	0	-83	-99	-99	37	0	58
LOWEST VALUE	0	-99*	0	-37	0.0*	-99*	0	0	-99	-99	-99	-11,903	-2,980	0
MEAN VALUE	182	80*	11	99	5.4	48	71	27	11	21	10	22,992	45,280	83,928
STD. DEVIATION	174	229	61	20	1.4	174	64	77	87	117	85	106,758	202,226	342,327
EXCEPTIONAL COMPANIES	299	529	130	184	216	276	205	284	149	269	210			
COMPANIES HAVING RESULTS	1630	1630	1630	1410	1630	1630	1630	1630	1630	1630	1620			
PERCENT EXCEPTIONAL	18	32	8	13	13	17	13	17	9	17	13			

usual range is less than 40%, and 20% of all insurers failed the test at the end of 1977.

Test 9 is the one-year-loss-reserve-development-to-surplus ratio, the percentage of current surplus represented by the previous year's deficient reserves or redundant reserves. As the NAIC report describes this test,

> The most up-to-date estimate of the losses that were outstanding a year ago is the sum of the current reserves for those losses still outstanding plus the payments on those losses made during the past year. The difference between this current estimate and the reserves that were established at the end of the prior year is the one-year reserve development. If the current estimate is greater, the prior year's reserves were deficient, as judged by one year's hindsight. If the current estimate is less, the reserves were redundant. The ratio of one-year reserve development to surplus is this deficiency or redundancy taken as a percentage of surplus. A positive test result indicates a deficiency, while a negative test result indicates a redundancy.[5]

Test 9 is used to measure the accuracy with which reserves were established one year prior. The test is also used to provide "an indirect indication of management's opinion of the adequacy of surplus." If management considers its surplus as adequate, it "frequently tends to overestimate reserves, for income tax and other reasons," according to the NAIC report. If management considers its surplus as inadequate, however, and fails to take advantage of such tax benefits available from adequate reserving (or even redundant reserving), this indication provides an additional warning. In any event, the usual range for Test 9 is less than 25%, and 10% of all companies failed it in 1977.

Test 10 is the two-year-loss-reserve-development-to-surplus ratio, the percentage of current surplus determined by the previous two years' deficient reserves or redundant reserves. Test 10 is similar to Test 9, and the comments made therein apply here as well for a two-year period. The usual range for the two-year ratio is also less than 25%, and 20% of all companies failed this test in 1977.

Test 11 is the estimated-current-loss-reserve-deficiency-to-surplus ratio, the percentage of surplus represented by the current loss reserve deficiency (or redundancy). This test is designed to provide an estimate

---

[5]*Ibid.*, pp. 21, 22.

of current reserve adequacy, and the usual range for deficiency to surplus is less than 25%. In 1977, 15% of all companies failed Test 11.

The above descriptions of the seven audit ratios directly affected by policyholder surplus are mere summaries. For specifics of actual calculations, it is necessary to use the NAIC instruction book. All of the tests or ratios indicate that policyholder surplus is a key measure used by regulators in judging the financial strength of a reinsurer (or insurer) from the very inception of the company throughout its continuing existence.

Sources of Additional Surplus

After the original stockholders' investment of capital and surplus, subsequent growth is derived not only from the earnings of reinsurance underwriting but from investment earnings on funds developed by such underwriting operations. These funds are subject to certain statutory restrictions, i.e., the amount of capital and unearned premium reserves must be invested in designated conservative investments. The remaining assets can be invested in a wide range of securities, real estate, and other properties. Any income from such investments, after investment expenses, then flows to policyholder surplus and is used to provide funds required in the reinsurance operation.

One cannot assume that the practice of accumulating surplus is a one-way street, since surplus is also the source of dividends paid to stockholders who are interested in a return on their investment. The accumulation of surplus is further depleted by the growth of the unearned premium reserve, by any underwriting losses, and by decreases in the value of investment portfolios. Should a company find that its surplus is being depleted too much, it can arrange to retrocede a portion of its business to reinsurers. This will reduce the unearned premium reserve and increase surplus by the amount of commission received from such reinsurers on the premium reserve ceded. This is not a panacea but a temporary improvement, giving the company time in which to put its house in order. Furthermore, care must be exercised to retrocede business only to reinsurers licensed in all states in which the ceding company is admitted, for otherwise no credit can be given for the transaction for the ceding company's Annual Statement.

There are other ways to increase liquidity — by using outside financing. One method consists of the usual corporate avenue for raising funds — selling additional stock, either common or preferred. This method, however, is not available to a mutual company. Another method (for a subsidiary) is to request its parent stockholder to make an additional contribution to surplus. Also, to a limited extent, a company can borrow funds by issuing debentures or notes. Such indebtedness is subject to a limitation of 5 % of the company's admitted assets, unless a higher percent is approved by the state insurance department. However handled, outside financing is usually not a viable approach, since the need for additional liquidity arises from an internal crisis situation, thus making the investment unattractive to investors.

The only other alternative for improving surplus is the drastic curtailment of new and renewal business, coupled with tight underwriting. Such techniques are beneficial over the long range rather than being an overnight cure. Perhaps the best preventive for an ailing surplus position is for management to dedicate itself to avoiding the problem from the outset.

Summary

Policyholder surplus refers to the balance which remains after a reinsurer's liabilities have been deducted from its assets. The original amount of capital and surplus which a reinsurer must have is determined by the laws of the state in which the company is licensed. The reinsurer also continues to be subject to regulatory rules regarding the size and makeup of the policyholder surplus.

Management, the ceding company, and regulators are all concerned with the financial strength of the reinsurer, and each keeps a keen eye on both the size and changes in size and structure of the company's policyholder surplus to test that financial strength.

Management of the reinsurance company must protect the interests of its policyholders (the ceding companies), while at the same time producing a profit for its investors. To accomplish this, the management team must be guided by a sound underwriting and investment philosophy.

From the ceding company's view, its most important concern is that the reinsurer be there when losses occur. It is essential, therefore, that the ceding company scrutinize the financial stability of its potential reinsurer. To aid the company in making such a financial analysis, the two most important tools for the company are A.M. Best's *Insurance Reports* and the reinsurer's Annual Statement filed in each state in which it conducts business.

An NAIC "Early Warning System" (which includes seven policyholder surplus tests in the total of eleven tests applied) was developed in the early 1970's to assist insurance departments in identifying property-liability companies which require particularly close surveillance and to determine the form that surveillance should take.

In order to increase the size of its surplus, the reinsurer has several avenues open for creating additional contributions. Among others, these can include the company's retained earnings and dividends and interest on investments. In addition, the company can sell additional stock (common and/or preferred).

But it must be remembered that just as policyholder surplus may be increased, the reverse will apply as well. Underwriting and investment losses, dividends paid to stockholders, commission penalties involved in the growth of the unearned premium reserve, and unadmitted retrocessional companies will all combine to decrease the amount of the policyholder surplus.

*   *   *   *   *   *

About the Author of Chapter 20

Marion A. Woodbury was born in Wilmington, North Carolina, on February 23, 1923. He attended the University of North Carolina and received his law degree from the Woodrow Wilson College of Law in 1955.

The first seven years of his insurance career were spent in New York and Alabama with Chubb & Son from 1949 to 1956. In 1957 he joined the Bankers Fire and Marine Insurance Company as assistant to the president, later serving as executive vice president and director, and becoming its president the following year, 1958. In 1959 he became vice president of the Reinsurance Corporation of New York, executive vice president in 1962, and president in 1965. In 1977 he organized the United Reinsurance Corporation of New York, which is managed by the The Reinsurance Corporation of New York, and serves as chairman of the board.

21

Regulation, Accounting, and Statistics

by C. Frank Aldrich*

Regulation

PATTERNS OF REGULATION AROUND THE WORLD

Insurance and reinsurance are the subjects of regulation by governmental bodies throughout the world. While the degree and form of such regulation vary considerably from one country to another, there are some general observations that are useful in providing a perspective. In most countries the source of regulation is an arm of the national government. The principal exception is the United States where the primary source of regulation is the fifty separate states and the District of Columbia. There are other exceptions, such as the systems of dual regulation by national and provincial governments in Canada and Australia, and the exclusive provision of property insurance by local governmental bodies in Switzerland and parts of West Germany.

The purposes of insurance regulation generally include the protection of buyers of insurance, most of whom are unsophisticated in insurance matters, from abuses as well as the risk that an insurance company may be unable to pay for losses due to insolvency. Another frequent purpose of regulation is to further a national interest: to foster domestic industry by protecting it from foreign competition. And yet most countries have a total insurance industry capacity grossly inadequate to cover peak exposures, such as large industrial plants and natural catastrophes. That lack of capacity provides an incentive for allowing reinsurance to be transacted across national boundaries with relative freedom. This relative freedom afforded reinsurance is nevertheless be-

---

* President, Kemper Reinsurance Company, Long Grove, Illinois 60049.

ing constantly eroded by steps (sometimes reasonable and sometimes unreasonable) such as deposit requirements for reserves, taxation imposed through ceding companies, and national reinsurance schemes. This last development is becoming increasingly widespread in developing countries, the usual result being that a government agency buys reinsurance in bulk for the country's entire insurance industry. Not infrequently another result is that the government agency takes the form of a company, which then becomes an international reinsurer seeking reciprocity for its purchases.

There is perhaps no country imposing more detailed regulation on insurance than that of the United States through its individual states. On the other hand, there are few (if any) countries less motivated than the U.S. by national protective interests in regulation, unless it be Great Britain. This lack of motivation may be attributable in part to the highly developed state of the industry in the United States which produces over 50% of the free world's insurance premiums, and to the substantial contribution made by Great Britain's insurance and reinsurance industry to that country's trade balance. But there are many of us who believe that the allowing of competition within a private enterprise system, subject to reasonable regulation, produced these conditions in the United States and Great Britain in the first place.

REGULATION IN THE UNITED STATES BY THE SEVERAL STATES

A primary purpose of regulating the insurance business by the states is to assure company solvency. Additionally, the regulators of insurance act as protectors of the general public to prevent fraud, overcharging, misleading advertising, and other harmful practices. To this end the state statutes provide for the licensing and regulation of agents and brokers (and adjusters in some states), for the regulation of rates and forms, and for the establishment of certain standards to be met by each insurer in its operations.

In the case of reinsurance, the regulation for company solvency is also the primary concern; concern for the buyer is minimal, however, since the parties to reinsurance contracts are recognized as sophisticated in insurance matters and well able to guard their own interests. Therein lies one reason why rates and forms of reinsurers are not subject to state regulation. A further reason is that regulation of contract terms or rates would not be practical since reinsurance contracts are "tailormade." Yet another reason is the need for capacity through international markets not subject to the regulators' jurisdiction. The regulation of rates and forms of primary companies is important to the reinsurer, since they influence significantly reinsurance exposures and the competitive climate in which such exposures are accumulated by the reinsured companies. It may even be argued that the reinsurer's pricing is indirectly regulated, since its charges may be limited by the premiums available from the original transaction. Conversely, the primary company's need for reinsurance from the reinsurance market may serve to temper overzealous limitations on pricing by regulators: when uneconomic pricing requirements are imposed by government, insurance and reinsurance capacity becomes limited or unavailable.

While the reinsurers are not subject to premium taxes on assumed business, they do pay indirectly their share of the substantial premium taxes levied on primary insurers by the various states. While the percentage of such taxes used by states for the operation of the state insurance departments is minimal (averaging 4 % annually), the revenue inuring to the states is another important purpose of such regulation.

The revenue income to states, the regional differences in exposure and loss patterns, and the fear of federal bureaucratic heavy-handedness are the main reasons why the states (and for the most part, with industry support) have fought to retain control over the regulation of the insurance business. Ever since the case of Paul vs. Virginia[1] in 1868 (recognizing federal jurisdiction of interstate commerce), and even since the McCarran-Ferguson Act[2] of 1945 declared insurance regulation to be the business of the several states, the battle has waxed and waned between those espousing state or federal regulations. At present, there is perhaps more pressure than at any time in the last twenty years to put at least financial regulation of the insurance business under federal control.

The use of licensing as a regulatory tool can be effective if properly administered by state insurance departments. The measure of control exercised determines by its amount and quality whether the industry is stifled, or allowed to operate virtually unchecked, or operates within a reasonable and prudent framework. A condition to licensing is that companies meet certain standards of solvency, practice, and service to the public. Annual or more frequent submission of financial and other data makes continuing surveillance possible. Reinsurers as well as primary companies come under the licensing requirements of the states in which they conduct business, if they elect to operate on an admitted basis.

The rules for licensing reinsurance companies as admitted or "authorized" reinsurers do not differ from those for primary companies.

---

[1] Paul vs. Virginia, 8 Wall. 168, 19 L. Ed. 35T (1868).

[2] Public Law 15, 79th Congress, 1945. McCarran-Ferguson Insurance Regulation Act.

But a reinsurer, other than in its state of domicile, may have as its principal objective in seeking to be licensed the recognition of its reinsurance as a credit to the company reinsured. Some states have special provision for a status of "approved" or "accredited" for a reinsurer without its having to become admitted. As with the laws setting out qualifications for licensing, the requirements for such accreditation vary widely. About half of the states have accreditation requirements relating to reinsurance which makes such "approved" status desirable. Some states are almost silent on the subject, but the majority require that the reinsurer   1) be licensed in at least one U.S. state, 2) meet the same capital and surplus minimum required of a domestic company in the state granting approval, and   3) obtain the approval of that state's insurance commissioner. For alien companies outside the U.S. and Underwriters at Lloyd's of London, some states require higher minimums, trust funds for the benefit of U.S. risks, and/or deposits with the state. Practice varies almost as much as the law. The State of Washington requires that an alien company be licensed in at least one state as a condition for approval, while no restriction is put on U.S. companies. Arkansas requires commissioner approval to operate as a non-licensed reinsurer in order to allow credit for reinsurance. Alabama requires the assuming carrier to have been licensed in at least one other state for three years. Like Alaska, Alabama requires like capital and surplus of a domestic insurer and for Lloyd's a $50 million trust fund for the U.S. Oregon, like Arkansas, permits admission on the commissioner's okay. New York is the only state at present which licenses reinsurance brokers, although most, if not all the states, license surplus lines brokers.

In the case of domestic or admitted (licensed) companies, the regulatory authorities have access to several methods of determining compliance with statutes: a) direct examination of the companies themselves, b) review of examinations conducted by other jurisdictions, c) review of Annual Statements, and d) requiring deposits of funds. Should such methods reveal financial deficiencies or non-compliance, the threat of suspension of activities or revocation of license is a powerful tool. Actual conservatorship or receivership is the ultimate weapon.

For non-admitted companies (in the main comprised of surplus lines or reinsurance companies), the enforcement of law is usually indirect. For the most part United States companies will voluntarily file Annual Statements or other detail on request, and approval or disapproval may follow analysis of that detail. Such companies in the majority of cases will follow the dictates of the jurisdiction. Again, withdrawal of approval is a respected antidote for non-compliance. Alien companies' annual reports do not conform to the standard United States Annual Statement format and many times are difficult to understand or translate both in language and accounting procedures. To accommodate the states and the companies, the NAIC has established the Non-Admitted Insurer Information Office (NAIIO) to obtain, analyze and report information on such companies as wish to become approved by that office. The NAIIO has now begun publishing analyses of alien companies' annual reports, showing all amounts in the United States dollars. The analyses will be updated annually and should prove useful. While not all states automatically approve those companies on the NAIIO list, most do. Many of those states which do not approve the listed companies nevertheless use the list as a starting or reference point in their reviews. Other sources of information used by regulators are the various publications in this country and abroad which give financial and other data on companies.[3] Federal agencies will frequently have information on companies registered with the SEC or those which are national or international in their operations.

To enforce compliance with regulations, or to protect the solvency of licensed companies, the most used method is the granting or withholding of credit for reinsurance. Before the ceding company can be relieved of the liability for unearned premiums and for reserves for loss and loss expense on ceded reinsurance, the assuming reinsurer must be either admitted (licensed) or approved by the domiciliary state (and in a few instances by a state other than the one of domicile). The withholding of such credit can produce serious penalties to the policyholder surplus of the ceding company. Such penalty can be cured either by the ceding company's withholding funds due its reinsurer to offset reserves or by the assuming reinsurer's putting up funds in the form of a letter of credit or certain deposits, but either of these methods can prove cumbersome and costly.

The New York State Insurance Department has promulgated a new regulation[4] dealing with credit for reinsurance which greatly expands its earlier regulation and allows much greater flexibility in the use of alien reinsurers. Objections to the new regulation center around two questions: whether an advantage is given the alien reinsurer over the licensed

---

[3] Some suggested publications: (1) *The Review*, International Insurance Intelligence, published by United Trade Press, Ltd., UTP House, 33-35 Bowling Green Lane, London EC1R ODA. (2) *Best's Insurance Reports*, (annual), A. M. Best Co., Ambest Road, Oldwick, NJ 08858. (3) *L'Argus International*, 18 Rue Cadet, 75009, Paris, France. (4) *Assecuranz-Compass*, A I Ediziun S.A., P. O. Box 46 CH-7200 Sehiers, Switzerland. (5) *Argus FC&S Chart* (annual), The National Underwriter Co., 420 E. 4th St., Cincinnati, Ohio 45202.

[4] Regulation No. 20 (11 NYCRR 125), Credit for Reinsurance from Unlicensed Insurers (Nov. 22, 1977). New York State Insurance Department, Two World Trade Center, New York, NY 10047.

or admitted reinsurer, and whether the alien company is subject to the same financial and solvency test requirements applicable to licensed companies. The burden of proof for the alien company's solvency is placed on the ceding company and entails a considerable amount of work to meet the reporting requirements.

An additional safeguard for reinsured companies are the recently introduced intermediary clauses under which the reinsurer assumes the credit risk for funds transmitted in either direction through an intermediary. Such clauses are now in use in most reinsurance of United States companies transacted through intermediaries. The NAIC Examiner Handbook now states that when an intermediary is involved, no credit for reinsurance ceded will be allowed unless the clause provides that "the reinsurer assumes all credit risks of the intermediary related to payments to the intermediary."

Analysis of the detail in Schedule F (discussed later in this chapter) can reveal much about a reinsured company, for valid and collectable reinsurance is vital to the solvency of companies. Two pages of general interrogatory questions in the Annual Statement analysing the effects of reinsurance ceded may also be revealing.

U.S. FEDERAL REGULATORY INTERESTS

Treasury Department Regulations. An insurer or reinsurer wishing to write surety on U.S. obligations, whether those obligations run to the U.S. government or not, must obtain a Certificate of Authority from the Treasury Department and be placed on either the primary insurers' or the reinsurers' list. Although being licensed by at least one state is required, state certification alone is not sufficient to qualify. But the procedures and qualifications are reasonable and follow substantially the standards of the states. Some of the differences will be touched on here.

Companies which by their charters are restricted to reinsurance and which are U.S. branches of alien companies may not be licensed for primary writing, but for reinsurance only. Reinsurance may not be used where the obligations run to the federal government. In such instance coinsurance is the method employed, although side agreements of reinsurance with hold harmless clauses are not prohibited. A condition to being on the Treasury Department list is compliance with a limit of risk on all contracts issued by a company, whether running to the U.S. Government or not. The limit is 10% of surplus to policyholders after deducting reinsurance with companies on the Treasury Department list.

Being on the list is extremely important for reinsurers, even if they do not plan to engage in surety business, as their clients will wish to take credit for reinsurance in Treasury Department filings.

Federal review of the financial condition of companies, while relying on the NAIC Annual Statement and state insurance department examination, does not necessarily reach the same conclusion on a company's policyholder surplus as does the state regulator. For example, the Treasury Department does not give full credit for participation in state mandated insurance plans, such as joint underwriting associations (JUA's) and similar reinsurance facilities, which can have an effect on policyholder surplus. Conversely, the federal examiner may allow addition of some non-admitted assets in determining "surplus" which states do not permit. While Schedule F in the Annual Statement provides credit for funds withheld and letters of credit received in determining an insurer's policyholder surplus, the Treasury Department only recognizes reinsurance with other listed companies in determining compliance with its 10% risk limit, and then only up to the amount for such reinsurer shown on the list.

Reinsurance and Antitrust. The McCarran-Ferguson Act, 15 USC §§1011-1015, provides a substantial shelter from federal antitrust concerns to the insurance industry as a whole. However, agreements or acts of boycott, coercion or intimidation are expressly excluded from the McCarran shelter. The McCarran shelter will also fail in the absence of a finding that the "business of insurance" is involved, or in the absence of a finding that a particular activity is state regulated.

Courts have tended to construe the term "business of insurance" narrowly in recent years, with a focus on the relationships between an insurer and its policyholders. In addition, reinsurance has been traditionally subject to little, if any, specific state regulations of the type contemplated by the McCarran Act. As a result, reinsurance activities are more subject to antitrust exposures arising from a failure of the McCarran shelter than the majority of insurance industry activities. When no clear reliance on the McCarran shelter appears justified, reinsurance activities must be evaluated under a standard, or basic, analysis. Except for types of activity which have been held to constitute *per se* antitrust violations (e.g., price-fixing, tying arrangements, monopolistic conduct), the appropriate analysis has been called a test of "reasonableness."

Reinsurance in joint underwriting and pooling arrangements has been deemed especially sensitive to antitrust exposures. Consent judgments in actions brought by the Justice Department against aviation insurance pools indicate areas of serious antitrust concern (see *U.S. v. Associated Aviation Underwriters,* 1967 C.C.H. Trade Cases paragraph 72,260 and *U.S. v. United States Aviation Underwriters, Inc.,* 1968 C.C.H. Trade Cases paragraph 72,571). The analysis of "reasonableness" as a test generally applied to any joint venture activities was set forth in a January, 1977, report of the Department of Justice to the Task Group on Antitrust Immunities as follows:

1. Does the creation of the joint venture eliminate any significant competition between the parties?

2. Are there any unreasonable collateral restraints?

3. Is the joint venture an essential facility to which all are entitled to access on reasonable and nondiscriminatory terms?

However, specific shelter for marine insurance association activities may be found in a special antitrust exemption at 48 USC §885.

Co-insurance is frequent, especially in the broker market. It is customary to expect a broker placement to be on the same terms for all reinsurers unless specifically advised to the contrary. Reinsurers operating on this basis must use special care to maintain competitive conditions and independence of individual company quotations, leaving it to the broker (who usually is also competing with other brokers or direct writers) to reconcile terms between some portion of the competing companies. Reinsurers must also use care, in exchanging views on industry problems directly or through broker channels, that such exchanges do not lead to suggestions of fixing terms by concert or boycott. They must also use care, even though sharing in contracts where terms may be influenced by agreements among foreign reinsurers to act in concert, that as reinsurers they are in no way party to such agreements to act in concert.

Accounting

Reinsurance accounting is controlled by requirements applicable to primary insurance accounting. These requirements, and the many excellent treatises concerned therewith, have not generally recognized many peculiarities of assuming reinsurance professionally. Perhaps the reason for this is that the U.S. insurance industry relied so heavily on non-U.S. sources of reinsurance that the twelve largest U.S. companies specializing in assuming reinsurance professionally reported in 1950 only $500,000 of earned premium, or only 0.7% of the total premium for the

U.S. industry. The importance of recognizing the peculiarities of rein-surance will be apparent from the fact that the figure for 1976 is over $2 billion, or 3.3% of the total.

An example of the unfortunate consequences that may flow from this downgrading of the significance of reinsurance is the manner in which company figures are most often reflected in publications of A. M. Best Company and others, moving from gross primary premiums writ-ten to net premiums written. For primary companies ceding normal amounts of reinsurance and occasionally exchanging reinsurance, the net will be less than the gross by the amount of net cost for reinsurance, and the figures will reasonably reflect an overview of the company's opera-tions, including the extent of reliance on reinsurance. For a reinsurer writing no primary business and retroceding normal proportions, the gross will be zero and the net will reasonably reflect the company's operations. But this method of summarizing a company's operations will not permit identification of the company writing a modest amount of primary business and a very large volume of reinsurance heavily retro-ceded. The burdens of such a company, which may be acting as issuing company for a reinsurance pool while retaining 5% or less, may be far beyond anything suggested by the summary figures.

Accounting Differences Between Primary Insurers and Reinsurers

Timing Differences. The first set of problems encountered arise out of the timing differences between primary insurers and reinsurers. No matter how much time lag may be experienced by the primary insurer in the documentation and entry of business transactions, there is an additional time lag experienced by reinsurers since they can only receive their infor-mation after it has been entered by the insurer and summarized for the report to the reinsurer. While this additional time lag ranges from forty-five or more days on monthly reporting reinsurance contracts to more than ninety days on quarterly reporting contracts, the reinsurer is required to close its books on the same calendar year basis as the insurer and make filings of Annual Statements for the calendar year by March 1 of the following year.

There have been a number of approaches in trying to make the ac-counting of reinsurance fit the mold established for primary insurance without reflecting distinctions that would otherwise flow from this addi-tional time lag. At one time it was popular to hold the books open until February in order to obtain from reinsured companies year-end reports or estimates to be entered as part of the prior calendar year figures.

However, the current March 1 deadline for the Annual Statement with penalties for delay makes this first approach an unpopular solution. Another approach is to estimate year-end figures for the reinsured and make preliminary entries subject to adjustment in the following year when reports are received. Yet another approach is to operate with fiscal year figures being reflected as if they were calendar year figures. At least one company, recognizing that complete figures are frequently received from foreign companies only once a year, went so far as to accumulate complete calendar year figures to be entered in the subsequent calendar year.

All of the above approaches have shortcomings, but each probably reflects a more accurate picture than the methods contemplated by primary insurance accounting. In any event, reserving practices of reinsurance companies take on added importance. Measurement of reinsurance reserves by yardsticks used for primary companies (such as those developed as part of the NAIC Early Warning tests) may not be appropriate for reinsurance companies. For example, under certain reinsurance arrangements, deposit premiums are paid to reinsurers periodically, and usually in advance. When such deposits are made, and when a minimum premium provision exists under the reinsurance agreement, and when the amount of the minimum premium is equal to or greater than the deposit premium, how are unearned premium reserves calculated? Most companies have found it advantageous to program their computers to calculate unearned premium reserves on some sort of pro rata method, based upon the time the premium is entered and the unexpired period of time remaining which the premium is intended to cover. If the minimum premium under the agreement is less than the deposit premium, the reinsurer may opt for pro rata accrual of earnings based upon the deposit amount and recognize at the same time that earned premium may be overstated. Or the reinsurer may wish to suppress the computer calculation of unearned in these cases in favor of a manually calculated and input unearned based upon the minimum premium amount.

By-Line Breakdowns. Another set of problems arises from attempts to force reinsurance into the by-line breakdowns provided for primary insurance. While in one sense the subject of reinsurance may be the pieces of a portfolio of primary business that can be divided into lines specified in the Annual Statement, frequently the indivisible total of such pieces may be radically different from the proportional parts of the pieces. This is particularly true of excess of loss reinsurance on a treaty basis, but the increasing use of sophisticated forms of proportional insurance (for example, various forms of deductibles in surplus treaties) is achieving the same results in proportional business.

The approaches to fit reinsurance into insurance accounting include the use of complex formulas for allocation between lines, the use of estimates if necessary information from the reinsured is otherwise unavailable, the reporting of excess of loss or other subdivision of reinsurance as a separate line of business, and the reporting of all reinsurance as a separate line. Numerous reinsurers do complete the Statement on a by-line basis when they have the ability to extract necessary data. But, for the most part, these data are not accurate but instead are approximations or formula extractions based on management's best estimates of the mix of business.

Agents Balances. Another question arises with respect to agents balances. One company which does not do business with agents nevertheless reflects agents balances of around $100,000,000, approximately the same as the difference between its assets and invested assets plus cash. Another shows assets exceeding invested assets plus cash by more than $75,000,000, with less than $20,000,000 agents balances. In both cases, the agents balances were made up principally of amounts due from reinsured companies, certainly a different quality of asset than the customary agents balances of a primary company. The difference between the two companies compared is probably attributable to a funds held account which is peculiar to the reinsurance business. The funds held approach tends to cause reinsurance companies to have a disproportionately high relationship of liabilities to liquid assets, another test in the NAIC Early Warning System.

Loss Expense Reserve. Another question which receives varying treatment by reinsurance companies is loss expense reserve, another Annual Statement entry on the liability page. Normally the reinsurer contracts to cover part of the reinsured's loss expense along with its loss. Many reinsurers treat such loss expenses as if they were their own, while others treat them as part of the reinsured loss and only consider their own additional loss expense as expense to the reinsurer. If the latter procedure is followed, which seems to be more logical, the proportions of such reserves in the Annual Statement will vary radically from those applicable to primary companies. Similarly, should salvage by the reinsured company be considered as salvage to the reinsurer, or as a reduction of the reinsurer's contract loss? The latter would seem to be the logical choice, and is probably the most frequent method employed by reinsurers. Here again, the figures in the Annual Statement will contrast with those of primary companies.

Loss Reserving Practices. Obviously reserving practices of reinsurers must vary from those of primary companies, and the importance of such reserves increases for reinsurers. The differing manner of handling or establishing reserves for reinsurers can lead to special questions in relation to the IRS and to the SEC. These entities are primarily concerned with the reporting of the financial conditions of companies and with taxable income. The establishing of larger than apparently warranted reserves would certainly raise questions. Consistent, reasonable methodology should be established to avoid criticism.

The National Association of Insurance Commissioners Examiner Handbook should be required reading for any insurance accountant. The Handbook sets forth guiding principles and details of statutory accounting with procedures to be followed during examinations by the state insurance departments. Instructions apply to the proper allocation of expenses, the computation of reserves, and the completion of numerous schedules and exhibits among other functions. Designed for primary companies, the manual is like the Annual Statement in not being the perfect tool when applied to reinsurance companies. But periodic revisions tend to bring it more in line with present industry practice.

As was stated, Schedule F in the Annual Statement is valuable in revealing reinsurance data. The present instructions for Schedule F call for a listing by individual company showing the required detail for each company. The instructions also call for separate grouping of affiliated and non-affiliated companies. While not mandatory, some companies further subdivide the listing into those authorized and those unauthorized. Instead of listing individual companies, an erroneous practice has developed in Schedule F: showing brokers, intermediaries, pools, syndicates, or managers. Such a showing is contrary to the instructions, and many states will not accept such listings.

Section 2 of Schedule F pertains to assumed reinsurance and need not be completed when the Annual Statement is submitted but must be completed later, usually by April 1 of the filing year. The detail involved in this section is revealing to competing companies, and the separate filing is an effort to achieve a degree of confidentiality. And the purpose of Part 1B of the Schedule F reflecting portfolio reinsurance is to alert regulators to any bulk transfer of liability which could have considerable effect on a company's policyholder surplus. A sample of Schedule F follows.

SCHEDULE F—PART 1A—SECTION 1

Ceded Reinsurance as of December 31, Current Year

Name of Reinsurer*	Location**	1 Reinsurance Recoverable on Paid Losses	2 Reinsurance Recoverable on Unpaid Losses	3 Premiums in Force	4 Unearned Premiums (Estimated)
Affiliates:					
Totals-Affiliates					
Non-affiliates:					
Totals-Non-affiliates					
Grand Totals					

SCHEDULE F—PART 1A—SECTION 2

Assumed Reinsurance as of December 31, Current Year (To be filed not later than April 1)

Name of Reinsured*	Location**	1 Reinsurance Payable on Paid Losses	2 Reinsurance Payable on Unpaid Losses	3 Unearned Premiums (Estimated)
Affiliates:				
Totals-Affiliates				
Non-affiliates:				
Totals-Non-affiliates				
Grand Totals				

*All companies should be listed in straight alphabetical order.
**Show the precise location of the reinsurance company.

SCHEDULE F—PART 1B

Portfolio Reinsurance Effected or Cancelled (—) during Current Year

Name of Company	1 Date of Contract	2 Amount of Original Premiums	3 Amount of Reinsurance Premiums
(a) Reinsurance Ceded			
Total Reinsurance Ceded by Portfolio			
(b) Reinsurance Assumed			
Total Reinsurance Assumed by Portfolio			

SCHEDULE F—PART 2

Funds Withheld on Account of Reinsurance in Unauthorized Companies
as of December 31, Current Year

Name of Reinsurer	1 Unearned Premiums (Debit)	2 Paid and Unpaid Losses Recoverable (Debit)	3 Total 1 + 2	4 Deposits by & Funds Withheld from Reinsurers (Credit)	5 Miscellaneous Balances (Credit)	6 Sum of 4 + 5 but not in excess of 3
Totals:						

NOTES: Total of Column 6 to agree with deduction taken in Item 15, Page 3
Securities held on deposit shall be valued in accordance with N.A.I.C. valuations.
Letters of credit are to be included in Column 4 and indicated by an asterisk(*).
Letters of credit are not to be included in assets or liabilities on Pages 2 or 3 or
supporting pages or exhibits.

ACCOUNTING PRACTICES IN OTHER COUNTRIES: LLOYD'S OF LONDON

For the insurer wishing to engage in international business, it is important to recognize that the high degree of uniformity of insurance accounting practices in the United States has been achieved through a system of regulation peculiar to this country. Outside the U.S., there are wide variations from one country to another, and often within a single country. Anyone who has attempted to convert a foreign financial statement to the U.S. form can also attest that the differences go far beyond terminology. However, such a conversion is useful for two reasons: to allow sensible underwriting as well as to provide guidelines for entering foreign reinsurance accounts into the accounting system of the United States reinsurer.

There is one accounting system which has been highly developed by Lloyd's of London and extensively emulated by others. That system is important because of its high degree of uniformity within Lloyd's, because of the importance of Lloyd's in international and United States reinsurance, and because its sharp differences from U.S. practices give perspective on those practices.

Period Covered as an Accounting Unit. A key element that distinguishes Lloyd's of London accounting from that of U.S. insurers is the period covered as an accounting unit. In the U.S. accounting applies to a calendar year unless a fiscal year is specified. In order to fit the activity into a calendar or fiscal year, we seek an earned premium appropriate to that year. To compute an earned premium, we calculate the premium that logically should be applied to future years, label it unearned premium, and subtract that amount from the sum of the previous year's unearned premium and the premium written during the year which has been accounted for—to arrive at the earned premium.

We fit losses to the calendar year by assigning them to the year of the occurrence, and then add estimated amounts for losses that have occurred but which are unknown and call this estimate incurred but not reported (IBNR). We charge expenses incurred during the calendar year, including those expenses related to unearned premium. This earned premium less losses and expenses is the statutory underwriting gain or loss.

We then produce a second result called generally accepted accounting principles (GAAP) by adding to statutory gain or loss the expenses related to unearned premium. Then we produce schedules to show whatever accuracy was achieved in estimating IBNR in the light of subsequent developments. Premium developed later is not allocated back to the year to which it applies, and there are limited provisions for showing development of losses in a subsequent year if the loss development generated the additional premium.

These procedures are scrutinized by several government bodies—by the Internal Revenue Service to make sure the estimates are not high enough to avoid taxation, by state insurance regulatory officials to make sure the estimates are not low enough to create a threat of insolvency to the insurer's customers, and by the Securities and Exchange Commission to make sure the estimates do not materially diverge from accuracy in a way that will mislead a buyer or seller of stock in the insurer. Neither the insurer nor any of the scrutinizing regulators have the means of truly measuring the accuracy of the estimates, though there are instances where the regulator's scrutiny is performed much later when much of the subsequent development has been recorded. As these procedures go forward from year to year, the owner of the results whether good or bad and whether recognized early or late is the same corporate entity. The owners of the corporate entity may change from time to time, and such changes occur throughout each calendar year.

The organization of Lloyd's of London is different from that of a corporate entity, and the accounting procedures recognize this difference. A group of individuals is syndicated for the purpose of underwriting during a calendar year contracts of insurance and reinsurance, none of which is to endure more than twelve months beyond the end of the calendar year. If the syndicate is to repeat such activity in the succeeding calendar year, it is reconstituted (this reconstitution may be virtually automatic by agreements that such will be the case in the absence of notice). The individuals included in the more than 200 syndicates elect a committee to regulate the total activity. There are numerous corporations involved with Lloyd's (such as corporations to manage the interests of the individuals in their activity, and corporations to perform specific functions), but the impact of the underwriting activity basically falls to the individual through the underwriting syndicates. The accounting practices at Lloyd's have been established to recognize this structure.

Syndicate Accounting. In order to report to the individuals in a 1978 syndicate, for example, an account is established into which all premiums, losses, and expenses are reflected for the activity covered by that syndicate. The only expenses accounted for are overhead, since the beginning point is the premium net of acquisition cost. This account is kept open until all activity is complete or until some earlier date on which the runoff is reinsured. Neither the committee of Lloyd's nor the British tax authority requires any estimate of IBNR for the 1978 syndicate until the end of 1980, and this estimate is then subject to audit by parties responsible to the committee. It has become customary for the runoff to be reinsured at this point, based on the audit, by a syndicate for a subsequent year under the same management, but this is subject to negotiation and there are instances where accounts have been left open to extinction. Where this happens, it may become necessary to reinsure the interest of a particular individual in order to close an estate or for some other purpose.

The above differences highlight the price paid for regulation in the U.S. in terms of uncertainties in order to achieve an early reporting of results for each calendar year. The differences also suggest that in the U.S. is rarely produced, even after full development, an accurate result of activities during a given period. On the other hand, the differences suggest the price paid by Lloyd's in terms of delayed information in order to achieve the accuracy of accounting to the individuals in each one-year syndicate. In England, the urgency of accounting for premiums and reported losses during the early part of the activity is diluted. There the individual underwriter has no real measure of results to assist in deciding whether to stay with the syndicate until shortly before notice is due on the fourth succeeding calendar year. Of course, efforts can be made to compare development of a syndicate year at the 12th or 24th month of the account with prior years at the same point, but such comparisons can be distorted by speedups or delays in the policy signing office maintained for the common benefit of all Lloyd's syndicates, or even by other circumstances. Similar circumstances may affect the accuracy of U.S. estimates, but there is in the U.S. a burden to try at the end of the year while at Lloyd's the first burden to try comes at the end of the third year.

This writer does not advocate one system over the other. They each have advantages and disadvantages. But the U.S. reinsurer should recognize in the Lloyd's system 1) that there is no unearned premium and no equity therein represented by prepaid expenses, 2) that IBNR adjusted annually is replaced by a closing estimate at the end of the third year representing all elements of ultimate profit and loss, 3) that there are no counterparts of the Annual Statement Schedules O and P, 4) that Lloyd's 1974 year, for example, is only somewhat overlapping with the U.S. 1974 year, 5) that subsequent premium development (ceded and assumed) is allocated back to the year of account to which it belongs, 6) that "allocation to year" is for the purpose of recognizing differences in equity rather than to satisfy regulators' scrutiny, 7) that ratios are different because the starting point is premium net of acquisition cost, 8) that reported results include investment income and capital gains on underwriting funds with the capital funds (deposits) and earnings thereon not treated on a syndicate basis, 9) that balances due from agents are not entered though they are taken into account in the audited closing estimate, and 10) that there are a host of other differences that flow from the basic differences in accounting approach.

These comments have been directed to accounting practices and should not be construed as having any relationship to the question of security. Lloyd's of London syndicates are backed by deposits from each individual as well as unlimited liability of each individual. The various syndicates are supported by each other through a centralized insolvency fund. While no figures are available for direct measure of the margins available for security, there has never been a loss from inability to pay.

IBNR RESERVES

From the comments above comparing U.S. and Lloyd's accounting, it will be apparent how important the IBNR estimate is in the U.S. It is even more significant for U.S. reinsurers than for insurers. The ten largest reinsurers in the U.S. at the end of 1977 had aggregate IBNR reserves equal to more than 45 % of their aggregate earned premiums, a proportion much higher than any representative group of primary insurers. This comparison becomes even more significant when coupled with the fact that outstanding reported loss figures for reinsurers as a group (in proportion to earned premiums) are larger than those of primary insurers. The reasons are that reinsurers stand behind the primary insurers and receive their reports of loss secondhand and thus with a greater delay, that reinsurers are involved with a larger proportion of large or unusual claims taking longer periods to resolve, and that reinsurers are frequently involved only with the excess portion of a loss which is the last part to be recognized and resolved.

Techniques used by reinsurers to deal with the IBNR vary substantially, with reinsurers generally recognizing that the techniques of insurers are inadequate for reinsurer purposes. Primary insurers generally use statistical data with substantial credibility for selected categories of business, and with a high degree of homogeneity as respects loss development patterns. Since the data usually involve large numbers of similar losses, any departures in statistical development from early estimates on individual IBNR cases may be offsetting if the primary insurer has used appropriate trend factors. For the net position of the primary carrier, credibility is also enhanced by any reinsurance which covers the large or unusual situation. Although the task is difficult for the primary carrier and requires much judgment to supplement the scientific approaches used, the reinsurer finds less opportunity for science and more need for judgement.

Even if the reinsurer's business is all quota share, it is still faced with a variety of approaches from its ceding companies. But any reinsurer is frequently concerned since it is an excess reinsurer with only a limited number of losses involved in the primary company's calculations, which number sharply limits credibility of any statistical approach even when the limited number from each reinsured is combined by the reinsurer with numbers from other reinsureds. For example, out of 10,000 claims handled by a ceding company (which should produce credibility for it), it may be that 100 have some reasonable probability of involving the reinsurer out of which 10 claims actually develop payments from the reinsurer (which do not produce credibility). Now, the ceding company will have established reserves on an estimated basis for all 10,000 claims not paid immediately, including the 100 which eventually may involve the reinsurer. If the reserves established for the 10 which do require payments from the reinsurer are less than the payments, the ceding company will have underreserved those claims, and the reinsurer will be called upon to pay more than expected from a scrutiny of the reinsured's reserves, to the detriment of the reinsurer. Thus, the lack of credibility proved adverse in this case to the reinsurer.

On the other hand, if the reserves established for the 90 which did not require payments from the reinsurer are more than the ceding company actually paid, the company will have overreserved those claims, to its benefit. If the underreserving amount were equal to the overreserving amount, the total reserves on the 100 claims would be accurate and adequate for the ceding company, but not the reinsurer. The reinsurer, to the contrary, suffers from the underreserving and the lack of credibility. So the ceding company benefits from accuracy because of the offset, but the reinsurer cannot benefit. Therefore, what is incurred but not enough reported (IBNR) must be viewed differently by reinsurer and reinsured, and this includes the loss incurred which is reported to the reinsured but which is not reported at all to the reinsurer.

So one of the techniques used by reinsurers, particularly with casualty lines where the reinsurer is providing excess coverage, is to review the reinsured's claim files. This review is important for the reinsurer to identify the claims with reserves that involve reinsurance, and to determine whether such reserves are adequate.

It is also important to identify the larger number of claims which have potential for adverse development sufficient to involve reinsurance. While each of such claims may be reasonably reserved based on current knowledge, reinsurance experience tells us that there will be adverse development on some of the claims, and the numbers of such cases (and their nature) will give clues to the kind of IBNR reserve to establish.

A prudent reinsurer will not conclude that its review of the reinsured's claim files has disclosed all claims reported to the reinsured with potential for adversity, and will know that all claims have not even been reported to the reinsured. The exercise of estimating IBNR is quite similar to the exercise of projecting losses for the purpose of establishing price. Thus, one approach is to establish initial IBNR reserves on the basis of the same projections, and to use the claim reviews to refine and improve projections for adjusting IBNR reserves and future prices. If the judgment used in reserving differs from that used in pricing, the inconsistency is difficult to rationalize.

The casualty excess of loss is the most difficult part of IBNR reserving. And the higher the level of attachment, the more the difficulty. But the lower levels of attachment, as well as pro rata casualty, may have an even greater impact on the reinsurer because of the frequency and volume. Property excess of loss has similarities but the time for development is much shorter. The special problem for reinsurers on pro rata property is the time lapse between the report of a loss to the reinsured and the reinsured's report to the reinsurer, which is associated with a time lapse in reporting of premiums; while there is a difference in these time lapses, a recognition of one without the other would be unrealistic. Some reinsurers recognize this situation by estimating both premiums and losses while others record accounts on a modified fiscal year basis. Marine property, both pro rata and excess, has lengthy delays in reporting attributable to delays by shipowners in appraising and repairing damages which are allowed to accumulate between dry-dockings. Special problems exist in other categories of business.

One of the categories with particular problems is catastrophe reinsurance. Here the existence of a natural loss occurrence is usually known to the reinsurer from the news media. News media reports are usually based on early and unreliable dramatic indications, with news value gone by the time reliable information is available, and loss figures estimated are usually economic loss having little relationship to insured loss figures. Nevertheless, it is possible to glean clues from news reports that can be related to the reinsurer's knowledge of its portfolio, and to the impact of prior natural catastrophe losses, in coming up with a sensible estimate at an early date. This estimate can be refined as reports start to come in, with adjustments made over the coming months. This same technique can be used for lesser natural catastrophe losses, and for major casualty losses.

Regardless of the combination of techniques employed in estimating IBNR, it is important to establish a defined methodology, to tract actual developments, and to relate those developments to the earlier estimates in identifying any deficiences in the methodology.

Statistics

We have been discussing accounting as it relates to the preparation of a conventional Annual Statement form for filing by the reinsurer with United States regulatory authorities. We also discussed the Lloyd's of London accounting practices and made some comparisons. We have also commented on IBNR reserves as an important element in accounting. An understanding of accounting as it applies to the ceding company is also important, since there are many occasions where the impact on the ceding company's Statement will be the crucial point in negotiations. This aspect of accounting has been covered in earlier chapters. But in this section we shall consider accounting further as it relates to the gathering of statistical data important to the operation of the reinsurer's business.

The purpose of gathering statistics is not so much to record the past as to develop tools useful in making decisions and predicting the future. When statistics are used to predict the future, there are a number of variants that must be recognized. For example, non-insurance statistics are not as reliable in predicting an insurance future as insurance statistics, even though the subject matter of the statistics is otherwise identical. This is because the purchase of insurance is a selective process which does not develop a true cross-section, and also because the existence of insurance may affect the reporting of events and even the occurrence of events. Every body of statistics must be treated as having less than 100% credibility. The future will probably emulate the past but not duplicate it, so trend factors must be applied to recognize this difference.

The primary insurance industry has highly developed statistical programs. Because of the numbers involved, there is high credibility in such categories as automobile and homeowners insurance. Such credibility exists even though the usefulness of averages from such lines has been eroded by the competitive process which constantly seeks to "beat the average" by careful underwriting. Such competition in the marketplace naturally leads to a variety of subclassifications, which in turn sharply reduce credibility for some of them. Nevertheless, there is available to reinsurers a vast body of statistics that can be valuable in their undertakings. As just one example, primary insurance excess limits factors, probably one of the least credible items flowing from primary statistics, receives wide usage in the reinsurance industry.

FACULTATIVE REINSURANCE STATISTICS

Facultative reinsurance may well be considered a first cousin to primary insurance. Moreover, the reinsurance of an insured single risk is the oldest form of reinsurance. With the advent of treaty reinsurance the scope and usage of facultative reinsurance changed. Today facultative reinsurance is mainly used when any one or combination of the following situations exist:

1. Capacity of the treaty program is insufficient for a given risk.
2. Treaty exclusions preclude the cession or inclusion of the particular risk under the treaty program.
3. While a certain risk may be acceptable under the treaty program, the reinsured nevertheless wishes to place the risk facultatively in order to protect the treaty reinsurers and to protect the rate basis of the treaty.
4. The reinsured is in need of the reinsurer's expertise in writing a class of exposure.

Since facultative reinsurance is similar to primary business in dealing with one risk at a time, many of the principles involved in primary business also apply to facultative reinsurance. Although both primary and facultative apply the law of large numbers, there are important differences between the two. Facultative reinsurers are frequently concerned only with excess layers. The variety of attachment points and limits in relation to a variety of original exposures by size and character tends to lead the facultative reinsurer out of the realm of credible statistics. There is only limited prospect of a single reinsurer developing sufficient business of this type to produce credible statistics from the various categories, and there is no program for accumulating statistics for reinsurance on an industrywide basis. Nevertheless, it may be useful for a reinsurer to code its contracts to permit accumulation of its own statistics in broad categories. For example, the coding may be directed to excess layers within PML, within the level above PML up to 200% of PML, etc. The choice of categories can probably be determined best by each reinsurer's considering its own posture in the market and its own approaches to pricing.

Another difference for facultative reinsurers may lead to a result just the opposite from that produced by deficiencies in credibility. The large, unusual, and difficult risks tend to gravitate to reinsurers. A limited number of reinsurers dealing with such risks regularly from a much larger number of insurers may result in a reinsurer's having a better statistical base for certain types of risks than is otherwise available. This improved credibility is an important factor in the fourth usage situation for facultative reinsurance mentioned above. Indeed, the possession of significant statistical data on an unusual category of risk can be a powerful tool in competing for business.

TREATY REINSURANCE STATISTICS

When it comes to treaty reinsurance, we move much further away from the applicability of the primary insurance industry statistical program. And the nature of treaty business is such that a first look suggests no reasonable possibility of developing credible statistics. The number of potential purchasers, instead of being tens or hundreds of millions is a little over 3,000 in the United States and 10,000 worldwide. When it is further recognized that each of the potential customers purchases a "tailormade" program to fit its own particular needs and desires, the task of gathering statistics looks impossible. Of course there are some patterns in what is purchased, such as first layers of catastrophe covers, second layers, etc. But here we see sophisticated buyers selecting the level for their first layer to fit what they perceive the market to be charging for first layers, thus destroying any similarity of the category.

However impossible it may seem to achieve credibility of statistics, it will behoove a reinsurer to accumulate summary information to enhance its knowledge of its own business. Having done so, it is also important that such summary information be used with judgment to avoid reliance of the type that may be deserved by credible statistics.

An essential information source is that available from the experience on each treaty. This comment may seem primitive in the field of statistics, but in a sense each treaty starts with a large number of individual policies as its subject matter. Also, a concept in treaty reinsurance is the spreading of a single client's results over a number of years. It should also be recognized that the accounting entry of transactions does not produce the contract experience automatically as a by-product. For one thing, calendar year insurance accounting does not allow the assignment of premium and losses to the period that is of importance in assessing the treaty. Nor does it make provision for entry of IBNR reserves to individual contracts. If the reinsurer makes provision for additional coding to recognize these factors, instead of relying entirely on a manual reconstruction of experience, the development of summary information will be enhanced. The reinsurer may also wish to bring together the experience on all contracts in a given program or for a given company or group to facilitate statistical review.

The primary classifications of insurance lose much of their meaning in the reinsurance business from a statistical viewpoint. Treaties usually cover more than one class of business and sometimes cover all classes. Often the treaty covers the infrequent unexpected occurrence, with little or no prior knowledge for predicting the probability that it will occur from one class or another. It is more important on treaty business to know what classes are included than to assign premiums and losses to the traditional primary classifications. This suggests additional coding to categorize the business by the various combinations of subject business (such as fire, homeowners, automobile), with a number of additional classes being recognized (such as excess, surplus lines, and reinsurance).

The type of company reinsured can also be an important factor. What is its size? Is it stock or mutual? Does it operate internationally, nationally, regionally, within a single state, or even more locally? Does it specialize by class of insurance or by classification of customer? Is it partly multiple line or full multiple line? Additional coding to identify such features may be helpful to the reinsurer in determining how well it is perceiving the different needs of various groups of customers.

The general nature of the treaty is certainly important. The variety may be as great as the number of treaties, but it seems feasible to categorize them into 1) quota share; 2) first surplus, second surplus, etc., and surplus treaties with deductibles; 3) catastrophe covers which are exposed to property business divided into several levels; 4) risk excess covers divided into several levels; 5) aggregate excess covers divided into several layers; and 6) perhaps others.

Statutory insurance accounting requirements force development of information on a calendar year basis. Schedules O and P in the Annual Statement measure the adjustments necessary to produce more accurate accident year figures (even though in neither case will a reinsurer's calendar year match the calendar year of its clients). Earlier additional coding was suggested to produce contract period figures for individual treaties. One final step of value is to code by underwriting year of account, permitting the measurement of results based on what was happening in the marketplace during a calendar year. Where business is developed through intermediaries, it is also important to recognize the source, and additional coding for this purpose is desirable.

What has been suggested above are the basic elements of a statistical plan for treaty reinsurance. The sophistication of the plan will vary from one company to another, as may the extent to which the variety of summary information available is actually produced from time to time. However, it seems worthwhile to develop a plan that preserves access to a significant variety of summaries. But it is worth repeating that the results will not constitute credible statistics—the purpose should be viewed as an enhancement to the reinsurer's knowledge of its own business and the development of tools to aid the exercise of judgment. A good human mind is still the most complete computer available for reinsurance —statistics and summaries developed by man-made computers may be considered as input to this best computer.

Summary

Worldwide, the purposes of insurance regulation are threefold: to protect buyers of insurance, most of whom are unsophisticated in insurance matters, from abuses; to protect buyers from the risk that an insurance company may be unable to pay for losses due to insolvency; and, in many countries to foster the domestic insurance business by protecting it from foreign competition. The relative freedom afforded reinsurers from regulation, especially across national boundaries, is being constantly eroded by such restriction as deposit requirements for reserves, taxation imposed through ceding companies, and national reinsurance schemes. This last development is becoming increasingly widespread in developing countries where a government agency will buy reinsurance from reinsurers in other countries for the country's entire insurance industry. The government agency sometimes becomes an international reinsurer seeking reciprocity for its purchases.

Regulation in the United States is more detailed than perhaps in any other country, but its purposes do not include fostering its domestic insurance industry by restricting foreign competition. Indeed, there are many who believe that competition is a more productive force than regulations designed to protect an industry. Concern for the reinsurance buyer in the U.S. is minimal, since the parties to a reinsurance contract are typically sophisticated and able to guard their own interests. Regulation of reinsurance forms and rates is not practical for at least two reasons: reinsurance contracts are tailormade, with no two alike; reinsurance capacity must often be sought through international markets, which are not subject to regulation. While the principal thrust of regulation in the United States is by the several states, there is regulation at the federal level such as the Treasury Department policing of maximum risk undertakings. Federal laws give a limited exemption from antitrust laws to the extent there is regulation by the several states, but the state regulation of reinsurance is such that the exemption has limited application.

Important accounting differences between primary insurers and reinsurers include those relating to 1) time lags, which are even greater for reinsurers than insurers, 2) by-line breakdowns provided for primary insurance, which are frequently not available to reinsurers, 3) agents balances, which may be balances due from ceding companies and may survive the usual ninety-day limit to qualify as an admitted asset, 4) loss expense reserves, recognizing that the reinsurer is usually obligated by contract to cover part of the ceding company's expenses as a part of the reinsurer's loss, and 5) loss reserving practices. The requirement that professional reinsurers follow rules primarily designed for insurance leads to some variances between reinsurers in methods used to achieve a reconciliation between such rules and the reinsurance business in areas where they don't neatly come together.

Accounting practices in other countries lack uniformity. Many insurers in the United Kingdom, and some in other nations, follow partially a very different system created by Lloyd's of London. A key element that distinguishes Lloyd's accounting from that of U.S. insurers is the period covered as an accounting unit. The period is up to twelve months for each contract commencing in a calendar year, and accounts are kept open until all activity is complete or until some earlier date on which the runoff is reinsured. Syndicates are reconstituted commencing with each calendar year of activity. At Lloyd's accuracy of reports is gained at the expense of speed, while in the U.S. earlier reporting is required and based heavily on estimates.

The U.S. reinsurer working with Lloyd's of London should recognize in the Lloyd's system 1) that there is no unearned premium and no equity therein represented by prepaid expenses, 2) that IBNR adjusted annually is replaced by a closing estimate at the end of the third year representing all elements of ultimate profit and loss, 3) that there are no counterparts of the Annual Statement Schedules O and P, 4) that Lloyd's 1974 year, for example, is only somewhat overlapping with the U.S. 1974 year, 5) that subsequent premium development (ceded and assumed) is allocated back to the year of account to which it belongs, 6) that "allocation to year" is for the purpose of recognizing differences in equity rather than to satisfy regulators' scrutiny, 7) that ratios are different because the starting point is premium net of acquisition cost, 8) that reported results include investment income and capital gains on underwriting funds with the capital funds (deposits) and earnings thereon not treated on a syndicate basis, 9) that balances due from agents are not entered though they are taken into account in the audited closing estimate, and 10) that there are a host of other differences that flow from the basic differences in accounting approach. Those not working with

Lloyd's may gain perspective regarding U.S. accounting by reviewing the differences in the Lloyd's system.

Estimating incurred but not reported (IBNR) losses is even more significant for U.S. reinsurers than for U.S. insurers because of higher proportions and greater delays. Reinsurers stand behind primary insurers and receive their reports of loss secondhand and thus with greater delay. Reinsurers are also involved with a larger proportion of large or unusual claims which require longer periods to resolve. Lastly, reinsurers are frequently involved only with the excess portion of a loss which is the last part to be recognized and resolved.

The purpose of gathering statistics is not so much to record the past as to develop tools useful in making decisions and predicting the future. Non-insurance statistics are not as reliable in predicting an insurance future as insurance statistics for two reasons: the purchase of insurance is a selective process which does not develop a true cross-section, and the existence of insurance may affect the reporting of events and even the occurrence of events. The reinsurer may find insurance statistics very useful. While the base for reinsurance in most categories is much smaller than for insurance, causing a loss of credibility in comparison, provision for gathering statistics is important, because there are no other statistics using the categories that may be significant to reinsurers. The future will probably emulate the past but not duplicate it, so trend factors must be applied to recognize this difference. Whatever the plan in gathering statistics for use by insurers and reinsurers, the purpose should be to enhance human knowledge and help in the exercise of judgment. A good human mind is still the most complete computer available for reinsurance—statistics developed by man-made computers may be considered as input to this best computer.

*   *   *   *   *   *

About the Author of Chapter 21

C. Frank Aldrich was born August 28, 1925, in Little Rock, Arkansas. He attended Little Rock Junior College, Louisiana State University, Washington University of St. Louis, and St. Louis University. He served in the U. S. Army. He entered private law practice for several years after graduation from St. Louis University Law School.

For over twenty years he has been in the insurance business. During that period he has been a member or chairman of many association committees dealing with such areas as reinsurance, marine insurance, group health insurance, rate regulations, and legal matters. He is a trustee of the U. S. Council of the International Chamber of Commerce. He also is chairman of the Industry Advisory Committee to the Subcommittee on Reinsurance, Syndicates, and Pools of the National Association of Insurance Commissioners.

From the formation of Kemper Reinsurance Company, he has served as its chief operating officer and currently is its president and chief executive officer.

A Suggested Reinsurance Glossary

The following terms are in general use by the insurance business in its reinsurance practices, according to the several sources used in their compilation (the twenty-one chapters appearing herein, written by twenty-three reinsurance experts; reinsurance glossaries published by The Reinsurance Association of America and General Reinsurance Corporation; and the publication of Rough Notes: *Insurance Words and Their Meaning*). While there are differences of opinion among authorities concerning the nuances and subtleties of many words herein (as will be the case in the formation of any dictionary of technical terms), the editor of this book believes the definitions given are reasonably meaningful as practiced generally in the trade. Accordingly, the editor accepts responsibility for any errors created in the compilation and hopes the definitions will nevertheless be helpful to the reader of this work. Anyone is given permission to quote from this glossary or reproduce it in whole or in part if the source of the quotation is cited in the use thereof.

ACCIDENT YEAR EXPERIENCE—Simplistically, the matching of all losses occurring (regardless of when the losses are reported) during a given twelve-month period of time with all premium earned (regardless of when the premium was written) during the same period of time. More specifically, the total value (losses paid plus loss reserves) of all losses occurring during the defined twelve-month time period (i.e., the date of loss falls within the time period) is divided by the EARNED PREMIUM (see its definition) for this same exposure period. As the experience is developing, loss reserves are used in the calculation, but the ultimate result cannot be finalized until all losses are settled. While any twelve-month period can be used to define the exposure period, the year beginning January 1 is normally used. The most accurate method uses EXPOSURE EARNED premium (see its definition under EARNED PREMIUM) as the denominator, whereas in practice ACCOUNTING EARNED premium (see its definition under EARNED PREMIUM) is frequently used as a matter of convenience.

CALENDAR YEAR EXPERIENCE—Simplistically, the matching of all losses incurred (not necessarily occurring) within a given twelve-month period, usually beginning on January 1, with all premium earned within the same period of time. Incurred losses will include the change in IBNR. More specifically, the total value of all losses incurred (not necessarily occurring) during the calendar year is divided by the ACCOUNTING EARNED premium for this same exposure period. Losses incurred are equal to the sum of losses paid, plus the outstanding loss reserves at the end of the year, less the outstanding loss reserves at the beginnning of the year. Once calculated for a given period, calendar year experience never changes.

POLICY YEAR EXPERIENCE—Simplistically, the segregation of all premiums and losses attributable to policies having an inception or renewal date within a given twelve-month period. More specifically, the total value (losses paid plus loss reserves) of all losses arising from (regardless of when reported) policies incepting or renewing during the year is divided by the fully developed earned premium for those same policies. The finally developed earned premium will always equal the written premium for those policies. POLICY YEAR EXPERIENCE resembles ACCIDENT YEAR EXPERIENCE in that, while the experience is developing, loss reserves are used in the calculation, but the ultimate result cannot be finalized until all losses are settled. POLICY YEAR EXPERIENCE is different in that premiums earned from policies incepting during a one-year period of time will earn over the course of both the year of inception and a later year(s). Similarly, losses to be included will be occurring over this same extended time period.

ACCOUNT EXECUTIVE—The individual, either as employee of a reinsurer or a reinsurance intermediary, who is responsible for all matters pertaining to the reinsurance account of a particular insurer.

ACQUISITION COSTS—All expenses incurred by an insurance or reinsurance company which are directly related to acquiring insurance accounts (insured, or reinsured) for the company.

ADMINISTRATION EXPENSES—Costs incurred in conducting an insurance operation other than loss adjustment expenses, acquisition costs, and investment expenses.

ADMITTED ASSETS—Assets recognized and accepted by state insurance laws in determining the solvency of insurers or reinsurers.

ADMITTED COMPANY— 1) An insurer licensed to conduct business in a given state. 2) A reinsurer licensed or approved to conduct business in a given state.

ADVANCE DEPOSIT PREMIUM—An amount paid by a reinsured to a reinsurer which is held for the payment of the reinsured's losses. At some time in the future, any balance in the fund remaining after paying losses and any agreed reinsurance expenses will be returned to the reinsured. Also known as BANKING PLAN.

ADVANCE PREMIUM—The amount charged at the start of a treaty, to be adjusted later. Also known as DEPOSIT PREMIUM or PROVISIONAL PREMIUM.

ADVERSE SELECTION—The conscious and deliberate cession of those risks, segments of risks, or coverages that appear less attractive for retention by the ceding company.

AGENCY REINSURANCE— 1) A designation that identifies the reinsurance of one or more of an agent's policies, with the agent acting for the ceding insurer under its authority. 2) A contract of reinsurance between an insurer and a reinsurer that concerns or is confined to business produced by a named agent of the ceding insurer, usually generated by that agent and administered directly with the reinsurer with permission of the insurer. While there are other reasons for the practice, the usual intent is to allow an agent to issue larger policies than the insurer would otherwise permit. Usually, agency reinsurance is written as proportional reinsurance on property or other first-party insurances.

AGENT COMMISSION—In insurance, an amount paid an agent for insurance placement services.

AGGREGATE EXCESS OF LOSS REINSURANCE—A form of excess of loss reinsurance which indemnifies the reinsured against the amount by which the reinsured's losses incurred (net after specific reinsurance recoveries) during a specific period (usually twelve months) exceed either an agreed amount or an agreed percentage of some other business measure, such as aggregate net premiums over the same period or average insurance in force for the same period. This form of reinsurance is also known as stop-loss reinsurance, stop-loss-ratio reinsurance, or "excess of loss ratio reinsurance."

AGGREGATE WORKING EXCESS—A form of per risk excess reinsurance under which the primary company retains its normal retention on each risk and additionally retains an aggregate amount of the losses which exceed such normal retention.

ALIEN COMPANY—An insurer or reinsurer domiciled outside the U.S. but conducting an insurance or reinsurance business within the U.S.

AMORTIZATION PERIOD—Synonymous with payback period, this term is used in the rating of per occurrence excess covers and represents the number of years at a given premium level necessary to accumulate total premiums equal to the indemnity.

ANNUAL STATEMENT—A summary of an insurance company's (or reinsurer's) financial operations for a particular year, including a balance sheet supported by detailed exhibits and schedules, filed with the state insurance department of each jurisdiction in which the company is licensed to conduct business. Also known as CONVENTION BLANK.

ARBITRATION CLAUSE—A provision sometimes appearing in reinsurance treaties whereby the parties agree to submit any dispute or controversy to an unofficial tribunal of their own choosing in lieu of the tribunals provided by the ordinary processes of law. Although the wording of the clause may vary, it normally provides for the appointment of two arbitrators, one selected by each party, who in turn appoint an umpire, and the decision of a majority of the arbitrators is binding on the parties to the reinsurance treaty.

AS IF—A term used to describe the recalculation of prior years of loss experience to demonstrate what the underwriting results of a particular program would have been if the proposed program had been in force during that period.

ASSUME—To accept all or part of a ceding company's insurance or reinsurance on a risk or exposure.

ASSUMED PORTFOLIO—The transfer of in-force insurance liability by an insurer to a reinsurer (or vice versa) by the payment of the unearned premium reserve on those policies alone, or by the concurrent transfer of liability for outstanding losses under those policies by the payment of the outstanding loss reserve by the insurer to the reinsurer (or vice versa). The former is a premium portfolio, the latter a loss portfolio.

ASSUMPTION ENDORSEMENT—Another name for CUT-THROUGH EN-DORSEMENT.

ATTACHMENT POINT—The amount at which excess reinsurance protection becomes operative; the retention under an excess reinsurance contract.

AUTHORIZED REINSURANCE—Reinsurance placed with a reinsurer which is licensed or otherwise recognized by a particular state insurance department.

AUTOMATIC TREATY—An agreement between reinsured and reinsurer (usually for pro rata reinsurance, and usually for one year or longer), whereby the ceding company is obligated to cede certain risks as provided in the agreement and the reinsurer is obligated to accept. See OBLIGATORY TREATY.

BALANCE—A concept in surplus share reinsurance dealing with the relationship between written premium under the treaty and the maximum limit of liability to which the reinsurer is exposed. The precise relationship will vary from treaty to treaty, but if the ratio desired for a specific treaty is achieved, the treaty if referred to as "balanced."

BANKING PLAN—An agreement in which the ceding company pays the reinsurer a premium over a specified number of years which is intended to fully fund a specific limit of liability. If the premium is not fully expended by payment of losses within the contract period, the unused portion is returnable, less a reinsurance expense. Also known as ADVANCE DEPOSIT PREMIUM PLAN.

BASE PREMIUM—The ceding company's premiums (written or earned) to which the reinsurance premium rate is applied to produce the reinsurance premium. Also known as SUBJECT PREMIUM, PREMIUM BASE, and UNDERLYING PREMIUM.

BASIC LIMITS—The minimum amounts of insurance for which it is the practice to quote premiums in liability insurance. Additional amounts are charged for by the addition of certain percentages of the premium for the minimum (or basic) limits.

BINDER (REINSURANCE)—A record of reinsurance arrangements pending the issuance of a formal reinsurance contract (which then replaces the binder). See COVER NOTE.

BORDEREAU—Furnished periodically by the reinsured, a detailed report of reinsurance premiums or reinsurance losses. A premium bordereau contains a detailed list of policies (bonds) reinsured under a reinsurance treaty during the reporting period reflecting such information as the name and address of the primary insured, the amount and location of the risk, the effective and termination dates of the primary insurance, the amount reinsured and the reinsurance premium applicable thereto. A loss bordereau contains a detailed list of claims and claims expenses outstanding and paid by the reinsured during the reporting period reflecting the amount of reinsurance indemnity applicable thereto. Bordereau reporting is primarily applicable to pro rata reinsurance arrangements and to a large extent has been supplanted by summary reporting.

BROKER—A reinsurance intermediary who negotiates contracts of reinsurance between a reinsured and reinsurer on behalf of the reinsured, receiving commission for placement and other services rendered. Under the terms of one widely used intermediary clause, premiums paid a broker by a reinsured are considered paid to the reinsurer, but loss payments and other funds (such as premium adjustments) paid a broker by a reinsurer are not considered paid to the reinsured until actually received by the reinsured.

BROKERAGE COMMISSION—An amount paid a broker for insurance or reinsurance placement and other services.

BROKERAGE MARKET—A collective reference to those reinsurers which accept business mainly through reinsurance intermediaries.

BUFFER LAYER—Used in casualty insurance to describe a stratum of coverage between the maximum policy limit which the primary underwriter will write and the minimum deductible over which the excess or umbrella insurer will cover.

BURNING COST—The ratio of actual past reinsured losses to ceding company's subject matter premium (written or earned) for the same period. Used to analyze past reinsurance experience or to project the future.

BURNING RATIO—In primary insurance, the ratio of losses suffered to the amount of insurance in effect. Thus, not a "loss ratio," which is the ratio of losses incurred to premiums earned.

CALENDAR YEAR EXPERIENCE— See ACCIDENT YEAR EXPERIENCE.

CAPACITY—The measure of an insurer's financial strength to issue contracts of insurance, usually determined by the largest amount acceptable on a given risk or, in certain other situations, by the maximum volume of business it is prepared to accept.

CAPTIVE INSURANCE COMPANY—A company which is wholly-owned by another organization (generally non-insurance), the main purpose of which is to insure the risks of the parent organization.

CARPENTER PLAN—A form of excess of loss reinsurance in which a ceding company spreads its losses over a three-to-five-year period, first introduced in the U.S. by a broker of that name. See SPREAD LOSS REINSURANCE.

CARRIER, REINSURANCE—An organization assuming insurance liability of another insurer.

CASUALTY CATASTROPHE COVER—Reinsurance which is not exposed on a policy limit basis, i.e., the deductible on the treaty is equal to or exceeds the reinsured's maximum net exposure on any one policy. Therefore, such treaties protect against the infrequent loss involving two or more insureds in the same loss occurrence. Another name for CLASH COVER.

CATASTROPHE NUMBER—Whenever a catastrophe occurs which produces losses within a prescribed period of time in excess of a certain amount (now $1 million), the amount of such losses is recorded separately from non-catastrophe losses, is numbered by the American Insurance Association, and may be treated differently in the statistical experience records of the state used in setting rate levels.

CATASTROPHE REINSURANCE—A form of excess of loss reinsurance which, subject to a specified limit, indemnifies the ceding company for the amount of loss in excess of a specified retention with respect to an accumulation of losses resulting from a catastrophic event or series of events. The actual reinsurance document is referred to as "a catastrophe cover."

CEDE—To pass on to another insurer (the reinsurer) all or part of the insurance written by an insurer (the ceding insurer) with the object of reducing the possible liability of the latter.

CEDING COMMISSION—In reinsurance, an allowance (usually a percentage of the reinsurance premium) made by the reinsurer for part or all of a ceding company's acquisition and other costs. The ceding commission may also include a profit factor for the reinsured.

CEDING COMPANY—A reinsured.

CERTIFICATE OF REINSURANCE—A short-form documentation of a reinsurance transaction.

CESSION— 1) The unit of insurance passed to a reinsurer by a primary company which issued a policy to the original insured. A cession may accordingly be the whole or a portion of single risks, defined policies, or defined divisions of business, all as agreed in the reinsurance contract. 2) The act of ceding where such act is necessary to invoke the reinsurance protection.

CLAIM EXPENSES—The costs incurred in processing claims: court costs, interest upon awards and judgments, the company's allocated expense for investigation and adjustments and legal expenses (excluding, however, ordinary overhead expenses of the company such as salaries, monthly or annual retainers, and other fixed expenses which are defined as unallocated loss adjustment expenses). Also known as Loss Expenses or Loss Adjustment Expenses.

CLAIMS-MADE BASIS—The provision in a contract of insurance or reinsurance that coverage applies only to losses which occur and claims that are made during the term of the contract. (Losses occurring before the contract term are sometimes covered by the addition of "prior acts" coverage to the contract. Losses reported after the contract term are sometimes covered by the addition of "tail" coverage.) Once the policy period is over in claims-made covers, the approximate extent of the underwriter's liability is known. On the other hand, the traditional "occurrence" liability insurance method provides coverage for losses from claims which occurred during the policy period, regardless of when the claims are asserted. With the traditional "occurrence" liability coverage method, the underwriter may not discover the extent of liability for years to come from losses asserted to have occurred within the policy period. With claims-made covers which are renewed, however, losses which occurred during any period when the policy was in force are again covered if reported during the renewal term. In summary, the traditional method is similar to claims-made if the latter has added to it both "prior acts" and "tail" coverage.

CLASH COVER—A casualty excess of loss agreement with a retention higher than the limits on any one reinsured policy. The agreement is thus only exposed to loss when two or more casualty policies (perhaps from different lines of business) are involved in a common occurrence in an amount greater than the clash cover retention. Also known as CONTINGENCY COVER.

COMBINATION PLAN REINSURANCE—A form of quota share and excess of loss reinsurance combined which provides that, in consideration of a premium at a fixed percent of the ceding company's subject premium on the business covered, a) the reinsurer will indemnify the ceding company for the amount of loss on each risk in excess of a specified retention, subject to a specified limit, and b) after deducting the excess recoveries on each risk, the reinsurer will indemnify the ceding company for a fixed quota share percent of all remaining losses.

COMBINED RATIO—Another name for OPERATING RATIO or TRADE RATIO.

COMMISSION— 1) AGENT COMMISSION—In insurance, an amount paid an agent for insurance placement services. 2) BROKERAGE COMMIS-SION—An amount paid a broker for insurance or reinsurance placement services. 3) CEDING COMMISSION—In reinsurance, an allowance (usually a percentage of the reinsurance premium) made by the reinsurer for part or all of a ceding company's acquisition and other costs. The ceding commission may also include a profit factor for the reinsured. 4) OVERRIDING COMMIS-SION— a) A fee or percentage of money which is paid to a party responsible for placing a retrocession of reinsurance. b) In insurance, a fee or percentage of money which is paid by the insurer to an agent or general agent for premium volume produced by other agents in a given geographic territory. 5) OVER-WRITING COMMISSION—Another name for OVERRIDING COMMIS-SION. 6) PRODUCER COMMISSION—The same as BROKERAGE COM-MISSION. 7) REINSURANCE COMMISSION—The same as CEDING COM-MISSION.

COMMUTATION CLAUSE—A clause in a reinsurance agreement which provides for estimation, payment, and complete discharge of all obligations including future obligations between the parties for reinsurance losses incurred. This clause is often found in contracts reinsuring workers' compensation and may be optional (which is usual) or mandatory.

CONFLAGRATION—A massive fire which destroys many contiguous properties.

CONFLAGRATION AREA—A geographic territory in which many properties are subject to damage by a sweeping fire.

CONFLAGRATION (EXCESS) COVER—See CATASTROPHE REIN-SURANCE.

CONTINGENCY COVER—Reinsurance protection against the unusual combination of losses. See CLASH COVER.

CONTINGENT COMMISSION—An allowance by the reinsurer to the reinsured based on a predetermined percentage of the profit realized by the reinsurer on the business ceded by the reinsured. Also known as Profit Commission.

CONVENTION BLANK—Another name for the ANNUAL STATEMENT form of NAIC.

COVER NOTE—A written statement issued by an intermediary, broker, or direct writer, indicating that coverage has been effected. See BINDER.

CREDIBILITY—The measure of credence or belief which is attached to a particular body of statistical experience for ratemaking purposes. Generally, as the body of experience increases in volume, the corresponding credibility also increases. This term would frequently be defined in terms of specific mathematical formulas.

CUMULATIVE LIABILITY—The accumulation of liability of a reinsurer under several policies from several ceding companies covering similar or different lines of insurance, all of which are involved in a common event or disaster.

CUT-OFF—The termination provision of a reinsurance contract stipulating that the reinsurer shall not be liable for loss as a result of occurrences taking place after the date of termination or after an agreed date following termination. A cut-off normally involves return of unearned premium in force at the cut-off date.

CUT-THROUGH ENDORSEMENT—An addition to an insurance policy between an insurance company and a policyholder which requires that, in the event of the company's insolvency, any part of a loss covered by reinsurance be paid directly to the policyholder by the reinsurer. The cut-through endorsement is so named because it provides that the reinsurance claim payment "cuts through" the usual route of payment from reinsured company-to-policyholder and then reinsurer-to-reinsured company, substituting instead the payment route of reinsurer-to-policyholder. The effect is to revise the route of payment only, and there is no intended increased risk to the reinsurer. Similar to the guarantee endorsement, the cut-through endorsement is also known as an Assumption Endorsement.

DEFICIT—As used in reinsurance, any excess of charges over credits at the end of any accounting period (which excess shall be a charge in the computation of the contingent commission for the succeeding period, or in computing various experience rated reinsurance arrangements).

DEPOSIT PREMIUM—When the terms of a treaty provide that the ultimate premium is to be determined at some time after the treaty itself has been written, the reinsurer may require a tentative or a deposit premium at the beginning. The tentative premium is readjusted when the actual earned charge has been later determined. See ADVANCE PREMIUM.

DIRECT WRITER— 1) In reinsurance, a reinsurer which negotiates with a ceding company without benefit of an intermediary or broker. 2) In insurance, a primary insurer that sells insurance through licensed agents who produce business essentially for no one else.

DIRECT WRITTEN PREMIUM—The gross premium income (written instead of earned) of a primary company, adjusted for additional or return premiums but before deducting any premiums for reinsurance ceded and not including any premiums for reinsurance assumed.

DOMESTIC COMPANY—An insurer conducting business in its domiciliary state from which it received its charter to write insurance (as opposed to a foreign company: an insurer conducting business in a state other than its domiciliary state; or an alien company: one domiciled ouside the U.S. but conducting business within the U.S.).

EARLY WARNING TESTS—Financial ratio and performance criteria designed by the National Association of Insurance Commissioners to identify insurance companies which may need close surveillance by state insurance departments.

EARNED PREMIUM—That portion of written premium equal to the expired portion of the time for which the insurance or reinsurance was in effect. Technically, the following definitions are appropriate:

ACCOUNTING EARNED—This is the most common and widely understood method. The unearned premium reserve at the beginning of the period is added to the premium written (booked) during the period, and the unearned premium reserve at the end of the period is subtracted. Accounting earned is the figure used in the Annual Statement.

EXPOSURE EARNED—This method calculates the premiums which were actually exposed to loss (earned) for the period. The date on which premiums were booked is disregarded. What is significant is the effective date and term to which the premium applies. The portion of the premium written which was exposed to loss (earned) is allocated to the exposure period whether the premiums were booked prior to the period, during the period, or after the period. The exposure earned premium eliminates the deficiency contained in accounting earned premium that results from timing problems in the recording of premium records.

ERRORS AND OMISSIONS CLAUSE—A clause in a reinsurance treaty (requiring some affirmative act by the ceding insurer to activate the reinsurance protection) which stipulates that, in the event of inadvertent error or omission, the reinsured shall not be prejudiced in the fulfillment of the agreement, provided that such error or omission shall be corrected as soon as it is discovered.

EXCESS JUDGMENT LOSS—The amount paid by a liability insurer in excess of applicable policy limits occasioned by the failure, on account of negligence or bad faith, to settle a claim for an amount within such policy limits.

EXCESS LIMITS PREMIUMS—In casualty insurance, premiums for limits of liability added to basic limits, calculated as multiples of basic limits premium. Excess limits premiums were the original (and remain a popular) basis of premium paid for casualty excess of loss reinsurance.

EXCESS OF LINE REINSURANCE—A form of per risk excess agreement under which the indemnity is not a fixed dollar limit but a multiple of the primary company's net retention.

EXCESS OF LOSS RATIO REINSURANCE—See AGGREGATE EXCESS OF LOSS REINSURANCE.

EXCESS OF LOSS REINSURANCE—A generic term describing reinsurance which, subject to a specified limit, indemnifies the ceding company against all or a portion of the amount in excess of a specified retention. The term includes various types of reinsurance, such as catastrophe reinsurance, per risk reinsurance, per occurrence reinsurance, and aggregate excess of loss reinsurance. It should never be confused with "surplus share" which always refers to a pro rata form of reinsurance. Also known as NON-PROPORTIONAL REINSURANCE.

EXCESS PER RISK REINSURANCE—A form of excess of loss reinsurance which, subject to a specified limit, indemnifies the ceding company against the amount of loss in excess of a specified retention with respect to each risk involved in each loss.

EXCLUSIONS—Those risks, perils, or classes of insurance with respect to which the reinsurer will not pay loss or provide reinsurance notwithstanding the other terms and conditions of reinsurance.

EXPENSE RATIO—Expenses (other than loss adjustment expenses) incurred during a specific period of time divided by premiums written during the same period.

EXPERIENCE RATING—Another name for PROSPECTIVE RATING and RETROSPECTIVE RATING.

EXPIRATION—The cessation of a reinsurance cover when the time period for which it was written has ended. A treaty written on a "continuous until cancelled" basis does not expire but will contain a provision for termination.

EXTRA CONTRACTUAL DAMAGES (EXTRA CONTRACTUAL OBLIGATIONS, E.C.O.)—In reinsurance, monetary awards required by a court of law against an insurer for its negligence to its insured. Such payments required of an insurer to its insured are extra-contractual in that they are beyond the insurance contract between insurer and insured. A reinsurance treaty may cover these damages and, if so, will specify covered situations, percentages applicable, and required premium charges.

EXTRACTION FACTOR—A fraction or percentage of a reinsured company's subject premium deducted from the reinsurance premium to recognize and measure that portion of any policies not covered by reinsurance when the policies are written by the reinsured on an indivisible premium basis. For example, if property excess reinsurance does not cover third party liability or burglary in a reinsured company's Homeowners Policy, an extraction factor would adjust the reinsurance premium accordingly.

FACULTATIVE CERTIFICATE OF REINSURANCE—A document formalizing a facultative reinsurance cession.

FACULTATIVE REINSURANCE—The reinsurance of part or all of (the insurance provided by) a single policy, with separate negotiation for each cession. The word "facultative" connotes that both the primary insurer and the reinsurer have the faculty or option of accepting or rejecting the individual submission (as distinguished from the obligation to cede and accept, to which the parties agree in treaty reinsurance).

FACULTATIVE SEMI-OBLIGATORY TREATY—A reinsurance contract under which the ceding company may or may not cede exposures or risks of a defined class to the reinsurer which is obligated to accept if ceded.

FACULTATIVE TREATY—A reinsurance contract under which the ceding company has the option to cede and the reinsurer has the option to accept or decline individual risks. The contract describes how individual facultative reinsurances shall be handled.

FINANCING FUNCTION—A purpose of reinsurance in some cases, i.e., whenever the reinsurer relieves the primary company of all or part of the company's responsibility for carrying an unearned premium reserve and the reinsurer allows a ceding commission to the primary company. Because the cash or other statutorily recognized assets being transferred (causing a change in assets) are less than the unearned premium reserve change (causing a change in liabilities), the primary company's policyholder surplus is increased by the amount of the reinsurance commission allowance.

FIRST LOSS RETENTION—The amount of loss sustained by the reinsured before the liability of the excess of loss reinsurer attaches, often referred to as NET RETENTION. See ATTACHMENT POINT.

FIRST SURPLUS TREATY—A term exclusive to pro rata reinsurance treaties which defines the amount of each cession as the amount of gross (policy) liability which exceeds, or is "surplus" to, an agreed net retention up to the limit of (reinsurance) liability. Often a maximum net retention is specified in the treaty, with the primary company having the option to choose a lesser retention on individual risks. The amount of first surplus reinsurance provided will be limited to a fixed multiple of the selected retention in each case. Larger policy surpluses are termed "second," "third," and so on, each being the amount of reinsurance afforded once the prior surplus reinsurance capacity plus the true net retention have been exceeded. See SURPLUS REINSURANCE.

FLAT COMMISSION—A stated commission percentage, payable by the reinsurer to the reinsured, which is not subject to further adjustment under a profit-sharing provision. Common in pro rata facultative reinsurance.

FLAT RATE— 1) A fixed rate not subject to any subsequent adjustment. 2) A reinsurance premium rate applicable to the entire premium income derived by the ceding company from the business ceded to the reinsurer (as distinguished from a rate applicable to excess limits).

FOLLOW THE FORTUNES—A concept inherent in any reinsurance relationship which, when expressed in an agreement, generally runs to a statement that the reinsurer "shall follow the fortunes of the ceding company in all matters falling under this Agreement" or shall do so "...in all respects as if being a party to the insurance," or similar language. Expressed or not, the concept speaks to a relationship under which the reinsured's duty — to treat reinsured policy rights and obligations as if there were no reinsurance — is extended into a right. This right is not open-ended: it cannot carry a reinsurer outside its agreement; neither is it fixed. Rather, it rests on mutual trust within the circumstances of each case. Accordingly, some reinsurers avoid "following the fortunes" clauses in their agreements, while those in use are normally found in pro rata treaties where the sharing nature of cessions makes proper implementation reasonably evident and self-controlling.

Historically, the "follow the fortunes" clause was designed to deal with "errors and omissions," particularly in the case of inadvertent omission by the ceding company of a specific risk on a bordereau, intending to permit the ceding company to include the risk on a bordereau upon discovery of the oversight with retroactive reinsurance. However, the courts have held that under the "follow the fortunes" language of a reinsurance treaty, the reinsurer adopts the language of the primary policy, and thus a third party creditor of the primary insurer has a right of action against the reinsurer under a reinsurance contract. Such a holding is an exception to the general rule of law applicable to reinsurance agreements that such agreements operate solely between the reinsured and the reinsurer and create no privity between the reinsurer and any third party, and afford no right of action by any third party against the reinsurer on the reinsurance agreement. The historical objective of the clause can be achieved by inserting an "errors and omissions" clause in any reinsurance agreement which is not fully automatic. Neither a "follow the fortunes" nor "errors and omissions" clause is necessary in an automatic reinsurance agreement.

FOLLOWING REINSURER—A reinsurer which follows the lead reinsurer on a cover being placed, accepting or rejecting the terms as presented.

FOREIGN REINSURER—A U.S. reinsurer conducting business in a state other than its domiciliary state, where it is known as a domestic company (as opposed to an alien reinsurer: one domiciled outside the U.S. but conducting business within the U.S.).

FRANCHISE COVERS—A contractual provision, common in hail insurance but also used elsewhere, stating that no loss is payable until the loss exceeds a certain amount but, when that amount is exceeded, then the whole loss is paid.

FRONTING—An arrangement whereby one insurer issues a policy on a risk for and at the request of one or more other insurers with the intent of passing the entire risk by way of reinsurance to the other insurer(s). Such an arrangement may be illegal if the purpose is to frustrate regulatory requirements.

FUNDS HELD ACCOUNT (or FUNDS WITHHELD)—The holding by a ceding company of funds representing the unearned premium reserve or the outstanding loss reserve applied to the business it cedes to a reinsurer.

GAAP (GENERALLY ACCEPTED ACCOUNTING PRINCIPLES)—A method of reporting the financial results of an insurer more in accordance with the going-concern basis used by other businesses. GAAP assigns income and disbursements to their proper period, as distinguished from the more conservative requirements of statutory accounting affecting insurers.

G.N.E.P.I. (Gross Net Earned Premium Income)—See SUBJECT PREMIUM.

G.N.W.P.I. (Gross Net Written Premium Income)—See SUBJECT PREMIUM.

GRADED SURPLUS TREATY—A surplus share treaty under which the capacity expressed as a number of lines varies according to class or the net retained line of the ceding insurer.

GROSS LINE—The amount of liability an insurer has written on a risk including the amount it has reinsured. Net line plus reinsurance equals gross line.

GROUND-UP LOSS—The total amount of loss sustained before deductions are applied for reinsurance covers which inure to the benefit of the cover being considered and before the application of a deductible, if any, because that base theoretically reflects changes in exposure.

GUARANTEE ENDORSEMENT—An addition to an insurance policy (between an insurance company and a policyholder covering the policyholder's mortgaged property) which requires that, in the event of the company's insolvency, the mortgagee and/or the policyholder be paid directly by the reinsurer either for any loss covered by reinsurance or (as is often provided) for the full insurance protection afforded by the insurance company. Since the full insurance protection afforded by the insurance company may be above the reinsurance which would be payable to a reinsured company, the reinsurer may be assuming an additional risk in such an endorsement. Similar to the cut-through endorsement, the guarantee endorsement is also known as a Mortgagee Endorsement.

HONORABLE UNDERTAKING—A clause used in some reinsurance treaties, the purpose of which is that the agreement not be defeated by a strict or narrow interpretation of the language in the treaty.

INCURRED BUT NOT REPORTED (IBNR)—The liability for future payments on losses which have already occurred but have not yet been reported in the reinsurer's records. This definition may be extended to include expected future development on claims already reported. See LOSS DEVELOPMENT.

INCURRED EXPENSE (OTHER THAN LOSS EXPENSE)—An expense which has happened but which may or may not have been paid.

INCURRED LOSS RATIO—The relationship between incurred losses and earned premium, usually expressed as a percentage.

INCURRED LOSSES— 1) In insurance accounting, an amount representing the losses paid plus the change (positive or negative) in outstanding loss reserves within a given period of time. 2) Losses which have happened and which will result in a claim under the terms of an insurance policy or a reinsurance agreement.

INDEXING—A procedure which adjusts retention and limit provisions of excess of loss reinsurance agreements in accordance with the fluctuations of a published economic index such as wage, price, cost-of-living, etc.

INSOLVENCY CLAUSE—A provision now appearing in most reinsurance contracts (because many states require it) stating that the reinsurance is payable, in the event the reinsured is insolvent, directly to the company or its liquidator without reduction because of its insolvency or because the company or its liquidator has failed to pay all or a portion of any claim.

INTERMEDIARY—A reinsurance broker who negotiates contracts of reinsurance on behalf of the reinsured, receiving a commission for placement and other services rendered. Under the terms of one widely used intermediary clause, premiums paid a broker by a reinsured are considered paid to the reinsurer, but loss payments and other funds (such as premium adjustments) paid a broker by a reinsurer are not considered paid to the reinsured until actually received by the reinsured.

INTERMEDIARY CLAUSE—A provision in a reinsurance contract which identifies the specific intermediary or broker involved in negotiating the contract, communicating information, and transmitting funds. The clause should state clearly whether payment to the broker does or does not constitute payment to the other party of the reinsurance contract. Currently a widely used clause provides that payments by the ceding company to the intermediary shall be deemed to constitute payment to the reinsurer(s) and that payments by the reinsurer(s) to the intermediary shall be deemed to constitute payment to the ceding company only to the extent that such payments are actually received by the ceding company.

INTERMEDIATE EXCESS—Used in property reinsurance to describe a cover exposed to both catastrophe (occurrence) losses and to policy limit exposures, excess the probable maximum loss.

INVESTMENT INCOME—Money earned from invested assets. May also include realized capital gains, or be reduced by capital losses, over the same period.

KENNEY RULE—The ratio of an insurer's net premium writings to its policyholder surplus which is considered safe by the author, Roger Kenney, a recognized authority on insurance company finances and author of the book, *Fundamentals of Fire and Casualty Insurance Strength*. For strictly fire insurance companies, the recommended ratio is 2 to 1: $2 of net premium writings for each $1 of policyholder surplus. For multiple line companies, the ratio is 3 to 1.

LAW OF LARGE NUMBERS—A mathematical concept which postulates that the more times an event is repeated (in insurance, the larger the number of homogeneous exposure units), the more predictable the outcome becomes. In a classic example, the more times one flips a coin, the more likely that the results will be 50% heads, 50% tails.

LAYER RATING—The prediction of loss frequency within a given layer (or band) of insurance.

LEAD REINSURER—The reinsurer recognized as the one of several reinsurers on a contract responsible for negotiating the initial terms of the contract. There may be joint leaders on a contract, and the contract may specifically provide to the lead reinsurer the power to bind others to limited changes in or enhancements of the contract during its term.

LEVERAGED EFFECT—The disproportionate result produced by inflation on a reinsurer's liability in excess of loss reinsurance compared with the ceding company's liability. In other words, inflationary increases in average claim costs of a reinsured usually produce even greater increases for its excess of loss reinsurer, since an increase affecting all losses (those within the retention limit and those above it) multiplies itself when affecting the excess of loss portion above that retention limit. For example, if the reinsured's retention limit average claim cost increases 8%, the reinsurer's increase can be as much as twice or three times that amount, or more. The increase on the reinsurer over the ceding company's increase is referred to as the leveraged effect. The effect is leveraged in that such increases fall more on the reinsurer, proportionately at least, than the reinsured.

LINE— 1) Either the limit of insurance to be written which a company has fixed for itself on a class of risk (line limit), or the actual amount which it has accepted on a single risk or other unit. 2) A class or type of insurance (fire, marine, or casualty, among others), also known as LINE OF BUSINESS. 3) The word "line" in reinsurance usually pertains to surplus reinsurance and means the amount of the reinsured's retention as respects each risk. Thus, reference to a "two-line" reinsurance treaty pertains to a treaty which affords reinsurance for 200% of the reinsured's retention.

LINE GUIDE—A list of the maximum amounts of insurance which a company is prepared to write on various classes of risks. Within the primary company, a line guide will usually include a suggested net retention for each class of risk and is used to instruct its agents and underwriters. Also known as Line Sheet.

LINE OF BUSINESS—The general classification of insurance written by insurers, i.e., fire, allied lines, and Homeowners, among others.

LINE SHEET—Another name for LINE GUIDE.

LLOYD'S (OR LLOYDS)—A kind of organization for underwriting insurance or reinsurance in which a collection of individuals assume policy liabilities as the individual obligations of each. When spelled with an apostrophe, the term refers to Lloyd's of London, the formal name of which is "Underwriters at Lloyd's, London."

LONG-TAIL LIABILITY—A term used to describe certain types of third-party liability exposures (e.g., malpractice, products, errors and omissions) where the incidence of loss and the determination of damages are frequently subject to delays which extend beyond the term the insurance or reinsurance was in force. An example would be contamination of a food product which occurs when the material is packed but which is not discovered until the product is consumed months or years later.

LOSS COST—In crop-hail insurance, the ratio of incurred loss to liability, or the dollars of loss per $100 of insurance in force. In reinsurance the total value of all losses divided by an exposure base. Also referred to as PURE PREMIUM.

LOSS DEVELOPMENT—The process of change in amount of losses as a policy or accident year matures, as measured by the difference between paid losses and estimated outstanding losses at one point in time and paid losses and estimated outstanding losses at some previous point in time. In common usage it might refer to development on reported cases only, whereas a broader definition would also take into account the IBNR claims.

LOSS INCURRED—See INCURRED LOSSES.

LOSS LOADING OR "MULTIPLIER"—A factor used to convert losses to premium and provide for the reinsurer's loss adjustment expense, overhead risk, and profit margin. Also known as Loss Conversion Factor.

LOSSES OUTSTANDING—Losses (reported or not reported) which have occurred but have not been paid.

LOSSES PAID—The amounts paid to claimants as insurance claim settlements.

LOSS RATIO—Losses incurred expressed as a percentage of earned premiums.

LOSS RESERVE—For an individual loss, an estimate of the amount the insurer expects to pay for the reported claim. For total losses, estimates of expected payments for reported and unreported claims. May include amounts for loss adjustment expenses. See INCURRED BUT NOT REPORTED (IBNR) and INCURRED LOSSES.

MANAGER—In reinsurance, any person, partnership or corporation representing an insurer or reinsurer and underwriting for the insurer's or reinsurer's account.

MFL (MAXIMUM FORESEEABLE LOSS)—The anticipated maximum property fire loss that could result given unusual or the worst circumstances with respect to the non-functioning of protective features (firewalls, sprinklers, a responsive fire department, ...), as opposed to PML (Probable Maximum Loss), which would be a similar valuation, but under the assumption that such protective features function normally.

MINIMUM PREMIUM—The least premium charge applicable, frequently used in excess of loss reinsurance contracts or catastrophe covers which contain a provision that the final adjusted premium may not be less than a stated amount.

MORTGAGEE ENDORSEMENT—Another name for GUARANTEE ENDORSEMENT.

NET LINE—The amount of insurance the primary company carries on a risk after deducting reinsurance from its "gross" line. See NET RETENTION.

NET LOSS—The amount of loss sustained by an insurer after making deductions for all recoveries, salvage, and all claims upon reinsurers—with specifics of the definition derived from the reinsurance agreement. Such net loss may or may not include claim expenses. As provided in the reinsurance agreement, net loss can be confined to the amount paid by the reinsured within applicable policy limits, or it can also include amounts paid by the reinsured for compensatory damages in excess of applicable policy limits because of failure of the reinsured to settle within applicable policy limits.

NET RETENTION—The amount of insurance which an insurer keeps for its own account and does not pass on to another insurer. In excess of loss reinsurance, the term "first loss retention" may be preferred. See NET LINE.

NONADMITTED ASSETS—Assets owned by an insurance company which are not recognized for solvency purposes by state insurance laws or insurance department regulations, e.g., premiums due and uncollected past ninety days, and furniture and fixtures, among others.

NONADMITTED COMPANY— 1) An insurer not licensed in a given state. 2) A reinsurer not licensed or approved in a given state.

NONADMITTED INSURANCE—Insurance protection placed in a nonadmitted insurer.

NONADMITTED REINSURANCE—Reinsurance protection bought by a ceding company from a reinsurer not licensed or authorized to transact the particular line of business in the jurisdiction in question. No credit is given the ceding company for such nonadmitted reinsurance in its Annual Statement unless it withholds funds or holds a letter of credit on behalf of such unauthorized reinsurer, as shown in Part 2 of Schedule F of the Statement.

NON-PROPORTIONAL REINSURANCE—Reinsurance under which the reinsurer's participation in a loss depends on the size of the loss. Also known as EXCESS OF LOSS REINSURANCE.

OBLIGATORY TREATY—A reinsurance contract under which the subject matter business must be ceded by the ceding company in accordance with contract terms and must be accepted by the reinsurer. Also known as AUTOMATIC TREATY.

OCCURRENCE— 1) In a non-insurance sense, an incident, event or happening. In insurance, the term may be defined as continual, gradual or repeated exposure to an adverse condition which is neither intended nor expected to result in injury or damage, as contrasted with an accident which is a sudden happening. In reinsurance, per occurrence coverage permits all losses arising out of one event to be aggregated instead of being handled on a risk-by-risk basis. 2) One basis or determinant for calculating the amount of loss or liability in insurance or reinsurance when an aggregation of related losses is to constitute a single subject of recovery. For example, in property catastrophe reinsurance treaties, occurrence is usually defined so that all losses within a specified period of time involving a particular peril are deemed an occurrence.

OPERATING INCOME /PROFIT—The sum of the net investment income and net underwriting income in any reporting period.

OPERATING RATIO—The arithmetic sum of two ratios: incurred loss to earned premium, and incurred expense to written premium. Considered the best simple index to current underwriting performance of an insurer.

OVERLINE—The amount of insurance or reinsurance exceeding the insurer's or reinsurer's normal capacity, inclusive of automatic reinsurance facilities.

OVERRIDING COMMISSION— 1) A fee or percentage of money which is paid to a party responsible for placing a retrocession of reinsurance. 2) In insurance, a fee or percentage of money which is paid by the insurer to an agent or general agent for premium volume produced by other agents in a given geographic territory.

OVERWRITING COMMISSION—Another name for OVERRIDING COMMISSION.

PARTICIPATE—To share in the writing of a risk.

PARTICIPATING REINSURANCE—The sharing of risks, as in quota share and surplus share reinsurance, which participate pro rata in all losses from the first dollar up. See PRO RATA REINSURANCE.

PAYBACK PERIOD—A term used in the rating of per occurrence excess covers which represents the number of years at a given premium level which would be necessary to accumulate total premiums equal to the indemnity. Synonymous with AMORTIZATION PERIOD.

PER RISK REINSURANCE—Reinsurance in which the reinsurance limit and the retention apply "per risk" rather than per accident, per event, or in the aggregate.

PML (PROBABLE MAXIMUM LOSS)—The anticipated maximum property fire loss that could result given the normal functioning of protective features (firewalls, sprinklers, a responsive fire department, ...), as opposed to MFL (Maximum Foreseeable Loss), which would be a similar valuation, but on a worst case basis with respect to the functioning of the protective features. Underwriting decisions would typically be influenced by PML evaluations, and the amount of reinsurance ceded on a risk would normally be predicated on the PML valuation.

POLICY PROFILE—A study which segregates an insurer's policies into various groupings (for example, by policy limit or policy premium).

POLICY YEAR EXPERIENCE—See ACCIDENT YEAR EXPERIENCE.

POLICYHOLDER—The party in whose name an insurance policy is issued.

POLICYHOLDER SURPLUS— 1) The net worth of an insurer as reported in its Annual Statement. For a stock insurer, the sum of its surplus and capital. For a mutual insurer, its surplus. 2) The amount by which the assets of an insurer exceed the organization's liabilities. Another name for SURPLUS TO POLICYHOLDERS.

POOL—Any joint underwriting operation of insurance or reinsurance in which the participants assume a predetermined and fixed interest in all business written. Pools are often independently managed by professionals with expertise in the classes of business undertaken, and the members share equally in the premiums, losses, expenses, and profits. An "association" and a "syndicate" (excluding that of Lloyd's of London) are both synonymous with a pool, and the basic principles of operation are much the same.

PORTFOLIO—A defined body of a) insurance (policies) in force (premium portfolio), b) outstanding losses (loss portfolio), or c) company investments (investment portfolio). (The reinsurance of all existing insurance as well as new and renewal business is therefore described as a running account reinsurance with portfolio transfer or assumption.)

PORTFOLIO REINSURANCE—The transfer of a portfolio via a cession of reinsurance; the reinsurance of a run-off. Only policies in force (or losses outstanding) are reinsured, and no new or renewal business is included. Premium or loss portfolios, or both, may be reinsured. The term is sometimes applied to the reinsurance by one insurer of all business in force of another insurer retiring from an agency, a territory, or from the insurance business entirely.

PORTFOLIO RETURN—If the reinsurer is relieved of liability (under a pro rata reinsurance) for losses happening after termination of the treaty or at a later date, the total unearned premium reserve on business left unreinsured (less ceding commissions thereon) is normally returned to the cedent. Also known as a RETURN PORTFOLIO or Return of Unearned Premium.

PORTFOLIO RUN-OFF—Continuing the reinsurance of a portfolio until all ceded premium is earned, or all losses are settled, or both. While a loss run-off is usually unlimited as to time, a premium run-off can be for a specified duration.

PREMIUM—The monetary consideration in contracts of insurance and reinsurance.

PREMIUM BASE—The ceding company's premiums (written or earned) to which the reinsurance premium rate is applied to produce the reinsurance premium. Also known as BASE PREMIUM, SUBJECT PREMIUM, and UNDERLYING PREMIUM.

PREMIUMS EARNED—When used as an accounting term, premiums earned describe the premiums written during a period plus the unearned premiums at the beginning of the period less the unearned premiums at the end of the period.

PRIMARY—An adjective applied in reinsurance to these nouns: insurer, insured, policy, and insurance—meaning respectively: 1) the primary insurer is the insurance company which initially originates the business, i.e., the ceding company; 2) the primary insured is the policyholder insured by the primary insurer; 3) the primary policy is the initial policy issued by the primary insurer to the primary insured; 4) the primary insurance is the insurance covered under the primary policy issued by the primary insurer to the primary insured (sometimes called "underlying insurance").

PRIORITY—The term used in some reinsurance markets outside the U.S. to mean the retention of the primary company in a reinsurance agreement.

PRODUCER COMMISSION—The same as BROKERAGE COMMISSION.

PROFESSIONAL REINSURER—A term used to designate an organization whose business is mainly reinsurance and related services, as contrasted with other insurance organizations which may operate reinsurance assuming departments in addition to their basic primary insurance business.

PROFIT COMMISSION—See CONTINGENT COMMISSION.

PROPORTIONAL REINSURANCE—Another name for PRO RATA REINSURANCE.

PRO RATA REINSURANCE—A generic term describing all forms of reinsurance in which the reinsurer shares a proportional part of the original losses and premiums of the ceding company. Also known as PARTICIPATING REINSURANCE and Proportional Reinsurance.

PROSPECTIVE RATING PLAN—The formula in a reinsurance contract for determining the reinsurance premium for a specified period on the basis, in whole or in part, of the loss experience of a prior period (as opposed to retrospective rating, which is based on loss experience for the same period). Also known as Experience Rating. See SPREAD LOSS REINSURANCE.

"PROTECTING THE TREATY"—Used to describe any action taken by an insurer to prevent heavy losses to its treaty reinsurer, which can lead to increased reinsurance rates or decreased participation in any profit-sharing arrangements with the reinsurer.

PROVISIONAL PREMIUM, RATE OR COMMISSION—The tentative amount which is subject to subsequent adjustment.

PUNITIVE DAMAGES—Damages awarded separately and in addition to compensatory damages, usually on account of malicious or wanton misconduct, to serve as a punishment for the wrongdoer and possibly as a deterrent to others. Sometimes referred to as "exemplary damages" when intended to "make an example" of the wrongdoer.

PURE LOSS COST—The ratio of reinsured losses incurred under a reinsurance agreement to the ceding company's subject earned premium for that agreement, before loading. Also known as BURNING COST.

PURE PREMIUM— 1) That part of the premium which is sufficient to pay losses and loss adjustment expenses but not including other expenses. 2) Also the premium developed by dividing losses by units of exposure, disregarding any loading for commission, taxes and expenses. 3) In crop-hail insurance, the ratio of incurred loss to liability, or the dollars of loss per $100 of insurance in force.

QUOTA SHARE REINSURANCE—A form of pro rata reinsurance (proportional) in which the reinsurer assumes an agreed percentage of each insurance being insured and shares all premiums and losses accordingly with the reinsured. Quota share reinsurance is usually arranged to apply to the insurer's net retained account (i.e., after deducting all other reinsurance except perhaps excess of loss catastrophe reinsurance), but practice varies. A quota share reinsurer may be asked to assume a quota share of a gross account, paying its share of premium for other reinsurance protecting that gross account.

RATE—The percent or factor applied to the ceding company's subject premium to produce the reinsurance premium, or the percent applied to the reinsurer's premium to produce the commission payable to the primary company (or, if applicable, the reinsurance intermediary).

RATE ON LINE—Premium divided by indemnity. A British term for the rate which, when multiplied by the indemnity, would produce the premium. Related to the American terms, "amortization period" and "payback period." This term is used extensively in judging the adequacy of rates for per occurrence excess covers, and is the inverse of AMORTIZATION PERIOD and PAYBACK PERIOD.

RECAPTURE—The action of a ceding company to take back reinsured risks previously ceded to a reinsurer.

RECIPROCITY—The mutual exchanging of reinsurance, often in equal amounts, from one party to another, the object of which is to stabilize overall results.

RECOVERIES—Amounts received from a reinsurer for a reinsured's losses.

REINSTATEMENT—The restoration of the reinsurance limit of an excess property treaty to its full amount after payment by the reinsurer of loss as a result of an occurrence.

REINSURANCE— 1) The transaction whereby the reinsurer, for a consideration, agrees to indemnify the ceding company against all or part of the loss which the latter may sustain under the policy or policies which it has issued. 2) When referred to as "a reinsurance," the term means the reinsurance relationship between reinsured(s) and reinsurer(s).

REINSURANCE ASSUMED—That portion of risk the reinsurer accepts from the original insurer or ceding company.

REINSURANCE CEDED—That portion of the risk that the ceding company transfers to the reinsurer.

REINSURANCE COMMISSION—Another name for CEDING COMMISSION.

REINSURANCE PREMIUM—An amount paid by the ceding company to the reinsurer in consideration for liability assumed by the reinsurer.

REINSURED—A company which has placed reinsurance risks with a reinsurer in the process of buying reinsurance. Also known as CEDING COMPANY.

REINSURER—An organization which assumes the liability of another by way of reinsurance.

RETAINAGE—Contract balances held in suretyship by an obligee for payment to a contractor upon completion of the contract.

RETENTION—The amount which an insurer assumes for its own account. In pro rata contracts, the retention may be a percentage of the policy limit. In excess of loss contracts, the retention is a dollar amount of loss.

RETROCEDENT—The ceding reinsurer in a retrocession, where the assuming reinsurer is known as the retrocessionnaire.

RETROCESSION—The transaction whereby a reinsurer cedes to another reinsurer all or part of the reinsurance it has previously assumed.

RETROCESSIONNAIRE—The assuming reinsurer in a retrocession, where the ceding reinsurer is known as the retrocedent.

RETROSPECTIVE RATING PLAN—The formula in a reinsurance contract for determining the reinsurance premium for a specified period on the basis of the loss experience for the same period (as opposed to prospective rating, which is based on loss experience for the prior period). Also known as Experience Rating.

RETURN PORTFOLIO—The reassumption by a ceding company of a portfolio of risks previously assumed by reinsurer. See ASSUMED PORTFOLIO.

RISKS— 1) In fire insurance, the physical units of property at risk instead of perils or hazards. In reinsurance, each insurance company makes its own rules for defining units of hazard or single risks. 2) Also, the different types of properties or insurable interest, e.g., non-hazardous risks and protected risks.

RUN-OFF—A termination provision of a reinsurance contract stipulating that the reinsurer shall remain liable for loss under reinsured policies in force at the date of termination, as a result of occurrences taking place after the date of termination.

SECOND SURPLUS—A supplementary treaty to a FIRST SURPLUS TREATY.

SEMI-AUTOMATIC TREATY—See FACULTATIVE SEMI-OBLIGATORY TREATY.

SINGLE RISK REINSURANCE—See FACULTATIVE REINSURANCE.

SLIDING SCALE COMMISSION—A commission adjustment on earned premiums under a formula whereby the actual commission varies inversely with the loss ratio, subject to stated maximum and minimum percentages.

SOCIAL INFLATION—The increasing of insurance losses caused by higher jury awards, more liberal treatment of claims by workers' compensation boards, legislated rises in benefit levels (in some cases retroactively), and new concepts of tort and negligence, among others.

SPECIAL ACCEPTANCE—The specific agreement by the reinsurer to include under a reinsurance contract a risk which is not automatically included within the terms thereof.

SPECIAL COVERS—A general term used to describe reinsurance agreements written to protect the primary company against certain unusual situations, usually contingent in nature, rather than for the repayment of normal losses suffered under the primary company's policies.

SPECIAL EXCEPTION—See SPECIAL ACCEPTANCE.

SPREAD LOSS REINSURANCE—A type of excess of loss property reinsurance which provides for a periodic adjustment of the reinsurance premium rate based on the reinsured's experience for preceding years (usually five) plus a loading for the purpose of compensating the reinsurer for a) its expenses, b) the possibility of unusual losses, c) those losses occurring at the end of the period of the treaty which the reinsurer might not have a chance to recoup if the treaty is not renewed, d) a catastrophe possibility, and e) the reinsurer's profit. In casualty reinsurance, adjustments to the above may be required for such other factors as economic and social inflation. Also known as CARPENTER PLAN.

STATUTORY ACCOUNTING PRINCIPLES (SAP)—Those principles required by state law which must be followed by insurance companies in submitting their financial statements to state insurance departments. Such principles differ from generally accepted accounting principles (GAAP) in some important respects, e.g., SAP requires that expenses must be recorded immediately and cannot be deferred to track with premiums as they are earned and taken into revenue. See GAAP.

STOP LOSS REINSURANCE—See AGGREGATE EXCESS OF LOSS REINSURANCE.

SUBJECT PREMIUM—The ceding company's premiums (written or earned) to which the reinsurance premium rate is applied to produce the reinsurance premium. Also known as BASE PREMIUM, PREMIUM BASE, UNDERLYING PREMIUM and Subject Matter Premium Income.

G.N.E.P.I. (Gross Net Earned Premium Income)—The usual rating base for excess of loss reinsurance. It represents the earned premiums of the primary company for the lines of business covered net, meaning after cancellations, refunds, and premiums paid for any reinsurance protecting the cover being rated, but gross, meaning before deducting the premium for the cover being rated.

G.N.W.P.I. (Gross Net Written Premium Income)—Gross written premium less only returned premiums and less premiums paid for reinsurance which inure to the benefit of the cover in question. Its purpose is to create a base to which the reinsurance rate is applied. Same as G.N.E.P.I., except premiums are written instead of earned.

SURPLUS LIABILITY—That portion of a reinsured company's gross liability on any one risk which exceeds the amount the company is willing to retain net for its own account.

SURPLUS REINSURANCE—A form of pro rata reinsurance indemnifying the ceding company against loss for the surplus liability ceded. Essentially, this can be viewed as a variable quota share contract wherein the reinsurer's pro rata share of insurance on individual risks will increase as the amount of insurance increases, in order that the primary company can limit its net exposure regardless of the amount of insurance written. First surplus is the amount of surplus on each risk that must apply first to the first surplus contract. Second surplus, third surplus, etc., reinsurances are the remaining portions of the surplus that must apply to each such respective contract after deducting the amount(s) ceded to the underlying surplus contract or contracts.

SURPLUS RELIEF— 1) The result of reinsurance ceded on a portfolio basis to offset extraordinary drains on policyholder surplus. 2) A designation of a reinsurance the main purpose of which is to finance new or in-force business, or both. See FINANCING FUNCTION.

SURPLUS TO POLICYHOLDERS— 1) The net worth of an insurer as reported in its Annual Statement. For a stock insurer, the sum of its unassigned surplus and capital. 2) The amount by which the assets of an insurer exceed the organization's liabilities. Another name for POLICYHOLDER SURPLUS.

SYNDICATE—An association of individuals or organizations to pursue certain insurance objectives. For example, individual underwriters in Lloyd's of London associate in separate syndicates to write marine insurance, reinsurance, life insurance, etc., entrusting the administrative details of each syndicate to a syndicate manager. See POOL.

TARGET RISKS—Risks designated in reinsurance treaties or contracts by the reinsurer that are specifically excluded (e.g., high valued bridges, tunnels, fine arts collections), because they normally are of such size and capacity demand as to require individual acceptance, lest "blind" cessions under automatic reinsurance overline the reinsurer.

TRADE RATIO—The combination of loss incurred to earned premiums ratio and incurred expense to written premiums ratio. Also known as Combined Ratio and OPERATING RATIO.

TREATY—A reinsurance agreement between the ceding company and the reinsurer, usually for one year or longer, which stipulates the technical particulars applicable to the reinsurance of some class or classes of business. Reinsurance treaties may be divided into two broad classifications: a) the participating type which provides for sharing of risks between the ceding company and the reinsurer; and b) the excess type which provides for indemnity by the reinsurer only for loss which exceeds some specified predetermined amount. For different forms, see QUOTA SHARE, EXCESS OF LOSS, FIRST SURPLUS, SECOND SURPLUS, SPREAD LOSS, STOP LOSS, CATASTROPHE.

TREATY REINSURANCE—A standing agreement between reinsured and reinsurer for the cession and assumption of certain risks as defined in the treaty. While most treaty reinsurance provides for automatic cession and assumption, it may be optional or semi-obligatory and is not necessarily obligatory.

TRENDING—The necessary adjustment of historical statistics (both premium and losses) to present levels or expected future levels in order to reflect measurable changes in insurance experience over time which are caused by dynamic economic and demographic forces and to make the data useful for determining current and future expected cost levels.

TURN—Referred to as "the turn," this word describes the excess of reinsurance commission received by a ceding company over its actual costs incurred in producing the business ceded. The excess is considered a profit to the ceding company.

UBERRIMAE FIDEI—Literally, of the utmost good faith. A defining characterization or quality of some (contractual) relationships, of which reinsurance is universally recognized to be one. Among other differences from ordinary relationships, the nature of reinsurance transactions is dependent upon a mutual trust and a lively regard for the interests of the other party even if inimical to one's own. A breach of utmost good faith, especially in regard to full and voluntary disclosure of the elements of risk of loss, is accepted as grounds for any necessary reformation or redress, including rescission.

ULTIMATE NET LOSS— 1) In reinsurance, the unit of loss to which the reinsurance applies, as determined by the reinsurance agreement. In other words, the gross loss less any recoveries from other reinsurance which reduce the loss to the treaty in question. 2) In liability insurance, the amount actually paid or payable for the settlement of a claim for which the reinsured is liable (including or excluding defense costs) after deductions are made for recoveries, and certain specified reinsurance.

UNAUTHORIZED INSURER, REINSURER—An insurer not licensed, or a reinsurer neither licensed nor approved, in a designated jurisdiction.

UNAUTHORIZED REINSURANCE—Reinsurance placed with a reinsurer which does not have authorized status in the jurisdiction in question.

UNDERLYING—The amount of loss which attaches before the next higher excess layer of insurance or reinsurance attaches.

UNDERLYING PREMIUM—The ceding company's premiums (written or earned) to which the reinsurance premium rate is applied to produce the reinsurance premium. Also known as PREMIUM BASE, BASE PREMIUM, and SUBJECT PREMIUM.

UNDERWRITING CAPACITY—The maximum amount of money an insurer or reinsurer is willing to risk in a single loss event on a single risk or in a given period. The limit of capacity for an insurer or reinsurer may also be imposed by law or regulatory authority.

UNDERWRITING INCOME—The excess of premiums earned by a reinsurer during any reporting period over the combined total of expenses and losses incurred by the reinsurer during the same period.

UNEARNED PREMIUM RESERVE—The sum of all the premiums representing the unexpired portions of the policies or contracts which the insurer or reinsurer has on its books as of a certain date. It is usually based on a formula of averages of issue dates and the length of term.

WARRANTED NO KNOWN OR REPORTED LOSSES (WNKORL)—A statement made on application for excess or catastrophe reinsurance, which is being back-dated, to protect the reinsurer from placement of reinsurance after a loss has occurred.

WORKING EXCESS—A contract covering an area of excess reinsurance in which loss frequency is anticipated, as opposed to loss severity. Thus, a working cover would usually have a low indemnity and would attach above a relatively low retention.

Index